INDIAN AESTHETICS

An Introduction

Edited by

V.S. SETURAMAN

TRINITY
PRESS
(An Imprint of Laxmi Publications Pvt. Ltd.)
An ISO 9001:2008 Company
BENGALURU • CHENNAI • COCHIN • GUWAHATI • HYDERABAD
JALANDHAR • KOLKATA • LUCKNOW • MUMBAI • RANCHI • NEW DELHI
BOSTON (USA) • NAIROBI (KENYA)

INDIAN AESTHETICS

Printed and bound in India

First Published : 1992, *Reprinted* : 2005, 2011, 2014, 2015, *Edition* : 2017

ISBN : 978-93-5138-056-6

PUBLISHED IN INDIA BY

TRINITY PRESS

(An Imprint of Laxmi Publications Pvt. Ltd.)
An ISO 9001:2008 Company
113, GOLDEN HOUSE, DARYAGANJ, NEW DELHI-110002, INDIA
Telephone : 91-11-4353 2500, 4353 2501
Fax : 91-11-2325 2572, 4353 2528
www.laxmipublications.com info@laxmipublications.com

Branches

Bengaluru	080-26 75 69 30
Chennai	044-24 34 47 26
Cochin	0484-237 70 04, 405 13 03
Guwahati	0361-254 36 69, 251 38 81
Hyderabad	040-27 55 53 83, 27 55 53 93
Jalandhar	0181-222 12 72
Kolkata	033-22 27 43 84
Lucknow	0522-220 99 16
Mumbai	022-24 93 12 61
Ranchi	0651-220 44 64

C—14202/017/06

Printed at : Ajit Printing Press, Delhi.

CONTENTS

Preface

This book tries to meet the long felt need for an introduction to Indian Poetics for Indian students studying literary theory at the post-graduate and research levels. The only other book in the field so far, *Introduction to Indian Poetics,* edited by Raghavan and Nagendra, which comprised essays in English by twentieth-century Indian scholars, contained none of the basic Sanskrit texts; nor did it include the work of later critics and theoreticians like Ananda K. Coomaraswami, Rabindranath Tagore or Sri Aurobindo.

The present book consists of three sections along with an Introduction and some Appendices.

Section I: contains extracts from some of the basic Sanskrit texts in poetics such as Bharata's *Natyasastra*, Bhāmaha's *Kavyalankara*, etc.

Section II: consists of essays on Indian poetics by scholars like P.V. Kane, M. Hiriyanna, S. Kuppuswami Sastri and R. Gnoli. All these essays had been included in *Introduction to Indian Poetics*, edited by Raghavan and Nagendra. Essays 11-16 have been added by the present editor.

Section III: contains essays on art and poetry by well-known modern philosophers and aestheticians like Rabindranath Tagore and Sri Aurobindo. The opening article by Mulk Raj Anand provides an over-view of Hindu Art based on Ananda Coomaraswamy's appraisal of it.

The Appendices comprise essays by the present editor on Sri Aurobindonian Aesthetics, the role of Indian aesthetics in the teaching of literature and schools of criticism in Sanskrit. A glossary is also appended.

The book does not purport to be exhaustive or even authoritative. It is just an attempt to introduce to our students some of the concepts of Indian poetics. It is assumed that they are already acquainted with Western aesthetics and poetics from Plato down to Derrida. This book, it is hoped, will help them to see how "modern" the speculations of some of our aesthetic philosophers are — and how relevant and insightful.

The works of later theorists like Vāmana, Kshemendra and Sankuka have not been included since no satisfactory translations of these texts are available.

The editor acknowledges with gratitude the valuable help rendered by Dr Kunjunni Raja who not only went through the introduction but also gave positive suggestions regarding the selections.

He is also grateful to Prof. G.B. Mohan Thampi, Vice-Chancellor, University of Kerala, for so readily granting permission to select passages/selections from his *Response to Poetry* (New Delhi: People's Publishing House Pvt. Ltd., 1968). It was indeed gracious of him to have helped in addition with his suggestions which were as valuable academically as they were spontaneous.

V.S. SETURAMAN

General Introduction

What the ancients thought about the name and nature of poetry may be had from the Riks of the Vedas and the texts of the Upanishads. The Vedic texts declared that the poets were 'gods', - *Kavi* was the term they employed. While invoking the foremost of the Gods - Ganapati - they addressed him as the poet's poet - (कविं कवीनां). A human being could become a poet only in so far as he attained to the nature and status of a god.

The poet was the Seer of Truth having a subtle, profound and penetrating consciousness. he was also a creator / or maker in as much as he was *Kavikratuh*: (कविक्रतु:) the builder, fashioner and lastly he embodied the principle of Delight - (कविर्हि मधुहस्त्य:). He saw the principle of beauty in all things and was filled with utter ecstasy and raised the earth to the level of Heaven and established this principle of joy everywhere (Rig Veda III, 38, 2&3).

Thus the Vedic conception of a poet took into account all aspects of poetry: its creation, its manifestation and its impact upon the reader. The poet was in conscious control of the Word. He had the *Vak*; he knew the four levels of *Vak*; and *Vak* chose to reveal Herself to him.

The Vedic *Kavi* was also a yogi in the sense that he was absolutely conscious of the process of creation. Apart from the normal consciousness which we call *jāgrat* (the waking state), the Upanishads spoke of subtler states such as *swapna*, (the dream state), suṣupti (deep sleep) and *turiya* (the transcendental state) not to mention infraconscious levels. The Upanishadic Seer-Poet could withdraw, ingather or collect, contain and concentrate his consciousness and come out to express his vision and experience. His mental and other instrumental faculties could receive the inspiration in a state of wise passiveness and transcribe it without distortion. He had the *Word*. He could also see objectively what he had created and evaluate it. He could thus *give* us the vision and he knew the way to get back to the source and testify to the authenticity of the transcript.

The most significant example of what we have been describing is, of course, Valmiki, whose *Ramāyana* spontaneously sprang out of the pathos-filled fountain of the poet's heart. He says:

पादबद्धोऽक्षरसमः तन्त्रीलयसमन्वितः ।
शोकार्तस्य प्रवृत्तो मे श्लोको भवतु नान्यथा ।।

The observation makes it clear that (1) genuine great poetry is not *made* (constructed out of one's cleverness (चमत्कार) but is a spontaneous emanation from a heart filled with रसः (2) that the great artist is also a great art critic - the *Kavi* and *Sahṛdaya* are one and it is only the most sensitive critic that can respond to the *charm* of great poetry. One here recalls the Rig Vedic definition of the nature of the identity between the artist and the critic:

सं गच्छध्वं. सं वदध्वं सं वो मनांसि जानताम् ।
देवाः भागं यथा पूर्वे सं जानाना उपासते ।।

समानोमन्त्रः समितिः समानी समानं मनः सहचित्तमेषाम् ।
समानं मन्त्रमभिमन्त्रये वः समानेन वो हविषा जुहोमि ।।

समाना वः आकूतिः समानाहृदयानि वः ।
समानमस्तु वो मनः यथा वः सुसहासति ।।

And (3) most significantly the form (of poetry) which includes diction, versification and *music* is determined by the inspiration and the *laya* is as important as any other element and it determines the meaning of the utterance. Every Vedic scholar who has learnt his texts in the traditional way will tell us about the importance of intonation / *swara* and how it determines the meaning. (Students of Indian Scriptures will recall the story of the war between the Devas and Asuras and how Asuras by articulating wrongly the phrase *Indraśatru* made it a Bahuvrihi compound instead of Tatpurusha compound which would have helped them to get what they wanted).

The concept of *rasa* is referred to in the phrase शोकार्तस्य प्रवृत्तो मे etc. *Rasa* is the source of inspiration. The term is rendered as taste/essence. Tradition makes God Almighty himself as the first and foremost of creative artists; and Taittiriya Upanishad describes him as Rasa रसो वै सः. He is also the greatest of critics who felt that what He created was good and made Him happy. Rasa is therefore supposed to constitute art experience and the critic is one who is capable of रसानुभव.

Bharata was the first art critic to define रस for us. He must have had in mind *nātyasāstra* and drama when he defined art emotion. He said that *rasa* is achieved as a result of the functioning of the *vibhavas* the objective condition causing an emotion (a lover on the stage), (2) the *anubhavas* (bodily gestures/expression by which the emotion is expressed and (3) *vyabhichari bhavas* - secondary emotion and sensations which feed the dominant emotion. *Vibhavas* include persons (characters) as well as the circumstances that cause or excite the emotions. A love-lorn woman on the stage as a character in a play or a dancer expressing by gestures the feelings and sensations of a love-lorn woman exciting a response in the spectator is an example. The implication may be described in the following way. To get the art experience the artist has to be disinterested, (surely unselfish) objective and capable of contemplating life-experiences without being affected by them. What he embodies in his work of art is this emotion re-collected in a state of tranquillity where all disagreeables get evaporated and life experience and life emotions and sensations get transformed. What art communicates is thus the emotion of an emotion. There is the substratum of peace, delight and in the process what is particular and individual gets universalized. There is the freedom from involvement in life-emotions of pain and pleasure and its pathological consequences caused by selfishness, struggle, personal loss or gain etc. Art emotion, therefore, cannot cause excitement or depression or grief. It takes us beyond the dualities of life to a state of delight against the background of peace. It is for this reason that it was often compared by enthusiastic critics to spiritual Delight (*Brahmananda*) though they knew that it was not that. Brahmananda is the state of *jāgrat suṣupti*: the aesthetic joy, though akin to it is the joy of *jāgrat swapna*. It is temporal; it lasts as long as we are in the world of art (one recalls Keats's line, 'Was it a vision, or a waking dream?'). It teases us out of all thought and helps us to attain to a calm of mind all passion spent, 'as doth eternity'. The artist not only has this delight himself, but communicates it. How does he communicate it? He communicates, rather induces in the reader (with the necessary sensibility) the same state by first choosing a life experience and then judiciously idealizing it and embodying it in appropriate language. The artist is thus both an imitator and a creator (art is both mimesis and poesis). The starting point is perhaps the imitation of life experience; but the artist's imagination (प्रतिभा, as it was called by Indian aestheticians), is a kind of *dṛṣti* (दृष्टि) which helps him to see differently and transform it. He creates a new world (The English poet-critic Sidney uses the terms brazen and golden worlds to describe the real world and the world of art), a world free from the laws of destiny which govern our own. Hence the well-known verse of Ananda Vardhana

अपारे काव्यसंसारे कविरेव प्रजापतिः

In the infinite world of poetry the poet is indeed the Creator. He transforms the world as it pleases him. He has the vision. But how does he give it a concrete shape? He has *also* the words and the rhythm. In his inspired state the poem (unwritten, not yet articulated) is born. The state chooses for him the words and their order.

Indeed, our language philosophy distinguishes, as has been mentioned earlier, four levels of *Vak: Para / Pasyanti / Madhyama* and *Vaikhari*. It is only the *vaikhari vak* that is *heard*. The other *Vāks* are not heard. They are, so to say, concealed, hidden. It is only the wise that know them. Bhartṛhari used the term *sphota* or dispersion and he made it clear that it provided a bridge between the preverbal state of inspiration and vision and the verbal expression of it. *Sphota*, which may also be rendered *utterance*, is manifested through sounds temporally though it is in itself beyond time. What is articulated and heard is *dhvani*/ sounds but this dhvani is only the manifesting agent of *sphota*, which is unheard. To Bhartṛhari again the unit of speech is utterance, not *words* and the perception of the whole must precede the division and analysis of the utterance into words. This explains how utterance is capable of giving us more than a sum of what the individual words of the utterance can. The creative artist, who is conscious, is poised between the unheard and the heard like Janus, allowing the inspiration to choose the words and their order. The critic too can proceed from the articulated words to the unheard melodies and recover the experience; and he does so by his sensitive response to the suggestive power of words. He can respond effectively only if he is a *Sahṛdaya*, one who can feel, think in the same way as the artist. He is one with the author; achieves an identity with the artist, hears with the inner as well as the outer ear. He recovers from the

Vachya (articulated words) through their significative power the experience in its entirety and the joy that follows.

Suggestion is therefore the link between the words on the page on the one hand and the vision or experience on the other. It is called *Vyanjana*, more appropriately rendered as the significative power of words (which have sounds/meaning etc. as constitutive elements). In all articulated utterances there are three distinctive elements: 'expression, suppression and impression'. Comprehending consists in our getting the meaning not only from 'expression' but also from what is suppressed. In poetry, more than denotation, it is connotation, suggestion and rhythm that help us to get at the experience; and the *Sahṛdaya* proceeds from lexical meanings and association of words on the page, through his response to their evocative, significative power, and arrives at the experience. The words that can be articulated (*vachya*) can express only a fraction of the '*experience*'. It is their capacity for 'suggestion' that takes us to the experience in its entirety. Dhwani functions through denotative and connotative meanings of words even as Atman functions through the *Sarira* or the body. They belong to different orders of reality. The right response helps the *Sahṛdaya* to make the 'hermeneutical' leap. Hence the critics words like *Sphutatwa*, *avabhasa*. The significance belongs to the non space-time dimension. When the poet Kalidasa invokes Parvati and Parameshawara for *vagartha pratipatti*, he is only praying to our first parents to enable him to achieve a synthesis between *vak* and *artha*.

वागर्थाविव सम्पृक्तौ वागर्थप्रतिपत्तये ।
जगतःपितरौ वन्दे पार्वतीपरमेश्वरौ ।।

In the words of one of the best exponents of our poetics, S. Kuppuswami Sastri,

> Genuine poetry is looked upon as spontaneous emanation from a rasa-filled heart. A beautiful thought clothes itself in a beautiful garb without any conscious effort on the part of the poet. This is the highest test of true poetry. Another writer, Bhavabhuti observes: 'In the case of the wise men of this world word runs after sense; but in the case of primeval sages, sense rushes after their word' . . . .
>
> To examine this statement in the light of our definition of *vyangya*/ suggestion in poetry is to see how sense is always

aggressive and in the hands of an ordinary man it shapes its language. But in the case of *rishis* or seers sense follows the sound. That is why it is often said that the poet can create new words, invest old words with new meanings, enrich them, force them to yield more.

It is only for purposes of discussion and analysis that we speak of form and content. In any successful work of art they are inseparable. It is the power of suggestion (*Vyanjana*) that fuses the form and content. The diction and its collocations are called *gunas*. Other decorative devices, embellishments such as simile/metaphors, are the *alankaras*. Style or *riti* includes '*deviation*' (*vakrokti*) in expression, and *auchitya*. The synthesizing factor is *dhvani* /or suggestion and so it is called the soul of poetry; it is that that leads us straight to *rasanubhava*. These elements themselves constitute the body of poetry.

In spite of so much discussion of the nature of poetry by language philosophers, theoreticians and rhetoricians, there is very little of practical criticism in Sanskrit poetics. Such applied criticism as is available is to be seen only in commentaries on texts.

Among later Indian critics three names stand out prominently. They are Ananda Coomaraswamy, Rabindranath Tagore and Sri Aurobindo. Ananda Coomaraswamy takes us back to the spiritual basis of Indian art revolting against the philistinism of the late XIX and early XX centuries. Tagore was the first to stress the principle of joy and freedom in art and to show that

> the beauty of a poem is bound by strict laws, yet it transcends them. The laws are its wings, they do not keep it weighed down, they carry it to freedom. Its form is in law but its spirit is in beauty. Law is a first step towards freedom and beauty is the complete liberation which stands and shines on the pedestal of law. ('Sadhana')

Sri Aurobindo's synthetic vision has not only recovered for us the salient principles of ancient Indian aesthetics but their potentialities too. His application of these principles has helped him to attempt a revaluation of both Indian and Western literature bringing out their relevance to us.

Acknowledgements

The publishers wish to acknowledge the following sources to which they have applied for copyright permission.

Section I

Karnataka University Press for S Krishnamurthi's translation of Anandavardhana from *Dhvanyaloka* and Kuntaka from *Vakrokti Jivita.*

Harvard University Press, Massachusetts for Mason and Patwardhan's translation of Abhinava Gupta from *Locana.*

Section II

Macmillan India Ltd. for the first ten items of section II from *An Introduction to Indian Poetics* (ed) Raghavan and Nagendra.

Theosophical Society Press, Madras for Kunjunni Raja's "Bhartrhari's Discussion About the Nature of the Sphota" and "Theory of Dhvani"

Mohan Tampi for "Rasa : Aesthetic Experience," "The Mode of Aesthetic Experience" and "The Obstacles to Aesthetic Experience"

OUP India for "The Word and the World" by B.K. Matilal

Section III

Asia Publishing House for "The Aesthetic Hypothesis" by Mulk Raj Anand.

Macmillan London for "Shakuntala: Its Inner Meaning" by Rabindranath Tagore

Sri Aurobindo Ashram for "The Soul of Poetic Delight and Beauty" by Sri Aurobindo.

SECTION - I

Basic Sanskrit Texts with English Translations

Introduction

The theory of Rasa is associated with Bharata, though there are references to it in the Vedas and in Vālmiki. The contexts in the Vedas and the Upanishads where Rasa is mentioned, are not exactly aesthetic. The word means sap or essence and refers to the experience of the Supreme Reality which is one of self-existent delight. The Vedic poetry does contain a number of *ṛks* on speech, *Vāk*, especially in the tenth *mandala*, (or Ṛg Veda) and the seers knew perhaps a lot about inspiration and the need for *sahṛdayatwa* in understanding and enjoying poetry. Valmiki's slokas, spontaneously emanating from his being overpowered by an intense feeling of pathos, and his own appreciation of it, indicate that he was, at one stroke, both a poet and a critic. The Karunārasa of the epic *Ramayana* has made all the later critics and poets look upon him (Valmiki) as the father of the theory of Rasa.

It is, however, only in *The Natyasastra* of Bharata (see section A, selections i & ii) that the theory of Rasa is stated in all its ramifications. We do not know when Bharata lived. Scholars like A.B. Keith place him in the first or the second part of the first century B.C. The references to various aspects of dramaturgy in the book show that dramatic technique must have been highly developed when it was written, and Bharata himself must have been a teacher of theatre arts, music and dancing. The extracts are intended to give us an idea of the theory of Rasa. He defines Rasa in his well known aphorism: Vibhāva anubhāva vyabhichāri samyogāt Rasa nishpattihi. *Vibhāvas* are causes or mainsprings of emotion:

a) the characters in a drama that excite our feelings;
b) setting: spring, garden, fragrance, moonlight:

Anubhavas are the effects of emotions that develop the main sentiment such as anxiety, anger, depression, through which love (which is the principal emotion) is expressed.

A blending of these bhavas rousing in the reader/spectator/a certain emotion, accompanied by a thrill and a sense of joy is Rasa. The contributing factors are also described by Bharata in detail. He speaks of eight different types of Rasas and their development is aided by poetry, music, and other histrionic devices called nātyadharmi, all brought under abhinaya. The points to be noted are:

1. The emotion generated — the Rasa is the emotion resulting from a contemplation of the feelings and emotions of characters, situations etc. They may be considered the objective correlative of the Rasa.
2. It is not personal. There is a certain amount of distancing and the delight that it communicates is against the background of peace, or, at any rate, absence of any agitation or disturbance.

These are elaborated and discussed by Abhinavagupta who also discusses in his commentary the cognitive value of art. (It is for this reason that the selections from his *Abhinavabharati* follow the selection from Bharata).

Between Bharata and Anandavardhana there were many literary critics or aestheticians, but they were all interested not so much in *Rasa* theory as in the nature of poetic form, the qualities of style, as the selection from Bh a maha will make it clear. Bh a maha, in particular, held that alankaras or figures, mattered most in poetry and he brought Rasa also under Alankara. Besides, he felt that the function of poetry was to inculcate moral principles.

The next important critic was Dandin for whom lucidity, sweetness, richness and grandeur, constituted poetry. To Vamana, style or *Riti* was the soul of poetry.

The most important critic and aesthetic philosopher after Vamana, was, of course, Anandavardhana, the author of *Dhvanyaloka*. The metaphorical title must reveal how the work is a spirited statement of defence of suggestion as the soul of poetry. Earlier critics had given some thought to it, but it was Anandavardhana who formulated the theory in categorical terms. He related it to the Indian theories of meaning (see extracts from Professor Kunjunni Raja's book of the same title). The subject was not new to the aestheticians because the Indian semanticists classified meaning under several heads:

1. denotation
2. indirect indication by means of metaphors etc.

3. A third power was *sphota* or the meaning of the utterance as a whole. They called it *t a tparyasakti*. Anandavardhana thinks of a fourth power, the power of suggestion, which may be related to sphota. But to him and his commentator this meaning

belonged to a different order or dimension and goes beyond literal sense and intention, conscious or unconscious. Anandavardhana also granted that *Rasa* cannot be directly expressed; it is only through Dhvani that Rasa gets expressed. This leads him to discuss the concept of appropriateness and the interrelationship between different elements of poetry.

It was, however, left to his commentator Abhinavagupta to establish once and for all the validity of the theory of Anandavardhana by resolving many of the intricate problems involved in the theories of Rasa and Dhvani and integrating the several strands of truth. He discusses both in his *Locana* and in his *Abhinavabharati* the nature of Rasa, the barriers to the realization of Rasa, how the Sahrdaya gets over the obstacles and realizes the experience. This realization is considered *Alaukika* or transcendental. It is ineffable and cannot be expressed. It is a peculiar kind of cognition similar to but not identical with yogic knowledge and realization. The nearest that we have to this kind of knowledge and realization in Western criticism is the 'sublime' and the 'transport' caused by it as described by Loginus in the treatise *On the Sublime*.

Kuntaka must have been a contemporary of Abhinavagupta. Kuntaka held that a certain deviation from the ordinary mode of expression of ideas constituted the essence of poetry. He recognized the importance of suggestion and Rasa, but he felt that aesthetic pleasure is derived from 'deviation', clever and dexterous choice of words and ideas. He distinguished six varieties of deviation. The extract from *Vakrokti Jivita* will not only illustrate how sometimes the choice and the change made in the incidents in the plot add to the beauty of the whole, but provide an instance of admirable practical criticism. (Abhinava too concentrated on the *whole* as might be seen in the selection from *Locana*).

Mahimbatta, who came after Kuntaka, is a powerful logician and is the founder of the Anumana school. He felt that the principle of suggestion was only a variety of inference. His stress is on ratiocination, immediate inference. Mahimbatta and Kshemendra, whose *Aucityavicara* discusses propriety or 'keeping', are discussed in detail in section B.

1

From *Natyasastra*

Bharata

पूर्वरङ्गविधिं श्रुत्वा पुनराहुर्महत्तमाः ।
भरतं मुनयः सर्वे प्रश्नान् पञ्चाभिधत्स्व नः ।।२।।
ये रसा इति पठ्यन्ते नाट्ये नाट्यविचक्षणैः ।
रसत्वं केन वै तेषामेतदाख्यातुमर्हसि ।।२।।
भावाश्चैव कथं प्रोक्ताः किं वा ते भावयन्त्यपि ।
संग्रहं कारिकां चैव निरुक्तं चैव तत्त्वतः ।।३।।
तेषां तु वचनं श्रुत्वा मुनीनां भरतो मुनिः ।
प्रत्युवाच पुनर्वाक्यं रसभावविकल्पनम् ।।४।।
अहं वः कथयिष्यामि निखिलेन तपोधनाः ।
संग्रहं कारिकां चैव निरुक्तं च यथाक्रमम् ।।५।।
न शक्यमस्य नाट्यस्य गन्तुमन्तं कथंचन ।
कस्माद्बहुत्वाद्भावानां शिल्पानां वाप्यनन्ततः ।।६।।
एकस्यापि न वै शक्यमन्तं ज्ञानार्णवस्य हि ।
गन्तुं किं पुनरन्येषां ज्ञानानामर्थतत्त्वतः ।।७।।
किंत्वल्पसूत्रग्रन्थार्थमनुमानप्रसाधकम् ।
नाट्यस्यास्य प्रवक्ष्यामि रसभावादिसंग्रहम् ।।८।।
विस्तरेणोपदिष्टानामर्थानां सूत्रभाष्ययोः ।
निबन्धो यः समासेन संग्रहं तं विदुर्बुधाः ।।९।।
रसा भावा ह्यभिनया धर्मी वृत्तिप्रवृत्तयः ।
सिद्धिस्वरास्तथातोद्यं गानं रङ्गश्च संग्रहः ।।१०।।
[उपचारस्तथा विप्रा माण्डपश्चेति सर्वशः ।
त्रयोदशविधो ह्येष ह्युद्दिष्टोनाट्यसंग्रहः ।।११।।]
अल्पाभिधानेनार्थो यः समासेनोच्यते बुधैः ।
सूत्रतः सा तु विज्ञेया कारिकार्थप्रदर्शिनी ।।१२।।

नानानामाश्रयोत्पन्नं निघण्टुनिगमान्वितम् ।
धात्वर्थहेतुसंयुक्तं नानासिद्धान्तसाधितम् ॥१३॥
स्थापितोऽर्थो भवेद्यत्र समासेनार्थसूचकः ।
धात्वर्थवचनेनेह निरुक्तं तत्प्रचक्षते ॥१४॥
संग्रहो यो मया प्रोक्तः समासेन द्विजोत्तमाः ।
विस्तरं तस्य वक्ष्यामि सनिरुक्तं सकारिकम् ॥१५॥
श्रृङ्गारहास्यकरुणा रौद्रवीरभयानकाः ।
बीभत्साद्भुतसंज्ञौ चेत्यष्टौ नाट्ये रसाः स्मृताः॥१६॥
एते ह्यष्टौ रसाः प्रोक्ता द्रुहिणेन महात्मना ।
पुनश्च भावान्वक्ष्यामि स्थायिसंचारिसत्त्वजान्॥१७॥
रतिर्हासश्च शोकश्च क्रोधोत्साहौ भयं तथा ।
जुगुप्सा विस्मयश्चेति स्थायिभावाः प्रकीर्तिताः ॥१८॥
निर्वेदग्लानिशङ्काख्यास्तथासूयामदश्रमाः ।
आलस्यं चैव दैन्यं च चिन्ता मोहः स्मृतिर्धृतिः॥१९॥
व्रीडा चपलता हर्ष आवेगो जडता तथा ।
गर्वो विषाद औत्सुक्यं निद्रापस्मार एव च ॥२०॥
सुप्तं विबोधोऽमर्षश्चाप्यवहित्थमथोग्रता ।
मतिर्व्याधिस्तथोन्मादस्तथा मरणमेव च ॥२१॥
त्रासश्चैव वितर्कश्च विज्ञेया व्यभिचारिणः ।
त्रयस्त्रिंशदमी भावाः समाख्यातास्तु नामतः ॥२२॥
स्तम्भः स्वेदोऽथ रोमाञ्चः स्वरभङ्गोऽथ वेपथुः ।
वैवर्ण्यमश्रु प्रलय इत्यष्टौ सात्त्विकाः स्मृताः ॥२३॥
आङ्गिको वाचिकश्चैव आहार्यः सात्त्विकस्तथा ।
चत्वारोऽभिनया ह्येते विज्ञेया नाट्यसंश्रयाः॥२४॥
लोकधर्मी नाट्यधर्मी धर्मीति द्विविधः स्मृतः ।
भारती सात्वती चैव कैशिक्यारभटी तथा ॥२५॥
चतस्त्रो वृत्तयो ह्येता यासु नाट्यं प्रतिष्ठितम् ।
आवन्ती दाक्षिणात्या च तथा चै[illegible]

पञ्चालमध्यमा चेति विज्ञेयास्तु प्रवृत्तयः ।
दैविकी मानुषी चैव सिद्धिः स्याद्द्विविधैव तु ।।२७।।
शारीराश्चैव वैणाश्च सप्त षड्जादयः स्वराः ।
ततं चैवावनद्धं च घनं सुषिरमेव च ।।२८।।
चतुर्विधं च विज्ञेयमातोद्यं लक्षणान्वितम् ।
ततं तन्त्रीगतं ज्ञेयमवनद्धं तु पौष्करम् ।।२९।।
घनस्तु तालो विज्ञेयः सुषिरो वंश एव च ।
प्रवेशाक्षेपनिष्क्रामप्रासादिकमथान्तरम् ।।३०।।
गानं पञ्चविधं ज्ञेयं ध्रुवायोगसमन्वितम् ।
चतुरस्रो विकृषटश्च रङ्गःत्रयस्रश्च कीर्तितः ।।३१।।
एवमेषोऽल्पसूत्रार्थो निर्दिष्टो नाट्यसंग्रहः ।
अतः परं प्रवक्ष्यामि सूत्रग्रन्थविकल्पनम् ।।३२।।

तत्र रसानेव तावदादावभिव्याख्यास्यामः। नहि रसादृते कश्चिदर्थः प्रवर्तत इति।

तत्र विभावानुभावव्यभिचारिसंयोगाद्रसनिष्पत्तिः ।

को दृष्टान्तः। अत्राह–यथा हि नानाव्यञ्जनौषधिद्रव्यसंयोगाद्रसनिष्पत्तिर्भवति, यथा हि गुडादिभिर्द्रव्यैर्व्यञ्जनैरोषधिभिश्च षाडवादयो रसा निवर्तन्ते, तथा नानाभावोपगता अपि स्थायिनो भावा रसत्वमाप्नुवन्तीति। अत्राह–रस इति कः पदार्थः। उच्यते। आस्वाद्यत्वात्। कथमास्वाद्यते रसः। यथा ही नानाव्यञ्जनसंस्कृतमन्नं भुञ्जाना रसानास्वादयन्ति सुमनसः पुरुषा हर्षादींश्च अधिगच्छन्ति तथा नानाभावाभिनयव्यञ्जितान् वागङ्गसत्त्वोपेतान् स्थायिभावानास्वादयन्ति सुमनसः प्रेक्षकाः, हर्षादींश्चाधिगच्छन्ति तस्मान्नाट्यरसा इत्यभिव्याख्याताः। अत्रानुवंश्यौ श्लोकौ भवतः–

यथा बहुद्रव्ययुतैर्व्यञ्जनैर्बहुभिर्युतम् ।
आस्वदयन्ति भुञ्जाना भक्तं भक्तविदो जनाः ।।३३।।
भावाभिनयसंबद्धान्स्थायिभावांस्तथा बुधाः ।
आस्वादयन्ति मनसा तस्मान्नाटयरसास्मृताः।।३४।।

अत्राह किं रसेभ्यो भावानामभिनिर्वृत्तिरूताहो भावेभ्यो रसानामिति। उच्यते केषांचिन्मतं परस्परसंबन्धादेषामभिनिष्पत्तिरिति। तन्न। कस्मात्। दृश्यते हि भावेभ्यो रसानामभिनिर्वृत्तिर्न तु रसेभ्यो भावानामभिनिर्वृत्तिरिति।

भवन्ति चात्र श्लोकाः

नानाभिनयसंबद्धान्भावयन्ति रसानिमान् ।
यस्मात्तस्मादमी भावा विज्ञेया नाटचयोक्तृभिः।।३५।।
नानाद्रव्यैर्बहुविधैर्व्यञ्जनं भाव्यते यथा ।
एवं भावा भावयन्ति रसानभिनयैः सह ।।३६।।
न भावहीनोऽस्ति रसो न भावो रसवर्जितः ।
परस्परकृता सिद्धिस्तयोरभिनये भवेत् ।।३७।।
व्यञ्जनौषधिसंयोगो यथान्नं स्वादुतां नयेत् ।
एवं भावा रसाश्चैव भावयन्ति परस्परम् ।।३८।।
यथा बीजाद्भवेद्वृक्षो वृक्षात्पुष्पं फलं यथा ।
तथा मूलं रसाः सर्वे तेभ्यो भावा व्यवस्थिताः।।३९।।

तदेषां रसानामुत्पत्तिवर्णदैवतनिदर्शनान्यभिव्याख्यास्यामः–तेषामुत्पत्तिहेतवश्चत्वारो रसाः। तद्यथा शृङ्गारो रौद्रो वीरो बीभत्स इति।

अत्र–

शृङ्गाराद्धि भवेद्धास्यो रौद्राच्च करुणो रसः ।
वीराच्चैवाद्भुतोत्पत्तिर्बीभत्साच्च भयानकः ।।४०।।

श्रृङ्गारानुकृतिर्या तु सा हास्यस्तु प्रकीर्तितः ।
रौद्रस्यैव च यत्कर्म स ज्ञेयः करुणो रसः ।।४१।।
वीरस्यापि च यत्कर्म सोऽद्भुतः परिकीर्तितः ।
बीभत्सदर्शनं यत्र ज्ञेयः स तु भयानकः ।।४२।।

अथ वर्णाः-

श्यामो भवति श्रृङ्गारः सितो हास्यः प्रकीर्तितः ।
कपोतः करुणश्चैव रक्तो रौद्रः प्रकीर्तितः ।।४३।।
गौरो वीरस्तु विज्ञेयः कृष्णश्चैव भयानकः ।
नीलवर्णस्तु बीभत्सः पीतश्चैवाद्भुतः स्मृतः ।।४४।।

अथाधिदैवतानि-

श्रृङ्गारो विष्णुदैवत्यो हास्यः प्रमथदैवतः ।
रौद्रो रुद्राधिदैवत्यः करुणो यमदैवतः ।।४५।।
बीभत्सस्य महाकालः कालदेवो भयानकः ।
वीरो महेन्द्रदेवः स्याददद्भुतो ब्रह्मदैवतः ४६।।

एवमेतेषां रसानाम् उत्पत्तिवर्णदेवतान्यभिव्याख्यातानि। इदानीं विभावानुभावव्यभिचारिसंयुक्तानां लक्षणनिदर्शनानि अभिव्याख्यास्यामः, स्थायिभावांश्च रसानामनुक्रमिष्याम इति।

तत्र श्रृङ्गारो नाम रतिस्थायिभावप्रभव उज्ज्वलवेषात्मकः। यथा यत्किंचिल्लोके शुचि मेध्यमुज्ज्वलं दर्शनीयं वा तच्छृङ्गारेण उपमीयते। यस्तावदुज्जवलवेषः स श्रृङ्गारवानित्युच्यते। यथा च गोत्रकुलाचारोत्पन्नान्याप्तोपदेशसिद्धानि पुंसां नामानि भवन्ति तथैवैषां रसानां भावानां च नाट्याश्रितानां च अर्थानां आचारोत्पन्नान्याप्तोपदेशसिद्धानि नामानि भवन्ति एवमेष आचारसिद्धो हृद्योज्ज्वलवेषात्मकत्वाच्छृङ्गारो रस इति। स च स्त्रीपुरुषहेतुक उत्तमयुवप्रकृतिः। तस्य द्वे अधिष्ठाने-संभोगः, विप्रलम्भश्च। तत्र

संभोगस्तावद् ऋतुमाल्यानुलेपनालंकारेष्टजनविषयवरभवनोपभोगोपवनगमनानुभवनश्रवणदर्शनक्रीडालीलादिभिर्विभावैरुपद्यते। तस्य नयनचातुरीभ्रूक्षेपकटाक्षसंचारललितमधुराङ्गहारवाक्यादिभिः अनुभावैरभिनयः प्रयोक्तव्यः। व्यभिचारिणस्त्रासालस्योग्रजुगुप्सावर्जम्। विप्रलम्भकृतस्तु निर्वेदग्लानिशङ्कासूयाश्रमचिन्तौत्सुक्यनिद्रासुप्तस्वप्नविव्वोकव्याध्युन्मादापस्मारजाड्यमरणादिभिरनुभावैरभिनेतव्यः। अत्राह–यद्ययं रतिप्रभवः श्रृङ्गारः कथमस्य करुणाश्रयिणो भावा भवन्ति। अत्रोच्यते–पूर्वमेवाभिहितं संभोगविप्रलम्भकृतः श्रृङ्गार इति। वैशिकशास्त्रकारैश्च दशावस्थोऽभिहितः ताश्च सामान्याभिनये वक्ष्यामः।

करुणस्तु शापक्लेशविनिपतितेष्टजनविप्रयोगविभवनाशवधबन्धसमुत्थो निरपेक्षभावः। औत्सुक्यचिन्तासमुत्थः सापेक्षभावो विप्रलम्भकृतः। एवमन्यः करुणोऽन्यश्च विप्रलम्भ इति। एवमेष सर्वभावसंयुक्तः श्रृङ्गारो भवति। अपि च

सुखप्रायेष्टसंपन्न ऋतुमाल्यादिसेवकः।
पुरुषः प्रमदायुक्तः श्रृङ्गार इति संज्ञितः ॥४७॥

अपि चात्र सूत्रानुबद्धे आर्ये भवतः–

ऋतुमाल्यालंकारैः प्रियजनगान्धर्वकाव्यसेवाभिः ।
उपवनगमनविहारैः श्रृङ्गाररसः समुद्भवति ॥४८॥
नयनवदनप्रसादैः स्मितमधुरवचोधृतिप्रमोदैश्च ।
मधुरैश्चाङ्गविकारैस्तस्याभिनयः प्रयोक्तव्यः ॥४९॥

[इति शृङ्गाररसप्रकरणम्।]

अथ हास्यो नाम हासस्थायिभावात्मकः। स च विकृतपरवेषालंकारधाष्टर्यलौल्यकुहकासत्प्रलापव्यङ्गदर्शनदोषोदाहरणादिभिः विभावैरुत्पद्यते। तस्यौष्ठनासाकपोलस्पन्ददृष्टिव्याकोशाकुञ्चनस्वेदास्य-

रागपार्श्वग्रहणादिभिरनुभावैरभिनयः प्रयोक्तव्यः। व्यभिचारिणश्चाव-
हित्थालस्यतन्द्रानिद्रास्वप्नप्रबोधासूयादयः। द्विविधश्चायम् – आत्मस्थः
परस्थश्च। यदा स्वयं हसति तदात्मस्थः। यदा तु परं हासयति
तदा परस्थः। अत्रानुवंश्ये आर्ये भवतः–

'विपरीतालंकारैर्विकृताचाराभिधानवेषैश्च ।
विकृतैरङ्गविकारैर्हसतीति रसः स्मृतो हास्यः ॥५०
विकृताचारैर्वाक्यैरङ्गविकारैश्च विकृतवेषैश्च ।
हासयति जनं यस्मात्तस्माज्ज्ञेयो रसो हास्यः ॥५१॥'
स्त्रीनीचप्रकृतावेष भूयिष्ठं दृश्यते रसः ।
षड्भेदाश्चास्य विज्ञेयास्तांश्च वक्ष्याम्यहं पुनः ॥५२॥
स्मितमथ हसितं विहसितमुपहसितं चापहसितमतिहसितम् ।
द्वौ द्वौ भेदौ स्यातामुत्तममध्याधमप्रकृतौ ॥५३॥

तत्र–

स्मितहसिते ज्येष्ठानां मध्यानां विहसितोपहसिते च ।
अधमानामपहसितं ह्यतिहसितं चापि विज्ञेयम् ॥५४॥

अत्र श्लोकाः–

ईषद्विकसितैर्गण्डैः कटाक्षैः सौष्ठवान्वितैः।
अलक्षितद्विजं धीरमुत्तमानां स्मितं भवेत् ॥५५॥
उत्फुल्लाननेत्रं तु गण्डैर्विकसितैरथ ।
किंचिल्लक्षितदन्तं च हसितं तद्विधीयते ॥५६॥

[अथ मध्यानाम्–]

आकुञ्चिताक्षिगण्डं यत्सस्वनं मधुरं तथा ।
कालागतं सास्यरागं तद्वै विहसितं भवेत् ॥५७॥
उत्फुल्लनासिकं यत्तु जिह्मदृष्टिनिरीक्षितम् ।
निकुञ्चितांसकशिरस्तच्चोपहसितं भवेत् ॥५८॥

[अधमानाम्–]

अस्थानहसितं यत्तु साश्रुनेत्रं तथैव च ।
उत्कम्पितांसकशिरस्तच्चापहसितं भवेत् ।।५९।।
संरब्धसाश्रुनेत्रं च विकृष्टस्वरमुद्धतम् ।
करोपगूढपार्श्वं च तच्चातिहसितं भवेत् ।।६०।।
हास्यस्थानानि यानि स्युः कार्योत्पन्नानि नाटके ।
उत्तमाधममध्यानामेवं तानि प्रयोजयेत् ।।६१।।
इत्येष स्वसमुत्थस्तथा परसमुत्थितश्च विज्ञेयः ।
द्विविधस्त्रिप्रकृतिगतस्त्रयवस्थभावो रसो हास्यः ।।६२।।

[इति हास्यरसप्रकरणम् ।]

अथ करुणो नाम शोकस्थायिभावप्रभवः। स च शापक्लेशविनिपतितेष्टजनविप्रयोगविभवनाशवधबन्धविद्रवोपघातव्यसनसंयोगादिभिर्विभावैः समुपजायते। तस्याश्रुपातपरिदेवनमुखशोषणवैवर्ण्यस्त्रस्तगात्रतानिः श्वासस्मृतिलोपादिभिरनुभावैरभिनयः प्रयोक्तव्यः। व्यभिचारिणश्चास्य निर्वेदग्लानिचिन्तौत्सुक्यावेगभ्रममोहश्रमभयविषाददैन्यव्याधिजडतोन्मादापस्मारत्रासालस्यमरणस्तम्भवेपथुवैवर्ण्याश्रुस्वरभेदादयः। अत्रार्ये भवतः–

इष्टवधदर्शनाद्वा विप्रियवचनस्य संश्रवाद्वापि ।
एभिर्भावविशेषैः करुणरसो नाम संभवति ।।६३।।
सस्वनरुदितैर्मोहागमैश्च परिदेवितैर्विलपितैश्च ।
अभिनेयः करुणरसो देहायासाभिघातैश्च ।।६४।।

[इति करुणरसप्रकरणम् ।]

अथ रौद्रो नाम क्रोधस्थायिभावात्मको रक्षोदानवोद्धतमनुष्यप्रकृतिः सङ्ग्रामहेतुकः। स च क्रोधधर्षणाधिक्षेपावमानानृतवचनोपघातवाक्पारुष्याभिद्रोहमात्सर्यादिभिर्विभावैरुत्पद्यते। तस्य च ताडन-

पाटनपीडनच्छेदनप्रहरणाहरणशस्त्रसंपातसंप्रहाररुधिराकर्षणाद्यानि कर्माणि। पुनश्च रक्तनयनस्वेदभ्रुकुटीकरणावष्टम्भदन्तौष्ठपीडनगण्डस्फुरणहस्ताग्रनिष्पेषादिभिरनुभावैरभिनयः प्रयोक्तव्यः। भावाश्चास्य–असंमोहोत्साहावेगामर्षचपलतौग्र्यगर्वविकृतेक्षणस्वेदवेपथुरोमाञ्चगद्गदादयः। अत्राह – यदभिहितं रक्षोदानवादीनां रौद्रो रसः किम् अन्येषां नास्ति। उच्यते – अस्त्यन्येषामपि रौद्रो रसः किंतु अधिकारोऽत्र गृह्यते। ते हि स्वभावत एव रौद्राः। कस्मात्। बहुबाहवो बहुमुखाः प्रोद्धूतविकीर्णपिङ्गलशिरोजा रक्तोद्वृत्तविलोचना भीमासितरूपिणश्चैव। यच्च किंचित्समारभन्ते स्वभावेन चेष्टितं वागङ्गादिकं तत्सर्वं रौद्रमेवैषाम्। श्रृङ्गारश्च तैः प्रायशः प्रसभं सेव्यते। तेषां चानुकारिणो ये पुरुषास्तेषामपि सङ्ग्रामसंप्रहारकृतो रौद्रो रसोऽनुमन्तव्यः। अत्रानुवंश्ये आर्ये भवतः–

युद्धप्रहारघातनविकृतच्छेदनविदारणैश्चैव ।
सङ्ग्रामसंभ्रमाद्यैरेभिः संजायते रौद्रः ।।६५।।
नानाप्रहरणमोक्षैः शिरःकबन्धभुजकर्तनैश्चैव ।
एभिश्चार्थविशेषैरस्याभिनयः प्रयोक्तव्यः ।।६६।।
इति रौद्ररसो दृष्टो रौद्रवागङ्गचेष्टितः ।
शस्त्रप्रहारभूयिष्ठ उग्रकर्मक्रियात्मकः ।।६७।।

[इति रौद्ररसप्रकरणम्।]

अथ वीरो नामोत्तमप्रकृतिरुत्साहात्मकः। स चासंमोहाध्यवसायनयविनयबलपराक्रमशक्तिप्रतापप्रभावादिभिर्विभावैरुत्पद्यते। तस्य स्थैर्यधैर्यशौर्यत्यागवैशारद्यादिभिरनुभावैरभिनयः प्रयोक्तव्यः। भावाश्चास्य धृति मतिगर्वावेगौग्र्यामर्षस्मृतिरोमाञ्चप्रतिबोधादयः। अत्रार्ये रसविचारमुखे–

उत्साहाध्यवसायादविषादित्वादविस्मयान्मोहात् ।
विविधादर्थविशेषाद्वीररसो नाम संभवति ।।६८।।

स्थितिधैर्यवीरगर्वैरुत्साहपराक्रमप्रभावैश्च ।
वाक्यैश्चाक्षेपकृतैर्वीररसः सम्यगभिनेयः ॥६९॥

[इति वीररसप्रकरणम् ।]

अथ भयानको नाम भयस्थायिभावात्मकः। स च विकृतरवसत्वदर्शनशिवोलूकत्रासोद्वेगशून्यागारारण्यगमनस्वजनवधबन्धदर्शनश्रुतिकथादिभिः विभावैः उत्पद्यते। तस्य प्रवेपितकरचरणनयनचपलपुलकमुखवैवर्ण्यस्वरभेदादिभिरनुभावैरभिनयः प्रयोक्तव्यः। भावाश्चास्यस्तम्भस्वेदगद्गदरोमाञ्चवेपथुस्वरभेदवैवर्ण्यशङ्कामोहदैन्यावेगचापलजडतात्रासापस्मारमरणादयः।

अत्रार्याः–

विकृतरवसत्त्वदर्शनसङ्ग्रामारण्यशून्यगृहगमनात् ।
गुरुनृपयोरपराधात्कृतकश्च भयानको ज्ञेयः ॥७०॥
गात्रमुखदृष्टिभेदैरूरुस्तम्भाभिवीक्षणोद्वेगैः ।
सन्नमुखशोषहृदयस्पन्दनरोमोद्गमैश्च भयम् ॥७१॥
एतत्स्वभावजं स्यात्सत्त्वसमुत्थं तथैव कर्तव्यम् ।
पुनरेभिरेव भावैः कृतकं मृदुचेष्टितैः कार्यम् ॥७२॥
करचरणवेपथुस्तम्भगात्रसंकोचहृदयकम्पेन ।
शुष्कौष्ठतालुकण्ठैर्भयानको नित्यमभिनेयः ॥७३॥

[इति भयानकरसप्रकरणम् ।]

अथ वीभत्सो नाम जुगुप्सास्थायिभावात्मकः। स चाहृद्याप्रशस्ता प्रियावेक्षानिष्टश्रवणदर्शनोद्वेजनपरिकीर्तनादिभिर्विभावैरुत्पद्यते। तस्य च सर्वाङ्गसंहारमुखविकूणनोल्लेखननिष्ठीवनोद्वेजनादिभिरनुभावैरभिनयः प्रयोक्तव्यः। भावाश्चास्य–अपस्मारोद्वेगावेगमोहव्याधिमरणादयः। अत्रार्ये भवतः–

अनभिमतदर्शनेन च गन्धरसस्पर्शशब्ददोषैश्च ।
उद्वेजनैश्च बहुभिर्बीभत्सरसः समुद्भवति ।।७४।।
मुखनेत्रविकूणनया नासाप्रच्छादनावनमितास्यैः ।
अव्यक्तपादपतनैर्बीभत्सः सम्यगभिनेयः ।।७५।।

[इति वीभत्सरसप्रकरणम् ।]

अथाद्भुतो नाम विस्मयस्थायिभावात्मकः। स च दिव्यजनदर्शनेप्सितमनोरथावाप्त्युपवनदेवकुलादिगमनसभाविमानमायेन्द्रजालसंभावनादिभिर्विभावैरुत्पद्यते। तस्य नयनविस्तारानिमेषप्रेक्षणरोमाञ्चाश्रुस्वेदहर्षसाधुवाददानप्रबन्धहाहाकारबाहुवदनचेलाङ्गुलिभ्रमणादिभिरनुभावैरभिनयः प्रयोक्तव्यः।

भावाश्चास्य – स्तम्भाश्रुस्वेदगद्गदरोमाञ्चावेगसंभ्रमप्रहर्षचपलतोन्मादधृतिजडताप्रलयादयः। अत्रानुवंश्ये आर्ये भवतः–

यत्त्वतिशयार्थयुक्तं वाक्यं शिल्पं च कर्म रूपं वा ।
तत्सर्वमद्भुतरसे विभावरूपं हि विज्ञेयम् ।।७६।।
स्पर्शग्रहोल्लुकसनैर्हाहाहारैश्च साधुवादैश्च ।
वेपथुगद्गदवचनैः स्वेदाद्यैरभिनयस्तस्य ।।७७।।

[इत्यद्भुतरसप्रकरणम् ।]

शृङ्गारं त्रिविधं विद्याद्वाङ्नेपथ्यक्रियात्मकम् ।
अङ्गनेपथ्यवाक्यैश्च हास्यरौद्रौ त्रिधा स्मृतौ ।।७८।।
धर्मोपघातजश्चैव तथार्थापचयोद्भवः ।
तथा शोककृतश्चैव करुणस्त्रिविधः स्मृतः ।।७९।।
दानवीरं धर्मवीरं युद्धवीरं तथैव च ।
रसं वीरमपि प्राह ब्रह्मा त्रिविधमेव हि ।।८०।।
व्याजाच्चैवापराधाच्च वित्रासितकमेव च।
पुनर्भयानकं चैव विद्यात्त्रिविधमेव हि ।।८१।।

बीभत्सः क्षोभणः शुद्ध उद्वेगी स्याद्द्वितीयकः ।
विष्ठाक्रिमिभिरुद्वेगी क्षोभणो रुधिरादिजः ।।८२।।
दिव्यश्चानन्दजश्चैव द्विधा ख्यातोऽद्भुतो रसः ।
दिव्यदर्शनजो दिव्यो हर्षादानन्दजः स्मृतः ।।८३।।

The Sentiments

The sages question

1-3. After hearing about the rules regarding the Preliminaries, the great sages continued their inquiries and said to Bharata, "Answer five of our questions. Explain how the Sentiments enumerated by experts in dramatic art attain their special qualities. And why are the *bhāvas* (States) so called, and what do they *bhāvayanti* (make us feel)? Besides these, what are the real meanings of terms such as, Digest (*saṃgraha*)[1] Memorial Verse (*kārikā*) and Etymology (*nirukta*)?"

Bharata answers

4. At these words of the sages, Bharata continued speaking and mentioned in reply to their question the distinction between the Sentiments and the States.

5.7. And then he said "O sages, I shall tell you in detail and in due order about the Digest (*saṃgraha*), the Memorial Verse (*kārikā*) and the Etymology (*nirukta*). I am not able by any means to exhaust all the topics about drama (*nāṭya*); for science (*jñāna*), and arts and crafts (*Śilpa*) connected with it are respectively manifold and endless in number. And as it is not possible to treat exhaustively (lit. to go to the end of) even one of these subjects which are [vast] like an ocean, there cannot be any question of mastering them all.

1-3 For a possible chronological implication of *Samgraha, kārikā, nirukta, sūtra* and *bhāsva* mentioned in this chapter see Skt. Poetics, Vol. I. pp.28 ff.

8. [Hence] I shall tell you about the Digest on Sentiments, States and such other matters, which has its contents embodied in a small number of Sutras (short rules) but which promotes inference [about the understanding of the subject].

Digest, Memorial Verse and Etymology defined

9. When subjects taught in detail have been compressed and brought together in [a number of] Sutras and their Bhasyas (commentary), these latter constitute according to the learned a Digest (*samgraha*).

10. The Digest [of the Natyaveda treats] the Sentiments, the States, the Histrionic Representation (*abhinaya*), the Practice (*dharmi*), the Styles (*vṛtti*), the Success (*siddhi*), the notes (*svara*), the instrumental music (*ātodya*), songs and the stage.

11. When a rule (lit. meaning) is explained (lit. uttered) briefly in the manner of a Sutra by means of a minimum (lit. small) number of words it is called the memorial Verse (*kārikā*) which shows the meaning [of the rule clearly].[1]

12. The Etymology (*nirukta*) is that which arises in connexion with various nouns, is helped by dictionaries and rules of grammatical interpretation, includes the meaning of the root involved as well as the reasons modifying it, and is helped by various findings [of Śastras].

13. When the meaning [of a noun] is established from a consideration of its root [and *pratyaya* or affix], words expressing [such] meaning in brief are called the Etymology.

14. O the best of the Brahmins, [the subjects included into] the Digest (*saṃgraha*), which I mentioned earlier, will now be discussed in detail with the necessary Memorial Verses (*kārikā*) and Etymologies connected with them.

---

[1] One additional characteristic of the *kārika* is that it should be generally composed in metres like *āryā* or śloka, *e.g.* the *Samkhyakārika*.

The eight Sentiments

15. The eight Sentiments (*rasa*)[1] recognised in drama are as follows: Erotic (*śringāra*), Comic (*hāsya*), Pathetic (*karuṇa*) Furious (*raudra*), Heroic (*vira*), Terrible (*bhayanaaka*) Odious (*bibhatsa*) and Marvellous (*adbhuta*)[2]

16. These eight are the Sentiments named by Brahman; I shall now speak of the Dominant, the Transitory and the Temperamental States.

The Dominant States

17. The Dominant States (*sthāyibhāva*)[1] are known to be the following: love, mirth, sorrow anger, energy, terror, disgust and astonishment.

18-21. The thirtythree Transitory States (*vyabhicāribhāva*)[1] are known to be the following: discouragement, weakness, apprehension, envy, intoxication, weariness, indolence, depression, anxiety, distraction, recollection, contentment, shame, inconstancy, joy, agitation stupor, arrogance, despair impatience, sleep, epilepsy, dreaming, awakening, indignation, dissimulation, cruelty, assurance, sickness, insanity, death, fright and deliberation. These are defined by the names.

The eight Temperamental States

22. Paralysis, Perspiration, Horripilation, Change of Voice, Trembling, change of Colour, Weeping and Fainting are the eight Temperamental States.[2]

---

15. [1] *rasa* — A.K. Coomaraswamy is for translating the word as 'flavour' (MG. p. 17).

[2] The later writers on Skt. poetics add one more *rasa* (*śānta*) to this number.

17. [1] *sthāyibhāva* — Keith translates the term as 'dominant emotion' (Skt. Drama) and Haas as 'Permanent State' (DR.) and others as 'permanent mood' (*e.g.* S.K. De, Skt. Poetics, Vol. II. p. 26).

18-21. [1] These are also known as *sañcāri-bhāva*.

22. [1] *sāttvika bhāva* — The word *sāttvika* cannot be properly translated into English. Keith does not make any such attempt (see Skt. Drama). Haas translates the *sāttvika-bhāva* as 'Involuntary States'. But this seems to be very misleading, for the NŚ. take *sattva* to be connected with *manas*. (see VI. 94), and most of the later writers follow

(continued...)

23. The four kinds of Histrionic Representation are Gestures (*āṅgika*)[1], Words (*vācika*)[2], Dresses and Make-up (*āhārya*)[3] and the Representation of the Temperament (*sāttvika*).[4]

The two Practices

24 The Practice of Representation (*dharmi*)[1] in a dramatic performance is twofold: realistic (*lokadharmi* , lit. popular) and coventional (*nāṭyadharmi*, lit. theatrical).

The four Styles

And the Verbal (*bhārati*), the Grand (*sāttvati*) the Graceful (*kaiśiki*) and the Energetic (*ārabhati*) are the four Styles (*vṛtti*)[2].

The four Local Usages

25-26. Āvanti, Dāksinātyā, Odramāgadhi and Pānçcālamadhyamā are the four Local Usages (*pravrtti*)[1] in a dramatic performance.

---

[1] (_Continued)

this work in this respect. So the author of the ND. (III. 153) writes अवहितं मन सत्त्व तत्प्रयोजन हेतुरस्येति सात्त्विकः ममोऽनवधाने हि न शक्यन्त एव स्वरभेदादयो नाट्येन दर्शयितुम्. The NŚ. has also a definition of *sāttva* which is also as follows: देहात्मकं भवेत् सत्त्व (XXIV.7). The author of the BhP. elaborately defines the term *sāttva* and discusses the psychological process connected with its use; see (pp. 13-14). Viśvanātha in his SD.(164) defines *sāttva* as follows: सत्त्वं नाम सात्मविश्राम- प्रकाशकरो कश्चनान्तरो धर्मः

23 (B.24, G.23). [1] *āṅgikā* – means Gerstures of speical kind definedin the *śāstra* see NS.VIII-XII.

[2] *vācika* – means Words suitable for representation of the different States (*bhāva*) composed by the playwright.

[3] See NS.XXIII. [4] See NS.XXIV.

24 (B.25-26a, G.24-25a). [1] *dharmi* – This word has not been very correctly used. But the meaning is clear; for details about *dharmi* see NS.XIII 69-81.

[2] Haas translates vṛttis as Styles of Procedure (DR.p.67). The four Styles are translated by him as Eloquent (*bhārati*), Grandiose (*sāttvati*) Gay (*kaisiki*) and Horrific (*arabhaṯi*). We follow Keith's translation (Skt. Drama, p.326). For details about vṛttis see NŚ.XXIII.ff.

are the four Local Usages (*pravrtti*)[1] in a dramatic performance.

The Success.

The Success[2] in the Dramatic Performance is of two kinds: divine (*daivikī*) and human (*mānusī*).

The Notes

27-29. And [musical] notes such as, Ṣaḍja, Ṛṣabha etc. are seven in number, and they fall into two groups: human (śārīrā lit. from body) and instrumental (*vaiṇava* lit. from the Vinā).

The four kinds of musical instruments

The musical instruments are of four kinds: stringed (*tata*) covered (*avanaddha*), solid (*ghana*), and hollow (*suṣira*). Among these, the stringed (*tata*) means an instrument with strings, the covered (*avanaddha*) means a drum, the solid (*ghana*) a cymbal and the hollow (*suṣira*) a flute.

The five kinds of Dhruvās

29-30. Songs which relate to Dhruvas are of five kinds: entering (*pravésa*), casual (*ākṣepa*), going out (*niṣkrama*), pleasing (*prāsādika*) and intermediate (*āntara*). And the playhouse is of the three types: oblong (*vikṛṣṭa*), square (*caturasra*) and triangular (*tryasra*)

31. So much about the Digest on drama giving its contents (lit. meaning by a small number of Sūtras (concise rules). I shall now speak about the contents of the Sūtra-work[1].

25-26. [1] *pravṛtti* — Haas translates this word as 'Local Characteristics', (See DR. p. 74). The five geographical names (Avanti, Dākṣhinātya, Oḍra, Magadha and Pañcāla) probably show that these were the parts of India where dramatic show was current at the time when tradition recorded in this NŚ, arose. Omission of the north-eastern part of India, including Bengal and Assam, probably shows that at that time these places were still in many respects outside the pale of Aryanized India. And the omission of the north-western India from this list may be explained on the assumption that it being on the way of the new immigrants who frequently poured into this country the formation of any established usage was difficult. For details about *pravṛttis* see NŚ.XIV. 36-56.

[2] *siddhi* (success) — For details about the Success see NŚ. XXVII. 1ff.

31. [1] The original of the next passage till the beginning of 33 is in prose.

The Sentiments explained

In that connexion I shall first of all explain the Sentiments (*rasa*). No meaning proceeds [from speech] without [any kind of] Sentiment. The Sentiment is produced (*rasa-niṣpattiḥ*) from a combination (*saṃyoga*)[2] of Determinants (*vibhāva*), Consequents (*anubhāva*) and Transitory States (*vyabhicāri-bhāva*). Is there any instance (*dṛṣṭānta*) [parallel to it]. [yes], it is said that, as taste (*rasa*) results from a combination of various spices, vegetables, and other articles[3], and as six tastes (*rasa*) are produced by articles such as, raw sugar or spices or vegetables, so the Dominant States (*sthāyibhava*), when they come together with various other States (*bhāva*) attain the quality of the Sentiment (*i.e.* become Sentiment). Now one enquires, 'What is the meaning of the word *rasa*"? It is said in reply to this [that rasa is so called] because it is capable of being tasted (*āsvādyate*). How is *rasa* tasted? [In reply] it is said that just as well-disposed persons while eating food cooked with many kinds of spices enjoy (*āsvādayanti*) its tastes (*rasa*) and attain pleasure and satisfaction, so the cultured people taste the Dominant States (*sthāyi-bhāva*) while they see them represented by an expression of the various States with Words, Gestures and the Temperament and derive pleasure and satisfaction. Thus is explained [the Memorial Verse ending with] *tasmān nātyarasā iti*[4]. For in this connexion there are two traditional couplets:

32-33. Just as connoisseur of cooked food (*bhakta*) while eating food which has been prepared from various spices and other articles, taste it, so the learned people taste in their mind the Dominant States (such as love, sorrow etc.) when they are represented by an expres sion of the States with Gestures. Hence these Dominant States in a drama are called the Sentiments.[1]

---

[2] The NŚ. nowhere explains the terms *niṣpatti* and *saṃyoga* of this definition and does not include the *sthāyibhāva* in it (the def.). Hence the theory of *rasa* has come to be interpreted differently in later times by Lollaṭa, Śankuka, (Bhaṭṭa) Nāyaka and Abhinavagupta. For a brief exposition of their views see Viṣṇupada Bhaṭṭācārya — Sāhityamimāṃsā (Bengali), Calcutta, 1948. pp. 33 ff.

[3] G. adds here one sentence more (*tathā..........niṣpattiḥ*).

[4] See below 33-34.

32-33. [1] For a discussion on Bharata's theory of *rasa* see Skt. Poetics, Vol.II. pp. 25 ff.

The relation between the Sentiments and the States

Now one enquires, "Do the States (*bhāva*) come out of the Sentiments (*rasa*) or the Sentiments come out the States?" On this point, some are of opinion that they arise from their mutual contact. But this is not so. Why?

"It is apparent that the Sentiments arise from the States and not the States from the Sentiments. For [on this point] there are [traditional] couplets such as:

34-35. The States are so called by experts in drama, for they cause to originate (*bhāvayanti*) the Sentiments in connexion with various modes of dramatic representation. Just as by many articles of various kinds auxiliary cooked food (*vyañjaña*) is brought forth, so the States along with different kinds of Histrionic Representation will cause the Sentiments to originate.

36. There can be no Sentiment prior to (lit. without) the States and no States without Sentiments [following it], and during the Histrionic Representation they are produced from their mutual relation.

37. Just as a combination of spices and vegetables imparts good taste to the food cooked, so the States and the Sentiments cause one another to originate (*bhāvayanti*).

38. Just as a tree grows from a seed, and flowers and fruits [including the seed] from a tree, so the Sentiments are the source (lit. root) of all the States, and likewise the States exist [as the source of all the Sentiments][1]

The eight Sentiments from the four original ones

Now we shall describe the origins, the colours, the [presiding] deities, and examples of these Sentiments. Sources of these (eight) Sentiments are the four[original]Sentiments *e.g.* Erotic, Furious, Heroic and Odious.[2]

---

38. [1] B adds one prose sentence more after this passage.

[2] The original of this passage till the beginning of 39 is in prose.

[3] Bhoja criticises this view of the author of the NŚ. in his Śr. Pr. See Ramaswamy Sastri Bh. P. Introduction p.28; V. Raghavan, Śr. Pr. 27.

39. The Comic [Sentiment] arises from the Erotic, the Pathetic from the Furious, the Marvellous from the Heroic, and the Terrible from the Odious.

40-41. A mimicry of the Erotic [Sentiment] is called the Comic, and the result of the Furious Sentiment is the Pathetic, and the result of the Heroic Sentiment is called the Marvellous, and that which is Odious to see results in the Terrible.

42-43. The Erotic Sentiment is light green (*śyāma*), the Comic Sentiment white, the pathetic (Sentiment) ash-coloured (*kapota,*) the Furious Sentiment red, the Heroic (Sentiment) light orange (*gaura*), the Terrible (Sentiment) black, the Odious (Sentiment) blue and the Marvellous (Sentiment) yellow.

The Presiding deities of the Sentiments

44-45. Viṣṇu is the god of the Erotic, Pramathas of the Comic, Rudra of the furious , Yama of the Pathetic, Siva (Mahā Kāla) of the Odious, Yama (Kāla) of the Terrible, Indra of the Heroic, and Brahman of the Marvellous Sentiments.

[1]Thus have been described the origins, the colours and the deities of these (Sentiments). Now we shall explain the Determinants (*vibhava*), the Consequents (*anubhāva*), the Transitory States (*vyabhicārin*), their combination, and their definitions and examples.

We shall now enumerate the Dominant States in different Sentiments.

The Erotic Sentiment

Of these, the Erotic (*śringāra*) Sentiment proceeds from the Dominant State of love (*rati*) and it has as its basis (lit. soul) a bright attire; for whatever in this world is white, pure, bright and beautiful is appreciated in terms of the Dominant State of love (*śringāra*). For example, one who is elegantly dressed is called a lovely person (śringarin). Just as persons are named, after the custom of their father or mother or family in accordance with the traditional authority, so the Sentiments, the States and other objects connected with drama are given names in pursuance of the custom and the

---

44-45. [1] The original of this passage till the beginning of 46, is in prose.

traditional authority. Hence the Erotic Sentiment has been so named on account of its usually being associated with a bright and elegant attire. It owes its origin to men and women and relates to the fullness of Youth. It has two bases: union (*sambhoga*) and separation (*vipralambha*), of these two, the Erotic Sentiment in union arises from Determinants like the pleasures of the season, the enjoyment of garlands, unguents, ornaments [the company of) beloved persons, objects (of senses), splendid mansions, going to a garden, and enjoying [oneself] there, seeing the [beloved one], hearing [his or her words], playing and dallying [with him or her]. It should be represented on the stage by Consequents such as clever movement of eyes, eyebrows, glances, soft and delicate movement of limbs and sweet words and similar other things. Transitory States in it do not include fear, indolence, cruelty and disgust. [The Erotic Sentiment] in separation should be represented on the stage by Consequents such as indifference, languor, fear, jealousy, fatigue, anxiety, yearning, drowsiness, sleep, dreaming awakening, illness, insanity, epilepsy, inactivity, [fainting], death and other conditions.

Now it has been asked, "If the Erotic Sentiment has its origin in love, why does it [sometimes] manifest itself through pathetic conditions?" [In reply to this] it is said, "It has been mentioned before that the Erotic Sentiment has its basis in union as well as in separation. Authorities on *ars amatoria* (*vaiśika-śāstra*) have mentioned ten conditions [of the persons separated from their beloved ones, which are pathetic], We shall discuss them in the chapter on the Common Histrionic Representation. The Pathetic Sentiment relates to a condition of despair owing to the affliction under a curse, separation from dear ones, loss of wealth, death or captivity, while the Erotic Sentiment based on separation relates to a condition of retaining optimism arising out of yearning and anxiety. Hence the Pathetic Sentiment, and the Erotic Sentiment in separation differ from each other. And this is the reason why the Erotic Sentiment includes conditions available in all other Sentiments.

46. And the Sentiment called Erotic is rich in pleasure, connected with desired objects, enjoyment of seasons, garlands and similar other things, and it relates to [the union of] man and woman.

There are besides two Āryas related to the preceding Sūtra:

47-48. The Erotic Sentiment arises in connexion with favourable seasons. garlands, ornaments, enjoyment of the company of beloved ones, music and poetry,and going to the garden and roaming there. It should be represented on the stage by means of serenity of the eyes and the face, sweet and smiling words, satisfaction and delight, and graceful movements of the limbs.

The Comic Sentiment

[1]Now the Comic (*hāsya*) Sentiment has as its basis the Dominant emotion of laughter. This is created by Determinants such as showing unseemly dress or ornament, impudence, greediness, quarrel, defective limb, use of irrelevant words, mentioning of different faults, and similar other things. This (the Comic Sentiment) is to be represented on the stage by Consequents like the throbbing of the lips, the nose and the cheek, opening the eyes wide or contracting them, perspiration, colour of the face, and taking hold of the sides. Transitory States in it are indolence, dissimulation, drowsiness, sleep, dreaming, insomnia, envy and the like. This (Sentiment), is of two kinds: self-centred and centred in others. When a person himself laughs it relates to the self-centred (Comic Sentiment), but when he makes others laugh it (the Comic Sentiment therein) is centred in others.

There are two traditional Āryās here:

49. As this makes one laugh by an exhibition of oddly placed ornaments, uncouth behaviour, words and dress and strange movement of limbs, it is called the Comic Sentiment.

50. As this makes persons laugh by means of uncouth behavior, words, movement of the limbs and strange dress, it is known as the Comic Sentiment.

51. This Sentiment is mostly to be seen in women and persons of the inferior type, and it has six varieties of which I shall speak presently.

52. They are: Slight Smile (*smita*), Smile (*hasita*), Gentle Laughter (*vihasita*), Laughter of Ridicule (upahasita), Vulgar Laughter (*apahasita*) and Excessive Laughter (*atihasita*). Two by two they belong respectively to the superior, the middling and the inferior types [of persons].

---

[1] The original of this passage till the beginning of 49 is in prose.

53. To persons of the superior type belong the Slight Smile (*smita*) and the Smile (hasita), to those of the middling type of Gentle Laughter (*vihasita*) and the Laughter of Ridicule (*upahasita*) to those of the inferior type the Vulgar Laughter (*apahasita*) and the Violent Laughter (*Atihasita*).

There are Ślokas on this subject:

54. The Slight smile (*smita*) of the people of the superior type should be characterised by slightly blown cheeks and elegant glances, and in it the teeth should not be visible.

55. Their Smile (*hasita*) should be distinguished by blooming eyes, face and cheeks, and in it the teeth should be slightly visible.

Of persons of the middle type

56. The Gentle Laughter (*vihasita*) should have slight sound, and sweetness, and should be suitable to the occasion and in it the eyes and the cheeks should be contracted and the face joyful.

57. During the Laughter of Ridicule (*upahasita*) the nose should be expanded, the eyes should be squinting, and the shoulder and the head should be bent.

Of persons of the inferior type

58. The laughter on occasions not suitable to it, the laughter with tears in one's eyes, or with the shoulder and the head violently shaking, is called the Vulgar Laughter (*apahasita*).

59. The Excessive Laughter (*atihasita*) is that in which the eyes are expanded and tearful, sound is loud and excessive, and the sides are covered by-hands.

60. Comic situations which may arise in the course of a play, for persons of the superior, middling or inferior type are thus to be given expression to.

61. This Comic Sentiment is of two kinds: self-centred and centred in others; and it relates to the three types of persons: superior, middling and inferior, and has thus [on the whole] six varieties.

The Pathetic Sentiment

[1]Now the Pathetic (*karuṇa*) Sentiment arises from the Dominant State of sorrow. It grows from Determinants such as affliction under a curse, separation from dear ones, loss of wealth, death, captivity, flight [from one's own place], [dangerous] accidents or any other misfortune. This is to be represented on the stage by means of Consequents such as, shedding tears, lamentation, dryness of the mouth, change of colour, drooping limbs, being out of breath, loss of memory and the like. Transitory States connected with it are indifference, languor, anxiety, yearning, excitement, delusion, fainting, sadness, dejection, illness, inactivity, insanity, epilepsy, fear, indolence, death, paralysis, tremor, change of colour, weeping, loss of voice and the like.

On this point there are two Āryās:

62. The Pathetic Sentiment arises from seeing the death of a beloved person, or from hearing something very unpleasant and these are its Determinants.

63. This is to be represented on the stage by Consequents like weeping loudly, fainting, lamenting and bewailing, exerting the body or striking it.

The Furious Sentiment

[1]Now the Furious (*raudra*) Sentiment has as its basis the Dominant State of anger. It owes its origin to Rākṣasas, Dānavas and haughty men, and is caused by fights. This is created by Determinants such as anger, rape, abuse, insult, untrue allegation, exorcizing, threatening, revengefulness, jealousy and the like. Its actions are beating, breaking, crushing, cutting, piercing, taking up arms, hurling of missiles, fighting, drawing of blood, and similar other deeds. This is to be represented on the stage by means of Consequents such as red eyes, knitting of eyebrows, defiance, biting of the lips, movement of the cheeks, pressing one hand with the other, and the like. Transitory States in it are presence of mind, determination, energy, indignation,

---

61. [1] The original of this passage till the beginning of 62 is in prose.

63. [1] The original of this passage till the beginning of 64 is in prose.

restlessness, fury, perspiration, trembling, horripilation, choking voice and the like.

Now one enquires, "Is it to be assumed from the [above] statement about Rākṣasas that they only give rise to the Furious Sentiment, and that this Sentiment does not relate to others?" [Reply] "No, in the case of others too this Sentiment may arise. [But in the case of Rākṣasas] it is to be understood as their special function. They are naturally furious,[2] for they have many arms, many mouths, standing and unkempt hairs of brown colour, and prodigious physical frame of black complexion. Whatever they attempt, be it their speech, movement of limbs are any other effort, is by nature furious. Even in their love-making they are violent[3]. It is to be easily inferred that persons who imitate them give rise to the Furious Sentiment from their fights and battles.

On these points there are two Āryās:

64. The Furious Sentiment is created by striking, cutting, mutilation and piercing in fights, and tumult of the battle and the like.

65. It should be represented on the stage by special acts such as the release of many missiles, cutting off the head, the trunk and the arms.

66. Such is the Furious Sentiment viewed [by experts];it is full of conflict of arms, and in it words, movements and deeds are terrible and fearful.

The Heroic Sentiment

[1]Now the Heroic (*vīra*) Sentiment, relates to the superior type of persons and has energy as its basis. This is created by Determinants such as presence of mind, perseverance, diplomacy, discipline, military strength, aggressiveness, reputation of might, influence and the like. It is to be represented on the stage by Consequents such as firmness, patience, heroism, charity, diplomacy and the like. Transitory States

---

[2] G. considers this passage till end of this sentence as an *āryā*

[3] Cf. Bhaṭṭikāvya, VIII. 98.

66. [1] The original of this passage till the beginning of 67 is in prose.

in it are contentment, judgement, pride agitation, energy (*vega*), ferocity, indignation, remembrance, horripilation and the like.

There are two Āryās [on these points]:

67. The Heroic Sentiment arises from energy, perseverance, optimism, absence of surprise, and presence of mind and [such other] special conditions [of the spirit].

68. This Heroic Sentiment is to be properly represented on the stage by firmness, patience, heroism, pride, energy, aggressiveness, influence and censuring words.

The Terrible Sentiment

[1]Now the Terrible (*bhayānaka*) Sentiment has as its basis the Dominant State of fear. This is created by Determinants like hideous noise, sight of ghosts, panic and anxiety due to [untimely cry of] jackals and owls, staying in an empty house or forest, sight of death or captivity of dear ones, or news of it, or discussion about it. It is to be represented on the stage by consequents such as trembling of the hands and the feet, horripilation, change of colour and loss of voice. Its Transitory States are paralysis, perspiration, choking voice, horripilation, trembling, loss of voice, change of colour, fear, stupefaction, dejection, agitation, restlessness, inactivity, fear, epilepsy and death and the like.

On these points there are two traditional Āryās:

69. The Terrible Sentiment is created by hideous noise, sight of ghosts, battle, entering an empty house or forest, offending one's superiors or the king.

70. Terror is characterised by looseness of the limbs, the mouth and the eyes, paralysis of the thighs, looking around with uneasiness, dryness of the drooping mouth, palpitation of the heart and horripilation.

71. This is [the character of] natural fear; the artificially shown fear also should be represented by these conditions. But in case of the feigned fear all efforts for its representation should be milder.

---

68. [1] The original of this passage till the beginning of 69 is in prose.

72. This Terrible Sentiment should be always represented by tremor of the hands and the feet, paralysis, shaking of the body, palpitation of the heart, dryness of the lips, the mouth, the palate and the throat.

The Odious Sentiment

[1]Now the Odious (*bībhatsa*) Sentiment has as its basis the Dominant State of disgust. It is created by Determinants like hearing of unpleasant, offensive, impure and harmful things or seeing them or discussing them. It is to be represented on the stage by Consequents such as stopping the movement of all the limbs, narrowing down of the mouth, vomiting, spitting, shaking the limbs [in disgust] and the like. Transitory States in it are epilepsy, delusion, agitation, fainting, sickness, death and the like.

On these points there are two traditional Āryās:

73. The Odious Sentiment arises in many ways from disgusting sight, tastes, smell, touch and sound which cause uneasiness.

74. This is to be represented on the stage by narrowing down the mouth and the eyes, covering the nose, bending down the head and walking imperceptibly.

The Marvellous Sentiment

[1]The Marvellous (*adbhuta*) Sentiment has as its basis the Dominant State of astonishment. It is created by Determinants such as sight of heavenly beings or events, attainment of desired objects, entrance into a superior mansion, temple, audience hall (*sabhā*), a seven-storied palace and [seeing] illusory and magical acts. It is to be represented on the stage by Consequents such as wide opening of eyes, looking with fixed gaze, horripilation, tears [of joy] perspiration, joy, uttering words of approbation, making gifts, crying incessantly hā, hā, hā, waving the end of *dhoti* or *sārī*, and movement of fingers and the like. Transitory States in it are weeping, paralysis, perspiration, choking voice, horripilation, agitation, hurry, inactivity, death and the like.

On this point there are two traditional Āryās;

---

72. [1] The original of this passage till the beginning of 73, is in prose.

[1] The original of this passage till the beginning of 75, is in prose.

75. The Marvellous Sentiment is that which arises from words character, deed and personal beauty.

76. This is to be represented on the stage by a gesture of feeling [sweet] smell, joyful shaking of limbs, and uttering of ha, ha, ha, sounds, speaking words of approbation, tremor; choking voice, perspiration and the like.

The three kinds of the Erotic, the Comic and the Terrible Sentiments

77. The Erotic Sentiment is of three kinds, viz, of words, dress, and action. And the Comic and the Terrible Sentiments are likewise of three kinds, viz, of limbs, dress and words.

The three kinds of the Pathetic Sentiment

78. The Pathetic Sentiment is of three kinds, viz. that arising from obstruction to lawful deeds, from loss of wealth and from bereavement.

The three kinds of the Heroic Sentiment

79. The Heroic Sentiment is likewise of three kinds, viz. that arising from making gifts, from doing one's duty (*dharma*) and from fighting [one's enemy].

The three kinds of the Terrible Sentiment

80. The Terrible Sentiment is also of three kinds, viz, feigned fear, fear from a wrong action, and fear from an apprehension of danger.

The three kinds of the Odious Sentiment

81. The Odious Sentiment is of three kinds, viz. nauseating, simple, and exciting. Of these the Sentiment from a sight of stool and worms is nauseating, and the sight of blood and similar objects is exciting.

The two kinds of the Marvellous Sentiment

82. The Marvellous Sentiment is of two kinds, viz. celestial and joyous. Or these the celestial is due to seeing heavenly sights, and the joyous due to joyful happenings.

83. These are the eight Sentiments and their definitions, I shall hereafter speak of the characteristics of the States.

2

From *Abhinava Bharati – I*

Abhinava Gupta

एतदुक्तं भवति–'एतादृशा वै रामादयो न कदाचन प्रमाणपथमवतार्यन्ते। यदागमेन वर्ण्यन्ते तदा तद्विशेषबुद्धिर्यद्यपि रामायणप्रायादेकस्मान्महावाक्यादुल्लसति, तथापि वर्तमानतयैव विशेषाणां सम्भाव्यमान अर्थक्रियासामर्थ्यात्मकस्वालक्षण्यपर्यवसानम्'। न च तेषां वर्तमानता इत्यपगता तावद्विशेषबुद्धिः।

कथास्वपि हृदय एव तावत् साधारणीभावो विभावादीनां जातः। तत्रापि कथामात्रे साधारणीभावः सम्भवति यद्यपि, तथापि 'एवं ये कुर्वन्ति तेषामेतद् भवति' इति वाक्यवद् रञ्जनातिशयाभावान्न चित्तवृत्तेनिमग्नता भवति।

काव्ये तु गुणालङ्कारमनोहरशब्दार्थशरीरे लोकोत्तररसप्राणके हृदयसंवादवशात् निमग्नाकारा तावद् भवति चित्तवृत्तिः। किन्तु सर्वस्य प्रत्यक्षसाक्षात्कारकल्पा तत्र न धीरूदेति।

नाट्ये तु–पारमार्थिकं किञ्चिदद्य मे कृत्यं भविष्यति इत्येवम्भूताभिसन्धिसंस्काराभावात् सर्वपरिषत्साधारणप्रमोदसारापर्यन्तसरसत्वेन आदरणीयलोकोत्तरदर्शनश्रवणयोगी भविष्यामि इत्यभिसन्धिसंस्कारात्, उचितगीतातोद्यचवर्णाविस्मृतसांसारिकभावतया विमलमुकुरकल्पीभूतनिजहृदयः 'सूत्रधाराद्यभिनयावलोकनोद्भिन्नप्रमोदशोकादितन्मयीभावः, पाठ्याकर्णन–पात्रान्तरप्रवेशवशात् समुत्पन्ने देशकालविशेषावेशानालिङ्गिनि सम्यङ-मिथ्या-संशय-सम्भावनादिज्ञानविज्ञेयत्वपरामर्शानास्पदे रामरावणादिविषयाध्यवसाये, तत्संस्कारानुवृत्तिकारणभूततत्सहचरहृद्यवस्तुरूपगीतातोद्यप्रमदा–

नुभवसंस्कारसूचितसमनुगततदुक्तरूपरामाध्यवसायसंस्कार एव भवन् सचमत्कारतदीयचरितमध्यप्रविष्ट - स्वात्मरूपमतिः स्वात्मद्वारेण विश्वं तथा पश्यन्, प्रत्येकंसामाजिकोदेशकालविशेषणापरामर्शेन, एवं कारिणामिदं इति 'लीढात्मकविधिसमर्पितं संविज्जातीयमेव संविद्विशेषरञ्जक प्राणवल्लभाप्रतिम - रसास्वादसहचर - रम्यगीतातोद्यादिसंस्कार - वशेन हृदयाभ्यन्तरनिखातं तत 'एवोत्पुङ्खशतैरपि म्लानिमात्रमप्यभजमानं भजन्, तत्तच्छुभाशुभप्रेप्साजिहासासततस्यूतवृत्तित्वादेव शुभमाचरत्यशुभं समुज्झति। इदानीमुपायसंवेदनालाभात्।

These personages i.e., Rāma, etc., have never descended into the sphere of our means of knowledge. When these [Rāma, etc.,] are described in the scriptures, even if the idea of the particularity of each of them (*tadviśeṣabuddhi*) arises from a Great Sentence such as the Rāmāyaṇa, etc., nevertheless, only when these are [felt as] contemporary (*vartamāna*), do they amount to a real individuality (*svālakṣaṇya*) animated by the power (*sāmarthya*) of a corresponding Causal Efficiency (*arthakriyā*). Now, this contemporaneity does not exist and therefore there is no contradiction in the idea of their particularity (personality) being accepted in drama.[1] This state of generality of the Determinants, etc.,

---

[1] a) The perception of the particular names and shapes of Rāma, etc., (therefore of their qualification of time, space, etc.), does not involve that they cannot be perceived in a generalised form. A personality, etc., inserts itself into our practical life (develops, so to say, his Causal Efficiency) only when it is contemporary with us, i.e., connected with the present and therefore with the practical interests, etc., of our own Ego. When these personalities are not contemporary they cannot develop their natural Causal Efficiency. In the aesthetic perception, they are independent from the concepts both of reality and non reality and are thus perceived as "generalized". In this sense, their particularity (*viseṣa*) is not contrasting with the concept of generality.

(Continued...)

occurs also in proper poems; in this case, it penetrates directly into the heart.[1] Even if this state of generality can also occur in mere tales (*kath ā m ā tre*), nevertheless in this case (cf. for example the sentence, "Such-and-such happens to people who do so-and-so") it has only a weak power of colouring and therefore the corresponding mental movement does not obtain a state of conviction (*nirnaya*). But owing to the consent of the heart every mental movement remains completely submersed, in the case of a poem (let us remember that poetry is made up of words embellished by Qualities and Ornaments and consists of, and is animated by, a Rasa of a non ordinary nature).[2] Not in every person, however, does arise through poetry an idea similar to a direct perception. In drama this difficulty does not arise.[3] [What is the true nature of drama?] In drama there is the absence of the mental trace of the intention, 'Today I must do something practical', and the presence, in its place, of the intention. 'Today I am going to enjoy venerable sights and sounds of a non-ordinary character, which arouse, in the end, a state of freedom from wordly interests[4] and whose essence is

---

[1](...Continued)

b) In this context, *sv ā laksanya* is simply a synonym of *svar ū pa*, one's own form or shape, one's own peculiar nature and thus individuality, etc. *Sv ā laksanya* is commented on by A.G. in this way in the *Dh. A .L.*, p.538. The Causal Efficiency (*arthakriy ā* ; on this concept, cf. p. 36, n.7) in the sense of practical or pragmatical functionality belongs to the real individuality (*i.e.*, contemporary with the spectator) only. The generalized image of the aesthetic experience has no practical efficiency, *i.e.*, does not insert itself in practical life. The concept of Causal Efficiency in connexion with the one of individuality (in the sense of a particular essence contrasting with the general essence, the *s ā m ā nyalaksana*) has a Buddhist origin and, freely interpreted, became part of the common philosophical vocabulary.

2 Cf. *supra*, p. 54

3 Some individuals whose aesthetic sensibility (consent of the heart, etc.) is poor need visual illustration of what is suggested by the power of the poem; such visual illustration (consisting of the actors, etc.) contributes to bring about the immersion of the spectator in the events represented to the exclusion of everything else. Cf. *supra*, p. 84, n. 3.

4 The type of drama to which A.G. refers in these lines in the *n ā tya*, which is, in general, inspired by the fact and personages taken from the *Mah ā bh ā rata* and the *R ā m ā yana*. A.G. observes that the murders, deaths and tragical occurrences

(continued...)

genreralized pleasure shared by all the spectators'. During the spectacle, the spectator forgets about the *sams a rika* existence and immerses himself in the Tasting of the vocal and instrumental music which accompanies the play being acted.[1] The heart of such a spectator has, of course, to be as clear as a spotless mirror; only if it is, will he be able to identify himself with the mental states of Sorrow, Delight, etc., aroused by the sight of the [four species of] Representation (gesticulation, etc.,). By listening to the play which is being performed the spectator enters into the life of a character different from himself, and, for this reason, there grows up in him a cognition whose object is R a ma, R a vana, etc.[2] This cognition is not circumscribed by space and time and is free from all notion of the things which are the matter of real, mistaken, uncertain, probable, etc., forms of knowledge. The spectator is accompanied by the impressions of this cognition (whose object is R a ma, etc.,) for several days; they are evidenced, in their turn, by impressions of the direct perception of the vocal and instrumental music and of the images of the women. These pleasure-producing things accompanying the spectacle are themselves the cause of the continuation of these impressions. The spectator, whose awareness of his own self (*sv a tmar u pa = svar u pa*, identity, etc.,) is lost in the events represented endowed with *camatk a ra*, continues, by means of his own self to see everything in this light.[3] The spectators, therefore, remain in possession of a particular form of consciousness afforded to them by the following affirmation, which

[4](...continued)
which are recounted, f.i., in the Mah a bh a rata give the reader a feeling of the vanity of human life (cf. *Dh. A .L.*, p. 530: *yadyapi dharm a rthak a m a n a m sarvasvam t a drñ n a sti yad anyatra navidyate, tath a piparyantavirasatvam atraivavalokyat a m).*

1 Colouring power (*ra n jakatva*) *par excellence* belongs to the music accompanying the performance of the play.

2 In other words, the spectator lives the life of the characters represented (R a ma, R a vana, etc.).

3 Cf. *Mrcchaka tik a* , III, 5: *yat satyam virate 'pi gitasamaye gacch a mi srnvanniva.* "To tell the truth, although the song is ended, I seem to hear it as I walk."

remains, as it were, on their lips to be licked and tasted (*liḍhātmaka*)[1]: 'Such-and-such happens to people who do so-and-so'. This form of consciousness is free of every spatial and temporal specificaion. By virtue of the perception of Rasa, aroused by the traces of all the pleasure-producing things — vocal and instrumental music, etc., — which accompany its Tasting (Rasa colours the consciousness in a special way, differing from that of the heart's beloved), this form of consciousness remains deeply fixed in the heart, like an arrow, in such a way that by no possible effort can it be disregarded, let alone extracted.[2]

Thus the subject who enjoys it (and this happens simply because the mind is naturally desirous of attaining to the good and abandoning the bad) does good and avoids evil.[3]

---

1 Cf. the verse quoted in the *Rasapradipa* by Prabhākara Bhaṭṭa, Benares 1925: *sāmājikās tu lihate rasam pātram naṭo mataḥ*

2 I have not been able to find the word *utpunkha* in any dictionary. The sense, however,shows, without any possibility of doubt, that *utpunkha* is a synonym of *utpāṭana*, which denotes the act of extracting an arrow (*punkha* is the shaft or feathered part of an arrow). The same expression is to be found in the *Ī.P.V.V.*, I, p. 37: *prasiddhiśatapūrṇe jivaloke kasyacit kācid eva prasiddhiḥ "lineva pratibimbiteva likhitevāntarnikhāteva ca (Mālatimādhava,* 5, 10)" *iti nyāyena hṛdayabhittau utpāṭanaśatair api hṛdayam anunmūlya nāpasarpati.*

3 A.G. accepts the traditional Indian view of art as a means of instruction, but tends to give the word instruction a meaning of his own. Such instruction, according to A.G. is of a different character from any other, and of an unmistakable nature. *DhĀ.L.*, p. 190: *vyutpādanaṃ ca śāsanapratipādanābhyāṃ śāstretihāsakṛtābhyāṃ vilakṣaṇam yathā rāmas tathāham ityupamānātiriktām rasāsvādopāyasvapratibhāvijṛmbhārupām vyutpattim ante karotiti kam upālabhāmahe* "The knowledge imparted by poetry differs from the injunctions and instruction of religious treatises and historical narrative. However, if it is meant that poetry ultimately produces instruction consisting in the enrichment of one's aesthetic sensibility (this being the instrument which allows of the tasting of Rasa), different from ordinary analogy (as with Rāma, so with me), we have no objection to make." *A.Bh.*, I, p. 41: *nanu kiṃ guruvad upadeśaṃ karoti, netyāha, kintu buddhiṃ vivardhayati, svapratibhām evam tādṛśam vitarati.* Elsewhere (*DhĀ.l.*, p. 40) A.G. says that the principal element is not knowledge (for in that case there would be confusion with works on ethics and historiography) but pleasure (*priti, ānanda*). The pleasure and knowledge, both *sui generis*, aroused by poetry are not distinct from each other but two aspects of the same thing (*na caite pritivyutpattibhinnarūpe eva, dvayor apy ekaviṣayatvāt*, *DhĀ.L.*, p. 336).

3

From *Abhinava Bharati – II*

Abhinava Gupta

आम्नायसिद्धे किमपूर्वमेतत्संविद्विकासेऽधिगतागमित्वम् ।
इत्थं स्वयंग्राह्यमहार्हहेतुद्वन्द्वेन किं दूषयिता न लोकः ।।
ऊर्ध्वोर्ध्वमारुह्य यदर्थतत्त्वं धीः पश्यति श्रान्तिमवेदयन्ती ।
फलं तदाद्यैः परिकल्पितानां विवेकसोपानपरम्पराणाम् ।।
चित्रं निरालम्बनमेव मन्ये प्रमेयसिद्धौ प्रथमावतारम् ।
सन्मार्गलाभे सति सेतुबन्धपुरप्रतिष्ठादि न विस्मयाय ।।
तस्मात्सतामत्र न दूषितानि मतानि तान्येव तु शोधितानि ।
पूर्वप्रतिष्ठापितयोजनासु मूलप्रतिष्ठाफलमामनन्ति ।।

तर्ह्युच्यतां परिशुद्धतत्त्वम् ।

उक्तमेव मुनिना न त्वपूर्वं किञ्चित्। तथाह्याह – "काव्यार्थान् भावयन्ति" इति (ना.शा.अ – ७) तत्काव्यार्थो रसः।

यथा हि 'रात्रिमासत। * 'तामग्नौ प्रादात्' इत्यादावर्थितादिलक्षितस्याधिकारिणः प्रतिपत्तिमात्रादतितीव्रप्ररोचितात्प्रथमवृत्तादनन्तरमधिकैवोपात्तकालतिरस्कारेणैवास्ते (से) प्रददानीत्यादिरूपा संक्रमणादिस्वभावा यथादर्शनं प्रतिभाभावनाविध्युद्योगादिभाषाभिर्व्यवहृता प्रतिपत्तिस्तथैव काव्यात्मकादपि शब्दादधिकारिणोऽधिकाऽस्ति प्रतिपत्तिः ।

अधिकारी चात्र विमलप्रतिभानशालिहृदयः। तस्य च "ग्रीवाभङ्गाभिरामम्।" इति (शाकु. अ.२) "उमापि नीलालक" इति (कुमा-३.६२) 'हरस्तु किञ्चित' (कुमा-३.६७) इत्यादिवाक्येभ्यो वाक्यार्थप्रतिपत्तेरनन्तरं मानसी साक्षात्कारात्मिकाऽपहसिततत्तद-

वाक्योपात्तकालादिविभागा तावत्प्रतीतिरुपजायते। तस्यां च यो मृगपोतकादिर्भाति तस्य विशेषरूपत्वाभावाद्भीत इति त्रासकस्यापारमार्थिकत्वाद्भयमेव परं देशकालाद्यनालिङ्गितम्। तत एव 'भीतोऽहं भीतोऽयं शत्रुर्वयस्यो मध्यस्थो वा' इत्यादिप्रत्ययेभ्यो दुःखसुखादिकृतहानादिबुध्यन्तरोदयनियमवत् तया विघ्नबहुलेभ्यो विलक्षणं निर्विघ्नप्रतीतिग्राह्यं साक्षादिव हृदये निविशमानं चक्षुषोरिव विपरिवर्तमानं भयानको रसः। तथाविधे हि भये नात्माऽत्यन्ततिरस्कृतो न विशेषत उल्लिखितः।

एवं परोऽपि। तत एव न परिमितमेव साधारण्यम्। अपि तु विततम्। व्याप्तिग्रह इव धूमाग्न्योः। भयकम्पयोरेव वा तदत्र साक्षात्कारायमाणत्वे परिपोषिका नटादिसामग्री। यस्यां वस्तुसतां काव्यार्पितानां च देशकालप्रमात्रादीनां नियमहेतूनामन्योन्यप्रतिबन्धबलादत्यन्तमपसरणे स एव साधारणीभावः सुतरां पुष्यति। अत एव सर्वसामाजिकानामेकघनतयैव प्रतिपत्तेः (त्तिः) सुतरां रसपरिपोषाय। सर्वेषामनादिवासनाचित्रीकृतचेतसां वासनासंवादात्। सा चाविघ्ना संवित्। चमत्कारस्तज्जोऽपि कम्पपुलकोल्लुकसनादिर्विकारः। चमत्कारो यथा–

"अज्ज वि हरी चमक्कइ कहविण मंदरेण दळिआइं।
चंदकळादळसच्छीआइं ळच्छीए अंगाइं॥"

तथा हि–स चातृप्तिव्यतिरेकेणाविच्छिन्नो भोगावेश इत्युच्यते। भुञ्जानस्याद्भुतभोगस्पन्दाविष्टस्य च मनःकरणं चमत्कार इति। स च साक्षात्कारस्वभावो मानसोऽध्यवसायो वा सङ्कल्पो वा स्मृतिर्वा तथात्वेन स्फुरत्य(न्न)स्तु। यदाह

"रम्याणि वीक्ष्य मधुरांश्च निशम्य शब्दान्-
पर्युत्सुको भवति यत्सुखितोऽपि जन्तुः।

तच्चेतसा स्मरति नूनमबोधपूर्वं
भावस्थिराणि जननान्तरसौहृदानि ।। "(शाकु. ५–) इत्यादि ।

(अत्र हि स्मरतीति या स्मृतिरुपदर्शिता सा न तार्किकप्रसिद्धा। पूर्वमेतस्यार्थस्याननुभूतत्वात्। अपि तु प्रतिमानापरपर्यायसाक्षात्कारस्वभावेयमिति।) सर्वथा तावदेषास्ति प्रतीतिरास्वादात्मा यस्यां रतिरेव भाति। तत एव विशेषान्तरानुपहितत्वात्सा रसनीया सती न लौकिकी न मिथ्या नानिर्वाच्या न लौकिकतुल्या न तदारोपादिरूपा। तथैव चोपचयावस्थासु देशाद्यनियन्त्रणादनुकारोऽप्यस्तु। भावानुगामितया करणात् विषय सामग्र्यपि भवतु विज्ञानवादावलम्बनात्। सर्वथा रसनात्मकवीतविघ्नप्रतीतिग्राह्यो भाव एव रसः।

तत्र विघ्नापसारका विभावप्रभृतयः। तथा हि–लोके सकलविघ्नविनिमुक्ता संवित्तिरेव चमत्कारनिर्वेशरसनास्वादनभोगसमापत्ति लयविश्रान्त्यादिशब्दैरभिधीयते। विघ्नाश्चास्यां प्रतिपत्तावयोग्यता–संभावनाविरहो नाम स्वगतत्वपरगतत्वनियमेन देशकालविशेषावेशो निजसुखादिविवशीभावः प्रतीत्युपायवैकल्यं स्फुटत्वाभावो अप्रधानता संशययोगश्च।

तथाहि–संवेद्यमसंभावयमानः संवेद्ये संविदं विनिवेशयितुमेव (यो) न शक्नोति का तत्र विश्रान्तिरिति प्रथमो विघ्नः। तदपसारणे हृदयसंवादो लोकसामान्यवस्तुविषयः। अलोकमान्येषु तु चेष्टितेष्वखण्डितप्रसिद्धिजनितगाढारूढप्रत्ययप्रसरकारी प्रख्यातरामादिनामधेयपरिग्रहः। अत एव निस्सामान्योत्कर्षोपदेशव्युत्पत्तिप्रयोजने नाटकादौ प्रख्यातवस्तुविषयत्वादि नियमेन निरूपयिष्यते। न तु प्रहसनादाविव। तच्च स्वावसर एव वक्ष्याम इत्यास्तां तावत्।

What shall we do?

Why repeat truths disclosed already in the Thought handed down by Tradition and thus behave as no one has behaved before? This double, serious and indissimulable error will certainly be imputed to me by audience.

Tireless, the mind of man climbs ever higher to gaze on truth. What is the point of dwelling on the doctrines which have succeeded each other on the ladder of thought?

The first attempts to establish the reality of things are, I suppose, doubtful and vacillating: but as we advance doggedly along this road, we cease to be amazed by built bridges, city foundations, or anything else.

A rich and fruitful harvest may be culled by posterity from the inheritance of thought left to it by its predecessors. Thus the doctrines of the sages of antiquity will only be refined by us here and not refuted.

Let us then state what is the true nature of Rasa purified of previous mistakes. It has already been stated by Bharata, and we shall add nothing new. For he has said "The mental states are called *bhāva*, because they bring into existence (*bhāv*) the essence of poetry". Thus Rasa is simply the essence of poetry. That is to say, immediately after the first perception of the literal sense of the following expressions. "They lay by night," "He gave it (*scil.*, the omentum) to the fire"[1], there occurs (in a qualified person (*adhikārin*), characterised by a certain pragmatic requirement (*arthitā*), etc., and possessed of a keen interest in the object of perception involved) a second perception eliminating the temporal data, etc., contained in the first. This second perception consists in a transfer (*saṃkramaṇa*), etc., of the literal sense and is presented in the form: "I give", etc. According to different systems, this perception is called propulsion (*bhavanā*), command (*vidhi*), order (*niyoga*), etc.[2]. A similar

---

1 Two quotations taken from revelation (*śruti*) (from the Taittiriya Brāhmaṇa?). Cf. p. 64, n. 1.

2 In other words, some scriptural sentences (*e.g.*, those quoted) awaken in the believer the need to give the omentum to the fire himself, etc. In this sense, their literal meaning undergoes a transformation: the past tense and the third person, etc.,

(continued...)

thing may be said to happen in the case of poetry: there occurs in a qualified person a perception transcending the words of the poem. The qualified person is in this case any person whose heart possesses a mirror-like power of intuition (*pratibhāna*)[1]. In such a person

---

[2](...continued)
used in these sentences are turned into the present tense, etc. There arises in the heart of the believer the form of consciousness (*pratipatti*), "I give the omentum to the fire", etc. This passing from one sense to another is given the names of propulsion (*bhāvanā*), order and command (*vidhi, niyoga*). The terms *bhāvanā, vidhi,* and *niyoga*, are proper to the liturgical speculations of *mimāṃsā* (the term *bhāvanā* used by Bhaṭṭa Nāyaka was probably taken from the terminology of the *pūrvamimāṃsā*). The terms *vidhi* and *niyoga*, observes J., *T.Ā.*, I, p. 167, are used above all by the followers of Prabhākara; Kumārila's disciples prefer instead the word *bhāvanā*. The shift of sense involved, of course, presupposes the adherence of the subject to the sacred writings, his desire to attain certain ends, etc. This shift of sense is clearly explained in three *śloka* quoted by H.C.., p. 98 (surely taken from a work on poetics earlier than A.G., perhaps the *Hṛdayadarpaṇa of Bhaṭṭa Nāyaka*).

"In the sentences 'Śamba regained his health when he praised the Sun God', etc., there occurs at first the perception of their literal sense, and then (and on this there is no matter of doubt) there arises in the mind of the perceiving subject a perception which eliminates the temporal data, etc., assumed by the sentence in question. This perception is presented in the following form: 'Everyone who praises the Sun regains his health; so I too will praise the Sun, so as to free myself from disease'". Cf. *I.P.V.V.*, I. p. 24; *I.P.V.*, I. p. 27.

1 a) Not everybody, A.G. observes, has the intrinsic capacity to taste a poem. Individuals possessed of aesthetic sensibility are called possessed of heart, those who have the consent of the heart (*sahṛdaya, hṛdayasaṃvādabhāk*). The fact of being possessed of heart is defined in the following way (*Dh.A.L.*, p. 38):

"The faculty of self-identification with the events represented (the Determinants, etc.,) demands that the mirror of the mind should be made completely clear, by means of repeated acquaintance with and practice of poetry. The possessed of heart, those who possess the consent of their own hearts, are these who have this faculty. For it has been said: 'the tasting of that which finds the consent of the heart arouses the Rasa. The body is pervaded by it, as dry wood by the fire'". The mind and heart must be mirror-like (*viśada, vimala*), ready to receive all the images which are reflected in them: *vimalamukurakalpibhūtanijahṛdayaḥ*, *A.Bh.*, p. 37. In the *T.Ā.*, III, 200, A.G. says:

"When the ears are filled with the sound of sweet song or the *nostrils* with the *scent* of sandal-wood, etc., the state of indifference (non-participation, impersonality, etc.), disappears and the heart is invaded by a state of vibration (*spandamānatā*; for the significance of the term *spanda*, cf. p. 74, n. 1). Such a state is precisely the so-called power of beatitude, thanks to which man is 'gifted with heart'". According to

(continued...)

hearing the following phrases, "There he (*scil.*, the deer) is now, gracefully by the bending of his neck ..."[1], "Even Umā, dropping the golden *karṇikāra* ..."[2] "The firmness of Hara ..."[3], there appears, immediately after the perception of their literal sense, a perception of a different order (an inner (*mānasi*) perception, consisting in a

---

[1](...continued)
the śaiva of Kashmir, heart is consciousness itself, thought, beatitude, etc. (cf. p. 87, n.2).

Elsewhere (*A.Bh.*, II, p. 339), A.G. says that poetic sensibility is the faculty of entering into identity with the heart of the poet (*kavihṛdayatādātmyāpattiyogyatā*). Of course, people whose nature is "gentle (*sukumāra*)" will have a greater feeling for erotic poetry; people of bolder nature will [sic] heroic poetry, etc. Every individual has a particular nature (tendencies, innate instincts, beginningless root desires, *vāsanā*), according to which he will feel himself more drawn to some poets than to others. "Sensibility" (*sahṛdayatva*) also plays an important role in religious experience, but in this case we may not talk of aesthetic sensibility, the more correct term being religious sensibility; cf. *P.T.V.*, p. 45 ff.

b) The word *pratibhāna* (= *pratibhā*) has the double sense of creative imagination, artistic genius, inspiration (*kārayitri pratibhā*) and of aesthetic sensibility, of consent of the heart conceived in the terms of an active power which permits the manifestation of Rasa (*bhāvayitri pratibhā*). In this case, *pratibhā* is just used in this very sense. I translate: power of intuition. The division of the concept of *pratibhā* in *kārayitri pratibhā* (creative intuition and intelligence) and in *bhāvayitri pratibhā* (contemplating intuition has first been explicitly stated by Rājaśekhara, *Kāvyamimāṃsā, IV.*) *Pratibhā* means also intuitive cognition, etc., cf. p. 58, n. 3.

1 Kālidāsa, *Abhijñānaśakuntalā*, I, 2: "There he (*scil.*, the deer) is now, gracefully by the bending of his neck casting a glance ever and anon at the chariot which pursues him, by (the contraction of) the hinder half (of his body repeatedly drawing himself into the fore (part of his) body through fear of the descent of the arrow; strewing the road with grass half-chewed which drops from his mouth kept open from exhaustion. See! by reason of his lofty boundings he goes chiefly in the air, and little on the ground" (Monier Williams, *Śakuntalā*, Hertford, 1853, p. 9).

2 Kālidāsa, *Kumārasaṃbhava*, III, 62: "Even Umā, dropping the golden *Karṇikāra* flowers which glowed among her black tresses, deeply bowed her head (while the flowers which adorned them fell from her ears) before Śiva".

3 *Op. cit.*, III, 67: "The firmness of Hara, even, was somewhat shaken – like the sea when the moon is just about to rise; he cast his eyes in desire towards the face of Umā, towards her lips, red as the fruit of the *bimba*".

direct experience (*sākṣātāra*)[1] which completely eliminates the temporal distinctions, etc., assumed by these sentences. In fact, the young deer, etc., which appears in this perception is devoid of its particularity (*viśeṣa*), and at the same time, the actor, who, (playing the role of the deer,) frightens (the spectators) (*trāsaka* ...), showing to be afraid, is unreal (*apāramārthika*). As a result, what there appears in simply and solely Fear — Fear in itself, uncircumscribed by time, space, etc.[2]. This perception of Fear is of a different order from the ordinary perceptions ("I am afraid, he — my enemy, my friend, anybody — is afraid"); for these are necessarily affected by the appearance of fresh mental movements (of shunning, etc.)[3], consisting of pleasure, pain, etc., and just for this reason are full of obstacles (*vighna*). The sensation of the Fear above mentioned, on

1 Like the sensations of pleasure, pain, etc., aesthetic experience is an inner or mental perception (*mānasapratyakṣa*, *i.e.*, it is perceived through the mind or inner sense. Such a perception is self-knowing (*svasaṃvedanasiddha*). In the *A.Bh.*, p. 291, A.G. observes that the fact of tasting (*āsvādana*; aesthetic perception being conceived as a particular form of tasting) is of a mental order: it differs from the fact o eating, which is a purely material act (*rasanavyāpārād bhojanād adhiko yo mānaso vyāpāraḥ sa evāsvādanam*). The mind of he who tastes must be *ekāgra*, absorbed in the object of the tasting to the exclusion of all else. On the contrary, he who eats may be also *anyacitta*: he can also think of other things, etc. Aesthetic tasting is of a non-ordinary nature (*alaukika*), *sui generis*, cf. *infra*, with reference to the concept of beatitude, p. 87, n. 2. The mind is the organ of tasting; during the tasting the mind must be free of all obstacles, devoid, that is to say, of any other sensory perceptions, etc. The subject is immersed in a *camatkāra* set apart from any distinctions of "self" or "others". Aesthetic tasting is a "generalised" perception and free, therefore, of obstacles (in the *A.Bh.*, I, p. 291 the expression *āsvādāyanti manasā*, *N.Ś.*, VI, v. 36, is commented upon in the following manner: *ā samantāt sādhāraṇībhāvena nirvighnapratipattivaśān manasā indriyāntaravighnasaṃbhāvanāśūnyena svādayanti svaparavivekaśūnyasvādacamatkāraparavaśā. ...*).

2 In other words, the spectator (and hence the state of consciousness by which he is pervaded) is not in the real time and space either of the deer or of the actor as such. In aesthetic experience, these two temporal and spatial orders cancel each other out. On the one hand, therefore, the deer, etc., is without any temporal or spatial determination (viz. it is not felt as an element of ordinary life but is perceived in a generalised form); similarly, the actor and hence the impression of fear which he suggests is not perceived as a constituent element of practical life. The state of consciousness which does occur is, therefore, unaffected by space and time; it is a generalized Permanent Mental State, a Rasa.

3 "Shunning, etc.", *i.e.*, shunning, accepting and disregarding.

the contrary, is the matter of cognition by a perception devoid of obstacles (*nirvighna*), and may be said to enter directly (*niviś*) into our hearts, to dance (*viparivṛt*)[1] before our eyes: this is the Terrible Rasa. In such a Fear, one's own Self is found to be in a state neither of complete occultation (*tiraskṛ*) nor of particular emergence (*ullikh*)[2]; and the same thing happens with the other Selves. As a result of this, the state of generality involved is not limited, (*parimita*), but extended (*vitata*) — as happens at the moment in which is formed the idea of the invariable concomitance (*vyāpti*) between smoke and fire or, in fact, between trembling and fear[3]. The

---

1 *Viparivrt* signifies to move, to vibrate in various ways, to revolve, etc. A.G. comments on the word *viparivartamānasya* in the following way (*I.P.V.*, II, p. 140): *vicitratvenā viśvasya bhedābhedātmanā parivartamānasya spandanena sphurato* ...

2 In first case there would not be aesthetic cognition, but mystical cognition, characterized by the total absence of discursive thought and distinct apprehensions (*vikalpa*). In the second case ordinary discursive cognition would occur. Cf. pp. 100, ff.

3 The best explanation of this passage is to be found in *I.P.V.*, II, 4, 12:

"But, according to this system, at the time of forming the idea of invariable concomitance, the images of smoke and fire are common to all perceivers, who can possibly have their existence at that place (*i.e.*, in the kitchen, etc.), as according to those who admit the existence of an external objective world. For, in relation to these images, the Lord (*i.e.*, Iśvara, the unlimited Ego, etc. has made the subjects one". In other words two or more subjects which see the same thing are in the same psychic condition, etc., *i.e.*, they form a single knowing subject. Such a conception is in contradiction to the doctrine of the *vijñānavādin*, who maintain that mental series (*saṃtāna*) *are independent one of the other* (*I.P.V.*, I, 5, 4-5). During the aesthetic experience, the practical "personalities" of the spectators, different each from the other, are momentarily eliminated; to these there succeeds a state of consciousness, a "knowing subject" which is unique, "generalised", not circumscribed by any determination of space, time, etc. Rasa, aesthetic pleasure, is simply this new state fo cinsciousness. A.G. observes that the pleasure given by a spectacle increases when there are a large number of spectators. In other words, when each spectator is conscious that the spectacle is being seen at the same time by a number of other people. *T.Ā.*, X, v. 85 ff.:

"The spectators who watch, absorbed, a spectacle of dancing, of singing, etc., feel that it is a real sea of nectar (J. comments: "anyone, in fact, can observe that spectacles seen by many people at the same time generate a greater pleasure than those which are seen by a single individual). It is for this reason that those who teach the true nature of spectacles of wrestling and acting, say that, in these, a real state of

(continued...)

combination of actors etc., thus serves to nourish (*paripus*) the sensation of having the event represented directly in front of one

---

[3](...continued)
identity of all knowing subjects takes place; this state generates a perception of a full and perfect beatitude. If the mere consciousness of what they see on the stage (without, that is, the realisation that the spectacle is seen by other people) were sufficient to satisfy the spectators taken one by one, how then can the different state of consciousness, which arises when they are together, be explained? And how could it still be sustained that a state of identity of knowing subjects exists? When, instead, the spectator is aware that the spectacle is seen at the same time by all the others also, one can say with reason that it appears in a different form from the arid aspect it had before (this spectacle, then, observes J., takes on another nature which generates a very high *camatk ā ra*)".

The annullment of every distinction between one's own Self and the Self of other people, and the actuation of a generalised state of consciousness also occurs, observed A.G., during certain religious ceremonies (for example, the tantric *cakra*), which must be celebrated in common. *T.A*., XXVIII, v. 373 ff.:

"The consciousness, which consists of, and is animated by, all things, on account of the difference of bodies, enters into a state of contraction. But, in public celebrations, it returns to a state of expansion since all the components are reflected in each other. The flow of one's own consciousness in ebullition (*i.e.* when it is tending to come out of itself) is reflected in the consciousness of all the bystanders, as if in so many mirrors, and, inflamed by these, it abandons without effort its state of individual contraction. Just for this reason, in meetings of many people (at a spectacle of dancers, singers, etc.), fullness of joy occurs when every bystander, not only one of them, is identified witht he spectacle. The consciousness, which, considered separately also, is innatedly (sic) made up of beatitude, reaches, in these circumstances during the execution of dances, etc. a state of unity, and so enters into a state of beatitude which is full and perfect. In virtue of the absence of any cause for contraction, jealousy, envy, etc. (the causes of contraction are the *vighna*, obstacles; cf. pp. 77 ff.) the consciousness finds itself, in these circumstances, in a state of expansion, free of obstacles, and pervaded by beatitude. When, on the other hand, one of the bystanders does not concentrate on the spectacle he is looking at, and does not share, therefore, the form of consciousness in which the other spectators are immersed, this consciousness is disturbed, as at the touch of an uneven surface. This is the reason why, during the celebration of the *cakra*, etc., no individual must be allowed to enter who does not identify himself with the ceremonies and so does not share the state of consciousness of the celebrants; this would cause, in fact, a contraction of the consciousness".

Everything, observes J., *T.A*., IX, p. 133, is consciousness, and consciousness is one. The diversity (*bheda*) is nothing but an illusion aroused by the *m ā y ā* of Thought, of Śiva. In aesthetic experience, etc., when all the spectators are absorbed in the same thing to the exclusion of all other things, this diversity ceases momentarily to exist, to give place to the manifestation of unity, of the unlimited consciousness.

(*sāksātkārāyamāṇatva*)[1]; this combination — in which the real limiting causes (*niyamahetu*) (time, space, the particularized cognizing subject, etc.) on the one side, and those afforded by the poem on the other, cancel each other out and completely eliminate each other — readily nourishes (puṣ) the state of generality in question. Therefore this very density (*ekaghanatā*) [2] of the spectator's perception nourishes the Rasa of all of them readily, because the latent impressions of their minds concord with each other, the minds being varied by beginning less latent impressions[3] . This (form of) consciousness without

---

1 *i.e.,* that the perception of events represented (in other words, aesthetic perception) is like a direct cognition (*sākṣātkārāyamāṇa = sākṣātkārakalpa, pratyaksakalpa, cf. infra*, p.84 n.3). The direct cognition or experience (*sākṣātkāra, pratykṣa*) is in a necessary connexion with the concept of reality. In this sense, aesthetic perception, which is not dependent on the concepts of reality and unreality, is not a direct perception, but, A.G. says, is "like" a direct perception (cf. *A.Bh.*,I, p.43: the drama is *pratyakṣakalpanuvyavasāyaviṣayo lokaprasiddasatyādivilakṣaṇatvat*. On the meaning of the word *anuryavasaya, cf. infra*, pp. 106 ff.). In other terms, it is a direct perception *sui generis*, free of every relation with practical reality, etc.

2 The word *ekaghanatā* derives from *ghana*. "*Ghana,* from *ghan,* to strike, hinder, etc., has a primary sense of "dense mass", implying a condensation of multiple factors without extension in space" (A.K. Coomaraswamy, *The Transformation of Nature in Art*, Harvard 1934, p.209). Hence *ekaghana* comes to mean "dense", "compact", "uniform", etc., in the sense of a state of consciousness which does not allow the interference of "obstacles" (*vighna*). On the obstacles, ef. pp.77 ff.

3 A.G. replies with this argument to the objection of Bhaṭṭa Nāyaka, according to whom the spectator can identify himself only with a person similar to himself but not with a being of non-ordinary nature, as Rāma, deity, etc. The identification and therefore the state of generality required for the aesthetic experience postulates an affinity of nature (latent impressions, tendencies, instincts, etc.) between the spectator and the person represented. A.G. replies to this objection sayting that no being (animal or deity) exists with which man has not affinity of nature. The *saṃsāra* is beginningless and every man, before being that which he actually is, has been all the other beings as well. The consciousness of the spectator thus possesses (in other words, is varied by....) the latent impressions of all the possible beings and therefore is susceptible of identifying himself with each of them. The same concept is expounded in the *Dh. Ā.L.*, p.187 *rāmādicaritaṃ tu na sarvasya hṛdayasaṃvāditi mahat sāhasam citravāsanaviśiṣṭatvac cetasaḥ yad āha "tāsām anāditvam āśiṣo nityatvāt", "jātideśakālavyavahitānām apy ānantarayaṃ smṛtisaṃskārayar ekarūpatvāt" iti (Yogasūtra*, IV, 9, 10).

obstacles is called camatkāra[1]; the physical effects (trembling, horripilation, vibrations of joy (*ullukasana*), etc., are also *camatkāra*. For example: "Viṣṇu is still today in a state of a *camatkāra*: how, oh how is it that limbs of Lakṣmi, which are like the borders of a limb of the moon, have not been convulsed by mount Mandara?". That is to say, what is called *camatkāra* is an uninterrupted (*acchinna*) state of immersion (*āveśa*) in an Enjoyment, characterized by the presence of a sensation of inner fullness (*tripti*). It might be said indeed that *camatkāra* is the action proper to a tasting (*cam*) or enjoying subject, *i.e.*, to a person immersed in the inner movement (*spanda*)[2] of a magic (*adbhuta*) enjoyment. This may be presented under the aspect either of a form of mental cognition (*mānasādhyavasāya*), consisting of a direct perception (*sākṣātkāra*)[3], or of

---

1 The term *camatkāra* means aesthetic experience, the state of fruition of the Rasa. *Camatkāra* is aesthetic experience or Tasting. This word pervades the whole of Indian aesthetics and religions speculation, from the *Yogavasiṣtha* to the *Agnipurāṇa*, from Abhinava to Jagannātha. It is compounded of the *camat* and *kāra: camat*, which occurs only in this expression, is probably no more than an interjection, expressing surprise or wonder, while *kāra* (from *kṛ* means the act of emitting such an interjection, of finding oneself in this state of consciousness. This sense of wonder or surprise at the presence of somethingwhich suddenly invades our fields of consciousness is never absent from the word *camatkāra* (in this connexion cf. for example Ruyyaka's commentary on the *Vyaktiviveka* of *Mahimabhaṭṭa*, p. 53: *ālekhyalekhyādau santamasāvasthite pradipādinā prakāśite jhaṭiti adbhutārthaprakāśanāc camatkāro jāyate tadvad rasādau*). Traditional etymology prefers the derivation of *camat* from *cam*, taste, eat and hence enjoy (*bhuj*). According to this interpretation *camat* is the present participle of *cam*. The fact of being *camat* (camattvam), in this sense, means being immersed in the Tasting or enjoyment of something, particularly of an aesthetic or mystical kind. A.G. accepts both interpretations.

2 *Spanda* means movement, vibration, energy, etc. According to the *śaiva* schools of Kashmir, consciousness is vibration, the ceaseless force from which springs all that exists. The modes of discursive thought are the fruits of the solidification of this first, incandescent principle. This force manifests itself in the instinctive motions of consciousness (fear, joy, etc.). It is the energy that consents to go from word to word, from thought to thought. It is the first moment of will (*icchā*), the initial motion of the spirit, which is presupposed by any form of consciousness.

3 *I.e.*, it is a mental or inner perception (*mānasapratyakṣa*; see *supra*, p. 38, n.2; p. 66, n. 4. *Adhyavasāya* is used in the sense of *anuvyavasāya* (*N.Ś.*, I, I.4); cf *infra*, pp. 106 ff.

imagination (*samkalpa*), or of a form of memory, which, nevertheless, is manifested in a different manner to its ordinary nature. For as Kālidāsa has said: "Often a man, in the act of admiring in happiness beautiful shapes or listening to sweet sounds, feels in himself a strange, intense disquiet. Does he, perhaps, recall, in his soul, affections of his past lives, affections which remain fixed in his spirit without his knowedge?"[1]. The form of memory referred to in this stanza by means of the expression, "Does he, perhaps, recall ...", is not of the same kind as ordinary memory as recognised by logicians (*tārkika*). The object of such memory, indeed, has never been perceived in the past. In fact, we might say that its nature is that of direct percepion, *i.e.*., of that form of direct perception otherwise known as intuition. In any case, it is beyond question that it is a form of perception, in which appears [a Permanent Mental Movement, (in this case) Delight] consisting of, and animated by, a Tasting. For this reason, i.e., because it is not limited by further specifications, this perception can be the object of a Tasting: that is to say, it is neither a form of ordinary (*laukika*) cognition, nor is it erroneous, nor ineffable, nor like ordinary perception, nor does it consist of a super-imposition (*āropa*) of the latter[2]. To conclude, we

---

1 Kālidāsa, *Śakuntalā*, V, 96. This stanza is quoted by A.G., also in *I.P.V.V.*, III, p. 252. The disquiet, to which Kālidāsa alludes, is, observes A.G., an unobjectified desire; it corresponds to what is, metaphysically, the desire which induces consciousness to deny its original fullness and to crumble in time and space.

2 A. Bh., I, p.36: "With regard to the personages moving on the stage, one has neither the idea of being concerned with reality, nor of being concerned with a similitude as in the case of two similar things , nor with an illusion, as when a piece of mother-of-pearl reminds one of a piece of silver , nor with a super-imposition as when wrong knowledge follows the denying of the right , nor with an ascertainment as when one says 'this peasant is a cow [i.e., is foolish as a cow] , nor with a comparison as between a face and the moon , nor with a copy as in the case of a painted image , nor with an imitation as in the case of masters and disciples, who seek to explain the scriptures in the same way , nor with a sudden apparition as in magic , nor with a skilfully conjured-up apparition as in sleight-of-hand, etc. In all these cases, that which emerges does not appear, in fact, in a generalized form and, therefore, the subject does not actively share in what he sees. In consequence, the tasting of Rasa does not take place."

The words *āropa* and *adhyavasāya* are used in the sense given them by the Buddhists, according to whom discursive knowledge is an arbitrary and illusory super-imposition on reality, on the thing *in se* (cf.I.P.V., p.40).

may say equally: a) that it consists of a state of intensification (*upacaya*)[1] – using this term to indicate that it is not limited by spatial data, etc.; b) that it is an imitation[2] – using this expression to mean that its operation temporally follows that of real life; and c) that it is a combination of different elements[3] – this conception being interpreted in the light of the doctrine of the *vijñānavādin*. From whichever point of view it is examined, Rasa is, in any case, simply and solely a mental state which is the matter of cognition on the part of a perception without obstacles and consisting in a Tasting.

The elements which eliminate the obstacles to aesthetic perception are the Determinants, etc. To specify: here, the words *camatkāra*, Immersion (*nirveśa*), Tasting (*rasanā*), Sampling (āsvādana), Enjoyment (bhoga), Accomplishment (*samāpatti*), Lysis (*laya*), Rest (*viśrānti*), etc., mean simply a form of consciousness completely free from any obstacles. The obstacles to Tasting are seven in number[4]: 1) unbecomingness (*ayogyatā*) of perception, called lack of verisimilitude (*saṃbhāvanāviraha*); 2) immersion in temporal or spatial determinations which are exclusively one's own or exclusively those of another; 3) the fact of being at the mercy of sensations of

---

1 Lollaṭa's doctrine.

2 Śankuka's doctrine.

3 Bhaṭṭa Nāyaka's doctrine. The different elements are the Determinants, etc. Cf. (*supra*, p.62) the stanza "Rasa is, it is said, the essence of poetry...". Bhaṭṭa Nāyaka says that Rasa is not perceived but enjoyed. Well, says A.G., this theory is also true if it is interpreted in the light of the *vijñanavāda*, the idealistic Buddhism, according to which everything that exists is pure consciousness or perception (according to which, therefore, every fruition, etc., is simply a form of perception).

4 In the following lines A.G. explains the *vighna*, the obstacles to aesthetic perception. The *vighna*, obstacles, are all the extraneous elements which break the unity of a state of consciousness (desires for gain, worry of all kinds, etc.). The same conception is met with in connexion with religious experience. The *vighna* are defined in the I.P.V.V., I, p.18: *vighnanti vilumpanti kartavyam iti vighnāḥ adhyātmikādayo 'navadhānadoṣādayas trividhopaghātaḥ tadadhiṣṭhātāraś ca devatāviśeṣāh* "The obstacles obstruct or hinder what one does; this is why they are called obstacles. They are of three kinds (inherent in the perceiving subject, etc.): lack of attention, etc. The divinities which preside over them are also called obstacles". Their principal source is lack of attention (*anavadhāna*), i.e., the absence of a total rest of the whole being on the object of perception.

pleasure, etc., which inhere solely in one's own person; 4) defective state (*vaikalya*) of the means of perception; 5) lack of evidence (*asphuṭatva*); 6) lack of preeminence (*apradhānatā*) and 7) the fact of allowing admission to doubts.

1) A man who considers that what constitutes the object of congnition (*saṃvedya*) [the subject of perfomance] is lacking in verisimilitude is obviously not able to immerse (*viniviś*) his consciousness in it[1]. Thus the spectator will not be able to rest in it[2]. This is the first obstacle. The means by which it is eliminated are the consent of the heart[3] and the representation of an event of an ordinary nature (*lokasāmānya*)[4]. If there is any question of representing on the stage events which transcend ordinary life (*alokasāmānya*), it is necessary to resort to the device of bringing on to the stage people whose names are famous — Rāma, etc — to produce in the spectator a flow of trust (*pratyaya*) deeply rooted in himself, aroused by the uninterrupted fame (*prasiddhi*) which the character represented has enjoyed since antiquity[5]. For the same reason, it is said that *nāṭaka*[6], etc., whose purpose is the illustration (*vyutpatti*) and teaching (*upadeśa*) of deeds transcending ordinary life, necessarily requires to deal with famous events, etc. This requirement however, is absent in the case of comedies (*prahasana*). All this will

---

1 In other words, to identify oneself with it, to partake actively in the events represented.

2 I.e., identifying oneself in it to the exclusion of everything else.

3 Cf. p.65, n.1.

4 An event of an ordinary character finds a more ready response in the spectator's heart.

5 If the same extraordinary events (crossing of the ocean, etc.) which are, in fact, attributed to a legendary figure (Rāma, etc.) were referred to an ordinary man, they would arouse the incredulity of the spectators. Dh.A.L., p.331: "But when such undertakings are referred to Rāma, etc., they lose all appearance of falsehood: for they are rooted in the spectator's confidence, the cumulative result of the uninterrupted fame enjoyed from antiquity by the character in question".

6 Cf. p.79, n.1.

be explained at a suitable time and place[1]. What has been said will suffice for the present.

---

1 A.Bh., ch.XVIII. The appropriate subjects for the ten kinds of play are described and commented upon in N.Ś., XVIII. *Nāṭaka* are plays on elevated subjects. *Daśarūpa*, Haas, p.4: "[The ten chief varieties of drama] are: the *Nāṭaka*, the *Prakaraṇa*, the *Bhāṇa*, the *Prahasana*, the *Ḍima*, the *Vyāyoga*, the *Samavakāra*, the *Vīthi*, the *Aṅka* (= *Utsṛṣṭikāṅka*), and the *Īhāmṛga*". Cf.Ind. Th., p.139 ff. In the A.Bh., p.27, A.G. makes the general remark: "It is not fitting to imitate an event of actual life; for in this case the spectators would be affected by passions (hatred, partisanship, indifference, etc.) [extraneous to aesthetic experience] and would thus be unable to identify himself with the event represented. Pleasure being thus absent, instruction would be absent as well. Besides, in the case of an actual event, the relation between the action (its merit, etc.) and the fruits which result from it is discerned by direct experience; it is, therefore, useless to put it on the stage".

4

From *Kavyalankara*

Bhamaha

प्रणम्य सार्वं सर्वज्ञं मनोवाक्कायकर्मभिः ।
काव्यालङ्कार इत्येष यथाबुद्धि विधास्यते ॥१॥
धर्मार्थकाममोक्षेषु वैचक्षण्यं कलासु च ।
प्रीतिं करोति कीर्त्तिं च साधुकाव्यनिबन्धनम् ॥२॥
अधनस्येव दातृत्वं क्लीबस्येवास्त्रकौशलम् ।
अज्ञस्येव प्रगल्भत्वमकवेः शास्त्रवेदनम् ॥३॥
विनयेन विना का श्रीः का निशा शशिना विना ।
रहिता सत्कवित्वेन कीदृशी वाग्विदग्धता ॥४॥
गुरूपदेशादध्येतुं शास्त्रं जडधियोऽप्यलम् ।
काव्यं तु जायते जातु कस्यचित्प्रतिभावतः ॥५॥
उपेयुषामपि दिवं सन्निबन्धविधायिनाम् ।
आस्त एव निरातङ्कं कान्तं काव्यमयं वपुः ॥६॥
रुणद्धि रोदसी चास्य यावत्कीर्त्तिरनश्वरी ।
तावत्किलायमध्यास्ते सुकृती वैबुधं पदम् ॥७॥
अतोऽभिवाञ्छता कीर्तिं स्थेयसीमा भुवः स्थितेः ।
यत्नो विदितवेद्येन विधेयः काव्यलक्ष्मणि ॥८॥
शब्दश्छन्दोभिधानार्था इतिहासाश्रयाः कथाः ।
लोको युक्तिः कलाश्चेति मन्तव्या काव्यवैखरी ॥९॥
शब्दाभिधेये विज्ञाय कृत्वा तद्विदुपासनम् ।
विलोक्यान्यनिबन्धांश्च कार्यः काव्यक्रियादरः ॥१०॥
सर्वथा पदमप्येकं न निगाद्यमवद्यवत् ।
विलक्ष्मणा हि काव्येन दुःसुतेनेव निन्द्यते ॥११॥
नाकवित्वमधर्माय व्याधये दण्डनाय वा ।
कुकवित्वं पुनः साक्षान्मृतिमाहुर्मनीषिणः ॥१२॥

रूपकादिरलङ्कारस्तस्यान्यैर्बहुधोदितः ।
न कान्तमपि निर्भूषं विभाति वनिताननम् ॥१३॥
रूपकादिमलङ्कारं बाह्यमाचक्षते परे ।
सुपां तिङां च व्युत्पत्तिं वाचां वाञ्छन्त्यलङ्कृतिम् ॥१४॥
तदेतदाहुः सौशब्द्यं नार्थव्युत्पत्तिरीदृशी ।
शब्दाभिधेयालङ्कारभेदादिष्टं द्वयं तु नः ॥१५॥
शब्दार्थौ सहितौ काव्यं गद्यं पद्यं च तद्द्विधा ।
संस्कृतं प्राकृतं चान्यदपभ्रंशं इति त्रिधा ॥१६॥
वृत्तदेवादिचरितशंसि चोत्पाद्यवस्तु च ।
कलाशास्त्राश्रयं चेति चतुर्धा भिद्यते पुनः ॥१७॥
सर्गबन्धोऽभिनेयार्थं तथैवाख्यायिकाकथे ।
अनिबद्धं च काव्यादि तत्पुनः पञ्चधोच्यते ॥१८॥
सर्गबन्धो महाकाव्यं महतां च महच्च यत् ।
अग्राम्यशब्दमर्थ्यं च सालङ्कारं सदाश्रयम् ॥१९॥
मन्त्रदूतप्रयाणाजिनायकाभ्युदयैश्च यत् ।
पञ्चभिः सन्धिभिर्युक्तं नातिव्याख्येयमृद्धिमत् ॥२०॥
चतुर्वर्गाभिधानेऽपि भूयसार्थोपदेशकृत् ।
युक्तं लोकस्वभावेन रसैश्च सकलैः पृथक् ॥२१॥
नायकं प्रागुपन्यस्य वंशवीर्यश्रुतादिभिः ।
न तस्यैव वधं ब्रूयादन्योत्कर्षाभिधित्सया ॥२२॥
यदि काव्यशरीरस्य न स व्यापितयेष्यते ।
न चाभ्युदयभाक्तस्य मुधादौ ग्रहणं स्तवे ॥२३॥
नाटकं द्विपदीशम्यारासकस्कन्धकादि यत् ।
उक्तं तदभिनेयार्थमुक्तोऽन्यैस्तस्य विस्तरः ॥२४॥
प्रकृतानाकुलश्रव्यशब्दार्थपदवृत्तिना ।
गद्येन युक्तोदात्तार्था सोच्छ्वासाऽऽख्यायिका मता ॥२५॥
वृत्तमाख्यायते तस्यां नायकेन स्वचेष्टितम् ।
वक्त्रं चापरवक्त्रं च काले भाव्यर्थशंसि च ॥२६॥

कवेरभिप्रायकृतैः कथनैः कैश्चिदङ्किता ।
कन्याहरणसंग्रामविप्रलम्भोदयान्विता ।।२७।।
न वक्त्रापरवक्त्राभ्यां युक्ता नोच्छ्वासवत्यपि ।
संस्कृते संस्कृता चेष्टा कथाऽपभ्रंशभाक्तथा ।।२८।।
अन्यैः स्वचरितं तस्यां नायकेन तु नोच्यते ।
स्वगुणाविष्कृतिं कुर्यादभिजातः कथं जनः ।।२९।।
अनिबद्धं पुनर्गाथाश्लोकमात्रादि तत्पुनः ।
युक्तं वक्रस्वभावोक्त्या सर्वमेवैतदिष्यते ।।३०।।
वैदर्भमन्यदस्तीति मन्यन्ते सुधियोऽपरे ।
तदेव च किल ज्यायः सदर्थमपि नापरम् ।।३१।।
गौडीयमिदमेतत्तु वैदर्भमिति किं पृथक् ।
गतानुगतिकन्यायान्नानाख्येयममेधसाम् ।।३२।।
ननु चाश्मकवंशादि वैदर्भमिति कथ्यते ।
कामं तथास्तु प्रायेण संज्ञेच्छातो विधीयते ।।३३।।
अपुष्टार्थमवक्रोक्ति प्रसन्नमृजु कोमलम् ।
भिन्नं गेयमिवेदं तु केवलं श्रुतिपेशलम् ।।३४।।
अलङ्कारवदग्राम्यमर्थ्यं न्याय्यमनाकुलम् ।
गौडीयमपि साधीयो वैदर्भमिति नान्यथा ।।३५।।
न नितान्तादिमात्रेण जायते चारुता गिराम् ।
वक्राभिधेयशब्दोक्तिरिष्टा वाचामलङ्कृतिः ।।३६।।
नेयार्थं क्लिष्टमन्यार्थमवाचकमयुक्तिमत् ।
गूढशब्दाभिधानं च कवयो न प्रयुञ्जते ।।३७।।
नेयार्थं नीयते युक्तो यस्यार्थः कृतिभिर्बलात् ।
शब्दन्यायानुपारूढः कथञ्चित्स्वाभिसन्धिना ।।३८।।
मायेव भद्रेति यथा सा चासाध्वी प्रकल्पना ।
वेणुदाकेरिति च तां नयन्ति वचनाद्विना ।।३९।।
क्लिष्टं व्यवहितं विद्यादन्यार्थं विगमे यथा ।
विजहुस्तस्य ताः शोकं क्रीडायां विकृतं च तत् ।।४०।।

हिमापहामित्रधरैर्व्याप्तं व्योमेत्यवाचकम् ।
साक्षादरूढं वाच्येऽर्थे नाभिधानं प्रतीयते ।।४१।।
अयुक्तिमद्यथा दूता जलभृन्मारुतेन्दवः ।
तथा भ्रमरहारीतचक्रवाकशुकादयः ।।४२।।
अवाचोऽव्यक्तवाचश्च दूरदेशविचारिणः ।
कथं दूत्यं प्रपद्येरन्निति युक्त्या न युज्यते ।।४३।।
यदि चोत्कण्ठया यत्तदुन्मत्त इव भाषते ।
तथा भवतु भूम्नेदं सुमेधोभिः प्रयुज्यते ।।४४।।
गूढशब्दाभिधानं च न प्रयोज्यं कथञ्चन ।
सुधियामपि नैवेदमुपकाराय कल्पते ।।४५।।
असितर्तितुगद्रिच्छित्स्वःक्षितां पतिरद्बिदृक् ।
अमिद्भिः शुभ्रदृग्दृष्टैर्द्विषो जेघ्नीयिषीष्ट वः ।।४६।।
श्रुतिदुष्टार्थदुष्टे च कल्पनादुष्टमित्यपि ।
श्रुतिकष्टं तथैवाहुर्वाचां दोषं चतुर्विधम् ।।४७।।
विड्वर्चोविष्ठितक्लिन्नच्छिन्नवान्तप्रवृत्तयः ।
प्रचारधर्षितोद्गारविसर्गहदयन्त्रिताः ।।४८।।
हिरण्यरेताः संबाधः पेलवोपस्थिताण्डजाः ।
वाक्काटवादयश्चेति श्रुतिदुष्टा मता गिरः ।।४९।।
अर्थदुष्टं पुनर्ज्ञेयं यत्रोक्ते जायते मतिः ।
असभ्यवस्तुविषया शब्दैस्तद्वाचिभिर्यथा ।।५०।।
हन्तुमेव प्रवृत्तस्य स्तब्धस्य विवरैषिणः ।
पतनं जायतेऽवश्यं कृच्छ्रेण पुनरुन्नतिः ।।५१।।
पदद्वयस्य संधाने यदनिष्टं प्रकल्पते ।
तदाहुः कल्पनादुष्टं स शौर्याभरणो यथा ।।५२।।
यथाऽजिह्लददित्यादि श्रुतिकष्टं च तद्विदुः ।
न तदिच्छन्ति कृतिनो गण्डमप्यपरे किल ।।५३।।
संनिवेशविशेषात्तु दुरुक्तमपि शोभते ।
नीलं पलाशमारब्धमन्तराले स्रजामिव ।।५४।।

किञ्चिदाश्रयसौन्दर्याद्धत्ते शोभामसाध्वपि ।
कान्ताविलोचनन्यस्तं मलीमसमिवाञ्जनम् ॥५५॥
आपाण्डुगण्डमेतत्ते वदनं वनजेक्षणे ।
सङ्गमात्पाण्डुशब्दस्य गण्डः साधु यथोदितः ॥५६॥
अनयान्यदपि ज्ञेयं दिशा युक्तमसाध्वपि ।
यथा विक्लिन्नगण्डानां करिणां मदवारिभिः ॥५७॥
मदक्लिन्नकपोलानां द्विरदानां चतुःशती ।
यथा तद्वदसाधीयः साधीयश्च प्रयोजयेत् ॥५८॥
एतद्ग्राह्यं सुरभिकुसुमं ग्राम्यमेतन्निधेयं
धत्ते शोभां विरचितमिदं स्थानमस्यैतदस्य ।
मालाकारो रचयति यथा साधु विज्ञाय मालां
योज्यं काव्येष्ववहितधिया तद्वदेवाभिधानम् ॥५९॥

1. After prostrating before the Lover of All and the All-knowing, by mental, vocal and bodily acts, this work, called *kāvyālaṅkāra*, is composed to the best of (my) capacity.

The word सार्वः in the sense of सर्वेभ्यो हितः is evolved in the manner stated in Verse 53 of Chapter VI *post*.

2. Composition of good poetry produces ability in (or makes one able, or capable in the pursuit of) *Dharma, Artha, Kāma,* and *Mokṣa*; also in Arts. It also confers Pleasure and Fame.

Locana p.12. substitutes for the last word निबन्धनम् the word निषेवणम्. The meaning will be that the advantages enumerated above will result to one who studies *Kāvyas*. The word निषेवणम् includes composition also. See commentary to Sāhityadarpaṇa N.S. Ed, p.4, where this verse is quoted in the text.

3. The knowledge of *Śāstras* possesed by one who is not a poet is like the pauper's charitableness, the eunuch's dexterity in arms, and the fool's self-confidence.

4. What is wealth without modesty. What is Night without the Moon. What is cleverness in speech (eloquence) without the capacity to compose good (literary) works.

5. Even the dull-witted can learn *Śāstra* (Science) with the help of a teacher. Poetry however is to him who has a natural capacity and that too, not invariably.

6. Even to those who have passed away to *Svarga* (the other world) but who have composed good literary works there surely exists (there) a body consisting of their works which is both beautiful and free from disease (or decay).

7. Further, as long as his imperishable Fame continues to last in (besiege) this and the Upper World, so long does he, the blessed one, continue to occupy a place among the *Devas.*

8. Therefore should the wise one, who aims at Fame which shall last as long as the world, direct his endeavours towards (the acquisition of) the essentials of Poetry.

The last word काव्यलक्ष्मणि is found in O.L., and fits in better than काव्यलक्षण: , another reading.

9. Those that resort to *Kāvya* should regard (the essentials to be) the following:- Grammar, Metre (*i.e.*, Science of metre), the nature of words (as conveying primary and secondary sense), meanings of words, the stories in *Itihāsas*, the ways of the world, Logic and the Arts.

The readings in O.L. are काव्यतैर्वशी and काब्यवैखरी . Both are equally unintelligible. We may have काव्यगैर्ह्यमी Locana p.10 in explaining its text भाक्तमाहु स्तामन्ये and its वृत्ति points out that as per Udbhaṭa (Bhāmaha's commentator) Bhāmaha intends to include in अभिधान both the primary and secondary meanings of words:- 'भट्टोद्भटो बभाषे – शब्दानामभिधाव्यापारो गुण- वृत्तिश्च' If अभिधानम् is merely the word then the word अर्थ in the text will refer to 'meanings' and would mean "proficiency in the Lexicon."*

10. The desire to compose *kāvya*, should be entertained (only) after learning Grammar and the meanings of words and after having served the masters therein and after having studied other (*Kāvyas*), works.

*The use of the word शब्दाभिधेये in the next verse means "the word and meaning," hence the word अभिधान here may simply mean "the word" in this verse.

11 Never shall be spoken even a word which is faulty. By a work which is bad, one gets a bad name, as by a bad son.

In verse (ii): By गदमदचरयमश्चानुपसर्गे (3.1.100). मत् is added when there is no उपसर्ग। (Ex-गद्यम्); when there is उपसर्ग as here, we have एयत् (ऋहलोर्ण्यत् 3.1.124).

12 Not being an author does not lead to evil or disease or punishment. But being a bad author is, according to the wise, nothing less than death.

In verse 12 Rājaśekhara in Kāvya Mīmāṁsā - p.21. Line 4 gives expression to the same verse. He says वरम् अकविः न पुनः कुकविस्स्यात्। कुकविता हि सोच्छ्वासं मरणम्।

Introduction to verses 13, 14 and 15:- These three verses start and conclude a discussion as to the utility of accepting two groups of *Alaṅkāras* viz., *Śabdālaṅkāras* and *Arthālaṅkāras.* These three verses are bodily quoted by Mammaṭa in the opening portion of chapter VI of *Kāvyaprakāśa.* Mammaṭa in that chapter explains that the division of *Kāvyas* into शब्दचित्रम् and अर्थचित्रम् is not intended to be mutually exclusive. There are many cases in which both occur. In fact, in practically all cases, by some little ingenuity the presence of both may be proved. In such cases, says Mammaṭa, the author's intention is our guide in determining whether the passage should be considered as coming under *Śabdālaṅkāra* or *Arthālaṅkāra.* The author's intention could be easily ascertained, if we direct our attention to discover what the author mainly relies upon for the beauty (चमत्कृतिः) of the passage. To support his view that both may lead to चमत्कृति, he quotes these verses from Bhāmaha.

13. Some *Ālaṅkārikas* vehemently maintain that only *Rūpaka* etc., constitute its (*kāvya's*) ornaments. (Because) a damsel's face, though beautiful, does not shine, if it should be devoid of ornaments.

This is the view of one School. They argue as follows:- The beauty of a *Kāvya* consists in its *Rasa* which depends upon विभावs etc. These result from the meanings of words. Words, as such, are *functus officio*, as soon as the meanings have been produced. Therefore the *Alaṅkāras* that relate to meanings may conduce to the beauty of the *Rasa* and not the *Alaṅkāras* that relate merely to the word or the sound. In the example, the natural beauty of the face corresponds to the grammatical correctness of the nouns and verbs and the beauty in their disposition also. But the face is beautified by ornaments which are separate. The expression '*Alaṅkāras* like *Rūpaka* etc.' denotes all *Arthālaṅkāras*.

14. Some people are of opinion that Figures of Speech like *Rūpaka* are external, They maintain that the proper disposition of nouns and verbs constitutes the (real) ornaments of speech. That (kind of) excellence in the disposition of words is this beauty (*Sauśabdya*). The meanings are not so.

This is the antagonistic view. This School argues as follows:- The beauty of a poem lies primarily in the disposition of the words. Again it is the language (consisting of the words) that first attracts one and then the meaning arises. The word काव्यम् itself means कविकर्म and consists in the selection of proper words and in properly stringing them together. In common parlance also we say "Poetry is read", "Poetry is Heard" etc., which cannot apply to meanings. In fact we also say "Poetry is understood", "Poetry is not understood", thereby sharply contrasting 'meaning' with 'Poetry' which necessarily means the collection of words. This being so, what enhances the beauty of the words must be the real ornament. So *Śabdālaṅkāra* is superior to *Arthālaṅkāra*. In fact, it is after the words have functioned and produced a meaning, *Arthālaṅkāras* can come in. So these ornaments are very much on the outside (बाह्यम्), व्युत्पत्तिः = सन्निवेशः, Read तत्सौशब्द्यमेतत् (That verbal beauty is this *i.e.*, what is properly called as *Alaṇkāra*). सौशब्द्यम् means काव्यस्य शोभनत्वम् . = शब्दनिर्माण सौष्ठवम् . अर्थव्युत्पत्तिः = अर्थालङ्कारः

नेदृशी = न शाब्दवत्स्वतश्चमत्कारिका, अपि तु विभावाद्युत्कर्षमुखेनैवेत्यर्थः.
The last line यदेतदाहुः etc., is the reason for upholding *Śabdālaṅkāra*.
- Bālabodhinī.

15. We however accept both, as we accept the distinction of *Śabdālaṅkāra* and *Arthālaṅkāra*.

Intro. Classification based on 'Structure' and 'Language':-

16. Word and meaning taken together constitute *Kāvya*. It is of two kinds, Prose and Verse. It is further distinguishable into Sanskrit, Prakrit and Dialect

Intro. Classification based on subject-matter -

17. (Again) *Kāvya* is divided by the wise, four-fold, (thus):- real narratives of gods etc., stories put together (fiction), facts relating to Arts and those relating to the Sciences.

This classification includes Dramas and Grammar under the category of *kāvya*. Later writers restrict the word to words and meanings accompanied with *Rasa*, *Guṇa* or *Alaṅkāra*. Pratihārendu Rāja in his commentary *Laghu Vṛtti*, p. 78, explains that Bhāmaha uses this word in an extended sense (भक्त्या) *i.e.*, analogically.

Classification based on the nature of the composition:-

18. *Kāvyas* again are divisible into five groups thus:-
(1) Those that are built up by divisions called *Sargas*;
(2) Those that should be acted or exhibited on the stage;
(3) *Ākhyāyikās* (explained below);
(4) *Kathās* (explained below);
(5) Unconnected composition.*

(a) *The reader will note that kāvya is divided with reference to four different bases of classification into 2,3,4, and 5 divisions progressively.

Intro. Verses, 19 to 28 both inclusive describe *Mahākāvya* (No. 1 of the previous Stanza).

19. *Mahākāvya* is that which is made up of (parts called) *Sargas*; which treats of the Big and is big; is devoid of vulgarity of expression; has (profound) significance; contains Figures of Speech and treats of the good.

20. It also consists of (the description of) state-councils, messengers, travels, war and the good fortunes of the Hero. It contains also the five *Sandhis*. It does not require much commentary and has a prosperous ending.

Vāgbhaṭa in *Kāvyānuśāsana* N. S. Ed., p. 15 explains the *Sandhis* as follows:- (1) मुखसन्धिः = The seed of the plot, just indicated, proceeding from various *Rasas*. (2) प्रतिमुखसन्धिः = The sprouting of the seed made partially visible. (3) गर्भ- सन्धिः = The full development of the same culminating in the attainment of the desire or the reverse; also the search after it. (4) विमर्शसन्धिः = The investigation of the same. (5) निर्व- हणसन्धिः = The conclusion - the gathering up of all the threads and bringing the plot to an end.

21. While describing the four-fold objects of human existence it relates chiefly to the acquisition of wealth, conforms to the ways of the world and contains separately the various *Rasas*.

22. After having first placed the *Nāyaka* (Hero) by extolling his ancestry, prowess, knowledge etc., do not narrate his destruction with the object of enhancing the glory of another.

(1) Here *Nāyaka* apparently refers to the rival (प्रतिनायक) Bhāmaha's view obviously is that if you first describe a person and extol his virtues and thereby enlist the reader's sympathy on his side it would be *mal adroit* or inharmonious to describe later on his destruction with the object of enhancing the glory of the Hero (2) Daṇḍin (*Kāvyādarśa Parichheda I*, Verses 21 and 22) attacks this view. His language suggests his posteriority to Bhāmaha.

23. If he (the person first described) is not intended to dominate the whole poem and (further) is not to participate in the (final) success, it is useless to describe him at the beginning.

Intro. Verse 24 describes the second group - *Nāṭakas* on verse 18 *ante.*

24. *Nāṭaka* consists of *Dvipadi, Samyā, Rāsaka, Śkandhaka etc.* It has been described as intended to be acted. Its amplifications have been described by others.

Intro. Verse 25 and up to the last quarter of the verse 29 define *Ākhyāyikā*, No.3 and *Kathā* No.4 of verse 18 *ante.*

25. *Ākhyāyikā* is a prose composition treating of an elevated subject-matter and characterised by agreeable words, meaning and style in harmony with the context. It is divided into parts called *Ucchvāsas.*

In it the Hero himself narrates his own exploits.

26-7 It (*Ākhyāyikā*) should consist of verses in the *Vaktra* and *Aparavaktra* metre. It must contain fore-casts of events on appropriate occasions. It must be marked (distinguished) by some narratives of the poet's own creation (original stories). It must treat of the abduction of damsels, of war, of separation (of lovers) and of success. Even if the verses *Vaktra* and *Aparavaktra* are not employed and there are no divisions into *Ucchvāsas* (it does not matter).

28-9 *Kathā* is acceptable if composed in Sanskrit. It may also be in a dialect. In it, the history of the Hero is narrated by others not by himself. How could a well-born (person) narrate his own exploits?

The reading संस्कृते instead of संस्कृतम् which is found in the printed text is in deference to the opinion of some Pandits as giving a more intelligible meaning. The above view is in consonance with that of Daṇḍin who says 'कथा हि सर्वभाषाभिः संस्कृतेन च बध्यते' - (*Kāvyādarśa I.* 38.)

This refers to the fifth sub-division of verse 18.

Anibaddha (unconnected composition) consists only in *Gāthās* and verses.

Unconnected composition means that the various *Ślokas* are not connected with each other but deal with separate subjects.

30. All this (i.e. whatever has been described before) becomes important (commendable) if characterised by indirect or disguised statement (or cleverness of speech).

I have translated वक्रस्वभावोक्त्या as speech characterised by indirectness (lit. crookedness). It would be incorrect, I thought, to translate the passage as 'speech characterised by वक्रोक्ति and स्वभावोक्ति', for, Bhāmaha later, disregards स्वभावोक्ति as an *Alaṅkāra* at all. (See Verse II. 93). In I 34, I(36) and II(85) Bhāmaha shows a partiality for वक्रोक्ति.

31. There are some wise ones who regard that there is another kind of composition known as *Vaidarbha* which is different and superior. The other (*Gauḍī*) though consisting of elegant meaning is not so (*i.e.* superior).

The word अन्यत् = the other

32. Is there (really) any difference (between the two) because this is called *Gauḍīya* and the other *Vaidarbha*? This nomenclature is due to unintelligent people following (blindly) the lead of others.

33. Works like *Aśmakavaṁsa* etc., are known as *Vaidarbhi* (in style). Be it so; for a name is largely of one's own choice. P.V. Kane in his introduction to *Sāhityadarpaṇa* p. XX surmises that there was a work known as *Aśmkavaṁśa*.

34. If a composition should be devoid of suggestion or cleverness of statement but is merely clear, smooth and elegant, then, (if it differs from ordinary speech at all) it differs merely as music does, by being pleasant to the ear.

What Bhāmaha condemns as mere song, Vāmana in his *Kāvyālaṅkārasūtra* recognises as a distinct source of enjoyment under the name of *Vaidarbhi* (1, 2, 11 and 20). गेयम् has been described by some a distinct kind of composition. Vāgbhaṭa, in *Kāvyānuśāsana* p. 18, mentions eleven varieties of this. The general characteristic of the whole group is there given 'पदार्थाभिनयस्वभावानि डोम्बिकादीनि गेयानि रूपकाणि चिरन्तनैरुक्तानि'. As this kind is included in dramas it has no connection with the गेय in question.

35. Even *Gauḍīya* is superior if it has *Alaṅkāra*, is devoid of vulgarity, has full and proper meaning and is simple. There is no separate thing as *Vaidarbhī*.

I have translated न्याय्यम् as "having a proper meaning." Its literal meaning is 'just'.

36. Beauty of words is not exclusively produced by the first method. We accept as ornaments of speech cleverness in words and cleverness in meanings.

Locana p. 208 - In support of the position that *Atiśayokti* may be found mixed up in many as *Alaṅkāra*, Abhinavagupta quotes the second half of the above verse and explains as follows:- There is वक्रता (lit. crookedness) in words and also in meanings. This consists in stating (things) in a manner transcending the ordinary method (लोकोत्तीर्णेन रूपेण); and this constitutes *Alaṅkāra* of an *Alaṅkāra*. The purport is, that all *Alaṅkāras* have this peculiarity in common - that the statement is not the ordinary prosaic statement, but an arresting or catching one. What constitutes the special peculiarity of each *Alaṅkāra* consists in something over and above the fundamental strikingness of expression (See also note to Chap.II 85 *post.*)

37. Poets do not employ (language susceptible of the following defects, viz.,) *Neyārtha*, *Kliṣṭa*, *Anyārtha*, *Avācaka*, *Ayuktimat* and *Gūḍhasabdābhidhāna*.

38. Prose order.-यस्यार्थः कृतिभिः (=कुशलैः) बलाद्युक्तो नीयते तन्नेयार्थम्. That is *Neyārtha* whose proper meaning has to be forcibly dragged out by clever people. It transcends the laws of language and is somehow made to result from one's desire.

युक्तः may also be taken as an adjective of अर्थः as meaning "proper". There is considerable difference of opinion among *Ālaṅkārikas* as to the nature of this defect. One view seems to be this. The cardinal rule regarding speech (शब्दन्याय) is that all the words necessary to give the full meaning intended by the speaker should be employed. If such words are not employed there is a violation of the laws of language (शब्दन्यायानुपारूढः). Thus insufficient words constitute this defect. This view receives some support from Daṇḍin who without describing the defect as such, describes its absence as a *Guṇa* viz., *Arthavyakti*. He says अर्थव्यक्तिरनेयत्वमर्थस्य. His use of the word अनेयत्वम् and his example emphasise the above meaning of *Neyārtha*). Other writers define *Neyārtha*)as the artificial imputation of meanings to words by the speaker, *i.e.*), an artificial *Śakti* so to speak-a meaning other than the accepted one.

39. For example (take the statement) "Auspicious as deceit". This is an improper supposition. But (people) lead these words to some sense by introducing the meaning *Veṇudākeḥ* without using the word.

If we take वेणदाके: as वेणुदारे: then we can guess a meaning. A *Veṇudāri* is mentioned as the son of Bāṇāsura. Being an *Asura* he must excel in *Māyā* (deceit). Deceit is never auspicious (= भद्रा). So the statement 'मायेव भद्रा' = 'auspicious as deceit' is an improper supposition. If however you introduce the sense of वेणुदारे: (of *Veṇudāri*) and understand the *Māyā* as belonging to *Veṇudāri*, then there is some sense. Because probably his deceit was useful for some good purpose. No such story however is available.

Intro. Examples of *Kliṣṭa* and *Anyārtha* of verse 37 are given in this.

40. That defect is called *Kliṣṭa* (Difficult) in which the meaning is obstructed. *Anyārtha* is where the (accepted) meaning is absent, thus:- "They disported (with) his sorrow in play". This is nonsense and is caused by (the syllable) *Vi*.

(i) Vāmana (see *Vāṇi Vilāsa* Edition) says in II.1.13 'कल्पितार्थं नेयार्थम्' and in *Sūtra* 21 says 'व्यवहितार्थप्रत्ययं क्लिष्टम्' and gives as example of the latter 'दक्षात्मजादयित (= चन्द्र वल्लभ = (कान्त) वेदिकानाम् *i.e.*, चन्द्रकान्तवेदिकानाम् . Mammaṭa however would call this a case of *Neyārtha*, for his illustration of it is 'वस्त्रवैदूर्यचरणैः' (2) The *Śloka* gives no illustration of *Kliṣṭa*. It merely defines the same. It however defines and illustrates *Anyārtha*. In the example the intended meaning is. "They removed his sorrow by playing with him." तास्तस्य शोकं क्रीडायां जहुः (=removed). But by using the word 'विजहुः' the meaning is changed. The prefix 'वि' changes the root-meaning 'to play'. So instead of 'removed' we get the meaning 'disported' which is a different meaning (अन्यार्थम्) got by abandoning the legitimate meaning (विगमे) and the mischief is done by the particle वि (विकृतम्).

41. The sky is overcast by (*Himāpahāmitradharāḥ* meaning) clouds. That expression which is not (universally accepted as) connected with the intended meaning is inexpressive.

The word हिमापहामित्रधरा:-is made to evolve the meaning 'clouds' in this way-हिम is Snow. Its अपह (destroyer) enemy is Fire. That which is unfriendly (अमित्र) to Fire is water. That which carries or supports (धर) water is a Cloud. The prose order of the second half is 'साक्षाद्वाच्येऽर्थेऽरूढमभिधानं न प्रतीयते'. This verse is attributed to Daṇḍin on the authority of *Śārṅgadhara Paddhati*. The full verse is – 'विजितात्मभवद्वषि- गुरुपादहतो जनः। हिमापहामित्रधरैर्व्याप्तं व्योमाभिनन्दति ।।' *Vide* Trivedi's Introduction to *Pratāpa Rudrīya* p. XXIX. The same verse is given as an illustration to *Doṣa, Kliṣṭa* in *Sarasvatī Kaṇṭhābharaṇa* p.8.

Intro. This and the succeeding two verses refer to the *Doṣa, Ayuktimat* (unintelligent).

42. The employment, as messengers, of clouds, Winds, the Moon; also the Bee, *Hārita* (a bird of that name) *Cakravāka* (bird) or the parrot is the *Doṣa* known as "*Ayuktimat*".

Cloud messenger obviously refers to Kālidāsa's *Meghadūta*. A.B. Keith in his classical Sanskrit Literature (p.36) mentions the *Pavana-dūta* of Dhoyika (12th century) as the earliest imitation of *Meghadūta*. If Bhāmaha should be deemed to refer to that work, then, Bhāmaha should be later than the 12th century or Dhoyika's date must be much earlier than the 12th century. There is an इन्दुदूतम् published in part XIV of the *Kāvyamālā* series. Its author is not explicitly stated in the Poem. Possibly his name was Vinaya; for the last quarter of the last verse is "प्रभूतोदन्तं लेखं लिखति विनयो लेखलेखानतानाम्".

43. Those that cannot speak and those that are of indistinct utterance–how can these, going to distant places perform their function as messengers? Such descriptions do not fit in with reason.

44. If these are addressed by one from an excess of longing, as if he were mad,–be it so. It is on some such supposition it has to be

understood that these can be employed (as messangers) by intelligent people.

45. Poets never employ a word with a hidden meaning. It does not help even learned people.

Intro. The following is an example of words with hidden meanings.

46. Let (God *Subrahmaṇya*) the son of Fire destroy your enemies completely by his fierce and (dazzlingly) white and fearful glances- He who is the borer of a mountain, the Lord of the inhabitants of *Svarga*, and has more than two eyes.

(1) The above meanings which are hidden are got at thus.- असित = *Lit.* not white, therefore black. This is the conventional meaning of the word. ऋति = way- or path; from the root ऋ(गतौ) = to go. So असितर्ति = He who has (*i.e.*, leaves behind him) a black path- Fire. तुक् = अपत्यम् = son. (So the whole means "Son of Fire". God *Subrahmaṇya* is according to the Purāṇas the son of Fire also. अद्रिच्छित् = Breaker or Borer of a mountain, here the mountain called *Krauñcha.* स्वःक्षितां पतिः = The Lord (पतिः) of those that live in *Svarga.* अद्विदृक् = not having (only) two eyes; hence "many-eyed". अमिद्धिः अस्निग्धैः or रूक्षैः = Fierce. शुभ्रदृग्दृष्टैः = Glances which are white; because while looking on in anger the black cornea of the eye will go up making the eye appear white. द्विषः = Enemies. जेघ्नीयिषीष्ट = पुनः पुनर्वध्यात्. Frequentative of हन् = to kill, meaning 'completely destroy'. (2) The above is taken from Ratneśvara's commentary on *Sarasvatī kanṭhābharaṇa.* Note the difference between this *Doṣa* and *Avācaka* No.4. *ante* described in verse 41. There the intended meaning (वाच्यार्थ) was not traceable to the words directly साक्षादरूढम् *e.q.*, हिमापहामित्रधराः does not directly lead to "clouds" whereas here, each of the above, no doubt leads directly to the meaning which however is not apparent *i.e.*, is not the ordinary meaning but is hidden.

47. Four other defects of Speech are also mentioned viz., *Srutiduṣṭa* (= offensive to the ear), *Arthaduṣṭa* (= of improper or objectionable meaning), *Kalpanāduṣṭa* (= objectionable construction *i.e.*, such a joining together of words as gives rise to an objectionable sense) and *Śrutikaṣṭa* (= painful to the ear- cacaphony).

Intro. This and the following verse enumerate words that are offensive to the ear.

48. विट्, वर्चस् and विष्ठित (mean "Excrement"), क्लिन्न (means wet), छिन्न (= Broken or cut), वान्त (= vomited), प्रवृत्ति, प्रचार (Roaming, wandering), धर्षित (= seduced, outraged), उद्गार (= belching; vomiting, ejection), विसर्ग (= emission), हद (= voiding excrement), यन्त्रित (= restrained, bound etc.).

49. Also हिरण्यरेता: (because of the word रेतस् which means semen). संबाध: (= the vulva), पेलव (= thin). The 1st two letters पेल mean in the *Lāṭa* dialect the scrotum and hence objectionable. (see notes to *Sāh. Darpaṇa* N.S. Edition p.395. See however Kālidāsa using 'परिबाधापेलवैरङ्गैः '), उपस्थित (= placed over another–the objection being apparently to the part उपस्थ which means "genitals"), अण्डज (born from an egg-the objection is to the part अण्ड which means scrotum) and also words like वाक्काटव etc. These are known as words which are offensive to the ear.

The literal meaning of the word वाक्काटवम् is "Harshness or incisiveness of speech". The objection of the word lies in the fact that a portion of the word is काट which is said mean the male organ. In explaining *Sūtra* 20, Vāmana in his *Kāvyālankārasūtra* p.49. 50.11.1 gives this word as an example of the *Doṣa* व्रीडादायिन् (= producing a feeling of shame because of possessing an indecent meaning). According to him this kind of indecency may be hidden (*i.e.*,) may not be apparent because the word may have a meaning other than this one and widely acknowledged and gives as an example the word सम्बाध whose well-known meaning is सङ्कट = stress, crowd; but which has a very much less known application to 'genitals'.

Intro. This illustrates No.2 in Verse 47 *ante*.

50. That must be known as of 'improper significance' the sound of which when uttered produces ideas of indecent things.

51. Simple and indecent and therefore not translated. This is used by Mammaṭa in his *Kāvyaprakāśa*. See p.405, Jhalkikar's Edition. Here the word हन्तुम् means sexual intercourse and the words following emphasise that meaning.

52. If two words are so placed in juxtaposition that out of them a combination results capable of an indecent meaning it is a case of *Kalpanādusṭa* (Improper juxtaposition) as "स शौर्याभरणः".

This word means "One whose ornament is valour". This meaning is no doubt fine, but in bringing together the two words we get the combination याभ which means sexual intercourse.

Intro. This gives an example of *Śrutikaṣṭa*:-

53. Words like अजिहृ लदत् are harsh of sound; The wise dislike them. Some object to the word गण्ड also.

Intro. This provides for exceptions in some cases:-

54. Sometimes even objectionable words shine by the position given to them; just as (mere) green leaves look pretty when interposed amidst the flowers of garlands.

Vāmana (*Kāvyālaṅkārasūtra* p.41) adds the following *Vṛtti* to *Sūtra* No.6.-'रचनागुम्फितमप्युद्वेजयति '. The commentary *Kāmadhenu* explains that the view of Bhāmaha in the above verse is repudiated - विशिष्टसन्दर्भगर्भगतमपि सहृदयहृदयोद्वेगमावहति.

55. Some objectionable (words) attain a grace on account of the place they occupy; just as collyrium, which is really dirt, when applied to the eyes of a beautiful damsel.

56. Oh Lotus-eyed one! This, your face has cheeks slightly pale. Here the word गण्ड becomes unobjectionable by being yoked to the word पाण्डु.

57. Similarly (i.e. by indications such as these) even improper words may be connected. As for instance 'मदवारिभिर्विक्लिन्न - गण्डानां करिणाम्' = Of elephants whose cheeks are wet with flow of ichor.

Here the words क्लिन्न and गण्ड both of which are objectionable cease to be so, on account of their connection with the flow of the ichor of an elephant.

58. Of elephants there are four hundred whose cheeks are wet with ichor. Thus, one may employ words both proper and improper.

59. Just as a man who strings up a garland uses one kind of flower because it is sweet-smelling and rejects another because it is ordinary; again knows that one (particular) flower will look pretty when intervowen in a particular manner or that only a (particular) place is suited for a particular flower just as such a man strings up discriminating correctly - so should one (composing *Kāvya*) dispose of words with close attention.

5

From *Dhvanyaloka*

Anandavardhana

एवं वाच्यव्यतिरेकिणो व्यङ्ग्यस्यार्थस्य सद्भावं प्रतिपाद्य प्रकृत उपयोजयन्नाह –

यत्रार्थः शब्दो वा तमर्थमुपसर्जनीकृतस्वार्थौ ।
व्यङ्क्तः काव्यविशेषः स ध्वनिरिति सूरिभिः
कथितः ॥१३॥

यत्रार्थो वाच्यविशेषः वाचकविशेषः शब्दो वा तमर्थं व्यङ्क्तः स काव्यविशेषो ध्वनिरिति। अनेन वाच्यवाचकचारुत्व-हेतुभ्य उपमादिभ्योऽनुप्रासादिभ्यश्च विभक्त एव ध्वनेर्विषय इति दर्शितम् ।

यदप्युक्तम् – 'प्रसिद्धप्रस्थानातिक्रमिणो मार्गस्य काव्यत्वहानेर्ध्वनिर्नास्ति' इति तदप्ययुक्तम् । यतो लक्षणकृतामेव स केवलं न प्रसिद्धः, लक्ष्ये तु परीक्ष्यमाणे स एव सहृदयहृदयाह्लादकारि काव्यतत्त्वम् । ततोऽन्यच्चित्रमेवेत्यग्रे दर्शयिष्यामः ।

यदप्युक्तम् कामनीयकमनतिवर्तमानस्य तस्योक्तालङ्कारादिप्रकारेष्वन्तर्भावः इति, तदप्यसमीचीनम्; यतो वाच्यवाचकमात्राश्रयिणि प्रस्थाने व्यङ्ग्यव्यञ्जकसमाश्रयेण व्यवस्थितस्य ध्वनेःकथमन्तर्भावः, वाच्यवाचकचारुत्वहेतवो हि तस्याङ्गभूताः, न तु तदेकरूपा एवेति प्रतिपादयिष्यमाणत्वात् ।

परिकरश्लोकश्चात्र –

'व्यङ्ग्यव्यञ्जकसंबन्धनिबन्धनतया ध्वनेः ।
वाच्यवाचकचारुत्वहेत्वन्तःपातिता कुतः ॥'

ननु यत्र प्रतीयमानस्यार्थस्य वैशद्येनाप्रतीतिः स नाम मा भूद्ध्वनेर्विषयः। यत्र तु तत्प्रतीतिरस्ति, यथा समासोक्त्याक्षेपानुक्तनिमित्तविशेषोक्तिपर्यायोक्तापह्नुतिदीपकसङ्करालङ्कारादौ, तत्र ध्वनेरन्तर्भावो भविष्यतीत्यादि निराकर्तुमभिहितम् – 'उपसर्जनीकृतस्वार्थौ' इति। अर्थो गुणीकृतात्मा, गुणीकृताभिधेयः शब्दो वा यत्रार्थान्तरमभिव्यनक्ति स ध्वनिरिति। तेषु कथं तस्यान्तर्भावः। व्यङ्ग्यप्राधान्ये हि ध्वनिः। न चैतत्समासोक्त्यादिष्वस्ति। समासोक्तौ तावत् –

उपोढरागेण विलोलतारकं तथा गृहीतं शशिना निशामुखम्।
यथा समस्तं तिमिरांशुकं तया पुरोऽपि रागाद्गलितं न लक्षितम्॥

इत्यादौ व्यङ्ग्येनानुगतं वाच्यमेव प्राधान्येन प्रतीयते, समारोपितनायिकानायकव्यवहारयोर्निशाशशिनोरेव वाक्यार्थत्वात्।

आक्षेपेऽपि व्यङ्ग्यविशेषाक्षेपिणो वाच्यस्यैव चारुत्वं प्राधान्येन वाक्यार्थ आक्षेपोक्तिसामर्थ्यादेव ज्ञायते। तथाहि तत्र शब्दोपारूढो विशेषाभिधानेच्छया प्रतिषेधरूपो य आक्षेपः स एव व्यङ्ग्यविशेषमाक्षिपन्मुख्यं काव्यशरीरम्। चारुत्वोत्कर्षनिबन्धना हि वाच्यव्यङ्ग्ययोः प्राधान्यविवक्षा। यथा –

अनुरागवती सन्ध्या दिवसस्तत्पुरस्सरः।
अहो दैवगतिश्चित्रा तथापि न समागमः॥

अत्र सत्यामपि व्यङ्ग्यप्रतीतौ वाच्यस्यैव चारुत्वमुत्कर्षवदिति तस्यैव प्राधान्यविवक्षा।

यथा च दीपकापह्नुत्यादौ व्यङ्ग्यत्वेनोपमायाः प्रतीतावपि प्राधान्येनाविवक्षितत्वान्न तया व्यपदेशस्तद्वदत्रापि द्रष्टव्यम्। अनुक्तनिमित्तायामपि विशेषोक्तौ –

आहूतोऽपि सहायैरोमित्युक्त्वा विमुक्तनिद्रोऽपि ।
गन्तुमना अपि पथिकः सङ्कोचं नैव शिथिलयति ।।

इत्यादौ व्यङ्ग्यस्य प्रकरणसामर्थ्यात्प्रतीतिमात्रम्। न तु तत्प्रतीतिनिमित्ता काचिच्चारुत्वनिष्पत्तिरिति न प्राधान्यम्।

पर्यायोक्तेऽपि यदि प्राधान्येन व्यङ्ग्यत्वं तद्भवतु नाम तस्य ध्वनांवन्तर्भावः। न तु ध्वनेस्तत्रान्तर्भावः। तस्य महाविषयत्वेनाङ्गित्वेन च प्रतिपादयिष्यमाणत्वात्। न पुनः पर्यायोक्ते भामहोदाहृतसदृशे व्यङ्ग्यस्यैव प्राधान्यम्। वाच्यस्य तत्रोपसर्जनीभावेनाविवक्षितत्वात्।

अपह्नुतिदीपकयोः पुनर्वाच्यस्य प्राधान्यं व्यङ्ग्यस्य चानुयायित्वं प्रसिद्धमेव।

सङ्करालङ्कारेऽपि यदालङ्कारोऽलङ्कारान्तरच्छायामनुगृह्णाति, तदा व्यङ्ग्यस्य प्राधान्येनाविवक्षितत्वान्न ध्वनिविषयत्वम्। अलङ्कारद्वयसम्भावनायां तु वाच्यव्यङ्ग्ययोः समं प्राधान्यम्। अथ वाच्योपसर्जनीभावेन व्यङ्ग्यस्य तत्रावस्थानं तदा सोऽपि ध्वनिविषयोऽस्तु, न तु स एव ध्वनिरिति वक्तुं शक्यम्। पर्यायोक्तनिर्दिष्टन्यायात्। अपि च सङ्करालङ्कारस्य क्वचित् सङ्करोक्तिरेव ध्वनिसम्भावनां निराकरोति।

अप्रस्तुतप्रशंसायामपि यदा सामान्यविशेषभावात् निमित्तनिमित्तिभावाद्वा अभिधीयमानस्याप्रस्तुतस्य प्रतीयमानेन प्रस्तुतेनाभिसम्बन्धः तदाभिधीयमानप्रतीयमानयोः सममेव प्राधान्यम्। यदा तावत्सामान्यस्याप्रस्तुतस्याभिधीयमानस्य प्राकरणिकेन विशेषेण प्रतीयमानेन सम्बन्धस्तदा विशेषप्रतीतौ सत्यामपि प्राधान्येन तस्य सामान्येनाविनाभावात्सामान्यस्यापि प्राधान्यम्। यदापि विशेषस्य सामान्यनिष्ठत्वं तदापि सामान्यस्य प्राधान्ये सामान्ये सर्व-

विशेषाणामन्तर्भावाद्विशेषस्यापि प्राधान्यम्। निमित्तनिमित्तिभावे चायमेव न्यायः।

यदा तु सारूप्यमात्रवशेनाप्रस्तुतप्रशंसायामप्रकृतप्रकृतयोः सम्बन्धस्तदाप्यप्रस्तुतस्य सरूपस्याभिधीयमानस्य प्राधान्येनाविवक्षायां ध्वनावेवान्तर्भावः। इतरथात्वलङ्कारान्तरत्वमेव। तदयमत्र संक्षेपः –

(१) व्यङ्ग्यस्य यत्राप्राधान्यं वाच्यमात्रानुयायिनः ।
समासोक्त्यादयस्तत्र वाच्यालङ्कृतयः स्फुटाः ॥

(२) व्यङ्ग्यस्य प्रतिभामात्रे वाच्यार्थानुगमेऽपि वा ।
न ध्वनिर्यत्र वा तस्य प्राधान्यं न प्रतीयते ॥

(३) तत्परावेव शब्दार्थौ यत्र व्यङ्ग्यं प्रति स्थितौ ।
ध्वनेः स एव विषयो मन्तव्यः सङ्करोज्झितः ॥

तस्मान्न ध्वनेरन्यत्रान्तर्भावः ।

इतश्च नान्तर्भावः, यतः काव्यविशेषोऽङ्गी ध्वनिरिति कथितः। तस्य पुनरङ्गानि – अलंकारा गुणा वृत्तयश्चेति प्रतिपादयिष्यते। न चावयव एव पृथग्भूतोऽवयवीति प्रसिद्धः। अपृथग्भावे तु तदङ्गत्वं तस्य न तु तत्त्वमेव। यत्रापि वा तत्त्वं तत्रापि ध्वनेर्महाविषयत्वान्न तन्निष्ठत्वमेव।

'सूरिभिः कथित' इति विद्वदुपज्ञेयमुक्तिः, न तु यथाकथञ्चित्प्रवृत्तेति प्रतिपाद्यते। प्रथमे हि विद्वांसो वैयाकरणाः, व्याकरणमूलत्वात्सर्वविद्यानाम्। ते च श्रूयमाणेषु वर्णेषु ध्वनिरिति व्यवहरन्ति। तथैवान्यैस्तन्मतानुसारिभिः सूरिभिः काव्यतत्त्वार्थदर्शिभिर्वाच्यवाचकसम्मिश्रः शब्दात्मा काव्यमिति व्यपदेश्यो व्यञ्जकत्वसाम्याद्ध्वनिरित्युक्तः। न चैवंविधस्य ध्वनेर्वक्ष्यमाणप्रभेदतद्भेदसङ्कलनया महाविषयस्य यत्प्रकाशनं तदप्रसिद्धालङ्कारविशेषमात्र-

प्रतिपादनेन तुल्यमिति तद्भावितचेतसां युक्त एव संरम्भः। न च तेषु कथञ्चिदीर्ष्यया कलुषितशेमुषीकत्वमाविष्करणीयम्।

तदेवं ध्वनेस्तावदभाववादिनः प्रत्युक्ताः। अस्ति ध्वनिः।

स चासावविवक्षितवाच्यो विवक्षितान्यपरवाच्यश्चेति द्विविधः सामान्येन। तत्राद्यस्योदाहरणम्—

सुवर्णपुष्पां पृथिवीं चिन्वन्ति पुरुषास्त्रयः।
शूरश्च कृतविद्यश्च यश्च जानाति सेवितुम्॥

द्वितीयस्यापि—

शिखरिणि क्व नु नाम कियच्चिरं किमभिधानमसावकरोत्तपः।
तरुणि येन तवाधरपाटलं दशति बिम्बफलं शुकशावकः॥

यदप्युक्तं भक्तिर्ध्वनिरिति तत्प्रतिसमाधीयते—

भक्त्या बिभर्ति नैकत्वं रूपभेदादयं ध्वनिः।

अयमुक्तप्रकारो ध्वनिर्भक्त्या नैकत्वं बिभर्ति, भिन्नरूपत्वात्। वाच्यव्यतिरिक्तस्यार्थस्य वाच्यवाचकाभ्यां तात्पर्येण प्रकाशनं यत्र व्यङ्ग्यप्राधान्ये स ध्वनिः। उपचारमात्रं तु भक्तिः।

मा चैतत्स्याद्भक्तिर्लक्षणं ध्वनेरित्याह—

अतिव्याप्तेरथाव्याप्तेर्न चासौ लक्ष्यते तया॥२४॥

नैव भक्त्या ध्वनिर्लक्ष्यते। कथम्? अतिव्याप्तेरव्याप्तेश्च। तत्रातिव्याप्तिर्ध्वनिव्यतिरिक्तेऽपि विषये भक्तेः सम्भवात्। यत्र हि व्यञ्जकत्वकृतं महत्सौष्ठवं नास्ति तत्राप्युपचरितशब्दवृत्त्या प्रसिद्ध्यनुरोधप्रवर्तितव्यवहाराः कवयो दृश्यन्ते। यथा—

परिम्लानं पीनस्तनजघनसङ्गादुभयत
स्तनोर्मध्यस्यान्तः परिमिलनमप्राप्य हरितम्।

इदं व्यस्तन्यासं श्लथभुजलताक्षेपवलनैः
कृशाङ्ग्याः सन्तापं वदति बिसिनीपत्रशयनम् ।।

तथा–

चुम्बिज्जइ सअहुत्तं अवरुन्धिज्जइ सहस्सहुत्तं वि ।
रमिअ पुणो वि रमिज्जइ पिए जणे णत्थि पुणरुत्तम् ।।
[चुम्ब्यते शतकृत्वोऽवरुध्यते सहस्रकृत्वः ।
रन्त्वा पुनरपि रम्यते प्रिये जने नास्ति पुनरुक्तम् ।।
इतिच्छाया]

तथा–

कुविआओ पसण्णाओ ओरण्णमुहीओ विहसमाणाओ ।
जह गहिआ तह हिअअं हरन्ति उच्छिन्तमहिलाओ ।।
[कुपिताः प्रसन्ना अवरुदितवदना विहसन्त्यः ।
यथा गृहीतास्तथा हृदयं हरन्ति स्वैरिण्यो महिलाः ।।
इतिच्छाया]

तथा–

अज्जाएँ पहारो णवलदाए दिण्णो पिएण थणवट्टे ।
मिउओ वि दूसहो ब्विअ जाओ हिअए सवत्तीणम् ।।
[भार्याया प्रहारो नवलतया दत्तः प्रियेण स्तनपृष्ठे ।
मृदुकोऽपि दुःसह इव जातो हृदये सपत्नीनाम् ।।
इतिच्छाया]

तथा–

परार्थे यः पीडामनुभवति भङ्गेऽपि मधुरो
यदीयः सर्वेषामिह खलु विकारोऽप्यभिमतः ।
न सम्प्राप्तो वृद्धिं यदि स भृशमक्षेत्रपतितः
किमिक्षोर्दोषोऽसौ न पुनरगुणाया मरुभुवः ।।

इत्यत्रेक्षुपक्षेऽनुभवतिशब्दः। न चैवंविधः कदाचिदपि ध्वनेर्विषयः।

यतः-

उक्त्यन्तरेणाशक्यं यत्तच्चारुत्वं प्रकाशयन् ।
शब्दो व्यञ्जकतां बिभ्रद् ध्वन्युक्तेर्विषयी भवेत् ॥२५॥

अत्र चोदाहृते विषये नोक्त्यन्तराशक्यचारुत्वव्यक्तिहेतुः शब्दः।

किञ्च-

रूढा ये विषयेऽन्यत्र शब्दाः स्वविषयादपि ।
लावण्याद्याः प्रयुक्तास्ते न भवन्ति पदं ध्वनेः ॥२६॥

तेषु चोपचरितशब्दवृत्तिरस्तीति। तथाविधे च विषये क्वचित्सम्भवन्नपि ध्वनिव्यवहारः प्रकारान्तरेण प्रवर्तते। न तथाविधशब्दमुखेन। अपिच-

मुख्यां वृत्तिं परित्यज्य गुणवृत्त्यार्थदर्शनम् ।
यदुद्दिश्य फलं तत्र शब्दो नैव स्खलद्गतिः ॥२७॥

तत्र हि चारुत्वातिशयविशिष्टार्थप्रकाशनलक्षणे प्रयोजने कर्तव्ये यदि शब्दस्यामुख्यता तदा तस्य प्रयोगे दुष्टतैव स्यात्। तस्मात्-

वाचकत्वाश्रयेणैव गुणवृत्तिर्व्यवस्थिता ।
व्यञ्जकत्वैकमूलस्य ध्वनेः स्याल्लक्षणं कथम् ॥२८॥

तस्मादन्यो ध्वनिरन्या च गुणवृत्तिः ।

अव्याप्तिरप्यस्य लक्षणस्य। न हि ध्वनिप्रभेदो विवक्षितान्यपरवाच्यलक्षणः, अन्ये च बहवः प्रकारा भक्त्या व्याप्यन्ते; तस्माद्भक्तिरलक्षणम्।

कस्यचिद्ध्वनिभेदस्य सा तु स्यादुपलक्षणम् ।

सा पुनर्भक्तिर्वक्ष्यमाणप्रभेदमध्यादन्यतमस्य भेदस्य यदि नामोपलक्षणतया सम्भाव्यते, यदि च गुणवृत्त्यैव ध्वनिर्लक्ष्यत इत्युच्यते, तदभिधाव्यापारेण तदितरोऽलङ्कारवर्गः समग्र एव लक्ष्यत इति प्रत्येकमलङ्काराणां लक्षणकरणवैयर्थ्यप्रसङ्गः । किं च–

लक्षणेऽन्यैः कृते चास्य पक्षसंसिद्धिरेव नः ॥१९॥

कृतेऽपि वा पूर्वमेवान्यैर्ध्वनिलक्षणे पक्षसंसिद्धिरेव नः; यस्माद्ध्वनिरस्तीति नः पक्षः। स च प्रागेव संसिद्ध इत्ययत्नसंपन्नसमीहितार्थाः संवृत्ताः स्मः ।

येऽपि सहृदयहृदयसंवेद्यमनाख्येयमेव ध्वनेरात्मानमाम्नासिषुस्तेऽपि न परीक्ष्यवादिनः। यत उक्तया नीत्या वक्ष्यमाणया च ध्वनेः सामान्यविशेषलक्षणे प्रतिपादितेऽपि यद्यनाख्येयत्वं तत्सर्वेषामेव वस्तूनां प्रसक्तम्। यदि पुनर्ध्वनेरतिशयोक्त्यानया काव्यान्तरातिशायि तैः स्वरूपमाख्यायते तत्तेऽपि युक्ताभिधायिनं एव।

इति श्रीराजानकानन्दवर्धनाचार्यविरचिते सहृदयालोके

प्रथमोद्द्योतः ॥

So far, the existence of suggested meaning apart from the explicit has been set forth; and now it is made to serve the purpose on hand in the following text:

That kind of poetry, wherein the (conventional) meaning renders itself secondary or the (conventional) word renders its meaning secondary and suggests the (intended or) implied meaning, is designated by the learned as DHVANI or 'Suggestive Poetry'.

The kind of poetry wherein not only meaning, i.e., specific meaning but also word, i.e. specific word, goes to suggest only the said (implicit) meaning, is signified by the name DHVANI or Suggestive poetry. By this it is shown how the province of Suggestive Poetry is quite distinct from that of the sources of charm in explicit meaning, such as the figure simile on the one hand, and from that of the sources of charm in distinctive sound, such as the figure alliteration on the other.

The *prima facie* view already mentioned, viz, "Suggestion does not exist indeed; for, a species of poetry opposed to all well-known canons will necessarily cease to be poetry", is unsound. The reason is that it is unfamilar only to writers on poetics and if one were to examine the best specimens of literature, it alone would emerge as the most intrinsic principle of poetry delighting all refined critics. We shall show later on that all else is only 'puzzling picture'.

The other objection, viz, "since it is not distinct from a source of charm, it naturally comes under the causes of charm already enumerated", is also fallacious. How can suggestion which is grounded on the relation of the suggested sense to the suggesting word be ever comprehended by a theory which is based on the relation of only the conventional sense to the denotative word? It will be expounded later that the sources of beauty in conventional meanings and expressions can only be ancillary and never identical with it.

Here is a mnemonic verse:

> *Suggestion, indeed, is conditioned by only the relation between the suggested and the suggester; when such is the case, how can it ever be subsumed under the source of beauty in the expressed and the expression?*

Perhaps some might argue in the following strain: 'Such instances (of figures of speech) wherein no implicit meaning is clearly discernible may by all means be regarded as incapable of subsuming suggestion. But suggestion can certainly be subsumed under such figures of speech as Condensed Metaphor, Paraleipsis, Metonymy, Periphrasis, Fancied Denial, Ellipsis implying a Simile, and Merging of Figures, since we have a clear perception of the implicit meaning in these. It is in order to refute such an argument that the words, 'renders itself or its meaning secondary' etc, have been included in the text. The idea is that when in a work of poetry an explicit meaning renders itself secondary or when a word renders its own denotative meaning secondary and each of these suggests anoth - sense, we call it Suggestive Poetry. How can this suggestion be brought under the said figures? Suggestion is possible only when the suggested element is exclusively important. This is not so in Condensed Metaphor and the like. In an instance of Condensed Metaphor such as -

> *The twilight (heroine's face) with twinkling stars (shining pupils) was illumined (kissed) by the moon (the hero) glowing red (overcome by emotion) so suddenly (with such love) that the entire mass of darkness (black garment) disappearing in the east (slipping even in front), due to illumination (love) was not at all noticed.* -

it is the explicit meaning alone which appears as prominent and the suggested sense is only secondary to it. The main subjects of description are the night and the moon. And the behaviour of a heroine and that of a hero are attributed to them (only secondarily).

Even in Paraleipsis, we find beauty more in the explicit than in the particular idea it hints at. That the explicit is relatively more important than the implicit in this figure is brought out even by its title - 'the pointer'. In an instance of Paraleipsis in poetry, that which stands out as the chief element is the very act of hinting at and it will be of the nature of a disavowal s .rving the purpose of conveying speciality; and it will be found expressed openly, in so many words, though all the while it will be hinting at the suggested idea. Between the expressed and the suggested, which of them is intended to be relatively more important can be settled only by determining the relative excelence of cha.'m. For example -

> *Twilight is full of love (red colour),*
> *And the day chases her face to face;*
> *But, oh, look at the decree of Fate*
> *The twain do never meet!*

Though a suggested idea is understood here, charm is felt to exist only in the expressed. Hence that alone should be taken to be primarily intended.

Just as in figures like Ellipsis implying a simile and Fancied Denial, although we find a suggested simile, we do not designate these figures by that name because the explicit aspects in them are intended to be more important, so also in Paraleipsis the same consideration should be kept in sight.

The same is true of Metonymy in which (the effect alone is mentioned and) the cause is omitted:

The friends are calling outside;
'Coming' is his reply form inside
All his sleep is gone by.
Still the traveller rolls in langour
Though with a mind to go.

In instances like this, we simply get at the suggested idea by force of context and we do not come across any charm therein. Hence the suggested idea is not of primary importance.

So also in Periphrasis, if the suggested idea were to be regarded as primarily important, it might by all means be brought under suggestion: but suggestion will not be subsumed under it. For not only the province of suggestion is wider but its importance also is greater (than that of the expressed) as it will be explained later. In the figure Periphrasis as illustrated by Bhāmaha, we do not have at all any exclusive importance attached to the suggested idea, since the expressed one is not intended there to be secondary.

So far as Fancied Denial and Ellipsis implying a simile are concerned, it is well known that the expressed element alone is primary therein and that the suggested element is secondary to it.

In Merging of Figures too, when one figure favours the shade of another figure, the suggested alone is not primarily intended and hence it cannot be reckoned to subsume suggestion. In instances where two figures may be said to exist simultaneously, the expressed and the suggested get equal importance. If in an instance the expressed is secondary and the suggested has primary importance, then it might, of course, be brought under suggestion. But it is not possible to say even then that it is itself identical with suggestion. The argument given in connection with Periphrasis is applicable here also. What is more, the very expression we use to signify this figure, viz., 'Merging of Figures' prevents often even our imagining that it might be the same as suggestion.

So also in the figure, Vicarious Reference, in instances where the expressed extraneous idea and the implied contextual idea are related to each other either as universal and particular or as cause and effect, the expressed and the implied get equal importance of course. In other words, when the expressed extraneous idea is a universal and it is related to the implied contextual idea which happens to be its particular, the universal itself gets equal importance since its relationship with the particular is one of inseparable inherence. Similarly, even when the extraneous particular happens to be its relationship with the particular is one of inseparable inherence. Similarly, even when the extraneous particular happens to be related to the contextual universal, notwithstanding the importance accruing to the universal (by its sheer relevancy), the particulars are comprehended by the universal. The same logic applies also to instances where the expressed and the implied are related to each other as cause and effect. Even in instances of Vicarious Reference where the relation is of similarity, if the extraneous expressed idea bearing similarity is not intended as primarily important, it comes, of course, under the category of suggestion. Otherwise (i.e. if it is intended as primarily important), it will just be one of the figures.

The following mnemonic verses sum up the position:-

1 *Wherever we find the implied meaning unimportant and merely ancillary to the expressed, we should clearly conclude that such instances contain only figures like the Condensed Metaphor.*

2 *In places where we have just a glimmer of the implied, or where the implied is just a handmaid to the expressed, or where its primary importance is not clearly discernible, there is no Suggestive Poetry.*

3 *Only those instances wherein we find both the word and the meaning solely directed towards the implied meaning should be regarded as real instances of Suggestive Poetry admitting of no confusion whatever.*

It is thus established that suggestion cannot be subsumed under other heads.

Another reason why it cannot be so subsumed is the statement that 'it is only the full-limbed species of poetry which gets the designation of DHVANI or Suggestive Poetry'. It will be explained hereafter that the limbs (of poetry) are figures, qualities, and varieties of diction. Looking upon each component part as the whole itself is quite unheard of. When considered collectively, it will be but a part of the whole and never identical witht he whole. Even if identity were possible in some instances, Suggestive Poetry cannot be looked upon as conditioned by its limbs mentioned, since its sphere is very extensive.

The expression, "*is designated by the learned*" brings out the fact that this designation was first devised by the learned and that it has not gained currency in a haphazard fashion. The foremost among the learned are grammarians because grammar lies at the root of all studies. They indeed refer to articulate letters by the term DHVANI or Suggester. In the same way, since the element of suggestion is common (to both), not only the word and its meaning but its essential verbal power and also that which is usually referred to by the term poetry, has been given the same designation, viz, DHVANI by other learned men whose insight into the fundamental truth about poetry is profound and who are followers of the principles laid down by grammarians. A treatment, then, of such a comprehensive concept as suggestion, with all its divisions and subdivisions yet to be explained in the sequel, is not at all on a par with the enumeration of the well known, specific figures of speech and hence the enthusiasm of persons imbued in their minds with the value of suggestion is quite proper. None need display jealousy to show somehow that they are all men of deranged minds.

The advocates of the view that suggestion is non-existent have been thus refuted. Suggestion does exist.

Broadly considered, it will be two-fold: (1) with unintended literal import and (2) with intended but further-extending literal import. The following is an example of the first kind:

Three persons will gather
Flowers of gold from the earth:
The bold, the learned,
And he who knows how to serve.

The following illustrates the second:

On which mountain and for how long
Did this one perform penance?
And what might be its name?
For, the young parrot pecks
The fruit so red as your lips.

The counterview that metaphorical indication itself is suggestion is answered in what follows:-

Suggestion does not bear identity with indication because there is difference in nature between the two.

Suggestion which has been explained above does not bear identity with logical implication or indication since the two have different natures. Suggestion is the uni-directional communication of a sense other than the expressed by both the expressed sense and the expression while at the same time the implied sense will be exclusively important. But indication is merely metaphorical application.

One might perhaps urge - "Indication may not be identical with suggestion; but it can at least be regarded as a differentia of the latter". This view is countered below:

Nor is this a differentia of that as both the fallacies of Too Wide and Too Narrow would result (if one were to hold such a view).

Nor is suggestion determined by indication. 'Why'? '*Because of the fallacy of Too Wide and also of the fallacy of Too Narrow*'.

The fallacy of Too Wide is there inasmuch as indication can exist even in such instances as are devoid of suggestion. Even in instances where no excessive charm due to suggestion is present, poets are seen to employ words with metaphorical applications in pursuance of established usage as in the following example:

This bed of lotus-leaves bespeaks
The torment of the damsel that slept thereon.
Faded as its two ends with pressure
Of her buxom breasts and burly hips.
The part that spanned her slender waist
Remains green without such pressure.
And here it is in disorder
By the movements of her tense creeper-like arms.

To take another example:

The beloved one is kissed for the hundredth time,
Is embraced for the thousandth time,
And with but a brief pause, is fondled again;
Yet there is no tautology for lovers.

Here is another example:

Angry or pleased, in tears or in smiles,
In whatever state they are caught,
Wanton women steal one's heart.

This is also an example:

Though it was but a mild blow
Which the husband gave
On the bosom of his youngest wife,
It became a smarting blow as it were
On the hearts of his other wives.

The following is still another example:

If that which suffers pain for others' sake
And remains sweet though broke in twain,
If that whose various deformities too
Are held to be ever pleasing,
Falls on a barren soil and fails to grow,

Is it the mistake of the sugar-cane,
And not at all of the worthless desert?

In this last example, the word ***suffers*** *is an instance of indication. Such instances can never be regarded as instances of suggestion. For –*

Only that word, which conveys a charm incapable of communication by any other expression and which is pregnant with suggestive force, becomes a fit instance for the title "Suggestive".

In the illustrative examples given above the word does not become a source of suggesting any charm uncommunicable by other expressions. Moreover–

Words which signify by common usage meanings other than what they primarily denote, as for instance the word lāvaṇya, do not become instances of Suggestion.

But in such words anyway, there is metaphorical application. Even if the title 'Suggestion' should be possible of application towards them, it would be on the basis of an entirely different consideration. Words of the kind mentioned will have nothing to do with it.

If one gives up the primary denotative power of a word and understands a sense (secondarily conveyed by it) through its indicative power, it is because of a purpose. In conveying this purpose, the word does not move falteringly at all (as it moves falteringly when indicating a meaning secondarily). 17.

In order to justify secondary usage, one will have to posit a purpose, namely, the communication of a meaning imbued with great charm. If the word were to convey this purpose too in a secondary way only, then the very employment of the word would be fallacious. But it is not so in fact.

Therefore -

The fact is that indication is grounded on the

primary denotative force of words. How can it ever be a definition of suggestion whose sole support is suggestivity? 18

Hence suggestion is one thing and indication another.

The definition (that suggestion is indication) contains the fallacy of *Too Narrow* also. Indication does not cover instances of suggestion like 'that with intended but further-extending literal import' as also numerous other instances. Hence, indication cannot be a definition of suggestion.

(At the most), it might serve as a pointer to one of the species of suggestion.

One could only fancy that indication might serve, if at all, as a pointer to just a single species from among the numerous varieties of suggestion pointed out in the sequel. With all this, if one were to assert dogmatically that suggestion is indeed defined by indication, that way, one might say that the act of defining individual figures is an utter waste since the primary denotation of words defines the entire group of all individual figures. What is more-

If one were to say that the definition of suggestion has already been propounded by others, it would only substantiate our own position.

Even if it be true that the definition of suggestion has already been propounded by earlier writers, it would only mean a substantiation of our own position. For, our position is that suggestion exists; and in case it has been established already, we should consider ourselves to be extremely fortunate inasmuch as our object has already been realised without any labour at all on our part.

Even those, who assert that the nature of suggestion is within the experience of only the perceptive critics and that it is inexpressible, betray only their lack of discernment. (The reason is not far to seek). We have already propounded the general definition of suggestion; and definitions of its several varieties will be set forth hereafter. If inspite of all these, it should be thought of as "inexpressible", then this would be true of everything in the world. If, on the other hand, they are only giving expression to the all-surpassing nature of suggestion by means of this exaggeration, then they also might be regarded as but stating the truth itself.

6

From *Locana*

Abhinava Gupta

सद्भावमिति । सत्तां साधुभावंप्राधान्यं चेत्यर्थः। द्वयं हि प्रतिपिपादयिषितम्। प्रकृत इति लक्षणे। उपयोजयन् उपयोगं गमयन्। तमर्थमिति चायमुपयोगः। स्वशब्द आत्मवाची। स्वश्चार्थश्च तौ स्वार्थौ; तौ गुणीकृतौ याभ्याम्; यथासंख्येन तेनार्थो गुणीकृतात्मा, शब्दो गुणीकृताभिधेयः। तमर्थमिति। 'सरस्वती स्वादु तदर्थवस्तु' इति यदुक्तम्। व्यङ्क्तः द्योतयतः। व्यङ्क्त इति द्विवचनेनेदमाह यद्यप्यविवक्षितवाच्ये शब्द एव व्यञ्जकस्तथाप्यर्थस्यापि सहकारिता न त्रुट्यति, अन्यथा अज्ञातार्थोऽपि शब्दस्तद्व्यञ्जकः स्यात्। विवक्षितान्यपरवाच्ये च शब्दस्यापि सहकारित्वं भवत्येव, विशिष्टशब्दाभिधेयतया विना तस्यार्थस्याव्यञ्जकत्वादिति सर्वत्र शब्दार्थयोरुभयोरपि ध्वननं व्यापारः। तेन यद्भट्टनायकेन द्विवचनं दूषितं तद्गजनिमीलिकयैव। अर्थः शब्दो वेति तु विकल्पाभिधानं प्राधान्याभिप्रायेण। काव्यं च तद्विशेषश्चासौ काव्यस्य वा विशेषः। काव्यग्रहणादुगुणालङ्कारोपस्कृतशब्दार्थपृष्ठपाती ध्वनिलक्षण 'आत्मे'त्युक्तम्। तेनैतन्निरवकाशं श्रुतार्थापत्तावापि ध्वनिव्यवहारः स्यादिति। यच्चोक्तम्–'चारूत्वप्रतीतिस्तर्हि काव्यस्यात्मा स्यात्' इति तदङ्गीकुर्म एव। नाम्नि, खल्वयं विवाद इति। यच्चोक्तम्–'चारुणः प्रतीतिर्यदि काव्यात्मा प्रत्यक्षादिप्रमाणादपि सा भवन्ती तथा स्यात्' इति। तत्र शब्दार्थमयकाव्यात्माभिधानप्रस्तावे क एष प्रसङ्ग इति न किञ्चिदेतत्। स इति। अर्थो वा शब्दो वा, व्यापारो वा। अर्थोऽपि वाच्यो वा ध्वनतीति, शब्दोऽप्येवम्। व्यङ्ग्यो वा ध्वन्यत इति व्यापारो वा शब्दार्थयोर्ध्वननमिति। कारिकया तु प्राधान्येन समुदाय एव

काव्यरूपो मुख्यतया ध्वनिरिति प्रतिपादितम्। विभक्त इति। गुणालङ्काराणां वाच्यवाचकभावप्राणत्वात्। अस्य च तदन्यव्यङ्ग्यव्यञ्जकभावसारत्वान्नास्य तेष्वन्तर्भाव इति। अनन्यत्र भावो विषयशब्दार्थः। एवं तद्व्यतिरिक्तः कोऽयं ध्वनिरिति निराकृतम्। लक्षणकृतामेवेति । लक्षणकाराप्रसिद्धता विरुद्धो हेतुः; तत एव हि यत्नेनलक्षणीयता। लक्षयेत वप्रसिद्धत्वमसिद्धो हेतुः। यच्च नृत्तगीतादिकल्पं, तत्काव्यस्य न किञ्चित्। चित्रमिति विस्मयकृद्वृत्तादिवशात्, न तु सहृदयाभिलषणीयचमत्कारसाररसनिःष्पन्दमय मित्यर्थः। काव्यानुकारित्वाद्वा, चित्रम्, आलेखमात्रत्वाद्वा कलामात्रत्वाद्वा। अग्र इति।

प्रधानगुणभावाभ्यां व्यङ्ग्यस्यैवं व्यवस्थितम् ।
द्विधा काव्यं ततोऽन्यद्यत्तच्चित्रमभिधीयते ।।

इतितृतीयोद्द्योते वक्ष्यति। परिकरार्थं कारिकार्थस्याधिकावापं कर्तुं श्लोकः परिकर श्लोकः। यत्रेत्यलङ्कारे। वैशद्येने ति। चारुतया स्फुटतया चेत्यर्थः। अभिहितमि ति भूतप्रयोग आदौ व्यङ्क्त इत्यस्य व्याख्याततत्वात्। गुणीकृतात्मे ति। आत्मेत्यनेन स्वशब्दस्यार्थो व्याख्यातः। न चैतदिति। व्यङ्ग्यस्य प्राधान्यम्। प्राधान्यं च यद्यपि ज्ञप्तौ न चकास्ति; 'बुद्धौ तत्त्वावभासिन्यां' इति नयेनाखण्डचर्वणाविश्रान्तेः, तथापि विवेचकैर्जीवितान्वेषणे क्रियमाणे यदा व्यङ्ग्योऽर्थः पुनरपि वाच्यमेवानुप्राणयन्नास्ते तदा तदुपकरणत्वादेव तस्यालङ्कारता। ततो वाच्यादेव तदुपस्कृताच्चमत्कारलाभ इति। यद्यपि पर्यन्ते रसध्वनिरस्ति, तथापि मध्यकक्षानिविष्टोऽसौ व्यङ्ग्योऽर्थो न रसोन्मुखीभवति; स्वातन्त्र्येणापि तु वाच्यमेवार्थं संस्कर्तुं धावतीति गुणीभूतव्यङ्ग्यतोक्ता। समासोक्ताविति।

यत्रोक्तौ गम्यतेऽन्योऽर्थस्तत्समानैर्विशेषणैः ।
सा समसोक्तिरुदिता संक्षिप्तार्थतया बुधैः ।।

इत्यत्र समासोक्तेर्लक्षणस्वरूपं हेतुर्नाम तन्निर्वचनमिति पादचतुष्टयेन क्रमादुक्तम्। उपोढोरागः सान्ध्योऽरुणिमाप्रेमचयेन। विलोलास्तारका ज्योतींषि नेत्रत्रिभागाश्च यत्र। तथेति। झटित्येव प्रेमरभसेन। गृहीत माभासितं परिचुम्बितुमाक्रान्तं च। निशाया मुखं प्रारम्भो वदनकोकनदं चेति। यथेति। झटिति ग्रहणेन प्रेमरभसेन च। तिमिरं चांशुकाश्च सूक्ष्मांशवस्तिमिरांशुकं रश्मिशबलीकृतं तमःपटलं, तिमिरांशुकं नीलजालिका नवोढाप्रौढवधूचिता। रागाद्रक्तत्वात् सन्ध्याकृतादनन्तरं प्रेमरूपाच्च हेतोः। पुरोऽपि पूर्वस्यां दिशि अग्रे च। गलितं प्रशान्तं पतितं च। रात्र्या करणभूतया समस्तं मिश्रितम्; उपलक्षणत्वेन वा। न लक्षितं रात्रिप्रारम्भोऽसाविति न ज्ञातं, तिमिरसंवलितांशुदर्शने हि रात्रिमुखमिति लोकेन लक्ष्यते न तु स्फुट आलोके। नायिकापक्षे तु तयेति कर्तृपदम्। रात्रिपक्षे तु अपिशब्दो लक्षितमित्यस्यानन्तरः। अत्र च नायकेन पश्चाद्गतेन चुम्बनोपक्रमे पुरो नीलांशुकस्य गलनं पतनम्। यदि वा 'पुरोऽग्रे नायकेन तथा गृहीतं मुखमि'ति सम्बन्धः। तेनात्र व्यङ्ग्ये प्रतीतेऽपि न प्राधान्यम्। तथाहि नायकव्यवहारो निशाशशिनावेव श्रृङ्गारविभावरूपौ संस्कुर्वाणोऽलङ्कारतां भजते, ततस्तु वाच्याद्विभावीभूतादसनिःष्यन्दः। यस्तु व्याचष्टे – 'तया निशयेति कर्तृपदं, न चाचेतनायाः कर्तृत्वमुपपन्नमिति शब्देनैवात्र नायकव्यवहार उन्नीतोऽभिधेय एव, न व्यङ्ग्य इत्यत एव समासोक्तिः' इति। स प्रकृतमेव ग्रन्थार्थमत्यजद्व्यङ्ग्येनानुगतमिति। एकदेशविवर्ति चेत्थं रूपकं स्यात्, 'राजहंसैरवीज्यन्त शरदैव सरोनृपाः' इतिवत्, न तु समासोक्तिः; तुल्यविशेषणाभावात्। गम्यत इति चानेनाभिधाव्यापारनिरासादित्यलमवान्तरेण बहुना। नायिकाया नायके यो व्यवहारः स निशायां समारोपितः; नायिकायां नायकस्य यो व्यवहारः स शशिनि समारोपित इति व्याख्याने नैकशेषप्रसङ्गः। आक्षेप इति।

प्रतिषेध इवेष्टस्य यो विशेषाभिधित्सया ।
वक्ष्यमाणोक्तविषयः स आक्षेपो द्विधा मतः ।।

तत्राद्यौ यथा–

अहंत्वां यदि नेक्षेय क्षणमप्युत्सुका ततः ।
इयदेवास्त्वतोऽन्येन किमुक्तेनाप्रियेण ते ।।

इति वक्ष्यमाणमरणविषयो निषेधात्माक्षेपः। तत्रेयदस्त्वित्येतदेवात्र म्रिये इत्याक्षिपत्सच्चारुत्वनिबन्धनमित्याक्षेप्येणाक्षेपकमलङ्कृतं सत्प्रधानम्। उक्तविषयस्तु यथाममैव–

भो भोः किं किमकाण्ड एव पतितस्त्वं पान्थ कान्या गतिः
तत्ताद्दक्तृषितस्य मे खलमतिः सोऽयं जलं गूहते ।
अस्थानोपनतामकालसुलभां तृष्णां प्रति क्रुध्य भोः
त्रैलोक्यप्रथितप्रभावमहिमा मार्गः पुनर्मारवः ।।

अत्र कश्चित्सेवकः प्राप्तः प्राप्तव्यमस्मात्किमिति न लभ इति प्रत्याशाविशस्यमानहृदयः केनचिदमुनाक्षेपेण प्रतिबोध्यते। तत्राक्षेपेण निषेधरूपेण वाच्यस्यैवासत्पुरुषसेवातद्वैफल्यतत्कृतोद्वेगात्मनः शान्तरसस्थायिभूतनिर्वेदविभावरूपतया चमत्कृतिदायित्वम्। वामनस्य तु 'उपमानाक्षेपः' इत्याक्षेपलक्षणम्। उपमानस्य चन्द्रादेराक्षेपः; अस्मिन्सति किं त्वया कृत्यमिति। यथा–

तस्यास्तन्मुखमस्ति सौम्यसुभगं किं पार्वणेनेन्दुना
सौन्दर्यस्य पदं दृशौ यदि च तैः किं नाम नीलोत्पलैः ।
किं वा कोमलकान्तिभिः किसलयैः सत्येव तत्राधरे
ही धातुः पुनरुक्तवस्तुरचनारम्भेष्वपूर्वो ग्रहः ।।

अत्र वयङ्ग्योऽप्युपमार्थो वाच्यस्यैवोपस्कुरुते। किं तेन कृत्यमिति त्वपहस्तनारूप आक्षेपो वाच्य एव चमत्कारकारणम्। यदि

वोपमानस्याक्षेपः सामर्थ्यादाकर्षणम्। यथा–

> ऐन्द्रं धनुः पाण्डुपयोधरेण शरद्दधानार्द्रनखक्षताभम्।
> प्रसादयन्ती सकलङ्कमिन्दुं तापं रवेरभ्यधिकं चकार ।।

इत्यत्रेर्ष्याकलुषितनायकान्तरमुपमानमाक्षिप्तमपि वाच्यार्थमेवालङ्करोतीत्येषा तु समासोक्तिरेव। तदाह–चारुत्वोत्कर्षेति। अत्रैव प्रसिद्धं दृष्टान्तमाह–अनुरागवतीति। तेनाक्षेपप्रमेयसमर्थनमेवापरिसमाप्तमिति मन्तव्यम्। तत्रोदाहरणत्वेन समासोक्तिश्लोकः पठितः। अहो दैवगतिरिति। गुरुपारतन्त्र्यादिनिमित्तोऽसमागम इत्यर्थः। तस्यैवेति। वाच्यस्यैवेति यावत्। वामनाभिप्रायेणायमाक्षेपः, भामहाभिप्रायेण तु समासोक्तिरित्यमुमाशयं हृदये गृहीत्वा समासोक्त्याक्षेपयोः युक्त्येदमेकमेवोदाहरणं व्यतरद्ग्रन्थकृत्। एषापि समासोक्तिर्वास्तु आक्षेपो वा, किमनेनास्माकम्। सर्वथालङ्कारेषु व्यङ्ग्यं वाच्ये गुणीभवतीति नः साध्यमित्यत्राशयोऽत्र ग्रन्थेऽस्मद्गुरुभिर्निरूपितः।

एवं प्राधान्यविवक्षायां दृष्टान्तमुक्त्वा व्यपदेशोऽपि प्राधान्यकृत एव भवतीत्यत्र दृष्टान्तं स्वपरप्रसिद्धमाह–यथा चेति। उपमाया इति। उपमानोपमेयभावस्येत्यर्थः। तयेत्युपमया। दीपके हि 'आदिमध्यान्तविषयं त्रिधा दीपकमिष्यते' इति लक्षणम्।

> मणिः शाणोल्लीढः समरविजयी हेतिदलितः
> कलाशेषश्चन्द्रः सुरतमृदिता बाललना।
> मदक्षीणो नागः शरदि सरिदाश्यानपुलिना
> तनिम्ना शोभन्ते गलितविभवाश्चार्थिषु जनाः ।।

इत्यत्र दीपनकृतमेव चारुत्वम्। 'अपह्नुतिरभीष्टस्य किञ्चिदन्तर्गतोपमा' इति। तत्रापह्नुत्यैव शोभा। यथा–

नेयं विरौति भृङ्गाली मदेन मुखरा मुहुः ।
अयमाकृष्यमाणस्य कन्दर्पधनुषो ध्वनिः ॥ इति ।

एवमाक्षेपं विचार्योद्देशक्रमेणैव प्रमेयान्तरमाह–अनुक्तनिमित्तायामिति ।

एकदेशस्य विगमे या गुणान्तरसंस्तुतिः ।
विशेषप्रथनायासौ विशेषोक्तिरिति स्मृता ॥

यथा–

स एकस्त्रीणि जयति जगन्ति कुसुमायुधः ।
हरतापि तनुं यस्य शम्भुना न हृतं बलम् ॥

इयं चाचिन्त्यनीमित्तेति नास्यां व्यङ्ग्यस्य सद्भावः । उक्तनिमित्तायामपि वस्तुस्वभावमात्रत्वे पर्यवसानमिति तत्रापि न व्यङ्ग्यसद्भावशङ्का । यथा–

कर्पूर इव दग्धोऽपि शक्तिमान्यो जने जने ।
नमोऽस्त्ववार्यवीर्याय तस्मै कुसुमधन्वने ॥

तेन प्रकारद्वयमवधीर्य तृतीयं प्रकारमाशङ्कते – अनुक्तनिमित्तायामपीति । व्यङ्ग्यस्येति । शीतकृता खल्वार्तिरत्र निमित्तमिति भट्टोद्भटः, तदभिप्रायेणाह नत्वत्र काचिच्चारुत्वनिष्पत्तिरिति । यत्तु रसिकैरपि निमित्तं कल्पितम् – 'कान्तासमागमे गमनादपि लघुतरमुपायं स्वप्नं मन्यमानो निद्रागमबुद्ध्या सङ्कोचं नात्यजत्' इति तदपि निमित्तं चारुत्वहेतुतया नालङ्कारविद्भिः कल्पितम्, अपि तु विशेषोक्तिभाग एव न शिथिलयतीत्येवम्भूतोऽभिव्यज्यमाननिमित्तोपस्कृतश्चारुत्वहेतुः । अन्यथा तु विशेषोक्तिरेवेयं न भवेत् । एवमभिप्रायद्वयमपि साधारणोक्त्या ग्रन्थकृन्न्यरूपयन्न त्वौद्भटेनैवाभिप्रायेण ग्रन्थो व्यवस्थित इति मन्तव्यम् । पर्यायोक्तेऽपीति ।

पर्यायोक्तं यदन्येन प्रकारेणाभिधीयते ।
वाच्यवाचकवृत्तिभ्यां शून्येनावगमात्मना ।।

इति लक्षणम् । यथा-

शत्रुच्छेददृढेच्छस्य मुनेरुत्पथगामिनः ।
रामस्यानेन धनुषा देशिता धर्मदेशना ।। इति ।

अत्र भीष्मस्य भार्गवप्रभावाभिभावी प्रभाव इति यद्यपि प्रतीयते, तथापि तत्सहायेन देशिता धर्मदेशनेत्यभिधीयमानेनैव काव्यार्थोऽलंकृतः। अत एव पर्यायेण प्रकारान्तरेणावगमात्मना व्यङ्ग्येनोपलक्षितं सद्यदभिधीयते तदभिधीयमानमुक्तमेव सत्पर्यायोक्तमित्यभिधीयत इति लक्षणपदम्, पर्यायोक्तमिति लक्ष्यपदम्, अर्थालङ्कारत्वं सामान्यलक्षणं चेति सर्वं युज्यते। यदि त्वभिधीयत इत्यस्य बलाद्व्याख्यानमभिधीयते प्रतीयते प्रधानतयेति, उदाहरणं च 'भम धम्मिअ' इत्यादि, तद़ालङ्कारत्वमेव दूरे सम्पन्नमात्मतायां पर्यवसानात्। तदा चालङ्कारमध्ये गणना न कार्या। भेदान्तराणि चास्य वक्तव्यानि। वदाह-यदि प्राधान्येनेति। ध्वनावि ति। आत्मन्यन्तर्भावादात्मैवासौ नालङ्कारस्स्यादित्यर्थः। तत्रेति। यादृशोऽलङ्कारत्वेन विवक्षितस्तादृशे ध्वनिर्नान्तर्भवति, न तादृगस्माभिर्ध्वनिरुक्तः। ध्वनिर्हि महाविषयः सर्वत्र भावाद्व्यापकः समस्तप्रतिष्ठास्थानत्वाच्चाङ्गी। न चालङ्कारो व्यापकोऽन्यालङ्कारवत्। न चाङ्गी, अलङ्कार्यतन्त्रत्वात्। अथ व्यापकत्वाङ्गित्वे तस्योपगम्येते, त्यज्यते चालङ्कारता, तर्ह्यस्मन्नय एवायमवलम्ब्यते केवलं मात्सर्यग्रहात्पर्यायोक्तवाचेति भावः। न चेयदपि प्राक्तनैर्दृष्टमपि त्वस्माभिरेवोन्मीलितमिति दर्शयति-न पुनरिति। भामहस्य यादृक्तदीयं रूपमभिमतं तादृगुदाहरणेन दर्शितम्। तत्रापि नैव व्यङ्ग्यस्य प्राधान्यं चारुत्वाहेतुत्वात्। तेन तदनुसारितया तत्सदृशं यदुदाहरणान्तरमपि कल्प्यते तत्र नैव व्यङ्ग्यस्य प्राधान्यमिति सङ्गतिः।

यदि तु तदुक्तमुदाहरणमनादृत्य 'भम धम्मिअ' इत्याद्युदाहियते, तदस्मच्छिष्यतैव। केवलं तु नयमनवलम्ब्यापश्रवणेनात्मसँस्कार इत्यनार्यचेष्टितम्। यदाहुरैतिहासिकाः–'अवज्ञयाप्यवच्छाद्य शृण्वन्नरकमृच्छति' इति भामहेन ह्युदाहृतम् –

'गृहेष्वध्वसु वा नान्नं भुञ्ज्महे यदधीतिनः।
विप्रा न भुञ्जते' इति।

एतद्धि भगवद्वासुदेववचनं पर्यायेण रसदानं निषेधति। यत्स एवाह–'तच्च रसदाननिवृत्तये' इति। न चास्य रसदाननिषेधस्य व्यङ्ग्यस्य किञ्चिच्चारुत्वमस्ति येन प्राधान्यं शङ्क्येत। अपि तु तद्व्यङ्ग्योपोद्बलितं विप्रभोजनेन विना यन्नभोजनं तदेवोक्तप्रकारेण पर्यायोक्तं सत्प्राकरणिकं भोजनार्थमलङ्कुरुते। न ह्यस्य निर्विषं भोजनं भवत्विति विवक्षितमिति पर्यायोक्तमलङ्कार एवेति चिरन्तनानामभिमत इति तात्पर्यम्। अपह्नुतिदीपकयोरि ति। एतत्पूर्वमेव निर्णीतम्। अत एवाह–प्रसिद्धमि ति। प्रतीतं प्रसाधितं प्रामाणिकं चेत्यर्थः। पूर्वं चैतदुपमादिव्यपदेशभाजनमेव तद्यथा न भवतीत्यमुया छायया दृष्टान्ततयोक्तमप्युद्देशक्रमपूरणाय ग्रन्थशय्यां योजयितुं पुनरप्युक्तं 'व्यङ्ग्यप्राधान्याभावान्न ध्वनिरि'ति। छायान्तरेण वस्तु पुनरेकमेवोपमाया एव व्यङ्ग्यत्वेन ध्वनित्वाशङ्कनात्। यत्तु विवरणकृत् – दीपकस्य सर्वत्रोपमान्वयो नास्तीति बहुनोदाहरणप्रपञ्चेन विचारितवांस्तदनुपयोगि निस्सारं सुप्रतिक्षेपं च।

मदो जनयति प्रीतिं सानङ्गं मानभङ्गुरम्।
स प्रियासङ्गमोत्कण्ठां सासह्यां मनसः शुचम्॥ इति।

अत्राप्युत्तरोत्तरजन्यत्वेऽप्युपमानोपमेयभावस्य सुकल्पत्वात्। न हि क्रमिकाणां नोपमानोपमेयभावः। तथा हि –

राम इव दशरथोऽभूद्दशरथ इव रघुरजोऽपि रघुसदृशः ।
अज इव दिलीपवंशश्चित्रं रामस्य कीर्तिरियम् ।।

इति न न भवति। तस्मात्क्रमिकत्वं समं वा प्राकरणिकत्वमुपमां निरुणद्धीति कोऽयं त्रास इत्यलं गर्दभीदोहानुवर्तनेन। सङ्करालंङ्कारेऽपीति ।

विरुद्धालंक्रियोल्लेखे समं तद्वृत्यसम्भवे ।
एकस्य च ग्रहे न्यायदोषाभावे च सङ्करः ।।

इति लक्षणादेकः प्रकारः। यथा ममैव-

शशिवदनासितसरसिजनयना सितकुन्ददशनपङ्क्तिरियम् ।
गगनजलस्थलसम्भवहृद्याकारा कृता विधिना ।। इति ।

अत्र शशी वदनमस्याः तद्वद्वा वदनमस्या इति रूपकोपमोल्लेखाद्युगपद्द्वयासम्भवादेकतरपक्षत्यागग्रहणे प्रमाणाभावात्सङ्कर इति व्यङ्ग्यवाच्यताया एवानिश्चयात्का ध्वनिसम्भावना। योऽपि द्वितीयः प्रकारः-शब्दार्थालङ्काराणामेकत्रभाव इति तत्रापि प्रतीयमानस्य का शङ्का। यथा-स्मर स्मरमिव प्रियं रमयसे यमालिङ्गनात् इति।

अत्रैव यमकमुपमा च। तृतीयः प्रकारः- यत्रैकत्र वाक्यांशेऽनेकोऽर्थालङ्कारस्तत्रापि द्वयोः साम्यात्कस्य व्यङ्ग्यता। यथा-

तुल्योदयावसानत्वाद्गतेऽस्तं प्रति भास्वति ।
वासाय वासरः क्लान्तो विशतीव तमोगुहाम् ।। इति ।

अत्र हि स्वामिविपत्तिसमुचितव्रतग्रहणहेवाकिकुलपुत्रकरूपणमेकदेशविवर्त्तिरूपकं दर्शयति। उत्प्रेक्षा चेवशब्देनोक्ता। तदिदं प्रकारद्वयमुक्तम् ।

शब्दार्थवर्त्त्यलङ्कारा वाक्य एकत्र वर्त्तिनः ।
सङ्करश्चैकवाक्यांशप्रवेशाद्वाभिधीयते ।। इति च ।

चतुर्थस्तु प्रकारः यत्रानुग्राह्यानुग्राहकभावोऽलङ्काराणाम् । यथा–

प्रवातनीलोत्पलनिर्विशेषमधीरविप्रेक्षितमायताक्ष्या ।
तया मृहीतं नु मृगाङ्गनाभ्यस्ततो गृहीतं नु मृगाङ्गनाभिः ।।

अत्र मृगाङ्गनावलोकनेन तदवलोकनस्योपमा यद्यपि व्यङ्ग्या, तथापि वाच्यस्य सा सन्देहालङ्कारस्याभ्युत्थानकारिणीत्वेनानुग्राहकत्वाद् गुणीभुता, अनुग्राह्यत्वेन हि सन्देहे पर्यवसानम् । यथोक्तम्–

परस्परोपकारेण यत्रालङ्कृतयः स्थिताः ।
स्वातन्त्र्येणात्मलाभं नो लभन्ते सोऽपि सङ्करः ।।

तदाह – यदालङ्कार इत्यादि । एवं चतुर्थेऽपि प्रकारे ध्वनिता निराकृता । मध्यमयोस्तु व्यङ्ग्यसम्भावनैव नास्तीत्युक्तम् । आद्ये तु प्रकारे 'शशिवदने'त्याद्युदाहृते कथञ्चिदस्ति सम्भावनेत्याशङ्क्य निराकरोति – अलङ्कारद्वये ति । सममि तिं । द्वयोरप्यान्दोल्यमानत्वादिति भावः । ननु यत्र व्यङ्ग्यमेव प्राधान्येन भाति तत्र किं कर्तव्यम् । यथा–

होइ ण गुणाणुराओ खलाणँ णवरं पसिद्धिसरणाणम् ।
किर पहिणुसइ ससिमणं चन्दे पिआमुहे दिट्ठे ।।

अत्रार्थान्तरन्यासस्तावद्वाच्यत्वेनाभाति, व्यतिरेकापह्नुती तु व्यङ्ग्यत्वेन प्रधानतयेत्यभिप्रायेणाशङ्कते – अथे ति । तत्रोत्तरम् – तदा सोऽपी ति । सङ्करालङ्कार एवायं न भवति, अपि त्वलङ्कारध्वनिनामायं ध्वनेर्द्वितीयो भेदः । यच्च पर्यायोक्तेनिरूपितं तत्सर्वमत्राप्यनुसरणीयम् । अथ सर्वेषु सङ्करप्रभेदेषु व्यङ्ग्यसम्भावनानिरासप्रकारं साधारणमाह – अपि चेति । 'क्वचिदपि सङ्करालङ्कारे चे'ति

सम्बन्धः, सर्वभेदभिन्न इत्यर्थः। सङ्कीर्णता हि मिश्रत्वं लोलीभावः, तत्र कथमेकस्य प्राधान्यं क्षीरजलवत्।

अधिकारादपेतस्य वस्तुनोऽन्यस्य या स्तुतिः।
अप्रस्तुतप्रशंसा सा त्रिविधा परिकीर्त्तिता ॥

अप्रस्तुतस्य वर्णनं प्रस्तुताक्षेपिण इत्यर्थः। स चाक्षेपस्त्रिविधो भवति–सामान्यविशेषभावात्, निमित्तनिमित्तिभावात्, सारूप्याच्च। तत्रप्रथमे प्रकारद्वये प्रस्तुताप्रस्तुतयोस्तुल्यमेव प्राधान्यमिति प्रतिज्ञां करोति – अप्रस्तुते त्यादिना प्राधान्यमि त्यन्तेन। तत्र सामान्यविशेषभावेऽपि द्वयी गतिः– सामान्यमप्राकरणिकं शब्देनोच्यते, गम्यते तु प्राकरणिको विशेषः स एकः प्रकारः। यथा–

अहो संसारनैर्घृण्यमहो दौरात्म्यमापदाम्।
अहो निसर्गजिह्मस्य दुरन्ता गतयो विधेः ॥

अत्र हि दैवप्राधान्यं सर्वत्र सामान्यरूपमप्रस्तुतं वर्णितं सत्प्रकृते वस्तुनि क्वापि विनष्टे विशेषात्मनि पर्यवस्यति। तत्रापि विशेषांशस्य सामान्येन व्याप्तत्वाद्व्यङ्ग्यविशेषवद्वाच्यसामान्यस्यापि प्राधान्यम्, न हि सामान्यविशेषयोर्युगपत्प्राधान्यं विरुध्यते। यदा तु विशेषोऽप्राकरणिकः प्राकरणिकं सामान्यमाक्षिपति तदा द्वितीयः

प्रकारः। यथा–

एतत्तस्य मुखात्कियत्कमलिनीपत्रे कणं पाथसो
यन्मुक्तामणिरित्यमंस्त स जडः शृण्वन्यदस्मादपि।
अङ्गुल्यग्रलघुक्रियाप्रविलयिन्यादीयमाने शनै-
स्तत्रोड्डीय गतो हाहेत्यनुदिनं निद्राति नान्तः शुचा ॥

अत्रास्थाने महत्त्वसम्भावनं सामान्यं प्रस्तुतम्, अप्रस्तुतं तु जलबिन्दौ मणित्वसम्भावनं विशेषरूपं वाच्यम्। तत्रापि सामान्-

यविशेषयोर्युगपत्प्राधान्ये न विरोध इत्युक्तम्। एवमेकः प्रकारो द्विभेदोऽपि विचारितः, यदा तावदित्यादिना विशेषस्यापि प्राधान्यमित्यन्तेन। एतमेव न्यायं निमित्तनैमित्तिकभावेऽतिदिशंस्तस्यापि द्विप्रकारतां दर्शयति–निमित्तेति। कदाचिन्निमित्तमप्रस्तुतं सदभिधीयमानं नैमित्तिकं प्रस्तुतमाक्षिपति। यथा–

ये यान्त्यभ्युदये प्रीतिं नोज्झन्ति व्यसनेषु च ।
ते बान्धवास्ते सुहृदो लोकः स्वार्थपरोऽपरः ।।

अत्राप्रस्तुतं सुहृद्बान्धवरूपत्वं निमित्तं सज्जनासक्तया वर्णयति नैमित्तिकीं श्रद्धेयवचनतां प्रस्तुतामात्मनोऽभिव्यङ्क्तुम्; तत्र नैमित्तिकप्रतीतावपि निमित्तप्रतीतिरेव प्रधानीभवत्यनुप्राणकत्वेनेति व्यङ्ग्यव्यञ्जकयोः प्राधान्यम्। कदाचित्तु नैमित्तिकमप्रस्तुतं वर्ण्यमानं सत्प्रस्तुतं निमित्तं व्यनक्ति। यथा सेतौ–

सग्गं अपारिजाअं कोत्थुहलच्छिरहिअं महुमहस्स उरम् ।
सुमरामि महणपुरओ अमुद्धअन्दं च हरजडापब्भारम् ।।

अत्र जाम्बवान् कौस्तुभलक्ष्मीविरहितहरिवक्षःस्मरणादिकमप्रस्तुतनैमित्तिकं वर्णयति प्रस्तुतं वृद्धसेवाचिरजीवित्वव्यवहारकौशलादिनिमित्तभूतं मन्त्रितायामुपादेयमभिव्यङ्क्तुम्। तत्र निमित्तप्रतीतावपि नैमित्तिकं वाच्यभुतम्; प्रत्युत तन्निमित्तानुप्राणितत्वेनोद्धुरकन्धरीकरोत्यात्मानमिति समप्रधानतैव वाच्यव्यङ्ग्ययोः। एवं द्वौ प्रकारौ प्रत्येकं द्विविधौ विचार्य तृतीयः प्रकारः परीक्ष्यते सारूप्यलक्षणः। तत्रापि द्वौ प्रकारौ–अप्रस्तुतात्कदाचिद्वाच्याच्चमत्कारः, व्यङ्ग्यं तु तन्मुखप्रेक्षम्। यथास्मदुपाध्यायभट्टेन्दुराजस्य–

प्राणा येन समर्पितास्तव बलाद्येन त्वमुत्थापितः
स्कन्धे यस्य चिरं स्थितोऽसि विदधे यस्ते सपर्यामपि ।
तस्यास्य स्मितमात्रकेण जनयन् प्राणापहारक्रियां
भ्रातः प्रत्युपकारिणां धुरि परं वेताल लीलायसे ।।

अत्र यद्यपि सारूप्यवशेन कृतघ्नः कश्चिदन्यः प्रस्तुत आक्षिप्यते, तथाप्यप्रस्तुतस्यैव वेतालवृत्तान्तस्य चमत्कारकारित्वम्। न ह्यचेतनोपालम्भवदसम्भाव्यमानोऽयमर्थो न च न हृद्य इति वाच्यस्यात्र प्रधानता। यदि पुनरचेतनादिनात्यन्तासम्भाव्यमानतदर्थविशेषणेनाप्रस्तुतेन वर्णितेन प्रस्तुतमाक्षिप्यमाणं चमत्कारकारि तदा वस्तुध्वनिरसौ। यथा ममैव–

भावव्रात हठाज्जनस्य हृदयान्याक्रम्य यन्नर्तयन्
भङ्गीभिर्विविधाभिरात्महृदयं प्रच्छाद्य संक्रीडसे ।
स त्वामाह जडं ततः सहृदयम्मन्यत्वदुःशिक्षितो
मन्येऽमुष्य जडात्मता स्तुतिपदं त्वत्साम्यसम्भावनात् ।।

कश्चिन्महापुरुषो वीतरागोऽपि सरागवदिति न्यायेन गाढविवेकालोकतिरस्कृततिमिरप्रतानोऽपि लोकमध्ये स्वात्मानं प्रच्छादयल्ँलोकं च वाचालयन्नात्मन्यप्रतिभासमेवाङ्गीकुर्वन्स्तेनैव लोकेन मूर्खोऽयमिति यदवज्ञायते तदा तदीयं लोकोत्तरं चरितं प्रस्तुतं व्यङ्ग्यतया प्राधान्येन प्रकाश्यते। जडोऽयमिति ह्यद्यानेन्दूदयादिर्भावो लोकेनावज्ञायते, स च प्रत्युत कस्यचिद्विरहिण औत्सुक्यचिन्तादूयमानमानसतामन्यस्य प्रहर्षपरवशतां करोतीति हठादेव लोकं यथेच्छं विकारकारणाभिर्नर्तयति। न च तस्य हृदयं केनापि ज्ञायते कीदृगयमिति, प्रत्युत महागम्भीरोऽतिविदग्धः सुष्ठुगर्वहीनोऽतिशयेन क्रीडाचतुरः स यदि लोकेन जड इति तत एव कारणात्प्रत्युत वैदग्ध्यसम्भावननिमित्तात्सम्भावितः, आत्मा च यत एव कारणात्प्रत्युत जाड्येन सम्भाव्यस्तत एव सहृदयः सम्भावितस्तदस्य लोकस्य जडोऽसीति यद्युच्यते तदा जड्यमेवंविधस्य भावव्रातस्याविदग्धस्य प्रसिद्धमिति सा प्रत्युत स्तुतिरिति। जडादपि पापीयानयं लोक इति ध्वन्यते। तदाह–यदा त्विति। इतरथा त्विति। इतरथैव पुनरलंकारान्तरत्वमलङ्कारविशेषत्वं न व्यङ्ग्यस्य

कथंचिदपि प्राधान्य इति भावः। उद्देशे यदादिग्रहणं कृतं समासोक्तीत्यत्र द्वन्द्वे तेन व्याजस्तुतिप्रभृतिरलङ्कारवर्गोऽपि सम्भाव्यमानव्यङ्ग्यानुवेशः सम्भावितः। तत्र सर्वत्र साधारणमुत्तरं दातुमुपक्रमते – तदयमत्रेति। कियद्वा प्रतिपदं लिख्यतामिति भावः। तत्र व्याजस्तुतिर्यथा–

किं वृत्तान्तैः परगृहगतैः किन्तु नाहं समर्थ-
स्तूर्णीं स्थातुं प्रकृतिमुखरो दाक्षिणात्यस्वभावः ।
गेहे गेहे विपणिषु तथा चत्वरे पानगोष्ठ्या-
मुन्मत्तेव भ्रमति भवतो वल्लभा हन्त कीर्तिः ।।

अत्र व्यङ्ग्यं स्तुत्यात्मकं यत्तेन वाच्यमेवोपस्क्रियते। यत्तूदाहृतं केनचित्–

आसीन्नाथ पितामही तव मही जाता ततोऽनन्तरं
माता सम्प्रति साम्बुराशिरशना जाया कुलोद्भूतये ।
पूर्णे वर्षशते भविष्यति पुनः सैवानवद्या स्नुषा
युक्तं नाम समग्रनीतिविदुषां किं भूपतीनां कुले ।।

इति, तदस्माकं ग्राम्यं प्रतिभात्यत्यन्तासभ्यस्मृतिहेतुत्वात्। का चानेन स्तुतिः कृता? त्वं वंशक्रमेण राजेति हि कियदिदम्? इत्येवंप्राया व्याजस्तुतिः सहृदयगोष्ठीषु निन्दितेत्युपेक्ष्यैव।

यस्य विकारः प्रभवन्नप्रतिबन्धस्तु हेतुना येन ।
गमयति तमभिप्रायं तत्प्रतिबन्धं च भावोऽसौ ।। इति ।

अत्रापि वाच्यप्राधान्ये भावालङ्कारता। यस्य चित्तवृत्तिविशेषस्य सम्बन्धी वाग्व्यापारादिर्विकारोऽप्रतिबन्धो नियतः प्रभवंस्तं चित्तवृत्तिविशेषरूपमभिप्रायं येन हेतुना गमयति स हेतुर्यथेष्टोपभोग्यत्वादिलक्षणोऽर्थो भावालङ्कारः। यथा–

एकाकिनी यदबला तरुणी तथाह-
मस्मिन्गृहे गृहपतिश्च गतो विदेशम् ।
कं याचसे तदिह वासमियं वराकी
श्वश्रूर्ममान्धबधिरा ननु मूढ पान्थ ॥

अत्र व्यङ्ग्यमेकैकत्र पदार्थे उपस्कारकारीति वाच्यं प्रधानम्। व्यङ्ग्यप्राधान्ये तु न काचिदलङ्कारतेति निरूपितमित्यलं बहुना।

यत्रेति काव्ये। अलङ्कृतय इति। अलङ्कृतित्वादेव च वाच्योपस्कारकत्वम्। प्रतिभामात्र इति। यत्रोपमादौ श्लिष्टार्थप्रतीतिः। वाच्यार्थानुगम इति। वाच्येनार्थेनानुगमः समं प्राधान्यमप्रस्तुतप्रशंसायामिवेत्यर्थः। न प्रतीयत इति। स्फुटतया प्राधान्यं न चकास्ति, अपि तु बलात्कल्प्यते, तथापि हृदये नानुप्रविशति। यथा–'देआ पसिअणिआतासु' इत्यत्रान्यकृतासु व्याख्यासु। तेन चतुर्षु प्रकारेषु न ध्वनिव्यवहारः सद्भावेऽपि व्यङ्ग्यस्य अप्राधान्ये श्लिष्टप्रतीतौ वाच्येन समप्राधान्येऽस्फुटे प्राधान्ये च। क्व तर्ह्यसावित्याह–तत्परावेवेति। सङ्करेणालङ्कारानुप्रवेशसम्भावनया उज्झित इत्यर्थः। सङ्कारालङ्कारेणेति त्वसत्, अन्यालङ्कारोपलक्षणत्वे हि क्लिष्टं स्यात्। इतश्चेति। न केवलमन्योन्यविरुद्धवाच्यवाचकभावव्यङ्ग्यव्यञ्जकभावसमाश्रयत्वान्न तादात्म्यमलङ्काराणां ध्वनेश्च यावत्स्वामिभृत्यवदङ्गिरूपाङ्गरूपयोर्विरोधादित्यर्थः। अवयव इति। एकैक इत्यर्थः। तदाह–पृथग्भूत इति। अथ पृथग्भूतस्तथा मा भूत्, समुदायमध्यनिपतितस्तर्ह्यस्तु तथेत्याशङ्क्याह – अपृथग्भावे त्विति। तदापि न स एक एव समुदायः, अन्येषामपि समुदायिनां तत्र भावात्; तत्समुदायिमध्ये च प्रतीयमानमप्यस्ति, न च तदलङ्काररूपं, प्रधानत्वादेव। यत्त्वलङ्काररूपं तदप्रधानत्वान्न ध्वनिः। तदाह–न तु तत्वमेवेति। नन्वलङ्कार एव कश्चित्त्वया प्रधानताभिषेकं दत्त्वा ध्वनिरित्यात्मेति

चोक्त इत्याशङ्क्याह–यत्रापि वेति। न हि समासोक्त्यादीनामन्यतम एवासौ तथास्माभिः कृतः, तद्विविक्तत्वेऽपि तस्य भावात्, समासोक्त्याद्यलङ्कारस्वरूपस्य समस्तस्याभावेऽपि तस्य दर्शितत्वात् 'अत्ता एत्थ' इति 'कस्य वा ण' इत्यादि; तदाह–न तन्निष्ठत्वमेवेति । विद्वदुपज्ञेति । विद्वद्भ्य उपज्ञा प्रथम उपक्रमो यस्या उक्तेरिति बहुव्रीहिः। तेन 'उपज्ञोपक्रमं, इति तत्पुरुषाश्रयं नपुंसकत्वं निरवकाशम् । श्रूयमाणेष्विति । श्रोत्रशष्कुली सन्तानेनागता अन्त्याः शब्दाः श्रूयन्त इति प्रक्रियायां शब्दजाः शब्दाः श्रूयमाणा इत्युक्तम् । तेषां घण्टानुरणनरूपत्वं तावदस्ति; ते च ध्वनिशब्देनोक्ताः । यथाह भगवान् भर्तृहरिः–.

यः संयोगवियोगाभ्यां करणैरुपजन्यते ।
स स्फोटः शब्दजाश्शब्दा ध्वनयोऽन्यैरुदाहृताः ।। इति ।

एवं घण्टादिनिर्ह्रादस्थानीयोऽनुरणनात्मोपलक्षितो व्यङ्ग्योऽप्यर्थो ध्वनिरिति व्यवहृतः। तथा श्रूयमाणा ये वर्णा नादशब्दवाच्या अन्त्यबुद्धिनिर्ग्राह्यस्फोटाभिव्यञ्जकास्ते ध्वनिशब्देनोक्ताः। यथाह भगवान् स एव–

प्रत्ययैरनुपाख्येयैर्ग्रहणानुगुणैस्तथा ।
ध्वनिप्रकाशिते शब्दे स्वरूपमवधार्यते ।। इति ।

तेन व्यञ्जकौ शब्दार्थावपीह ध्वनिशब्देनोक्तौ । किञ्च वर्णेषु तावन्मात्रपरिमाणेष्वपि सत्सु । यथोक्तम्–

अल्पीयसापि यत्नेन शब्दमुच्चारितं मतिः ।
यदि वा नैव गृह्णाति वर्णं वा सकलं स्फुटम् ।। इति ।

तेषु तावत्स्वेव श्रूयमाणेषु वक्तुर्योऽन्यो द्रुतविलम्बितादिवृत्तिभेदात्मा प्रसिद्धादुच्चारणव्यापारादभ्यधिकः स ध्वनिरुक्तः । यदाह स एव–

शब्दस्योर्ध्वमभिव्यक्तेर्वृत्तिभेदे तु वैकृताः ।
ध्वनयः समुपोहन्ते स्फोटात्मा तैर्न भिद्यते ।। इति ।

अस्माभिरपि प्रसिद्धेभ्दः शब्दव्यापारेभ्योऽभिधातात्पर्यलक्षणारूपेभ्योऽतिरिक्तो व्यापारो ध्वनिरित्युक्तः। एवं चतुष्कमपि ध्वनिः। तद्योगाच्च समस्तमपि काव्यं ध्वनिः । तेन व्यतिरेकाव्यतिरेकव्यपदेशोऽपि न न युक्तः । वाच्यवाचकसंमिश्र इति । वाच्यवाचकसहितः संमिश्र इति मध्यमपदलोपी समासः । 'गामश्वं पुरुषं पशुम्' इतिवत्समुच्चयोऽत्र चकारेण विनापि । तेन वाच्योऽपि ध्वनिः वाचकोऽपि शब्दो ध्वनिः, द्वयोरपि व्यञ्जकत्वं ध्वनतीति कृत्वा । संमिश्यते विभावानुभावसंवलनयेति व्यङ्ग्योऽपि ध्वनिः, ध्वन्यत इति कृत्वा । शब्दनं शब्दः शब्दव्यापारः, न चासावभिधादिरूपः, अपि त्वात्मभूतः, सोऽपि ध्वननं ध्वनिः। काव्यमिति व्यपदेश्यश्च योऽर्थः सोऽपि ध्वनिः, उक्तप्रकारध्वनिचतुष्टयमयत्वात् । अतएव साधारणहेतुमाह – व्यञ्जकत्वसाम्यादि ति । व्यङ्ग्यव्यञ्जकभावः सर्वेषु पक्षेषु सामान्यरूपः साधारण इत्यर्थः । यत्पुनरेतदुक्तं 'वाग्विकल्पानामानन्त्यात्' इत्यादि, तत्परिहरति–न चैवं विधस्येति । वक्ष्यमाणः प्रभेदो यथा-मुख्ये द्वे रूपे । तद्भेदा यथा–अर्थान्तरसंक्रमितवाच्यः, अत्यन्ततिरस्कृतवाच्य इत्यविवक्षितवाच्यस्य, असंलक्ष्यक्रमव्यङ्ग्यः संलक्ष्यक्रमव्यङ्ग्य इति विवक्षितान्यपरवाच्यस्येति । तत्राप्यवान्तरभेदाः। महाविषयस्ये ति – अशेषलक्ष्यव्यापिन इत्यर्थः। विशेषग्रहणेनाव्यापकत्वमाह । मात्रशब्देनाङ्गित्वाभावम् । तत्र धवनिस्वरूपे भावितं प्रणिहितं चेतो येषां तेन वा चमत्काररूपेण भावितमधिवासितमत एव मुकुलितलोचनत्वादिविकारकारणं चेतो येषामिति । अभाववादिन इति । अवान्दरप्रकारत्रयभिन्ना अपीत्यर्थः ।

तेषां प्रत्युक्तौ फलमाह–अस्तीति । उदाहरणपृष्टे भाक्तत्वं सुशङ्कं सुपरिहरं च भवतीत्यभिप्रायेणोदाहरणदानावकाशार्थं भाक्तत्वालक्षणीयत्वे प्रथमं परिहरणयोग्येऽप्यप्रतिसमाधाय भविष्यदुद्द्योतानुवादानुसारेण वृत्तिकृदेव प्रभेदनिरूपणं करोति–स चेति । पञ्चधापि ध्वनिशब्दार्थे येन यत्र यतो यस्य यस्मै इति बहुव्रीह्यर्थाश्रयेण यथोचितं सामानाधिकरण्यं सुयोज्यम् । वाच्येऽर्थे तु ध्वनौ वाच्यशब्देन स्वात्मा तेनाविवक्षितोऽप्रधानीकृतः स्वात्मा येनेत्यविवक्षितवाच्यो व्यञ्जकोऽर्थः। एवं विवक्षितान्यपरवाच्येऽपि । यदि वा कर्मधारयेणार्थपक्षे अविवक्षितश्चासौ वाच्यश्चेति । विवक्षितान्यपरश्चासौ वाच्यश्चेति। तत्रार्थः कदाचिदनुपपद्यमानत्वादिना निमित्तेनाविवक्षितो भवति । कदाचिदुपपद्यमान इति कृत्वा विवक्षित एव, व्यङ्ग्यपर्यन्तां तु प्रतीतिं स्वसौभाग्यमहिम्ना करोति । अत एवार्थोऽत्र प्राधान्येन व्यञ्जकः, पूर्वत्र शब्दः । ननु च विवक्षा चान्यपरत्वं चेति विरुद्धम् । अन्यपरत्वेनैव विवक्षणात्को विरोधः? सामान्येनेति । वस्त्वलङ्काररसात्मना हि त्रिभेदोऽपि ध्वनिरुभाभ्यामेवाभ्यां सङ्गृहीत इति भावः । ननु तन्नामपृष्ठे एतन्नामनिवेशनस्य किं फलम्? उच्यते–अनेन हि नामद्वयेन ध्वननात्मनि व्यापारे पूर्वप्रसिद्धाभिधातात्पर्यलक्षणात्मकव्यापारत्रितयावगतार्थप्रतीतेः प्रतिपत्तृगतायाः प्रयोक्त्रभिप्रायरूपायाश्च विवक्षायाः सहकारित्वमुक्तमिति ध्वनिस्वरूपमेव नामभ्यांमेव प्रोज्जीवितम् ।

सुवर्णपुष्पामिति। सुवर्णानि पुष्प्यतीति सुवर्णपुष्पा, एतच्च वाक्यमेवासम्भवत्स्वार्थमिति कृत्वाविवक्षितवाच्यम्। तत एव पदार्थमभिधायान्वयं च तात्पर्यशक्त्यावगमय्यैव बाधकवशेन तमुपहत्य सादृश्यात्सुलभसमृद्धिसम्भारभाजनतां लक्षयति। तल्लक्षणाप्रयोजनं शूरकृतविद्यसेवकानां प्राशस्त्यमशब्दवाच्यत्वेन गोप्यमानं

सन्नायिकाकुचकलशयुगलमिव महार्घतामुपयद्ध्वन्यत इति। शब्दोऽत्र प्रधानतया वयञ्जकः अर्थस्तु तत्सहकारितयेति चत्वारो व्यापाराः।

शिखरिणी ति। न हि निर्विघ्नोत्तमसिद्धयोऽपि श्रीपर्वतादय इमां सिद्धिं विदध्युः। दिव्यकल्पसहस्रादिश्चात्र परिमितः कालः। न चैवंविधोत्तमफलजनकत्वेन पञ्चाग्निप्रभृत्यपि तपः श्रुतम। तवेति भिन्नं पदम्। समासेन विगलिततया प्रतीयेत, तव दशतीत्यभिप्रायेण। तेन यदाहुः– 'वृत्तानुरोधात्त्वदधरपाटलमिति न कृतम्' इति, तदसदेव; दशतीत्यास्वादयति अविच्छिन्नप्रबन्धतया, न त्वौदरिकवत्परं भुङ्क्ते; अपि तु रसज्ञोऽत्रेति तत्प्राप्तिवदेव रसज्ञताप्यस्य तपःप्रभावादेवेति। शुकशावक इति तारूण्यादुचितकाललाभोऽपि तपस एवेति। अनुरागिणश्च प्रच्छन्नस्वाभिप्रायख्यापनवैदग्ध्यचाटुविरचनात्मकविभावोद्दीपनं व्यङ्ग्यम्।

अत्र च त्रय एव व्यापाराः–अभिधा तात्पर्यं ध्वननं चेति। मुख्यार्थबाधाद्यभावे मध्यमकक्ष्यायां लक्षणायास्तृतीयस्या अभावात्। यदि वाकस्मिकविशिष्टप्रश्नार्थानुपपत्तेर्मुख्यार्थबाधायां सादृश्याल्लक्षणा भवतु मध्ये। तस्यास्तु प्रयोजनं ध्वन्यमानमेव, तत्तुर्यकक्ष्यानिवेशि, केवलं पूवत्र लक्षणैव प्रधानं ध्वननव्यापारे सहकारि। इह त्वभिधातात्पर्यशक्ती। वाक्यार्थसौन्दर्यादेव व्यङ्ग्यप्रतिपत्तेः केवलं लेशेन लक्षणाव्यापारोपयोगोऽप्यस्तीत्युक्तम्। असंलक्ष्यक्रमव्यङ्ग्ये तु लक्षणासमुन्मेषमात्रमपि नास्ति। असंलक्ष्यत्वादेव क्रमस्येति वक्ष्यामः। तेन द्वितीयेऽपि भेदे चत्वार एव व्यापाराः ।।१३।।

अत्र एवोभयोदाहरणपृष्ठ एव भाक्तमाहुरित्यनुभाष्य दूषयति। अयं भावः– भक्तिश्च ध्वनिश्चेति किं पर्यायवत्ताद्रूप्यम्? अथ पृथिवीत्वमिव पृथिव्या अन्यतो व्याबर्तकधर्मरूपतया लक्षणम्?

उत काक इव देवदत्तगृहस्य सम्भवमात्रादुपलक्षणम्? तत्र प्रथमं पक्षं निराकरोति–

भक्त्या बिभतीति। उक्तप्रकार इति पञ्चस्वर्थेषु योज्यम्–शब्देऽर्थे व्यापारे व्यङ्ग्ये समुदाये च। रूपभेदं दर्शयितुं ध्वनेस्तावद्रूपमाह – वाच्येति। तात्पर्येण विश्रान्तिधामतया प्रयोजनत्वेनेति यावत्। प्रकाशनं द्योतनमित्यर्थः। उपचारमात्रमिति। उपचारो गुणवृत्तिर्लक्षणा। उपचरणमतिशयितो व्यवहार इत्यर्थः। मात्रशब्देनेदमाह – यत्र लक्षणाव्यापारात्तृतीयादन्यश्चतुर्थः प्रयोजनद्योतनात्मा व्यापारो वस्तुस्थित्या सम्भवन्नप्यनुपयुज्यमानत्वेनानाद्रियमाणत्वादसत्कल्पः। 'यमर्थमधिकृत्य' इति हि प्रयोजनलक्षणम्। तत्रापि लक्षणास्तीति कथं ध्वननं लक्षणा चेत्येकं तत्त्वं स्यात्। द्वितीयं पक्षं दूषयति – अतिव्याप्तेरिति। असाविति ध्वनिः। तयेति भक्त्या। ननु ध्वननमवश्यम्भावीति कथं तद्व्यतिरिक्तोऽस्ति विषय इत्याह – महत्सौष्ठवमिति। उत एव प्रयोजनस्यानादरणीयत्वाद्व्यञ्जकत्वेन न कृत्यं किञ्चिदिति भावः। महद्ग्रहणेन गुणमात्रं तद्भवति। यथोक्तम् – 'समाधिरन्यधर्मस्य क्वाप्यारोपो विवक्षित' इति दर्शयति। ननु प्रयोजनाभावे कथं तथा व्यवहार इत्याह – प्रसिद्ध्यनुरोधेति। परम्परया तथैव प्रयोगात्।

Abinava here comments only on the *Kārikā*. The *Vṛtti* is so similar as to need no separate comment. **That meaning:** here he puts (the proven existence of the suggested meaning) to use. (The compound *upasarjanikṛtasvārthau* ("subordinating their own meaning") is to be analysed as follows:) *sva* = self; *svārthau* = self and meaning; *upasarjani- kṛtasvārthau* = subordinating itself and its meaning. Here we must pair off the terms in order, viz., the meaning subordinates itself and the word subordinates its meaning. **That meaning:** viz., the meaning that he has already referred to in speaking of "Sarasvati, pouring forth this sweet matter" (1.6 *K*).

Suggest: i.e., indicate. Here he uses the dual form, [rather than the singular], for while it is true that in the *avivakṣitāvācya* type of *dhvani* a word is the suggestor, the cooperation of its [literal] meaning cannot be wholly dispensed with; otherwise, a word of whose meaning we are ignorant might be a suggestor. And in the *vivakṣitānyaparavācya* type there must be the cooperation of words, because the meaning [which is there predominant] could not be suggested if the denoted sense were not furnished by a word or words. Accordingly, the operation of suggestion always belongs to both word and meaning. So when Bhaṭṭanāyaka criticizes the dual here, he is overlooking the obvious facts. But [we must remember that] in stating the alternative "word or sense" our author means [to include the notion of] predominance.

The type of poetry: One may analyse the compound (*kāvyaviśeṣa*) as a *karmadhāraya* or as a genitive *tatpuruṣa*. By using the word "poetry" he shows that that soul which has been characterized as *dhvani* falls in the area of words and meanings embellished by the poetic qualities and figures of speech so that there is no occasion for applying the word *dhvani* to the "material inference" (*arthāpatti*) [of the Mimāṃsā].

As for what has been said that "then the apprehension of beauty (*cārutvapratiti*) will be the soul of poetry," we are quite willing to accept it. The only dispute is about a name [viz., whether to call the soul of poetry *cārutvopratiti* or *dhvani*]. But when it is said that "If the soul of poetry is [nothing more than] the apprehension of beauty, the soul of poetry could arise from any means of cognition, such as visual perception and the like," we reply that the statement is nonsense. The context is an effort to define the soul of poetry, which is an entity consisting of words and meanings. How would there be any occasion [for bringing in visual perception]?

[The five meanings of *dhvani*.]

That in which: we may consider the reference to be to the sense, or the word, or to the operation [of word and sense]. And the sense may be either the literal sense, for it suggests (*dhvanati*), as does the word, on the suggested sense, for it is suggested (*dhvanyate*), [while] the operation is an alternative [because it is] the suggesting (*dhvanana*), of word and sense. But the *Kārikā* would convey by the word *dhvani* primarily the sum total of these elements in the form of poetry.

L **Is different:** *dhvani* cannot be included in them because the life of poetic qualities and figures lies in the nature of word and literal sense. Whereas the essence of *dhvani* lies in the nature of the suggestor and the suggested, which are different from that. The word **habitat** (*viṣaya*) shows that it exists in no other place. In this way the deprecation is silenced that took the form of "What is this thing called *dhvani* that it should differ from these?" (1.1a *A*).

The makers of definitions: [In inferring the non-existence of *dhvani*] its being not well known to the makers of definitions is a reason contradictory to what is sought to be proved (*viruddho hetuḥ*). In fact this is all the more reason for trying to frame a definition. On the other hand, its not being well known in the poetry itself would be a "falsely assigned reason" (*asiddho hetuḥ*). And the suggestion that it might be something like dancing and singing (cf. 1.1b *L*) [is nonsense because that] would have nothing to do with poetry.

Citra: it is called "display" because its use of meters and other [embellishments] causes admiration, while it lacks the exudation of that nectar of true beauty that is sought by the sensitive audience. Or it may be called *citra* in that word's sense of "picture," as an imitation of poetry, or because it is a mere written design, or because it is simply one of the arts.

In what follows: viz., in Chapter Three [verse 41, which Abhinava here quotes].

1. Cf. 1.9 Intro. *L* and note 1. 2. Cf. 1.2 *L*, note 2. 3. This would apply to the topiary verses, e.g. verses composed in the shape of a sword or lotus, with which the Indians, like the ancient Greeks, amused themselves. 4. The last suggestion is not quite clear to me. Perhaps Abhinava feels that any of the sixty-four arts may be called *çitra* in the sense of bright, interesting, amusing.

1. For these figures of speech see the Index.

Where: viz., in a figure of speech. **Clearly:** he means both with beauty and clarity. **Specified:** The *Vṛtti* uses the past tense because it has already dealt with the word "suggest" [in. 1.13b]. **Subordinating itself:** the *Vṛtti* explains the sense of *swa* ("own") of the *Karikā* by *atman* ("itself"). **Which it is not:** this predominance of the suggested sense is not. That is to say its predominance does not appear as we are understanding the verse, because we spend our enjoyment in an unbroken relishing [of both literal and suggested meanings] on the principle of [what was said in 1.12 *K*]: "in the minds of those in whom the real [meaning] appears." But [in a second stage], when a man of discrimination seeks the enlivening element, since it is the suggested meaning that gives life to the literal, he will decide that he is presented with a figure of speech, because the suggested is helping out that [literal sense]. And so he will say that he received his delight from the literal meaning as helped out by that [suggestion]. Although in a final [third] stage, there is indeed *rasadhvani*, nevertheless this suggested meaning in the second stage does not point to *rasa*; for its own part it simply hastens to ornament the literal meaning. And so the *Vṛtti* speaks of the suggested meaning as being subordinated.[3]

L Samāsokti

Where in a statement a second meaning is understood because of epithets common to both meanings the wise call that *samāsokti*, because the meaning is composite. (Bhāmahas 2.79)

In the four quarters of this verse the author has given successively the basic characterization of *samāsokti*, the reason for it, its name, and the explanation of the name.

Reddening (literally, possessing redness): [in the case of the moon this means] assuming the red color of twilight; and [in the case of a lover it means] assuming the feelings of love. **With trembling *tārakā***: in which the lights of heaven are trembling and in which a portion of the eye is trembling. **So**: i.e., suddenly [of the moon] and with a rush of love [of the lover]. **Seized**: illumined [of the moon with respect to the night] and seized in order to kiss [of the lover with respect to his beloved]. **The face of night**: the beginning [of the night] and the lotus face [of the woman]. **Thus**: suddenly [of the night] and with a rush of love [of the woman]. **Cloak of darkness**: Of the night *timirāṃśukam* means *timiram* (darkness) and *sūkṣmāśavaḥ* (feeble rays), i.e., her mass of darkness spangled with a few rays [of the stars]; of the beloved *timirāṃśuka* means the dark veil appropriate to a newly wed bride who is shy. [In place of *mohād* (in confusion) Abhinava reads *rāgād*, which he explains as follows:] *Rāgād* [in the case of the night] means "from redness", that is immediately following the redness produced by twilight; and [in the case of the woman] it means "from love", that is, because of love. **In the east** [in connection with night] and [in connection with 'the woman] in front of her. **Fallen:** vanished in the one case and fallen in the other. **By her:** by the night as instrument (Pāṇ. 2.3.18) the mass of darkness is spangled [with starlight], or we may take the pronoun to be an instrumental of identification (Pāṇ. 2.3.21). **Unnoticed:** it was not realized that this was the beginning of night, for people recognize the face, or beginning, of night when they see a mass of darkness spangled with starlight, but not when a clear light [as of the moon] is present. In the case of the woman, on the other hand, "by her" will be an instrumental of agent ["unnoticed by her"]. In the case of the night the word *api* in *puro 'pi* = even in front of her] must be transposed to follow *upalakṣitam* [i.e., "was not even noticed by people"]. And here [in the case of the woman] the veil falls, or drops, in front, as the lover coming from behind begins to kiss her. Or we may take the syntax to be that the lover [standing] in front seizes her face.

So although we understand a suggested sense in this stanza, it is not predominant. That is to say, the [superimposed] behavior of lover and beloved in ornamenting the moon and night, which thus take the form of *vibhāvas* of the erotic flavor, acts as an ornament or figure of speech. But then from the literal sense [of moon and night] which has been turned into a *vibhāvas*, there issues forth a stream of *rasa*.

Here someone has said, "The word 'by her', viz., by the night, expresses agency, and since agency is impossible on the part of an insentient being, the behavior of lovers which we infer is given by the denotative force of 'night' and 'moon' and not by a suggestion. That is why the stanza forms a compouind utterance(*samāsokti*)." This explicator has ignored the clear sense of the text with which we are concerned, [for the *Vṛtti* has clearly said] "accompanied by a suggestion." At that rate the figure would be *ekadeśavivarti rūpakam* (a partial metaphor) like the couplet:

> The pond kings were fanned
> by autumn with her wild geese.
>
> (Udbhata, 1.*12 Indurāja = 1.24 *Vivṛti*)

It would not be a *samāsokti* because it would not contain epithets that apply [in each instance] equally to both [the denoted and the suggested sense]. Furthermore, the denotative function is ruled out [in Bhāmaha's definition of *samāsokti* just quoted] by the phrase "is understood' [rather than "is stated"]. But let us not run on at too great length on a subordinate matter.

Here it might be thought that Ānanda should have written *samāropitanāyika-vyavahārayoḥ* rather than *samāropitanāyikā-nāyakayoḥ*.[8] However there is no need for an *ekaśeṣa* compound [viz., *nāyakayoḥ*] if we explain the meaning to be that the behavior of a lady toward her lover is superimposed on night and the behavior of a lover toward his lady is superimposed on the moon.

In ākṣepa: [The figure has been defined thus:]

The denial (or holding back) of an intended [statement] out of a wish to convey some special [suggestion] is *ākṣepa* (denial, hint, censure), which is of two types depending on whether the statement was about to be spoken or has been made. (The first half of this verse is Bhāmaha 2.68)

An example of the first type is this:

> If in my longing
> I should lose sight of you but for a moment...
> But I say no more.
> Why say that which would pain you?
>
> (Bhāmaha 2.69)

Here we have *ākṣepa* in the form of withholding the death that the lady was about to speak of. The words "But I say no more," while they suggest the statement "I will die," are themselves the cause of the beauty in the verse. So [we must say that] the *ākṣepa*(the hinting reticence) as embellished by what it hints at is the predominant element. An example of [the second type, where] a statement that has been made [is denied or censured] is a verse of mine:

> "My dear traveler, what causes this sudden collapse?"
> "What else can I do who have such thirst,
> When the miserly road here hides its water?"
> "Your thirst is mistimed, good sir, and misplaced.
> Vent your anger on it. The glory and greatness of the desert road are famous throughout the world."

In this verse a servitor is present. His heart is torn by desire and he asks why he receives nothing from his lord. Some one puts him to a right way of thinking by this censure. Here it is the literal meaning, expressing distress at the lack of recompense from service with a bad master, being transformed by a censure in the form of a denial into the *vibhāva* indifference (*nirveda*) which is the basic emotion of the favor of peace (*śāntarasa*), which gives beauty to the stanza.

Vāmana, in different fashion, defines *ākṣepa* as censure of the simile. It amounts to saying, "When this is present, of what account are you?" He gives an example:

> When we have the fair clarity of her face,
> who would care for the full-orbed moon;
> or who would care for water-lily flowers
> before the vast beauty of her eyes?
> What price would you pay for the tender, lovely opening
> of a leaf, when you see her lower lip?
> Ah me! but God shows a stubborn zeal
> for tautological creation.
>
> (Vāmana 4.3.27.1)

In this stanza the simile, although it is suggested, merely serves the literal sense. The expressed censure, in its casting away [of the simile] with a "who would care for it?" is the source of all the charm.

Or again, *ākṣepa* [here simply hint, not censure] of the simile may be brought in by the inherent capability] of the literal sense], as in this example:

> Lady Autumn beautifies the moon
> although his face is made imperfect
> by its mark, and bearing on her cloud a rainbow like a wound
> left by a lover's nail, has made the sun grow hot.
>
> (Vāmana, ibid. vs.2)

In this stanza, although a simile is hinted at, namely a lover who is pained by jealousy, it serves only to beautify the literal meaning.

But the stanza [which Ānanda] here [quotes, viz., "The sunset is flushed with red," etc.] is really an instance of *samāsokti* [if one follows the normal definition, as of Bhāmaha].

So he says: "[depends on] which is the more charming", and apropos of this quotes a well-known example: **The sunset is flushed with red.** Note that he has not yet finished his consideration of *ākṣepa* and that it is as an example of *ākṣepa* that he quotes this *samāsokti* couplet.

Ah, but such is the way of fate: The [suggested] sense is that there is no union [of the lovers] because of some such obstacle as their subjection to their parents. **This:** i.e., the literal sense.

Realizing that the figure of speech here is *ākṣepa* according to Vāmana's definition and *samāsokti* according to Bhāmaha's, our author by joining the two figures has given this single example. Let it be an example of *samāsokti* or of *ākṣepa*, what does it matter to us? All that we are trying to demonstrate is that in figures of speech the suggested sense is always subordinate to the literal. This is how my teacher [Bhaṭṭatauta] explained the intention of the present passage.

L Having thus provided an example of where [the literal] is intended to be predominant, he now gives an example, acceptable both to his followers and his opponents, of how the name [of a figure of speech] derives from its predominant element: **and as in**, etc. **[Although we apprehend] a simile:** he means that we apprehend a relation of subject and image. **By that name:** viz., "simile." For example, in *dipaka* — of which the definition runs thus, '*Dipaka* is held to be threefold, as it falls at the beginning, middle or end' (Bhāmaha 2.25) — the beauty of the verse is occasioned by the operation of the *dipaka*, [not by the suggested simile] as in this example:

A jewel placed against the whetstone,
a victorious warrior wounded by the sword,
the moon when left with its last digit
a young woman thin from exercise of sex,
an elephant in rut, a river
drawn back from its lovely sandbanks in the autumn,
and the rich who spend their wealth by giving to the poor:
all these by lessening grow resplendent.

(Bhartṛhari, *Nitiś*. 11)

Apahnuti has been defined: "The denial of what one really accepts, if it contains to some extent a simile, is *apahnuti*" (Bhāmaha 3.21).

In this figure it is the denial itself that is charming, as in:

> **This is not the buzzing of a bee,**
> **busy in her drunken joy;**
> **it is the twanging of the string**
> **as Cupid pulls his bow.**

(Bhāmaha 3.22)

L After considering *ākṣepa* in the above manner, he now speaks of the subject that immediately followed it in the order of his initial statement: **and in that type of *viśeṣokti*.** [The figure in general is thus defined:] "The praise of one quality in the absence of others, if made in order to reveal some excellence, is traditionally known as *viśeṣokti*" (Bhāmaha 3.23). An example is the following:

> Alone the god of the flowered bow
> conquers all three worlds,
> whose body Siva destroyed
> but left him still his strength

(Bhāmaha 3.24)

As the reason in this case [viz., the reason why incineration should not lead to impotence] is inconceivable, there is no suggestion [of a reason]. Even where the reason is explicitly stated, since the statement amounts to no more than giving the nature of the object, there is no question of a suggested sense. For example:

> I give my praise to him
> who like camphor grows stronger with burning,
> against whom no man prevails,
> the god of the flowered bow.

(Bālarāmāyaṇa 3.11)

Accordingly, our author passes over these two varieties and examines only a third type [as a possible case of a predominant suggested sense]: **when the reason is not expressed.**

[We merely apprehend] the suggestions viz., according to Bhaṭṭodbhata, the discomfort caused by the cold, this being the reason [for the traveler's remaining curled up in his bedding]. Conformably with this interpretation, our author says, **there arises no particular beauty here.** Some men of taste have imagined a different reason here, namely that the traveler does not uncurl his limbs because he wishes to bring back sleep, thinking that a dream would be a quicker means of union with his beloved than setting forth [on his farther journey]. But the experts in figures of speech have not taken even that reason as a source of beauty here, but have taken the source of beauty to be the words "does not uncurl his limbs," which form part of the *viśeṣokti* itself, as embellished by the suggested reason. Otherwise this would not be an example of *viśeṣokti* at all. So our author here accommodates both views by speaking generally [i.e., by not mentioning the precise nature of the suggested reason]. It should not be thought that the text is based exclusively on the view of Udbhaṭa.

L **In *paryāyakta*:** It has been defined thus "*Paryāyakta* is when something is said in a different manner, namely through an understanding that lacks the operation of denoter and denoted" (Udbhaṭa, 4.6 Indurāja = 4.11 *Vivṛti*). An example is this:

> The sage Rāma, who had strayed into evil ways
> in his rage to cut down his foes,
> was instructed in the path of duty by this bow.

In this stanza, although we understand [the suggestion] that the might of Bhiṣma overcame the might of Paraśu Rāma, it is merely as helped out by this suggestion that the literally used phrase "was instructed in the path of duty" ornaments the final meaning of the verse.

When what is said is distinguished by a *paryāya* (periphrasis), that is, speaking in a different manner, which consists in a giving to understand, [that is, when it is distinguished] by a suggestion, then the literally used words themselves form a *paryāyokta* (statement of periphrasis). Here "when something is said" forms the definition, "statement of periphrasis" is the thing to be defined, and the general characteristic of this thing is as a figure of speech based on meaning (*arthālankāra*). And so everything is here in order. On the other hand, if one forces on the phrase "when something is said" the unnatural interpretation that it means "when something is apprehended as the chief element," and if one offers as an example such verses as "Go your rounds freely, pious monk" (cf. 1.4b *A*), then the statement of periphrasis will cease to be a figure of speech at all, for it will end up as the soul [of poetry, namely *dhvani*]. In that case it should not be included in figures of speech. Furthermore, in that case we should have to list subvarieties of it [just as injunction, prohibition, etc., were listed as subvarieties in 1.4b, c, d, e *A*]. Our author says this in the words **if the suggestion is predominant.** That is, by including it in *dhvani, paryāyokta* would be the soul of poetry, not one of the *alankaras* (ornaments, figures of speech). **In it:** *dhvani* cannot be included in that sort of statement which is intended as a figure of speech. We have not defined *dhvani* as something [subordinate] of that sort. For *dhvani* has a wide range. As it exists in all [sorts of statements], it is widely spread (*vyāpaka*), being the principal element on which all the [*guṇas* and *alankāras*] are placed. A figure of speech is not widely spread any more than any other ornament, [e.g., a bracelet is worn only on the wrist, an anklet on the ankle]. And it is not the principal, as it is subordinate to the object which it ornaments. Or, if you assume that the suggestion here is both of widely spread type and principal, and that there is no figure of speech here, why then you would be accepting our own position but out of mere spite continuing to call it a *paryāyokta*.

Our author now shows that even this much [viz., that the suggestion can sometimes be predominant] was not understood by the ancients but was first revealed by himself: **furthermore.** Bhāmaha furnished his illustration of *paryāyokta* in accordance with the nature he conceived the figure to have. Now in his illustration the suggested element is not predominant because it is not the source of any special beauty. Accordingly, we may agree that in such other illustrations as may be composed along the same lines, there is likewise no predominance of the suggested sense. If you disregard the illustration just given and give as an illustration some such verse as "Go your rounds freely, gentle monk," you will have become our author's pupil [for you will be talking about *dhvani*]. But one must say that you have behaved in an unmannerly fashion by educating yourself in his doctrine with disregard of the rules and by an illicit hearing of it. The experts in sacred history say:

> He who shows no respect to the teacher
> but listens in hiding to his teaching
> goes straight to hell.

The illustration which Bhamaha gives is this:

> Neither at home nor when abroad
> do we eat food that is not eaten
> by learned brahmins.

(Bhāmaha 3.9)

This statement of the blessed Krishna by a periphrasis averts his being given poison. As Bhāmaha says himself, "This is to avoid his being given poison." Now there is nothing charming in this suggestion of the averting of poison by which we might suppose it to be predominant. Rather, the statement of periphrasis itself, viz., that he does not eat without the prior eating of brahmins, as embellished by this suggestion, ornaments the matter under discussion, namely his eating of food. The intention of the statement is not to say "Give me unpoisoned food". And so *paryāyokta* is simply a figure of speech according to the opinion of the ancients. This is what it all comes down to.

In *apahnuti* and *dipaka*: These are figures which he has already discussed: so he says, **as is well known.** He means the matter has already been proved with valid means of proof. Previously he brought up these figures to serve as illustration of how a figure does not take its nature from the [subordinate] simile, etc., [which it might contain,] whereas now he mentions them in a different way to show that they are not dhwani because their suggestions are not prominent. This mentioning of them a second time is to keep the order of his original list so that he may make his text all of one piece. But the matter on both occasions is basically the same, for one might suspect them of being *dhvani* from the fact that they suggest a simile.

As for the statement of the author of the *Vivaraṇa*, based on an examination of many instances, that a [suggestion of] simile does not always accompany a *dipaka*, it is unhelpful, without merit, and can easily be refuted: In the stanza:

> Infatuation creates desire;
> and that, love with its loss of pride;
> that, yearning to gain the beloved;
> and that, unbearable pain of heart.
>
> (Bhāmaha 2.27)

one can easily imagine a relation of subject and simile between the terms even though the terms are produced successively. One cannot say that such a relation of similarity is impossible among successive objects, for we have the verse:

> Daśaratha was like Rāma,
> Raghu like Daśaratha and Aja like Raghu
> and the whole race of Dilipa like Aja;
> marvellous is the glory of Rāma,

where one cannot say that it does not exist. So why worry whether sequentiality or contemporaneity hinders the [suggestion of] simile? Enough of trying to milk a mule.

L In the figure sankara. One type of *sankara* is defined thus:

> When contradictory figures appear,
> when they cannot function together,
> and when there is neither right
> nor wrong
> in accepting just the one,
> we have sankara.
>
> (Udbhata 5.11 Indurāja = 5.20 *Vivṛti*)

An example is a verse of mine:

> Moon faced she is,
> dark water lily-eyed
> and with teeth of white jasmine:
> God has given her forms of beauty
> from sky, river and earth.

Either metaphor or simile may appear here, depending on whether we analyse "moon-faced" as "having a moon for her face" [by Pāṇini 2.1.72], or as "having a face like the moon" [by Pāṇini 2.1.56]. As both figures cannot be entertained at the same time and as there is no compelling reason to accept or reject one of the other, we have here the figure *sankara.* As there is no evidence that one of the components is denoted and the other suggested, what possibility is there here of *dhvani*?

And what chance is there in the second type, where a figure of sound and a figure of sense occur in one [sentence]? As in:

> Remember as Kāma your lover,
> in whose embrace you have found delight.

where we have the figure of sound *yamaka* and the figure of sense simile.

In the third type too, where more than one figure of sense is found in a single portion of a sentence, in as much as both are equally presented literally], how can either be suggested? As in:

They rise and sink together,
So when the bright sun has set,
the weary day for rest
enters as it were the cave of night

(Bhāmaha 3.48)

For in this stanza the partial metaphor [viz., "the cave of night"] implies a full metaphor of a well-bred man eager to perform the appropriate duty [of self-immolation] on the fall of his master. [The partial metaphor is directly expressed] and poetic fancy is also directly expressed, viz., by the term,"as it were." These two types are embodied in the following definition: "When figures of sound and sense occur in one sentence or one portion of a sentence, we have the figure *sankara*" (Udbhaṭa, 5.12 Induraja = 5.22 *Vivṛti*).

The fourth type is where there is a relation of assistance between the figures. As in this:

These glances of the long-eyed maid
that tremble like water-lilies in the wind:
did she borrow them from the does of the wood,
or did the does borrow them from her?

(Kumārasambhava 1.46)

Although a likening of Pārvatī's glances to the glances of female deer is here suggested, the simile becomes subordinate from its role as assistant in giving rise to the figure *sandeha* (poetic doubt), for by its assistance we end up with the figure sandeha. This [fourth type of *sankara*] is defined: "Where figures are placed in mutual assistance and lack independent being, that too is the figure *sankara*" (Udbhaṭa, 5.13 Induraja = 5.25 *Vivṛti*).

This is what our author refers to in the words **when a figure,** etc., And so the existence of *dhvani* in the fourth type is ruled out. We have already stated that there is no possibility of *dhvani* in the second and third types. But in regard to the first type, exemplified in "Moonfaced she is," one might suspect the possibility. This he now rules out: **Where either of two figures. Equal:** because our mind sways between the two.

But now, when the suggested sense appears to be predominant, what are we to do? Take the example:

The masses have no care of quality
but easily, fall for reputation.
The moonstone sweats at sight of the moon
but not as my true love's face.

Hence the figure *arthāntaranyāsa* (substantiation) appears, literally expressed, but *vyatireka* (contrast) and *apahnuti* (feigned denial) appear by suggestion and are predominant. Having this in mind, he says, but if, etc. He answers the problem with **then we may assign it**. That is to say, this is not *sankara* at all, but is the second type of *dhvani* called *alankāradhvani* (suggestion of a figure of speech). What was said under the subject of *paryāyokta* [viz. that *dhvani* is of wider range than the figure and is always predominant] may be equally applied here.

Now he gives a general means of denying the possibility of a [predominant] suggested sense in any form of *sankara:* **furthermore.** One must construe by changing the position of the particle *api*. The sense is, "everywhere in the figure *sankara,*" as distinguished from any particular variety. For fusion means a mingling, a complete commixture. How would one element predominate any more than in the mixture of milk and water?

The praise of something different,
that is, other than the matter in hand
is called *aprastutapraśaṃsā*.
It is threefold.

What is meant is a description of extraneous matter which hints at the matter in hand. The hint is threefold, as it is based on a relation of general and particular or a relation of cause and effect, or on similarity. In the sentence beginning **When by a relation** and ending with **equally important** our author sets forth the thesis that in the first two of these types the extraneous matter and the matter in hand are equally important.

In the type based on a relation of general and particular there are two methods of procedure. One method is where a general statement which is extraneous is literally expressed and the particular, which is the matter in hand, is suggested; as in the following:

Ah, the cruelty of worldly life,
the malignity of misfortune!
Ah, the tragic ways of fate
deceptive in its very nature.

Here the power of fate in its general form, which is extraneous to the poet's real intention, and which is stated throughout the verse, ends up in [a suggestion of] the matter in hand, which is a particular disaster that has befallen someone. Here the general statement, which is literally expressed, is as important as the particular, which is suggested, because the species is logically included in its genus; for there is no contradiction in the simultaneous importance of general and particular.

When a particular which is extraneous suggests a general statement which is germane, we have the second type; as in the following:

It is not so much that at first the fool imagined
a drop of water upon a lotus leaf
to be a pearl; but hear what happened next:
as he tried to take it slowly on his finger tip
with gentle motion, it melted at his touch.
At this he cried, "Alas, it has flown away!"
and now he cannot sleep from inner grief.

(*Bhallaṭaśataka* 94)

In this stanza the matter intended by the poet is the general principle that people imagine greatness in what is really nothing, while the extraneous subject is particular, that of imagining a pearl in a drop of water. Here too there is no contradiction in the simultaneous importance of the general and the particular, as has been said. In this way our author has dealt with the first type in its two varieties in the passage from "**to begin with**" to "**all particulars are included in the general.**"

Extending the same principle to the type based on a relation of cause and effect, our author shows that it too has two varieties: **where the relation is one of cause and effect.** Sometimes a cause, which is extraneous, is presented literally in order to suggest an effect, which is the matter in hand. For example:

They who take joy in your success
and stay with you in adversity

are your true relatives and friends;
other seek only their own benefit.

Here the speaker states explicitly a cause which is extraneous to his real intent. The cause is that good men by their faithful attachment are friends and relatives to us. He states this in order to suggest what he really intends, namely that his own words should be trusted. Although we apprehend the effect here, our apprehension of the cause becomes important from its giving life to the effect; so both cause and effect are important.

Sometimes an effect, which is extraneous, being literally presented suggests a cause which is the matter in hand. An example will be found in the *Setubandha:*

I remember before the churning of the sea
heaven without its pārijāta trees,
Viṣṇu without his Lakshmi by his side
or the kaustubha jewel upon his breast, and Śiva
without the lovely moon within his locks.

(*Setubandha* 4.20)

Here Jāmbavān describes his memory of Viṣṇu's breast without the *kaustubha* jewel or Lakṣhmi, and so on, which are matters extraneous to, and at the same time a cause of, what is his real intention. He does this in order to suggest the result, namely that his service of the elder gods, his longevity, and his skill in negotiations fit him to be accepted as an advisor. Here the suggested and the literal senses are equally important, for although we apprehend the cause to be important, the effect, which is literally presented, raises itself [into importance] by its giving life to that cause.

After dealing with these two types, each of which is twofold, he examines the third type, which is based on similarity. Here too there are two varieties. Sometimes the charm [and therefore the importance] comes from the extraneous matter which is literally presented, while the suggested matter is subservient. An example is this verse by my teacher Bhaṭṭendurāja:

He who brought you back to life
and by his strength supported,
who carried you upon his back
and even gave you worship:

that man you kill with but a smile.
O brother zombie, you show yourself
to be the prince of gratitude.

Here, although some other ingrate is suggested by the power of similarity, the charm and interest of the stanza lie in the anecdote of the zombie (vetāla) which is extraneous. The sense is not impossible as would be a reproach against an insentient being, and the anecdote is not without attraction. So the predominance here lies in the literal sense.

But if the matter in hand is charming and is suggested by a literal description of an extraneous subject possessing properties such as insentiency which render it impossible for the described purpose, then we have a case of *vastudhvani*. An example is a verse of my own:

Troop of delights, who storm the hearts of men
and make them dance in many an antic step;
concealing your own intention as you play;
men call you brute and stupid, in their ignorance
thinking themselves intelligent thereby.
That title of stupidity, I think,
if given to *them* would be honorific,
for it would seem to liken them to you.

Here the germane matter, which is revealed by suggestion, is the extraordinary way of life of a man while he is being despised by the world as a fool. What is meant is a great man, who has rolled back the curtains of darkness by an eye of deep penetration and who lives a worldly life on the principle of "unimpassioned yet as though with passion," concealing his real self and accepting the reproaches of men as he causes their tongues to wag.

[The literal meaning.] A delight, such as a garden or moonrise, is despised by men as being a brute thing, but it can make the heart of an absent lover grieve with yearning, or make the heart of another overflow with joy. Of what sort its own heart may be no one knows. In fact it is vastly deep and intelligent, utterly void of pride and skilful at play. Now if people for that reason call it brute and stupid when it stands rather in honor because of its implied intelligence, and for the same reason honor themselves as intelligent when they are, rather, worthy of being considered stupid, then the expression "you are brute and stupid," being established as an epithet of the troop of delights, which we have seen are really intelligent, will, rather, be an honorific. What is hinted at is that men are worse than stupid. He indicates all this in the sentence **but ... if.**

Otherwise: otherwise it will just be another figure of speech, that is, the particular figure of speech [*aprastutapraśaṃsā*], but never when the suggested element is predominant.

In the list [of seven figures of speech] with which our author began [his discussion (1.13c A)], the words "and the like" refer to any other figure where a suggestion may be imagined, that is, to *vyājastuti* (trick praise), etc. **Here then,** etc. His feeling is that it is useless to write on each particular figure.

Among such figures [we may give] an example of *vyājastuti:*

What good is done by telling on other wives?
And yet, being a chatterbox by nature
and a southerner as well,
I can't keep still.
She's in everybody's house,
in the market, at the crossroads and at drinking bouts;
she runs about like a drunkard, does your mistress.
Oho, but her name is Fame.

(Vidyā?)

Here it is the literal meaning that is embellished by the suggestion in the form of praise. Another critic has offered the following as an example of the figure.

The great earth, lord, engirdled by the sea,
was wedded to your grandsire;
she next became your mother, while today
to raise a family you keep her as your wife.
After a full century, without reproach,
she will be married to your son.
Say is this decent in a line of kings
who know the rules of proper conduct?

This stanza strikes one as obscene, because it causes one to think of highly indecent things. And what does the praise amount to? That you are king by hereditary succession. What is so great about that? The praise of this art will be reproved in any company of sensitive artists and deserves to be ignored.

[To explain the term "etc." in his remark "*vyājastuti*, etc.," Abhinava takes up another figure of speech, *bhāva* (expression of inner feeling):]

In an alteration [of a given state of mind], arising from an [apparently] unconnected cause, gives us to understand the intention and its connection with that cause, we have the figure *bhāva*.

(Rudrata 7.38)

Here too if the literal sense is predominant, the case is one of a figure of speech, *bhāva*. That is to say, if an alteration of a state of mind appears, such as the speaking of certain words not normally connected [with their apparent cause], and gives us to understand for what reason the intention embodied in that state of mind [has arisen] — here the reason may be such as aim of enjoying the pleasures of love without stint — we have the figure of speech, *bhāva*. For example:

> As I am a weak woman,
> young and left in the home
> while my husband has gone abroad,
> with no one here but my blind and deaf mother-in-law,
> how can you be so foolish, traveler,
> as to ask to spend the night?

(Rudraṭa 7.41)

Here a suggestion embellishes the literal sense of each word and so the literal sense is predominant. On the other hand, if the suggested sense were predominant, we should not have a figure of speech at all, as we have shown before. So enough of many words.

Where: i.e., in a poem. **Ornaments:** it is because they are ornaments that they act only to embellish the literal sense.

Appears only faint: that is, where there is a vague impression, as in the simile, etc. [suggested by the figure *dipāka*, etc.]. **Follows along with the literal:** the meaning of following along with the literal is the having of equal importance with it, as in *aprastutapraśaṃsā*. **Not felt to be:** where its predominance does not appear clearly, but must be forced on it and so does not really enter the heart, as in the verse, "Turn back, I beg you," as explained by other commentators. By these two verses he shows that in four cases we are not justified in speaking of *dhvani*: where the suggested sense, although it is present, is not predominant [being a mere ornament], where it is faintly perceived, where it is equally important with the literal, and where its predominance is not clear. Where then are we justified? He tells us, **only where word and sense are subordinate.** He adds, **where there is no fusion.** By "fusion" he means the possibility of inserting any figure of speech. It is wrong to interpret as "without the figure called *sankara* (fusion)," for then it would be difficult to take the proviso as prohibiting other figures.

And for this reason too: not only by reference to the contradiction of denoter-denoted to suggestor-suggested can it be shown that the figures of speech and *dhvani* are not identical, but because there is a contradiction between the nature of a whole and of a part, as there is between that of master and servant. **Its parts:** that is, taken singly, as he goes on to say: **if taken by itself.** Very well, then, let us not take [a figure of speech] by itself but regard it in the context of the whole. In defense against this proposal he says, **if taken together with the whole. It is then not the whole itself** because other constituents are included in the whole; and among its constituents is the suggested sense which is not a figure of speech because of its predominance. He makes this point with the words: **not the whole itself.**

Now it may be objected against our author that he has consecrated an occasional instance [of what appears to be a figure of speech] with predominance and has recognized it as the soul of poetry, *dhvani*. With this in mind, he now says, **even where one of these,** etc. He has not consecrated any one of the figures, such as *samāsokti,* as *dhvani* itself, because each figure may exist separately from *dhvani* and because *dhvani* is found in the absence of all figures of speech, *samasokti* and the rest, as in the stanzas "Mother-in-law sleeps here" (1.4c A) and "Who would not be angry" (1.4f A). He makes this point with the words, **is not limited to it.**

Was invented by men of knowledge. The compound *vidvad-upajñā* is a *bahuvrihi* modifying *uktiḥ,* literally, "a term of which the *upajñā* or first use was by men of knowledge." Accordingly, the neuter gender demanded by Pan. 2.4.21 when *upajñā* is used in a *tatpuruṣa* is here inapplicable.

The sounds of speech which are heard: According to the process [described in the Nyāya-vaiśeṣika] it is the last sound of a chain of sounds that enters the orifice of the ear, so the heard sounds are sounds born of sounds, [not the original sounds produced by the organs of speech]. These sounds in form are like the reverberations of a bell, and it is these sounds that are called *dhvani*. As the master Bhartṛhari has said:

Others have expressed the view that the *sphoṭa* is born from conjunction and disjunction with the organs of articulation; the *dhvanayaḥ* (plural) are the sound-born sounds. (*Vākyapadiya* 1.102)

In the same way, the suggested meaning has been called *dhvani* as it too is often characterized by a reverberation analogous to the pulsations of a bell. Again, the phoneme is heard, technically called *nādaśabdas*, manifest the semantic unit which we comprehend as soon as we cognize the final phoneme. These phoneme-manifestors are called *dhvani*s. As the same master says:

The true form [i.e., the semantic context] in the word that is manifested by the *dhvani* is determined by a series of cognitions [viz, the cognitions of the successive phonemes] which are unnameable [that is to say, each phoneme-cognition in itself is unassignable to this word or that], but favorable to the final [word-identifying] cognition. (*Vākyapadiya* 1.83)

So we too use the term *dhvani* for the word and the [literal] sense which manifest [the suggested meaning].

Further more, it is in the *varṇas* (the phonemes produced by the conjunction and disjunction of the vocal organs) that the differences of prosodical length (eg., a and ā, and i) reside, as has been said.

Either the mind does not perceive a sound if it is pronounced too softly, or it perceives clearly the whole phoneme [eg., we never hear half an ā]. (Kumārilla *Ślokavartika, Sphoṭavāda,* ve 10)

As these same differences are heard in the secondary sound, [or *dhvani*, that reaches the ear], it is only such other elements of the speaker's speech, such as its slow or rapid delivery, elements over and above the well-defined operations of articulation [e.g., prosodical length, aspiration, closure, etc.] that are more particularly called *dhvani*. As Bhartrhari has said:

The derivative *dhvani*s (i.e., the sounds which reach the ear) after they have manifested the word continue to carry in themselves the variations in speed of utterance, but the nature of the phonemes is not altered by them. (*Vākyapadiya* 1.77)

In like manner we [poeticians] apply the word *dhvani* to an operation over and above the well known operations of denotation, sentence-meaning and secondary usage. Thus we have four senses of *dhvani*; and by combining them we may speak of a whole poem as *dhvani*. It is for this reason that statements both of its difference [from poetry, as in "*dhvani* is the soul of poetry," 1.1.K] and of its identity [as in 1.13 K, which Abhinava interprets as speaking of "poetry, as a distinctive type of literature, which the wise call *dhvani*"] are not improper.

[Abhinava now gives a highly artificial analysis of the compounds *vācya-vācaka-sammiśra* and *śabdātmā*, which we translated as **a mixture of denotative and denoted entities** and as **verbal entity** respectively.] *Vācya-vācaka-sāmmiśra* is a compound from which the penultimate member has been dropped. It stands for *vācya-vācaka-sahita-sammiśra*, "possessing mixtures as well as denotative and denoted elements." The sense of addition is given without the use of "and," as in "ox, horse, man, beast." By this analysis one can see that the denoted sense can be called *dhvani* and the denoted word can be called *dhvani*, for both of them are suggestive inasmuch as both hint at (*dhvanati*) the suggested sense. As they form a mixture when they are combined with the *vibhāvas*, and *anubhāvas*, the suggested sense also, [which consists of such a mixture,] can be called *dhvani*, for it is what is hinted at (*dhvanyate*). The word *śabda* in the compound *śabdatma* means *śabdana*, "a putting into words," or verbal operation, and that not in the form of the denotative operation but in the form of the *ātman*, "the soul," of poetry. This [suggestive operation] can also be called *dhvani*, for it is a hinting. Finally the object "which is designated as a 'poem'" can also be called *dhvani* because it is composed of the four other types of *dhvani* in the manner just described.

And so he states the reason common [to both the grammatical and the poetical traditions for the use of the same term *dhvani*]: **because of the similarity in its being a manifestor.** The relation of manifestor and manifested, present in general in all four-senses [of poetic *dhvani*], is common [to the term as used by the grammarians]. This is the meaning.

It was objected [in 1.1c A] that because the possibilities of speech are endless, [there may well be some small variety which has hitherto remained unknown and which might be called *dhvani*]. He answers that objection with **now this being the nature of *dhvani*, etc. The types which we shall soon describe:** there are two main types. **The subtypes:** for example, the subtype "where the literal is shifted to another sense" (*arthāntarsaṇkramitavācya*) and that "where the literal is entirely set aside" (*atyantatiraskṛtavācya*), both of these belonging to the main type "where the literal meaning is not intended" (*avivakṣitavācya*);

and the subtypes "where the suggested meaning is produced without apparent sequence" (*asaṃlakṣyakramavyangya*) and that "where the sequence is apparent" (*saṃlakṣsyakramavyangya*), these belonging to the type "where the literal is intended but is subordinated to a second meaning" (*vivakṣsitānyaparavācya*). And even among these subtypes there are further divisions. **The range of which is immense:** the sense is that it covers the whole of poetry. By the word **individual** he indicates the restricted nature [of a figure of speech]; by the word **mere**, its being subordinate. **Saturated** (*bhāvita*): that is whose minds are intend on the nature of *dhvani*, or, it may mean, whose minds by being perfumed with its charm, cause them to show such symptoms of emotions as closing their eyes (cf. 1.1 A). **Those who deny the existence of *dhvani*:** that is, those divided into all those categories (described in 1.1 a, b, C A).

He states the result of refuting [the position of those who deny the existence of *dhvani*]: **there is such a thing.** Now, that *dhvani* should be no more than secondary usage (*lakṣaṇā*) [which was the fourth objection to the *dhvanivada* set forth 1.1 d A] can be easily explained and answered only after giving examples. So despite the fact that one would expect straight away a refutation of the view that *dhvani* is secondary usage [the fourth objection], or that it is indescribable [the fifth objection, cf. 1.1 e A], the author of the *vrtti* here sets forth the two main varieties of *dhvani* in order to be able to give examples. In doing so he follows [the system set forth by the *karikas* in] the next chapter **and it is ...**

To fit the five meanings of "*dhvani,*" the grarmmatical agreement [of the compound *avivakṣita-vācya* with *dhvani*] can be achieved by taking it as a *bahuvrihi* which has simultaneous instrumental, locative, ablative, dative, and genitive relations to its exocentric member]. When "*dhvani*" has the sense of *vācya* (the literal meaning) *dhvani* itself will be referred to by the element *vācya* in the compound. The *avivakṣitavācya* [*dhvaniḥ*] with the that type of *dhvani* (i.e., *vācya*, literal meaning) by which that literal meaning itself is not intended, that is, is not intended to predominate [in the final meaning]. Such a *dhvani* will be a suggestor. The same sort of analysis can be made of *vivakṣitāṇyaparavācya*. Or, in the one option [of the five] where "*dhvani*" means *artha* (the literal meaning), we can analyse the compounds as *karmadhārayas* (simple adjective compounds). *Avivakśitavācyaḥ* will then be an unintended literal meaning. *Vivakṣitānyapravācyaḥ* will be "a meaning which is literal and which is subordinated to something else which is intended [to predominate]." In these two types, sometimes [viz., in *avivakṣitavācya]* the literal sense is not intended for such reasons as that it makes no sense in the context; sometimes [viz., in *vivakṣitānyaparavācya*] it is intended in-so-far as it does make sense in the context, but by the power of its beauty it extends our apprehension to a suggested sense. It is on this account that in the second type a meaning is primarily the suggestor, in the first type a word. But is it not a contradiction to say that a meaning is intended and then say that it is subordinated to something else? No, because what is meant is that it is intended only insofar as it is subordinated to a second meaning.

In general of two sorts: His view is that although there are three kinds of *dhvani* — *vastudhvani*, *alankarādhvani,* and *rasadhvani* — they are included in these two sorts. But we may ask what benefit accrues, after giving the name *dhvani*, from adding these [particular] names [for its two main varieties]. The benefit is this. The first name indicates the cooperation in the operation called *dhvanana* (suggestion) of the apprehension on the part of the auditor of meanings implied by the three other operations of denotation, sentence-meaning, and secondary usage, while the second name indicates the cooperation of what is wished to be said, that is, of the intention on the part of the poet. In this way the true nature of *dhvani* is rendered more apparent.

flower of gold: the compound *suvarṇapuṣpām* [is an *upapada* compound agreeing with *pṛthivī;* it] means "which flowers forth in gold pieces." As the sentence thus embodies an impossible meaning, the literal sense must be unintended. Accordingly, after setting forth the literal sense of the words by denotative power (*abhidhā*) and giving us the syntax by the power of sentence-meaning (*tātparya-śakti*), the stanza, abandoning this sense because of the obstacle [of impossibility], gives us by the power of secondary usage (*lakṣaṇā*) a meaning which is related by similarity, namely that the three men easily partake of great wealth. The purpose of this secondary usage is that the praise of the warrior, man of knowledge and servant, which hides because of its not being expressed literally, should rise to the highest value by being suggested, just as the breasts of a beautiful woman [are the more beautiful from being half hidden]. The primary manifestor of the suggestion here is the word [*suvarṇapuṣpam*], but the literal meaning cooperates. All four semantic operations are in use.

On what mountain: for not even such mountains as Śriparvata, which give unobstructed success of the highest order, furnish such success as this. The time spent there must have been measured in millenia of divine aeons. And no form of austerity, such as sitting amid five fires has been recorded as being productive of such reward. The word *tava* has been given separately lest it be understood with weakened force as it would be if placed in compound. His intention is to bring the action of biting into close relation with "you". Accordingly, those who say that the author failed to use the expression *tvad-adhara-pāṭalaṁ* simply because it would not fit into the meter are mistaken.

Bites: [the suggestion is that] he tastes it in an unbroken continuity; [that] he does not eat it like a glutton, but rather acts like a connoisseur. Hence it is suggested [that] he has gained his refined taste, just like the other reward from his austerity. **Little parrot**: From this indication of his youth, we see that he has gained his reward at the proper time. This also must derive from his austerity. We have in this stanza a suggestion made by a lover which stimulates the [*ālambana*] *vibhāva* i.e., the lady who is the object of his love]. It takes the form of a clever compliment which transmits his own hidden desire [viz., to kiss the lady's lip].

In this stanza there are only three semantic operations, viz, denotation sentence-meaning, and suggestion, [as opposed to the four operations contained in the preceding stanza], for here the third, or middle-stage, operation of metonymy (*lakṣaṇā*) is missing as there is no blocking of the primary meaning, etc. Or, by a different interpretation, we may say that the third operation, *lakṣaṇā*, does intervene. We may suppose that the primary meaning is blocked by the impossibility of taking literally these improbable questions [directed to a parrot] and that a secondary meaning of the lover as obtaining the chance to taste his lady's lip], based on similarity, ensues. But the purpose of the *lakṣaṇā* is still that which is being suggested, which enters in the fourth stage. There is this difference however, that in the former verse (Three men reap the earth) *lakṣaṇā* was the chief semantic power to cooperate with suggestion, while here the chief powers are denotation and the power of sentence-meaning for it is because of the beauty of the literal sense that we apprehend the suggestion. This shows that the operation of *lakṣaṇā* is helpful only to a very small extent. In that variety of suggestion where the sequence is not noticed at all (*asaṃlakṣyakramavyangya*) [=*rasadhvani*] there is no apprehension of *lakṣaṇā* at all, for the sequence [from the literal to suggested meaning is not apparent, as we shall show. So we may take it that in the second type of *dhvani* also [at least as here exemplified] all forms of semantic operation are present.

And so it is only giving examples of both [major types of *dhvani*] that has comments on and refutes the view expressed [in 1.1k] by "some say it is *bhākta* (secondary operation)." What he has in mind is this. Are *bhākta* and *dhvani* identical, the two words being merely synonyms? Or does *bhākti* define *dhvani* marking it off from what is other than *dhvani* as *pṛthivitva* (earthness) marks off from earth what is other than earth? Or is it an *upalakṣaṇa* (occasional characteristic), as a crow may be Devadatta's house because a crow may be perched on it? [The *Kārikā*] begins by denying the first possibility **not identical with bhakti.** The [*Vṛtti's*] phrase, **of the sort just mentioned** should be referred to the five meanings of *dhvani*: word, literal meaning, operation, suggested meaning and poem. To show the difference [of the two concepts] he begins by stating the nature of *dhvani*; **[where a meaning other than] the literal**, etc. **To the final sense**; i.e., the sense that permits our apprehension to come to the sense which is the purpose [of the poet's employing just those particular words]. **Is revealed:** he means, is suggested. **Merely a subordinate operation** (*upacāra*): that is, secondary usage (*guṇavṛti*), metonomy *lakṣaṇā*) To use an associated sense is to speak in transgression [of the literal sense]. By the word "merely" he is referring to cases where a fourth semantic operation, of the nature of suggestion, may be inferred as possible from the mere fact that the third operation has been employed but where this fourth operation, being neither useful nor important, is as good as absent. For the definition of a [primary] purpose is "that with a view to [the acquiring or avoiding of] which one starts about an action." Inasmuch as secondary usage is found even in such cases, how can one say that the suggestive operation and the operation of *dhvani* are one and the same thing?

[The *Kārikā*] then rules out the second possibility: **because the definition would be too wide**, etc. **Nor is it**, viz., *dhvani*, **defined by that**, viz., by secondary operation. It may be objected that the suggestive operation must take place[wherever a secondary operation is employed], so how can one distinguish the area [of *dhvani* from that of *lakṣaṇā*]? To provide against this, [the *Vṛtti*] says: **without any great beauty.** He means, for the reason that the purpose in question is of no importance and nothing is therefore accomplished by the suggestion of it. By the use of the word "great" [he admits that there is some beauty in such cases but that] there is only enough to qualify as a *guṇa* (poetic quality), as shown by the definition [of the quality, aptness (*samādhi*)]: "the imposition of the property [of one thing] on some [other] thing should be called aptness."

But if there is no real purpose in using such expressions, how is it that an author uses them? He answers this objection: "because of *prasiddhyanurodha*," for such has been the usage through a long succession [of writers]. But I would say that *prasiddhi* implies [not that there is no purpose but] that the purpose is too obvious. Although the purpose appears in clear form, it stands in need of something hidden, like buried treasure [in order to be in the domain of *dhvani*]. For in the case of the secondary usage (*upacāra*) illustrated by "speaks" [in the first of Ananda's illustrative verses] the purpose is the apprehension by the auditor of "making something quite clear." If the author had used the obvious literal expression, would the verse lose an element of beauty? Or by his using this covert expression is any element of beauty added? With this in mind our author will say [that *dhvani* reveals] "a beauty which cannot be conveyed by any other form of expression".

[In the second verse quoted by Ānanda] the Prakrit word *avarundhijjai* means *ālingate* (there is embracing). "Tautology" is used in its secondary sense of something to be avoided, because the literal meaning [viz., repetition of words] is impossible in the context.

[For the third of the quoted verses Abhinava furnishes a Sanskrit translation of the Prakrit and then adds:] In this verse 'catch' is used in the secondary sense of receive, "carry away" in the sense of subjecting to their power.

[The fourth verse:] Here a husband in the course of normal love-play gives a light stroke of a fresh vine to the breast of his youngest wife. As this indicates the favor she has attained with him, it proves from its very softness hard to bear in the heart of her fellow wives, who no longer share in his love-play. That a light stroke given to one person should have its effect on another and be hard to bear "even although so soft," is startling. In this stanza giving is used in the secondary sense of rewarding.

[The fifth verse:] Although the word "suffers" is used in its primary sense with respect to the virtuous man, who is the subject really intended, still, with respect to the extraneous subject sugar cane, which is being praised, as the "suffering" of pressure is impossible, the word is used in a secondary sense of undergoing pressure, so that the whole expression made up meaning nothing more than as "squeezed."

Now in such cases of course there is some purposes, so how can we avoid saying, that there is *davani*? It is in response to such an objection that our author says: **Instances like those**, etc.

7

From *Vakrokti Jivita*

Kuntaka

यथा रघुवंशे मृगयाप्रकरणे–

अत्र हि तरङ्गिणीतीरलेखास्वाखेटवाटोद्यतेन प्रमाद्यता दशरथेन राज्ञा स्थविरान्धतपस्विबालवधो व्यवधीयतेति एकवाक्यशक्यप्रतिपादनोऽप्ययमर्थः पुनः परमार्थसरससरस्वतीसर्वस्वायमानप्रतिभाविधानकुशलेन कविना तादृश्या प्रकरणविच्छित्त्या विस्फारितश्चेतनचमत्कारकारणतामधितिष्ठति।

तथाहि – यद्यत्रानेकनक्तन्दिनानुबन्धिविविधमृगयाव्यापारपरवशीकृतान्तःकरणकवलितसकलतदितर (व्यापार) व्यावृत्त्यवसरंप्रसरदभ्यासरससोदरात्मकमृगयानुरागगरिमातः प्राण्येतादृग्रूपो न प्रतिहन्येत, तदा सदाचारसंपादनचणे त्रिभुवनाभयदीक्षाधिकारिणि किरणमालिनः कुले तिलकायमानस्याखिलविद्यापारावारपारदृश्वनः कीर्तिधनस्य धन्य (दशरथ) नाम्नो धरित्रीपतेः पवित्रितत्रिदिवाधिपाधासनस्य तथाविधाकरणीयकरणं महर्षिणाप्युदाहियमाणमनुपपन्नप्रायमेव प्रतिभासेतापाततः। इदं च तत्रैव सकलमुन्मीलित मनागुदाहियते।

व्याघ्रानभीरभिमुखोत्पतितान् गुहाभ्यः
फुल्लासनाग्रविटपानिव वायुरुग्णान्।
शिक्षाविशेषलघुहस्ततया स धन्वी
तूणीचकार शरपूरितवक्त्ररन्ध्रान् ॥२५॥

अपि तुरगसमीपादुत्पतन्तं मयूरं
न स रुचिरकलापं बाणलक्षीचकार।

सपदि गतमनस्कश्छिन्नमाल्यानुकीर्णे
रतिविगलितबन्धे केशहस्ते प्रियायाः ।।२६।।

लक्ष्यीकृतस्य हरिणस्य हरिप्रभावः
प्रेक्ष्य स्थितां सहचरीं व्यवधाय देहात् ।
आकर्णकृष्टमपि कामितया स धन्वी
बाणं कृपामृदुमनाः प्रतिसंजहार ।।२७।।

इत्यादि। एतैर्हि विचित्रवाच्यवाचकौचित्यचारुभिर्वाक्यविशेषैर्विविधव्यापारपारवश्यमतितरां प्रतीयते। यथा–

स ललितकुसुमप्रवालशय्यां
ज्वलितमहौषधिदीपिकासनाथाम् ।
वनरतिरतिवाहयांबभूव
क्वचिदसमेतपरिच्छदस्त्रियामाम् ।।२८।।

अत्र वनरतिरिति विशेषणवक्रता वने स्थित्या विलासगृहकेलीपर्यङ्के प्रेयसीं समेत्य मधुगोष्ठीप्रभृत्युपभोगप्रतीतिप्रत्याख्यातप्रतीतिं प्रतिपादयन्त्या प्रस्तुतरसावेश एव वितन्यते। त्रियामेति वचनवक्रतोल्लेखेन चिरतरसमयमन्ध (कारः) समुन्मील्यते। रूढिवक्रतामहिम्ना च निर्भरान्धकारनिवारितरुचिरव्यापारप्रकारान्तरसान्तरायकारित्वात् तत्प्रतिकूलता प्रतिपाद्यते। अत एवातिवाहयांबभूवेति क्रियावक्रत्ववैचिञ्येण दारुणदेहवेदनां शयनगतः अपगमयामास, परमपरिश्रमविधाने निद्रा रसदायिनीत्यभिननन्द। यथा च

इति विस्मृतान्यकरणीयमात्मनः
सचिवावलम्बितधुरं धरापतिम् ।
परिवृद्धरागमनुबन्धसेवया
मृगया जहार चतुरेव कामिनी ।।२९।।

अत्र जहारेति क्रियावक्रत्वविच्छित्त्या, मृगयाया करणीयेतर-भावनासुविकलान्तःकरणत्वमङ्कुरितं महीभर्तुः । तथा

अथ जातु रुरोर्गृहीतवर्त्मा
विपिने पार्श्वचरैरलक्ष्यमाणः ।
श्रमफेनमुचा तपस्विगाढां
तमसां प्राप नदीं तुरङ्गमेण ।।३०।।

अत्र तपस्विगाढामिति विशेषणवक्रतया विविधधर्माचारपराय-णतापससंकुलां तमसां पश्यन्नपि शब्दश्रवणमात्रात् शरं व्याकृष्य शरमोक्षमविकलान्तः करणः कथमकुर्वतेति प्रकाश्यते ।

"अपथे पदमर्पयन्ति हि श्रुतवन्तोऽपि रजोनिमीलिताः" इत्यनेन न्यायेन परधाराधिरूढदुर्धरव्यसनरागान्धकारकवलितविवेकदृष्टयस्तथा विधा अशुद्धाध्वनि सञ्चरन्त इत्युपपत्तिरप्युपपादिता। उत्तरकथोप-कारोऽप्येकदेशस्यास्त्येव। तथा हि–

दिष्टान्तमाप्स्यति भवानपि पुत्रशोका-
दन्ते वयस्यहमिवेति तमुक्तवन्तम् ।।३१।।

इति विशीर्णतापसवितीर्णशापस्य तापसं प्रति प्रतिवचनं कौसल्यापतेः –तथा हि

शापोऽप्यदृष्टतनयाननपद्मशोभे
सानुग्रहो भगवता मयि पातितोऽयम् ।
कृष्यां दहन्नपि खलु क्षितिमिन्धनेद्धः
बीजप्ररोहजननीं दहनः करोति

अत्र शाप इति एवंविधापचारप्राग्भारप्रभवो भवतु नाम। सा-नुग्रह इति अनुग्रहः पुनरयमनुपपन्न एवास्यामवस्थायाम्। भगव-तेत्यनर्थदर्शनेन सहजदयालुना। यदि वा भगवता शापोऽपि इति

शापानुग्रहयोर्दहनवारिणोरिवैककालमेकविषयवर्तित्वमसतोरपि भगवत् (स्वरूप) संपत्सामर्थ्यादेव संभाव्यते, अदृष्टतनयाननपद्मशोभे मयि एतस्मादेवानुग्रहादवश्यंभाविनः सुचिरकालाभिकाङ्क्षितस्य सुनावलम्बनतनोर्जीवितफलस्य विलोकनोत्कण्ठापारवश्यात् (सार्थक्यम्) इत्यलमतिप्रसङ्गेन।

अस्या एव प्रभेदान्तरमुन्मीलयति–

कथावैचित्र्यपात्रं तद्वक्रिमाणं प्रपद्यते ।
यदङ्गं सर्गबन्धादेः सौन्दर्याय निबध्यते ।।९।।

"यदङ्गंसर्गबन्धादेःसौन्दर्याय निबध्यते" = "यत्" – जलक्रीडादिप्रकरणं ("सर्गबन्धादेः") महाकाव्यप्रभृतेः ("सौन्दर्याय") – उपशोभानिष्पत्त्यै ("निबध्यते") निवेश्यते।

अयमस्य परमार्थः–प्रबन्धेषु जलकेलिकुसुमापचयप्रभृति प्रकरणं प्रक्रान्तसंविधानकानुबन्धि निबध्यमानं निधानमिव कमनीयसंपदः संपद्यते।

यथा रघुवंशे–

अथोर्मिलोलोन्मदराजहंसे
रोधोलतापुष्पवहे सरय्वाः ।
विहर्तुमिच्छा वनितासखस्य
तस्याम्भसि ग्रीष्मसुखे बभूव ।।३३।।

इत्यादि। जलक्रीडास्पर्शानन्तरलक्षितत्वात् अखिलमदविकल (ललना) विलासमूलाध्यास्यमानोत्सवाकुलस्य (कुमुदकन्या) कन्दुकक्रीडालक्षणमुत्सवान्तरमुत्तरकथोपकार्युपपद्यते, तद्विदामाह्लादमावहति च।

तथा हि राज्ञः करा (स्फालनाभ्युक्षणा) दिवारिविहाररसपरवशान्तःकरणस्य (करारविन्दा) दलंकरणमलक्षितपतनमुत्पन्नकुतूहला कुमुद्वती नाम नागकन्या जगृहे। ततस्तस्मिन्नादरोद्रेकादन्विष्टेऽप्यनासादिते पाथोन्तर्वर्तिनं नागनायकमानीय निवेदितं कुमुदमुद्दिश्य दशाननान्तकनन्दनः समधत्त धनुषि धन्वी गारुत्मतमस्त्रम्। अथ परित्राणपर्याकुलः कुमुदः कुमुद्वतीं स्वसारमाभरणेन समं करकमलालंकारिणा विदेहनन्दिनीनन्दनस्या (र्पयामास)।

अत्र सूक्तानि कानिचिदुदाहियन्ते।

अवैमि कार्यान्तरमानुषस्य
विष्णोः सुताख्यामपरां तनुं त्वाम्।
सोऽहं कथं नाथ तवाचरेय
माराधनीयस्य धृतेर्विघातम् ।।३४।।

कराभिघातोत्थितकन्दुकेय
मालोक्य बालातिकुतूहलेन।
हृदात्पतज्ज्योतिरिवान्तरि
क्षाददत्त जैत्राभरणं त्वदीयम् ।।३५।।

तदेतदाजानुविलम्बिना ते
ज्याघातरेखाकिणलाञ्छनेन।
भुजेन रक्षापरिघेण भूमेरुपैतु
योगं पुनरंसलेन ।।३६।।

इमां स्वसारं च यवीयसीं मे
कुमुद्वतीं नार्हसि नानुमन्तुम्।
आत्मापराधं नुदतीं चिराय
शुश्रूषाया पार्थिव पादयोस्ते ।।३७।।

एतेषु भुजङ्गराजवाक्येषु आद्ये 'विष्णो'रिति रूढिवक्रतया वक्तृप्रभावात् पर्यङ्कीभूय भुवनाधारेण अनन्तेन निषेव्यमाणस्य सकलाज्ञापालनसंपादने सज्जो भुजङ्गान्तरो भविष्यतीति प्रतिपाद्यते। 'स' इति संवृतिवक्रत्वेन यः सततमेव तव वास्तव्यविषयः स एवेत्यभिव्यज्यते। कथम् इति पदवक्रतया (त्वयि) भक्तिरिति विधेयतानियन्त्रितस्य मम न केनापि प्रकारेण दुश्चरितापन्नं शीलमाशङ्क्यमिति।

द्वितीयेऽपि "औत्पातिकज्योतिरिवान्तरिक्षात्" इत्युपमया न कथं किसलयितदिगन्तरालतरलितमरीचिमण्डलतया यावदस्माकं अकारणकमहाभयसंशयसंपादनमपीत्यवगम्यते।

तृतीयेऽपि तदेतदिति संवृतिवक्रतया यस्य त्वत्पितुरुरस्थलमिव कौस्तुभस्य भद्रजयविभूष्यताविषयः इति "रक्षापरिघेण भूमेः" इति रूपकेण निवारितनिखिलवसुन्धरादुःखस्य त्वद्बाहोरलंकरणम्, 'शुश्रूषया पादयो'रिति चरणशुश्रूषापवित्रेण पाणिना संपादितपरिणयोत्सवां 'यवियसी'मिति द्रुततरतारुण्यावतारितत्वदनुरागप्राग्भाराम्। अत एव नार्हसि नानुमन्तुमपि। तदर्ह्यर्हस्यैव गत्यन्तराभावादिति प्रतीयते।

"अतिथिं नाम काकुत्स्थात् पुत्रमाप कुमुद्वती" ।।३८।।

इत्यनन्तरप्रकरणे कथोपकारोऽपि प्रकटमेव वारिविहारस्य दर्शितः। नस्मादेव च तदवसरनिदानतया निदाघवर्णनमपि अत्र–

अथास्य रत्नग्रथितोत्तरीय-
मेकान्तपाण्डुस्तनलम्बिहारम् ।
निश्वाससहार्यांशुकमाजगाम
घर्मः प्रियावेषमिवोपदेष्टुम् ।।३९।।

इत्यादिना निबध्यमानं न कथावैचित्र्यमात्रमतिक्रामति। (अस्मिन् समस्त) प्रबन्धे प्रकरणं प्रक्रान्तसंविधानमपि (नानाप्रियकार्यतन्तुमिलितरूपकारणं प्रसक्तम्। अस्या निदर्शनान्यपि स्वयमन्यान्युदाहरणणीयानि।

जलक्रीडादिकाख्यानमपि संदर्भसुन्दरम् ।
प्रबन्धस्य कथाप्राणपरिस्पन्दपरं सुखम् ।।४०।।

[इत्यन्तरश्लोकः]

पुनरप्यस्याः प्रभेदान्तरमुद्भावयति–

यत्राङ्गिरसनिष्यन्दनिकषः कोऽपि लक्ष्यते ।
पूर्वोत्तरैरसंपाद्यः साङ्गादेः कापि वक्रता ।।२०।।

"साङ्गादेः कापि वक्रता" अङ्गादेः "=अङ्गसर्गादेः प्रकरणस्य" सा कापि="अलौकिकी" "वक्रता" – वक्रभावो भवतीति संबन्धः। "यत्राङ्गिरसनिष्यन्दनिकषः कोऽपि लक्ष्यते" "यत्र" – यस्यां अङ्गी यः "रसः" प्राणरूपः, तस्य निष्यन्दः प्रवाहः तस्य, काञ्चनस्येव निकषः परीक्षोपलवद्विषयविशेषः "कोऽपि" अभूत – निर्माणनिरुपमो लक्ष्यते (निकष) योजने (काञ्चनस्य रेखो) "दयैरिव विशेषः। किं विशिष्टः "पूर्वोत्तरैरसंपाद्यः"– प्राक्परवृत्तिभिरङ्गाद्यैः संपादयितुमशक्यः।

इदमत्र तात्पर्यम्। प्रधानरससर्वस्वक्रीडानिकेतनं तत्किमपि प्रकरणं (यत्र) प्रकटतरं च वक्रताविच्छित्तिर्विद्योतते। यदीयलावण्यातिशयं मनाङ्मात्रमपि पूर्वाण्यपराणि वा प्रकरणान्तराणि नानुकर्तुं शक्नुवन्ति।

An example may be had in the hunting episode described in *Raghuvamsa*:- Here Dasaratha is seen indulging himself in a hunting excursion on the banks of river. In the course of his sport, he bungles and commits the murder of a son of an old and blind sage. The incident is such that it can be stated in a short sentence like this. But the poet (namely, Kālidāsa) is such a creative genius that one might well deem him as the embodiment of the Muse of *rasas* at their best; he gives a delightful turn to it investing it with episodal beauty which exquisitely appeals to the readers.

To explain: It cannot even be pleaded justifiably that the king was completely preoccupied by his many-sided hunting sport demanding his whole attention day and night and that he was oblivious of everything else at that time except for some sweet memories called up occasionally by force of his habit; and that in his zeal to display his great skill in hunting, he could shoot down any animal. For the plea fails when the animal shot is of this nature (i.e., a human boy). And more so in the case of such a personality as Dasaratha whose sole concern is to set a model of good conduct for others, who is expected to afford all the three worlds protection from danger, who is the best scion of the great dynasty descended from the Sun-god, who is well versed in all the lores of study, who should value glory as superior to all else, who bears such a fair name and is a king sharing the throne of Indra, the King of heaven. That such a person should commit such a misdeed would indeed apparently be most unjustified as expressed by the great sage himself (the dead boy's father). All this has been very beautifully revealed there in the poem itself. A few verses only are cited below:

Highly trained as he was in the art of archery,
By a deftness of hand he could fearlessly shoot
Into mouths of tigers pouncing upon him from their dens
Like so many branches of blossomed ***'āsana'*** *tree*
Blown down by the gale; and turn
Their open mouths into quivers for his arrow.[1] (25)

Though the peacock sprang close to his horse,
He wouldn't shoot it with its lovely plumes

[1] Raghuvamśa, IX.63.

As he remembered his beloved's loose hair
With broken wreaths afar during amours.[1] (26)

That archer, so mighty as the king of gods,
Seeing its mate curling up into the body
Of the deer against which he took aim,
Withdrew his arrow in great pity
Though it was about to be shot,
Being fully drawn up to his ear
As he was himself a lover still.[2] (27)

and so on. In the descriptions, each containing a delightful and varied fancy, we get a full picture of the king's engrossment in the diverse forms of hunting. Further:-

The king was so fond of the forest
Alone, without his retinue,
On a bed of soft flowers and leaves
With luminous herbs serving as lamps.[3] (28)

The epithet of the king, viz. 'fond of the forest' is an example of artistic epithet. The stay of the king in the forest suggests that he preferred the forest to the palace at night, even with all its comforts of lovely bed in a beautiful room, company of beloved and wine party, etc. This indeed adds to the charm of his present interest in hunting. The singular number in the word 'triyama' (lit, three watched') for the night shows that he did not feel it to be dragging long; on the on the other had, he felt it to pass in a short while as it were. So it is an example of artistic use of 'number'. There is also the beauty of significant name instanced in this very usage. The result is the suggestion that the darkness was so dense that it shut out all possibility of any other engagement more delightful, and acted as a hindrance to all else. That is why even the predicate 'passed' is significant with beauty. It suggests that relaxing in bed, he overcame

---

[1] Op.cit. IX.67.

[2] Op.cit.IX.57.

[3] Op.cit.Ix.70.

his fatigue; and appreciated how sleep acts as a balm on the limbs only after hard physical exercise. We might take also another verse in this context:-

When the king was thus free from other cares
With the burden of state resting on ministers,
Hunting attracted him as a sly damsel
Adding to his zest by repeated acts.[1] (29)

Here we have a beautiful artistic use in the verb 'attracted'. It suggests that hunting made him averse to all other duties by its extreme attraction. Then comes the verse:-

On his horse, foaming in fatigue,
Once he reached the river Tamasa,
Full of ascetics engaged in ablutions,
In hot pursuit of a spotted deer
In the wild, unseen by his men.[2] (30)

The epithet 'full of ascetics' is full of artistic significance. Though the king was seeing with his own eye several ascetics engaged in religious austerities on the Tamasa river, how he shot his arrow in the direction from which he heard a sound without any hesitation or second thought is rather astounding. This idea is suggested by the said epithet. In accordance with the adage,

"Even the learned tread a wrong path
When blinded by a fit of passion" [3].

that such great personalities also can tread wrong paths with their eye of discrimination blinded by the overwhelming darkness of uncontrolled passion rising to a high pitch, is also implied indirectly by this very epithet. And, of course, it also serves to promote the later development in the story itself. Later we read (about the

---

[1] Op.cit.IX.69. [2] Op.cit.IX.72.

[3] Op.cit.IX.74.

curse of the sage):-

Like me, you too will die in old age
Only by grief on a son's account.[1] (31)

Being so cursed by the very old and dying sage, Daśaratha replies:-

This curse, O sage, is like a blessing in my case,
Denied the sight of a son's lovely lotus-face!
Though fire lit by faggots burns down
The earth to be tilled, it assists
In making it still more fertile.[2] (32)

The significance of some expressions here may be indicated:— The expression 'cause' suggests the king's acceptance of it as a proper punishment for his grave misdeed. But the expression 'like a blessing' underscores that the blessing is something which is most unreasonable or unexpected in the circumstances. The expression 'O sage' shows how he is by nature so compassionate, whatever be the tragedy coming to his notice. We might interpret this in another way too:- The juxtaposition of the words 'curse' and 'venerable sage' suggests that though, normally, the two traits, viz cursing and blessing, are diametrically opposed to each other like fire and water, their simultaneous co-existence in this person is rendered possible only on account of his extraordinary good nature. 'As I haven't had the pleasure of seeing the lotus-face of a son so long, as the fruit of this blessing indeed, now I am bound to have that joy, very much longed for, of a son's birth, a joy which I consider to be the fulfilment of a supreme craving in my life'. We shall put an end now to this incidental digression.

Another type of this very beauty of episode is explained in the following:-

When integrated with the beauty of the plot, even the conventional themes, that come to be described in court-epics and so forth conforming to set patterns, attain a novel artistic beauty. (9)

---

[1] Op.cit.IX.79.

[2] Op.cit.IX.80.

Novel artistic beauty is attained even when the conventional themes like water-sports are described as an integrated part of a whole pattern supplied by the art of plot-construction.

The substance is this:- Themes or incidents such as water-sports and flower-gathering should also be so described that they come within the general pattern of the plot as a whole, if they have to yield their best aesthetic relish.

We have an example of this in the *Raghuvamsa*:-
Then he desired to sport with women
In the waters of the river Sarayu,
Cool in summer, rich with stately swans
Swimming along waves, with floating flowers.[1] (33)

and so forth. The king is so much lost in the delights of water-sport, entailing diverse blandishments of drunken damsels, that he discovers the loss of his armlet only at the end of the sport. This incident becomes helpful later on in providing a link with the next incident of ball-play of the sister of the Naga king, Kumuda (since she is said to catch the circular ornament falling down in the water, mistaking it to be her own ball thrown up in play). And this artistic connection brings great delight to connoisseurs.

To explain, fully:- As the king was engaged in the joyous activities of water-sport like splashing the water with his hands upon the ladies nearby, his armlet slipped down this arm without his noticing it. The daughter of the Naga king called Kumudvati caught it as it fell in the water out of curiosity. The king who valued the ornament very highly, arranged for a thorough search of it in the water; but the search ended in vain. The fishermen who were employed in this search brought him news that it must have been taken by Kumuda, the king of the netherworld, living within the waters. At once Kusa (the son of the destroyer of Ravana), a great archer that he was, fitted the Garuda missile to his bow to be shot against Kumuda. Soon Kumuda was seen in a fluster; and in a bid to save himself somehow, he came up to Kusa and surrendered into his lotus-like hands not only his own sister Kumudvati but also the armlet lost.

---

[1] Raghuvamśa, XVI. 54.

Some of the beautiful verses in this connection are cited below:-

I know indeed you are the son-prototype
of Lord Visnu who assumed a form human
For fulfilling his divine mission
Hence you are truly adorable to me.
How dare I cause any vexation to you? (34)
This girl at play had sent up her bull
Giving it a gentle stroke with her hand;
When she saw falling from above, thy armlet
Glittering so like a falling star,
And seized by great curiosity,
She caught it in her hand. (35)
May this ornament be reunited
With thy massive arm, reaching thy knee,
Scarred by the bowstring's brushings often
And like the bolt ensuring the earth's safety! (36)
I pray, don't refuse to accept
Kumudvati too, this young sister of mine,
Who desires to atone for her guilt
By services rendered at thy feet.[1] (37)

In this statement of the Naga King we have several types of artistic beauty combined:- In the first verse, the name 'Visnu' is full of beauty associated with a significant name. The special nature of the speaker here, viz., his being a Naga or serpent, suggests that even Lord Visnu is fond of a Naga only called Ananta who is the bearer of the weight of the universe and whom he allows to serve him by coiling up into a soft couch, and by carrying out all his commands. The pronoun "*so'ham*" too is richly significant, and partakes of 'beauty of concealment'. It suggests that he is the same one who is well known to the king as a denizen in his realm for a long time. The word 'how' carries its own beauty of expression. It reassures the king of the Nagas firm loyalty and removes effectively any doubt regarding misdeed on his part, since he is completely under the restraint imposed by his obedience to the king.

Raghuvamśa, XVI. 82-85.

In the second verse, the simile adduced of the ominously falling star from above suggests that the halo of glittering light surrounding the armlet and illumining all quarters was so astounding that it brought sudden fear and doubt even in grown-ups like Kumuda.

In the third verse, the demonstrative pronoun *'tadetad'* suggests that like the jewel *Kaustubha* adorning the chest of your father, this armlet of victory too formed an inseparable ornament. The metaphor of 'the bolt ensuring the earth's safety' suggests that the king has effectively relieved the entire earth from all distress and the arm of such a person certainly deserves to be adorned by all means. The phrase 'by services rendered at thy feet' is suggestive of the fact that she hopes to attain the rare privilege of holding his hand in marriage by virtue of the merit she gains by rendering service at his feet. The adjective 'young' suggests she has suddenly come under the overwhelming influence of love for him because of her stepping into youth. All these converge to justify the prayer — 'Don't refuse to accept'. It implies; 'You are bound to concede our prayer since you are left with no other go'.

In the next incident of the story also, when the poet says —

Kumudvati got a son, Atithi by name,
From Kusa, the scion of Kakutstha,[1] (38)

we can clearly see how the earlier incident of water-sport is connected with later events like this organically. Similarly, the earlier description of summer in the same canto is very well connected with this inasmuch as it prepares the ground for water-sports. Such descriptions are:—

Then came summer to teach as it were
Fair ladies how they should dress
With upper garments laced with gems,
With necklaces dangling about their breasts,
And silk so fine as to be blown away by breath![2] (39)

serve no other purpose except adding to the varied interest of story (by providing a proper motivation). Though in the whole wo

[1] Op.cit.XVII. 1.

[2] Op.cit.XVI. 43.

this forms but an incidental episode, it is seen to serve the purpose of gathering different loose threads of the story into a whole. Other illustrations in the art of episode-construction may be imagined by the readers themselves.

Descriptions of water-sports etc. should not only have a contextual beauty of their own, but should also be vitally connected with the plot as a whole to delight the readers most. **(40)**

This is a mnemonic verse.

Now, another type of this beauty of episode is explained:

Another type of beauty in respect of Acts etc., is instanced when the beauty is so exclusive to an Act that it cannot be attained by any other Act, either preceding or following, in the play and the Act thus serves as a touchstone in its own way of the ruling sentiment in the play. (10)

The beauty relating to an Act in a play or a canto in an epic — both being *prakaraṇas* or parts of a whole structure — is also unique or exclusively singular. In such a well devised act or canto, we observe as it were the exclusive quality of an extraordinary touchstone testing the delightful flow of the vital ruling sentiment as if it were gold brought to be tested; i.e. the quality of revealing the purity or otherwise of sentiment like the touchstone that of gold from the lines imprinted. And it is a singular quality which cannot be found in other acts of the same play, earlier or later.

The purport of the whole is this:- Not all acts are equally beautiful; only some unique ones will serve as a sporting-ground for the essence of the ruling sentiment; and the artistic beauty of that act alone strikes us most. Its artistic excellence will be such that it cannot be limited or repeated in any other act, earlier or later, even of the same play.

SECTION - II

Essays on Indian Poetics

1

Rasa — "Imaginative Experiences"

J.L. Mason and Patwardhan

We come now to the key word of all Sanskrit literary criticism, the word that Abhinava says sums up the whole of the critical literature: *rasa*. First what are the most simple meanings of the technical terms used in aesthetic experiences? How does the tradition regard a viewing of the *Śākuntalam* from the point of view of *rasa*? The *vibhāvas* (sources) belong to the characters represented on the stage. The *ālambana vibhāvas* (primary sources) will be Śakuntalā and Duşyanta — The uddipanavibhāvas (setting) will be the physical beauty of both the characters, the spring flowers, the trees etc. The *anubhāvas* (in which are included the more intimate *sāttvikabhāvas*) will also belong to the characters and are the physical indices of love (or more simply, "actions" as Bharata himself sometimes calls them), trembling, sweating, etc. These are the essential elements of the preliminary stage. Now we come to the more problematic three: the *vyabhicāribhāvas* (also called *sañcāribhāvas*) the *sthāyibhāva*, and finally *rasa* itself. *Vyabhicāribhāvas are* emotions that accompany the primary feelings of the character. They are liable to change and are not inherent to the character's personality. Examples are joy (*harşa*), longing (*autsukya*), etc., all of which belong exclusively to the characters. Dusyanta's longing for Śakuntalā is not shared by the audience. Now the *sthāyibhāva* (*rati*, there are eight or nine of them) is a state of mind which because it is more deeply felt, dominates all other emotions. It belongs to both the character and to the spectator. The difference is this: Once the character experiences the *sthāyibhāva*, he has reached the height of emotion. But the spectator can go farther, and in a sense deeper. For when "love" is awakened in him, it is not like the love that the original character felt. The spectators do not fall in love with Sītā. This *sthāyibhāva rati* is transformed (*pariņata*) into an extraworldly state (*alaukikāvasthā*), and this is what is called *rasa*. The *sahṛdaya* sympathises (*hṛdayasaṃvāda*) with the original character, and to a large degree he even identifies (*tanmayibhāva*) with the situation depicted. But he does not identify completely; he retains a certain *aesthetic distance*, the name for which is *rasa*. The actor in the opinion of Abhinavagupta

Abhinavagupta and most later writers does not experience *rasa,* nor does the original character, nor even the author. For *rasa* implies distance. Without this aesthetic distance, there cannot exist literature, only the primary world. This is what, in our opinion, lies behind Abhinava's famous comparison of drama to a dream: in both cases nothing in the real world "happens" or is affected. It would be as absurd for a spectator to fall in love with a character in a drama as it would be to expect the golden lady-bug of a dream to still be shining on our hand in the morning. The transparent but adamant glass partition that separates both is art.

Whereas *dhvani* was for a long time a much debated issue, with many prominent critics refusing to admit its existence let alone importance, *rasa* never met with any such controversy. Everybody admitted its existence. It has not been generally recognised that in fact Ānandavardhana said that the whole point of his work was not so much to show the existence of *dhvani* as to establish the importance of the suggestion of *rasa*. In our view, the major thrust of the *Dhvanyāloka* is directed towards a reordering of priorities in literary criticism and not towards trying to establish the superiority of one "school" over another. (It is very artificial to speak, as De and Kane do, of the "*rasa*" school, opposing it, without any justification, to the "*dhvani*" school). Mahimabhaṭṭa justly asks who would question the priority of *rasa*, but the question is not one of belief, but of practice. Ānanda is the first author to make *rasa* the pivotal point around which his discussion of literature revolves. Earlier writers are brief, for reasons that are not entirely clear. In fact, to the great detriment of Sanskrit literary criticism, later writers too, on the whole, tend to busy themselves once again with scholastic deliberation of figures of speech. But regardless of their practical pre-occupations, no writer would, we think, ever have denied the importance of *rasa*. The later tradition compares a poem without *rasa* to a marriage without love! Judging Sanskrit criticism by the standards of universal application, there can be no doubt that *rasa* is the greatest contribution that India has made to world literature. For *rasa* is no less than the reader's reaction to, his personal involvement with literature. It is true that there is some confusion in its use in the D.Ā. and the *Locana*. Often it is used to mean simply the *sthāyibhāva*, or even simply "emotion", or whatever important takes place when literature is appreciated. Abhinava is not unaware of this fact, and seems to take a particular delight in the richness of the "associations" the word calls up. He does not seem to wish to restrict its meaning too narrowly. *Rasa* has so many connotations in Sanskrit that it would indeed be limiting to always apply its purely technical sense of the experience of the reader. Ānanda and Abhinava used it as the nucleus of an entire new vocabulary that soon dominated the whole of Sanskrit literary criticism. Of course when Bharata says that a poem has *rasa*, he does not mean this literally. It is the poem's capacity to elicit a deep response from a sensitive reader. *Rasa* is after all not an objective "thing" in the real world. It is a private experience. This is perhaps why later writers tend to compare it to religious experiences for ecstatic experiences are essentially private, inner happenings more or less invisible to a third party and which are liable to evaporate under rigorous questioning. Abhinava says that a *rasa*, too roughly handled, will fade like a flower.

There has been a tendency, as we noted earlier, for the post-Abhinava writers to remain relatively silent on the issue of *rasa*. No doubt it is due partly to awe; the silence of admiration faced with a nearly perfect mind. For there is no doubt that no later writer has written anything more profound on *rasa* than Abhinavagupta. But there seems more to it than this. Perhaps the desire to abdicate reason when faced with the mysterious or the inexplicable is a natural reaction. In part it must be the natural respect we feel for that which we cannot understand fully and surely *rasa* belongs to this category of experience. But there is also a sense in which we simply retreat from an exacting task. Ānanda already noticed that many sincere critics admitted the importance of suggestion (including *rasa*), but said that it lay beyond the realm of speech, and one would do well to simply keep quiet about it. There is a fine verse from the anthologies on this theme.

"I respect the person who (in the face of great poetry) is forced into silence. His visibly thrilled body bears testimony to the intention of the poet which is beyond the reach of words, but which vibrates in his language that overflows with emotion."

The Poet Hṛṣikeśa in fact addresses a stanza to Ānanda:
"This nectar (of suggestion) which is a fusion of both word and meaning, bathes the minds of sensitive readers with the oozings of bliss. It is the truth of poetry, shining without cessation. Clear to the heart, it is yet beyond words." But Abhinava, while he may have renounced reason at the last moment of his life, used his renowned intellect all the rest of it. He was very willing to bring his powerful

mind to bear on the problem of *rasa*, and he does so, as one might expect, in a most impressive way: "In the course of our ordinary life, we acquire a certain proficiency (*pāṭava*) through long practice (*abhyāsa*) in inferring people's mental moods (*cittavṛtti*), i.e. their basic emotions (*sthyāyyātma*) from observing certain signs (*linga*) consisting in causes, effects and accompanying elements (*sahacāra*). In watching a drama (or reading a poem — *adhunā*), a garden, or a glance, i.e. ordinary causes (effects, etc.) lose their ordinary characters of cause etc. and take on the essential nature of the function of awakening a permanent emotion (*vibhāvanā*), the function of leading the spectator to a recognition of this permanent emotion (*anubhāvanā*) and of adding colour (to the emotions in question — *samuparañjakatva*). And so they acquire the non-ordinary names of *vibhāvas* etc. Now it is through these things called *vibhāvas* etc., precisely in order to proclaim the fact that they are dependent upon the *saṃskāras* (latent impressions) of their nature as a cause etc. and whose essential characteristics will be given in the *bhāvādhyāya* (seventh chapter), when they, by assuming a leading or subordinate role, attain a unity, a joining, a fusion (*yoga*) in the mind of the spectator, that an emotional situation (*artha*) whose essence consists exclusively in aesthetic pleasure (*carvyamāṇataikasāra*) is brought to the state of aesthetic relish (*carvaṇā*) which is a form of consciousness (*saṃvedana*) free from worldly obstacles (i.e. worldly preoccupations). It is not something that is objectively existent (*siddhasvabhāva*) (for) it exists only for the duration of aesthetic relish (*tātkālika eva*) and does not persist for any time after the aesthetic emotion. It is completely different from the permanent emotions. It is *rasa*."

There are two places in the *Locana* where he gives similar statements about *rasa*. Both are difficult but important. In these passages Abhinava distinguishes the process whereby *rasa* is achieved from other more "mundane" (*laukika*) processes. In this he is only following the D.Āl., where the views of writers who claimed that suggestion is nothing more than secondary usage (*bhakti, guṇavṛtti, lakṣaṇā* or inference (*anumāna*), or *tātparya* are all refuted. The first passage contains Abhinava's famous example: *putras te jātaḥ*. "Now this (suggested sense such as *rasādi* is not "produced" the way joy is produced when (a man hears the words): "A son has been born to you", nor does it come about through lakṣaṇā. No, rather this (suggested sense) arises in the fully responsive reader as being relished by him through his awareness of the vibhāvas and anubhāvas, from the force of his sympathetic response, and through his identification. It is different from happiness etc. whose nature is well-known. Its sole essence consists in aesthetic enjoyment." The next passage is even more important for it brings in the NŚ and shows us how Abhinava interprets Bharata's *rasasūtra*: "Do you think that the apprehension of *rasa* is the apprehension of the mental mood of somebody else? Please don't be so foolish as to think so. For we know about another person's mental mood by inference. What aesthetic experience is involved in this? Aesthetic experience has for its very essence a transcendental delight, and consists in the aesthetic relish of the *vibhāvas* etc. in poetry. It should not be degraded to the level of recollection or inference. However the (literary critic) whose mind has been trained (*saṃskṛta*) by everyday inferences of causes from effects (and vice-versa) perceives the *vibhāvas* etc. not in an objective (i.e. indifferent, uninvolved) manner (*tāṭasthyena*) but by being completely overcome by sensitivity, *sahṛdayatva*, which is another name for sympathetic response of the heart. Because of the sprouting (*ankuribhāva*) of the relish of *rasa* which is heading towards completion (*pūrṇibhaviṣyat*) without employing the process of inference and recollection, (he perceives the *vibhāvas*) as having for their essence aesthetic relish which is the result of (literally: appropriate to, *ucita*) complete identification. Now this aesthetic relish was not formerly the product of some other valid means of cognition such that it could now be "recollected". Nor has it now arisen from any other valid means of cognition. For the (empirical) means of valid cognition such as direct perception (inference), etc., (simply) cannot operate in regard to something that is transcendental. And so the designation as *vibhāvas* etc. (in the case of kāraṇa etc. of *rasapratiti*) is an indication of the transcendental nature of *rasapratiti*. As has been said (NŚ. VII, p. 346, GOS edn.): "The word vibhāvas has an epistemological significance." In everyday life it is called a cause and not a *vibhāva*. The *anubhāvas* are also transcendental. As has been said: (NŚ. VII, p.347) "Since verbal and physical acting and the acting of involuntary physical reactions of certain mental states (such as stupefaction, perspiration, horripilation etc.) brings to our consciousness (*anubhāvayati*) (the working of the *sthāyibhāva* and the *vybhicāribhāvas*), therefore it (the acting) is called an *anubhāva*. For experience (*anubhāvana*) (of the *sthāyibhāva* and the *vyabhicāribhāvas*) is the complete identification (*tanmayibhavana*) with these mental moods. In everyday life we use the term *kārya* and not *anubhāva*. And so (in aesthetic experience) it is not another person's mental mood that is inferred.

With this in mind Bharata did not mention the word *sthāyi* in his *sūtra*: "*rasa* arises from the combination of the *vibhāvas*, *anubhāvas*, and *vyabhicāribhāvas*." Had he done so, far from being (helpful) it would have been a great (source of) error. It is quite proper to say that the *sthāyibhāvas* become *rasas* (or perhaps better: This is said in a metaphorical manner). Because (the final result) is the beautiful experience that takes place when one's latent impressions are aroused through the mental moods corresponding to the *vibhāvas* and *anubhāvas* that belong to the character. And further, because at the time of (the inferential) knowledge of the (aroused) mental mood in the (original) character, which (knowledge) is extremely useful (i.e. necessary) for the sympathetic response of the heart of the *sahṛdaya*, there is the apprehension of the mental mood such as love aroused in the (original character), with the help of the (*vibhāvas*) like bristling hair etc. Now (the reason that Bharata) mentioned the *vyabhicāribhāvas*), though they are mental moods (just like the *sthāyibhāvas*) among the *vibhāvas* and *anubhāvas* (in this *sūtra*) is that they are relished as subsidiary to the major mental mood (the *sthāyibhāva*). Therefore the emergence of aesthetic experience is the enjoyment (by the *sahṛdaya* of the mental mood evoked in him by the objective mental mood of the character portrayed), by suppressing the ordinary worldly emotions such as joy etc. which arise (in the character portrayed) from such causes as reunion with his dear relatives, etc. as described in a literary work ... What sort of thing is this that arises? Why it is *rasa*, something transcendental... Where else can such a thing be seen? (Reply:) the very fact that such a thing is not seen elsewhere shows that it is transcendental. Objection: if this is the case, then *rasa* would be unreliable (*apramāṇa*) (as a means leading to *vyutpatti*). Yes, so what? Since pleasure (*priti*) and instruction (*vyutpatti*) are achieved from the relish of aesthetic experience, what else is required?"

This brings us to the heart of the controversy about rasa that is alive today as it was in the eleventh century: there are eight *rasas*. Certainly in the case of love (*śṛṅgāra*) one can immediately understand why it would appeal to everybody: being in love is pleasant, hearing about love is pleasant, watching a play that deals with love is pleasant. Yes, we can all agree, this is what our best moments are like, they are full of the most unmysterious kind of pleasure. But there are other rasas as well, among them, in particular, karuṇa, where what we see on the stage is not pleasant, it is rather painful, and we often leave the theatre where a tragedy has been presented feeling deeply disquieted. We may even be struck by the incongruity of our friends' questions: "Did you enjoy the play?". "Well ...yes...but." And here we have struck the heart of the matter. How can we have enjoyed something that deals with a painful situation? Aristotle put forward the theory of *katharsis*. What did the Indians say? First we must dispose of a common misunderstanding: while it is true that most Indian plays end happily, this does not mean that Indian writers and critics were not alive to the importance of the tragic element in literature. They most emphatically did admit that *karuṇarasa* can be a dominant emotional mood in a poem or a play. In fact, we feel that there is a sense in which the Indians believed that the emotions associated with *karuṇa* (sadness, regret, nostalgia, a kind of emotional weariness) are the very essence of human life. Viśvanātha quotes a verse to the effect that love cannot reach its height until one has experienced separation. We don't think any culture has been more conscious than the Indian of the frailty of human existence, the tragedy inherent in simple everyday life:

"If you have really decided to go, then leave you must. But what is this hurry? Stay two or three minutes more, while I gaze at your face. In this world, our life is like water in a jug, swiftly rushing out. Who knows if we shall ever meet again."

This sense of "disquiet" is conveyed by Kālidāsa in what must be his most beautiful verse: *ramyāṇi vikṣya madhurāṇś ca niśamya śabdān* etc., and even Kṣemendra moves us:

"When he witnessed the death of his friend, he stood without moving. Then Kapiñjala let out a piteous cry resounding through the thicket of trees, and strong enough to break the stones of the mountain, piercing his own life, rendering him unconscious: O Puṇḍarika! Even now, long past, when the deer remember it, the grass drops from their mouths".

Abhinava in an obscure passage even says that śoka informs comedy, for it is the lightning flash of sorrow that illuminates the comic in our lives. Ānandavardhana says that *karuṇarasa* is the *pradhānarasa* of the whole Rāmāyaṇa. Even more to the point is Bhavabhūti's great *Uttararāmacarita*. What is the rasa of this play? On purely technical grounds, one can argue that it is *vipralambha-śṛṅgāra* since the lovers are eventually reunited, and the play ends with their happiness. It is in the terms of the NŚ, *sāpekṣabhāva*.

But this is only a technicality. The real *rasa* of the Uttarárāmacarita is *Karuna*, as the famous saying:

Kārunyam bhavabhūtir eva tanute, proves. Does the reader then experience sorrow, or more to the point, is the *karunarasa* of *Uttararāmacarita* duḥkhānuviddha? The most interesting discussion of this occurs in Dhanika's commentary on his brother's *Daśrūpaka: Kārikā* 43 says that *svāda* (aesthetic pleasure) comes from *ātmānanda*. "Objection: it is quite proper to say that *śṛṅgāra, vira, hāsya*, etc., which consist essentially in delight, arise because of the identification of the spectators with the matters presented in the drama (*kāvyārtha-sambheda*), from the joy of the Self. But in *karuṇa* etc. (i.e. in *vipralambhaśṛṅgāra* as well) which consists primarily in sorrow, how can joy arise? For when sensitive readers listen to a poem that consists essentially in *karuṇa*, they feel sorrow, shed tears, and do similar other things. If (*karuṇa*) were to consist in joy, this would surely not be the case. (Answer:) What you say is true. But this (aesthetic joy) in karuṇa etc. is such that it consists in both pleasure and pain, as when women, in the act of love hit (their lovers) pretending to repulse them (*kuṭṭamita*). The compassion of a poem is different from the compassion found in the ordinary world. The explanation is that sensitive readers (*rasikas*) become more and more deeply attracted towards this aesthetic experience of grief whereas they tend to shun the real experience. For if (*karuṇa*) were to consist exclusively in sorrow the way worldly *karuṇa* does, then nobody would feel like going (to plays in which *karuṇarasa*, was present). And thus large and important works such as the *Rāmayaṇa* etc. which consist exclusively in *karuṇarasa*, would fall into oblivion. There is nothing wrong if spectators shed tears upon listening to the description of a tragic event, just as there is nothing wrong with people being plunged in grief and shedding tears over the actual down fall and death of people in the real world. Therefore, *karuṇa*, like all the other *rasas*, consists in joy." Abhinava's answer to the above question also seems to be no, that *karuṇarasa* is not painful. Why? Because literature is not the real world. Nothing really takes place. The world of the past is transformed into art, and in watching this transformation (where all terms are from a different order of reality, *vibhāva* belongs only to art, not to the real world, where we say *kāraṇa*), we somehow (for it is never explained precisely how this is achieved) touch the very core of our being. In doing so, we experience a bliss that has its parallel only in the world of mysticism. One distinction is that *rasas* and *vibhāvas* are magical. That is they exist for the duration of a play. Abhinava explains that they have no parallel in the real world. *Rasa* is not *kārya*, and therefore *vibhāvas* are not *utpādaka-kāraṇas*. *Vibhāvas* are not *jñāpakahetus* because *rasa* is not *jñāpya*. The opponent asks Abhinava: "But there is nothing in the whole world like this." "Ah", says Abhinava, "at last you have understood" *rasa* is *alaukika*. It is above and beyond its constituent parts. *Rasa* is not something we know, but something we feel: *rasyamāna-taikaprāṇo hy asau na prameyādisvabhāvaḥ*. So Abhinava says: "*rasanā ca bodha-rūpaiva*. Aesthetic experience consists exclusively in knowledge." But Abhinava qualifies this knowledge as being in a class by itself, not comparable to any other kind of knowledge: *kintu bodhāntarebhyo laukikebhyo vilakṣaṇaiva*. Abhinava makes it clear in this passage,that in the theatre, we live neither in the time or space of the original characters, nor of the actors. We are, in a sense, outside both time and space altogether: *ata evobhayadeśakālatyāgaḥ*. There is no parallel to what takes place in a literary experience. Nor can we duplicate it. This is why Abhinava says it is like a wondrous flower (*adbhutapuṣpavat*), it is *sui generis*, nobody can create it at will. Just as you cannot tell somebody to fall in love, so also, you cannot tell someone to create *rasa*. Or even to experience it. *Rasa* is not subject to our will (*aniyata*). It just happens. What we see in the theatre suggests emotions, e.g. love, that are not bound by time: *deśakālāniyamena tatra* (i.e. in the theatre) *ratiṃ gamayanti*. Abhinava puts all of these ideas together in a marvellous passage at the beginning of the first volume of the A.Bh.

2

The Main Aspects of Indian Aesthetics*

M. Hiriyanna

It is usual for every prominent philosopher in the West to regard the question of beauty as a part of the problem he is attempting to solve. Hence aesthetics has come to be recognized there as a regular part of philosophy. The intrinsic relation implied in this between aesthetics and philosophy is not denied in India; but the former of these studies is carried on by a distinct class of thinkers — Ālaṃkārikas as they are called, or literary critics — who are not, generally speaking, professional philosophers. This separation of aesthetic problems, in the matter of investigation, from those of general philosophy may at first sight appear not only strange but also defective; a little reflection, however, will show that it is not really so. Before explaining this point, however, it is necessary to state that when we say that Indian philosophers have not troubled themselves with questions of beauty, what is meant is only that they do not deal with beauty in art and not also [sic] beauty in nature. The latter is certainly included; but, while it is explicit in some systems, it is only implicit in others. The exact view which they hold in this respect will become clear as we proceed. As regards their neglect of beauty in art, the reason is that its pursuit cannot, according to them, directly minister to the attainment of the final goal of life, which is the prime concern of Indian philosophers. Perhaps some among them thought that its pursuit might even tend to lead man away from that goal, in which case their attitude towards art would be like that of Plato towards the same.

So far from being a defect, the separation of aesthetics in this sense from general philosophy has many positive advantages. It has thereby been able to get rid of the constraint which particular types of metaphysical thought may impose upon it. When a philosopher holds a particular view of reality, he is bound to square his theory of art, if he formulates one, with it; and the consequence is that we have as many theories of art in the West as there are theories of reality. This cannot be helped in the case of beauty in nature, but there is no

---

* From *Art Experience*.

reason for acquiescing in such diversity of views in a theory of art. That is the view of Indian aestheticians. Thus the postulation by Indian aestheticians of what is called Vyāngyārtha (suggested sense), which is not only not recognized by any school of philosophy but is definitely opposed, shows the freedom with which aesthetic investigation has been carried on in India[1]. They have succeeded in this in evolving a theory of meaning which, as we shall try to point out, certainly sheds new light on the nature of art. Where it is not necessary to devise such a new theory, Indian aestheticians select one or other of the views held by the philosophic schools according to the needs of the case. Such eclecticism results in a more detached view (from the aesthetic standpoint) than would be the case if a particular philosophic point of view were adopted in its entirety. This does not, however, mean that there is a dull uniformity in the Indian theory of art. There is as much diversity in it as in any Western treatment of the subject; but the important point is that the diversity is based upon purely artistic considerations and is, therefore, more genuine.

There is another reason to support the Indian practice. Reality, as represented in art, as is generally admitted, is a unity in diversity, so that there is no room for any divergence of opinion in regard to it so far as art is concerned. The aim of art is not to discover the nature of reality but to secure for us the highest experience of life. It does not pronounce any final opinion on the tenability or otherwise of the view of reality it thus uses. In other words, aesthetics unlike ethics for instance, is alogical. While it is closely connected with psychology it regards logic, or more properly epistemology, as irrelevant to its purpose. Art is a short cut to the ultimate value of life, by-passing logic. Even supposing it is not admitted that reality, as represented in art, is necessarily a unity in diversity, the view of reality that may be accepted in its stead does not matter, for it is to serve but as the medium through which the value is realized, art being concerned less with facts than with values.

Nature and art

We have distinguished nature from art. The question will naturally arise here whether there is any need for seeking beauty in art, if it is found in nature. As G.E. Moore has stated in his *Principia Ethica*,

1 See Jayaratha's commentary on Ruyyaka's *Alaṃkārasarvasana*, p.10, Nirnayasagar Press Edition.

when other things are the same, beauty which is found in actual objects is decidedly better than that in imaginary ones. It is therefore necessary to point out why art is necessary, though in certain respects the beauty which it presents may be inferior to that in nature. As regards the latter, two views are possible:

(i) We may hold, with the idealists, that nature as a whole is beautiful, but that when it is looked at in parts, it may or may not be so. That is, though nature may, in reality, be beautiful, there may appear ugliness in it when we take a partial view of it as, ordinarily speaking, we are bound to do. This means that, though in the case of those few who can take a synoptic view of nature, art may be superfluous, it is not so in the case of the many. As an old Vedantic stanza has it, it is only when man has overcome selfishness and realized the highest truth, he will be in rapt ecstasy wherever he may turn, for he sees the glory of Being everywhere. Till then, therefore, he can have an experience of complete beauty only in art. Further, even as regards the parts that appear beautiful in nature, there is no certainty that they will continue to be so for long. For there may come to be a change in our attitude towards them, when their appeal will become non-aesthetic. Or the situations in nature may themselves so change in course of time that they will cease to appear beautiful. Hence it is that we require the creations of art which are not subject to these defects — a change in the presentations of nature or in our attitude towards them. This is the need for art according to the idealistic view of nature.

(ii) The second view of nature is that though it may be beautiful, that feature is inevitably associated with ugliness and that the latter element cannot be eliminated from it without, at the same time, eliminating the former also. According to this pessimistic view, art becomes even more necessary. In fact, it is the sole means, in this view, of satisfying the quest for unmixed joy which somehow actuates all men or, to state the same otherwise, the need for escaping from the struggles and perplexities of everyday life.

Whatever the worth of these two metaphysical theories in themselves may be, the point that is important for us now is that there is a need for art in either case. To state this need in terms applicable to both the views, it is the presence on the one hand, of evil in life and, on the other, of an ideal within us that has led to the invention of art. Here we may observe, in passing, we have another instance of Indian aesthetics transcending the differences that characterize the metaphysical schools. Art is a device for the provisional attainment of the final ideal of life, whether or not we look forward to a state which eventually renders it superfluous.[1]

Art experience

The aim of art is implicit in what we have said so far. It is to secure for man a unique form of experience which, according to one view, can never be attained in actual life and, according to the other, can be attained only when self-perfection is achieved. But either way, it is an ultimate value in the sense that it is sought for its own sake and not as a means to anything else.[2] The characteristics of this art experience are two:

(1) The first is unselfishness. It is true that all or nearly all men, in virtue of their social nature, show more or less of unselfishness in their behaviour; but it may be the result of habit or of prudential, and therefore eventually of selfish, considerations. Such outward unselfishness is not what is meant here. Even when it is spontaneous and therefore quite genuine, it is not complete. The selflessness signified by art experience, on the other hand, is not only spontaneous but also complete. Man grows so unselfish then that he becomes virtually unconscious of his private self. This is the meaning of saying that art experience consists in the disinterested contemplation of beauty. The intrusion of any personal aim is sure to vitiate it, and make the pursuit of art unsuccessful.

(2) The second characteristic, which is probably a consequence of the first, is that it yields a kind of joy which is pure and unstained by even the least pain. This is a further indication of the transcendental character of art experience; and it shows that the aesthetic attitude stands higher than that of common or everyday life which is invariably characterized by more or less of mental tension.

On account of these excellences, art experience is regarded as identifiable with the ultimate goal of life as it is conceived by the idealists. When we take the ideal of life, as it is conceived by others,

---

1 There is an ultimate ideal according to the second view also; but it is a state transcending joy as well as suffering. Positivistically speaking, this means that man may cultivate detachment to such an extent that he will ignore nature altogether. But there is nothing resembling aesthetic pleasure then, unless we understand the aesthetic end itself in an uncommon way.

2 Self-realisation in Advaita is value-realisation, for the Self is the ultimate value.

art experience affords the same escape from worldly concerns as that ideal, when attained, does; but it also does more for, while the latter does not represent a state of supreme joy, the former does. According to both, it is one of the only two such values recognized by Indians — Ātmānanda[1] and Rasānubhava.[2]

The content of art

But what is the means whereby the artist is able to secure for us such experience? All art is a blend of form and content; and it is through certain excellences characterizing either that he succeeds in inducing in us the artistic attitude. In the case of poetry, for example, the content is constituted by the figurative ideas and sentiments it expresses; and the form, by the musical language through which they find expression. Of these, the form varies much from one art to another; and it is also technical. We shall not refer to it here at any length and shall confine our attention mainly to the content. We shall only observe, in passing, that the legitimate function of form is to subserve the content; and if it assumes greater importance, the work in which it does so marks a lapse from the best type of art.

The content of art may be defined generally as the meaning which it expresses. The excellences that may characterize it are many, and they have been classified in various ways. But these details, while they are undoubtedly helpful in indicating to us their character in a concrete manner, can never be exhaustively enumerated. As one Indian literary critic observes[2], they can only be indicated generally. This general character of the content of art is that it must be drawn from actual life, but that it should also be judiciously idealized. The purpose of the idealization is two-fold. In the first place, it is that, having its source in the artist's imagination, it may appeal to the same faculty in the spectator and not to his intellect merely. In the second place, it is that the particular things of common experience may thereby be transformed into general ones, and thus readily induce a detached attitude in the spectator which, as we have pointed out, is a salient feature of all art experience. But it is necessary to add that the things represented in art will not become false or fictitious through such idealization. For a spectator to mistake them for real

---

1 Spiritual bliss. 2 Aesthetic enjoyment.

2 Cf. Vāgbhaṭa in his Alaṃkāra, p.77, N.S. Press edn.

objects, as we do in illusions, will be to lapse from the truly aesthetic attitude,because he will then cease to remain detached. But at the same time, they cannot be viewed as unreal or false because then they will cease to interest him. Thus the things depicted in art assume a unique character which the spectator can describe as neither real nor unreal. In brief, we do not take a logical view of them. We neither believe nor disbelieve in their reality. We merely entertain them[1].

This is the general view of the content of art which is prevalent everywhere. Indian aestheticians also held the same opinion for a long time; but a profound change in this respect, the germs of which seem to have been there all along, was introduced about the 9th century A.D. The change was to look upon what had so far been regarded as the content of art, viz., the meaning also as only the outer vesture of art and to take emotion as its true content[2]. When the meaning in general was regarded as the content, it might be emotion or might not be; but now it is laid down that it should be only emotion.We have stated that the appeal of art should be to the imagination; and imagination always implies the presence of emotion in some degree or other. But it is not this emotion that we should think of now. It is the emotional character of the situation depicted by the artist that constitutes the true content of art, and the type of experience to which it gives rise in the spectator is called Rasa. A consequence of this change in the idea of the content of art was to deny that the expressed meaning can have any excellences of its own and to assert that, like the form, it also has them only in relation to the emotion which it is intended to subserve. The excellences of meaning may be the very best, according to earlier standards; but yet they may produce the exact opposite of artistic feeling in the spectator, if they are out of harmony with the emotion depicted. This rightly introduces a relativistic view into art criticism; and neither form nor meaning was hence forward regarded as beautiful in itself. The standards by which they were judged remained more or less the same, but they ceased to be taken as absolute.

---

1 Cf. 'Poetic Truth'.

2 Poetry was brought nearer music thereby.

We may point out before concluding this topic that the earlier view of art as consisting in the excellences characterizing its form and meaning was not abandoned. That view also was retained; but works answering to that description came to be assigned an inferior status. It is designated 'Citra', a term which, in all probability, signifies that its merit lies more in skill which appeals to our intellect rather than in affecting our life or soul.

The method of art

Now emotions cannot be directly communicated.We can, of course, talk of, say, love or fear; but these words, when used by themselves,merely convey the idea of the corresponding feeling and do not communicate it to the listener. Such communication of it is possible only through a proper portrayal of select aspects of its causes and consequences. That is, the artist is obliged, if he is to succeed in what is his foremost aim, to adopt an indirect method in dealing with his material. This method is called Dhvani (suggestion); and secondarily, the work of art also, which is characterized by it, is designated by the same term. It had always been recognized as important for the artist, but only as one of those at his disposal for conveying the appropriate sentiment to the spectator.We may instance, as illustrating this point, Alaṃkāras like Paryāyokti[1] and Samāsokti[2], which are mentioned in the earliest Alaṃkāra works. The discovery that was made later was that it was the sole method of the best type of art. This, we may add, was the direct consequence of recognising Rasa to be the aim *par excellence* of the artist. The method of art is thus as unique as its aim.

The method of Dhvani has naturally been extended to other spheres of art where direct communication is possible, viz., Alaṃkāras; and has led to a preference being shown to them when they are indirectly suggested, instead of being directly expressed. Owing, however, to the intimate connection between imagination on which Alaṃkāras are chiefly based and emotion on which Rasa is, the difference between them is not always quite definite. The one may easily pass into another. Hence the decision in any particular case depends upon the view one takes of it; and it accordingly becomes personal, illustrating the well-known saying that tastes differ.

---

1 & 2 Figures of speech.

Another extension of this theory of Dhvani is to those poetic representations, which can be regarded neither as Rasa nor as Alaṃkāra and are therefore indefinitely designated as *Vastu.*[1] The innovation thus introduced by the Dhvani canon here, like that in the case of Alaṃkāras, we may observe, is more in rearranging conclusions that had already been reached than in making any new additions. The above statements enable us to divide the subject of first-rate art in a triple way. It may be emotion, when the resulting experience is called Rasa-dhvani; it may be any other imaginative situation, in which case it will be Alaṃkāra-dhvani; or it may be a matter-of-fact representation, in which case it will be Vastu-dhvani.

The discovery that the Dhvani method is the secret of true art furnishes another instance of what we described above as the alogical character of art. The conclusions suggested by this method vary according to the persons concerned and the contexts to which they belong, although the premises given are the same.At best, the mental process involved resembles analogical reasoning. Some of the erroneous views current before the method of Dhvani was formulated, or after, are due to mistaking the method of art to be logical. Thus Mahima Bhaṭṭa tried to make out that the process involved in the so-called Dhvani was nothing but inferential; and others like Mukula Bhaṭṭa represented the secondary senses of words as derived through the Pramāṇa[2] known as Arthāpatti[3]. Both forgot that the Dhvani lacks the element of necessity, which is essential to what is strictly a logical process.

Art and morality

We have referred to two views of reality in explaining the need for art. Whichever of them we may adopt, the implication is the presence of evil in life. According to one of these views, evil is finally removable; according to the other also it is so, only its removal

1 Any part of the idea or subject matter.

2 A mode of proof, evidence.

3 Presumption, one of the sources of knowledge or modes of proof accepted by some philosophers.

involves the removal of good as well along with it. Overlooking this distinction which is really irrelevant for art, we may ask what the bearing of art is on the problem of evil, which it thus implicitly postulates[1].

It may appear that art cannot be unconnected with morality, since the experience which it yields is, as we have pointed out, essentially disinterested; and disinterestedness is the very root of all morality. It is, therefore, necessary to examine what precisely the significance of this attitude is. To begin with, the ethical attitude is more than one of mere detachment. It is essentially active; but activity is, from the very nature of the case, wholly excluded from art experience. Or to state the same otherwise, the ethical attitude is oriented towards some purpose, while the artistic is quite the reverse, its sole purpose being the transcendence of all purpose. It is an attitude of contemplation rather than of achievement. Even as regards the unselfishness, which it shares with the ethical attitude, there is a vital distinction. There are two points to be noted in connection with it. In the first place, the aesthetic attitude is induced by an external stimulus. When once it has arisen, it may be quite genuine; but we cannot overlook the fact that it is due to an external influence. Morality which springs from fear of punishment or hope of reward is really no morality at all. The unselfishness characterizing the ethical attitude, on the other hand, springs from inside and is quite spontaneous. It is only when it is the result of an inner urge that it will be of an enduring influence on life. But this latter feature is lacking in the case of the art attitude, which we chiefly owe to the power that all true works of art possess. That such an exalted attitude can be produced, without any arduous trouble on the part of the spectator, is indeed an excellence of it; but it is unfortunately fugitive. Sooner or later, it comes to an end for it cannot last longer than the outside stimulus which has evoked it. Even such short-lived experience may, through refining emotions, leave some good influence behind; but the point to be noted is that there is no guarantee that it will.In the second place, the disinterestedness of the aesthetic attitude marks a reaction to an imaginary situation and not to a real one. It results from the contemplation not of actual but fictitious

---

1 It is the problem of evil that gives rise to art as well as to philosophy.

situations created by the artist. Fiction facilitates detachment. The consequence of this again is unfavourable to true morality, whose proper sphere is actual life. Thus even though perfect selflessness may be a prominent mark of art experience, its influence on the moral side of man may be very little. When that experience ceases he may lapse into the former state of tension and perplexity, which has its source in a selfish outlook on life.

According to some, this is no defect at all; for art, they maintain, has nothing to do with morality and is ethically neutral. But if that is so, it ceases to be a human value; and its recognition of evil as a fact of life becomes virtually meaningless[1]. There has been much controversy in this respect among art critics; but if we take a comprehensive view of man's nature and his aims, it seems that art cannot be altogether divorced from morality[2]. Art is, no doubt, for its own sake. But, in the result, it should be more by being a criticism of life's values. This explains, for instance, the double standard of our judging a character appearing in a work of art. To take the case of Iago, as an example, we not only speak of him as a perfect creation of Shakespeare but also condemn him as wicked in the extreme. The practice of the best artists is our support here. And the close alliance, again, of art with religion in all countries and in all times appears to be for saving art from possible degeneration by its separation from morality[3]. Art, correctly conceived, cannot be merely a selfish escape from life; it must also influence life permanently or, at least, tend to do so. But the view that art is not connected with morality is not altogether baseless. The truth underlying it is that art has nothing directly to do with morality. It should influence character indirectly; and what is discountenanced is only direct instruction in that regard, for it will militate against the

1 It would also then cease to appeal to the whole being of man which, as an ultimate value,it is expected to do.

2 It would then amount to a selfish escape from the tedium of life — a view as blameworthy as pure asceticism is in ethics. Both are at bottom egoistic, being preoccupied with oneself and not caring in the least for society.

3 The association of art with religion, in all probability, is primarily to make the latter attractive; but it has undoubtedly helped to prevent the former from deteriorating.

primary purpose of art which is to raise man above all strife and secure a form of unique joyful experience[1].

When even the primary aim of art is to be attained indirectly, it is natural to ask: What is this indirect connection between art and morality? It cannot be due to the method of art, for fables and parables teach morality indirectly but are not art. It must be through the characters which it introduces or, what comes to the same thing, through the general significance of the plot, that art can exercise moral influence on the spectators[2]. The implied outlook of these characters on life and the world should be moral. 'That is a true poem,' says an old Indian authority, 'which treats of the doings of the good and the great.' The best examples of this are to be found in the great epics of the *Rāmāyāṇa* and the *Mahābhārata* whose indirect influence on Indian men and women has all along been greater than that of any other single factor. In a work of art where no such characters are found, say, a lyric poem, it is the artist's outlook on what he portrays that counts. The conclusion to be drawn from this is that art should not have a moral aim, but must necessarily have a moral view, if it should fulfil its true purpose[3]. This is not to make art didactic, for morality does not form either its content or its purpose according to this view.

In addition to this general moral view, there may be some aspect of the moral ideal dominating the conduct of the hero or of other characters, and be thus intimately woven into the structure of the plot[4]. It will then become an organic part of the content of art. A

---

1 In this sense, the following statement of Bhaṭṭa Nāyaka is correct: Kāvye rasayitā sarvo na boddhā na niyoga-bhāk. (Quoted in *Dhvanyāloka-locana* p.12. N.S. Press edn. 1928.)

2 It is not what the characters say that counts; but what they are and what they do.

3 No artist will present characters like Iago as examples to be followed. But this negative attitude towards them is not enough. He should do his best to leave the impression on us that they are warnings.

4 This is the meaning of Indian critics saying that any of the Puruṣārthas (principal objects of human life) may be the content of art. When either Artha (money) or Kāma (sensual enjoyments) forms the content, a general moral view is

(continued...)

very good example of it is found in Bhavabhūti's drama *Uttara-rāmacarita*. Here, as in any other great work of art, there is a general moral view pervading the whole piece. It includes not a single character which leads to any lapse from the high level that is expected in a play of which Rāma is the hero. But over and above this, there is Rāma's sense of public duty (as interpreted by him, of course) and his determination that it should have priority over all private obligations, which forms the very pivot on which the whole of the story here dramatized turns[1]. Unlike the general moral view, this is in the foreground of the picture. But it must be added that it, in no way, encroaches upon the artistic function of the play which is to awaken in us the emotion of love — not as the source of all life's joy, but as leading to pathos which so often and so inexplicably comes in its wake. This emphasis on the importance of public duty may be the main lesson of the story. But the story is not the end in dramatic art; it is only a means to the communication to the spectators of the Rasa in question.

That is, the creations of art must leave a moral influence on the spectator without his knowing that he is being so influenced. Though theoretically, the theme of art may be anything which has a basis in life, this additional requirement makes it necessary to restrict the scope of the artist's choice to the higher aspects of life. Otherwise, art not only ceases to exert any moral influence; it may turn out in the end to be a means of corrupting character and degrading ideals.

4(...continued)
expected to prevail; when Dharma (religion) becomes the content, there is this additional emphasis on morality.

1 There is no hesitation whatever before the dictate of reason that a ruler must put public good before private inclination and there is a majestic sadness in the banishment of Sitā as a consequence.

3

Highways of Literary Criticism in Sanskrit*

S.Kuppuswami Sastri

Law and liberty

I am tempted to read out a well-known passage from one of the greatest of the modern poets, whose imaginative vision is all-comprehensive and thoroughly Indian — I mean Rabindranath Tagore. 'When we come to literature we find that though it conforms to rules of grammar, it is yet a thing of joy, it is freedom itself. The beauty of a poem is bound by strict laws, yet it transcends them. The laws are its wings, they do not keep it weighed down, they carry it to freedom. Its form is in law, but its spirit is in beauty. Law is a first step towards freedom and beauty is the complete liberation which stands and shines on the pedestal of law[1]. The passage referred to is prose-poetry and, in a telling and beautiful way, it points out the synthesis between literary law and literary freedom.

How is this synthesis between law and liberty achieved? It is achieved through a particular doctrine of literary criticism; the achievement of this synthesis has been rendered possible by the recognition and acceptance of the principle of Vyañjanā — suggestion, though true it is that the acceptance of this principle has led to a number of wooden classifications in Sanskrit literature. What is this Vyañjanā? In technical language, it may be described as an extraordinary significative power which all works of art possess. In its narrow sense, what do we understand by it? Yesterday I referred to the dictum laid down by Benedetto Croce, the replacement of the concept 'all art is expression' by the concept 'all expression is art'. We have now to remind ourselves of it. In one sense, even from the point of view of the ordinary speaker, even an ordinary sentence has some artistic element in it, and it is the result of the inherent artistic capacity that every intelligent being possesses. This idea is developed by a modern scientific writer, Jespersen, in a thrilling manner in a

---

* From *Highways and Byways of Literary Criticism in Sanskrit.*

1 *Sādhanā, Realisation in Love*, pp. 98-99, Macmillan & Co., Ltd.

recent work of his, *The Philosophy of Grammar.* In all speech, he says there are three distinct things — expression, suppression and impression. It is important to note that impression is often produced by suppression also and suggestion, he says, is impression through suppression. Boredom we have when there is only expression, but it is only a question of degree. You cannot come across any human being of average intelligence, being such a hopeless bore as to express everything. One cannot do it. One has always to suppress something and the greatness of great writers and great speakers is said to lie in the larger or greater degree of suppression. This idea could easily be illustrated by a commonplace example.We go to the railway station and standing at the counter say 'Please, a second class ticket to Annamalainagar.' Even here there is a large amount of suppression. This helps us to realize the full meaning of the definition given by Jespersen that suggestion is impression through suppression.

Vyañjānā is suggestion, that is, suggestion in poetry; and it often means more than that. Poetry comes from a principle of suggestion. Even in ordinary sentences the element of suppression cannot be avoided. This truth was long ago recognized in India by the Naiyāyikas, who in their anxiety to be absolutely precise by expressing everything have become real bores and everywhere they inflict their hopeless boredom. They are precise, they want to measure thought quantitatively and so use the various and varied formulas[1] such as *Avaccheda*[2], *Avacchinna*[3], etc., and in every sentence of theirs these formulas are used to the best of their ability, so that they might express everything they want, and leave no scope for carrying any impression through suppression. Even they, however, cannot escape from the inevitable nature of language. In spite of their formulas, there is yet a residual element in a sentence which refuses to be expressed — the residual element of artistic sense inherently available in every being. Now let us illustrate this position. Taking an ordinary sentence, let us enquire whether it expresses anything which is not expressed by its constituent

---

1 These formed the subject of a course of lectures of Prof. S. Kuppuswami Sāstri — *Thought-meaning Devices in Indian Dialectics* — delivered under the auspices of the Madras University in 1929.

2 Delimitation

3 Delimited.

elements. That is to say, does the sentence express anything over and above the meaning of the words which compose the sentence? The answer is inevitably 'yes'. The relation between the various words is unexpressed and the question naturally arises, how is this idea conveyed? Saṃsarga[1] they say is Vākyārtha[2]. How is this Samsarga conveyed? It is mysterious and has not yet been satisfactorily explained. In sentences we have a juxtaposition of words and the element of the relation between the words is conveyed, we have to say, by suppression; in other words, the essential part of every judgement is conveyed by suppression. Now the question is, how is this conveyed? The philosophers are not artists and naturally they have strongly differed from the Ālaṃkārikas and vehemently criticized their principles. They accept Saṃsarga but they say that Saṃsarga is not something suggested and would hide their answer by a technical expression 'saṃsargamaryādayā avabhāsate'; and this element they later describe as the element of suppression in conveying judgement. The life of speech consists in this suppressed element and the greater the life that art has, the greater is the suppressed element in it. Ālaṃkārikas have developed the scheme of suppression. From all this we come to understand that Vyañjanā is not the peculiar discovery of critics, and that it is a principle accepted and recognized by every student of philosophy, of logic and of language. It is a principle raised to the rank of a special principle, an important doctrine in the realm of literary appreciation. Poetic art is a superior kind of art and in this art, this principle is employed to a very large extent and the acceptance of this principle renders possible the synthesis between law and liberty. In the first place, it is easily seen that this establishes a sort of connection between expression and impression, between the speaker and the hearer. On the other side, this principle can be developed in the light of a second equation. On the one side there is the artist's mind, the aesthetic sense of artistic expression, and on the other there is the art itself. There is also a third equation, the reader or the Sahṛdaya. And the synthesis may be connected with these three important factors. On

1 Relation — association.

2 Meaning of the sentence.

the part of the artist, there is much scope for anticipatory imagination, and on the part of the Sahṛdaya there is scope for anticipatory realization. Now what is the connecting link or relation between the two? It is the poetic expression and this may be described as a bridge which caries the art from the Kavi to the Sahṛdaya, and this bridge is composed of the element of suggestion.

Law in the sphere of poetic art reduces itself to the numerous literary rules. In the same sphere, liberty is to be understood as the principle which determines the free play of the artist's genius. What harmonizes the attitude of the poet and the attitude of the critic is Vyañjanā or suggestion; in the absence of this suggestion either art will groan under the weight of the doctrines of literary appreciation or it will run riot. In this way, the principle of suggestion may be understood to establish a synthesis between law and liberty.

In this connection we may also profitably consider another matter. This principle has also made it possible to achieve a beautiful synthesis between the two important factors of life, speech and thought, sound and sense. In the ancient poetic literature and in the works of old Ālaṃkārikas (writers on Poetics), one could easily see the great importance attributed to this synthesis, between Śabda[1] and Artha[2]. The ancient Indian culture looks upon Śabda and Artha as an inseparable pair representing the father and mother of the world. The simple Mangala-śloka with which Kālidāsa opens his immortal epic, *Raghuvaṃśa,* is very significant in this direction, very forcible and telling. It is not to be misunderstood, as the verse of a Vaidika introduced without a purpose. It suppresses, conceals behind it a very great truth for artists and critics. Here the greatest literary artist of India pays homage to the symbol of Śabda and Artha in the world and seeks to obtain the adequate appreciation of that ample and full synthesis between sound and sense, an appreciation which every genuine artist must possess. The phrase 'Vāgartha-pratipattaye'[2] does not merely connote the acquisition of the words and their meanings — this is a very small thing which could easily be acquired

---

1 Word. 2 Meaning.

2 Literally, acquisition of or the mastery over word and meaning.

through Kośas[1], as in olden days and through dictionaries, as in modern days. Here the poet is seeking to equip himself with that important synthesis of sound and sense which every literary artist must have. Without this synthesis, a genuine artist cannot produce a genuine work of art.

Genuine poetry is always looked upon as spontaneous emanation from a Rasa-filled heart. A beautiful thought clothes itself in a beautiful garb without any conscious effort on the part of the poet. This is the highest test of true poetry. Another writer, Bhavabhūti[2], remarks:

'In the case of the wise men of this world, word runs after sense; but in the case of primeval sages, sense rushes after their word.' It is an oft-quoted, probably a hackneyed verse, but it embodies a great truth. Consider this verse in the light of the point of view we have been emphasizing. The underlaying idea is the complete harmony between sound and sense. Sense is always aggressive; and in the hands of an ordinary man, it shapes its language. But in the case of gifted people, gifted artists, sense follows sound. The term 'Ṛṣi' is to be understood in the sense of a gifted artist. Another gifted literary critic who is said to have been a teacher of Abhinavagupta, I mean Bhaṭṭa Tauta, remarks that Kavi and Ṛṣi are synonyms 'Nānṛṣiḥ Kavirityuktam'[3]. Prophets and poets are made of the same stuff and their vision is identical. Shelley remarks that painters and poets would not fail to apprehend this vision. How is this effected in poetic expression? It is, as I have already stated, by the principle of Vyañjanā. The secret is suggestion. Sound and sense cannot be harmonized except through suppression. Mechanically speaking, that is purely from the linguistic point of view, it would mean that the two could not be harmonized. The relation between Śabda and Artha has been and is a riddle and the difference becomes accentuated when this great principle is forgotten. Articulation is the result of certain adjustments of the speech mechanism, and sense is quite different from this. Thus, organically, the two cannot be harmonized. It is the artistic instinct of suppression that

1 Lexicons.

2 *Uttararāmacarita*, I.10.

3 One who is not a seer cannot be a poet.

serves as the connecting link, bridges over the gulf between the two entirely distinct things, Sabda and Artha. Thus in this field also, we find that this principle is very important.

This now leads us to a consideration of certain other principles representing certain other highways of literary criticism. We are aware of the fact that literary art or an expression of literary art involves two important aspects — form and content. Every artist has to pay special attention to literary form and literary content. Now what is literary form, and what is literary content? This again leads us to the old synthesis of Śabda and Artha. What is literary form? Indian critics have analyzed literary form and they have laid down that this consists of Śabda and Artha, or Śabda and certain types of Artha. Ordinary words grouped in an artistic way with some ideas, that is, Vācyārtha—primary sense—constitute form. This alone, of course, will not do. It must be bright, free from defects, etc., The other elements associated with form are technically referred to as Guṇas, Alaṃkaras, Ritis, etc. The term Alaṃkāra stands for decorative devices. Guṇa is a term untranslatable. It is not merely quality or merit, but something more; a new Rūḍhi (usage) must be established before these words could be accepted. Riti cannot again be identified with style merely. This is a very vague term. Does it refer to ways of grouping words or thought? It is not very clear. In a general way Riti may be equated with style, for both are vague. I have devised a pedantic phrase which is probably the nearest approximation to the ideas expressed by the term Guṇa, ways of collocation; collocation of ideas or sense and of words approaches Guṇa. It must remembered that it is not merely collocation of words and ideas referred to here but the artistic collocation of artistic Śabda, Artha, absence of defects, presence of brightness, Riti, Guṇa and Alaṃkāra; these constitute literary form.

Now what about content? The sense which is beautiful, the sense that is charming constitutes content. A careful examination of our great works of art and our views and modes of appreciation would reveal this important fact — on one side the various aspects of form synthesize, and on the other the various aspects of content synthesize. And this has been rendered possible by the doctrine of Dhvani which sums up the synthesis of all conceivable modes of literary appreciation.

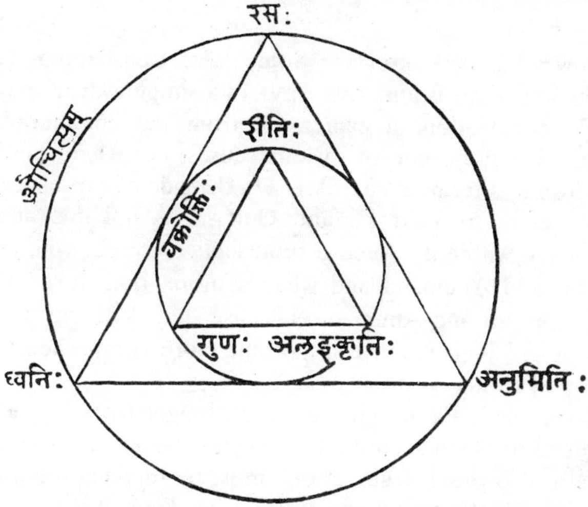

The above graph will form a key to the whole position. Dhvani, Rasa and Unnaya[1], these three stand for three important schools of thought in Sanskrit literary criticism. Dhvani is Vyañjanā, Rasa is a highway of criticism not only for Indian literature but also for the study of European literature, a sure and certain method. Emphasizing Rasa, one school accepts Dhvani or suggestion, while another school accepts Rasa, emphasizing Unnaya. Dhvani, the latter say, is a sort of inference, a quick anticipatory way of inference. These three run after Aucitya. Guṇas, Alaṃkāras and Ritis, these are emphasized in special ways. Are Ritis and Guṇas different? They are recognized as different in Alaṃkāra śāstra. Anṛju vāk means Vakrokti. This also runs after Aucitya.

The graph also represents their historical inter-relation. The bigger circle which encloses the bigger triangle stands for Aucitya which may be termed as 'adaptation' to be understood in its philosophical sense. Adaptation is understood in this sense as standing for the perfect harmony which parts bear to each other and to the whole. Dhvani, Rasa and Unnaya or Anumāna[2] obviously refer to the literary content,i.e.,artistic thought, whereas Guṇas, Alaṃkāras and Ritis refer to the literary form.

---

1 Inference.

2 Inference.

Now what is Vakrokti? Some have translated it as eccentric expression. This is a monstrosity. In a simple way, it may be understood as deviation in expression from the commonplace. This deviation may be due to various causes, but when the deviation is effective, it is termed Vakrokti. On the side of expression, the inner circle refers to Vakrokti and Guṇas. Alaṃkāras and Ritis are comprised within it. Aucitya represents the great synthesis of Rasa, Dhvani and Anumana and what is more, both form and content. Rasa, Dhvani and Anumana, because they deal with the sphere of content are bigger, more important more comprehensive than the sphere of form.

If speech fulfils its purpose, there ought to be some amount of suppression. Hence naturally thought is wider than speech. Philosophically also this is true. If one must be thinking, he must think in language. If this be so, and so far as we know it is so, can it be said that thought and speech are co-extensive? We have seen what the answer should be. And Indian metaphysicists hold that thought is always wider, more comprehensive than speech. If this is so in ordinary parlance, it is expressly and definitely so in the field of literary art. As a fiction, they are taken as co-extensive in one field, that is the field of law, both ancient and modern. The Mimāṃsakas assume that thought and form are co-extensive. But it remains only an assumption; in actual practice this view is always given up. The assumption is that Vidhi is straight-forward — 'Na Vidhau paraḥśabdārthaḥ': this is an attitude that is totally inimical to literary criticism. In this field, we accept that thought is always wider than form[1]; if not, the world would have been deprived of the pleasure of art; in the field of art, they are never co-extensive. This great synthesis of form and content is the greatest of our achievements in the realm of art and that we have been able to achieve through the doctrine of Vyañjana.

The graph also helps us to understand the various highways of literary criticism. Rasa-paddhati is the oldest and the most permanent; the most imperial highway of literary appreciation, the way of the great critic-artists, Vālmiki, Kālidāsa, the way of the great art-critics, Bharata, Ānandavardhana and Abhinavagupta. Historically

1 This is signified in the graph by the triangle of Rasa-dhvani-unnaya representing content, enclosing within itself Vakrokti, Rīti, Guṇa and Alaṃkāra, representing form.

also this is true. For if Vālmiki is the father of poetry and criticism, Rasa-paddhati becomes the most ancient highway of literary appreciation. Dhvani and Anumāna are placed side by side at the base of the triangle, because one cannot call one older than the other. The leading exponent of the Dhvani theory presupposes the Anumana theory and criticises it. It appears therefore possible that these two highways must have existed coevally. Mahima Bhaṭṭa is not the discoverer of Anumāna-paddhati. In the inner triangle the same historical sequence is observed. Bhāmaha, the oldest Ālaṃkārika available, emphasises, Alaṃkāra while Daṇḍin and Vāmana emphasize respectively Guṇa and Riti. These two authors are not far separated in time and, therefore, they are placed at the foot of the triangle. Further, Bhamaha throws out valuable hints regarding Vakrokti, even though it was reserved for Kuntaka to develop it systematically. According to Bhamaha, literary form and thought consist of Vakrokti:

> Saiṣā sarvaiva vakroktiranayārtho vibhāvyate[1].

Thus it will be found that the Vakrokti-synthesis which is less important only than the Aucitya-synthesis is older than the three other literary forms, Guṇa, Alaṃkāra and Riti.

II The central principle of literary criticism in Sanskrit

In fact, Vyañjanā may be regarded as the central principle of literary criticism in Sanskrit the pivotal doctrine round which the whole scheme of art-criticism in Sanskrit revolves. Now what is the secret of this principle? In a prosaic way, as I told you, it may be rendered by the term 'suggestion' and as to what suggestion is, I would like to remind you of the definition given by Jespersen: 'Suggestion is impression through suppression.' It is the suppressive element that is important in suggestion. We should also remind ourselves in this connection of the general principles laid down by Croce that all expression is art; not only poetical expression but all expression is art. One cannot, however low may be one's civilization or culture, provided one is equipped with some medium of expression, get away from being an artist in framing sentences. Now the principle of Vyañjanā is suggestion in poetry. Is it merely the suggestion that we

---

Kāvyālaṃkāra, II.85.

see in ordinary sentences? It is not merely that. It represents the centre of charm in poetry, the soul of charm in poetry and so it is not merely the suggestion we find in ordinary sentences. Then what is the secret of the force of Vyañjanā as an artistic principle? I refer to the suppressed element in the case of suggestion. Why should there be a suppressed element at all even in ordinary sentences? We wish to create a minimum degree of interest possibly in the minds of hearers. Without interesting the hearers to some extent at least, we cannot create anything like a desirable impression on the minds of the readers. Even to attract attention, a minimum degree of interest we should provide, and the element of suppression is necessary. Now this element of suppression may be enhanced in its value, this element of suppression may be intensified, may be improved upon in various ways; in poetic expression, it is this element of suppression and the principle of suggestion that rests upon it that prove all important. In fact it was discovered in the 9th and 10th centuries A.D. by Ānandavardhana and Abhinavagupta that this is the centre, the source of poetic charm. Well, what is the secret of this attraction? What is the secret of this force? Some people would say that there is an element of novelty in Vyañjanā or suggestion. The suggested idea is envisaged with a certain degree of novelty. What is suppressed and let out, and what is suppressed and suggested may appear novel, may appear new or may be envisaged with a certain outlook of freshness for the time being. Is it this element that is the real source of attraction? It is suggested by a Sanskrit writer that there is scope for some sort of intellectual quest in the process of Vyañjanā, quest provided it leads to conquest; and intellectual quest in Vyañjanā certainly leads to some conquest. Now these two things, quest and conquest are enough to create some interest. Well, is it because of the scope for quest and conquest that we have in Vyañjanā that it proves to be attractive? There is some truth in this explanation but it is not the whole truth. The same idea is expressed in some works on Sanskrit poetics in another way. Something is concealed for the time being; and concealing for a moment and withholding from your view might tend to enhance the degree of charm; like distance, concealing and withholding might lead to enhance its charm:' Gūḍham sat camatkaroti'[1]. Like the charms of

---

1 Concealment lends charm.

an attractive beauty which do not obtrude upon notice in an immodest way, but which are presented through a veil and in a properly concealed fashion, like the physical charms of a modest beauty then, the suggested element when it is presented, when it is disclosed after some degree of concealment, proves to be attractive. This is also true to some extent. But it is only a poetic way of presenting the other explanation. There is scope for quest and conquest here. But the fact is, as far as I have been able to gather, that Vyañjanā makes it possible for art, for every suggestive art, to re-live its life in itself through a purely artistic process and to find its fulfilment and consummation in a definitely artistic purpose. That is the secret of the force of the whole charm of Vyañjanā.

This requires amplification, and an amplification of this statement may involve a review of the whole literature on Sanskrit Poetics from the point of view of Vyañjanā. We may take a long and comprehensive view of the whole literature from this standpoint. Let us take this statement in parts and proceed to consider it. Vyañjanā is a wholly suggested, a wholly artistic, process. Can we not say that it is an intellectual process? Yes, in the language of the logic-ridden phraseology of the Ālaṃkārikas. Or can we not say in the technical sense of the logicians that it has a power attracted towards it? All these technicalities could be introduced in the course of a discussion of the nature of Vyañjanā and of a discussion of its place in art criticism. We have to remember in this connection one important fact. Such a view would enable you to see how to study in detail the learned criticisms in the Alaṃkāra śāstra and also how to study in detail all the discussions of relevant topics of this principle, namely Vyañjanā in art criticism. Many of you may be familiar with the learned arguments that are adduced to show that Vyañjanā or suggestion is not the ordinary *prima facie* significatory power which words possess. It is not the primary power by virtue of which words or expressions or phrases or sentences convey their *prima facie* meaning. Well, in a majority of instances, we are using so many words in a secondary sense. And can we not bring Vyañjanā or suggestion under the category of some secondary significatory power? Secondary significatory power is a sort of fiction which we have introduced in the philosophy of interpretation for purposes of convenience, the result of the superimposition of a certain subjective aspect made intentionally and consciously by the subject upon the expression that is used. You find a certain statement made and some phrases are loosely used, some expressions do not admit of strict interpretation, and consistently with the context, consistently with what you know about the intention of the speaker and consistently also with the general aim that is kept in view, you interpret and you seek to interpret correctly and to interpret him generously and favourably. Hearers are always supposed to be generous, except probably those who are to consider or interpret law. Other hearers are always supposed to be generous. A certain amount of generosity in interpretation is necessary in all inter-communication of thought. Life will not be worth living, if every hearer should insist upon exact precision and exact accuracy in every statement that you make in ordinary conversation. In writing even, it is possible only with due limitations. Now under such circumstances in order to find out the intention of the speaker, we take some of the phrases loosely used by him in a certain sense which those phrases do not primarily possess. Some hackneyed examples are cited in this connection. Take for instance a hamlet on the Ganges — we interpret it as a hut on the banks of the Ganges. Well, in such cases consistently with the context you reinterpret such phrases in a different way and the interpretation which you put upon them is attributed to some secondary significatory power which the phrase is supposed to possess. Well, can Vyañjanā or suggestion be brought under that? No; the reason is this: you deliberately resort to a certain process of interpretation, because you feel some difficulty in understanding the phrase in its literal sense. The phrase used cannot be construed strictly and your conscious experience of some hitch or difficulty is at the root of the secondary interpretation that is adopted. That is what I mean when I say that it is a sort of fiction which you create for purposes for interpretation. That is not suggestion. Behind that, however, there is another element. Well, fancy for a moment that the speaker who uses such a phrase uses it in that way with a purpose and in a deliberate manner, not as a result of some lapse. As it is, he deliberately uses the phrase then in a secondary sense. You are not justified in assuming that the speaker is a fool or thinking loose, that he has not got sufficient control over language to make himself intelligible in a direct and straightforward manner. You assume that he is a master of language. Under these circumstances there must be some object, some purpose the speaker must have in view in adopting this secondary mode of expression. He must have something in view, some purpose or Prayojana in view. What is it he wishes to suggest? He wishes to go a step further on the path of suppression. He wishes to conceal from the point of view for a little while a certain idea and at the same time he wishes that the idea should be understood in an agreeable way. As it is, the speaker wishes to suggest that the hut is pure, it is holy because it is situated on the bank of the river Ganga and it is very close to it. As it is, he wishes to emphasize the idea of the proximity to the river and so many other things that may be associated with its close proximity. That element is left to be gathered from the context and that element is left to be suggested; that element is not conveyed for the moment by the expression itself. This is Vyañjanā. This gives rise to a furious controversy in the philosophy of Alaṃkāra śāstra between the Ālaṃkārikas and the logicians. Well, why should not this element be brought under inference? It may be the case of an agreeable type of inference. Call it inference or call it suggestion, you cannot say that it is a regular type of syllogistic inference, you may treat it as a sort of immediate inference. A degree of mediacy is an essential feature of inferential process. Mediacy is the characteristic feature of inference and here in suggestion one feels that the degree of mediacy that is necessarily characteristic of inference is wanting, and we feel that there is a certain degree of immediacy which does not entitle us to bring it under inference. As a result, this process is taken to be a process associated with artistic expression itself but not with an ordinary process; it is taken to be an extreme process and it is described by Ālaṃkārikas as Lokottara[1]. In the course of the technical discussion of the nature of this Vṛtti[2], one is apt to forget the essential characteristic of the process called Vyañjanā. One is likely to be carried away by the glorifying description of the character of Vyañjanā. It is an extraordinary process. Abhinavagupta exalts this process as something extraordinary[3]. Why is it Lokottara? The simple idea behind the phrase Lokottara is this — it is essentially an

1 Extraordinary.

2 Significatory capacity of a word.

3 See *Locana,* Kuppuswami Sastri Research Institute edn. pp. 105-132.

artistic process; it is not a Laukika[1] process, it is not a process of the ordinary life, it is not the inartistic process with which we are familiar in this work-a-day world in our everyday task — it is an essentially artistic process. That is why it is described by the Ālaṃkārikas as a Lokottara-vṛtti and it is an artistic process for various reasons.

To appreciate adequately why Vyañjanā should be regarded as an essentially artistic people, you have to look at it from various points of view, and I propose to help you in looking at it from certain points of view. It is an essentially artistic process as it involves suppression, not of the everyday type but of the agreeable type. It is an essentially artistic process because it gives us an impression, not the ordinary commonplace impression which sentences give, not the impression of the craftsmanlike or mechanical type but a delicate impression described as artistic thrill. It is an essentially artistic process because it enables you to feel that you have done with certain matters with which students of Alaṃkāra śāstra are already familiar. It enables you to feel that you have done with the compartmental slicing of Sanskrit literature into literary genera such as epic, lyric, the metrical the non-metrical and so on. It enables you thus to feel that you have done with this sort of compartmental slicing up of literature and it enables you to take the right view of poetic art and view it as an organic and complete expression and put the right question which you should put to yourself in matters connected with literary production. Well, what is the right question which you should put to yourself? The question to be put is not what is the type under which it should be brought, not whether it conforms to certain time-honoured traditional classifications recognized by the classical schools of critics, not whether it conforms to rules deduced from such classification, not whether it conforms to the dead weight of the technique — that is not the right question to put, but the right question to put is what this artistic specimen expresses and how far it expresses it well and artistically? That is the right type of question to put. This point of view was emphasized adequately for the first time by certain Kashmirian critics under the leadership of Ānandavardhana, a great exponent of the Dhvani school. Prior to Ānandavardhana critics were carried away by the excesses of classification in Sanskrit literary criticism. Anandavardhana flourished in the latter part of the 9th

---

1 Worldly — such as we see in the world

century. If anybody before Anandavardhana investigated and envisaged the fruitfulness of this principle, namely the principle of suggestion, and vividly realized the importance of this principle being raised to the rank of the central principle of literary criticism, it was Vālmiki himself, the father of Sanskrit poetry, and Kālidāsa who followed Vālmiki in so many respects. Among the professional writers on literary criticism in Sanskrit, there is sufficient evidence to show that none clearly realized the importance of this principle before Ānandavardhana. This artists realized; the art critics were unconsciously biased in favour of this principle and they unconsciously recognized the importance of this principle but they never intentionally did anything to popularize this principle, to elucidate it and to explain and illustrate it: and we owe this great contribution to the genius of Ānandavardhana, that great artist and art critic.

It was he who inaugurated a certain way of classifying specimens of poetic art on the basis of this principle; in fact, it was he that was responsible for the re-classification of poetic expression under three heads. The three heads in Alaṃkāra literature are not very suggestive except to those who are familiar with the implications behind the names. The names are Uttama[1], Madhyama[2] and Adhama[3]. That specimen of poetry should be regarded as the best specimen, uttama, which allows the suggested element to reign supreme; it never lets itself to be subordinated to anything else — that should be regarded as the Kāvya of the best type. What about Madhyama kāvya? That specimen in which the suggested element is not raised to the supreme rank, is not allowed to reign supreme, and is either co-ordinated with some other element or subordinated to it but is at the same time allowed to preserve its minimum degree of agreeableness and beauty and attractiveness — that is regarded as the Madhyama. And then there are certain specimens of art which may be described as the result of amusing diversion in which poetic geniuses indulge either at the stage of practice or even after reaching the stage of perfection as a sort of amusement. They are readily described as lifeless *citras*[2] in poetry and such specimens give prominence only to certain

1 Best, first rate. 2 Second rate. 3 Inferior.

2 The inferior form of poetic composition based on figures and word-jugglery.

attractive features of literary form, and under such attractive features the beautiful suggested element is allowed to lie buried. Well, that is regarded as Adhama.

Ānandavardhana himself suggests that this re-classification is only a tentative device which he has suggested as a challenge to the traditional classification of literature into various genera, to the traditional method of compartmental slicings and cuttings. He indicates how the unity of poetry could be preserved by fixing your attention upon the central principle of Vyañjanā. You make it the leading principle of art criticism, adopt it as the source of literary charm and you can use it as a magic wand.

Some commentators and some traditional writers who came after Ānandavardhana were labouring under the misapprehension that he intended that this scheme should be adopted as an inflexible or rigid scheme of classification. Sometimes great masters provide the world with certain devices, and these devices are misused. Great artists provide the world with certain devices and with certain materials and their followers come to attach greater importance to the material than to the purpose itself. In that way, later writers, in the spirit of cavilling critics, proceeded to find fault with Ānandavardhana for giving an elastic or unnecessarily flexible scheme of classification which involves a lot of overlapping. It is not for purposes of a strict classification that Ānandavardhana provided the world of readers with this scheme. He never intended it to be a logical scheme. His scheme of classification is not intended to satisfy the demands of strict logic. It is more a challenge to the traditional process of slicing and cutting, and he himself makes it clear towards the end of his work. He indicates how this scheme could be re-arranged and could be re-exhibited in a slightly different fashion.

Take for instance what is known as the excellent specimen and compare it with what, in a technical sense, may be brought under Madhyama kāvya or a specimen of the middling type. Compare these two, you will find that you are likely to feel that Ānandavardhana has done a grave injustice to these two types. In this connection I should like to draw your attention to two specimens.

Suvarṇapuṣpām pṛthivim cinvanti puruṣāstrayaḥ
Śūraśca kṛtavidyaśca yaśca jānāti sevitum

This was brought under the first class. The suggestion is allowed to reign supreme here. Three classes of people are able to gather gold, as one would be able to gather flowers, wherever they go. They are in prosperity everywhere, that is the suggested idea. Who are these three classes of people? (1) The brave person, (2) the scholar, and (3) one who knows how to serve one's master. These three classes of people, wherever they go, thrive well. Now the simple idea that is suggested is that they meet with prosperity everywhere. That is not expressed in a straightforward way. That is certainly a suggested idea. That is allowed to reign supreme and for that reason it is Uttama kavya and so comes under the first rank. Now place it on one side and compare it for instance with another beautiful specimen which is likely to be brought under the technical Madhyama type.

Anurāgavati sandhyā divasastatpurassaraḥ
Aho daivagatiḥ kidṛk tathāpi na samāgamaḥ

The evening twilight is endowed with Rāga, is endowed with red colour. Her lover, the day, goes before her and quite close to her and love is reciprocated. What a fatality it is that they never come together! They are so anxious to marry each other, they are so anxious to be completely united with each other, but their desire is never allowed to fulfil itself and is never realized. The obvious meaning here is the relation between the *Sandhyā* and *Divasa* and behind it there is a suggested idea. The suggested idea is the relation of two lovers who reciprocate each other's love but who are never allowed to be united with each other. Such relation is described by the prince of Indian poets, by Kālidāsa, as reaching the supreme moment of the most spiritual aspect of love[1]. It is that aspect of coming together and separation, of complete reciprocation without fulfilment or consummation, it is this that represents the supreme spiritual moment of love. And students of Rasa know that Śṛngāra or love is essentially spiritual as conceived by Indians and in Indian culture.

The Indian conception of love is never to possess and is always to efface oneself and to forget oneself. That is why it is raised to the rank of a vehicle which can freely reach to God. Now in this aspect

---

1 *Mālavikāgnimitra*, III.15, Anāturotkaṇṭhitayoḥ, etc.

of love one could find something very attractive. Those who are sufficiently responsive to Rasa cannot miss the central idea in the suggested part of this verse. But still what is the position of that suggested idea? It is assigned a somewhat subordinate rank. It appeals certainly far better and with greater force than the idea on the surface. That is true. But what is the rank that is assigned to it? The intention of the poet is to describe *Sandhyā* and *Divasa*; from the context you have to assume that. In describing Sandhyā and Divasa, he has produced a work of art. A work of art the moment it leaves the artist's hands, is the property of art critics. We are not at all bound to interpret art in the same manner in which the artist himself intended it to be interpreted. That is the way of every good work of art, but still when we pay some attention to the context and so long as we are alive to the details of the circumstances under which this particular specimen of art was produced, we are hopelessly in the grip of historical criticism; and so long as we are within the grip of historical criticism, we have to realize that the position that is assigned to the suggested element is a subordinate position. Though we know from the circumstances of the case that the artist intends to present the idea beautifully, he seeks to present it by linking it up with some situation.

4

The Theory of Rasa*

S.N. Dasgupta

We must start the theory of Rasa or aesthetic emotion with Bharata's maxim, Vibhāvānubhāva-vyabhicāri-saṃyogād rasa-niṣpattiḥ: i.e. the Rasa is accomplished as a result of the conjunction of Vibhāva Anubhāva and Vyabhicāribhāva.

Before proceeding further it is necessary to explain a few of the technical terms that are continually associated with any discussion of Rasa:— (1) Vibhāva is the objective condition producing an emotion. Vibhāva may be of two kinds: (i) Ālambana and (ii) Uddipana. Ālambana-vibhāva means a person or persons with reference to whom the emotion is manifested. Uddipana-vibhāva means the circumstances that have excited the emotion. A man may feel attracted to a woman if the circumstances are cooperating with it. It is easier for a man to be attracted towards a woman of young age if they are thrown alone and there is a beautiful scenery before them, the moon peeping through the clouds, the fragrant breeze blowing, and the like. Any one of such circumstances may be regarded as Uddipana-vibhāva, whereas both the man and the woman are Ālambana-vibhāvas to each other. (2) Anubhāva means bodily expression by which the emotion is expressed. Thus the arch glances of a lady, her inviting smile, may be regarded as Anubhāva. (3) Vyābhicāri means a series of diverse emotions that feed the dominant emotion. A woman in love anxiously waiting at the rendezvous to meet her lover may feel disappointed that he is not coming, may be anxious that something might have happened to him, may be jealous that he might have been courted by another woman, may feel delight in remembering the coaxing words that he had whispered into her ears, and so on. Like pictures in a cinematograph, emotions of diverse sorts may be passing in quick succession, and may all at the same time be continuing the constitution of the same emotion.

---

*From *A History of Sanskrit Literature, Classical Period, Vol. I., University of Calcutta*, 1947, *pp*. 592-604.

The real discussion of Rasa was started by Abhinavagupta in his commentary on Bharata's maxim on Rasa. The real point of discussion and diversity of opinion was on the two words Samyoga (conjunction) and Rasa-niṣpatti (manifestation of Rasa or completion of Rasa). Before proceeding further it is necessary to say a few words about the foundation of Rasa. It is based upon a particular view of psychology which holds that our personality is constituted, both towards its motivation and intellection, of a few primary emotions which lie deep in the subconscious or unconscious strata of our being. These primary emotions are the amorous, the ludicrous, the pathetic, the heroic, the passionate, the fearful, the nauseating, the wondrous. Other aesthetic psychologists have in later times added to it the peaceful or intellectual, the devotional and the filial. These emotions are running through all natures in a permanent manner and may in that sense be called dominant emotions (Sthāyibhāva). These dominant states that determine the particular internal temperaments are regarded as the dominant characteristics of those emotional states. Emotional states, such as the amorous, the heroic and the others, show in their expressions the appearance of atomic formations, i.e., each emotion in its manifestation shows a composition of diverse sentiments constantly shooting out and changing like the kinetic atoms and gases, like the flamelets that continually come and go and thereby produce the appearance of the permanent, undivided whole of a flame; there are continually passing little flames of diverse sentiments that give expression to the permanent emotion of love or hate, heroism or anger. It should, however, be noted that no emotion is called Rasa unless it is aesthetically excited. When a young man falls in love with a young woman and his whole frame is shaken, we cannot speak of him as being the subject of Śṛngāra-rasa, or when his son is dead and he is crying in tears, we cannot speak of him that he is in the Karuṇa-rasa. Rasa is an emotion excited by artistic circumstances or situations.

Now, the question that puzzled the old Alaṃkāra writers was this: How can our dominant emotions be roused by aesthetic or artistic means? Some writers like Bhaṭṭa Lollaṭa held that while the Vibhāva, Anubhāva and Vyabhicāri are either ingeniously described or set forth vividly by mime, they cooperate together and in their conjunction Rasa is produced.

Mammaṭa, as a follower of Abhinavagupta, repudiates Bhaṭṭa Lollaṭa's view that Rasa is related to the Vibhāvas in the relation of the produced and the producer, as effect and cause. He says that if the vibhāvas are to be regarded as cause they must be regarded as the cause of agency or the efficient cause, —Nimitta-kāraṇa. But in the case of Nimitta-kāraṇa, we know that an action may remain intact even when the efficient agent is destroyed. There cannot be any Rasa unless there is also the Vibhāva and the Anubhāva. The Vibhāvas, etc., cannot also be regarded as a communicative agent, for a communicative agent presupposes the existence of the thing to be communicated, but the Rasa does not exist before. It can be lived through only when it is suggested by the vibhāvas and the Rasa has no other existence than being lived through and enjoyed. For, it should be remembered that the dominant emotions existing in the subconscious strata of the person are not themselves Rasas. They acquire that designation only when they are aesthetically presentable and enjoyable. Bhaṭṭa Lollaṭa cannot also explain the method as to how the Rasa produced in the player can infect the audience.

Śaṃkuka introduced the similitude of painting to explain the enlightenment of aesthetic emotion. He said that just as of a painted horse it can be said that it is not a horse and that it is a horse, so of an aesthetic experience we can say that it is both real and unreal. Bhaṭṭa Nāyaka said that Rasa is neither produced nor suggested nor created by anything. He held that a proper aesthetic creation has the peculiar function of generating in us a new spiritual creation and we have in us a special function by which we can enjoy it. These two functions are called by him Bhāvakatva and Bhojakatva. The enlightenment of Rasa is not the subject of ordinary psychology but of aesthetic psychology. For the presentation of the spiritual situation throbbing with exhilaration we are bound to admit two different functions, Bhāvakatva and Bhojakatva, without which the aesthetic experience cannot be explained.

Abhinavagupta combated the view with all the force that he can command. Abhinavagupta is unwilling to admit these two extraordinary functions. He holds that in the case of a truly poetic composition, after having grasped the full significance of the words and their meanings, there is a mental intuition as a result of which the actual temporal and spatial character of the situation is withdrawn from the mental field and the emotion suggested therein loses its individual character and also becomes dissociated from such conditions as might have led us to any motivation. The emotion is apprehended and intuited in a purely universal character and in consequence thereof the ordinary pathological symptoms of emotion lose their significance and through all the different emotions bereft of their pathological characters we have one enjoyment of joy. It is for this reason that in the experience of a tragedy we find as much enjoyment as in that of a comedy, for the experience of a grief would have been unpalatable if it was associated with its pathological consequences. These pathological consequences are always due to a sense of self-struggle, self-motivation, loss, and the like. But in the intuition of the Rasa we live through the experience of a pure sentiment bereft of all its local characters.

In the subconscious and unconscious regions there are always lying dormant various types of emotio-motive complexes. When through artistic creation a purely universal emotional fear, amour, etc., are projected in the mind they become affiliated to those types of emotio-motive complexes and this mutual affiliation or apperception or implicit recognition of identity immediately transforms the presented artistic universal into artistic joy or Rasa. It is for this reason that in experiencing artistic joy there is a kinship and identity among all art-enjoyers.

Abhinavagupta's teacher Bhaṭṭa Tauta, in his work *Kāvya-kautuka*, says that a dramatic play is not a physical occurrence. In witnessing a play we forget the actual perceptual experience of the individuals on the stage playing their different parts or manifesting their individuality as associated with their local names and habitations. The man who is playing the part of Rāma does not appear to us in his actual individual character and it does not also appear to us that he cannot be the Rāma about whom Vālmiki wrote. He stands somewhere midway between the pure actuality and the pure ideality. This together with all the scenic associations and those of music produces an experience which vibrates with exhilaration; and as a result thereof the whole presentation of actuality becomes veiled, as it were, in so far as it is an actual occurrence of presentative character. The past impressions, memories, associations, and the like, which were lying deeply buried in the mind, became connected with the present experience and thereby the present experience became affiliated and perceived in a new manner resulting in a dimension of new experience, revealing new types of pleasures and pains, unlike the pleasures and pains associated with our egoistic instincts and the success or failures of their strivings. This is technically called Rasāvādana, Camatkāra, Carvaṇā which literally means the experiencing of a transcendent exhilaration from the enjoyment of the roused emotions inherent in our own personality. A play or a drama is the objective content of such an experience. A drama or a play is not a physical occurrence. It is a pure spiritual enlightenment, a spiritual expression throbbing and pulsating with a new type of music, joyous and pensive. As a result of this experience, a unity is effected between the individual's own experience and the expression of the art. This experience is, therefore, nothing else but the enlightenment of a universal. Or it may also rather be said that it is a new creation involving the personality of the individual and the objective dramatic content as constituents — a new appearance, a revelation different from all other experience and all external objects. If this analysis be true, dramatic experience and art can no longer be regarded as imitative.

Bhaṭṭa Tauta thought that on the one hand all the equipments of the stage together with the music release from our mind the hold of the impression that such and such a person has taken a particular part, and it also makes us indifferent to the suggestion of an impossibility that the player before us cannot be Rāma. Being cut off from its connection on two sides, namely, the positive connection of the play with the present actor as a known individual with the actuality of all his bearings, and on the other hand the impossibility of connecting the actor with the realized Rāma's character having lost its force, the suggestive influence can very naturally surcharge the mind with new exhilarations and feelings which can, without any relation to anything else, modify the state of the mind. In this state the previous experiences existing in the mind of the audience as impressions work up independently in association with the suggestion of the dramatic performance. The affiliation, apperception, and integration of these roused impressions and expectations produce new joys and new intuitions. The aesthetic content of a drama is all that is illuminated in such a process.

Here we find that the universalization[1] of poetic art is of two kinds. First of all, the aesthetic composition by nature of its special

1 The universalisation which Abinavagupta elaborated is one of the original contributions of Bhaṭṭa Nāyaka.

suggestive force presents before our minds an aesthetic situation and an emotion that is devoid of all its local character. Secondly, the expression of this artistic enlightenment has a universal character in its manifestation in different minds. In the next stage this presented whole becomes commingled with various types of subconscious and unconscious feelings or emotio-motive complexes which are lying dormant in the minds of various people. It is easy to see that so far as these latter are concerned they are naturally different in different persons in accordance with the nature and diversity of experience. It is for this reason that the same artistic whole, though it be presented in the same manner in different minds, their artistic apperception of it would be different in accordance with the difference of diverse emotio-motive complexes, But neither in the universal whole presented to the mind nor in the motive complexes do we find any trace of any local character or colouration that is associated with the ego or the self in its practical commerce with the real objective world around it. It is, therefore, called transcendental, i.e., Alaukika, and its other name is Camatkāra. The word Camatkāra is in reality used in three different senses. It is sometimes used to denote the special aesthetic attitude of the mind produced by the commingling of the universal artistic situation and the stirred up emotio-motive complexes. It also means the aesthetic pleasure arising out of it; and thirdly, the bodily manifestation of such an enjoyment. In addition to this, it is also used to denote that special mental function by which the whole thing is enjoyed.

The view of Rasa expressed by Abhinavagupta had been accepted in later times as the almost unchallengeable gospel truth and as the last analysis of the aesthetic phenomenon propagated through literature.

5

Vāmana's Theory of Riti*

S.K. De

To Vāmana belongs the credit of being the first writer on Poetics who gave us a well thought out and carefully outlined scheme of Poetics, no longer naive or tentative, which in spite of its theoretic defects, is in some respects unique and valuable.

The enquiry as to what is the soul or essence of Poetry is for the first time definitely posed and systematically worked out by Vāmana; his predecessors, to whom the 'body' of poetry was more important, never having troubled themselves with this question. Vāmana lays down in clear terms: 'Ritirātmā Kāvyasya', 'the Riti is the soul of poetry'[1] and working out this figurative description he points out (on I.1.1.) that the word (Śabda) and its sense (Artha) constitute the 'body', of which the soul is the Riti. He defines the Riti as Viśiṣṭapada-racanā or particular arrangement of words. This particularity (Vaiśiṣṭya) of arrangement, again, rests upon certain definite combinations of the different Guṇas or fixed excellences of composition. For instance, of the three kinds of Riti proposed by Vāmana, the Vaidarbhi unites all the ten Guṇas, the Gaudi abounds in Ojas[2] and Kānti[2], the Pāñcāli is endowed with Mādhurya[2] and Saukumārya[2]. This is how Vāmana would distinguish the different Ritis from one another. On these three Ritis poetry takes its stand, just as painting has its substratum in the lines drawn on the canvas[3]. The Vaidarbhi is of course recommended, for it contains all the excellences; and as the genius of each diction is peculiar to itself, Vāmana rejects the view that the other two inferior dictions ought to be practised as steps

---

* From *History of Sanskrit Poetics*, Vol. II.

1 *Kavyalaṃkāra Sūtra*, I.2.6.

2 Names of poetic qualities which have been explained later.

3 Ibid. 1.13.

leading up to the Vaidarbhi. He argues that the proper diction cannot be attained by one who begins with the improper. If the weaver practises weaving with jute, he does not attain proficiency in the weaving of silk. It will be seen from this analysis of the three kinds of diction that the Vaidarbhi is the complete or ideal one which unifies all the poetic excellences, whereas the other two encourage extremes. The one lays stress on the grand, the glorious or the imposing, the other on softness and sweetness, whereby the former loses itself often in bombast, the latter in prolixity. It will be noticed also that the names of the different Ritis are derived from those of particular countries, and Vāmana expressly says in this connexion that the names are due to the fact of particular excellence of diction being prevalent in the writings of particular countries. This makes it probable that the theory of diction, peculiar to this school, originally arose from the empirical analysis of the prevailing peculiarities of poetic expression in different places and furnishes another proof of the general *a posteriori* character of the discipline itself.

It should be observed that the term Riti is hardly equivalent to the English word 'style', by which it is often rendered but in which there is always a distinct subjective valuation. Although Artha (i.e. sense or idea) is admitted as an element by Sanskrit writers, the Riti consists essentially of the objective beauty of representation (of the intended idea), arising from a proper unification of certain clearly defined excellences, or from an adjustment of sound and sense. It is, no doubt, recognized that appropriate ideas should find appropriate expression; or in other words, the outward expression should be suitable to the inward sense. Bharata goes further and formulates that in the drama the expression should also be in keeping with the temperament and character of the speaker to whom it is attributed. But at the same time, the Riti is not, like the style, the expression of poetic individuality, as it is generally understood by Western Criticism, but it is merely the outward presentation of its beauty called forth by a harmonious combination of more or less fixed literary 'excellences'. Of course, the excellences are supposed to be discernible in the sense or import, as much as in the verbal arrangement, but this subjective content is not equivalent to the indefinable element of individuality which constitutes the charm of a good style. If we accept the nomenclature of a modern analyst of style, we may say that the Sanskrit authors admit what he would call the 'mind'-in-style, as a subject of technical formulation, but not the 'soul'-in-style, which is elusive and which they leave to individual writers to evolve in their own way.

Vāmana, therefore, teaches that the Guṇas are essential in poetry, as they go to make up the Riti, which is the 'soul' of poetry[1]. The objection of the author of the *Ekāvali* is that to conceive the Guṇas, on the one hand, as the principal element and therefore as something fit to be adorned and to call them, on the other hand, properties that adorn poetry involves contradiction in terms. This raises only a scholastic quibble which does not bear serious examination. The Guṇas are, no doubt, spoken of as the attributes of the word and the meaning but this, as the commentator points out, is a loose or popular use of the term; for, strictly speaking, they are concerned directly with Riti. To the objection that these entities have no absolute existence, Vāmana replies that their existence is vouched by their cognition as such by men of taste and that these excellences are not found in all cases of recitation but depend upon the presence or absence of certain well-defined characteristics[2].

Vāmana enumerates the Guṇas as ten, which appears to have been the standard number from Bharata's time, but he really doubles the number by clearly differentiating between the Śabda-guṇas and the Artha-guṇas, and regarding each Guṇa as belonging respectively to Śabda and Artha. In other words, each Guṇa is looked at from two different points of view, and the distinction thus proposed between verbal and ideal excellences comes in, as technically put, according as the word or the idea is the denoter (Vācaka) or the denoted (Vācya). We find in Vāmana, for the first time, the definite classification of Guṇas of Śabda and Artha respectively. This sharp distinction, no doubt, clears away some of the vagueness surrounding definitions of Bharata's and Daṇḍin's individual Guṇas; and Vāmana, though widely differing from his predecessors in the peculiar connotation he attaches to some of them, is careful in distinguishing the allied Guṇas from one another.

---

1 *Kāvyālaṃkāra Sūtra,* I. 2. 6-8.

2 2.28 text and gloss.

His scheme of the Guṇas may be tabulated thus:

Śabda-guṇas	Artha-guṇa
i. ojas, or compactness of word structure (gāḍhabandhatva, where bandha means pada-racanā iii.1.4)	i. ojas, or maturity of conception (arthasya prauḍhiḥ)
ii. Prasāda, or laxity of structure (Saithilya)	ii. prasāda, clearness of meaning (artha-vaimalya) by avoidance of superfluity (anupayogi-parivarjanāt, as Abhinavagupta explains)
iii. Ślésa, or coalescence of words resulting in smoothness (maṣrṇatvam, yasmin sati bahūnyapi padāni ekavad bhāsante)	iii. Śleṣa or coalescence or commingling of many ideas (ghaṭanā)
iv. samatā, or homogeneity of manner, i.e., of construction (mārgābhedah, yena mārgeṇopakramas tasya atyāgah)	iv. samatā, or non-relinquishment of proper sequence of ideas (prakramābhedah)
v. samadhi, or symmetry due to orderly ascent and descent, i.e. when the heightening effect is toned down by softening effect, and *vice versa* (ārohāvaroha-krama)	v. samādhi, or grasping of the original meaning, arising from concentration of the mind (artha-drṣtih samādhi-kārāṇatvāt)
vi. mādhurya or distinctness of words (prthak-padatva) due to absence of long compounds (samāsadairghyani vṛtti)	vi. mādhurya, or strikingness of utterance (ukti-vaicitrya), i.e., in an impressive periphrastic manner for special charm.
vii. saukumarya, or freedom from harshness (ajaraṭhatva)	vii. saukumārya or freedom from disagreeable or inauspicious ideas (apārusya)

viii. udāratā, or liveliness in which the words seem as if they are dancing (yasmin sati nritāyantiva padāni) i.e. pada-vicchedāt	viii. udāratā, or delicacy i.e., absence of vulgarity (agrāmyatva)
ix. artha-vyakti, or explicitness of words whereby the meaning is easily apprehended (jhatiyartha-pratipatti-hetutva)	ix. artha-vyakti, or explictness of ideas which makes the nature of things clear (vastu-svabhāva-sphuṭatva)
x. kānti, or brilliance, i.e., richness of words (aujjvalya)	x. kānti, or prominence of the rasas (dipta-rasatva)

After the Guṇas Vāmana deals with the poetic figures or Alaṃkāras as elements of subsidiary importance. This definite differentiation of Guṇa from Alaṃkāra we meet for the first time in Vāmana; for Bhāmaha was indifferent to it, Daṇḍin does not accept it, and Udbhaṭa appears to have denied any difference. At the outset Vāmana states, no doubt, that poetry is acceptable from embellishment (Alaṃkāra); but he is careful to explain embellishment, not in the narrow sense of poetic figure, but in the broad and primary sense of beauty or charm[1]. He also points out that it is only in the secondary instrumental sense that the term alamkāra or embellishment is applied to simile and other poetic figures. In this view, Vāmana apparently develops logically Daṇḍin's teaching; but Vāmana does not make the presence of poetic figures a necessary condition. What makes poetry acceptable, in his opinion, is the presence of charm or beauty (i.e. Alaṃkāra in its broad sense of Saundarya), which he does not define and which is in some respects undefinable. The Riti and its constituent Guṇas come in as a *sine qua non* in the production of this beauty, but the poetic figures only contribute to its heightening. This distinction between the Guṇas and the Alaṃkāra as to their respective position in a formal scheme of Poetics, which is vaguely hinted at by Daṇḍin, is fully developed for the first time

1 Kāvyaṃ grāhyam alaṃkārāt, Saundarayam Alaṃkāraḥ

by Vāmana[1]. The Guṇas being essential to the Riti, are defined as those characteristics which create the charm of poetry — a function which is assigned to both Guṇas and Alaṃkāras by Daṇḍin — but Alaṃkāras are such ornaments as serve to enhance the charm already so produced. The Guṇas are said to be Nitya (permanent), implying that the Alaṃkāras are Anitya, for there can be charm of poetry without the Alaṃkāras but no charm without the Guṇas. In other words, the Guṇa stands to poetry in the Sāmavaya-relation[1], while the Alaṃkāra in Saṃyoga-relation, Saṃyoga being explained as mere conjunction and Samavāya implying inseparable connexion or inherence (Nitya-Saṃbandha). To put it in the usual figurative language, the Guṇa is related to the 'soul' of poetry (viz. Riti), while the Alaṃkāra rests merely on the 'body' (viz. Śabda and Artha). The Alaṃkāra, without the Guṇa, cannot of itself produce the beauty of a poem, but the latter can do so without the former.

The Riti-teachings mark a great advance on the Alaṃkāra-doctrine in many respects. There are many points which are common to both these systems; but, by clearly defining and working out the doctrine of Riti as that distinct characteristic of poetry which sharply separates it from dry philosophical or technical writings, the Riti school seems to have first suggested and started the enquiry (only hinted at by Bhāmaha's theory of Vakrokti) as to what constitutes the essential charm of poetry, and anticipated the theory of Vicchitti (or Ukti-vaicitrya) elaborated later by Kuntaka and other adherents of the Alaṃkāra-doctrine. The Dhvanikāra[2] pays an indirect compliment to the Riti school for having first perceived, however dimly, the true nature of poetry, although he does not agree with its peculiar theory of Riti. The Riti school also goes a step further than the Alaṃkāra school in including Rasa among the necessary characteristics (in Kānti as an Artha-guṇa). It is possible that Vāmana's partiality for the drama, which he considers to be the best form of composition and

---

1 *Kāvyālaṃkāra Sūtra,* I. 1.2

2 Dr. De, belongs to the school of scholars who consider the author of Dhvani text in verses (Dhvanikāra) and Ānandavardhana, the author of the prose gloss thereon, to be two different persons.

from which he supposes other forms of poetry to proceed[1], led him to realize the importance of Rasa, already worked out as fundamental in the drama by the dramaturgic Rasa school, and to incorporate it in one of the essential properties of poetry[2]. But, at the same time, it was perhaps his idea to make his definition of poetry comprehensive enough to cover a larger field and include those instances, e.g., which develop no Rasa. The Kāvya-śobhā (poetic beauty), a term which he probably borrows from Daṇḍin, or Saundarya which conveys the same general idea as the word 'beauty', is regarded as the ultimate test of all poetry; and this beauty, in his opinion, agreeing with the common-sense view of the matter, is realized by carefully worked-out diction, which avoids the damaging flaws by adopting primarily the so-called literary excellences, as well as the poetic figures for the secondary purpose of heightening the effect thus produced.

But the Riti-system, in spite of Vāmana's well-reasoned formulation and the advocacy of his followers, never appears to have wielded very great influence, and its existence was comparatively short-lived. There is no doubt that like the Rasa and the Alaṃkāra-systems, it left its impress on later theories, but it never found a serious champion after Vāmana among latter-day writers, and its theories never found unqualified acceptance. Its general doctrine of Riti began to be discredited and severely criticized from Ānandavardhana's time as too crude an explanation of the nature of poetry; and Mammaṭa, the foremost authority of the latest school, ingeniously combats and sets aside the leading views of Vāmana.

It may, however, be noted that some of the broad principles enunciated by the Riti school have been tacitly recognized by later theorists. The importance of Riti or diction, as such, became established as a stock-idea in Poetics: but it was accepted with grave modifications. It was accepted by the Dhvani school in so far as it contributed to the development of the Rasa-dhvani, and its chief characteristic was supposed to consist in an arrangement or disposition of words or letters for that purpose. This modification naturally diminished the value of all discussion and elaborate classification of the Ritis into different types, and the function of the three Ritis of Vāmana was

1 Kāvyālaṃkāra sūtra, I.3. 30-32.

2 ibid. III. 2.15 and Vṛtti.

made practically equivalent to the three Guṇas admitted by the authors of the *Dhvanyāloka;* but they do not yet appear to have lost all interest with later theorists. Even those writers, who do not subscribe to the doctrine either of the Riti school or of the Dhvani school, pay considerable attention to this question.

Abhinavagupta, however, thinks that the three Ritis of Vāmana, which, in his opinion, characterize an elevated, soft, and middling theme respectively through a peculiar combination of the Guṇas, have no separate existence from Guṇas and Alaṃkāras. Attention, therefore, was naturally directed to the Guṇas and Alaṃkāras more than to the Riti itself, of which they formed, in Vāmana's opinion, the constituent elements; and the Riti, if recognized at all, was recognized as consisting in a particular disposition of words, letters or syllables which favours the development of Rasa, and stands in the same relation to it as (in the usual figurative conceit) the conformation of the 'body' to the 'soul'[1]. It follows from this that the respective functions assigned to Guṇa and Alaṃkāra are not in relation to the Riti but to Rasa, which is one of the fundamental elements of poetry with the later schools. We have already noted that, after Ānandavardhana, the Guṇas are taken as inseparable attributes and causes of excellence[2] of the Rasa or the principal poetic mood in the composition (and not, as Vāmana thinks, of the Riti). The poetic figures, on the other hand, are only attributes of Śabdha and Artha, which constitute the 'body' of poetry, and therefore heighten the poetic mood or Rasa in an indirect way[3]. Vāmana's ideas about 'poetic charm' are also taken as axiomatic, but they appear in later theories in a somewhat different form as the Vicchitti, or Vaicitrya, or Kavi-prauḍhokti underlying all figurative expression.

In spite of these and other important contributions to the general theory of poetics, it is obvious that the fundamental doctrine of the Riti school could not have been accepted in its entirety. Nor could

---

1 Pada-saṃghaṭanā ritirangasaṃsthā-viśeṣavat/ upakartri rasādinām—Viśvanātha: *Sāhityadarpaṇa* ix. I.

2 aṅgino rasasya utkarṣa-hetavaḥ acalasthitayo guṇāh—Mammaṭa *Kāvyaprakāsa* viii. I.

3 *Ibid.* VIII. 2..

it have competed against that of the Dhvanikāra, because Vāmana comprehended poetry only from the formal point of view, whereas the former showed a deeper insight into its inner nature. The more or less objective definition of the Riti, given by this school, was hardly enough to satisfy the search for ultimate principles. Viśvanātha, following the Dhvanikāra and Ānandavardhana in this respect, states this objection when he says that the Riti is a particular kind of formal arrangement, a peculiar disposition or posture of parts; what is called the 'soul' or essence of poetry is something quite different. Again, the analysis of the several types of diction shows considerable ingenuity indeed, but it was found almost impossible, as Daṇḍin himself admitted very early, to label and classify all the modes of poetic expression with definite and unalterable characteristics. As the Riti school, therefore, tended to make invidious and essentially unprofitable (except as empirical facts) distinctions between the Vaidarbhi, Gauḍi and other kinds of diction with regard to whose exact significance there was bound to be inevitable difference of opinion, it naturally provoked criticism and opposition. In the same way, the endeavour to exhaust and classify all the literary excellences and flaws within clear-cut bounds on the basis of more or less formal analysis, was sure to prove unconvincing; and a protest against minute differentiation or endless multiplication of the Guṇas was rightly and definitely propounded by Mammaṭa, who following Ānandavardhana, reduced the number to three only, viz. Mādhurya, Ojas and Prasāda in relation to the ultimate factor of the poetic sentiment. The attempt, therefore, to stereotype the entire poetical output into so many ready-made dictions and fixed excellences, was bound ultimately to be discarded in favour of other and more penetrating principles.

6

Kuntaka's Theory of Poetry: Vakrokti*

S.K. De

At the outset of his work[1], Kuntaka lays down briefly that his object in writing a fresh treatise on poetics, when many others exist already in the field, is 'to establish the idea of Vaicitrya which causes extraordinary disinterested charm in poetry.' This pithy phrase, which sums up the characteristics of what he means by Vakrokti in poetry, practically forms the central principle of his poetic theory. For the Vakrokti, which he maintains to be essential in poetry, is taken as a kind of Vicitrā abhidhā[2] so that the Vakratva or Vakra-bhāva[3] underlying it becomes synonymous with Vaicitrya or Vicitra-bhāva. Indeed, Kuntaka does not appear to make any distinction between them but uses them as interchangeable terms. This Vakratva or Vaicitrya consists of a strikingness of expression which is different from the established or current mode of speech, such as we find in the Sāstras and the like. It is thus a deviation form the matter-of-fact manner of treatment established in the sciences and the scripture; or, more widely, from established usage in general. Mahimabhaṭṭa explains his stand-point clearly when he says that when, contrary to established usages, an idea is expressed with a view to attain strikingness, we have what is called Vakrokti.

Referring to the conventional definition that a word and its sense in their alliance constitute poetry, Kuntaka lays down the qualifications that this alliance must have the speciality of being characterized by what he calls Vakratva or Vaicitrya. He does not hold with Daṇḍin that mere word, however, charming, or mere idea constitutes poetry; what makes them into poetry is the presence of the Vaicitrya due to Vakrokti, which is therefore the essence of poetic speech.

---

* From the Introduction to his edition of the *Vakroktijivita*.

1 *Vakroktijivita*

2 Striking denotation.

3 The obliquity.

This Vakrokti is further described as Vaidagdhya-bhangi-bhaṇiti, which is explained in the Vṛtti (gloss) as a mode of expression (Bhaṇiti), depending on the peculiar turn (Bhaṅgi or Vicchitti) given to it by the skill of the poet (Vaidagdhya or Kavi-kauśala. Ultimate emphasis, is, therefore, laid (as Ruyyaka also points out) on Kavi-kauśala which is elsewhere designated more comprehensively as Kavi-vyāpāra or an act of the imagination on the part of the poet. The Vakra-kavi-vyāpāra or Kavi-vyāpāra-vakratva is, in Kuntaka's opinion, the ultimate source of poetry. The Vakrokti is thus a Bhaṇiti-prakāra — a mode of expression, or in the terminology of Ruyyaka an Ukti-vaicitrya — an extraordinary expression which rests entirely on the genius of the poet.

It follows from this exposition that Kuntaka, like Bhāmaha, cannot accept any composition involving mere Svabhāvokti[1], although Daṇḍin and others have given prominence to this particular figure, which consists in a description of the natural disposition of an object. When we make use of embellishment, what we embellish is the Svabhāva[2] of an object. If this Svabhāva itself is an embellishment, as it is in Svabhāvokti, what is there left to be embellished? To Kuntaka, a plain description of this Svabhāva (as he takes it) is obviously without the requisite strikingness; and he is naturally afraid, apart from technical objections, that the inclusion of this figure would admit even commonplace unadorned expressions into poetry. But this does not mean that Kuntaka entirely rejects the possibility of embellishing the svabhāva of an object. He includes it in the scope of a special kind of Vākya-vakratā[3] in which the Svabhāva of an object, whether Sahaja[4] or Āhārya[5] forms the legitimate theme for heightened expression, and allows it as one of the elements of the simpler Sukumāra-mārga[6].

Kuntaka also appears to agree with Bhāmaha that the Atiśaya[7], which he paraphrases in one place as Prakarṣa-kāṣṭhādhiroha[8], is

---

1 Natural description.

2 Nature.

3 Obliquity of sentence.

4 Natural.

5 Worked up.

6 Delicate (soft) style.

7 Striking quality

8 Climax of excellence.

involved in Vakrokti-vaicitrya; and he takes it as a necessary element in what he calls Vicitra-mārga[1]. But as this Vaicitrya, which consists in a departure from conventional usage, may be attained by wild or eccentric writing, it is laid down that it should be Tadvid-āhlāda-kāri or capable of pleasing the connoisseur. The Tadvid-āhlāda-kāritva[2] is defined as consisting of a pleasing enjoyment beyond what is afforded by the excellence of word, sense or embellishment. Thus the ultimate test of this Vaicitrya in poetry is Tadvid-āhlāda or the appreciation of the Sahṛdaya, the man of taste. The Tad-vid or Sahṛdaya plays an all important part in poetic theories. The sanskrit authors clearly assert that everyone is not capable of realizing the charm of poetry and demand a degree of culture and aesthetic instinct in the capable reader, the Rasika or the Sahṛdaya. He is the expert who must not only be initiated into the intricacies of theoretic requirements but must also possess the finer capacity of aesthetic enjoyment born out of wide culture and identification with the feelings and moods of the poet. Ānandavardhana discusses Sahṛdayatva at some length, and Abhinavagupta arrives at a concise definition of the Sahṛdaya thus — Yeṣām kāvyānuśilanābhyāsavaśād viśadibhūte mano-mukure varnaniyatanmayibhavana-yogyata te hrdaya-saṃvāda-bhājaḥ sahṛdayāḥ[3], a definition which became so much standardized that Hemacandra does not scruple to copy it literally.

Taking this broad connotation of Vakrokti, Kuntaka maintains that this Vakrokti constitutes the only possible embellishment or Alaṃkāra of poetry. No doubt, for the sake of convenience of treatment, one speaks conventionally of Alaṃkārya (that which is to be embellished, viz. Śabda and Artha) and its Alaṃkāra (embellishment, viz. the poetic figures); but this distinction in his opinion is not essential. The embellished speech itself in its entirety is poetry and the addition of poetic figures is not adventitious. His position appears to be that embellished word and sense constitute poetry; and

---

1 Striking style.

2 Capacity to please the connoisseur.

3 Those whose sensibilities, rendered transparent by a regular contemplation of poetry, are capable of identification with the described object — such persons with responsive hearts are called Sahṛdayas, the men of taste.

it is not proper to say that Alaṃkāras belong to Kāvya, for this statement would suggest that Kāvya may exist without them. Indeed, Vakrokti as a mode of expression being essential in poetry, it underlies and forms the substance of all poetic figures so called. In a sense, therefore, Kuntaka (like Daṇḍin uses the term Vakrokti as almost co-extensive with the generic term Alaṃkāra. As such, therefore, the Vakrokti is, as Kuntaka holds, the only Alaṃkṛti[1] possible to Śabda and Artha and all so-called poetic figures are but different aspects of the Vakrokti. As a matter of fact Kuntaka includes the Alaṃkāras in the province of Vākya-vakratā.

The Vakrokti being the only Alaṃkāra admissible, all other Alaṃkāras or poetic figures so analyzed by other writers can be properly included in its comprehensive scope. Kuntaka is conscious of the fact that the Kavi-vyāpāra, which is the source of Vakrokti, is in its nature undefinable; yet one can distinguish and classify its function into six different spheres. The Vakratva, created by Kavi-vyāpāra, may occur in the following cases: (1) in the arrangement of letters which is termed Varṇa-vinyāsa-vakratā. In this may be included among other things all matters which other writers would include in Anuprāsa[2] and Yamaka[3]. (2-3) In the substantive (Prātipadika) or the terminal (Pratyaya) part of a word, it is called respectively Pada-pūrvārdha-and pada-parārdha (or Prātyaya)-vakratā. In the former are included peculiar uses of Paryāya (synonym), Rūḍhi (conventional words), Upacāra (fancied identification founded on resemblance), Viśeṣaṇa (attributive words), Saṃvṛti (covert expressions), Vṛtti (i.e., Samāsa and Taddhita affixes), Bhāva (roots of words), Linga (gender) and Kriyā (verb). In the second group are dealt with the peculiar uses of Kāla (tense), Kāraka (case), Saṃkhyā (number), Puruṣa (person), Upagraha (voice) and particles and indeclinables. (4) In a sentence, it is called Vākya-vakratā. The Vākya-vakratā may be of infinite varieties for it depends on the fertile fancy of the poet. In this section is included the treatment of all poetic figures embracing those figures. This is the subject-matter of the third chapter. (5) In a particular topic (Prakaraṇa), it is called

---

1 Embellishment.

2 Alliteration.

3 Chiming, sustained assonance.

Prakaraṇa-vakratā. (6) In the composition as a whole, it is called Prabandha-vakratā. The fourth chapter is devoted to a consideration of these two subjects. With the exception of the introductory portion of the first chapter which deals with general principles, the whole of the work is devoted to the definition, classification and illustration of these varieties of Vakratā which form the different categories into which poetic speech is analyzed. But Kuntaka himself admits that Vakratva may be of infinite kinds, depending on the creative genius of individual poets.

Kuntaka appears to put much more stress on Riti than his master Bhāmaha does, and his treatment of Guṇas appertaining thereto is much more elaborate. In this he was probably influenced by the traditions of the Riti-school. He acknowledges three Mārgas[1] (a term used both by Daṇḍin and Vāmana as equivalent to Riti), and these correspond to the three Ritis of Vāmana and his followers. But he finds fault with the classification and nomenclature of Ritis adopted by these exponents of the Riti-theory. Kuntaka alludes to Daṇḍin's twofold and Vāmana's threefold classification of Ritis, but asserts that if Ritis are to be named and differentiated as Vaidarbhi, Gauḍi, etc., after different localities in which they are supposed to flourish, then one would be forced to admit infinite varieties of Ritis as there is infinite number of countries. In his opinion, a particular Riti cannot be established as a Deśa-dharama (the property or characteristic of a part of a country); for, it does not depend on particular regional characteristics, or special customs of a particular place, but on the peculiarities of Śakti (power), Vyutpatti (culture) and Abhyāsa (practice) of particular types of poets, which can never conform to mere geographical distribution. To classify Ritis, again, into good, bad or indifferent (Uttama, Adhama and Madhyama) and give them geographical names is futile; for the best kind of poetry alone, the Uttama Kavyā which appeals to the sensibilities of the Sahṛdaya, is to be accepted and there is no point in admitting or framing rules for the so-called Madhyama (indifferent) and Adhama (bad) Ritis. In these arguments Kuntaka anticipates the objections put forward by Mammaṭa and his followers against the Riti-theory generally; but Kuntaka admits the Riti to a distinct place in his

---

1 Ways of writing styles.

system, adopting however, a different basis of classification. In his opinion, the Kavi-svabhavā[1] alone furnishes the criterion for Kavi-prasthāna-bheda[2]; and the ritis are to be classified according to the essential difference in the Śakti[2], Vyutpatti[3] and Abhyāsa[4] of particular types of poets. One class of poets has special fitness for compositions characterized by Saukumārya, while others prefer Vaicitrya, these being the two extreme styles of composition. But there may be still other poets who would like to steer a middle course, thus favouring a mixed style.

Broadly speaking, the chief distinction between the Sukumāra and the Vicitra mārga seems to be that in the former the Kavi-kauśala is not Āhārya (adventitious or artificial) because of the prominence given to the Svabhāva of things, and consequently whatever ornamentation it possesses is effected with the least effort; while in the Vicitra mārga, the Vakrokti-vaicitrya, by which is meant Alaṃkāra-Vicitra-bhāva[5] predominates and poetic effort is subordinated to this object. In the Sukumāra style the natural powers of the poet find an unhampered scope and result in a kind of heightened expression; while in the Vicitra style the art is chiefly decorative, and through it the Bhaṇiti-vaicitrya attains a peculiar factitious charm. The Dhvani (or Pratiyamānatā[6] as it is called) is an element in both; but in the former the Rasa becomes an Anga of the delineation of Svabhāva, while in the latter the ornamentation is to be done in accordance with the underlying motives of Rasa. In Kuntaka's opinion, the Vicitra-mārga, which is favoured by all good poets, is the more difficult of the two, demanding greater skill and maturity of treatment.

To the Sukumāra-mārga belong the excellences of Mādhurya (sweetness due to fewness of compounds), Prasāda (perspicuity), Lāvaṇya (beauty arising out of proper arrangements of letters and

---

1 The temperament of the poet.

2 Difference of poetic styles.

2 Talent.

3 Culture.

4 Practice (training).

5 The striking quality of the figure.

6 Suggestiveness

words) and Ābhijātya (smoothness). The Vicitra-mārga is similarly characterized by four sets of excellences, which are designated by the same names but defined somewhat differently, viz., Mādhurya (compactness of skilful structure avoiding laxity), Prasāda (lucidity due to the use of expressive words and easy syntax), Lāvaṇya (beauty due to the arrangement of short and long syllables), and Ābhijātya (elevatedness which is neither too soft nor too hard). The Madhyama mārga, which stands midway between these two styles, combines the excellences of both (Ubhayātmaka). To these special characteristics Kuntaka adds Aucitya (I. 53-54) and Saubhāgya (I. 55-56) as excellences common to the three Mārgas. The Aucitya, which as a characteristic emphasizes the fitness of words and ideas, had been admitted by the Dhvani school chiefly in connection with Rasa, and discussed generally in a separate treatise by Kṣemendra; while the Saubhagya is an excellence which arises out of the realization of all the resources of a composition.

From the prominence thus given to the analysis of Alamkara, it will be clear that Kuntaka could not put enough emphasis on Rasa and Bhava as elements of poetry. The Rasa is dealt with topically in connexion with the poetic figures of the different Mārgas in which it is involved, as also in the treatment of Prakaraṇa-prabandha-vakratā[1]. Kuntaka admits the necessity of Rasa, but regards its delineation apparently as a special kind of realizing Vakratva in a composition. He quotes with approval an Antara-śloka[2] which lays down: Nirantara-rasodgāra-garbha-saundarya-nirbharāḥ/giraḥ kavinām jivanti na kathā-mātramāśritāḥ[3]. He admits that it is not the mere matter or plot but the beauty imparted to it by the continuous development of Rasa which can make the words of a poet live, and in this he follows the dictum of Ānandavardhana; but as he had already accepted the essentiality of Vakrokti, the Rasa could be comprehended only as an element of Vakrokti. It would appear that

---

1 The charm of episode and plot-structure.

2 An observation put pointedly in the form of a verse in the midst of prose gloss.

3 The utterances of (eminent) poets which are full of beauty, characterized by a continuous development of Rasa, do not live merely upon the theme.

while the theorists of the school to which Kuntaka belonged were indeed cognizant of that aesthetic delectableness which must be present in poetry and which in Sanskrit goes by the name of Rasa, but they could not yet harmonize it with their theory of Alaṃkara except indirectly as an embellishment of the language or of sense. Thus in the figure Rasavat, which was recognized by old poetics (Bhāmaha III.6; Daṇḍin II. 280 ff.) and which helped to smuggle in, as it were, the idea of Rasa into their systems, the moods and feelings are roused not for their own sake but only to adorn the expressed thought. Kuntaka substantially follows this tradition, but as in the meantime the Dhvanikara and Ānandavardhana had already worked out the importance of Rasa and indicated its position as an essential element in poetry, he had to assign to Rasa a definite place in his system, and could no longer regard the Rasavat, etc., as convenient figures of speech in which the Rasas could be included.

While discussing the kind of Vākya-vakratā in which the Svabhāva of an object forms the theme, Kuntaka gives directions as to how sentient objects can be described and made attractive through the proper development of sentiments like love. He appears to accept the theory of Ānandavardhana that the Rasas cannot be Sva-śabda-vācya[1] and gently ridicules those writers (e.g. Udbhata) who hold views to the contrary. In this connexion he points out how charming results can be produced in poetry by nourishing Rasas and Bhāvas, and cites verses from the *Vikramorvaśiya* and *Tāpasa-vatsarāja* as illustrations of Vipralambha śṛṇgāra[2] and Karuṇa rasa[3] respectively. He also comments upon the Rasoddipana-sāmarthya[4] of *Kumāra-sambhava* and *Vikramorvaśiya*. Incidentally, he considers in detail the claims of the so-called Rasālaṃkāras (Rasavat, Preyas, Urjasvin and Samāhita) to be included in the list of Alaṃkara as they were done by older writers who comprehended all ideas of rasa in these figures. Kuntaka could not regard them in the same light as they

1 Described by their name.

2 Love in separation.

3 Pathetic sentiment.

4 Capacity to evoke rasa.

were viewed by older theorists like Bhāmaha and Daṇḍin nor could he regard them with Ānandavardhana as cases of Guṇibhuta-vyangya in which the suggested sense (here Rasa) is subordinated to the expressed poetic figures. He maintains that, like Svabhāvokti, they are not Alaṃkāras but Alaṃkarya, i.e., in these so-called poetic figures, the Rasa is developed for its own sake and not merely as an embellishment of the expressed thought. He criticises severely the older views of Bhāmaha, Daṇḍin, Udbhaṭa and others, commenting in detail upon their definitions. But he is at the same time careful in laying down that even the Rasavat, in which Rasa is independently developed, is only an aspect of Vakratā depending on Kavi-kauśala. If not theoretically invulnerable, this view is interesting as indicating that the importance of Rasa, first advocated in poetic theories by the Dhvanikāra[1], appears to have influenced thinkers belonging to other traditions of thought. The Dhvanikāra attempted to reconcile the older idea of Rasavat as involving the Rasas secondarily by admitting it in his second division of poetry; but Kuntaka brushes aside all older views in this respect, and thinks that the case of Rasavat should be considered as one in which the poet has an opportunity of creating a kind of Vakrokti in which the Rasa supplies the principal charm.

Thus Kuntaka, recognizing the importance of Rasa in poetry, had to allow it to form an element of the two kinds of style, the Sukumāra and the Vicitra. He lays down in general terms that Vicchitti is Sarasatva-sampaducitā[2]. He also allows the Rasas to play an important part in what he calls Prabandha and Prakaraṇa-vakratā, i.e., in Vakratā, occurring in the composition as a whole or in its constituent episodes. In a Prakaraṇa[3], for instance, the special kind of Vakrāta-vicchitti (or the ingenious and charming turns) introduced in the incidents of a traditional plot is justified in so far as it contributes to the development of Rasas. Sometimes the Prakaraṇa-vakratā may be such that the aṅgi or dominant Rasa is developed in an act of a drama (e.g. in *Vikramorvaśiya* Act IV) to a climax which it has never attained either

---

1 Author of the Dhvani theory.

2 Endowed with Rasa.

3 Context or part of the theme.

before or after. Sometimes a single Rasa like Karuṇa is developed and sustained thoughout the play with constant repetition of the theme, but the Vakratā is thereby not rendered tiresome because it is woven with new surprises and made brilliant with Rasa and Alaṃkara. In a Prabandha[1], again, the Aṅgi rasa of the original story may be abandoned in favour of another Rasa to impart new charm to the plot. Thus in the *Veṇisaṃhāra* the dominant Śānta rasa of the *Mahābhāratha* is rejected in favour of Vira rasa.

Similar remarks apply to Kuntaka's treatment of the element of Dhvani in poetry. It is clear that Kuntaka who admits not the essentiality of Rasa or Dhvani — subject, of course, to what has been said in the foregoing paragraph about the importance of Rasa to Kuntaka, — but that of Vakrokti, can comprehend tham only in some aspects of Vakratā. Ruyyaka explains that all ideas of Dhvani are acknowledged by Kuntaka in the special form of Vakrokti, called Upacāra-vakratā, the peculiarity of his view consisting in this recognition of the concept of the 'suggested sense' and in the attempt to incorporate it in Vakrokti. From Kuntaka's treatment of Upacāra-vakratā it appears that the Upacāra-vakratā lies at the root of such pleasing figures as Rūpaka and therefore of metaphorical expression generally; and that, generally speaking, the Upacāra consists of a supposed or fancied identification of two objects, however distinct, on the basis even of the slightest resemblance. The term Upacāra, no doubt, is often used loosely as identical with Lakṣaṇā (Indication or Transferred Sense); but the above interpretation agrees with the idea of Upacāra expounded by a majority of theorists, and is put concisely by Viśvanātha (p. 47) as 'the arrest of the apprehension of difference between the two objects, absolutely distinct, by means of the greatness of their resemblance'. As such, therefore, it is admittedly involved in figures like Rūpaka (metaphor) and forms the basis of metaphorical expression in general. As an instance of Upacāra-vakratā, Kuntaka cites the case of application to immaterial objects of words which denote material objects, as in the phrase 'particle of abuse'. The word 'particle' applicable to material objects in the sense of 'little' bears a pleasing charm to the Sahṛdaya, when it is applied, through the analogy of 'littleness', to such immaterial objects as 'abuse'.

1 Whole work.

Kuntaka's Upacāra would come under the comprehensive domain of transferred expression known as Lakṣaṇā and would be included by the writers of the Dhvani school in the province of Lakṣaṇa-mūla-dhvani or suggestion based upon Transference of Indication.

The author of the *Vakroktijivita*, therefore, may be classed (together with Bhāmaha, Daṇḍin Udbhaṭa and Vamana) among those who hold (according to the classification of the Dhvanikāra and Ānandavardhana) that Dhvani or suggestion is Bhākta[1]; or, in other words, among those who maintain that the suggested sense is not the essence of poetry but is only a secondary element. Kuntaka acknowledges the concept of Dhvani but denies its independent existence as 'the soul of poesy' by including it under various forms of Vakrokti.

But in spite of the opinions of Ruyyaka, Vidyādhara and Jayaratha, it appears that Kuntaka is more fully alive to the importance of Dhvani in poetry than they would make us believe, and assigns to it a larger part in his scheme of Poetics than allowing it to be comprehended in all its aspects in Upacāra-vakratā merely. At the very outset of his work he defines Vacaka[2] śabda and Vācya artha[2] comprehensively as including in its scope not only Lakṣaka śabda[3] and Lakṣya artha[4] but also Vyañjaka[5] and Vyaṇgya[6] word and sense, thus expressly recognizing the three Vṛttis, including Vyañjanā, in poetry. He acknowledges the element of Dhvani in the Sukumāra mārga but more explicitly in the Vicitra mārga. The two cases of Lakṣaṇā-mūla-dhvani[7], recognized by the Dhvani School, are acknowledged by Kuntaka. The Paryāya-vakratā, again, where words with a double meaning lead to the suggestion of a metaphor or simile, is expressly stated by Kuntaka to fall within the province of what is called the Śabda-śakti-mūla-dhvani[8]. Thus Kuntaka admits

---

1 Included in Lakṣaṇā — transference.

2 Denoting word. 2 Denoted meaning.

3 Indicating word. 4 Indicated meaning

5 suggesting word. 6 Sugessted meaning.

7 Dhvani based on transference.

8 Dhvani based on the power of the word.

most of the broad divisions of Dhvani elaborated by the Dhvani-theorists.

Again, Kuntaka recognizes Pratiyamānatā generally in those cases of Vākya-vakratā where the Svabhāva of an object forms the theme and guardedly uses the term, Gocaratva[1], instead of Vācyatva[2], so as to include the possibility of Vyaṇgyatva[3]. He thus clearly indicates that such descriptions are possible not only through express words but also through suggestive expressions. In other words, he accepts in a general sense what is known as Vastu-dhvani[4]. In this way, he appears to acknowledge Alaṃkāra-dhvani, as elsewhere he acknowledges Rasa-dhvani and Vastu-dhvani. In one passage, while discussing the figure Parivṛtti[5], which he would consider to be Alaṃkārya (and not an Alaṃkāra), he gives his opinion that this so-called figure is charming when it involves suggestion, and speaks categorically in this connexion of the three forms of suggestion of Vastu, Alaṃkāra and Rasa recognized by the Dhvani school.

Indeed, Kuntaka belongs to that group of authors who, having flourished after Ānandavardhana's time, do not deny the concept of Dhvani, but try to explain it in terms of already recognized ideas. Like Mahimabhaṭṭa who attempts to settle the process of Suggestion by the technical logical process of Inference, Kuntaka lived in the interval between Ānandavardhana who first championed the Dhvani-theory and Mammaṭa whose classical text-book raised the theory to almost exclusive authority. Like Mahimabhaṭṭa again, Kuntaka, as a follower of Bhāmaha, Udbhaṭa and the Alaṃkāra school, started a vigorous but short-lived reactionary movement which wanted to go back to the old position in a somewhat original way by an attempt to reconcile new ideas with the old. In this lies the historical

1 Being the object of expression.

2 Express denotation.

3 Suggestiveness.

4 Suggestion of the object.

5 A figure of speech based on the exchange of two similar or dissimilar things.

importance of Kuntaka's work. But like the Anumāna-theory of Mahimabhaṭṭa, still again, Kuntaka's theory of Vakrokti never appears to have received liberal recognition in the hands of later theorists, all of whom, since Mammaṭa's time, accepted without question the Dhvani-theory of Ānandavardhana. If later writers refer to his Vakrokti, it is only to criticize and reject it; and in attempting to revive and extend Bhāmaha's old theory in the face of the more widely received theory of the Dhvanikāra and Ānandavardhana, Kuntaka was apparently fighting on behalf of a cause already doomed.

7

Imagination in Indian Poetics*

T.N. Sreekantaiya

Dve vartmani girām devyāḥ śāstram ca kavikarma ca
Prajñyopajñam tayorādyam pratibhodhavamantimam[1].

Bhaṭṭa Tauta

It has been observed that Indian Poetics and Western Poetics view their subject-matter from somewhat different, if complementary, angles — the latter deals with poetry as the expression of the poet's mind while the former is chiefly occupied with its culmination as a unique experience of the reader. The great contribution of India to Comparative Poetics is the doctrine of Rasa-Dhvani, the process by which the reader re-creates for himself and re-lives the poet's original experience. Western poetics, on the other hand, studies how the multitudinous impressions of the external world melt, alter and combine in the crucible of the poet's mind and emerge as a harmonious whole, shining with the added gleam — 'the light that never was, on sea or land'. It is the poet's Imagination that works this magic and accordingly its study occupies an important place in Western schools of Poetics. A philosophical critic like Coleridge or Croce builds a style of Aesthetics with Imagination as its key-stone. Professional psychologists like Ribot and Spearman devote special treatises to the analysis of the 'Creative Imagination'. Even an off-hand answer in the West to the question 'What is Poetry?', is more likely than not to contain this omnipotent word. Have the Indian theorists nothing to say on this aspect of the problem?

The exact equivalent of Imagination in Sanskrit Poetics is Pratibhā (also Pratibhāna). It is often rendered as 'fancy', 'genius', etc; but these terms do not convey all its implications. There was a time

---

* From *The Indian Historical Quarterly*, Vol. XIII, No. 1.

1 'The goddess of speech has two ways: Science and Poetry. The former is born of intellect and the latter of imagination.' I am indebted to Dr.V. Raghavan for this quotation.

when 'fancy' was considered to be entirely different from Imagination; Coleridge held this view. Though modern psychology knows no such distinction between the two, 'fancy' is still used in literary discussions to denote that aspect of Imagination which concocts superficial conceits having no deep basis in reality. 'Genius' is the innate supernormal capacity which lies at the root of all great work; the word Pratibhā and its equivalent Śakti are sometimes used in this sense in Sanskrit works. But since genius is a vague and general term, and moreover is always seen in poetry in the excellence of the poet's imagination, we need not feel any hesitation in equating Prabithā with Imagination.

Pratibhā literally means a flash across the mind — a revelation characterized by 'immediacy and freshness'. Many systems of Indian philosophy have developed doctrines of Pratibhā to explain the transcendental knowledge gained by immediate vision without resorting to the laborious and often inadequate exercise of the intellect. Aesthetics is but a branch of philosophy; and it has been clearly shown that important theories of Indian Poetics, especially those which explain the realization of Rasa, follow closely distinct schools of Indian philosophy[1]. The statements of our Ālaṃkarikas about Kavipratibhā too can be easily traced to the doctrines of intuitive knowledge developed by different schools of philosophy like the Āgama, the Nyāya and the Jaina. We may note here one obvious illustration. It was in Kashmir, the home of the Pratyabhijñā school, that Indian aesthetic thought reached its fullest height; writers like Abhinavagupta achieved eminence in both fields of speculation. No wonder then that statements regarding the nature of Pratibhā in poetry should in many cases be a reflection of the Śaivāgama view. Indeed, Abhinavagupta's stanza:

Yadunmilanaśaktyaiva viśvamunmilati kṣaṇāt
Svātmāyatanaviśrāntām tām vande pratibhām śivām

— *Dhvanyālokalocana,*
end of ch. 1.

---

1 See *Indian Aesthetics* by Prof. M. Hiriyanna, Proceedings of the First All-India Oriental Conference, Poona, Vol. II; also included as the first essay in *Art Experience.*

which describes Parā Partibhā — the Supreme Power of Śiva ever residing in Himself and revealing the entire creation in the process of self-revelation — can equally well apply to Kavipratibhā, the poet's imaginative vision to which the whole universe becomes open. We may be certain that Abhinavagupta intended his lines to characterize both the Pratibhās.

But let us dally no further with this subject of philosophical origins and correspondences which, though fascinating, cannot be discussed with any competence by the present writer. We shall confine our attention to the views on Pratibhā as manifested in Poetry. It is customary for the majority of Ālaṃkārikas to dismiss this subject with a few remarks while discussing the requisites of the poet. But Rājaśekhara with his usual interest in topics which are somewhat out of the beaten track devotes a whole chapter and even more of his *Kāvyamimāṃsā* to Pratibhā. He has many interesting things to say about it; one of his most valuable contributions to the subject is the recognition of the Responsive (Bhāvayitri) Imagination of the reader beside the usual Creative (Kārayitri) Imagination of the poet. A writer who deserves far greater tribute, however, is Kuntaka. It may be said that his *Vakroktijivita* is nothing but a treatise on the function of Imagination in Poetry. At the outset he admits the ultimate supremacy of the poet's Imagination, he regards it as the source of every proper charm in a poem and holds it to be the very life of every poetic element, especially of Alaṃkāras. Again and again, almost on every other page of the *Vakrotijivita* the word Pratibhā (or some equivalent of it) is brought in to explain this or that charm of poetry. And, alone of all Ālaṃkārikas it is Kuntaka that has something direct to say about the shaping of the poet's conception in the course of expression. In fact, the very pivot of his system, the Vakra-kavivyāpāra (the striking activity of the poet), seems to mean nothing but Kavipratibhā-vyāpāra, since every mode (Prakāra) of its working is the transcending of the matter for the achievement of something imaginative.

Among the other Ālaṃkārikas that we can consult with great profit there are of course the two master-minds, Ānandavardhana[1] and Abinavagupta; the hints and chance-remarks that they drop off

1 The author of the present paper belongs to the school which makes no distinction between the Kārikā and the Vṛtti portions of the *Dhvanyāloka*; Ānanada-vardhana is taken as the author of both.

and on illumine the whole regions of the subject of Pratibhā. Then, there is Abhinavagupta's own teacher Bhaṭṭa Tauta. Unfortunately, we possess only a few fragments from his still unrecovered *Kāvya-kautuka,* but they are quite precious. Lastly, we must not forget to mention Mahima Bhaṭṭa, the chief critic of the Dhvani school. In his *Vyaktiviveka* there is a short passage on the nature of Pratibhā introduced incidentally in the discussion of the figure Svabhāvokti. It is so significant that we cannot help regretting the loss of his philosophical work *Tattvoktikośa* in which he had specifically expounded Pratibhā-tattva.

It is the creative aspect of Imagination — its power to conceive ever-new thoughts and images and to express them in living words — that easily catches one's attention. The celebrated definition given by Tauta points out particularly this feature of Pratibhā. The full passage, so far as it has been preserved for us in quotations (e.g. *Kāvyā nuśāsana*, 2nd Edn., p.3), runs as follows:-

Prajñā navanavollekhaśālinī pratibhā matā
Tadanụprāṇanājīvadvarṇanānipuṇaḥ kaviḥ
tasya karma smṛtam kāvyam — [1]

In a passage probably inspired by the foregoing, Abhinavagupta characterizes Pratibhā in fuller terms:

Pratibhā apūrvavastunirmāṇakṣama prajñā tasyā viśeṣaḥ
rasāveśavaiśadysaundaryakāvyanirmāṇākṣamatvam[2]
(*Dhvanyāloka-locana,* p.29).

Abhinavagupta points out here that it is Imagination from which all creative work springs; Poetic Imagination is but one variety of it.

---

1 The faculty that creates ever-new forms is called Pratibhā. One who is deft in portrayal or representation under the inspiration of this Pratibhā is a poet. His work is called Poetry.

2 Prathibhā is that faculty of the mind which is capable of original creation. Its special form is the capacity to create Poetry rendered beautiful by lucidity of vision under the inspiration of Rasa.

But poetry has often come to trouble with philosophers for the very thing that critics grow enthusiastic over — its power to create a world of Imagination. To the matter-of-fact mind poetry seems to offer mere Appearance in place of Reality; it is at best 'pretty falsehood'. In our own country there have not been want of puritans who laid down Kāvyālāpāṃś ca varjayet[1], thus ruling out all poetry; and commentators have had to resort to ingenious interpretations of this injunction to save their favourite works of poetry from its anathema. More generous-hearted thinkers even have suffered poetry only so long as it subserved the interests of morality. But poetry is autonomous: A poet's Imagination has a way of looking at Reality which is as legitimate as the method of reason[2]. In fact, the Imagination and the Intellect are the two spiritual eyes of a human being and he needs both of them. Āandavardhana gave expression to this fundamental truth in the following supplication to the Deity:

> yā vyāpāravati rasān rasayitum kācit kavinām navā
> dṛṣṭiryā pariniṣṭhitārthaviṣayonmeṣā ca vaipaściti
> te dve apyavalambya viśvamaniśam nirvarṇayanto vayam
> śrāntā naiva ca labdhamabdhiśayana tvadbhaktitulyam sukham[3].

Here Anandhavardhana is no doubt subordinating both the imagination of the poet and the intellect of the philosopher to the religious attitude but we are not concerned with it for the present. What is to be noted is that he gave both Poetry and Philosophy an equal status in the interpretation of Life. His use of the word dṛṣṭi 'the eye (of Imagination)'

---

1 Poetry should be avoided.

2 'What distinguishes poetic from religious or philosophic apprehension is not that it turns away from reality, but that it lies open to and in eager watch for reality at doors and windows which with them are barred and blind. The poet's soul resides, so as to speak, in his senses, in his emotions, in his imagination, as well as in his conscious intelligence; and we may provisionally describe poetic apprehension as an intense state of consciousness in which all these are vitally concerned.' (C.H. Herford; *Is there a Poetic View of the World* ?).

3 Dhvanyāloka III. p. 227, 1928 edn.

is very significant, especially with the illuminating commentary of Abhinavagupta on this passage[1].

What is the individual way in which the poet's Imagination vies with the world? We find an eloquent answer to this question in the one available passage dealing with Pratibhā from Mahima Bhaṭṭa's writings. That Mahima Bhaṭṭa was a Naiyāyika is obvious from his elaborate attempt to reduce Dhvani to a type of anumāna; hence it is not surprising that he should have described Pratibhā in terms of the Nyāya philosophy making use of its distinction between the samanyarūpa and the viśeṣarūpa of an object. We shall, however, refrain here from entering these philosophical waters, and only note what Mahima Bhaṭṭa has to say directly on Pratibhā[2]. According Mahima Bhaṭṭa, it is the unique nature of an object that is revealed by the words which flow from the Pratibhā of a poet. When he sits in concentration, brooding over word and sense that will be in harmony with his dominant poetic mood, all at once there wells up in him an insight which touches the essence of things; this is Pratibhā[3]. It is verily the third eye of Lord Śiva, which reveals to him all things past, present and future. There is great truth in this view. To the ordinary man, occupied with the practical affairs of the world, one object looks much like another. Since he is chiefly interested in making everything that he comes across serve his personal ends, he has neither the time nor the inclination for seeing a thing as it really is. But before the disinterested gaze of the poet the objects of the world shed as it were their mark of familiarity and generality; and each thing reveals

---

1 ...काचिदिति लोकयात्रापतितबोधावस्थात्यागेन उन्मीलयन्ती। अत्त एव ते कवय: वर्णनायोगात्। नवेति क्षणे क्षणे नूतनैर्विचित्रैर्जगन्त्यासूत्रयन्ती। दृष्टिरिति प्रतिभारूपा। ...ते द्वे अपीति। न ह्येकया दृष्ट्या सम्यङ् निर्वर्णनं भवति ...

2 Vyaktiviveka, Trivandrum edn. p. 108

3 विशिष्टमस्य यद्रूपं तत् प्रत्यक्षस्य गोचरम् ।
स एव सत्कविगिरां गोचरः प्रतिभाभुवाम् । यत;
रसानुगुणशब्दार्थचिन्तास्तिमितचेतसः ।
क्षणं स्वरूपस्पर्शोत्था प्रज्ञैव प्रतिभा कवेः ।
सा हि चक्षुर्भगवतस्तृतीयमिति गीयते ।
येन साक्षात्करोत्येष भावांस्त्रैकाल्यवर्तिनः ।

its own unique self. The poet's Imagination seizes its individual qualities — the qualities which give even the meanest object great significance and make the ugliest appear most charming — and represents in fit words such a vision of reality.

Hence, a poet need not go beyond the commonality of life to create Beauty. There is Beauty before him if he can but look at it with the right eyes; and a bare, unadorned representation of it can become true poetry — indeed, it may surpass in charming descriptions cloaked in adventitious finery. This seems to be the real significance of admitting Svabhāvokti in poetry. Whether it should be technically brought under the Alaṃkāras proper or not is a problem of minor importance. What we should specially bear in mind in our present discussion is the fact that in Svabhāvokti the poet adds nothing of his own; he represents a thing as he sees it. No doubt his vision is fresh and selects only the unique features of the object he is describing; but there can be no art without selection.

That fidelity to life, as it is, has a place in poetry is further recognized by the theorists in the inclusion of Vastu along with Alamkara and Rasa under Dhvani. Abhinavagupta takes care to point out that even the other two kinds of Dhvani ultimately resolve into Rasa; but that vastu (unadorned fact)[1] should be given at all the status of Dhvani under appropriate conditions is surely significant. This point becomes still clearer when we observe its further division into Kavipraudhoktiniśpanna, 'evolved by the poet's imaginative expression' and Svataḥ sambhavi 'existing in actuality'. In Western Poetics there has been a long drawn quarrel over the question whether Poetry is essentially 'Imagination' or 'Creation' (Mimesis or Poesis). In India, the problem did not long remain unsolved (though in the earlier stages of poetics there was some fight over Svabhāvokti). Both the modes came to be admitted because both of them could achieve Rasa prakāśa, the most important aim of poetry. Neither 'Imagination' nor 'Creation' — or to use our own terminology, neither 'Svabhāvokti' not 'Vakrokti' — is an end in itself; it is only a means to the realization of Rasa, and has to be justified only in relation to this end.

---

1 It must be remembered, that Vastu becomes poetic only when it is suggested. Again, Vastu can signify a supernatural fact as well as a natural fact. All suggested sense which is neither Rasa nor Alaṃkāra is termed Vastu.

So far we have been stressing the nature of Imagination as a kind of Dṛṣṭi — a way of looking at the universe. Now we have to revert to its more familiar aspect — Sṛṣṭi (Creation), and make an attempt to understand more exactly what it means. The poet is often compared to the Creator, sometimes to the detriment of the latter. The poetic world is said to be free from the laws of Destiny and created by the poet without the least material cause. That is to say, the poet is supposed to weave it out of the shapes and sounds that his own Imagination bodies forth. But, in art as in life, something cannot come out of nothing. The poet's Imagination must feed on something outside it, be the food as rare and tenuous as 'the aerial kisses of shapes that haunt thought's wildernesses'. Psychologists have shown that even the most original Imagination can only work on the impressions of the world it has received; it may produce new modes of combination, but no new elements[1]. Indian theorists too were not unaware of this even when they grew eloquent over the Poet's creative magic. For instance, when Ānandhavardhana says:

Apāre Kāvyasaṃsāre kavireva prajāpatiḥ
Yāthāsamai rocate visvam tathedam parivartate[2]

he admits clearly that the poet works upon the material presented by the world and does not create his poem out of the void. Note especially the word parivartate, 'transforms': it holds the key to the secret of poetic creation.

It is Kuntaka, however, that has devoted some space to the discussion of this problem. He remarks unequivocally:

Yanna (?) varṇyamanasvarupāḥ padārthāḥ kavibhirabhūtāḥ santaḥ kriyante, kevalam sattāmatreṇa parisphuratāṃ caiṣām

---

1. *Readings in Psychology*, p. 339. Cf. also '...... all so-called inspirations occur strictly within the limit of the individual's capacity, training and previous cognitions.' J.E. Downey, *Creative Imagination*, p. 158.

2 In this infinite world the Poet is the creator. He transforms the world as it pleases him.

Compare the implications of this with the statement of Croce: 'The philosophy of language, in a word, is identical with the philosophy of poetry and art, science of intuition-expression, aesthetics; which embraces language in its whole extension........ ' (Aesthetics, *Encyclopaedia Britannica* XIV, Edn.)

tathāvidhaḥ ko'pyatiśayaḥ punarādhiyate, yena kāmapi sahṛdayahṛdayahāriṇim ramaṇiyatām adhiropyate (*Vakroktijivita*, p. 140)

By this means that the poet does not set about creating nonexisting objects, but taking them as they occur bleak in life he endows them with some special charm in the process of describing them. Then, Kuntaka goes on to say, this special charm contributed by the poet conceals effectively the original character of the object, and in the form revealed through the poet's Imagination the object shines like some new creation. It is this which entitles the poet to the appellation of Creator. These remarks of Kuntaka apply to Utpādya[1] as well as Prasiddha[2] themes. For even when a poet invents an incident he does not create it absolutely. What he does is to fuse together the various features of the things that, owing to the inherent relation between one and another, spring at the moment to his Imagination of their own accord. As a result of this integration we perceive indeed a new thing, but in reality it is only its Atiśaya[3] that has been the original work of the poet. Kuntaka's account of this process is a little obscure here and there, but there is no uncertainty about his general position.

By thus questioning the poet's title to the rank of creator in the absolute sense, we are not, by any means, reducing the marvel of poetic creation. The picture as it emerges from the poet's imagination does indeed look new, because he has endowed it with a transcendental charm. And the elements which have gone to make it may seem incredible when viewed separately, but somehow they have become welded into a most harmonious whole. Thus does Ānandavardhana characterize the poet's speech, comparing it with the enchanting graces of one's beloved.

In almost every definition of Pratibhā, we observe that Artha and Śabda, Abhidheya and Abhidhāna, Darśana and Varnanā, or Prakhyā and Upākhyā — i.e., the conception (or intuition) and its verbal expression are both attributed to the imaginative activity. That is as it should be. A conception, however original it might be, leads but a shadowy

---

1 created by imagination.

2 Well-known (historical and legendary)

3 Extraordinary element.

existence until it is embodied in appropriate words. There are philosophers who hold that one possessed an intuition only to the extent one is able to express it, at least to oneself[1]. However this may be, there is no doubt that a poet truly becomes a poet only when he has woven his rich conceptions into verbal patterns. Bhaṭṭa Tauta, as quoted by Hemacandra, has something significant to say on this point.

'It is said that a Kavi is necessarily a seer (Ṛṣi); and a seer is one who has vision (Darśana). Vision is the intuition (Prakhyā) of the Reality underlying the manifold objects of the universe and their qualities. To be termed 'Kavi' in the Sastras, it is enough if one possesses this vision of Reality. But in common parlance the term 'Kavi' becomes current if one possesses expression (Varṇanā) as well as vision. Thus, though the Ādi-Kavi (i.e., Vālmiki), being a sage, ever possessed vision, the world did not accord him the appellation of 'Kavi' until his Expression was born (i.e., until he composed the *Rāmāyaṇa*).

In the famous invocatory stanza of the *Locana*, describing Sārasvatatattva (the truth of poetry), Abhinavagupta suggests that expression (Upākhyā) follows intuition (Prakhyā) : Kramāt parakhyopākhyāprasarasubhagam, the significance of the word Kramāt (one after another) here being explained by the commentator as, Prathamam hi prakhyā tadanantaramupākhyeti kramah. (i.e., first the intuition and then the expression)[2].

If this is understood to mean that the intuition is perfect before it is expressed in words, it needs modification. For, as Kuntaka has rightly observed, a conception taking its rise in the Imagination of the poet will not have attained perfection at the very first flash. At best it will be like a precious stone dug out of the mine, with its native appearance hardly to be distinguished from that of a bit of stone. It needs polish before it can shine with full lustre; this it undergoes in

1 Cf.'......intuition is only intuition in so far as it is, in that very act, expression. An image that does not express, that is not speech, song, drawing, painting, sculpture or architecture — speech at least murmured to oneself, song at least echoing within one's own breast, line and colour seen in imagination and colouring with its own tint the whole soul and organism — is an image that does not exist.' (Croce: Aesthetics, *Encyc. Brit.*, XIV th Edn.)

2 Kaumudi on *Dhvayāloka Locana*, Kuppuswami Sastri Research Institute edn. p.7.

the process of expression. That is to say, it is in being expressed that an intuition defines itself. Theorists recognise a stage called Avekṣana (examination)[1] in poetic composition, in which the poet removes one expression and inserts another because his mind is still in hesitation, indicating that the conception itself has not become quite definite. Śabdapāka (perfect expression) is said to occur when the words in a composition become irreplaceable. But in reality this Śabda-pāka is nothing but Artha-pāka (perfect intuition).

Works on Poetics usually indulge in some discussion concerning the various requisites of the poet: Śakti or Pratibhā (Imagination), Vyutpatti (culture comprising both Bahujñatā[2] and Ucitānucita-viveka[3]) and Abhyāsa (practice). Among these Pratibhā is admitted to be the very seed of poetry — without it poetry cannot arise, and even if composed somehow is sure to become the laughing stock of the world. The question that is hotly debated is 'Can Pratibhā alone produce Poetry?' Mammaṭa who represents one school of opinion says that all the three together (Samuditāḥ) form the cause (not causes) of Poetry: But others, of whom Jagannātha Paṇḍita has perhaps discussed this question most elaborately, hold that Pratibhā is the sole cause. No doubt, as Ānandavardhana has pointed out, the poet's Imagination can work such magic that faults of taste and the failure of the critical faculty may remain unnoticed in particular contexts, while the poverty of this Imagination at once springs to the eye. It is also true that we rarely find in the same poet a union of great intellect, study and application with innate imaginative power. Yet no poet that lacks the knowledge of life and the balance of mind which are connoted by the term Vyutpatti can hope to become a great poet. Without these requisites his poetry becomes unequal, and on the whole unsatisfactory, even though it may be excellent in parts.

We must however bear in mind that it is one thing to admit the desirability of Vyutpatti in the poet and quite another to hold that

---

1 पदाधानोद्धरणमवेक्षणम् । Vāmana, *Kāvyālaṃkārasūtra*, I. iii. 15.

2 Varied knowledge.

3 Discrimination.

without it and other accessories like Abhyāsa poetry cannot arise at all. For, Pratibhā is ever the only direct source of Poetry. A poet who lacks it lacks everything. Vyutpatti and Abhyāsa contribute but indirectly to the creation of poetry by regulating and refining the working of the poet's Pratibhā.

How does a person become endowed with this all important Pratibhā? Its springs are hidden in mystery; most writers refer its origin to the ante-natal Saṃskāra of the poet.[1] But Jagannātha traces it to at least two different sources: it may be due either to some super-natural cause (Adṛṣṭa) such as the favour of a deity or holy man or to an exceptional kind of culture (Vyutpatti) and practice (Abhyāsa) — the latter cause being evidenced by the sudden outburst of poetry in persons in an advanced stage of life who were till then innocent of it.

At this point we may invoke the help of modern psychology to throw some light on this problem. It observes that everyone can exercise his Imagination if he can but control the secret of it. The imaginative individual differs from the unimaginative in the freedom with which he uses the material at his disposal. The richer and more vivid that material and the more subtle his sense of relationship, the greater the possibilities for creative synthesis[2]. It is said that the ordinary man suppresses most of his impressions and impulses because he is incapable of managing them without confusion. He never gives them a chance to rise above the threshold of consciousness. Hence his vision becomes conventional and matter-of-fact. But in a poet most of these inhibitions are relaxed; hence his impressions freely flow into his consciousness. This accounts for the wealth of imagery that the poet has at his command. Again, much of the poet's constructive work takes place in his sub-conscious mind. This fact explains the shock of surprise the poet himself feels when a splendid thought or image flashes across his mind. His poem seems to compose itself for him. If one is averse to give credence to ante-natal Saṃskāras and supernatural blessings, this is the only explanation that one

1 Cf. पूर्ववासनागुणानुबन्धि प्रतिभानमद्भुतम् (*Kāvyādarśa*, I.104); जन्मान्तरागतसंस्कारविशेषः कश्चित् (Vāmana, *K.A. Sūtra*, *Vṛitti* on I.iii.16); अनादिप्राक्तनसंस्कारप्रतिभानमय (*Abhinavabhārati* on *Nāṭya Śāstra* vol.I, p.346); etc.

2 Downey, *Creative Imagination*, p. 164.

can accept of the creative mystery. It can also help one to understand the exceptional cases of poetic outburst mentioned by Jagannātha Paṇḍita — how at the end of a long period of silence a person suddenly finds his tongue and begins to sing. Probably a great intellectual or emotional crisis has loosened many of his inhibitions, and all the wealth of experience which had been till then locked up comes back to his consciousness in fresh associations to be moulded into poetry.

It is very interesting here to turn to what Hemacandra, following Jaina philosophy, has to say on the coming into play of Pratibhā. He divides Pratibhā into two classes: innate (Sahajā) and conditioned (Aupādhiki), the latter being caused by incantations, divine blessing, etc. But both kinds spring into activity in much the same way. The soul is luminous by nature like the sun. But certain Karmas (called Jñānāvaraṇiyakarmas) veil it like a cloud and prevent it from shining. When they are removed (Kṣaya) or suppressed (Upaśama) Pratibhā bursts forth in splendour. If this process takes place of its own accord we have 'innate' Pratibhā, but if supernatural aids are necessary to remove the veil we have the 'conditioned variety'. The correspondence between Hemacandra's view and that of modern psychology becomes striking once we equate the Āvaraṇa (veil) of Hemacandra with the 'inhibitions' of the latter school in this particular respect.

So far, we have deliberately refrained from dwelling on the most important condition of the poet's imaginative activity — the lever which sets it in motion. In the creative period of Indian aesthetics the critics of the Dhvani theory were one with its champions in acclaiming Rasa the soul of poetry. It is Rasānubhava[1] from which poetry springs and it is Rasaprakāśa[2] at which it aims. No wonder then that Rasa controls the working of the poet's Imagination too. Now we understand the significance of the expressions, 'Rasāveśa-vaiśadya'[3] — and 'Rasānuguṇaśabdārthacintā[4] — in the definitions of Pratibha given by Abhinavagupta and Mahima Bhaṭṭa respectively. For the very awakening of the poet's Imagination there must be an initial emotional thrill in his heart. The faggots must be lit

1 Experience of Rasa.

2 Ilumination of Rasa.

3 Clarity of vision resulting from the inspiration of Rasa.

4 Contemplation of the word and the meaning conforming to Rasa.

before the flame can shoot up. Again, the Imagination of a poet who is genuinely under the influence of Rasa can conceive only such fancies and images and order them only in such ways as are most in harmony with his predominant emotional mood. If through carelessness his fancy breaks loose and produces conceptions which bring a break in the Rasapratiti[1], he has to cancel them ruthlessly for the sake of achieving harmony. A poet has to be doubly watchful in the matter of Alaṃkāra for, Alaṃkāras more than anything else are the specific creatures of Imagination[2]. An Alaṃkāra has a place in poetry when it can be conceived by the poet as he is borne along the current of Rasa and does not put forth any extraneous effort for its development. An Alaṃkāra (ornament) justifies its name only when it is developed with care and in place.

Ānandavardhana again and again stresses this point. A poet's fancy may have the power to mint a hundred images; but he must use only those that are in harmony with the Rasa. Alas, then, as now, there were not wanting poets who snapped their fingers at Rasa and indulged their fancy to the utmost in heaping Alaṃkāra on Alaṃkāra.

What has been said just now must not of course be taken to mean that Ānandavardhana is averse to the full play of Imagination. All that he wants to stress is that Rasa should be its guiding star. Once this is admitted, he yields to none in appreciating the supreme importance of Imagination in poetry. Nor is he prone to judge the propriety of an Alaṃkāra by a cast-iron rule. He knows that there tumbles into the imagination of an inspired poet conception after conception, each of which leaves the reader gaping with wonder. The poet does not go seeking after them; they crowd at his door eager to get a nod from him[3]. In fact, it is on the supernormal excellence of a poet's Pratibhā, as revealed in his poetry, that his greatness depends.

---

1 Perception of Rasa.

2 That a specific activity of the Imagination is at the basis of every Alamkāra is fully recognized by our Ālamkārikas from Kuntaka onwards. (See S.K.De: *Varoktijivita*, Introduction, Sec. 7, where the matter is fully discussed.) As we have noted already, the fight over Svabhāvokti too ultimately revolves round this point. *I.H.Q., March, 1937.*

3 अलङ्कारान्तराणि हि निरूप्यमाणदुर्घटनान्यपि रससमाहितचेतसः प्रतिभानवतः कवेरहं पूर्विकया परापतन्ति। *Dhvanyāloka* (1928 *edn*). pp. 86-87

As Ānandavardhana has pointed out in his comment here, the world has indeed seen numberless poets of the most varied types; but it is some five or six like Kālidāsa that have been accorded the epithet 'mahākavi'. It is the exceptional quality of their Imagination that has won for them this rank.

At the outset of the present enquiry we observed the bias of Indian Poetics towards the reader's point of view. Nowhere else has the reader of poetry received such an exalted position. He is the Sahṛdaya — one with a kindred heart — in whom the outpouring of the poet's heart finds its goal and fulfillment. The poet and he are the two aspects of a single entity — the Sārasvata-tattva[1]. Hence the reader too needs Imagination to understand poetry and re-live it. Rājaśekhara calls it Bhāvayitri pratibhā (Responsive Imagination) distinguishing it from the Kārayitri pratibhā (Creative Imagination) of the poet. It is this which enables the reader to respond to and realize the poet's effort and conception[2]. There are critics who hold that the same person cannot be both a poet and a critic because he either lacks the power to compose poetry or cannot enjoy the poetry of another through jealousy or complete self-regard. It is also said that a poet cannot appreciate properly his own poetry either, but has to leave it to the enjoyment of the Rasika (one who has the capacity to enjoy Rasa),probably because he cannot rise above his personal concern in the poem and regard it objectively. But these views cannot stand much examination since they militate against the very conception of Sahṛdayatva. Poetry fails in its purpose if the same experience does not animate both the poet and the reader. It may be the misfortune of some poets not to be able to enjoy properly the work of another poet or even their own. But this is due to extra-poetic causes and does not concern us at present. What we are anxious to point out is the similarity that exists between the reader's appreciative activity and the poet's own creative activity. There is no

---

[1] *Cf.* सरस्वत्यास्तत्त्वं कविसहृदयाख्यं विजयते *Mangala-śloka of Dhvanyāloka Locana*

[2] भावकस्योपकुर्वाणा भावयित्री। सा हि कवेः श्रममभिप्रायं च भावयति। तथा खलु फलितः कवेर्व्यापारतरुः। (*Kāvyamimāṃsā*, p. 13).

doubt that there is some difference between the reader and the poet, since the former's Imagination is less active and less original than the latter's. While the poet's Imagination has to seek, select and build and so create poetry, the reader's has simply to re-experience what is given to it. But the latter is none the less a creative act. Unless the reader, by imaginative response, feels the very glow that thrilled the poet's heart, he cannot hope to re-live the experience that the poet once lived through and expressed in words. The appreciation of Poetry is not a cold intellectual apprehension. The reader has to feel the original inspiration in every fibre of his being.

Again, we must not forget the essentially suggestive nature of art. A poet can never hope to make explicit (Vācya) through words his glimpse of beauty. He can, at best, point in its direction; and the reader has to use his own eyes to visualize it. The enjoyment of poetry is no listless passivity. The reader has to meet the author at least half way. Abhinavagupta utters but the bare truth in remarking that the very life of Dhvani lies in the cooperation of the reader's Imagination with the poet's.

We can draw to a close now. There can be no apter conclusion to this enquiry than a quotation from the *Vakroktijivita* (p.129) indicating almost all the aspects of the subject — Sukṣmārthadarśana, apūrvārtha-nirmāṇa and kavisahṛdaya-pratibhā-sahakāra [i.e., intuition of the subtle aspects of things, creation of something new and the co-operation of the reader's imagination with the poet's].

> Linam vastuni yena sūkṣmasubhagam tattvam girākṛṣyate
> nirmātum prabhavenmanohoramidam vācaiva yo vā bahiḥ
> vande dvāvapi tāvaham kavivarau vandetarām tam punar
> yo vijñyataparisramóyamanayorbhāravatārakṣamaḥ

'He who with his words draws out the subtle and beautiful attributes hidden within things, he who can by his mere words incarnate them externally in a beautiful form, these two great poets I salute, and indeed I salute more the (connoisseur) who knows the labour of the above two and is a fit person to receive the burden unloaded by them.'

8

Use and Abuse of Alaṃkāra*

V. Raghavan

Poetry is not mere thought. 'While great poetry must necessarily embody it, very genuine poetry, at times, may do no more than give to the merest airy nothings a local habitation and a name.' 'Poetry does not reveal truth in logic but in light.' Mere thoughts and emotions are proper subjects for the science of psychology, etc. Facts, by themselves, are unattractive; sometimes reality appals us; but poets teach us as they charm.

True, as Leigh Hunt says, 'there are simplest truths often so beautiful and impressive that one of the greatest proofs of the poet's genius consists in leaving them to stand alone, illustrated by nothing but the light of their own tears or smiles, their own wonder, might or playfulness.' But, as he himself points out elsewhere, 'in poetry, feeling and imagination are necessary to the perception and presentation even of matters of fact.' The so-called figure of natural description, the Svabhāvokti, is a plain statement only in a comparative degree. Plain fact or feeling is always embellished in some manner and given some catching power. Even the natural description of a poet has its strikingness; Bāṇa says that Jāti[1] must be Agrāmya[2]. Bhāmaha also excludes ordinariness in expression in his description of poetry[3]. So poetry requires not only to be useful, but primarily attractive. All poetic expression involves some kind of expressional deviation of beauty[4], some out-of-the-way-ness. This expressional

---

* Adapted from *Some Concepts of Alaṃkāra Śāstra* and *Bhoja's, Śṛngāra Prakāśa*.

1 Natural description.

2 Free from vulgarity or insipidity.

3 अग्राम्यशब्दमर्थ्यं च सालङ्कार सदाश्रयम् ।
अलङ्कारवदग्राम्यम् अर्थ्यं न्याय्यमनाकुलम् ।

4 Cf. Bain: A figure of speech is a deviation from the plain and ordinary mode of speaking, for the sake of greater effect: it is an unusual form of speech.' *Rhetoric and Composition*, I.

deviation, this striking disposition of words and ideas, is Alaṃkāra; this constitutes the beautiful poetic form. It will be easier to dissociate love from its physical aspect than to keep the concept of poetry aloof from its form.

If we try to arrive at a clear definition of poetry with an objective differential, certainly the definition will revolve round the concept of Alaṃkāra, the word Alaṃkāra being taken here in the widest sense of that term in which Bhāmaha, Daṇḍin and Vāmana and Bhoja following them understood it. Alaṃkāra is the beautiful in poetry, the beautiful form[1]. Examining the field of poetic expression, Bhāmaha found Alaṃkāra omnipresent in it. When we reach the stage of Appayya Dikṣita, who has given as many as one hundred and twentyfive Alaṃkāras we see that the whole range of poetry is almost 'Vyāpta'[2] with Alaṃkāra in general, is 'Avinābhūta'[3] with Alaṃkāra. If Alaṃkāra is understood in this large sense as emphasizing the need for a beautiful form in poetry, it is not very improper for the subject of poetics to be called Alaṃkāra-śāstra.

Thus, Alaṃkāra, properly understood and properly employed, can hardly be a subject for wholesale condemnation. This is said not only in view of the large sense in which we have tried to explain it above. Taking the figures as such, the best definition we can give of them is that, in a great poet, they form the inevitable incarnations in which ideas embody themselves.

They should properly be compared to the Alaṃkāras of damsels which Bharata speaks of under Sāmānyābhinaya[4], Bhāva[4], Hāva[4] etc. and not to the Kaṭaka[5] and Keyūra[6].

Ānandavardhana says in Chapter II[7] that, though Alaṃkāras are only the Śarira, the outer body, they can be made the Śariri, the soul,

---

1 सौन्दर्यमलङ्कारः : Vamana; I. i. 2.

2 Pervaded by.

3 Inseparably connected.

4 Spontaneous expression and its modes in an emotional condition such as love.

5 Bracelet.

6 Armlet.

7 Of his *dhvanyāloka*. The writer, along with his Professor S. Kuppuswami Sastri, belongs to the school which takes Ānandavardhana as author of both parts of the text.

sometimes, i.e., when Alaṃkāras are not expressed but suggested; when simile, contrast, etc., are richly imbedded in an utterance and in the coming together of words in an expression, Alaṃkāras flash forth.

Abhinavagupta says here: As a matter of fact, Alaṃkāras are external ornaments on the body but can sometimes be like the Kuṃkuma[1] smeared for beauty on the body, when they are organic and structural. Far, far away is the hope to make this Alaṃkāra the very soul. But even this is possible in a way, says Ānandavardhana: Just as in the mere play of children there is some temporary greatness for the child which plays the role of the king, so also, when this Alaṃkāra is suggested it attains great beauty and partakes of the nature of the soul.

It must be noted here that Abhinavagupta compares the Suśliṣṭa Alaṃkāra[2] to Kuṃkumālaṃkaraṇa,[3] and raises it above the level of the altogether external jewel worn, the Kaṭaka. Bhoja realized the insufficiency of the comparison with Kaṭaka, etc., the external and detachable jewels. Alaṃkāra as ornament of a woman also, was understood by Bhoja in a large sense. Bhoja classified Alaṃkāras into those of Śabda[4], Bāhya[5], those of Artha[6], Ābhyantara[7] and those of both Śabda and Artha – Bāhayābhyantara[8]. The first, the most external, the verbal figure of Śabdālaṃkara, Bhoja compared to dressing, garlanding and wearing Kaṭaka, etc. The third, he compared to bath, treating the hair with fragrant smoke, smearing the body with Kuṃkuma, Candana[9], etc. Beginning from outside, these are more intimate with the body. The second, the purely Ābhyantara Alaṃkāras, the Arthālaṃkāras, Bhoja compared to cleaning the teeth,

---

1 Saffron.

3 Organic.

3 Adornment of smearing with saffron.

4 Word.

5 External.

6 Meaning.

7 Internal.

8 External-internal (combined).

9 Sandal-paste.

manicuring, dressing the hair, etc. These last are most intimate; nothing not forming part at all of the body is here superimposed.

Albeit the importance of form, one should not misunderstand rhetoric as poetry. It is possible to sacrifice poetry at the altar of figure. There is such a thing as Aucitya, appropriateness, harmony and proportion, which is the ultimate beauty in poetry. The final ground of reference for this Aucitya, the thing with reference to which we shall speak of other things as being appropriate, is the soul of poetry, Rasa. The body becomes a carcass when there is no soul there, when life is absent from it. Of what use are ornaments on a carcass?

Kṣemendra[1], the systematiser of Aucitya, says: 'Enough with Alaṃkāras; of what use are the Guṇas[2] if there is no life there? Ornaments are ornaments; excellences are excellences; but Aucitya is the life of the Rasa-ensouled Kāvya.'

What is this Aucitya? It is the clear statement of the proper place and function of Alaṃkāra, as of other elements.

Thus Alaṃkāras have their meaning only if they keep to their places. Just as a pearl-garland can beautify only a full bosom and otherwise cannot be a beautifying factor, only an Alaṃkāra appropriate to Artha and through it, to Rasa, can be of any beauty.

Kṣemendra proceeds to show how some poets have observed this rule of Aucitya of Alaṃkāra and how some have not. He points out the conceptual flaws in the latter, going against the main subject and sentiment. The Pratyudāharaṇas[3] are cases of abuses in so far as the authors of those verses have written those figures with an effort, merely because they desired to add figures. When the great poet is concentrating on Rasa, the sense of harmony and appropriateness attends on him, innate in him like instinct; there is hardly any room for impropriety. But when concentration is on figure, error creeps in. We shall consider two examples: the broken minister of the Nandas, stealing into the enemy's city over which he had once ruled like a king, looking like a serpent stilled by incantation, and consumed by his own inner fire, sees a dilapidated garden and

---

1 A writer on Poetics of the latter half of the 11th century.

2 Poetic qualities.

3 Counter illustrations.

describes it[1]. The plight of the garden resembles his own pitiable state and with great appropriateness in the conceiving of the similes, Viśākhadatta has drawn a mere description nearer to the context, harnessed it for Rasa and heightened the effect of the situation. On the contrary, we shall now cite a verse from the *Bhoja Campū*[2] where the poet has created a figure not only not in harmony with the main idea and the context but also so inappropriate as to make, as Kṣemendra says, the hearts of the Sahṛdayas shrink.

There is Hetu-Utprekṣā[3] here; the poet imagines that Brahmā presented himself before the Ādikavi[4], as if jealous of the appearance of [his spouse] Vāṇi [speech or poesy] in another person. As a matter of fact, it is to bless and give Vālmiki his favour to sing the whole *Rāmāyaṇa* that the god descended.

One can make Alamkara render the help its name means if one introduces it in such a manner that it will be conducive to the realization of the chief object, namely Bhāva and Rasa; that is, Alaṃkāra must be Rasabhāva-para[5]. That which is adorned by an Alaṃkāra is the Rasa. Even as the ordinary ornament, the jewels, putting them on or laying them down, suggest to us the mental state of the person, so also does figure suggest the Bhāva. Thus, whatever, remaining in a functionary place, aids to embellish and add to the main theme's beauty is Alaṃkāra. Rasa also can thus be employed as a decorative, as an Alaṃkāra, to adorn a Vastu [idea] or Rasa.

Raymond[6] expresses a similar opinon on Alaṃkāra; 'The one truth underlying all the rules laid down for the employment of figures

---

1 विपर्यस्तं सौधं कुलमिव महारम्भरचनं
सरः शुष्कं साधोर्हृदयमिव नाशेन सुहृदाम् ।
फलहीनना वृक्षा विगुणनृपयोगादिव नयाः
तृणच्छन्ना भूमिर्मतिरिव कुनीतैरविदुषः । Mudrārākṣasa, VI. 11.

2 वाणीविलासमपरत्र कृतोपलंभम् अंभोजभूरसहमान इवाविरासीत् ।

3 A figure, of speech, Poetic conceit, in which a cause is fancied.

4 The first poet, Vālmiki.

5 Devoted to or subserving Rasa and Bhāva.

6 *Poetry as a Representative Art.*

is that nothing is gained by any use of those which do not add to the effect of the thought to which they give expression. Language is to express our thought to others, and in ordinary conversation we use both plain and figurative language, but when a man wants to give another the description of a scene he has seen, he does not catalogue one and all of the details of that sight, but brings only his own idea of the landscape by adding to such of the details as have struck him many more ideas and emotions that have been arounsed in him.' Thus he transports his mental image to the hearer and if the representation is comparatively plain, we have Svabhāvokti[1]. 'On the other hand, if he realises that it is hard for the hearer to understand him fully, he gains his end by repeating the statement, or by adding illustrative images to the mere enumeration of facts.'

Compare Rudraṭa:

Samyak Pratipādayitum Svarūpato vastu taṭsamānamiti
vastvantaramabhidadhyāt vaktā yasminstadaupamyam[2]

'Thus the poet puts extra force into his language and in order to do so, inasmuch as the force of language consists in its representative character, he will augment the representation by multiplying his comparisons: his language becomes figurative.

From the verse of Rudraṭa quoted above, we see that a complex situation or an anxiety for clearer or more effective expression necessitates figures. Similarly a thought that is too simple, too ordinary or too small to impress or get admiration by itself, needs figurative embellishment. We shall consider this view of Ānandavardhana with his rules for the employment of these figures in such secondary and ordinary moods and thought. Even as he grants high flights in supreme moments, he grants even the bare Śabdacitra[3] ample provision in Rasābhāsa[4]. Heroic deeds, unselfish love,

1 Natural description — a figure of speech.

2 To communicate the nature of an idea most effectively, if the poet should mention another as being similar to it, that is simile.

3 Figures of sound — alliteration, etc.

4 A semblance or improper manifestation of Rasa.

sacrifice — things great in themselves — appeal to us even when directly expressed with minimum figure. But ordinary things must have purple patches.

All these facts about decoration by figure in poetry are realized by Ānandavardhana who has formulated rules for the proper employment of Alaṃkāra. Western writers also have laid similar conditions regarding ornament. Pater says: 'And above all, there will be no uncharacteristic or tarnished or vulgar decoration, permissible ornament being for the most part structural or necessary.' He continues: 'The artist, says Schiller, may be known by rather what he omits and, in literature too, the true artist may be best recognized by his tact of omission. For, to the grave reader, words too are grave; and the ornamental word, the figure, the accessory form or colour or reference is rarely content to die to thought precisely at the right moment, but will inevitably be stirring a long "brain-wave" behind it of perhaps quite alien associations.' 'As the very word ornament indicates what is in itself non-essential so the "one beauty" of all literary style is of its very essence and independent of all removable decoration; that it may exist in its fullest lustre in a composition utterly unadorned, with hardly a single suggestion of visibly beautiful things,' 'The ornaments are "diversions" — a narcotic spell on the pedestrian intelligence. We cannot attend to that figure — that flower there — just then — surplusage! For, in truth, all art consists in the removal of surplusage.'

Such strictures had to be passed by Ānandavardhana also; for, when he was thinking out the essence of poetry, Sanskrit poetry had deteriorated into an artificial stage. A blind tribe, Gaḍḍarikā-pravāha[1], was following a beaten path and was hardly proof to errors of taste. Not poetry, but the imitation thereof, was being assiduously produced. To guide such poets not gifted with Śakti[2] enough to posses an innate sense of Aucitya, Ānandavardhana lays down his rules for the employment of Alaṃkāra. As has already been pointed out, Alaṃkāra is subordinated to Rasa; it has to aid the realization of Rasa. It shall suit the Bhāva and be such as come to the poet along with the tide of the Rasa. It shall not monopolise the poet's

---

1 Sheep,gregarious.

2 Poetic genius or talent.

energy nor shall it be so prominent or continued as to monopolise the reader's mind. Says Ānandavardhana:

i] Alaṃkāra shall be intended to suggest Rasa.
ii] It shall be born along with the poet's delineation of Rasa.
iii] It shall be naturally and easily introducible.
iv] The poet shall not stop to take a fresh and extra effort to effect it.

Such a figure is allowed as proper in Dhvani[1]. This is the permissible structural figure that Pater speaks of. Such Alaṃkāra is born almost of itself. Such is the poet's genius that when the figure is actually found there, it is a wonder *Āścaryabhūta*, as Ānandavardhana says. This Alaṃkāra properly functions to heighten Rasa.

Though a perusal of an Alaṃkāra text-book gives the impression that Alaṃkāras are artificial, elaborate and intellectual exercises requiring great effort in turning them out precisely, things that must rather be avoided than handled with all their 'chhidras'[2], they are not really so difficult of effecting for a master poet. With him, as emotion increases, expression swells and figures foam forth.

We have many instances in the *Rāmāyaṇa* where we clearly see this connection between emotion and figure, though not as a rule. There is at least a strong tendency to wax figurative in forceful situations. The description of lamenting Ayodhyā on Bharata's return from the forest and Sitā's condemnation of Rāvaṇa on seeing him out of his guise are two of the striking examples. There is, further, a tendency in the *Rāmāyaṇa* to employ figures profusely in descriptions. The opening canto of the Sundarakāṇḍa contains a figure in almost every verse, surcharged as the canto is with Adbhutta-rasa[3].

But there are also places in the epic of high strung emotion where figures are not employed at all and the sublimity or pathos of the situation (e.g. Rāma weeping on the loss of Sitā in the closing cantos of the *Āraṇyakāṇḍa*) is left to itself to appeal to us with its own grandeur and beauty.

---

1 The superior form of poetry based on suggestion.

2 Loopholes.

3 The marvellous sentiment.

In Kālidāsa, we have many instances of figures rushing to the poet's pen in moments of overflowing Rasa. Every line is a figure in Purūravas's description of Urvaśi who has captivated his heart. And in the *Mudrārākṣasa* we have a similar situation with abundant figures, when, in the glee of his success, Cāṇakya exclaims as he hears that Rākṣasa has come. But to write such figures, the poet must be lost in Rasa and must have infinite Pratibhā[1]. Those who do not naturally get these figures in such an appropriate manner can employ figures effectively, if they do so with discrimination, — Samikṣā.

What is this Samikṣā[2]? Ānandavardhana formulates it into the following principles:

(i) Alaṃkāras must be ancillary, — Aṅgabhūta.
(ii) They must never become main, — Pradhāna or Aṅgin.
(iii) The main theme shall always be kept in view and figures, in consequence, must be taken and thrown away in accordance with the requirements of the main idea.
(iv) They must not be too much elaborated or overworked.
(v) Even if they are worked out, a good poet must take care to give them, on the whole, the position of Aṅga[3] only.

To conclude, poetry is neither pure emotion and thought nor mere manner. A beautiful idea must appropriately incarnate itself in a beautiful expression. This defines Alaṃkāra and its place and function. The function of Alaṃkāra is to heighten the effect; it is to aid the poet to say something more pointedly. Whether the poet exalts or does the opposite, Alaṃkāra is to help him. As such, these Alaṃkāras should flow out of Rasa. Even as emotion is depicted, these must come off, without the poet consciously striving after them. They must be irremovable, structural, organic, Rasākṣipta[4] and Apṛthag-yatna-nirvarttya[5].

Figures are thus legitimate, though a proper use of them is a gift which only the greater among the poets are endowed with. Be it a

---

1 Poetic genius.

2 Discrimination.

3 An ancillary.

4 Brought forth by Rasa.

5 Not to be executed by a separate effort.

Śabdālaṃkara or an Arthālāṃkāra, be it a sound-effect or a striking turn of the idea, it is not 'Bahiranga'[1] for Rasa, so long as it is useful for Rasa. Effective expression, the embodiment of the poet's idea, is Alaṃkāra. It is not as if it were in some separate place, like jewels in a box, to be taken and added.

The purposiveness of Alaṃkāra is inevitable like the purposiveness of poetry. But this does not mean that one should judge Alaṃkāra and poetry from a purely utilitarian point of view. There is simply beautiful poetry, which is nothing but the poet's desire to express taken shape. 'These very decorations' carry the emotional motive of the poet which says "I find joy in my creations; it is good." 'When in some pure moments of ecstasy we realize this in the world around us, we see the world not as merely existing but as decorated in its forms, sounds, colours and lines, we feel in our hearts that there is one who through all things proclaims "I have joy in my creation."[2] Nature is the creation of God's Līlā[3], Poetry, of the poet's Līlā.

---

1 External.

2 Tagore, *The Creative Ideal.*

3 Play.

9

Aucitya in Sanskrit Poetics*

V. Raghavan

One of the noteworthy points in the Sanskrit systems of literary criticism is that, in an inquiry into a comprehensive philosophy of the literary art, they do not separate poetry and drama, nor prose and verse. Bharata, in his *Nāṭya Śāstra*, defines drama as imitation of the three worlds or representation of the actions of men of various nature. *Nāṭya Śāstra* I.107, 113, 120, etc. Consequently Bharata sets forth a system of ideas of *Loka Dharmi* 'the way of the world,' which stands for the realistic elements in Bharata's Stage[1]. In the concept of *Prakṛti*, Bharata studies the various kinds of human nature. In the concept of Pravṛti he studies the provincial, racial and national characteristics in dressing and other activities. He elaborately deals with dress and make-up, which he says, must be appropriate to the mood and sentiment. He devotes separate sections to correct speaking in the drama according to the emotions (XIX), to the musical notes and tunes appropriate to the varying sentiments and moods (XXIX,1-4). Bharata analyses the text of the drama and points out how the verbal qualities of sweetness, harshness, etc., and the flights of fancies expressed in the form of figures of speech have to be appropriate to the mood or sentiment portrayed (XVII, 108-123). At the end of each topic, Bharata thus points out what suits what. In judging drama, therefore, the ground of reference for success of the art is the world. Bharata emphasizes that one has to know the infinite variety of human nature — *Prakṛti* and *Śila*, in which is *Nāṭya* or drama based.

Drama is the representation of moods, *Bhāva-anukirtana*. Out of these moods flow everything — actions, character, dress, nature of one's speech, etc. It is to this factor of *Rasa* which is at the root of

---

* Adapted from *Some Concepts of Alaṃkara Śastra* and Bhoja's *Śṛingāra Prakāśa*

1 See author's *Loka Dharmi*, Journal of Oriental Research, Madras VIII. 1, 1934. pp. 57-74.

all the other things that these latter have again to be referred for finding out whether in representing them, there is appropriateness. Things cannot be estimated by themselves, in isolation, and labelled good or bad, appealing or otherwise. Excellence (*Guṇa*) or Defect (*Doṣa*) does not inherently pertain to anything, eternally, but anything, according to the situation where it occurs, is either suitable or not; and in this suitability or otherwise lies Excellence or Defect. Improper placing, says Bharata, like placing a necklace at the foot and an anklet round the neck, can only produce laughter. It is a serious breach of propriety for a writer to describe a forlorn lady suffering from separation from her lord as having her body fully decked with jewels. In the realm of artistic expression the same rule holds good. A poet commits the greatest crime against *Rasa* if he introduces heavy verbal ornamentation in places where *Rasa* has to be effectively portrayed and where the absence of any figure is itself the perfection of art. The proper placing of things in such a manner as to suit *Rasa* and the avoiding of things not suitable to it form the essence of artistic expression. This is propriety, *Aucitya*. Thus the first work in the history of Sanskrit Poetics contains implicitly as much of this theory of poetry, Aucitya, as of the other theory of poetry, *Rasa*, explicitly, even though emphasis on both these — *Aucitya* and *Rasa* — was again systematically laid only in the ninth, tenth and eleventh centuries.

Aucitya is harmony and in one aspect it is proportion between the whole and the parts, between the chief and the subsidiary. This perfection is all the morals and beauty in art. At the final stage of its formulation as a theory explaining the secret of poetic appeal, *Aucitya* is stated to be the *Jivita*, life-breath, of poetry. This *Aucitya*, proportion and harmony on one side and appropriateness and adaptation on the other, cannot be understood by itself but presupposes that to which all other things are harmonious and appropriate, viz, *Rasa*, the 'soul'of poetry.

Poet Māgha, in his epic-poem *Śiśupālavadha* clarifies this law of *Aucitya* with an illustration from the science of polity. The King has to achieve his purpose with an eye on expediency, time and circumstance being the deciding factors of his policy. There is no inherent good in either Power or Forbearance by themselves but all the goodness of a policy consists in its effectiveness, in using that which is suited to the time. Thus adaptation is the only policy good for the king. The case is similar to that of a poet with whom the main concern is *Rasa* and *Bhāva* and an understanding of their subtle nature. In portraying his characters and their actions, it will not do if the poet sticks to one quality throughout, say *Prasāda* or *Ojas*. When the forceful sentiments of Heroism (*Vīra*), Wonder (*Adbhuta*) and The Terrible (*Raudra*) *Rasa*s appear, he has to adopt the quality *Ojas* to suit the vigour, energy and blaze (*Dīpti*) of those *Rasa*s and when the key of emotion is lowered and quiet emotional effects have to be produced, the requisite quality for the poet is *Prasāda*. This is the *Aucitya* of *Guṇa*.

It is again in respect of *Guṇas*, the qualities of style, that we have the next glimpse of the idea of *Aucitya* in certain parts of the treatises of Bhāmaha and Daṇḍin. In one way, the greatest *Guṇa* or Excellence of poetry is *Aucitya* and it comprehends all other *Guṇas*; and the greatest *Doṣa* or Flaw comprehending other flaws, is its absence, *Anaucitya*. Thus when the *Rīti*, Style, is not suited to the *Rasa*, there is *Rīti-anaucitya*, the flaw called *Arītmat*. The *Gauḍī* style which may not suit *Śṛṅgāra*, love, cannot be condemned altogether as eternally unsuited to all poetry. It can effectively suggest the forceful sentiments of *Vīra*, *Adbhuta*, and *Raudra* and in their case, the *Vaidarbhī* style suited to *Śṛṅgāra* may be inappropriate, *Anucita*. There may be harsh sounds and heavy, long and swollen utterances in a highly worked-up emotion like *Raudra*, the Terrible; the harsh sounds which suggest this *Rasa* must be avoided in Śṛṅgāra *Rasa* which is suggested by sweet assonances and delicate sound effects. Therefore it is that the flaws, *Doṣas*, given as such in separate sections by Bhāmaha and Daṇḍin, are, to use a word which came into currency only after Ānandavardhana, *Anitya*, contingent. That is, in certain circumstances *Doṣas* cease to be so; there are no fixed *Guṇas* or *Doṣas*; what is *Guṇa* in one case is *Doṣa* in another and vice versa.

The principle behind these observations is *Aucitya*, adaptation. Again, in chapter IV, the same writer, Bhāmaha speaks of such flaws in poetry as *loka-virodha*, going against factors of the world and nature which is a result of the non-observance of the *Aucitya* of *Prakṛti*, etc. In this context, he also points out that redundance, *Punarukti*, which is generally a flaw in expression, turns out to be an effective way of expression in fear, sorrow, jealousy, joy and wonder.

It is in the same section on *Doṣas* that the principle of *Aucitya* is implied in Daṇḍin's work also (Ch. IV). Each and every *Doṣa* is given by Daṇḍin with a qualification that in certain circumstances, it ceases to be *Doṣa* and turns out to be a *Guṇa*. Thus *Apārtha*, the meaningless, generally a flaw, is the most proper means of successfully portraying a madman's raving, a child's sweet prattle or the speech of a sick man. Similar is the flaw *Viruddhārtha* or *Vyartha*, the contradictory. *Punarukta*, redundance, is no flaw but is an effective way of expressing compassion or any stress of emotion which needs repetition. *Samśaya* or the use of doubtful or ambiguous words, may generally be a flaw but when such words are wilfully used, as is often needed in the world, they are perfect *Guṇas*.

Bhoja developed the same idea by constituting under the head *Guṇa* a special class called the *Vaiśeṣika Guṇas*, comprising those flaws, such as the above noticed ones, which become excellences sometimes. As a matter of fact, all *Guṇas* and *Doṣas* are *Vaiśeṣika*. 'It all depends,' says the discerning critic in literature, as one says in this complex world. If this analysis of *Doṣas* and *Guṇas* means or impels anything, it is the doctrine of *Aucitya* as the only ruling principle holding good in the realm of poetry for ever. It is only a clearer statement of what Daṇḍin has said that we have in Ānandavardhana and Abhinavagupta, who say that *Doṣa* or Flaw is contingent and that there is no separate Excellence of Flaw (*Dhvanyāloka* II. 12; III. 3-4).

In the first half of the 8th century, King Yaśovarman of Kanauj mentioned by name for the first time, so far as our present knowledge goes, the concept of *Aucitya* in a verse in the prologue to his drama *Rāmābhyudaya*. Yaśovarman here refers to a number of good features which a drama should have. First among them are Aucitya of expression, i.e., speech written according to the nature and level or rank of the characters, and *Aucitya* of *Rasa*, i.e., delineation of characters in their proper moods with an eye to developing the *Rasa* in the proper place. These two comprise the external and internal *Aucitya* or *Aucitya* of expression and *Aucitya* of the content, i.e., the *Rasa*.

There are these large epic poems (*Mahākāvyas*) whose component parts, like descriptions of cities, mountains, seasons, sunrise, sunset, etc., came to be overdone by the later poets, losing sight of the needs of the story. This Lollaṭa, a commentator on Bharata, strongly criticised, in three verses of his, drawing attention to an aspect of *Aucitya*, viz;, proportion and strict relevancy of every detail. Ornaments hide beauty if they are not structural or organic; similarly,'descriptions' have logically to emerge out of the story and the complex course of its *Rasa* as necessity. Descriptive cantos should not stand out like outhouses and isolated places for the poet's mind to indulge at length in excess. This is true of the drama as much as of the epic poem. In a drama, the sub-plots, the *Patākā* and the *Prakari*, and the *Sandhyaṅgas*, the ideas or striking points in the theme of the play, should not be considered as having any virtue by themselves but should be seen to their relevance to *Rasa*.

From the point of view of the perfect agreement between the parts and the chief element of *Rasa*, *Aucitya* can also be rendered in English as 'Sympathy', which as a word in art-criticism means 'mutual conformity of parts'.

The work of Rudraṭa is very important in the history of Poetics, as it stands at a transitional point when the older modes of evaluation were giving place to the new criticism of *Rasa* and *Dhvani*; and although still bearing the older name of *Kāvya-alaṃkāra* and dealing at length with figures, it foreshadows the later developments and prepares the way for Ānandavardhana. On the present subject Rudraṭa speaks of many of the ideas of *Aucitya* which receive more pointed treatment in the *Dhvānyaloka*. In respect of figures (*Alaṃkāras*), Rudraṭa realises the importance of *Rasa* to suit which *Alaṃkāra*s exist. If otherwise, these latter have little meaning. The idea that *Rasa* and *Rasa-aucitya* control *Alaṃkāra* is stated by Rudraṭa who, apart from the dramatist Yaśovarman noticed above, is the first writer on Poetics to mention the word *Aucitya*. After dealing with some figures of soul, Rudraṭa says that these figures must be introduced after bestowing due thought on propriety, *Aucitya*, with reference to the main theme. They have to be now cast away and now taken up and must be sparsely used with much advantage. They must not be thickly overlaid upon the theme through the whole length of it. (II.32). This is *Aucitya* of *Alaṃkāra* which Ānandavardhana elaborates in Ch II of his work.

The word *Aucitya* again occurs at the end of the next chapter in Rudraṭa's work where too Rudraṭa points out the danger of sustained rhymes and other sound effects, adding that they must be approached only by him who knows *Aucitya*. Rudraṭa speaks of the adaptation aspect of *Aucitya* also, implicitly like Daṇḍin, while dealing with *Doṣas*, which, in certain cases, become *Guṇas*, (VI.8; 29-30). Rudraṭa sums up that almost all kinds of Flaws become Excellences when occasion needs the imitation (*Anukaraṇa*) of those flaws. That is, the poet and the dramatist have to depict an infinite variety of men and nature in diverse circumstances. When a mad man has to be represented, his nonsense has to be 'imitated'and it is itself 'sense' for the artist here.

We may draw attention here to what the American critic J.E. Spingarn says as if explaining the principle of *Aucitya* by which *Doṣas* become *Guṇas* as a result of circumstances like 'imitation'. Spingarn says, in his essay on the Seven Arts and the Seven Confusions, that in poetry and drama Flaw and Excellence are not absolute but always relative. He remarks: 'It is inconceivable that a modern thinker should still adhere to the abstract tests of good expression, when it is obvious that we can only tell whether it is good or bad when we see it in its natural context. Is any word artistically bad in itself? Is not "ain't" an excellent expression when placed in the mouth of an illiterate character in a play or story?' In Rudraṭa's words, Spingarn says that a *Grāmya* (colloquial) word becomes most appropriate in a case of *Anukaraṇa* — 'imitation'. Therefore in expression, in the world of thought, in the realm action and feeling, and in the region of ideas, that which is proper in the context, that which is useful to the Rasa, and that which has mutual harmony with the other parts, is the best and most beautiful.

In chapter XI, Rudraṭa again speaks of flaws of thought and emotion, where under the flaw '*Grāmya*' he mentions *Anaucitya* or inappropriateness in doings, in port, in dress and in speech with reference to country, family, caste, culture, wealth, age and position, All these *Doṣas* again are shown to become *Guṇas* (verses 18-23). We can illustrate this principle of *Aucitya* everywhere. Taking, for example, use of a Simile, *Nyūnopamā* or comparing with an inferior object and *Adhikopamā* or comparing with a superior object are ordinarily flaws of Simile, but these two are the very secret of success when a poet wants to satirize a person.

The idea of *Aucitya*, as well as the word, occurs in the *Dhvanyāloka* in an explicit manner, besides being implied in many places. Kṣemendra, who later expounded *Aucitya* in a systematic manner as the 'life' of poetry, took his inspiration from Ānandavardhana.

Ānandavardhana lays down that the 'soul' of poetry is *Rasa* or *Rasa-dhvani*. That *Dhvani* is the only artistic process by which *Rasa*, the 'soul', is presented by the poet and is got at by the sensitive reader or spectator (*Sahṛdaya*) and that everywhere things appeal most by being deftly concealed and suggested by suppression in a fabric of symbolism are the grounds on which Ānandavardhana formulates Dhvani as the 'soul'of poetry. That really *Rasa* or *Rasa-dhvani* is the 'soul',he expressly says even in the first chapter of his work. The most essential thing in *Rasa* is *Aucitya*. That ideas and figures or the artistic expression couched in figure and style are only the outer garment of *Rasa*, that they are subordinate and serviceable to *Rasa* and that they have meaning only as such, is the way in which Ānanadavardhana speaks of the *Aucitya* of theme (*Vastu*) and figure (*Alaṃkara*) in relation to *Rasa*. Figure by itself has no virtue. It has to be relevant, helpful to develop *Rasa* and never an overgrowth. The term *Alaṃkāra* or embellishment itself has meaning only then. The *Aucitya* of figures could be secured by observing the principles for their proper employment and the principles enunciated by Ānanda-vardhana have been explained in the study on the use and abuse of *Alaṃkāra*.

Similarly Ānandavardhana relates *Guṇa* (quality) to *Rasa* to which it belongs and explains the *Aucitya* of Guṇa. The quality of sweetness is inherent in *Śṛṅgāra* (love), *Vipralambha* (love in separation) and *Karuṇa* (pathos), whereas *Raudra* (the terrible) is attended by the quality of *Dipti*, a blazing up of the heart. Accordingly words and collocation used in the two different cases must be such as to agree with the mood and the atmosphere of the *Guṇa* and its *Rasa* or such as to suggest the *Guṇa* and the *Rasa*. Thus sweet sound effects, the soft letters with nasal conjunct consonants, suggest the more tender and sweet emotional moods whereas harsh combinations which jar in the above instances instil vigour and become very appropriate to or highly suggestive of the forceful *Rasa* of *Raudra*. The proper use of letters according to *Rasa*s is the *Aucitya* of Varṇa; Ānandavardhana will say that there is *Varṇa-dhvani* or the suggestiveness of letters and sounds in these instances. Collocation suggestive of *Rasa* or appropriate to *Rasa* is a case of *Aucitya* of *Sanghaṭanā*. Wherever there is suggestiveness of *Rasa* in the expression, be it the element of sound and letter, separate words, collocation, portions of the theme (*Prakaraṇa*) or even the work as a whole (*Prabandha*), there we have the *Aucitya* of those elements to the main thing, the *Rasa*. This is the relation between *Dhvani* and *Aucitya*.

Ānandavardhana's treatment of *Prabandha-dhvani*, dealing with the very substance of a poem or drama, and its suggestion of an overall meaning and significance is important. In respect of this the principles of *Aucitya* are: The story has to be built up, as the expression of a *Rasa*. If a story already available is handled, changes suitable to the *Rasa* must be made wherever the old story is not helpful to bring out the *Rasa*. If there are too many incidents, only those that are most expressive of the emotion must be chosen; there is no point in having too many illustrative incidents. Says Ānanda-vardhana: The Aṅgas or subsidiary themes and accessory emotional interests have to be developed only up to the extent proper to them and to their Aṅgin, i.e. the chief theme and its *Rasa*. Thus the major and minor episodes, the *Patākās* and *Prakaris*, in drama, or the 'descriptions'in a *Mahākāvya* have to obescrve the rule of *Aucitya* or proportional harmony. They must not make the reader forget the main thread and side-track him into grounds foreign in purpose to the main theme.

Lastly Ānandavardhana deals with the most intimate forms of Aucitya, viz., those relating to *Rasa* and those elements and conditions that evoke it, *Vibhāva*, *Anubhāva* and *Sañcāri-bhāva*. The *Aucitya* of character, the human substratum of the emotions, is part of these considerations of *Rasa*-aucitya. *Aucitya* is very often met with in this section in the third chapter of the *Dhvanyānloka*. It is in this section that Anandavardhana formulates that memorable verse which forms that greatest pronouncement on the concept of *Aucitya* and its place in poetry. He says here "Nothing hinders *Rasa* as *Anaucitya* or impropriety. *Aucitya* or propriety is the greatest secret of *Rasa*.

Ānandavardhana then goes to other kinds of *Aucitya* and points out how, not only the working out of a plot, not only the expression of an idea in figure, but even the words and the synonyms, the case, inflection, voice, etc., have to be suggestive of *Rasa*. That is, a poet should explore all the possibilities that his poor medium called language can afford. If a jingle can aid him, he seizes it; if a use in the passive voice is more effective than one in the active, he prefers it; if *Ātmanepada* or one form of a verb rather than the other suggests more, that he exploits. Thus every bit of the medium called language from sound, word, position of a word in a sentence, etc., has to be thoroughly exploited and capital use made out of it by the poet. There is the *Aucitya* of *Pada*, of a word, of a name or synonym. This is the *Pada-dhvani* of Ānandavardhana, dealt with in the beginning of Ch. III. The 'suggestive word'or the'proper word'of Ānandavardhana and Kṣemendra is like the 'inevitable word' or the 'strong word' mentioned by some English writers. Of *Aucitya* of *Vṛtti* and *Riti* also, Ānandhavardhana speaks in Ch.III which is devoted to the exploration of all possible suggestive means in the medium of language, the *Vyañjaka*.

Aucitya regarding *Rasa* itself, how the main *Rasa* has to be delineated, how the subsidiary *Rasas* are to be made to contribute to the main, which *Rasa*s are mutually compatible and which incompatible, how a *Rasa* like *Śṛṅgara* must not be so over-developed as to cloy, or *Karuṇa* which, when again and again developed, makes the heart 'fade', these are dealt with by Ānandavardhana in Ch. III. In this respect also, the pitfalls which may be called *Rasa-doṣas*, are already mentioned to some extent in Rudraṭa, who gives a *Doṣa* called *Virasa* which is the introduction or the flowing in of an irrelevant or contradictory sentiment into the current of the main *Rasa*, as also the fault of over-development of even the proper *Rasa*, Ānandavardhana's *Atidipti*.

Ānandavardhana puts together all these ideas relating to the handling of the *Rasas* and gives a systematic exposition of them. (III. 1719). Among the principles he enunciates here, the additional ones are the abrupt break in the continuity of the main *Rasa* (*akāṇḍa-vicchitti*), the abrupt introduction of a *Rasa* and the inappropriate atmosphere or tempo. The last-mentioned as the *Anaucitya* of *Vṛtti* is the error in respect of thought in the development of character and in the portrayal of actions and incidents and also of the general texture of the verbal expression. A mellow temper cannot suit a boisterous scene of conflict in *Vira* or *Raudra*; tumult and chaos go ill with the sweetness and quiet pleasantness of love or the tenderness and delicacy of *Vipralambha* and *Karuṇa*. Thus Ānandavardhana has shown how, in his own phraseology, *Aucitya* is the greatest secret of Rasa — *parā upaniṣat*; how in the fashioning of every part of the expression which is the body or the symbolic vehicle of *Rasa* or 'the empirical technique' as Abercrombie would call it, the only ruling principle of the poet is an all-round, all-comprehensive *Aucitya*, with reference to which alone, the choice of words, cases, meters, collocation, style and its qualities, figures, in fact every means of suggestion from the trifling jingle to the greatest becomes intelligible.

Rājaśekhara, author of *Kāvya-mimāṃsā*, speaks of *Aucitya* under poetic culture and learning and opines that all poetic culture is only the discrimination of the proper and the improper, *Ucita* and *Anucita*.

There is also an oft-quoted Sanskrit verse which gives this same idea, regarding the larger art of man's behavior in the world:'One is deaf even though he hears, blind even when he sees and dull despite having known the things; he is really a man who is wise with reference to the place, the time and the purpose on hand.' Rājaśekhara's wife, Avantisundari, also lays great emphasis on *Aucitya*; for she says that *Pāka*, ripeness or maturity of poetic power, is the securing of expression — ideas, words, conceptions, fancies, etc., — which is proper and appropriate to *Rasa*. Rājaśekhara says again at the end of the available portion of his work: 'The careful poet who has his eye on *Aucitya* employs even the so-called flaws and makes them excellences, whereas the careless one abuses even the excellences and spoils his expression by the absence of the sense of *Aucitya*.'

The place of Abhinavagupta in the further clarification and consolidation of ideas of *Aucitya* is important. As the author of the *Locana*, commentary on the work of Ānandavardhana, he lucidly expounds and elaborates the ideas of Ānandavardhana; on the other side, Abhinavagupta is the teacher in Poetics of Kṣememndra who is the author of the systematic tract of *Aucitya*. It is clear from Ānandavardhana's treatment of *Aucitya* in Ch. III, that *Aucitya* naturally emerges out of the doctrines of *Rasa* and *Dhvani* and that the three cannot be separated. Abhinavagupata takes his stand on this triple aspect of the 'life' of poetry — *Rasa* first, then *Dhvani* and then *Aucitya*. *Aucitya* presupposes something to which a thing is '*ucita*,' and that to which everything else is finally to be estimated as '*ucita*' is *Rasa*, the 'soul'of poetry.

On *Alaṃkārāucitya* about which Ānandavardhana speaks so much in Ch.II, *Abhinavagupta* says that the greatest *Aucitya* of *Alaṃkāra* is that the term has any meaning at all only when there is the 'Alaṃkārya', the thing to be adorned, namely the'soul'. Otherwise, it is like decorating the dead body. Decoration of a living body also is *Anaucitya* in certain cases; ornaments on the body of a recluse who has renounced life appear ridiculous — *anucita*. Thus figures of speech without *Rasa* and figures of speech in places which do not need them are bad.

The idea of *Aucitya*, like that of *Vakrokti*, was current as a very frequently used term in the circles of Kashmirian critics for a long time. *Vakrokti* rose out of *Alaṃkāra*, *Aucitya* in the wake of *Rasa* and *Dhvani*. *Aucitya* must have become more current after Ānandavardhana who has spoken of it so much and who has said that its presence and absence makes and unmake *Rasa* and poetry. It was so much in use that, by the time of Abhinavagupta, it must have been heading towards systematization, even as the concept of *Vakrokti* which, as old as Bhāmaha, was given so much life in the critical circles that it enlarged itself and through Kuntaka built itself into a whole theory. *Aucitya* also had assumed proportions and was in search of a writer for systematization. The critics were speaking of *Aucitya* as the essence of poetry very often, more often than *Rasa* even. Says Abhinavagupta in two places criticizing these critics: 'One cannot be indiscreetly using the word *Aucitya* by itself; *Aucitya* is un-understandable without something else to which things are *'ucita'* — appropriate. *Aucitya* is a relation and that to which things are or should be in that relation must first be grasped. That is *Rasa*, nothing less and nothing else.' Abhinavagupta then proves first that there is no meaning in *Aucitya* without *Rasa*. He proves that *Aucitya* presupposes *Rasa*, and *Dhvani* also. These observations of Abhinavagupta clearly show that critics there were who were speaking of *Aucitya* as the only thing enough to explain poetry, which according to them was beautiful words and ideas set in perfect harmony-*Aucitya*. These critics had omitted the word *Rasa* from their vocabulary and dispensed with *Dhvani*. Abinavagupta criticizes these poor critics who do not understand the implication of what they say.

Abhinavagupta thus takes his stand on the tripod of *Rasa*, *Dhvani* and *Aucitya*. If an *Alaṃkāra* is said to suit, to be *'ucita'to* a *Bhāva*, (feeling), it means that the *Alaṃkara* effectively suggests that *Bhāva;* if there is said to be *Guṇaucitya,* it means the *Rasa* there is suggested by the *Guṇa*. A word, a gender, a mere exclamation — these are said to be *'ucita',* and how? The test of Aucitya, its proof, is the suggestion of *Rasa*.

Another idea which Abhinavagupta points out is that the breach of *Aucitya* resulted in *'Ābhāsatā'*. A *Kāvya* which does not have *aucitya* is *Kāvyābhāsā,* not poetry but the semblance of poetry. Improper *Alaṃkāra* is *Alaṃkārabhāsā*. If there is *Aucitya* we have *Rasa* and sentiment; if there is *Anaucitya,* due to absence of *Prakiṛy-aucitya*, etc., we have *Rasābhāsa* and sentimentality.

Kuntaka was a younger contemporary of Abhinavagupta or wrote immediately after him. The word denoting the essence of poetry at that time seems to have been *Jivita* meaning 'life'. For we find the *Locana* itself rendering the 'Ātman' of Ānandavardhana as *'Jivita'* twice. Kuntaka uses the same word *'Jivita'* to praise his *Vakrokti* and soon Kşemendra is to use the same to signify the place of *Aucitya*. The two main facts recognized by Kuntaka in poetry are the utterance and its embellishment or strikingness called *Alaṃkāra* or *Vakrokti*. Besides these he recognizes certain general concepts which go to define his idea of poetry. Notable among these is the idea of *Sāhitya*. Along with *Sāhitya* Kuntaka mentions two 'Sādhāraṇa *Guṇas*' called *Aucitya* and *Saubhāgya*. These general excellences pertaining to all styles of poetry are to be distinguished from the '*Asādharāna Guṇas*' special qualities, which go to distinguish styles into the graceful (*Sukumāra*), the striking (*Vicitra)*,and the middling (*Madhyama*). The *Sādhāraṇa Guṇas*, *Aucitya* and *Saubhāgya,* are of greater importance. The first of these two *Sādhāraṇa Guṇas*, *Aucitya,* is thus defined by Kuntaka in two verses: (I. 53-54:) '*Aucitya* is that striking mode of expression by which the effectiveness or distinction of the idea on hand is manifestly promoted or achieved. That is *Aucitya* again which clothes the idea in an altogether fresh form of excelling charm.' Both these kinds of *Aucitya* are for heightening the power of expression, for developing the idea undertaken to be described. They are general and comprehensive, referring to all aspects. Kuntaka describes *Aucitya* succinctly as *ucita-ākhyāna,* proper expression (Vide pp.72-74. *Vakroktijivita*).

Kuntaka grasps the supreme importance of *Rasa* and character, i.e., *Prakṛti* or, as he often says, *Svabhāva.* He accepts the *Aucitya* pertaining to these which has been spoken of by Bharata and Ānandavardhana. Other items of *Aucitya* also are shown by Kuntaka and in respect of every element, the word (*Śabda*), the idea (*Artha*), etc., he points out that all *Aucitya* is for developing the idea (*Vastu*)or *Rasa*.

Following Ānandavardhana, Kuntaka says that letters or sounds must be appropriate to the context and that certain harsh letters like cerebrals and conjunct consonants unsuited to certain situations may help the idea and *Rasa* in other situations. On this *Aucitya* of *Varṇa*, the appropriateness, suggestiveness or beauty of letters or sounds, the following of Pope in his *Essay on Criticism* may be compared:

'Its not enough no *harshness* gives offence,
The sound must seem an echo of the sense.
Soft is the strain when Zephyr *gently* blows,
And the *smooth* stream in *smoother* numbers flows;
But when loud *surges lash* the sounding *shore*
The *hoarse rough verse* should like a *torrent roar*

Hear how Timotheus varied lays surprise,
And bid alternate Passions fall and rise.

Kuntaka adds that under all circumstances cacophony should be avoided, concatenation of very unpleasant sounds are not to be written at all. These sounds, by nature, says Abhinavagupta in his *Abhinavabhārati,* torture our ears, while there are other sounds that seem to pour nectar into our ears. The beauty of parts of speech like a suffix, participle, tense and mood, number, gender, etc., used aptly and suggestively, is then dealt with by Kuntaka.

Thus the idea of *Aucitya* looms large in Kuntaka. As a matter of fact, in almost all cases of Kuntaka's *Vakratā,* (Strikingness or Charm) the test or proof of the Strikingness or Charm is this *Aucitya* of the various elements with reference to the *Vastu* (theme) or *Rasa* (Sentiment) the depiction of which is the task of the poet. When we see Kuntaka equating *Pada-aucitya* with *Pada-vakratā* (p.76) we may well exclaim that his *Vakrokti* is only another name for *Aucitya*. As more than once pointed out already, many of the instances of Ānanda-vardhana's *Dhvani*, Abhinavagupta's *Vaicitrya* mentioned in the *Abhinavabharati* Kuntaka's *Vakrata* and Kṣemendra's *Aucitya* are identical. There is bound to be this close relation between *Aucitya*, *Dhvani* and *Vakrata.* Criticising Kuntaka's definition of poetry as *Śabda* and *Artha* set in *Vakrokti,* Mahima Bhaṭṭa says in his *Vyakti-viveka* (Ch.I) 'The out-of-the-way-ness' of poetic word and idea as distinguished from those of *Śastras* (learned treatise) and *Loka* (ordinary speech) must either be the *Aucitya* so very essential to *Rasa* which is 'soul' of poetry or be the *Dhvani* of Ānandhavardhana. If, therefore, the new *Vakrokti* is only *Aucitya*, nothing new is said. If this is denied, the only other possibility is that *Vakrokti* is nothing but a new name for *Dhvani* which really seems to be the fact. For the same varieties and the same instances as given by Ānandavardhana are given by Kuntaka.

Mahima Bhaṭṭa wrote in the same age, just after Abhinavagupta and Kuntaka. Mahima Bhaṭṭa accepts *Rasa* as supreme and also the *Aucitya* pertaining to *Rasa*, *Bhāva* and *Prakṛti.* Critics of the time were aware of only two things as especially distinguishing the poetic utterance from the ordinary or learned one, viz., *Aucitya* and *Dhvani.* Of these two, there is no need specially to speak of the former because Mahima Bhaṭṭa considers it as the supreme necessity in so far as *Kāvya* is accepted as utterance ensouled by *Rasa*. That is, according to Mahima Bhaṭṭa, there can be no opposition to *Aucitya*. It is only with *Dhvani* that he fights.

On the point of *Rasa* and the *Aucitya* of every element of expression to this *Rasa*, Mahima Bhaṭṭa is completely in agreement with Ānandavardhana. Ānandavardhana says that if there is one word which is *Nirasa,* devoid of *Rasa*, it is the greatest literary flaw, the *Apaśabda.* Similarly all flaws are comprised in one common flaw, viz., hindrance to the realization of *Rasa*. All Doṣas are hindrances to *Rasa* and Mahima Bhaṭṭa calls them by the common name *Anaucitya,* the absence of appropriateness. Certain ideas get certain writers as their brilliant exponents. Thus *Sāhitya* gets Kuntaka as its first great exponent. To Mahima Bhaṭṭa falls the share of expounding two ideas, *Svabhāvokti* and *Doṣas*. The most important part of Mahima Bhaṭṭa's work is chapter II devoted to a study of five important flaws of expression, on which the classic *Kāvyaprākāśa*, the model for later compilations, draws for its own chapter on *Doṣas* to a great extent. These five flaws, and all others also, are only the many varieties of *Anaucitya* which means hindrance to the realization of *Rasa*. For *Aucitya* of *Rasa* and Prakṛti is the greatest Guṇa most essential for *Kāvya*. The absence of this *Aucitya* is the greatest *Doṣa* within which every other flaw is included. *Aucitya* and *Anaucitya* pertain to the content i.e., *Rasa* and *Artha* or *Vastu* as well as to their outer garment, viz., the expression — *Śabda.* The former is *Ābhyantara* or *Antaraṅga*-internal while the latter is *Bahiranga,* external. Even the unsuggestive and inappropriate meter is a case of *Anaucitya* of the latter category. Under varieties of *Śabdānaucitya,* Mahima Bhaṭṭa says that five are to be specially noted; they are five flaws named *Vidheyāvimarśa* (subordination of an idea to be prominently predicated) *Prakramabheda, kramabheda* (two kinds of improper sequence of ideas), *Paunaruktya* (redundance) and Vācyāvacana (irrelevance and saying what is not required).

Kṣemendra was the pupil of Abhinavagupta. Among his works, it is his *Aucityavicāracarcā* with which we are concerned here. Although small in size it yet belongs to the class of '*Prāsthana-works*', works which expound a new path, like those of Bhāmaha, Daṇḍin, Vamana, Ānanadavardhana, Kuntaka and Mahimabhaṭṭa. As is clear from the foregoing survey, Kṣemendra is not the author of *Aucitya*, but, as in the case of *Vakroti* and Kuntaka, Kṣemendra worked out *Aucitya* into a system, elaborating that concept and applying it to all parts of the *Kāvya*. Kṣemendra only schematised the ideas of Ānandavardhana and Abhinavagupta in whose system he had his being. Abhinavagupta criticised those critics who glibly talked of *Aucitya* without reference to *Rasa* and *dhvani* which alone render *Aucitya* intelligible. Just as Kuntaka's *Vakrokti* proceeds only after accepting *Rasa* as supreme and accepts also *Dhvani,* so also Kśemendra's *Aucitya*. Kṣemendra first posits *Rasa* as the soul, the thing whose presence makes *Kāvya*; *Aucitya* is its life 'Jivita'. The term 'Jivita' was used by Abhinavagupta himself to denote *Rasa-dhvani* with *Aucitya*. Thus Abhinavagupta used both the words 'Ātman' and 'Jivita' as interchangeable and as meaning generally the essence, *sāra*. But Kṣemendra made a subtle distinction between Soul and Life, *Rasa* the soul and *Aucitya* the life.

These two metaphorical names and the relation between them in metaphysical speculations point to the intimate relation between *Rasa* and *Aucitya* and of how both come into existence together. It is to explain *Rasa*, by which *Kāvya* is already explained, that Kṣemendra offers *Aucitya*. In a verse or in a *Kāvya*, *Aucitya* gives Camatkāra (delectation), *Aucitya* which is the life of *Rasa*.

We had observed before that *Aucitya* is as unintelligible without *Dhvani* as without *Rasa*. *Dhvani* is all throughout implied in Kṣemendra's treatment. Showing the propriety of *Pada-aucitya*, a case of *Padadhvani* with Ānandavardhana, Kṣemendra says that the *Aucitya* in that word pleases us because that word in particular suggests the state of separation and the consequent suffering (*Vipralambha Rasa*).

Kṣemendra has elaborated and pointed out some more principles of *Aucitya* in the wider sphere of thought (*Artha* and *Artha-sandarbha*), like Deśa (place), Kāla (time) Svabhāva, (nature of a person), etc. These are comprehended in *Prakṛtyaucitya* of Bharata and the absence of the flaw of *Loka-āgama-virodha* of Bhāmaha and Daṇḍin. The *Pratibhaucitya* given by Kṣemendra concerns with the minor 'fancies' and not with poetic imagination or genius as a whole. Similarly innumerable items of *Aucitya* can be elaborated and illustrated from poetry. As for instance, the propriety of metre,

Vṛttaucitya, is an interesting study. Bharata has spoken of it in his chapters (XVI,XXXII) on *Vṛttas* (metres) and *Dhruvās* (stage-songs). Abhinavagupta quotes in his commentary on the *Nāṭya Śāstra,* Kātyāyana, an old writer on metres, on the appropriateness of certain metres to certain subjects, moods and situations. Kṣemendra reserves this subject for special treatment in another work of his, the *Suvṛtta-tilaka* (III. 7-16). Kṣemendra explains with illustrations what situations and subjects should be handled in what metres. Though there is bound to be a large amount of subjectivism and impressionism in this study, though, even as in the case of the relation of *Rāgas* (musical melodies) and *Rasas* (sentiments), in this enquiry also, it may be that one and the same metre has many emotional significances, there is some truth in some principles of *Vṛttaucitya* (propriety of metres) like the association of long metres like *Sragdharā* with descriptions of war and heroic fights (*Vīra*) and scenes of terror and horror (*Raudra*) and loathsome and repulsive sights (*Bibhatsa*) and the use of *Anuṣṭubhs* for narration, brief summing up and pointed speech.

The concept of *Aucitya* grew as a supplement to *Rasa* and *Dhvani* and was so developed by Ānandavardhana, Abhinavagupta and Kṣemendra. From the verses in the beginning of Kṣemendra's tract which set forth the doctrine of *Aucitya* in general, it is clear that like *Rasa* and *Dhvani, Aucitya* came up as a severe criticism of a merely physical or materialistic or jeweller's philosophy of poetry which made much only of the embellishments and fine diction (*Alaṃkāra* and *Guṇas*). This is true not of the critical literature of Kṣemendra's time; for *Rasa* had been established firmly as the soul of poetry in poetics. But it is true of literary practice, of what the poets themselves were doing. Kṣemendra's *Aucitya* is another and final criticism of the undue emphasis of formal elements in poetry.

The *Rasārṇavālaṃkāra* of Prakasavarsa is somewhat important as its author gives some valuable ideas on *Aucitya*. He defines *Aucitya* as the spirit of mutual help between sound and sense, between word and idea, *Śabda* and *Artha*, and as an element which makes poetry great. He adds that to *Sahṛdayas* (connoisseurs of poetry), *Anaucitya* is the greatest offence. Prakāśavarṣa gives a new twofold classification of *Aucitya*.

It is this *Aucitya* which Robert Bridges speaks of in his essay on Poetic Diction under the name 'keeping' a concept borrowed from Painting and which he describes as the harmonizing of medium. The following line of his explains his idea further: 'But in Aesthetics no

Property is absurd if it is in keeping.' Bridges speaks here of absurdity (*Doṣa*) ceasing to be so and becoming a *Guṇa* (*Vaiśeṣika*) because of *Aucitya* (keeping).

Three doctrines form the great and noteworthy contributions of Sanskrit *Alaṃkāra* literature to the world's literature on literary criticism. They are *Rasa*, *Dhvani* and *Aucitya*. *Aucitya* is a very large principle within whose orbit comes everything else. The *Aucitya*-rule of criticism is obeyed by all others, including *Rasa* and its *Dhvani*.

10

Tragic Pleasure or the Enjoyment of the Pathetic Sentiment*

Nagendra

In Indian Poetics, Tragic Pleasure or the enjoyment of the Pathetic Sentiment never assumed the form of a problem — as if the accompaniment of the word 'Rasa' or 'aesthetic bliss' ruled out the very possibility of controversy on the subject. Therefore we do not come across any sustained discussions or well-argued positive answers to the question. Yet the Indian mind was vitally conscious of the enigma and has in its usual philosophical way made an acute analysis and suggested impressive answers: the solutions are, however, only implicit and not explicit because the problem did not assume such proportions as in the West.

The general answer is that it is basically unwarranted to apply the natural cause-and-effect theory of normal human life to Poetry. Poetry is a peculiar unworldly phenomenon which cannot be defined in terms of ordinary human logic — it is an extraordinary creation of a supernatural, supernormal genius and as such the ordinary rules of life cannot govern it. Sorrow emanates from sorrow, fear proceeds from fear in usual life: but the poetic genius performs the miracle of affording pleasure from painful situations, of converting horror or terror into pleasure:

> *Hetutvam śokaharṣādergatebhyo loksaṃśrāyāt*
> *Śokaharṣādayo loke jāyantām nāma laukikāḥ.* (6)
> *Alaukikavibhāvatvam prāptebhyaḥ kāvyasaṃśrayāt*
> *Sukham sañjāyate tebhyaḥ sarvebhyo'piti kā kṣatiḥ.* (7)
>
> (*Sāhityadarpaṇa,* III. 6-7)

'In the worldly life, well-known causes of pleasure or pain might lead to painful experience, but in poetry they assume a supernatural character. And hence, what is the harm in believing that in Poetry they cause pleasure invariably?'

Adapted in English from *Raṣa-Siddhānta*

This is one simple stock answer to the much-vexed question of Modern Poetics. I need hardly remind the students of Western criticism that this explanation anticipates in its own way all those theories of the Aesthetes like Bradley and Clive Bell of the 20th century who emphasize the specific character of poetic experience and claim complete autonomy for poetry and art. In the words of Bradley:

> 'First this experience is an end in itself, is worth having on its own account, has an intrinsic value. Next, its poetic value is this intrinsic worth alone .... For its nature is to be not a part, nor let a copy of the real world as we commonly understand that phrase, but to be a world by itself, independent, complete, autonomous.'
>
> —*A.C. Bradley: Oxford Lectures on Poetry, page* 5.

These critics have, of course, used the word'experience' and not 'joy', but as I have explained in my introduction to Aristotle's Poetics[1], the aesthetes, directly or indirectly, believed in the principle of aesthetic joy.

This answer underlines the supernatural character of aesthetic joy and naturally it stands or falls by that. This is really true that in almost every country the literary thinkers of the past have claimed that the poet's genius is a supernatural phenomenon and his activity also is consequently supernatural. Plato himself believed in the theory of divine madness of the poet. But today, after all the advances in the sciences of the Mind and their Matter, it is too late to revive or even accept the theory except in a metaphorical sense. It does not require a serious effort to prove that between poetic genius and other genius or between poetic activity and the intellectual activities and consequently between poetic and other emotional-cum-intellectual experience, there is a difference only of quality and not of nature. Therefore, whereas it is not to be denied that the experience of poeticised sorrow is certainly different from that of actual sorrow, it is certainly not supernatural or peculiar in the sense that it cannot be defined in terms of the science of emotions. Without being a direct experience of sorrow, it still remains a psychic experience all right. And hence this answer does not go very far in solving the problem.

Another solution is suggested by the 'Theory of Universalization'

---

1 *Arastū Kā Kāvyaśtra*, Introduction pp. 91, 100 -

propounded by Bhaṭṭa Nāyaka in the 8th-9th century A.D. According to him, the poetic experience is never personal or individual, it is always universal. The emotional experiences are so portrayed in literature that they are freed from their personal limitations, they cease to be the experiences of the particular hero or the heroine and become the common experiences of all the receptive and responsive readers or play-goers. Freed from the limitations of time and space in this way, they are elevated and refined — their edges are rounded and stings lost. Thus, in their universalized form, pity and fear are both enjoyed.

> *Tasmāt kāvye doṣābhāvaguṇālaṃkāramayatvalakṣaṇena nāṭye caturvidhābhinayarūpeṇa nibiḍanijamohasankaṭatānivāraṇakāriṇā vibhāvādisādharaṇikaraṇātmanā abhidhāto dvitiyenāmmśena bhāvkatvavyāpārena bhāvyamāno raso ... bhogena paraṃ bhujyate*[1]

The gist of this quotation is that, according to Bhaṭṭa Nāyaka, the poet with the help of a certain functional quality called 'Bhāvakatava' which is very much akin to 'imagination,' lends poetic enchantment to the word and the meaning and presents the painful emotions like sorrow and anger also along with their subjects in a universalized form.

Thus the poet has at his command two positive inter-related faculties, namely the imaginative faculty and the faculty for universalization — they are inter-related because universalization also is ultimately effected by the faculty of imagination. Under the spell of imagination 'sorrow' loses its peculiarity; divorced from, personal associations it is freed from the sordid attributes of common physical experiences and a sublimation of the emotion takes place. In terms of Indian philosophy we can explain this process all the more effectively. All personal experience is limited and the feeling of limitation is by itself a painful experience. But when it transcends personal limits and is universalized, it is converted into a veritable pleasure because the feeling of universality is essentially pleasant. We find some vague indications of this answer in Aristotle's theory of Catharsis; only vaguer indications, and not the full-fledged explanation which has been offered by Professor Butcher on behalf of Aristotle on the

1 Abhinavagupta, *Abhinavabhārati*, Gaekwad's Oriental Series Vol. I. (1926),p. 277.

basis of the later advances in Western Criticism. 'The sting of the pain,' says Butcher, 'the disquiet and unrest, arise from the selfish element which in the world of reality clings to these emotions. The pain is expelled when the taint of egoism is removed.' (*Aristotle's Theory of Poetry and Fine Art* P. 268). Butcher is himself conscious that he has overdone the job and adds by way of explanation: 'If it is objected that the notion of universalizing the emotions and ridding them of an intrusive element that belongs to the sphere of the accidental and individual, is a modern conception, which we have no warrant for attributing to Aristotle, we may reply that if this is not what Aristotle meant, it is at least the natural outcome of his doctrine.' Bhaṭṭa Nāyaka's theory, however, is as complete in itself as it is convincing. One of the most effective processes of sublimation according to modern Psychology is 'the socialization of the Ego', which is in essence the same thing as the 'universalization of the personal experience'.

Allardyce Nicoll has spoken of the 'feeling of universality' almost in the same context while discussing the various causes of 'tragic pleasure':

'Part(of the tragic relief) too comes from that very sense of universality — which has been stated to be the fundamental characteristic of all high tragedy — some form of contact with the vast, illimitable forces of the Universe.'

— *The Theory of Drama*,p. 131.

The third answer is impled in the theory of Revelation, Abhivyakti-vāda of Abhinavagupta who was possibly a junior contemporary of Bhaṭṭa Nayaka. Drawing on the philosophical treasures of Saivite Philosophy, Abhinavagupta has propounded that Rasa or aesthetic bliss is not created, but is only revealed. There is no cause-and-effect relationship between Poetry and aesthetic bliss: therefore, the question of tragic scenes giving rise to sorrow or fear does not arise. According to Abhinavagupta the soul is the abode of eternal bliss, it is by nature blissful. But on account of its associations with the mundane life, its purity is tarnished and a sort of moss gathers over the crystal stream of perennial joy. There are various ways and means of removing this moss and restoring the original purity and blissful state of the Soul, such as the Yoga or devotion or other spiritual practices. As soon as the moss is removed, the stream of joy flows clear and crystal again. Poetry is also one of these ways and means; although its effect is less permanent, yet it does succeed in removing the moss. Thus poetry does not cause or create bliss, it only opens the veil and lays bare the eternal bliss which resides in the soul:

> *Asmanmate tu saṁvedanamevānandaghanamāsvādyate. Tatra kā duḥkhāśaṅkā. Kevalaṁ tasyaiva citratākaraṇe ratiśokādi-vāsanāvyapāraḥ*[1].

i.e. 'In our opinion the ever blissful consciousness itself is enjoyed in the form of aesthetic pleasure; there is no question of pain. The emotions like love and pathos are only to lend it variety.'

All good poetry which succeeds in doing this leads to bliss — irrespective of its theme. The theme may be tragic or comic or romantic — so long as it is successfully poeticized, it must restore our soul to its essential blissful state. That is how a successful tragedy also leads to pleasure in the same way as a successful romance does. This is obviously a metaphysical theory and we find its echoes in critics like Coleridge and Croce in the West.

Śārdātanaya, a critic of the 13th century, comes out with another explanation which is also based on Saivite philosophy. According to him, this world is a mixture of good and evil, of pleasure and pain. Evil and pain are unavoidable in life, yet the soul by means of its certain permanent attributes (Rāgā, Vidyā and Kalā) enjoys it. The impulse for bliss is so powerful in the soul that it breaks down all barriers and forces and painful elements also to yield bliss because bliss alone is the reality. By the same process the soul of the reader discovers joy even in tragic scenes.

All these critics have, on the whole, a positive outlook; they all believe in the pleasure of pain. But there is another remarkable work on Sanskrit dramaturgy — the *Nāṭyadarpaṇa* of Rāmacandra and Guṇacandra who flourished in the 12th century A.D. The two authors have boldly challenged the tradition and laid down in unmistakable terms that Rasa or aesthetic experience is not pleasant only, it is both pleasant and unpleasant: sukhaḍuḥkhātmako Rasaḥ. They believe that the reader or the play-goer takes delight in a poetic work

1 *Abhinavabhārati*: Gaekwad's Oriental Series, Vol. I. (Edn. 1956), p. 292.

or a drama not because the painful emotions portrayed in the theme are transmuted into pleasurable experiences, but because he is charmed by the art of the poet and the actor and is deceived into finding a kind of enjoyment in the performance. The painful emotion remains painful without doubt, but the marvel of the poetic and the histrionic art fills him with a sort of rapturous astonishment in which the consciousness of the painful element is merged for the time being. This is a fore-runner of the 'Formal Theory' of the West which propounds that the embellishments of poetry and stage lend enchantment to a tragic work and round off its painful edges.

To quote Nicoll once again:

> "There is the presence of the creative artistic power of the dramatist himself, and, particularly in the Greek and Elizabethan plays, the rhythm of the verse, to reave away our minds for a moment from the gloomy depths of the tragedy. A more detailed consideration of the use and of the value of verse in tragedy we may leave till later, but here it may be observed that verse in many cases acts as a kind of anaesthetic on our senses. The sharp edge of the pain is removed in the plays of Aeschylus and Shakespeare and though it becomes more poignant in some ways, yet it is reft of its crudeness and sordidness by the beauty of the language.'

The note in the *Nāṭyadarpaṇa* contains one more answer which is again implicit. It is said that the taste of a work of poetry or drama is very much like that of a saucy drink. Just as in this drink a number of spices of all tastes — sweet, bitter, sour — are mixed up and they all contribute to the 'ultimate taste', in the same way in human life all experiences — pleasant and unpleasant — are mixed up and contribute to the ultimate enjoyment of life. In ordinary parlance, the bitter, the sour and the sweet are all called Rasas or tastes — so also in poetry the pathetic, the horrible, the terrible, the humorous and the beautiful are called Rasas. Just as the mixture of the bitter improves the taste of the drink, in the same way the mixing up of the tragic or the pathetic enriches the ultimate aesthetic experience. This explanation is more pragmatic than philosophical. But it contains the germ of the famous 'Interest Theory' of Western Criticism. Human life is a mixed pattern of pleasure and pain — both of them are equally inevitable and the human mind is naturally interested in both: the funeral engages our attention as much as the marriage, may be a little more. By the same logic, man is attracted towards a tragic play, his interest in the inevitable gloom of life invariably draws him to a tragedy. It is not for the lighter entertainment or the pleasure, but for the inherent interest in life in all its vicissitudes, that he loves to read or witness a tragedy. We find echoes of this theory in Lucas:

> 'Life is fascinating to watch whatever it may be to experience. And so we go to tragedies not in the least to get rid of emotions but to have them more abundantly: to banquet not to purge.'
>
> — *Tragedy*, p. 52.

These are in brief the various answers suggested by Indian Poetics to the problem of tragic pleasure. One more could be found in the realm of philosophy. According to the Buddhist philosophy, pain is one of the Supreme Truths of life. The realization of truth is always a positive gain; it is a joyful experience in essence. Tragedy, which emphasizes the Supreme Truth in life, is a veritable means of this realization and ultimately results in a happy experience. In Western philosophy, quite obviously under the influence of Buddhism, Schopenhauer has given the same explanation:— according to him tragedy lays emphasis on the 'serious and miserable side of life' and helps us to understand better the ultimate reality — namely 'the utter vanity of living'. Schlegel also offers a similar explanation although his argument is a little different. His belief is that in tragedy we have the consciousness of 'a destiny soaring above this earthly life and we find something consoling and elevating.' Such consciousness is not unknown in Indian literature; for ages the Indian mind has been deriving solace from the consciousness of a destiny soaring above earthly life:

> Karamagati ṭāre nāhi ṭare
> Muni Basiṣtha se paṇḍit gyāni sodhi ke lagan dhare
> Sitā haraṇa, maraṇa Daśarath ko, bana men bipati pare

> 'Inevitable are the ways of Destiny:
> A seer like Vasistha made all calculations and everything was done most auspiciously,
> Yet Rama was robbed of his wife, lost his father and was miserably stranded in the jungle.'

This problem has been tackled in a more optimistic way — possibly by Burke, who explained that tragedy was enjoyable because of the atmosphere of nobility and magnanimity which pervaded it. There is a veritable fall in a tragedy but it is the fall of the mighty and the virtuous, which rouses not pity but admiration in the spectator. The hero suffers, but his suffering sublimates his character and the spectator also shares this process of sublimation of personality. No poetic work illustrates this argument better than the *Rāmāyaṇa* depicting the sufferings of Rāma who personifies nobility.

Such solutions, I may repeat, are found only in the realm of philosophy or philosophical poetry or ethics and ethical poetry; they are not accepted in Indian Poetics, directly or even indirectly for the simple reason that they are in contravention of the fundamental theory of Rasa which is based on the theory of 'Ānanda'.

These explanations cover almost all the answers offered by Western Poetics. There are a few more given by Russo, Hume and others, namely (a) that we find a sort of gratification in the distress of others, or (b) that pleasure and pain are sisters and in meeting with one we discern the form of the other, or (c) that we watch a tragedy to get out of boredom because it is better to be afflicted than to be bored. But they are not to be taken very seriously. The Indian critics have arrived at their conclusions, independently of course; in most of the cases they have forestalled the theories of their Western colleagues. Their way of thinking is, without doubt, more profound and their arguments have sounder philosophical basis. They have at times mystified their explanations by using certain metaphysical terms or by starting on premises which the modern mind may find difficult to accept as such. But that is not enough to reject them as unscientific. A scientific, rational and psychological reorientation is easily possible in almost every case and it has never caused me much difficulty in rationalizing them in the modern way.

In this context, one is naturally reminded of the great Aristotle and the solution offered by him in his famous theory of Catharsis. For Aristotle, the experience of reading or watching a tragedy is a process of psychic purgation. According to him 'by arousing pity and fear tragedy affects a purgation of these and kindred emotions with the result that the painful element is extracted and the mental equilibrium is restored.' The explanation is fairly convincing but it goes only half-way. To the Indian thinker, such an experience is negative. It is only the extraction of the painful element and not a positive enjoyment. It only prepares the ground for the aesthetic bliss to blossom forth. As it is, it is only a sort of relief and not an enjoyment. Contrary to this, the experience envisaged in Indian Poetics has a positive character. It is not just a relief from pain, but a veritable enjoyment; it is a self-fulfilment and since it is achieved after breaking through the hurdles of pain and sorrow, it is all the more profound and powerful. And that accounts for the poetic outburst of Bhavabhuti who asserted that there is only one sentiment, the Pathetic — *Ekorasaḥ karuṇa eva.*

Conclusion

Thus, for more than two thousands years, the Western and Eastern, the ancient and the modern, thinkers have been struggling to solve this problem. Yet it seems to be where it was — at least we have not found any unimpeachable answer which may be universally accepted. In the light of the above discussions, we can safely draw the following conclusions:-

(i) There is a grain of truth almost in every answer, even in the principle of malicious pleasure; the difference is only of the degree, i.e., some answers are comparatively more acceptable than others — that is all.

(ii) No single answer is complete in itself so as to meet all doubts and objections. If you believe in the existence of a Soul which is essentially blissful, then Abhinavagupta's argument should suffice. But this 'if' — this proviso — is not so simple, because how many can have this belief today and how can they have it? By the laws of general logic and general psychology, the solution given by Bhaṭṭa Nāyaka, without its metaphysical concepts, seems to be quite profound: many a Western thinker has accepted or echoed it in his own way. This solution combines in itself the principles of 'artistic synthesis' and 'universality' which are fairly convincing by themselves.

(iii) Therefore we shall have to combine several arguments together in one to evolve an adequate formula — because in actuality also several conditions combine together to convert pain into pleasure in a piece of art: for example (a) the sentiment of sorrow depicted in a work of art is not a direct but imaginative experience and there can be no doubt that its sting is considerably minimized as a consequence; (b) In Tragic Poetry, pathos is mostly associated with the great and the noble — this association with greatness and virtue relieves sorrow of all its sordid elements and lends it a peculiar grandeur. The tragic scenes generally represent the dignity of the human soul at its climax and they invariably refine and sublimate our emotional responses. The personal sufferings of Rama, for example, in the *Rāmāyana* are adorned with a divine halo by his unshaken fidelity to social duty. Such scenes emphasize the grave and the serious side of life and help in the realization of the deeper truths of human existence. Realization of truth is indeed an achievement which elevates the soul. Thus the pathetic contents in a piece of art help us in the enjoyment of life in its fullness.

(c) And lastly the artistic process removes the remnant of pain. Artistic creation is a process of synthesis: by effecting harmony in diffused elements, the artist creates a unity in diversity and imparts 'form' to the formless and the deformed. This is called artistic unity in Aesthetics: it brings about secretly a harmony of emotional experiences which in its turn give comfort to the psyche. I cannot, in this context, resist the temptation of reproducing a passage from one of my own earlier works: 'Experience is composed of sensations and it is never one solitary sensation but a system or pattern of sensations. When the sensations are coordinated and harmonized, our experience is pleasant and when they are discordant and dishevelled the experience is unpleasant. The sensations derived from art are not direct but reflex. This by itself relieves them of their sting to a considerable extent and, besides, they pass through a process of coordination and systematization during the artistic contemplations by the poet. Thus, they are invariably reduced to a pleasant harmony, because the poetic contemplation is essentially a process of effecting unity in diversity which at the level of the psyche is, without doubt, a gratifying experience. In this way, the painful experiences of life, when their basic sensations are coordinated and systematized, are converted into a unified happy experience in art'.

This is how the paradox of Tragic Pleasure can be resolved: at least that is how I have been able to satisfy myself.

11

Bhartṛhari's Discussion of the Nature of the Sphoṭa

Kunjunni Raja

Bhartṛhari begins the discussion on the *sphoṭa* theory with the observation that words or sentences can be considered under two aspects, as sound-patterns or as meaning-bearing symbols. He says that in meaningful language, linguists recognize two entities, both of which may be called words: one is the underlying cause of the articulated sounds, while the other is attached to the meaning:[1]

> *dvāv upādānaśabdeṣu śabdau śabdavido viduḥ*
> *eko nimittaṃ śabdānām apara 'rthe prayujyate.*

The former is the sound-pattern which is the external facet of the language symbol, while the latter is the semantic facet which expresses the meaning. Janus-like, words have two faces: the external face looks at the sounds (*dhvaṇi*), while the internal face looks at the meaning (*artha*). The underlying cause of the articulated sounds (*śabdānāṃ nimittaṃ*) is the sound-pattern which underlies instances of the utterance of the word; this abstract sound-pattern with the time-sequence still attached to it is called *prākṛta-dhvani* and is the external aspect of the language. The internal aspect, which is directly attached to the meaning is the *sphoṭa* which is partless, integral linguistic symbol.[2]

---

1 *Vakyapadiya*, I.44.

2 The term *upādānaśabda* stands for the speech-unit in language. It is only the linguist who recognizes these two aspects in it, for 'sound and signification, form and function, are inseparable in the life of language'. The underlying cause of the articulated sounds is the *prākṛta-dhvani* (which is the cause of *vaikṛta-dhvani*). The internal aspect which is attached to meaning is the sphoṭa. Some explain the former as the *sphoṭa* and the latter as the *dhvani* (G. N. Bhattacharya, 'A Study in the Dialectics of Sphota', Journal of the Dept. of Letters, Calcutta University, 1937, p. 13;

(continued...)

This fundamental dichotomy between form and content in language is mentioned by Pāṇini himself in the *sūtra*:[1] *svaṃ rūpaṃ śabdasyā-śabdasaṃjñā*, 'A word (in a grammatical rule) which is not a technical term denotes its own form'. On this *sūtra* Kātyāyana says:[2] *śabda-pūrvako hy arthe saṃpratyayas, tasmād arthanivṛttiḥ*. 'The understanding of the thing-meant is preceded by that of the word; hence in a grammatical context, the question of the thing-meant does not arise.' A word can signify its own form, as well as the thing meant by it. One is the name and the other is the thing-named. Bhartṛhari says[3] that every word, first of all, expresses its own class, thereafter it is fictionally superimposed on the form of the class of things. In grammatical discussions where the thing-meant is irrelevant, it is only the form that is signified by a word (which is not a technical term). Thus, by the rule[4] '*agni* (fire) has the suffix *eya* (*agner ḍhak*), it is only to the form of the word that the suffix is added, and not to the fire or even to words synonymous to it.

Bhartṛhari says: 'Just as a technical term like *vṛddhi*, while linked to its own form, is also attached to what is named by it, namely, the speech-entities symbolized by *ādaic* (i.e., *ā*, *ai*, and *au*), so likewise this word *agni* (in the *sūtra*), which linked to the word *agni* (in everyday use, i.e. the meaning "fire") is also attached to the sound *agni*, which in this context has the word *agni* as the thing-expressed. The word which is uttered in ordinary usage must certainly not be the one which partakes of the operation (of adding the suffix). But in conveying this other sense, its power (to convey the normal sense)

---

[2](...continued)
Suryanarayana Sukla's commentary on the verse). See also the explanation of the passage by Prof. J. Brough,' Audumbarāyaṇa's theory of Language' *Bulletin of the School of Oriental and African Studies* London Vol.xiv part 1.

1 Pāṇini, I. 1.68.

2 *Mahabhaṣya*, I, p. 176.

3 *VP*, III. 1.6:
svā jātiḥ prathamaṃ śabdaiḥ sarvair evābhidhiyate
tato 'rthajātirupeṣu tadadhyāropakalpanā.
For a discussion of the problem, see Brough, loc. cit.

4 Pāṇini, IV.2.33.

is not impeded.'[1] Bhartṛhari emphasizes again and again the fact that a word has a double power; it can convey an idea of the form of an expression as well as its content. He explains the problem by means of various illustrations. Language is similar to light and consciousness in so far as it can reveal itself and also reveal other things. Just as consciousness can be conscious of itself, while being conscious of other things,[2] and just as a light can reveal itself while revealing other objects,[3] so also every word has the power of referring to itself as well as to the external things symbolized by it.

The Buddhists also accept [4] this twofold power of words to express their own identity as well as the things symbolized by them; but this character is cognized only when they become the subject of conventional relation, and not at the time of perception. It is only in the determinate knowledge that follows a perception that the relation between word and meaning is understood. At the time of perception of the sounds of the words, it is only the sound that is known; the expressive power does not belong to the sound at that time.

The grammarians too accept that words will have to be taken as referring to themselves until the relation between the word and the meaning is known. Thus, Patañjali says that when we do not hear a word properly, we ask, 'What did you say?', thereby indicating that we have not understood the form of the word.[5]

Bhartṛhari's analysis envisages three aspects of the language situation:[6] (1) the *vaikṛta-dhvani*, the individual instance of the utterance in purely phonetic terms. It is the actual sounds spoken by

---

1 *VP*, I.59-61. See the translation by J. Brough, op. cit., p.29.

2 *VP*, I.50:
ātmarūpaṃ yathā jñāne jñeyarūpaṃ ca dṛśyate
artharūpaṃ tathā śabde svarūpaṃ ca prakāśate.

3 *VP*, I.55:
grāhyatvaṃ grāhakatvaṃ ca dve śakti tejaso yathā
tathaiva sarvaśabdānām ete pṛthag iva sthite.

4 Satkari Mookerjee, op.cit., p.296 ff.

5 *Mbh*, I, p.176; *VP*, I.57; J. Brough, op.cit., p.31.

6 J. Brough, op. cit., p.40.

the speaker and heard by the listener. It includes all the various differences in intonation, tempo, pitch, etc. depending on the individual speakers. (2) The *prākṛta-dhvani*, the phonological structure, the sound-pattern of the norm; or, from another point of view, the name of the class of which the various instances are members. This is indicated by the *vaikṛta-dhvani*. All the non-linguistic personal variations are eliminated at this stage. Both the speaker and the listener are conscious of the normal phonological pattern alone. The time-sequence is still present in this. The *prākṛta-dhvani* may be considered as the acoustic image of the normal expression, or the expression in the mind, keeping the time-order with it. (3) The *sphoṭa*, the integral linguistic symbol, which is the unit of meaning, but which cannot be pronounced or written. This is manifested by the *prākṛta-dhvani*. In fact it is the *prākṛta-dhvani* considered as an integral, meaning-bearing, linguistic sign.

The *sphoṭa* as explained by Bhartṛhari is something analogous to the linguistic sign, which in the terminology of de Saussure[1] has two facets: the *signifiant* and the *signifié,* that which means and that which is meant. In the Indian Philosophy these two are called, respectively, *śabda* and *artha*. W.M. Urban has shown [2] beyond any shadow of doubt the existence of a bi-polar relation between the *signifiant* and the *signifié*. The glossematic school of lingiustics under Prof. Hjelmslev also accepts this parallelism between the plane of content and that of expression in language. Prof. Hjelmslev says:[3] 'The sign is a two-sided entity, with a Janus-like perspective in two directions, and with effect in two respects: "outwards" expression — substance and "inwards" toward the content-substance.' 'The sign is, then — paradoxical as it may seem — a sign for content-substance and a sign for an expression-substance'. Explaining this view, André Martinet says:[4] 'According to the glossematicians language has recourse to two different types of substance for its two planes. On the

1 *Cours de Linguistique générale*, pp. 98 ff.

2 *Language and Reality*, pp. 66, 115.

3 *Prolegomena to a Theory of Meaning*, p. 36.

4 'Structural Linguistics', *Anthropology Today* edited by A.L.Kroeber, Chicago, 1953, p.582.

plane of expression the substance may be phonic and therefore perceptible to the auditory organ; (but it is also commonly graphic and therefore usually perceptible and any other perceptible object could be used, although may not be quite so conveniently, for the same purpose). On the plane of content the substance is of a mental, semantic nature.'

The modern linguist considers the linguistic sign as a functional term, based on the relationship between the *signifiant* and the *signifié*, the *śabda* and the *artha.* But to Bhartṛhari this *sphoṭa* is an independent entity which is revealed by the *prākṛta-dhvani*. And it is this *sphoṭa* or the linguistic sign (*le signe* of de Saussure) which conveys the sense.

The distinction between the actual sounds of speech uttered during each occurrence of the speech (*vaikṛta-dhvani*) and the engrams left behind by them in *la langue* or the phonematic pattern or the acoustic images (*images acoustiques, prākṛta-dhvani*) is accepted by the linguists also.[1]

Bhartṛhari emphasizes the fundamental truth that, strictly speaking, words are psychical entities (*śabdo buddhisthaḥ*)[2] which reveal themselves through the articulate sounds. As A.H. Gardiner says,[3] 'it is only inaccurately, though by a sort of necessary inaccuracy, that the name of "words" is given to the articulate sounds which pass between speaker and listener'. 'As words exist in the possession of every individual (of a linguistic community), they are psychical entities, comprising on the one hand an area of meaning, and on the other hand the image of a particular sound susceptible of being physically reproduced whenever wanted.'[4] Even earlier thinkers in India had recognized the fact that the word is something more than the audible sounds uttered by the speaker and heard by the listener; Vyāsa, in the *Yogasūtrabhāsya* states clearly that the word is to be

---

1 *Cours*, pp. 97-103, 141-69.

2 *VP*, I. 46: *śabdo 'pi buddhisthaḥ śrutināṃ kāraṇaṃ pṛthak.*

3 Gardiner, *Speech and Language*, p.69.

4 ibid., p.70.

grasped in the mind, though it is brought together by the sounds.[1] Even the Mimāṃsakas who considered the word as an aggregate of the permanent letters (*varṇas*) in a fixed order recognized that it is much more than the articulate sounds.

De Saussure also emphasized[2] the fact that both the aspects of the *sign*, the *signifiant* and the *signifié*, are mental: the former is the acoustic image or the psychical entity which belongs to *la langue*, and the latter is the idea (*idée*). The Indian grammarians too maintain the subjectivity of both the word and the meaning (*śabda* and *artha*). Nāgeśabhaṭṭa says[3] in the *Laghumañjūṣā* that in reality the meaning is only subjective and the word is also subjective.

The concept of *sphoṭa* is something more than what is generally implied by the term linguistic sign. The relationship between the word and the meaning is an essential factor for the *sphoṭa* concept as for the sign. There is no *sphoṭa* without meaning; it is the meaning-bearing nature of an expression that makes it a *sphoṭa* (when considered as a whole apart from its parts which are irrelevant). In fact the *sphoṭa* is the *signifiant* taken as a timeless and indivisible symbol denoting a meaning. The time-order of the *signifiant* is merely a means for revealing the timeless and partless *sphoṭa*.

Even though the *sphoṭa* is an integral symbol which is indivisible and timeless, it can be revealed only by means of the sound in a time-series pattern. The fact that the sound is produced serially is no argument for considering the *sphoṭa* to have a time sequence. The individual sounds of the letters that we hear in the course of revealing the *sphoṭa* seem to be present in the *sphoṭa* itself only because of our incapacity to hear the symbol apart from the sounds.

How the *Sphoṭa* is comprehended

The *sphoṭa* — the word or the sentence located in the minds (of the speaker and the listener) and taken as an integral symbol — is revealed by the sounds produced in a fixed order. The sounds are

---

1 *Yogasūtrabhāsya*, under *sūtra* III: 17: *padaṃ punar nādānu saṃhārabuddhinirgrāhyam.*

2 *Cours*, p. 98 f.

3 *Laghūmañjūṣā*, p. 45; S. Varma, 'Analysis of Meaning in Indian Semantics', p. 14. See also Kaiyaṭa on Pāṇini, V.2.94.

only the manifesting agencies and have no function other than that of revealing the symbol. Each sound helps in manifesting this *sphoṭa*, the first one vaguely, the next one more clearly and so on, until the last one, aided by the impressions of the preceding perceptions, reveals it clearly and distinctly. It is one and the same *sphoṭa* that is revealed by each one of these letters. Bhartṛhari says[1] that 'with the last sound, the word is grasped in the mind (of the hearer) where the seed has been sown by the sounds, and which has been brought to ripeness by the telling over in order (*āvṛtti*) of the sounds'.[2] This *sphoṭa* is one and indivisible; the sounds uttered to reveal this *sphoṭa* cannot be considered as parts of the essential word or *sphoṭa*, but only as diacritical marks to reveal the identity of the whole word. The process of revelation of the word by the sounds is from the indeterminate stage to the determinate stage; it begins from complete ignorance, passes through partial knowledge and ends in complete knowledge.

The process of comprehension of the *sphoṭa* is illustrated by the grammarians by means of various analogies. It is like a jeweller examining a precious stone by looking at it steadily for some time to enable him to determine its real value. He has a series of perceptions: the first one gives him a general knowledge of the gem; each subsequent perception helps in revealing the real nature of the gem, until the last perception, aided by the impressions of the previous ones, helps him to grasp the real value of the gem completely and clearly.[3] Bhartṛhari has given another analogy; it is that of a student trying to learn a verse by heart by reading it repeatedly.[4] It is the

---

1 *VP*, I.85:
nādair āhitabījāyām antyena dhvaninā saha
āvṛttiparipākāyāṃ buddhau śabdo 'vadhāryate.

2 J. Brough, op.cit.,p.39.

3 *Sphoṭasiddhi*, p.131: *yathā ratnaparikṣiṇaḥ parikṣamāṇasya prathamasamadhigamānupākhyātam anupākhyeyarūpapratyayopāhitasaṃskāra rūpāhitaviśeṣāyāṃ buddhau krameṇa carame cetasi cakāsti ratnatattvam.* See also Vācaspatimiśra (*Tattvabindu*, p.20 f.) for the same analogy.

4 *VP*, I.83:
yathānuvākaḥ śloko vā soḍhatvam upagacchati
āvṛtyā na tu sa granthaḥ pratyāvṛtti nirūpyate.

last reading, aided by the impressions left behind by the previous readings, that helps the student to know the verse fully.

Even though each letter causes a vague cognition of the indivisible *sphoṭa*, the letter also figures in the cognition. It is the cognition of the whole that is significant and therefore important. The whole taken as an integral symbol is something different from the parts that constitute it, and the parts may be considered as irrelevant and illusory. It is not the existence of the cognition of the parts that is denied, for we do undoubtedly cognize the individual letters; it is their significance that is in question.[1] The *sphoṭa* is the object of cognition; but it is in the form of the letters that this cognition takes place. This is an instance of a series of errors leading finally to the truth. Even invalid cognitions can sometimes lead one to a valid knowledge; a false hypothesis can be of help in getting at the truth. Bhartṛhari explains it by means of some examples.[2] Sometimes a tree may appear as an elephant when seen from a long distance, or a rope be mistaken for a snake in a place without sufficient light; but close and careful observation will ultimately reveal its real identity. In the final cognition the object and the form become one. This correct cognition can take place without any change in the circumstances. Standing in the same place and looking steadily at the object we get the correct cognition of the tree or the rope. So also in language the real object of utterance is the *sphoṭa*, though the form is that of the letters themselves.[3]

Even though each letter in the word or sentence has the capacity of revealing the same indivisible *sphoṭa*, every one of them is necessary, since the complete and distinct manifestation of the word is effected only with the perception of the last letter. Hence the subsequent letters in the word are not at all superfluous. According the Mimāṃsakas, when a word is uttered, the individual sounds reveal only the permanent letters or the sound-units (which are analogous

---

1 S. S. Suryanarayana Sastri, 'Vācaspati's Criticism of the Sphoṭa Theory', *Journal of Oriental Research*, Madras, 1932, pp.311-14.

2 *VP*, I. 90-1 and the commentary thereon. See also K. A. Subrahmania Iyer, 'The Doctrine of Sphoṭa', *Journal of Ganganath Jha Research Institute*, (Allhabad). Vol. V, pt, 1, pp. 121 ff.

3 See also *Tattvabindu*, p,21, for a similar analogy.

to the phonemes of modern linguists), and nothing more than these; these act as a stimulus to produce the reaction of recognition of the meaning. But according to the grammarians it is the whole indivisible word that is revealed by the sounds, or by the letters indicated by the sounds. The function of the letters in revealing the integral *sphoṭa* is based on the 'value' in differentiating one word from another. Thus, while uttering the word *gauḥ*, the function of the letter *g* is to distinguish the word from all other words that do not begin with the letter *g*. The essential nature of the function of letters in the building up of a word is noticed by Vyāsa in his *Yogasūtra-bhāṣya*.[1] He says: 'The power of speech has its function in the utterance of the various sounds and the ear has for its object only the series of sounds. It is the mind of the listener that grasps the sounds as a significant unit at the end of the final sound. As the individual sounds cannot co-exist, they do not naturally aid one another. One by one they come into being, and vanish without touching the word; so none of them can be considered to have attained the form of a unitword. On the other hand, each one of these letters may be said to have the essence of the word and the potential capacity to express almost everything, in so far as, by association with other letters, in various combinations, it can form different words. Though a universe of meanings can thus be attached to a single letter, this potential capacity is limited by convention on account of the order of sequence in which the letters are uttered. Thus, the potential capacity of the letters *g*, *au* and *ḥ* is restricted to the object having dewlap, horn, etc. when they follow one another in the particular sequence, *gauḥ*.[2] Of course, Vyasa was not fully conscious of the *sphoṭa* doctrine as developed by Bhartṛhari and Maṇḍanamiśra; that is why he is trying to explain the

---

1 *Yogabhāsya* on *sūtra* III.17:
tatra vāg varṇeṣv evārthavati. śrotraṃ ca dhvanipariṇāmamātraviṣayam. padaṃ punar nādānusaṃhārabuddhinirgrāhyam iti. varṇā ekasamayāsaṃbhavitvāt paraniranugrahātmānas te padam asaṃspṛśyānupasthāpyāvirbhūtās tirobhūtāś ceti pratyekam apadasvarūpā ucyante.

2 ibid.: *varṇaḥ punar ekaikaḥ padātmā sarvābhidhānaśaktipracitaḥ sahakārivarṇāntarapratiyogitvād vaiśvarūpyam ivāpannaḥ. pūrvaś cottareṇa uttaraś ca pūrveṇa viśeṣe 'vasthāpita ity evaṃ bahavo varṇāḥ kramākurodhino 'rthasaṃketenāvacchinnā iyanta ete sarvābhidhānaśaktiparivṛttā gakāraukāravisarjaniyāḥ sāsnādimantam arthaṃ dyotayantiti.*

function of the letters in conveying the meaning of the word. But a similar argument will explain how the individual letters reveal the word symbol or *sphoṭa*.

This is what we find in the *Sphoṭatattvanirupaṇa* of Śeṣakṛṣṇa,[1] where a reasonable explanation, on the basis of Vyāsa's remarks, is given about the function of the individual letters in revealing the integral word. He says that when a man utters the sound *ka* with the intention of saying *kamalam* (a lotus), we know that he is trying to utter a word beginning with *ka*. Thus, the whole word is vaguely suggested by the first syllable itself, for it gives a clue to the identity of the word. When he utters the next syllable *ma*, we have another clue and the word can more clearly be guessed, since it narrows the field. All the words that do not begin with *kama* are now excluded. Still the word is not quite clear, for we do not know whether he is going to say *kamalam* or *kamanam*. When the last sound *lam* is also uttered, the word is known fully and clearly. Thus, the function of the letters in a word is to build up the higher unit; they have no meaning of their own; their value consists in differentiating one word from another.

This conception of the function of the letters in the manifestation of the *sphoṭa* is analogous to the *Apoha* theory of the Buddhists;[2] for the value of each letter in the word is its being different from all the other possible letters. It may also be compared to the view of some modern linguists that the significance of the phonemes — the smallest significant units in a language — lies in their differentiation value. Bhartṛhari's statement that the individual letters in a word or sentence have no direct connection with the meaning, but are merely concerned with the manifestation of the linguistic sign or the *sphoṭa* which is the real meaning-bearer, is quite in keeping with the claim of modern linguists that the basic assumptions that underlie phonemics can be stated without any mention of mind and meaning, and that the

---

1 *Sphoṭatattvanirūpaṇa*, p.10: *tathā hi kamalam ity ukte kakāramakārān-ubhave 'pi kiṃ kamaliyaḥ sphoṭaḥ kamaniyo veti saṃdeho nāpagacchati tāvad yāvan na caramo lo no vānubhūyate. tasmād iṣattvaṃ saṃdigdhatvam niścitatvam eva sphuṭataratvam.* (Quoted by K. A. Subrahmania Iyer, op.cit.,p.136.)

2 The Apoha doctrine is discussed above; [see *Indian Theories of Meaning*, pp. 78-94, Ed.]

structural analysis of a language need not necessarily involve considerations of meaning.

The *sphoṭa* is not an imperceptible entity[1] assumed by the grammarian to explain how a temporal series of sound-patterns can express a unitary sense; it is something which is actually perceived in speech situations. The very fact that a word or sentence is cognized gradually from the vague indeterminate stage to the clear determinate stage shows that it is through perception that this cognition takes places; for, as Maṇḍanamiśra points out,[2] it is only in perceptive cognition that a gradual process from the indistinct to the distinct, through increasing degrees of clarity, is possible; in the case of other means of cognition we have either a clear knowledge, or no knowledge at all.

In fact one of the arguments adduced by the grammarians in favour of the *sphoṭa* theory is the experience that people have in actual speech situations about the word or the sentence as a single entity. Nāgeśabhaṭṭa says that the justification for the existence of the *sphoṭa* and for its unity is the realization 'This is one word, one sentence'.[3] In the *Sarvadarśanasaṃgraha* also it is stated that the acceptance of the *sphoṭa* is based on direct perception itself, since it is a common experience that a word like 'cow' is a unique entity, apart from the different letters we seem to hear in it.[4] The same idea

---

1 D. M. Datta's statement (*The Six Ways of Knowing*, p.250) that, 'In reality, however, corresponding to every word perceived, there is an unperceived, partless symbol which directly presents the meaning' does not seem to be accurate, for the *sphoṭa* is the perceived word itself, taken as a partless symbol.

2 *Sphoṭasiddhi*, verse 23:
pratyakṣajñānaniyatā vyaktāvyaktāvabhāsitā
mānāntareṣu grahaṇam athavā naiva hi grahaḥ.
(There is no vagueness in non-perceptual knowledge.)

3 *Mahābhāsyapradipoddyota*, vol.I, p.11: *idam ekaṃ padam ekaṃ vākyam iti pratyayaḥ sphoṭasattve tadekatve ca pramāṇam.*

4 *Sarvadarśanasaṃgraha*, p.299: *pratyakṣam evātra pramāṇaṃ, gaur ity ekaṃ padam iti nānāvarṇātiriktaikapadāvagateḥ sāravajaninatvāt.*

is stressed in the *Sphoṭasiddhi*[1] and the *Tattvabindu.*[2] Jayantabhaṭṭa also mentions[3] the grammarians' view that the *sphoṭa* is cognized through direct auditory perception.[4] In the discussion of the *sphoṭa* doctrine, Śaṃkara presents the grammarian as saying, 'I do not postulate a new entity called *sphoṭa*; I know it through perception[5]. Even the critics of the *sphoṭa* doctrine do not deny the common experience of the word or the sentence as a unique entity; they only try to explain it in a different way.

Thus, it is argued by Vācaspatimiśra in the *Tattvabindu*[6] that the unitariness that is commonly experienced regarding the word or the sentence is based on some limitation (*upādhi*) like that of the experiences of an army or a forest, and that it need not be real. Two such extraneous adjuncts which produce the notion of unitariness are given: being the content of a single cognition, and being the cause of the cognition of one idea.[7] The critics of the *sphoṭa* doctrine base their arguments mainly on these two points.

Śaṃkara criticizes the *sphoṭa* doctrine on the ground that the apprehension of a temporal or spatial series can be explained as due

---

1 *Sphoṭasiddhi*, p.171: *sphoṭātmā tu pratyakṣavedanīyaḥ.*

2 *Tattvabindu*, p.23: *sārvajanīnam api padam iti vākyam iti caikaviṣayānubhavam.*

3 *Nyāyamañjarī*, p.371: *śrautre pratyaye pratibhāsamānaḥ.*

4 G. N. Bhattacharyya 'A Study in the Dialectics of Sphoṭa', pp.44,68) criticizes Jayantabhaṭṭa for misinterpreting the grammarian's view. 'We do not subscribe to Jayanta's views when he says that *sphoṭa* is perceived by the auditory organ'; his argument that the *sphoṭa* is known through mental perception (*mānasa-pratyakṣa*) is based on a passage in the *Tattvabindu*, p.16; but from its commentary by Parameśvara, it is clear that the term *mānasapratyakṣa* in the passage refers to *prayatnabheda* and not to *sphoṭa.* See also Nāgeśa, *Uddyota* on *Mahābhāṣyapradīpa,* p.66 (Nirnaya Sagar Press ed.): *vastutas tu sphoṭa eva śrotragrāhyaḥ.*

5 *Brahmasutrabhāya* on I.3.28: *na kalpayāmy ahaṃ sphoṭaṃ* pratyakṣam eva tv enam avagacchāmi.

6 *Tattvabindu,* pp.50 ff.

7 *ekavijñānaviṣayatā* and *ekābhidheyapratyayahetutā.*

to the synthesizing activity[1] of the mind. He holds that 'though a series cannot be apprehended as a whole through perception, we have, after all the members of a series have been perceived one by one, a memory of all the members combined together. We have in experience, in all cases of temporal and spatial series, the knowledge of wholes which preserve the internal relation obtaining among their component members[2]. We have to accept it on the basis of such an experience. Śaṃkara says: 'That one comprehensive cognition which follows upon the apprehension of the successive letters of a word has for its object the entire aggregate of the letters constituting the word, and not anything else[3].' He illustrates this point with various analogies. 'The ideas which we have of a row, for instance, or a wood or an army, or of the numbers ten, hundred, thousand and so on, show that also such things as comprise several unities can become the objects of one and the same cognitional act[4].' The particular order of sequence determines the nature of the word; just as ants produce the idea of a row only when they march one after the other, so the letters also constitute the idea of a certain word only if they follow one another in certain order.

The *sphoṭa* theory itself presupposes something like this as the means of revealing the *sphoṭa*, namely a comprehensive cognition of the letters in their proper order. The theory has to accept that the intellect has the power to interpret a series of sense-data as a finished Gestalt. Śaṃkara and the Mimāṃsakas do not explain how simultaneity and succession are compatible in the same act of the mind; the Naiyāyikas who consider that the synthesis of the letters is based on memory (*samūhālambanasmṛti*) are also at a loss to explain this problem. Their difficulty is mainly due to the fact that to them the present is an instant. The modern psychologists have shown that even the present has a duration of its own and extends both backward

---

1 Śamkara calls it *samastapratyavamarśini buddhi* or the intellect having the power of holding together the separate memories into one whole. The same is mentioned by Vācaspatimiśra as the *ekavijñānaviṣayatā*.

2 D. M. Datta, op,cit.,p.253; see also *Brahmasūtrabhāsya,* on *sūtra* I.3.28.

3 Thibaut's translation of the *Brahmasūtrabhāsya,* p.209.

4 ibid., p.209.

into the past and forward into the future[1]. Thus, there is a simultaneous perception of all the letters of a word, though these are successively heard by us. The *sphoṭa* theory is quite in keeping with the modern Gestalt psychology which believes in the primacy of Gestalten. The earlier methods proceeded from the elements to the whole, from the sounds to the words, from words to sentences and finally to the meaning of discourse as a whole; but the present tendency among psychologists is the exact opposite, namely, from meaning as Gestalt to the sentence and words as elements[2]. The *sphoṭa* is the sentence or word considered as a linguistic sign, and perceived as a Gestalt *ab initio*.

The second argument advanced by the Mimāṃsakas against the *sphoṭa* theory is that the unity of the word or sentence is based on the unity of the meaning, and that, therefore, no new *sphoṭa* need be assumed to explain this unity (*ekābhidheyapratyayahetutā*). The grammarians reply[3] that this objection involves the fallacy of interdependence, since the conception of the word as a unitary entity depends on its conveying a single idea and the meaning depends on the word[4]. The Mimāṃsakas argue that their is no interdependence since the conception of the word is based on that of the meaning but not *vice versa*.[5] We learn the meaning of words and sentences from their use in actual speech contexts; and so much of the sound-pattern in a fixed order which is found applied to a particular sense is taken

---

1 S. C. Chatterjee, *The Nyāya Theory of Knowledge*, p. 365; James, *Principles of Psychology*, vol.I, pp.608-10. This is only another way of describing the problem, and does not explain it fully. See also M. Hiriyanna, 'An Indian View of Present Time', *Indian Philosophical Studies*, vol.I.

2 W. M. Urban, *Language and Reality*, p.63.

3 *Tattvabindu*, p.51.

4 ibid : *parasarāśrayaprsaktir durvārā. na khalu aviditspadarūpāvadhir artham avaiti.*

5 ibid., p.53: na hi padāvadhāraṇādhinaḥ saṃbandhabodhaḥ; kiṃ tu tadadhinaṃ padajñānam.

to be a word having that meaning. Kumārilabhaṭṭa says[1] that the meaning of a word is determined by usage and as such, those letters uttered in a particular order of sequence by one individual, which has expressed the sense to us when we have first learned the word from our elders will express the same sense at all future times. Hence, it is argued that there is no necessity for postulating the *sphoṭa*. The grammarian's point of view is that even though the meaning is learned from their function in actual usage, we do experience the word or the sentence as a unitary entity, as a whole, and not as an aggregate of the various letters comprising it. And there is no reason to consider this experience as false.

---

1 *Ślokavārttika*, Sphoṭa section, v.69:
yāvanto yādṛśā ye ca yadarthapratipadāne
varṇāḥ prajñātasāmarthyās te tathaivāvabodhakāḥ

12

Theory of Dhvani

Kunjunni Raja

Ānandavardhana uses the term *dhvani* for his theory of poetic suggestion. He says[1] that this term is taken directly from the grammarians; just as the sounds of utterances (*dhvani* in the grammarian's sense) reveal the integral linguistic sign (*sphoṭa*), so also a good poem with its sound, as well as the literal sense, reveals, over and above the literal sense, a charming sense which has great aesthetic value. On account of this similarity of function, the term *dhvani* is applied to suggestive poetry when the suggested sense predominates over the literal sense. The term is also used to denote the suggested sense or the function of suggestion.

In the *Dhvanyāloka*, Ānandavardhana establishes his theory that suggestion is the soul of poetry[2]. He says that beautiful ideas in poetry are of two kinds: literal (*vācya)* and implied (*pratiyamāna).* The latter is something like charm in girls which is distinct from the beauty of the various parts of the body; this implied sense is something more than the literal meaning and depends on the whole poem, and not merely on its parts.[3] The expressed sense is invariably an idea or a figure of speech; but the suggested sense may be of three kinds: an idea, a figure of speech, or an emotion. This suggested sense is not understood by those who merely know grammar and lexicon; it

---

1 *Dhvanyāloka*, p. 47 f.;*prathame hi vidvāṃso vaiyākaraṇāḥ vyākaraṇamūlaivātsarvavidyānām, te ca śrūyamāṇeṣu varṇeṣu dhvanir iti vyavaharanti. tathaivānyais tamatānusāribhiḥ sūribhiḥ kāvyatattvarthadarśibhir vācyavācakasaṃmiśraḥ śabdātmā kāvyam iti vyapadeśyo vyañjakatvasāmyād dhvanir ity uktaḥ*

2 ibid., p. 2: *Kāvyasyātmā dhvaniḥ*

3 Ibid., p. 14:
pratiyamānaṃ punar anyad eva vastv asti vāṇiṣu mahākavināṃ
yat tatprasiddhāvayavātiriktaṃ vibhāti lāvaṇyam ivāṅganāsu.

is understood only by men of taste who know the essence of poetry.[1] This suggested sense is the most important element in poetry; in fact it is the soul of poetry. In all good poetry prominence is found to be given to this element. Such poetry in which the words and their literal meanings occupy a subordinate position and suggest some charming sense (an idea, a figure of speech or an emotion) is called dhvani.[2] It is the highest type of poetry. In cases where the suggested sense is subordinate to the expressed sense, as in some of the figures of speech like *samāsokti* and *paryāyokta*,[3] there is no *dhvani*; this type of poetry too has some charm, though not much; this type is called *guṇibhūtavyangya*. Poetry which does not contain any suggested sense cannot be considered as good poetry, however charming the expressed sense may be. The quality of poetry depends on the importance given to the element of suggestion.

Strictly speaking, the doctrine of *dhvani* is only an extension of the *rasa* theory propounded by the ancient sage Bharata, according to which the main object of a dramatic work is to rouse a *rasa* or aesthetic emotion in the audience.[4] Ānandavardhana extended this theory to poetry also. Many of his predecessors had understood the importance of *rasa* in poetry; But no one had systematically delt with it before. There is no conflict at all between the theory of *dhvani* and the theory of *rasa*; the former stresses the method of treatment, whereas the latter deals with the ultimate effect. Suggestion, by itself, is not enough in drama or poetry; what is suggested must be charming, and this charm can come only through *rasa* or emotion. The emotion is not something which can be expressed directly by the words, it can only be suggested.

---

1 ibid., p.29:
śabdārthaśāsanajñānamāmātreṇaiva na vedyate
vedyate sa hi kāvyārthathatattvajñair eva kevalam.

2 ibid., p. 33:
yatrārthaḥ śabdo vā tam artham upasarjanikṛasvārthau
vyaṅktaḥ kāvyaviśeḥ sa dhvanir iti sūribhiḥ kathitaḥ

3 For details about these see *Sāhityadarpaṇā*, ch. X

4 On the *rasa* theory see A. Sankaran, *Theories of Rasa and Dhvani;* K.C. Pandey, *Indian Aesthetics.* (For detailed bibliography see P.V. Kane, *The History of Sanskrit Poetics*, p. 350.)

The whole theory of *rasa* realization in literature and drama is based on the well-known passage in the *Natyasastra*:[1] *vibhāvānubhāva-vyabhicārisaṃyogad rasniṣpattiḥ*. *Rasa* is realized in some way from the combination of the *sthāyibhāva* (permanent and dominant emotional mood) with the *vibhāva-s* (the objects of emotion such as the hero and the heroine, and the exciting causes such as the spring, flowers, moonlight and the lower), *anubhava-s*[2] (the external manifestations of emotion such as the movement of the eyebrows, glances and smile) and the *vyabhicaribhāva-s*[3] (accessory moods come and go helping in the manifestation of the *rasa*). Bharata mentions[4] eight dominant emotional moods, or *sthāyibhāva-s* that may be aroused by a dramatic representation into the state of aesthetic pleasure. There are *rati* (love), *hāsa* (laughter), *śoka* (sorrow), *krodha* (anger), *utsāha* (energy), *bhaya* (fear), *jugupsā* (repugnance) and *vismaya* (wonder); the *rasa-s* corresponding to these are respectively called *śṛṅgāra, hāsya, karuṇa, raudra, vira, bhayānaka, bibhatsa* and *adbhuta*. Later writers accept a ninth *rasa* called *śanta* corresponding to the *sthāyibhāva* of *nirveda* (detachment).[5] Really the *rasa* or the aesthetic pleasure derived from literature is one and the same in all cases; the division into the various *rasa-s* is based on the difference in the *sthāyibhāva-s* which contribute to the *rasa-s*[6]. This *rasa* is a condition produced in the spectator, is a single feeling and a pleasureable one.

The *sūtra* of Bharata, defining the process of *rasa* realization, is

---

1 vol. I,p.274. For details see P.V.Kane,op.cit., pp.340-56.

2 Eight of these *anubhāva-s* are called *sāttvikabhāva-s*; these are perspiration, tears, etc. See *Daśarūpa, IV. 3-6.*

3 Bharata mentions thirty-three such fleeting accessory moods like *nirveda* or detachment and *glāni* or fatigue. *Nātyaśāstra*, I, pp. 356 ff.

4 ibiid., p.349 ff.

5 cf. V.Raghavan, *The Number of Rasas*.

6 P.V. Kane, loc. cit.

interpreted differently by different scholars.[1] Lollaṭa, who is a Mimāṃsaka, believes that the *rasa* is *produced* in the hero or heroine; the spectator ascribes it to the actor because of the cleverness of acting, and the spectator's delight is based on the appreciation of the realistic acting.[2] Śaṅkuka, who is a Naiyāyika, considers *rasa* to be a matter of inference. The *sthāyibhāva* in the original hero is inferred to exist in the actor (though, actually it does not exist in him). The spectator forgets the difference between the hero and the actor, and infers the *rasa* in the actor. These two views fail to explain how the spectator gets aesthetic pleasure by witnessing tragedies. Bhaṭṭanāyaka's theory of the enjoyment of *rasa* lays stress on the subjective aspect of *rasa* as the aesthetic experience of the spectator. He distinguishes poetic language from ordinary language, and postulates for the former two functions, *bhāvakatva* and *bhojakatva* in addition to the primary function *abhidhā* (which includes *lakṣaṇā* also). *Bhāvakatva* is the power of universalization (*sādhāraṇikaraṇa*) which strips the *vibhāvā-s, sthāyibhāva-s* etc., of their individual and personal aspects and generalizes them in the minds of the spectators endowed with the power of imagination; and *bhojakatva* is the power by which the *sthāyibhāva* reaches its climax and is enjoyed by the specators (this experience is described as something which cannot be defined in words).

Abhinavagupta, following Ānandavardhana, maintains that *rasa* is realized through suggestion. According to him the *sthāyibhāva-s*, as well as the fleeting *vyabhicāribhāva-s*, are dormant in the minds of the spectators and are roused by the stimulus of *vibhāvā-s* etc., and reach the state of *rasa*. He says that *rasa* is suggested by the power of *vyañjanā* and that *rasa* realization is not indescribable. His view

---

1 Four main interpretations are by Lollaṭa, Śaṅkuka, Bhaṭṭanāyaka and Abhinavagupta. Jagannātha (*Rasgaṅgādhara*,p 28) refers to eight interpretations. About these various interpretations, see S.K. De.'The Theory of Rasa in Sanskrit Poetics', pp. 207-53. See also Huparikar, op. cit., p. 513.

2 See Abhinavagupta's commentary on *Nātyaśāstra,* ch. VI for a discussion of these views. The portion has been edited with English translation and notes by Raniero Gnoli in *The Aesthetic Experience According to Abhinavagupta*, Is. M.E.O., Rome, 1956. The original works of Lollaṭa, Śaṅkuka and Bhaṭṭanāyaka are not extant.

is similar to that of Bhaṭṭanāyaka whom he criticizes for postulating new functions for words; for *bhojakatva* is nothing but suggestion.[1]

Abhinavagupta mentions three different psychological stages in the realization of *rasa* in literature. ' The first stage involves the cognition of the formal or intellectual elements of the poem, and serves as a means to the second. The second stage consists of idealization of things in poetry or drama by the power of imagination in the reader or spectator. The third stage can be marked as the climax of the inexpressible affective (emotional) condition of the reader or spectator. When thus the formal or intellectual, imaginative and emotional elements of a poem blend into one predominant sentiment and, making a simultaneous appeal, awaken the *sthāyibhāva* of the reader or spectator, the relish of *rasa* is manifested as a unity in the heart, leaving no trace of the constituent elements; and this is why the *rasa dhvani* is called *asaṃlaksyakramā-vyaṅgya* or the suggested sense with imperceptible stages.'[2]

Criticisms against the Dhvani theory

The theory of *dhvani* has to pass through an ordeal of fierce criticism before it was accepted universally by the Ālaṃkārika-s.[3] The various schools of philosophy in India, like the Nyāya and the Mimāṃsā, do not recognize the suggestive power of words at all. Later grammarians, however, accept it as necessary from the stand-point of grammar.[4]

In the *Dhvanyāloka* Ānandavardhana himself refers to many of the views against the doctrine of *dhvani*,[5] some holding that it does not exist, some saying that it is included in *lakṣaṇā* and others considering *dhvani* to be something beyond the province of words,

---

1 *Rasagaṅgādhara*, p. 25: *bhogas tu vyaktiḥ, bhogakṛtvaṃ tu vyañjanād aviśiṣṭam.*

2 Huparikar, *The Problem of Sanskrit Teaching*, p. 525.

3 Jagannātha says (*Rasgaṅgādhara*, p. 425) that the *Dhvanyāloka settled the principles to be followed in poetics.*

4 *Laghumāñjuṣā*, p. 160: *vaiyākaraṇānām apy etatsvikāra āvaśyakaḥ.*

5 *Dhvanyāloka*, I. I.2

which is known only to men of literary taste. He has also referred to the criticisms of the Naiyāyikā-s who want to include *dhvani* under inference.[1] Manoratha, a contemporary of Ānandavardhana, seems to have ridiculed the idea of *dhvani* as absurd.[2] In Jayaratha's commentary on the *Alaṃkārarvasva,* twelve anti-*dhvani* theories are mentioned.[3] We shall consider here the main arguments against *dhvani*.

(a) Dhvani and Anumāna

The Naiyāyikā-s reject the suggestive power of words. Mahimabhaṭṭa in his *Vyaktiviveka* written with the specific purpose of proving that *dhvani* is included in *anumāna* or inference,[4] says that the implied sense in literature is always conveyed by the expressed sense through the process of inference itself and that there is no necessity to accept a new potency for words. Mahimabhaṭṭa is not the discoverer of this anti-*dhvani* theory, for Ānandavardhana himself anticipates this objection and criticizes it in the third chapter of the *Dhvanyāloka*.[5] Ānandavardhana's main argument against the inference theory of poetic charm is that inference depends on the knowledge of *vyāpti* or an invariable concomittance between the middle and the major terms of a proposition. In literature there is no such invariable relation between the primary sense and the suggested sense, and therefore, the latter cannot be inferred from the former. There cannot be valid inference when there is the fallacy of undistributed middle (*anaikāntikatva*). Ānandavardhana illustrates his point by

---

1 ibid., pp. 201 ff.

2 ibid., p. 8 and the commentary *Locana* thereon: *granthakṛtsamānakālabhāvinā* manorathanāmnā.....

3 p.9. See V. Raghavan,*Bhoja's Śṛṅgāra Prakāśa*,pp. 149. ff.

4 *Vyaktiviveka*, I.1:
anumāne 'ntarbhāvaṃ sarvasyāpi dhvaneḥ prakāśayitum
vyaktivivekaṃ tanute praṇmya mahimā parāṃ vācam.

5 *Dhvanyāloka*, p.201: *vyañjakatvaṃ śabdānāṃ gavamkatvam, tac ca liṇgatvam ataś ca vyaṅgyapratitir lingipratitir eveti liṅgalingibhāva eva teṣāṃ vyaṇgyavyañjakabhāvo nāparaḥ kaścit.*

means of an analogy[1]. He says that the relation between the expressed sense and the implied sense is something similar to that between a light and pot; the light reveals the pot, even though there is no invariable relation between the two. Again, in inference the minor term becomes related to the major term through its relation to the middle term. Thus a degree of mediacy is an essential feature of inferential process, but 'in suggestion one feels that the degree of mediacy that is necessarily characteristic of inference is wanting'[2].

In the *Nyāyamañajari,* Jayantabhaṭṭa refers to the *dhvani* theory as one adopted by a wiseacre, and dismisses it as unworthy of serious consideration by scholars[3]. According to the later Naiyāyika-s, the *vyangyārtha* or the suggested sense of a word is really inference from its primary and secondary meanings and is not separate from them[4].

Precision and accuracy are the chief objects of logic and it should always demand the use of a word in its plain, primary and unambiguous sense. The secondary meaning is also accepted, since it can be ascertained with a fair amount of accuracy through the primary meaning. But the suggested meaning is too vague and fleeting and subjective to have any place among logical meanings[5]. Logic whose only appeal is to reason, takes accuracy and precision as indispensable and recognizes only as much of the suggested sense as can reasonably be inferred from the expressed sense; the subtle and subjective suggestions implied in language are not subjects of logical discussion. In the *Tractatus*, Wittgenstein laid down that 'whatever can be said, can be said clearly. And what we cannot speak about,

---

1 ibid.; see also *Locana* thereon: *pradipālokādau lingaingibhāvaśūnye 'pi hi vyangyavyañjakabhāvo 'sti.*

2 S. Kuppuswami Sastri, *Highways and Byways of Literary Criticism in Sanskrit*, p. 38.

3 *Nyāyamañjari*, p. 45:
yam anyaḥ paṇḍitaṃmanyaḥ prapede kaṃcana dhvanim...
athavā nedṛśi carcā kavibhiḥ saha śobhate

4 *Śabdaśaktiprakāśikā*, pp. 144-54

5 D.M. Datta, *The Six Ways of Knowing*, p. 284 f.

we must leave in silence'. Great poetry is written on the fringe of that silence; it aims at conveying the inexpressible, by means of suggestion. Logicians may dismiss it altogether as unreal, or include a part of it in inference and reject the rest; but the literary critic has to pay special attention to it, for the suggested sense plays an important part in poetry where the appeal is more to the emotion and sentiment than to reason. A philosophy of language[1] which would eliminate whole areas of human discourse as meaningless and unintelligible has little significance for human culture. It is only through the power of language to suggest things which cannot be expressed directly, that it can convey philosophical truth. In *Introduction to Metaphysics*, Bergson says:[2] ' Language is incapable of apprehending and expressing reality. But language may be used in another way, not to represent, but to bring the hearer to a point where he himself may transcend language and pass to incommunicable insight. It is a dialectical ladder which, when we have ascended, may be kicked away.' This insight and intuition cannot be expressed directly by words, but they can be communicated through the power of suggestion.

(b) Dhvani and Arthāpatti

The view that *dhvani* is to be included in *arthāpatti*[3] is similar to the previous one; for *arthāpatti* is a kind of immediate inference based on the universal relation between the absence of the major and the absence of the middle terms. Jespersen defines suggestion as impression through suppression. He says:[4] ' In all speech activity there are three things to be distinguished: expression, suppression and impression. Expression is what the speaker gives, suppression is what he does not give, though he might have given it, and impression is what the hearer receives. It is important to notice that an impression is often produced not only by what is said expressly, but also by what is suppressed.

1 As that of Wittgenstein. See W.M. Urban, *Language and Reality*, p. 12.

2 See Urban, loc cit.

3 Mentioned by Jayaratha in the *Vimarśini* commentary on *Alaṃkārasarvasva*, p. 9.

4 *The Philosophy of Grammar*, p. 309.

Suggestion is impression by suppression'. Prof. Kuppusvami Sastri says that this kind of suggestion has to be accepted by all schools of thought and that in the case of ordinary sentences, the individual words give only their isolated meanings, leaving the *saṃsarga* or the mutual relation of the words to be conveyed by suppression or suggestion[1]. The Naiyāyikā-s call this *saṃsargamaryādā,* while the Bhāṭṭa Mimāṃasakas consider it as based on *lakṣaṇā*. There is apparent contradiction between the juxtaposition of words in a sentence and their not being related to serve some purpose; hence the *saṃsarga* is cognized through a process of inference of the *arthāpatti* type. We may note here that even in *lakṣaṇā* the transferred sense is obtained through *arthāpatti;* and Mukulabhaṭṭa actually quotes the well-known example of 'the fat boy who does not eat during the day' as a variety of *lakṣaṇā*[2].

The Bhāṭṭa Mimāṃsaka-s accept *śrutārthāpatti* to explain elliptical sentences. This has to be distinguished from *dhvani*, for here the expressed sense itself is incomplete. *Arthāpatti,* being a means of valid knowledge, implies accuracy and definiteness of the sense cognized through it; but in poetic suggestion the implied sense is rather vague and can be fully understood only by men of literary taste who can appreciate the context of situation.

(c) Dhvani and Lakṣaṇā

Some of the Ālaṃkārika-s like Mukulabhaṭṭa tried to include *vyañjanā* or the suggestive power under *lakṣaṇā* itself. They accept that at times it is possible to convey, through sentences, ideas different from the literal sense; but all such instances can be included in *lakṣaṇā* itself. According to Mukulabhaṭṭa,[3] one variety of *lakṣaṇā* mentioned by the Mimāmsaka scholar Bhartṛmitra is that wherein the expressed literal sense indirectly leads to some other idea (*abhidheyena saṃbandha*). Thus even instances of *arthāpatti* will

---

1 op. cit., pp.20-2.

2 *Abhidhāvṛttimātṛkā*, p. 19.

3 ibid., p. 17.

come under *lakşaṇā*. Mukulabhaṭṭa defines *lakşaṇā*[1] in such a way that all instances where the expressed sense indicates other ideas are included in it, and he says that *dhvani*, propounded as a new doctrine by some literary critics, actually falls within the sphere of *lakşaṇa* itself[2].

Ānanadavardhana refers to this anti-*dhvani* theory and says that *lakşaṇā* and *dhvani* differ from each other with regard to their nature and subject matter. *Lakşaṇā* operates when there is some kind of inconsistency in the primary sense; it indicates the secondary metaphorical sense after cancelling its primary sense; but in suggestion the primary sense need not be discarded[3]. This argument is based on the assumption that *lakşaṇā* involves the impossibility of the literal sense and not merely the inconsistency of the literal sense with the intention of the speaker. For we know that in cases of *ajahatsvārthā lakşaṇā*, the literal sense is not completely rejected.

Lakşaṇā is based on the primary sense of a word and is its extension;[4] it is part of the primary sense itself and some have called it the tail of the primary sense (*abhidhāpuccha*). *Dhvani*, on the other hand, depends on suggestion; and suggestion can occur even in cases where there is absolutely no expressed sense, as in the case of emotion suggested by the sound of music[5] or the sight of dances. The emotive element in language can never be explained in terms of the expressive or the metaphorical senses of words. In *lakşaṇa* the implied sense is always indicated indirectly through the primary sense of the word; but in the case of *dhvani* it is possible for both the

---

1 ibid., p. 3: *arthāvaseyasya punar lakşyamāṇatvam ucayte.*

2 ibid., p. 21: *lakşaṇāmārgāvagāhivtvaṃ tu dhvaneḥ sahṛdayair nūtanatayopavarṇitasya vidyate.*

3 *Dhvanyāloka*, p. 192: *vyañjakatvamārge tu yadārtho 'rthāntaraṃ dyotayati, tadā svarūpaṃ prakaśayann evāsāv anyasya prakāśakaḥ pratiyate pradipavat.*

4 ibid., p. 55: *vācakatvāśrayeṇaiva guṇavṛttir vyavasthitā.*

5 ibid., p. 194:*gitadhvaninām api vyañjakatvam asti rasādivişayam, na ca teśāṃ vācakatvaṃ lakşaṇā vā kathaṃcil lakşyate.*

meanings to occur almost simultaneously.[1] Again, the suggested sense is determined by the contextual factors, the intonation, the facial expression, gestures, etc., whereas *lakṣaṇā*, as well as *abhidhā*, are independent.[2]

Even the subjects of *lakṣaṇā* and *dhvani* are different. The meaning conveyed by *lakṣaṇā* is always an idea; but the suggested sense can be an idea, a figure of speech or an emotion.

Even though *dhvani* is different from *lakṣaṇa* there is an element of suggestion in all cases of deliberate and intentional metaphors. The motive element under-lying the deliberate use of metaphors comes under suggestion[3]. Ānandavardhana says that *lakṣaṇā* operates only when there is inconsistency of the primary sense and that its function is exhausted when this inconsistency is removed by resorting to the secondary meaning which is related to the primary sense. The motive element which prompted the use of the metaphor cannot be explained by *lakṣaṇā* itself. In the example *gaṅgāyaṃ ghoṣaḥ* (The village is on the Ganges) the primary meaning of the word *gaṅgā* is the river Ganges; this cannot apply in the sentence, for the village cannot be on the stream itself. This hitch is at the root of the secondary interpretation adopted. The term *gaṅgā* is interpreted as indicating 'the bank of the Ganges'. Thus, the discrepancy is removed and with that the power of *lakṣaṇā* is also exhausted. The ideas of holiness and purity that are suggested by the statement cannot be implied by *lakṣaṇā* itself, because this 'overtone' of the word does not depend on the three conditions of *lakṣaṇā* (inconsistency of the primary sense, direct relation of the implied sense to the primary sense and a clear purpose or the sanction of popular usage behind the transfer); it is determined by the emotional atmosphere which envelops the word and is something elusive. Even in the absence of *lakṣaṇā* the

---

1 In *asaṃlakṣyakrama-vyaṅgya* even though the emotion is based on the primary sense, the sequence is not felt.

2 See Huparikar, op.cit., pp. 493 ff.

3 *Dhvanyāloka*, p. 54:
mukhyāṃ vṛttiṃ parityajaya guṇavṛyārthadarśanam
yam uddiśya phalam tatra śabdo naiva skhaladgatiḥ.
See also *Kāvyaprakāśa*, II. 13-18; *Sāhityadarpaṇa*,. II.15. For the use of the term *skhaladgati* in the sense of *lakṣaṇā* see Dharmakirti, *Pramāṇavārttika*, II.37.

word *gaṅgā* can suggest the qualities of purity and sanctity;[1] *lakṣaṇā* does not give the suggested sense, but it points the way to the richness of the ideas associated with the word. What might be left unnoticed in ordinary cases is emphasized by the *lakṣaṇā* because the inconsistency of the meaning (or the strangeness of the collocation of words) produces a break in the flow, and makes the listeners think about the purpose behind it. Thus, *lakṣaṇā* leads the way to the land of suggestion.

(d) Dhvani and Abhidhā

The Mimāṃsaka-s of the Prābhākara school who follow the *anvitābhidhāna* theory of verbal comprehension consider *dhvani* to be included in the primary function *abhidhā* itself; for according to them the meaning of a word is what is conveyed by it. There is no restriction to the scope of the significative force of a word. In a sentence a word conveys not only its own individual meaning, but also its relation to the other words in the sentence. The *saṃsarga* or the mutual relation of the word-meanings suggested by their juxtaposition in a sentence is also included in the primary meaning itself. In certain contexts a word may suggest new ideas beyond its normal sense, but all those come under *abhidhā* itself. Just as the range of an arrow can be extended farther and farther depending on the force with which it is discharged, the meaning of a word can be extended to any length.[2]

---

1 Thus , sanctity and purity can be implied even in the sentence *gangātire ghoṣaḥ (the village* is on the bank of the Ganges).

2 *Locana*, p. 188: *prābākaradaśane 'pi dirghadirgho vyāpāraḥ; p.*. *18: yo 'py anvitābhidhanavādi yatparaḥ śabdaḥ sa śabdārtha iti hṛdaye gṛhitvā śaravad abhidhāvyāpāram eva dirghadirghām icchati...*

Abhinavagupta explicitly states that it is the view of the followers of Prabhākara and that it is based on the *anitābhidhāna* theory. Govinda, in the *Pradipa* commentary on the *Kāryaparakāśa*, referred to it as the view of Bhāṭṭa-s; and Jhalakikara refers to this theory as that of *bhaṭṭamatopajivinaḥ* (in his edition of the *Kāvyaprakāśa*, V.47). S.K. De pointed out this mistake in the second volume of his *Studies in the History of Sanskrit Poetics*, p.192. See also V. Raghavan, *Bhoja's Śṛngāra Prakāśa*, p.150. Still this mistake has crept even into the work of Professor P.V. Kane. In his notes on *Sāhityadarpaṇa* he refers to this theory as that of 'some followers of Kumārila' (p.64). Trivedi, in his notes on *Ekāvali* (p.370) alludes to it as the view of Lollaṭa.

Ānandavardhana and his followers attack this view from the standpoint of the *abhihitānvaya* theory. The suggested sense cannot be conveyed by the power of *abhidhā*, for it is only the definite conven-tional sense, which is directly related to the word, that is conveyed by *abhidhā*. The power of the primary function of the word is exhausted when this task is performed.[1] Even the sentence meaning cannot be expressed by the words through the primary function alone. Another function has to be accepted to explain suggested meanings. The primary sense is directly related to the word but the suggested sense is, at times, known only indirectly through the expressed sense.[2]

Moreover, suggestion need not always depend on words; the melody of music, gestures, etc. are suggestive of sense. The primary sense is definite and fixed; but the suggested sense changes according to the changes in the contextual factors. The primary sense of a word can be objectively learned by any one from a lexicon; but the suggested sense in poetry can be fully appreciated only by men of taste.[3]

(e) Dhvani and Tātparyavṛtti

Some of the Ālaṃkarika-s like Dhanika and Dhanaṃjaya include *dhvani* under *tātparyavṛtti*, a function of the sentence postulated to explain the verbal comprehension arising from a sentence. The direct relation of the word is to its isolated meaning; in a sentence the primary function of the words is exhausted, when the isolated meanings of the individual words are presented. The mutual relation of the isolated word-meanings or the *saṃsarga* as it is called, is not conveyed by the words directly. It is not expressed, it is only

1 Śabara on *sutra* I.1.25: *padāni hi svaṃ svam artham abhidhāya nivṛttaavyāpārāṇi; Kāvyaprakaśa*, II. 10: *viśeṣyaṃ nābhidhā gacchet kṣiṇaśaktir viśeṣaṇe*. See also *Locana*, p. 16.

2 *Dhvanyāloka*, p. 188 f. : *vācyo hy arthaḥ sākṣāc chabdsya sambandhi taditaras tv abhidheyasāmārthyākṣiptaḥ saṃbandhisaṃbandhi; avācakasyāpi gitaśabdāde rasādilakṣaṇārthāvagamadarśanāt, aśabdasyāpi ceṣṭāder arthaviśeṣaprakāśanaprasiddheḥ*

3 ibid., p. 29: *vedyate sa tu kāvyārhatttvajñair eva kevalam*. See L. Renou, 'The Dhvani in Sanskrit Poetics', *The Adyar Library Bulletin*, vol. 18, p. 21 f.

suggested. This is done according to them by the *tātparyavṛtti*. Can poetic suggestion also be included in this?[1]

Tātparyavṛtti is postulated to explain the literal meaning of a sentence, whereas *vyañjāna* comes at the next stage. The power of the former is exhausted by establishing the logical connection of the word meanings, and cannot give further suggestions. Abhinavagupta says[2] that when an expression gives its other sense, we cannot regard both these distinct senses as conveyed by the same power. The former proceeds directly from the words, while the latter comes from this literal sense. *Tātparya* pertains to the expressed sense, whereas *dhvani* pertains to non-expressive factors also such as music, gesture, etc.

Dhanaṃjaya and Dhanika oppose the *dhvani* theory and include it under *tātparya*[3]; according to them the power of *tātparya* is not exhausted in giving the logical connection of the word-meanings, but can extend to any length. Some of the later Ālamarika-s have accepted *tātparya* almost as synonymous with suggestion.

(f) Dhvani and Varokti

In the *Vakroktijivita*, Kuntaka denied the independent existence of *dhvani*, and included it under *vakrokti* or 'a striking mode of speech'.[4] His *vakrokti* is all pervading and is almost analogous to *dhvani* itself.

Classification of Dhvani

The main division of *dhvani* is into two types:[5] *avivakṣita*-vācya and *vivakṣitānyapara-vācya*. The former is based on *lakṣaṇā* and is also

---

1 *Kāvyaprakāśa*, II. 6: *padārthānāṃ samanvaye tātparyātho viśeṣavapur apadārtho 'pi vākyārthaḥ samullasatity abhihitānvayavādināṃ matam.* This *tātparyavṛtti* is the same as *saṃsargamaryādā* of the Naiyāyika-s. See Kuppuswami Sastri, op.cit., p. 20f.; Huparikar, op.cit., pp. 504-11.

2 *Locana*, p. 13; also *Dhvanyāloka*, pp. 118 ff.

3 *Avaloka* commentary on the *Daśarupaka*, p. 157:
etāvaty eva viśrāntis tātparyasyeti kiṃkṛtam?
yāvatkāryaprasāritvāt tātparyaṃ na tulādhṛtam.

4 *Vakroktijivita*, I. 10: *vakroktir eva vaisagdhyabhangibhaṇitir ucyate.*

5 A fairly detailed classification of dhvani is given in the the *Dhvānyāloka*, chs. I and II; *Kāvyaprakāśa*, IV;*Sāhityadarpaṇaṇ, IV, etc.*

called *lakṣaṇāmūla*; in this type the literal meaning is not intended. The motive element in all cases of intentional metaphors comes under this. Corresponding to the two varieties of *lakṣaṇā* namely *jahallakṣaṇā* and *ajahallakṣaṇā*, the *avivakṣita-vācya* type of *dhvani* is also subdivided into two: *atyantatiraskṛta-vācya* where the literal sense is completely set aside and *arthāntarasaṃkramita-vācya* where the literal meaning is shifted. This second sub-variety comprises cases where a word is used in an enhanced or diminished sense. Edgerton compares this with the 'emphasis' of classical western rhetoricians;[1] though in fact the point of view here is somewhat different.[2] What Empson calls the pregnant use of words of the type 'A is *A* ' comes under this variety of *dhvani*.[3] The ancient Mimamsakas also recognized the use of *lakṣaṇā* for praising an object and gave examples like 'Dirty clothes are not clothes' (*yan malinam avāsas tat*).[4] This pregnant use of words is found in negation also; for negation can be partial. Thus, in the previous example the word *avāsas* (not clothes) means only 'not clothes in the fullest sense of the term'.[5] When Shelley says to the skylark, 'Bird thou never wert', he does not mean that the skylark does not belong to the class *Aves*.[6] Around the logical meaning of each word there floats an emotional atmosphere which envelops and penetrates it.[7] The pregnant use of the word can either bring all the feeling tones associated with it along with the logical sense, or can deprive all feeling tones from the sense of the word. And such use by which the normal sense is either enhanced or

---

1 F. Edgerton, 'Indirect Suggestion in Poetry: A Hindu Theory of Literary Aesthetics', *Proceedings of the Amercan Philosophical Society* ,vol 76 p.700. 1936.

2 J. Brough, 'Some Indian Theories of Meaning' *Transactions of the Philological Society*, 1953 p.174.

3 The *Structure of Complex Words*, p.351.

4 *vide supra*, p.237.

5 Thus the term *avidya* is explained as 'imperfect knowledge' rather than 'absence of knowledge'.

6 See Ogden and Richards, *The Meaning of Meaning* p. 238.

7 Vendryes, *Language*, p.182.

diminished can produce a suggestion of praise or blame. An example of this type of *dhvani* given by Ānandavardhana is: 'Only when favoured by the rays of the sun are lotuses *lotuses*'.[1] Here '*lotuses*' carries the meaning 'lotuses in the full sense of the word; lotuses with all the qualities of beauty which make them worth being called lotuses'.

The second division of *dhvani*, *vivakṣitānya-paravācya* is sometimes also called *abhidhāmūla* as it is based on *abhidhā* or the primary meaning of the word. In this type the literal sense is in fact intended, but subserves the implied sense. This is also divided into two sub-varieties; *saṃlakṣyakrama-vyangya* where the stages of realizing the suggested sense from the expressed sense can be well perceived, and *asaṃlaksyakrama-vyangya* where the stages in the realization of the suggested sense are imperceptible. The latter is more important and is concerned with the suggestion of poetic emotion. The permanent moods (*sthāyibhāva-s*) latent in the readers are roused along with the understanding of the expressed sense in the form of the *vibhāva-s* (causes of emotion), *anubhāva-s* (after-effects of emotion) and *vyabhicāribhāva-s* (transient moods); the intermediate steps between the understanding of the expressed sense and the realization of *rasa* are not perceived. In this case the *rasa* or *bhava* is suggested by the express mention of the *vibhāva-s*, etc., and it occupies the principal position in the poem. If the suggested emotion is subordinate to the expressed sense, it is included in the *guṇibhūta-vyangya*[2] variety of poetry. And if the *vibhavā-s*, etc. are not expressly mentioned, they have to be gathered from the context and hence the stages in the realization of the emotions will be perceptible[3].

---

1 *Dhvanyāloka*, p. 62: *ravikiraṇānugrhitāni kamalāni kamalāni.*

2 *Guṇibhūta-vyangya* is that type of poetry where the charm of the suggested sense is not more striking than that of the expressed one. It is divided into eight varieties on the basis of the suggested sense being obvious, abstruse, subordinate to the expressed sense, subordinate to another factor, of doubtful importance, of insufficient importance, not beautiful or brought about by intonation. See *Kāvyaprakāśa*, V.1-2:

agūdham aparasyāngaṃ vācyasiddhyangam asphuṭam
saṃdigdhatulyaprādhānye kākvākṣiptam asundaram
vyangyam evaṃ guṇibhūtavyangyasyāṣṭau bhidāḥ smṛtāḥ

3 Then it becomes an instance of *saṃlakṣyakrama-vyaṇgya*,

The type of *dhvani* called *saṃlakṣyakrama-vyangya* is again subdivided into *vastu-dhvani* where a fact is suggested and *alaṃkāra-dhvani* where the suggested element is a figure of speech. It can again be classified from another point of view, into that based on words (*śabda-śaktimūla*) and that based on the meanings *(arthaśakti-mūla*); in the former the actual words used are vital to the suggestion and cannot be substituted by their synonyms, while in the latter it is the contextual factors and the social and cultural background that are important in bringing out the suggestion. Or it may be based on both at the same time. (*ubhayaśaktimūla*).

In the *Sāhityadarpana,* Viśvanātha criticizes[1] Ānandavardhana for including under poetry suggestions of a fact or a figure of speech. He says that the suggestion of poetic emotion alone can be considered as the soul of poetry and refuses to recognize any piece of poetry in which emotional elements are absent. Every statement implies many other ideas which are not actually expressed. Thus, the statement 'Devadatta went to the village' implies that he was being attended by a servant[2] (in the social context of that time in India), but there is no poetry in that. Ānandvardhana himself was fully conscious of the importance of emotional elements in poetry. The facts and the 'figures of speech' suggested must ultimately lead to the realization of *rasa*. He says that the real function of the figures of speech in poetry is to serve in the development of *rasa*[3]. Abhinavagupta makes the idea clear by saying that really the suggestion of *rasa* (*rasa-dhvani*) alone is the soul of poetry and that the suggestion of ideas and figures of speech (*vastu-dhvani* and *alaṃkāra-dhvani)* ultimately terminates in the development of *rasa*[4].

Sabdasaktimula-dhvani is based on words and gives the feeling tones of a word. Sapir says that it is very difficult to come to any scientific conclusion regarding feeling tones. 'To be sure there are

---

1 p.4 He defines poetry as *vākyaṃ rasātmakam* (p. 5)

2 ibid,: *anyathā devadatto grāmaṃ yātiti vākye todbhṛtyasya tadanusaranarū-pavyangyāvagater api kāvyatvaṃ syāt.*

3 *Dhvanyaloka* p.85 f.

4 *Locana*, p.27 : *rasa eva vastuta ātmā, vastvalamkāradhvani tusarvathā rasam prati paryavasyete.*

socially accepted feeling tones or ranges of feeling tone for many words over and above the force of individual association, but they are exceedingly variable and elusive things at best'.[1] It is determined mainly by the frequency with which it is used in emotional contexts.[2] According to Mammaṭa and Viśvanātha, in the case of a homonymous word or expression having more than one primary sense, when the contextual factors restrict it to one of the senses possible, the other sense that still lurks in it is conveyed by the power of suggestion.[3] This they give as an example of *vyañjanā* based on words. Jagannātha Paṇḍita has rightly rejected[4] this view on the ground that all the senses in such cases are primary and are brought to the mind of the listener through the power of *abhidhā* itself. The contextual factors can only restrict its application, they cannot deprive it of its primary senses. So there is no necessity to bring in *vyañjanā* here.

Jangannātha Paṇḍita says[5] that in the case of *yogarūḍha* words like *pankaja* (lotus, mud-born), where the etymological meaning is applicable it is restricted in its use by the popular usage; the power of *abhidha* expresses its popular meaning. Sometimes the etymological sense is also conveyed by the power of suggestion, by a subtle supplementation.

' We seem at times to glimpse behind a word another sense, deeper and half-hidden and to hear faintly the entry of another

---

1 E. Sapir, *Language,* p.41.

2 See V.K. Gokak, *The Poetic Approach to Language*, p. 21. On the emotive elements in language, see Ullmann, op. cit., pp 96 ff., Ogden-Richards, op. cit. pp. 149 ff.]

3 1 Kāvyaprakāśa II 19:
anekarthasya sabdasya vacakatve niyantrite
Sāṃyogādyair avācyārthadhikṛdoyāprtir añjanam.
Sahityadarpaṇa, II 14. On the contextual factors *vide supra,* pp. 48 ff

4 *Rasagangadhara,* pp. 110 ff.

5 ibid., p.118:
yogarūdhasya śabdaya yoge rūdhyā niyantrite
dhiyaṃ yogaspṛṣo'rthasya yā sūite vyañjanaiva sā.

meaning, in and with which others begin to sound, and all accompany the original meaning of the word like the sympathetic chimes of a bell. Hence that deep and sonorous ring in words which is lacking in artificial and invented languages; and hence also the multiplicity, the indefiniteness, the strange suggestiveness and evasiveness of so much poetry.'[1] Hugo von Hofmannsthal says that this is a peculiarity of oriental poetry: ' It leads us into the innermost nature of oriental poetry, into the very mystery and being of language. For this mysteriousness is the deepest element in eastern language and poetry alike, in so far as every thing in it is metaphorical, everything remotely descended from ancient roots. The original root is sensuous, primitive, concise and strong but the word moves away from it by subtle transitions to new related meanings and then meanings only remotely related; yet in the remotest meaning there is still some echo of the original sound of the word, still some darkly mirrored image of the first sensuous impression'.[2]

The ancient etymological meaning that lurks behind the normal meaning can be brought back to life by a subtle supplementation. Examples can be found in all good poetry. In the *Kāvyaprakāśa*, Mammaṭa refers to the use of the words *kapālin* by Kālidāsa in the *Kumārasaṃbhava* verse[3]:

dvayaṃ gataṃ saṃprati śocaniyatāṃ
samāgamaprārthanayā kapālinaḥ
kalā ca sā kāntimati kalāvatas
tvam asya lokasya ca netrakaumudi

(By seeking association with *kapālin* — Śiva, the holder of the begging bowl — two things have become pitable: the brilliant digit of the moon and thyself (Pārvati), moonlight to the eyes of the world). Here the term *kapālin* directly denotes Śiva; but etymologically it means 'the holder of the begging bowl', and therefore aptly suggests his poverty and worthlessness.

---

1 F. Wisemann,'Language Strata', *Logic and Language*, p.13.

2 Quoted by Wisemann, op. cit., p.13f.

3 V.71 see also *Kāvyaprakāśa*, V.47.

In the case of homonymous expression (śleṣa) if both the meanings are applicable in the context, the meanings are known through the primary sense *abhidhā*; but if one is contextual and the other noncontextual, the power of *abhidhā* might bring the recollection of both, but the contextual factors will restrict it to one of the meanings. The figure of speech such as simile that is suggested in such cases is through *śabdaśaktimūla-dhvani,* because the suggestion is based on the actual words used, and the words cannot be substituted by their synonyms.

Arthaśaktimūla-dyvani is based on the expressed meaning. The suggested sense need not be an idea or a figure of speech; under this type are included instances where the emotions and transient feelings are suggested from contextual factors, without the express mention of the *vibhāva-s*, *anubhāva-s* etc.[1] These are explained as coming under *vastu-dhvani* itself. Even though the primary sense of a word is definite and fixed it can suggest various other ideas through factors such as the peculiar character of the speaker, or the person addressed, the sentence, the presence of another person, the expressed meaning, the occasion, the place, the time, the intonation or the gestures[2]. The idea or the figure of speech suggested could be either feasible in itself (*svaṭaḥsaṃbhavi*) or invented by the imagination of the poet (*kavipraḍhoktiniṣpanna*).

From the point of view of the *vyañjaka-s* or the indicators of suggestion the different varieties of the type, *saṃlaksyakrama-vyaṅgya,* could be subdivided into *pada-prakāśya* or revealed by a word and *vākya-prakāśya* or revealed by the whole sentence.

---

1 Thus the bashfulness of Parvati is suggested in the *Kumārasaṃbhava* verse (VI.84):

evaṃvādini devarṣau pārśve pitur adhomukhi
lilākamalapatrāṇi gaṇayāmāsa pārvati.

See *Dhvanyadloka,* p.102 .

2 *Kāvyaprakāśa,* III 21-2

vaktṛboddavyakākūnāṃ uākyavācyanyasṃnidheḥ
prastāvadeśakālāder vaiśiṣityāt praibhājuṣām
yo 'rthasyānyārthadhihetur vyāpāro uyakir eva sā.
cf. *Sāhityadarpaṇa,* II.16-7.

The other type, *asaṃlakṣyakrama-vyangya,* is also classified[1] as arising from individual sounds, words or parts of words, sentences, 'stylistic structure' (*sanghaṭanā*) or the whole poem. Ānanda-vardhana recognizes the importance of taking the whole stanza or even the poem as a whole, in order that the overtones of the suggested sense are fully grasped.

Intonation

The importance of intonation as a factor in conveying the nuances of the natural sentences of every day speech was not unknown to the ancient Indian thinkers. In the *Nāṭyaśāstra,* Bharata refers[2] to the different varieties of tone, tempo and pitch to be employed by the actors to bring out the subtle meanings in their speeches. Even the early grammarians distinguished those variations of the sounds in length, etc., which actually formed an integral part of the words themselves and could, therefore, be studied objectively, and those variations which suggest certain syntactic over-meanings and the subtle shades in the speaker's intention. Thus the division of vowels into short, long and prolate, constitutes an integral part in the form of the words in Sanskrit; the distinction of the accents into high (*udātta*), low (*anudātta*) and circumflex (*svarita*), forms an integral part of the words in Vedic Sanskrit. They are part of the phonemic system, or the *prākṛta-dhvani* of the language (in Bhaṛtrhari's terminology). But other personal variations in the mode of utterance such as those in speech, pitch and intonation, as well as the peculiarities of manual gesture and facial expression cannot be put to a uniform objective analysis, even though they play an important part suggesting the shades of meaning. These are analogous to the *vaikṛta-dhvani* (again, in Bhaṛtrhari's terminology). The former plays an important part in bringing out the linguistic meaning, whereas the latter helps in suggesting emotive meanings, and the social-cultural meanings.

Bharata refers[3] to the two main types of *kāku* or intonation in a sentence: *sākānkṣa* or expectant and *nirākānkṣa* or non-expectant.

---

1 *Dhvanyāloka,* III, 2; see J. Brough, op.cit., p.175.

2 *Nāṭyaśātra*, vol. II. p. 391 f.

3 ibid., p. 391; *dvividhā kākuḥ sākāṅkṣā nirākāṅkṣā ceti, vākyasyasākānkṣatvanirākānkṣatvāt.*

The former intonation shows that the meaning of the sentence is not complete and that it requires something more to complete it, while the latter type of intonation shows that the sense is complete. Rājaśekhara deals with the problem of intonation in speech in greater detail:[1] he divides the expectant intonation into three sub-varieties as suggesting (*a*) an objection or disapproval (*ākṣeph-garbhā*) (*b*) question (*praśnagabhā*) and (*c*) doubt or uncertainty (*vitarkagarbhā*). The non-expectant intonation is also divided into three varieties: (*a*) denoting a statement (*vidhirūpa*), (*b*) giving an answer (*uttararūpa*) and (*c*) asserting a decision (*nirṇayarūpa*). He defines *kāku* or intonation as a quality in the mode of utterance, which brings out the intention of the speaker clearly.[2] With the change in intonation the same sentence can mean different things: a question, assertion or a doubt. Only the main varieties are given here, for there are innumerable distinctions in intonation, which suggest subtle shades of meaning, cognitive or emotive. In the *Śṛṅgāraprakāśa,* Bhoja also discusses[3] the importance of intonation in bringing out the *vivakṣā* or intention of the speaker. Later Alaṃ-kārika-s accept intonation as a means of suggesting meanings not actually expressed by words. Intonation brings to light all manner of emotional attitudes; irony, pathos, argumentativeness, menace and so forth.[4] One variety of *guṇībhūta-vyaṅgya* is based on intonation and is called *kākvākṣipta*.[5] More than one type of intonation may be combined in different ways to indicate various emotional attitudes.

It is of interest to note that the protagonists of the *dhvani* theory enlarge the term *artha* or meaning to include all that is conveyed by a poem. It includes not only the cognitive meaning, but also the emotive or volitional senses and the 'social-cultural' significance of utterances suggested with the help of contextual factors. Another

---

1 *Kāvyamimāṃsā*, p, 31 f.

2 ibid., p. 31: *abhiprāyavān pāṭhadharmaḥ kākuḥ.*

3 Dr.Raghavan, *Bhoja's Śṛṅgara Prakāśa*, pp. 13 ff.

4 A. Gardiner, op. cit., p.202.

5 *vide supra*, p.302, n.2.

important point to be noted is that Ānandavardhana and his followers accepted the grammarian's view about the unity of the sentence-meaning; 'the *dhvani*-theory to a large extent operated in terms of larger unities and not individual words'.[1] But at the same time 'it is possible from another point of view to indicate that the operative factor in producing the overtones of the implied meaning may on occasion be a single word or phrase'.[2] Many of the criticisms against the *dhvani* theory are due to the fact that the poets and the literary critics did not confine themselves to a relatively small portion of language behaviour which is definite, but tried to extend it to the totality of human experience, including the emotional. But at the same time 'it is possible from another point of view to indicate that the operative factor in producing the overtones of the implied meaning may on occasion be a single word or phrase.'[3] Many of the criticisms against the *dhvani* theory are due to the fact that the poets and the literary critics did not confine themselves to a relatively small portion of language behavior which is definite, but tried to extend it to the totality of human experience, including the emotional.

---

1 J.Brough, op.cit. p. 174.

2 ibid.

3 ibid.

13

Rasa as Aesthetic Experience
The Rasa-sutra

Mohan Thampi

Defining the drama Bharata says that it is an imitation of the affairs of the world and that it is rich in the portrayal of many states and situations. In what sense Bharata used the word *anukaraṇa* (imitation) need not detain us here (it has a specialized meaning as Aristotle's 'mimesis' has); what is relevant to our purpose is the conception that the drama is a rendering of the affairs of the world, i.e., human actions, situations and emotions. How are these actions, situations and emotions rendered in a work of literature and with what effect on the reader? Bharata's famous definition of *rasa* says: '*rasa* is realized by the union of *vibhāva*, *anubhāva*, and *vyabhicāri bhāva*. This definition is so cryptic that, not surprisingly, it gave rise to a great deal of controversy. Every later theorist tried to interpret the definition, in his own way in the light of his philosophy. The greatest controversy was centered on the interpretation of *saṃyoga* and *niṣpatti* which I have rendered as 'union' and 'realization' respectively. The 'union' referred to in the definition is not a union among *vibhāva*, *anubhāva* and *vyabhicāri bhāva* it is the fusion of these elements with the *sthāyibhāva*, the permanent emotion. In order to arrive at a satisfactory explanation of this definition it is necessary to establish the exact meaning of the terms employed therein. Let us begin with '*bhāvas*'.

The Bhāvas

Bharata says that the drama renders the *bhāvas* of all the three worlds. Here, evidently, he means states and things existing, and emotions. The *bhāvas* bring into being (*bhāvayanti*) *rasa* which is the *kāvyārtha* (the end or meaning of the poem). It is the functional aspect of the word *bhāva* which is emphasized. *Bhāvayanti* means 'to bring into being' and 'to make pervade'. The creative experience of the poet (*kaverantargatam bhāvam)* is objectively realized in the poem. By extension, we can also say, that *bhāvas* are those elements which make the essence of poetry, *rasa*, pervade the heart of the reader. In this sense *bhāva* includes *sthāyi*, *vibhāva*, *anubhāva*, *vyabhicari*, and *sattvik bhāvas*. Though Bharata's emphasis was on the functional aspect of the world, he seems to have realized that, in the last analysis, it is the mental states rendered in a poem which manifest its essence and that the characters and their actions (the *vibhāvas* and the *anubhāvas*) are only the vehicles of the mental states. He himself contracted the meaning by speaking of the *bhāvas* as though they included only the three varieties: eight *sthayins,* thirty three *vyabhicarins* and eight *sāttvik bhāvas*. They are the forty nine *bhāvas* capable of manifesting the *rasa* of the poem.

A point which we must bear in mind in this connection is the distinction between the dramatic or poetic *bhāvas* and the personal emotions and feelings experienced in ordinary life. The central problem faced by Bharata was that of giving practical instructions to all those concerned with the production of drama as to how certain recurrent and universal states and situations in which human beings find themselves could be represented on the stage. In his list of *bhāvas* we find dream, sleep, and death which cannot be described as emotions. But we cannot ignore the intimate relation between even these states like death and sleep and emotional situations. As emotions and moods most of the *bhāvas* have their equivalents in ordinary life. On the one hand, *bhāvas* mean all the elements having the energy or power to manifest *rasa*; on the other, they stand for emotions and moods.

The sthayibhāvas

Though the term *sthāyi* does not figure in Bharata's definition, for a correct understanding of the theory of *rasa*, it is necessary for us to elucidate the concept. The word figures in Bharata's explanation of the *rasa-sūtra.* The *sthāyibhāvas* are of the nature of *vāsanā* or *samskāra.* Every human being is born with a set of instinctual propensities inherited from earlier generations, and deposited on the bed of his consciousness. M. Hiriyanna says:

> Every deed we do has a double result. It not only produces the particular result which it was intended to produce, but also tends to establish in us a habit favourable to the repetition of the same deed in future. This habit is termed samskāra.

S.N. Das Gupta makes a subtle distinction between *vāsanā* and *saṁskāra:*

> (*Saṁskāra*) means the impressions (which exist subconsciously in the minds) of the objects experienced. All our experiences whether cognitive, emotional or conative exist in a subconscious state and may under suitable conditions be reproduced as memory (*smṛti*). The word *vāsanā* (*Yogasūtra* IV, 24) seems to be a later word .... It comes from the root '*vas*' to stay. It is often loosely used in the sense of *saṁskāra* .... But *vāsanā* generally refers to the tendencies of the past lives most of which lie dormant in the mind. Only those appear which find scope in this life. But *saṁskāras* are the subconscious states which are being constantly generated by experience. *Vāsanā*s are innate *saṁskāras* not acquired in this life.

These *saṁskāras* and *vāsanās* are organised around what we call emotions. Emotions are related to typical, recurrent and universal situations and generate definable modes of conduct. They are called *sthāyi* (permanent), because they always remain embedded in human organism. It is generally agreed that there are nine such emotions possessed by all human beings:

> In fact, on the basis of the principle that all beings 'hate to be in contact with pain and are eager to taste pleasure,' every one is pervaded by sexual desires (Delight); believes himself superior to others, whom he is thus led to deride (Laughter); grieves when he is forced to part from what he loves (Sorrow); gets angry against the causes of such separation (Anger); gets frightened when he finds himself powerless (Fear); but still is desirous of overcoming the danger which threatens him (Heroism); is attacked, when judging a thing to be displeasing, by a sense of revulsion directed just towards this ugly object (Disgust); wonders at the sight of extraordinary deeds done by himself or others (Astonishment); and, lastly, is desirous of abandoning certain things (Serenity).

I am not interested in verifying whether such a classification corresponds with the latest findings in psychology. I want only to point out that the Indian aestheticians conceived these emotions as being the permanent foci directing the psychic energy in various channels. It is true that in some men some emotions predominate and in others certain other emotions; but all are capable of experiencing these emotional states. In poetic experience the latent emotional traces are aroused. As the elements of a poem do not impinge on our egoistic interests, the emotional states aroused by them acquire the status of free emotions. They are not tied to our ego. They are evoked in our consciousness which acquires trans-personal orientation. The experience transcends the pleasure-pain feeling component which is invariably present in all emotional experiences of everyday life.

The concept of *sthāyin* is relevant also from the point of view of the structure of a poem. In every poem of some length, however complex it may be, a single emotion will predominate over others. Usually this emotion will be associated with the attitudes and destiny of the hero. It is this predominant emotion which gives structural unity to the whole composition by recurring again and again by binding the other elements in an organic whole. Jagannatha says that it is because this emotion pervades, dominates and unifies the entire work it is called permanent *(sthāyi)*. This idea is the same as formulated by Stephen C. Pepper in the following passage:

> Now, the principle of dominant emotion is the selection, for the single work of art or section of a work, of stimuli belonging to one emotional scheme of action patterns. The specific quality of that emotion will then be echoed and re-echoed through all parts of the work; and all details diverse in other respects as they may be, become organised and unified through the single emotion evoked by them. Furthermore the expressive power of each detail becomes intensified by the repeated evoking of the same emotion.

The vyabhicari bhāvas

Apart from these clearly organised dominant emotions there are innumerable transient moods and mental states which accompany them in any experience. They do not attain the intensity of emotions; nor do they last long. They do not have any independent status. They are concomitant moods which rise with the well-defined emotions and subside with them. In short, they are weak, mild, temporary and dependent. But the permanent emotions cannot be expressed in poetry without depicting these moods. The *sthāyins* are very subtle; they manifest themselves through these moods. Love is manifested in the agent's longing or joy or bashfulness. One of the reasons why Bharata did not include *sthāyi* in his definition of *rasa* may be that *sthāyi* being subtle cannot be directly expressed and can only be indirectly depicted with the help of the *vyabhicārins*. These transitory moods in poetry and their relations to the permanent or dominant emotion are compared to the beads on a thread. Themselves varied they reinforce the colour pattern of the thread. They cannot be labelled satisfactorily as there are innumerable shades and combinations. Bharata has mentioned thirty three such *bhāvas*. His list includes sleep, disease and death which cannot be described as moods. But we should remember that in listing the *bhāvas* Bharata's intention was not to exhaust the moods but only to give practical instructions to the producers and the actors as to how real life situations could be represented on the stage.

The *vibhāva* and the *anubhāva*

Emotions and moods can be expressed in poetry only through images, characters, and their actions. In real life some stimuli are necessary to cause the emotions to rise in our heart. These stimuli may be material, existing in the environment, or ideal, existing in the mind itself. These human and environmental stimuli, when described in a poem, are called *vibhāvas*. *Vibhāva* is considered to be synonymous with 'cause' but there is an important difference between the two. The following passage from Dewey brings out exactly this difference: 'In the direct outburst, an objective situation is the stimulus, the cause of the emotion. In the poem, objective material becomes the content and matter of the emotion, not just its evocative occasion. The term is translated as 'determinants' because these *vibhāvas* determine the emotions and moods to be aroused in the reader. They can be described as the 'objective correlatives' in the poem. They are called *vibhāvas* because they make emotions known to us in a special way. In the final analysis a poet's success in evoking emotions will depend on his ability to arrange the *vibhāvas* properly.

Anubhāvas are those effects which are found on the characters consequent upon their emotional agitations. Anger causes blood to rush into the face, and the agent may curse or strike the victim of his anger. The *anubhāvas* are so called because what is represented is made to be felt, experienced (*anubhāvayati*) by us. They make it possible for our self to immerse in the emotions evoked. This process of immersion is called *anubhāvanam* and that which causes this process is called *anubhāva*. In short, they are the signs of emotions in the characters. Some of the consequents (*anubhāvas*) may be deliberate (e.g., cursing, thrashing); others may be involuntary (blushing, sweating, etc.). The latter have a special technical term: *sāttvik bhāvas*. *Sāttva* is the internal character or the inner essence of mind. Bharata felt that to create an impression of verisimilitude the actors must enact sweating, blushing, etc., on the stage. These involuntary consequents are intimately related to moods and emotions; therefore they are considered to be of the nature of *vyabhicāri bhāvas*. Thus the *sāttvik bhāvas* have a dual character: they can be subsumed under both *anubhāvas* (consequents) and vyabhicarins (transient moods).

Meaning and aesthetic experience

In poetry the *vibhāvas* and other elements have their existence as words. Poetry is the most complex and valuable of all the arts. The complexity and value partly arise from the unique qualities of its mode of using language to achieve its effects. Poetry uses all the resources of words, including their sound value, to the fullest extent possible. It is this exploitation of the multiple resources of words and their meanings that accounts for the subtlety, complexity and depth of poetic experience. No other art can rival poetry in its ability to invest human experience with significance; no other art can so efficiently suggest subtle emotional nuances. The theory of *dhvani* (suggestion) was incorporated into the theory of *rasa* to explain the relation between the meaning of words and poetic experience.

If the theory of *rasa* explains the nature of aesthetic experience and its ingredients, the theory of *dhvani* (suggestion) explains the means adopted by the poetic language to achieve its ends. In other words, if the theory of *rasa* is about what poetry does to us, the theory of *dhvani* is about how poetry does that. This theory elucidated *rasa* from the semantic point of view and took in its fold all the earlier concepts like *alamkāra, riti, guna*, etc. It gave Indian aesthetics an entirely new orientation. True to the tradition of the Indian genius this theory attempted successfully a long needed synthesis of many earlier doctrines which moved only on the fringes of the poetic realm and which very often becomes subjects of futile controversy among writers who mistook the contributory factors of poetry for its very soul. After the learned and powerful exposition of this theory in Ānandavardhana's *Dhvanyāloka* it once and for all settled the path to be followed in literary criticism.

The theory of meaning is a highly developed department of Indian philosophy. The concept of *dhvani* evolved out of the grammatical and logical discussions of the relation between word and meaning.

It developed hair-splitting distinctions and a highly sophisticated technical terminology. It is not necessary for us to go into the details of this theory. I shall give an outline of the theory of *dhvani* with a view to show the link between meaning in poetry and poetic experience.

Words have three types of meaning. A word has a primary literal meaning fixed arbitrarily by convention. A word also has a secondary meaning which is derived from the context in which it is used. Apart from these primary and secondary meanings a tertiary meaning also may operate. The tertiary meaning is suggested by the primary or secondary meanings. Beauty in poetry consists in the predominance of the suggested tertiary meaning over the primary referential and the secondary contextual meanings. It may appear paradoxical that the essence of poetry is not what is directly expressed but what is indirectly suggested. All poets find out directions by indirections. They resort to metaphor, paradox, hyperbole and other figures of speech because the direct and straight way of expression is not adequate to objectify their experience. The suggested meaning cannot be considered to be the sum total of the component parts based on these meanings; but it also transcends them. It is like the loveliness of a beautiful woman which is not the total of the beauty of the separate limbs and features but something transcending them though based on and projected by them. *Rasa* in a poem is a qualitatively new product arising from a combination of *vibhāvas*, etc. *Rasa* is not in any one of the ingredients but a product of their proper functioning. We can say that it is a quality which appears when the *vibhāvas*, etc., begin to function.

No doubt, the suggested meaning will not become comprehensible if the referential and contextual meanings do not function. But in poetry the latter must be taken as a means to an end. Just as a man interested in perceiving objects in the dark secures a lamp as a means to realise his end, so also one who is interested in perceiving the suggested meaning shows interest in the primary referential meaning. It must be noted, however, that the means-end relationship of primary and suggested meanings in poetry has a peculiarity. As the lamp analogy makes it clear, in poetry means and ends coexist. Once the lamp is removed we cease to perceive the objects. We secure a lamp not to look at it but to look at other objects in its light. In the same way we understand the primary meaning of words in a poem not to rest on it but to relish the suggested meaning. The primary meanings of words are fixed by convention; but the suggested meanings are accessible only to men with trained poetic sensibility. A person may be a competent grammarian or a lexicographer; but if he lacks poetic sensibility the suggested meaning will elude him.

What this tertiary power of words suggests in poetry is nothing but *rasa*. By its very nature *rasa* can only be suggested. It cannot be explicitly stated. To express Macbeth's sense of tragic frustration Shakespeare does not make him explicitly state his mood; he makes his hero say that life is a tale told by an idiot full of sound and fury signifying nothing. When the sage Angira made the proposal of marriage between Uma and Siva the young maiden hung her head down and began counting the petals of lotus. Kalidasa does not say Uma was bashful. It is because poetry depends on the suggestive power of words that it cannot be paraphrased or translated in the same language. The wealth of emotional suggestions contained by lines like 'To be or not to be ...' and 'Put out the light and then put out the light ...' cannot be evoked by another set of English words.

All poetry is suggestive; but all suggestion is not poetry. In ordinary language suggestion can be a means of making the hearer infer some meaning not fixed by convention. 'It is getting dark' may be an instruction to put on the light. But such suggested meanings can be translated in words with conventional meanings. The differentia of poetic language is its use to communicate impersonal mental states. It may seem to refer to objects and ideas and indicate patterns of behaviour; but ultimately it aims at making you relish certain mental states. The poet may suggest only the rise or fall of a mood; he may suggest an object or a figure of speech. But the suggestion of moods, objects and figures of speech will ultimately terminate in the experience of *rasa*. Like *rasa*, *dhvani* also is a comprehensive concept. It stands for the suggesting words, the suggested meanings, the function of suggestion, the suggested experience and the poem which suggests. In poetry meanings are grasped as symbols of a complex experience. When we relish poetry we apprehend meanings in terms of experience. *Rasadhvani* (the suggestion of *rasa*, or the suggested *rasa*) is the soul of poetry.

The number of rasa

Rasa is so called because it is relished. It is another name for the reposeful consciousness established when our self rests on the aesthetic configuration. In this sense *rasa* is the *mahārasa* (the great or basic *rasa*). But it has been the practice of Indian critics to classify the experience according to the *sthāyin* (permanent emotion) evoked by the particular set of determining factors like the *vibhāvas*, etc. The *vibhāvas* determine and control the emotional content of the poem and the emotional response in the reader. Lear and Falstaff do not evoke same emotions though both become objects of our delightful contemplation. According to Bharata there are only eight *sthāyins.* They are love (*rati*), laughter (*hāsa*), anger (*krodha*), heroism (*vira*), fear (*bhaya*), disgust (*juguptsa*), and wonder (*vismaya*). The corresponding eight *rasas* are the erotic (*sr̥ngāra*), the comic (hāsya), the pathetic (*karuṇa*), the furious (*raudra*), the heroic (*vira*), the terrible (*bhayanaka*), the odious (*bibhatsa*), and the marvellous (*adbhuta*). Śānta (serentity) was added later. Abhinavagupta accepted only these nine *rasas* because only the *sthāyins* of these nine *rasas* are related to the four *puruṣārthas* (ends of human life). There were periodical attempts to enlarge the list. No sanctity was attached to the number prescribed by Bharata even though the majority of the traditionalists consider that nine *rasas* are enough to cope with the infinite variety of literary productions.

The division of aesthetic experience into eight or nine or more *rasas* is not of any consequence today from the point of view of comparative aesthetics, though it is of some use in practical criticism. But even in the field of practical criticism this division merely enables us to label the content of poems. A critic does not stop there. He has to bring out the essential individuality of the emotional pattern of the poems. Here the traditional division can be only of superficial value. Related to this is the vexed question whether the transient moods (*vyabhicārins*) also attain to the state of *rasa*. Considering the fact that all these moods are in one way or another related to this or that *sthāyin* we may say that they can also attain the state of *rasa*. States like anxiety and bashfulness can be portrayed only in the larger background of some permanent emotion, though the readers may have to supply the essentials of such a background. Rudrata was a theorist who realized early the futility of the attempt to fix the number of *rasas*. According to him any emotion or mood, even the subtlest nuance of an emotion, can become *rasa* if it is portrayed and apprehended in poetry as relishable. In this sense *rasas* are not eight or nine or twelve but infinite.

On the other hand, there were also interesting attempts to synthesize all *rasas* into a single *rasa*. Most of these attempts were motivated by a desire to reduce all mental states in poetic response to a single basic emotion. For instance Bhāvabhuti, the dramatist, considered that karuna (the pathetic) is the only *rasa* which undergoes, according to the situations, various transformations as water assumes various forms like whirlpools, bubbles, ripples and waves. It is true that the above idea is expressed by a character in his play *Uttarāramacarita* and therefore, to what extent this reflects the dramatist's aesthetic convictions may be disputed. However, considering the general poetic temperament of Bhāvabhūti, which is essentially tragic, we may take it as his attempt albeit a cursory one, at a *rasa* synthesis. There was another attempt to reduce all aesthetic responses to one basic experience of wonder. Bhoja, in his *Sṛṅgāraprakāśa* asserts that there is only one *rasa*, *sṛṅgāra* (love), and establishes a peculiar if original relation between ego and *rasa*. He argues that *rasa* is made enjoyable by the ultimate reality which is *ahamkāra* or the sense of 'I' in man. This 'I' is identified with a man's personality and culture. As this ego consciousness is the fundamental basis of all our delights, he calls it *rasa*. This transcendental indivisible *rasa* is described by him as *sṛṅgāra* because it takes man to the peak of perfection. The most valuable synthesis was achieved by Abhinavagupta. Basing himself on some *Nāṭyaśāstra* verses whose authenticity is controversial, he argued that *śānta* (serenity) is the basic *rasa* and that all other *rasas* are only different forms which *śānta* assumes. In the context of Richards's doctrine of the equilibrium of impulses in aesthetic experience Abhinavagupta's synthesis is particularly illuminating. I do not wish to say anything more on the concept of *śānta* at present as it will be discussed in CHAPTER V.

The realisation of rasa

Now we may go back to the *rasa-sūtra* and try to elucidate the process of *rasa*-realisation. The *rasa-sūtra* may be interpreted both objectively and subjectively. Objectively interpreted it will refer to the process of realising *rasa* (the essential totality of the aesthetic qualities) in the poem or on the stage. Subjectively interpreted it will refer to the reader's realisation of *rasa* (aesthetic experience). We are concerned with the latter process. A competent reader is expected to have (i) a large fund of experience, and (ii) a trained sensibility. He must be an able observer capable of making appropriate deductions from the interactions of images and characters in the poem. Experiences leave subtle impressions in our consciousness. What a reader gains from a poem will partly depend upon the clarity and variety of these subtle impressions. The reader's *pratibhā* (poetic sensibility), his susceptibility and sensitivity to thought-emotion complexes, gets strengthened by its repeated and discriminating exercise. As a result it becomes 'mirror-like'; even the subtlest and most minute emotional nuances and shades suggested in the poem are reflected exactly in the reader's heart and a perfect identification (*tanmayibhavana*) takes place between the reader's sensibility and the basic mental state realized in the poem.

Human experience in its infinite variety is the raw material of poetry. The poet selects an area of human experience, combines and recombines the component elements of that part of experience and fashions a pattern out of them. A poem is not a direct outpouring of the poet; it is an arrangement of words evoking sensuous images and through them ideas of certain characters and their states of mind. All the images and characters are unified by a single dominant emotional quality and a host of transient moods contribute to the impression of the dominant emotion. The poet does not describe emotional states; he suggests them by describing the actions and behaviour of the characters. He resorts to figures of speech, rhyme, rhythm, symbolisation and other rhetorical devices to objectify his experience. Once he objectifies his experience by concretely embodying it in an adequately individualised pattern of imagery it becomes universal. It becomes accessible to anybody who can translate the imagery into corresponding emotional states. Words in poetry are charged with meanings which unfold in the minds of the reader as emotional states. When the poet wants to suggest the emotional states of Parvati as she listened to the marriage proposal from siva he does not say that she was shy, but that she started counting the petals of the lotus which she held in her hand. It is as if the mood of maidenly bashfulness is incarnated in Kalidasa's verse and we perceive it directly. Such a mood has no spatial or temporal limitations because it is personally and empirically connected with none in the world. It is objectified, individualised and also universalised.

I mentioned that the two words *saṃyoga* and *niṣpatti* in the *rasa-sūtra* have been variously interpreted. Without going into the details of the controversy over the two words, we may explain them in the following way: when we read a poem we first reconstruct the meanings of the words in the form of images and characters. These images and characters are vehicles of emotions and moods and therefore they evoke the latent emotional traces in the reader. As the *vibhāvas*, etc., are objectified, individualised and universalised, the emotional states evoked in the reader snap their connection with his ego and are contemplated. The *samyoga* (*samyak yogam* — proper union) in the *sūtra* refers to the organic fusion of all the elements in the poem and to the fusion between the aesthetic focus and the reader. The *vibhāvas*, etc., reacting upon the sensibility of the reader, manifest the permanent emotional states which become objects of reader's contemplation. The manifestation and the concurrent delightful contemplation of permanent emotions are indicated by the word *niṣpatti*. *Rasa* is the relishing of the contemplated *sthāyins*. It is an autonomous activity in the sense that it is correlated neither with the past nor with the future. It lasts only as long as the tasting of the *vibhāvas* lasts. Abhinavagupta compares aesthetic experience to the perception of 'the magic flower' (*adbhutapuṣpa*), in the sense that the essence of both is solely the present. He does not mean that *rasa* has no temporal dimensions he merely denies its continuity with ordinary personal interests of our everyday life.

14

The Mode of Aesthetic Experience

Mohan Thampi

Once Thomas Mann and a friend came out of a movie weeping copiously. We should imagine that the film was a very 'moving' work of art. But Mann narrates the incident in support of his view that films are not works of art. He said: 'Art is a cold sphere[1].' This statement raised important problems about the nature of aesthetic experience and its relation to emotions. All experiences are processes of mutual interaction between organism and environment. No experience occurs in total isolation from environment. In this sense all experiences have continuity. But within this continuity differentiations can be made on the basis of the nature of the particular bit of environment impinging on the mind and the specific mode perception and interaction. To determine whether aesthetic experience has a special mode, it is necessary to clarify our ideas about the ontological status of work of art, for instance, a poem. After determining the mode of existence of a poem in the light of the Indian concept of *alaukika,* I shall discuss what I call the 'naturalism' of I.A. Richards and John Dewey who insist on the continuity of aesthetic experience with ordinary experience, and the 'isolationism' of Kant and the modern formalists who deny the role of emotions in art. Lastly, I shall expound the Indian concept of *alaukika* and expose the fallacy involved in the question, how tragedy delights.

The Mode of Existence of a Poem

Does a poem have any special ontological status as distinct from that of the common objects of perception? René Wellek has analysed most of the usual and unusual answers to this question and finds them unsatisfactory[2]. A poem is not identical with the printed black

---

1 W. K. Wimsatt, Jr., and Monroe C. Beardsley, 'The Affective Fallacy'; W. K. Wimsatt, Jr., *The Verbal Icon* (Kentucky, 1954), p. 31.

2 René Wellek, 'The Mode of Existence of a Literary Work of Art', *Critiques and Essays in Criticism*, ed. R. W. Stallman (New York, 1949), pp. 210-23.

impression because printing is only a way of recording the poem which exists outside of the printed matter. Neither is the poem identical with the sequence of sounds uttered by a reader because the reading of a poem is merely a 'performance'. The poem is neither the author's experience, because it is a thing of the past; nor is it a single readers's experience, because every reader adds some extraneous and instantaneous elements to the poem. Wellek believes that a poem exists as a 'potential cause of experience'[1]. He wants us to conceive of a poem as a set of norms and standards realised — always partially — in the experience of individual readers[2]. A poem's system of norms is made of the sound structure, the implied units of meaning, and the world of objects to which the meanings refer. There are variations in the experiential realisation of a poem by individual readers; but the basic identity of the structure of norms remains unchanged.

> The work of art, then, appears as an object of knowledge *sui generis* which has a special ontological status. It is neither real (like a statue) nor mental (like the experience of light or pain) nor ideal (like a triangle). It is a system of norms of ideal concepts which are inter-subjective. They must be assumed to exist in collective ideology, changing with it, accessible only through individual mental experiences based on the sound-structure of its sentences[3].

Now, this conclusion of Wellek is not wholly free from difficulties and obscurities. I doubt whether he has made his 'system of norms of ideal concepts which are inter-subjective' sufficiently clear. What is important for us, however, is his statement that a poem has a special ontological status and that our perception of it is *sui generis*.

The Indian theorists believe that the *vibhāvas* are *alaukika*, non-ordinary. As I have pointed out earlier, *vibhāvas* are the vehicles of feelings, the 'objective correlatives'. Every poem, even a short lyric,

---

1 Ibid., p. 218.

2 I. A. Richards defines a poem 'as a class of experiences which do not differ in any character more than a certain amount, varying from each character, from a standard experience. We may take as this standard experience the relevant experience of the poet when contemplating the completed composition' (*Principles of Literary Criticism*, London, 1926, pp.226-27).

3 René Wellek, *loc.cit.*, p.223.

is about a situation and the reaction of a character — or the poet as dramatist speaker — to that situation. In ordinary life our attitude to all objects and persons can be described in terms of attraction, repulsion or indifference. Men and things directly or indirectly, impinge on our life and our practical interests. A person, in ordinary life has *arthakriyā*, causal efficiency. *Arthakriyā* means the ability to produce practical effects[1]. Only when a person has causal efficiency can he be said to have real existence. A character in a poem does not have the real existence of ordinary men because he does not have this ability of *arthakriyā*. He does not impinge on our egoistic interests. Our attitudes of attraction, repulsion, and indifference are transcended when we contemplate a character like Macbeth. We are not concerned with the fact of Macbeth's historicity; even if he had an historical existence it is irrelevant to our appreciation of the play. Such characters and their actions exist merely to be imaginatively perceived and entertained by us. Susanne K. Langer calls a work of art a 'virtual entity'. 'Anything that exists only for perception, and plays no ordinary part in nature as common objects do, is virtual entity.'[2] A 'virtual entity' is estranged from actuality:

> Every real work of art has a tendency to appear thus dissociated from its mundane environment. The most immediate impression it creates is one of 'otherness' from reality — the impression of an illusion enfolding the thing, action, statement, or flow of sound that constitutes the work.[3]

The non-ordinary mode in which a work of art exists has been recognised by many theorists including Alexander and Beardsley. According to Beardsley, aesthetic objects are 'so to speak objects

---

1 *Abhinavabharati*, pp.35-6.

2 Susanne K. Langer, *Problems of Art* (New York, 1957), p.5.

3 Susanne K. Langer, *Feeling and Form* (New York, 1953), p.45.Also see, 'Art and Feeling' by Otto Baensch where he says: "The work of art must be an object existing for itself, separated out from the rest of the world of objects. It must exclude all other objects. It must have a frame within which separated feeling moves about as in a container. This is what has been called the self-sufficiency of the work of art, which was what inspired Schiller's speculations on freedom in pure appearance' (*Reflections on Art*, ed. Susanne K. Langer, p. 24).

manqués. There is something lacking in them that keeps them from being quite real, from achieving the full status of things or, better, that prevents the question of reality from arising.'[1] Alexander prefers Schiller's word *schein*, 'semblanace', to describe the specific status of the work of art. His position is set forth in the following statements:

> The work of art asks not to be believed as we believe in things of the practical world in which we live, submitting ourselves to it.
>
> We create an autonomous world, a blending of the physical with ourselves, and therefore a new reality within the so called real world; neither believed or disbelieved but entertained and therefore not acted upon.[2]

From the above presentation it is clear that Wellek, the Indian theorists, Susanne K. Langer, Beardsley and Alexander are agreed on the non-ordinary ontological status of a work of art. The relation between the perceptual field and the material medium on which the former is dependent varies in the different arts. Croceans would believe that a work of art exists purely in imagination. Collingwood goes to the extent of asserting that a work of art is an 'imaginary thing' and that the 'real' work of art is only a means by which the readers can reconstruct for themselves.[3] We are not justified in adopting a wholly subjectivistic position by believing that a poem exists as an 'imaginary experience'. This would entail the absurd conclusion that the structural identity of a poem as a linguistic construct can never be established. Though we do not identify a statue or a painting (as a work of art) with the physical properties of its medium, we are prepared to concede that without the material basis the art objects will not exist for appreciation by the community. In the case of poetry no such simple solution seems possible. When we read a poem our attention is concentrated not on the black

---

1 Monroe C. Beardsley, *Aesthetics: Problems in the Philosophy of Criticism* (New York, 1958), p. 529.

2 Samuel Alexander, *Beauty and Other Forms of Value* (London, 1933), p. 37.

3 R. G. Collingwood, *The Principles of Art* (Oxford, 1938), p. 139.

impression on the paper but on the reverberations of meanings evoked in us. We are really concerned with patterns of sound conventionally invested with meanings. Good poetry adds new dimensions to the meanings of words by charging them with emotional and intellectual associations of great human significance.

In India there was a controversy over the relative importance of words and meanings. Does a poem exist as a system of words or as a system of meanings or as *rasa*? It was the reflection in a poetics of the soul-body dichotomy in philosophy. Bhāmaha defined literature as the union of words and meanings.[1] This is an inane definition till we clarify the special aesthetic context of the 'union' *(sahitau)*. As such, Bhāmaha's definition is unilluminating because without union of word and meaning all language will be mere gibberish. Later there were intensive searches in different directions to find the differentia of the particular union of words and meanings in poetry. This unique union consists in the sensuous and symbolic qualities of words and meanings, the images and associations evoked by them and all the constituents competing and interacting in a fruitful tension suggesting *rasa*.[2] Panditarāja Jagannatha, after showing up the inadequacy of many definitions of a poem, emphasises the aspect of poetry as a structure of words, though his definition includes meanings, and delight giving meanings at that.[3]

In poetry words and meanings harmoniously coexist. Language in poetry is not means to an end like conveying information or issuing instructions. We know that in a good poem each word is inevitable and irreplaceable. When we say that a poem is an organic unity we mean that the nexus of the meanings of the words lies within it, making it autonomous and self-sufficient. In non-poetic use, language leads you away from itself; in poetry language pulls you towards itself. Poetry dissolves the means-end conflict. Paul Valery has drawn an interesting analogy to explain the difference between poetry and prose, which we might take to be the difference between imaginative

---

1 Śabdārtha sahitau kāvyam — *Kāvyālamkara*, I, 16.

2 tasmād etayoh śabdārthayoh yathā svam yasyām svasaṃpatsāmagri-samudāyah sahṛdaya hṛayāhlādakāri parasparaspardhayā parisphurati, sā kācid eva vākya vinyāsa sampat sāhitya, vyapadesabhāg bhavati — Kuntaka, *Vakroktijivitam*, quoted by V. Raghavan, *Sṛngara Prakāśa*, p. 100.

3 ramaniyārtha pratipādaka śabdam kāvyam — *Rasagangādhara*, I.

language and non-imaginative language:

> Walking, like prose, aims at the attainment of a perfectly definite objective. It is an activity directed towards reaching a specific end. Dancing consist in a means of actions, but their objective lies within themselves. It leads nowhere. It does envisage an end, but this end exists only as an ideal state of mind .... [A] poem is designed expressly to be reborn from its ashes, to become once more what it has just succeeded in being.[1]

Evidently, the idea that a poem exists merely as a system of meanings is unsatisfactory because a newspaper editorial also exists as a system of meanings. To indicate the special status of a poem we may use Alexander's phrase 'reality within reality' or Valery's 'language within language'. Poetry is imposing a formal pattern on language or, if it sounds too mechanical, we may say that poetry is carving out of language a formal pattern as a sculptor carves out of marble a statue. If marble exists outside the individual's mind in the material world, language exists outside the individual mind in a culture of a society.

Falstaff is an imaginary character; but *Henry IV* is not an imaginary play. In aesthetic theory the reality of the former is irrelevant; the reality of the latter is undisputed. Falstaff is imaginary but not in the sense of a quaint apparition in a dream; because the dream is a private experience whose authenticity is unverifiable and whose meaning, if it has any, is again private. But Falstaff has a structural identity available to all. He exists in the autonomous world of poetry and is accessible to anyone who can realise the system of meanings embodied in the play Henry IV.

The upshot of the above discussion is that if we ignore the multidimensional nature of poetry and go in search of simplified either/or type of answers, we are unlikely to arrive at truth. The question whether a poem exists as sounds, or words, or in the poet's mind, or in the reader's mind can have only one satisfactory answer, that is, that a poem exists as all these at once. If it is impossible for us to establish the locus of life in the heart or brain or in the stomach it is equally impossible to nail the poem to words or to meanings or to subjective experiences. A poem exists in different strata simultaneously. The verbal substructure of a poem shares its reality with

---

1 Paul Valery, *The Art of Poetry,* tr. Denise Folliot (London, 1958), p. 70.

other verbal patterns in language; but the autonomous world created by the substructure defies our ideas about reality or illusion. The logical status of its existence cannot be subsumed in the usual categories; hence the Indian theorists call it *alaukika,* non-ordinary.

Aesthetic experience and ordinary experience

The Naturalists : I.A. Richards

I.A. Richards categorically denies any qualitative difference between aesthetic experience and ordinary life experiences. He has built up a theory of value which has no necessity to distinguish between them to evaluate them. His value theory is quantitative, i.e., the larger the number of impulses are coordinate in an experience the more it is valuable. Poetic experience is more valuable than that of eating cherries simply because it coordinates a greater number of impulses. He tries to explode the assumption that there is a distinct kind of mental activity present in aesthetic experiences. The very title of the second chapter of his book *Principles of Literary Criticism* — 'The Phantom Aesthetic State' makes his intention clear. He considers that this assumption is 'a legacy from the days of abstract investigation into the Good, the Beautiful and the True.'[1] No doubt that an exaggeration of this distinction has led some thinkers to associate it with supra-mundane and extra-sensory experiences. Richards rendered a signal service to the discussion of the problem by lifting it out of the quagmire of pseudo-mysticism and transcendental jargon into which it was pushed by idealists and the aesthetes. The aesthetes denied any kind of relation between art and life. In combating their wrong notions Richards went to the other extreme of denying any distinctive quality which differentiates aesthetic experience from ordinary experience.

A.C. Bradley, in his famous inaugural lecture 'Poetry for Poetry's Sake' said that poetry is not a part or copy of the real world but a

---

1 I. A. Richards, *op. cit.*, pp. 11-12.

world by itself, independent, complete, autonomous'.[1] Richards hotly contests this view because he thinks that this way of formulating the problem introduces a severance between poetry and life .... 'The world of poetry has in no sense any different reality from the rest of the world and it has no special laws and no other worldly peculiarities'.[2] In another place he says; ' When we look at a picture, or read a poem, or listen to music, we are not doing something quite unlike what we are doing on our way to the Gallery or when we dressed in the morning'.[3] Despite the clarity and audacity it can be shown that Richards is not able to maintain his position without compromises. He admits that aesthetic experiences are different form non-aesthetic experiences by virtue of the difference in 'the connections between their constituents' and that they are a further development and a finer organisation of ordinary experience.[4] Even if one accepts his quantitative evaluation of experiences it can be argued that a quantitative increase leads to a qualitative change in experience. There is, of course, no way of knowing how many impulses are at work when we dress in the morning and how many when we read *Hamlet*. But if the number increases and the organisation goes on growing finer and finer a point may come when the entire consciousness gets a qualitatively different orientation.

Though it would appear that his theory of synaesthesis — the experience of equilibrium of impulses — does demarcate a special aesthetic realm within the wider context of man's total field of experience, the inference is negated by his two statements. He believes that synaesthesis can be brought about by non-poetic, non-artistic objects also. He also refuses to relate synaesthesis to the objective pattern and qualities of the work of art.[5] Apart from giving rise to pure impressionism and subjectivism in critical practice this theory makes poetry replaceable. It is ironical that the arguments

---

1 A.C. Bradley, *Oxford Lectures on Poetry* (London, 1909), p. 5.

2 Richards, op. cit., p. 78.

3 *Ibid.*, p. 16.

4 *Ibid.*, p. 18.

5 *Ibid.*, p. 248.

2 *Ibid.*, p. 249.

of Richards, who proceeds from a healthy regard for poetry's place in human civilisation, should negate the differentiating qualities and values of poetic experience and thus make poetry replaceable and dispensable.

Implicit modifications of Richards's explicit thesis are available here and there in his writings. He recognises the fact that certain characteristics of aesthetic experience like impersonality, disinterestedness, and detachment are of special service in promoting aesthetic communication, though they have nothing to do with the value of what is communicated.[2] He also recognises a readjustment of our impulses brought about by our change in our awareness of objects.

> The free impulses which are aroused have to adjust themselves to their new setting of other impulses due to our awareness that it is a picture which we are looking at.[3] To take another obvious example, the description of the theatrical presentation of a murder has a different effect upon us from that which would be produced by most actual murders if they took place before us.[4]

Here also Richards implicitly admits that the reality of the world of art is not the same as that the real world. Our awareness of the 'framing' of the work of art is accompanied by a qualitatively new orientation of impulses which has to be isolated from 'the accidents and irrelevancies of everyday existence'.[5] Richards's main explicit contention loses much of its force when considered in the context of these modifications which are cautious but which have far reaching consequences.

John Dewey

In a brilliant passage at the beginning of his book *Art as Experience* Dewey enumerates the principal social causes which tempted philosophers to effect and perpetuate a chasm between ordinary life experiences and aesthetic experience. Museums segregate art from temples and such other communal places. Nationalism, capitalism, economic cosmopolitanism, the impersonality of a world market, mass production — all these promote a kind of perverse aesthetic individualism

---

3 *Ibid.*, p. 110.

4 *Ibid.*, p. 110.

5 *Ibid.*, p. 145.

and the idea that art experience is something esoteric, and aloof and isolated from common life. Dewey outright rejects this isolationism and tries to establish that art experience is continuous with ordinary life. The similarity of his ideas with those of I.A. Richards is marked. As I.A. Richards believes that aesthetic experiences are only 'a further development' and 'a finer organisation' of ordinary experiences, Dewey maintains that works of art merely 'accentuate and idealise qualities found in ordinary life'.[1]

> Because experience is the fulfillment of an organism in its struggles and achievements in a world of things, it is art in a germ. Even in its rudimentary forms, it contains the promise of that delightful perception which is aesthetic experience.[2]

Dewey thinks that normal experience is prevented from running its course to fulfillment by extraneous interruption and inner lethargy. When the material expressed runs its course to fulfillment and when it is 'integrated within and demarcated in the general stream of experience',[3] it is called *an* experience. *An* experience is 'complete' in itself standing out because marked out from what went before and what came after'.[4] According to Dewey *an* experience of thinking has its own aesthetic quality; the experience of successful politicians like Caesar and Napoleon has also aesthetic quality.[5] This aesthetic quality which gives to an experience roundness and unity is emotional. There are no separate things called emotions in human experience. 'In fact emotions are qualities, when they are significant, of a complex experience that moves and changes.'[5] Dewey's conclusion is simply that

> [The] aesthetic is no intruder in experience from without, whether by way of idle luxury or transcendental ideality, but that it is the clarified and intensified development of traits that belong to every normally complete experience.[6]

---

1 John Dewey, *Art as Experience*, p. 11.

2. *Ibid.*, p. 19.

3 *Ibid.*, p. 35.

4 *Ibid.*, p. 36.

5 *Ibid.*, p. 38.

5 *Ibid.*, p. 41.

6 *Ibid.*, p. 46.

From the above paragraphs it is clear that Dewey is an uncompromising opponent of any theory which tries to isolate aesthetic experience from the general stream of human life. But it is necessary to point out an element of contradiction in his theory. He does not hesitate to differentiate between the humdrum experiences of ordinary life and *an* experience which has completeness, roundness and unity. To admit that aesthetic experience is *an* experience is to demarcate it from ordinary experiences. Sometimes Dewey wants us to believe that he uses the word 'aesthetic' adjectively, i.e., to qualify a phase of ordinary experience.[1] He talks as if aesthetic is only ordinary experience coloured by this aesthetic quality. He complicates the problem by stating that what gives an aesthetic experience its peculiar unity is only its emotional quality. But we know that emotions are frequent occurrences in our life. By themselves they cannot give unity and completeness to aesthetic experience.

It is interesting to observe that Dewey makes a distinction between emotion which is part of our daily life and emotion as felt in aesthetic experience though such a distinction runs counter to the general tenor of his thesis. In the chapter entitled 'The Act of Expression', he says that 'a person overwhelmed by emotion is thereby incapacitated for expressing it'.[2] He admits that artistic expression is not a 'direct emission of an emotion'.[3] The fact is that when we actively respond to the emotional situations depicted in a poem, we not only feel those emotions but also contemplate them. Dewey blames Kant for using the word 'contemplation' to describe art experience because he thinks that it is inept [sic] to suggest the excitement and passionate absorption which one feels while responding to poetry. No doubt, in ordinary parlance, the word has the connotations of inaction and mental passivity. But in aesthetics the word is used only to differentiate the attitude from the practical one. Dewey himself later concedes that the response to art is 'not practical, *if* by "practical" is meant an action undertaken for a specialised end outside the perception or for

---

1 See 'A Comment on Croce's and Dewey's Aesthetics' by Patrick Ramanell, *Journal of Aesthetics and Art Criticism,* Vol. VIII, no.2, December 1949, pp. 1225-27, for criticism of what Ramanell calls Dewey's adjectival and substantival analysis of experience.

2 Dewey, *op. cit.*, p. 69.

3 *Ibid.*, p. 67.

some external consequences'.[1] When we consider his contention about the continuity of art experience with the ordinary life experiences in the light of the above qualifications we find that it loses much of its force.

The isolationists : Kant

In a sense Kant can be considered the father of formalism in modern aesthetics. His aesthetic theory was not derived from an empirical study of aesthetic phenomena. It was designed to bridge the gulf between the cognitive faculties of imagination and understanding. Kant's formalism is the logical consequence of two of his doctrines: (i) his partial definition of beauty as 'purposiveness without purpose'; (ii) his distinction between 'free' or 'pure' or 'adherent' beauty.

The third moment of Kant's *Critique of Judgment* contains the statement that beauty is 'the form of purposiveness in an object so far as it is perceived apart from the presentation of a purpose'.[2] For instance, a flower or a landscape has no purpose in the sense that it is not there to make you appreciate its beauty; but it serves a purpose; it establishes, by virtue of its form, a free harmony between imagination which synthesises sense-data and understanding which conceptualises knowledge. The beautiful establishes this harmony merely by its form. 'The sole foundation of the judgment of Taste is the form of an object'.[3] Forgetting that to the extent we are able to use the knowledge of reality to change it, it is real knowledge, Kant declared that noumena in themselves are unknowable and thus caused the breach between phenomenon and noumenon. In the same way, in aesthetics, by rejecting content as irrelevant to aesthetic experience he caused a chasm between form and content which, in reality, constitute an inseparable unity both in creation and appreciation.

Kant says that the aesthetic interest is unconcerned with the sensuousness of the appeal of the beautiful objects; it is concerned

---

1 *Ibid.*, p. 256.

2 I. Kant, *Critique of Aesthetic Judgment*, tr. J. C. Meredith (Oxford, 1911), p. 67.

3 *Ibid.*, p. 62.

only with patterns or forms independent of the concepts of purpose, motive, perfection, etc. Thus a landscape is beautiful not by virtue of its green grass, multi-coloured foliage and flowers but merely by virtue of the arrangement, patterns, and shapes of grass, trees, flowers, etc. The fact is that we cannot conceive the shape or structure of a work of art apart from the sensuous material out of which it is created. There is no harmony without sound; there is no shape without substance. It may be that when we contemplate an arabesque or a sea shell we concentrate only on the form; but when this principle is applied to the major arts, particularly poetry, it breaks down. In poetry, form and content interpenetrate and, attention on the form alone, even if it is possible, will only result in emasculating our aesthetic experience of a richness which is available when we contemplate a poem as an organic whole. As Barrows Dunham has pointed out, 'Kant's theory amounts to a restricting of aesthetic experience to the enjoyment of a disembodied ghost.'[1]

Kant himself must have felt that his definition was too restrictive in practice. Therefore he distinguishes between 'free' or 'pure' beauty and 'dependent' or 'adherent' beauty; 'There are two kinds of beauty; free beauty or beauty which is merely dependent. The first presupposes no concept of what the object should be; the second does presuppose such a concept and, with it, an answering perfection of the object.'[2] We should expect that after making these two divisions, Kant would place 'pure beauty' on a higher pedestal. This would have led to the absurd conclusion that *Macbeth* is impure because of Shakespeare's preoccupation with concepts like ambition, crime, retribution, etc. Such a theory disables literary criticism because literature is not concerned with mere texture of words or the harmony of the sound-patterns; it is, above all, concerned with human values. But we find that Kant's moral nature compels him to declare unhesitatingly that poetry which has adherent beauty is richer spiritually than pure forms of beauty because it gives form to aesthetical ideas. By aesthetical ideas Kant means those intellectual reverberations in the mind which cannot be accurately reproduced in discursive prose.

---

1 Barrows Dunham, 'Kant's Theory of Aesthetic Form', *The Heritage of Kant*, eds. G. T. Whitney and D. F. Bowers (Princeton, 1939), p. 374. See also, Israel Knox, *The Aesthetic Theories of Kant, Hegel and Schopenhauer* (New York, 1936), pp. 31-9.

2 *Critique of Aesthetic Judgment*, p. 72.

Kant's exclusion of emotion from aesthetic experience leads to barren formalism. He categorically asserts that emotion and charm vitiate taste and are totally irrelevant to aesthetic experience.

> Emotion — a sensation where an agreeable feeling is produced merely by means of a momentary check followed by a more powerful outpouring of the vital force — is quite foreign to beauty.[1]
> Taste that requires an added element of charm and emotion for its delight, not to speak of adopting this as measure of its approval, has not yet emerged from barbarianism.[2]

It is true that Kant speaks of aesthetic feeling but this feeling is only 'pleasure', the state of the subject when he enjoys a work of art but has nothing to do with the interplay of various emotions in his mind when he reads a poem rich in emotional and spiritual content. The nature of the emotion which we feel when we read a poem must be investigated, no doubt. Whether its nature is the same as that of the emotion which we feel in our practical day-to-day experiences or a transformed state though organised by the same components which enter our real life emotions — these things require clarification because on this hinge many important aesthetic problems. It might be that Kant wanted to check the rising tide of sentimental emotionalism which identified beauty with anything that roused emotions. Sentimental emotionalism certainly cannot serve as a sound basis for a rational and coherent system of aesthetics. But in counteracting the vagueness of such romantic emotionalism which equates aesthetic experience with mere gush Kant threw the baby along with the bath-water. Mere disembodied form abstracted from sensuous and emotional experiences and meanings is like the grin of the Cheshire cat which exists only in the wonderland of psuedomystical aesthetics.

Clive Bell

In our own century this kind of aesthetic formalism found its staunchest exponents in Clive Bell and Roger Fry. When they regard our responses to work of art as distinct from our responses to non-artistic situations we may agree with them. But their esoteric formalism goes further

---

1 *Ibid.*, p. 65.

2 *Ibid.*, p. 65.

than this point and declares:

> The representative element in a work of art may or may not be harmful; always it is irrelevant. For, to appreciate a work of art we need bring with us nothing from life, no knowledge of its ideas and affairs, no familiarity with its emotions.[1]

The second part of the above statement represents the absurd extreme limit of formalism. It contains the starting idea that life is irrelevant to art.

Bell and Fry do not repudiate the role of emotion in art. But their emotion is a peculiar and exclusive aesthetic emotion; 'The starting point for all systems of aesthetics must be the personal experience of a peculiar emotion.'[2] This peculiar emotion is evoked by works of art which have 'significant form'. 'Significant form' is the quality common to all works of art. It results from a particular combination of lines, colours, sounds, etc. Bell's definition, as has been pointed out by his critics, does not escape from circularity; significant form is that form which evokes the unique aesthetic emotion and the unique aesthetic emotion is that which is evoked by significant form. The only way to escape from this vicious circularity is to relate the 'significance' to life as lived by human beings. But this is precisely what Bell refuses to do. According to Bell the intense and peculiar significance of the world of art is unrelated to the significance of life.[3] Significance is always a matter of value judgement. When artistic significance is cut off and isolated from significance in life we have no means of evaluating works of art. Bell's reduction of the complexities of aesthetic experience to single special aesthetic emotion cannot account for the variety of elements which enter art. There is no scope for internal differentiation within this aesthetic emotion. Such an absolutist position incapacitates and, in fact, invalidates all practical criticism.

It should be remembered, however, that Bell and Fry formulated their theories in the context of the graphic arts which had already

---

1 Clive Bell, *Art* (London, 1931), p. 25.

2 *Ibid.*, p. 6.

3 *Ibid.*, pp. 63-64 and 67.

shown tendencies towards abstraction and avoidance of representational elements. The advocates of 'pure poetry' and 'musical concept of poetry' reflect this extreme formalism in the field of literature. The absolutist position of Bell contradicts the experience derived from literature; therefore he regards literature as an impure art. 'We all agree that there is in literature an immense amount of stuff which is not purely aesthetic, which is cognitive and suggestive, which an intelligent bourgeois can understand as well as anyoneelse'.[1] The assumption that some arts are pure because of their freedom from the preoccupations of facts and ideas of life and other arts are impure because of the intrusion of life values in the exclusive realm of art is the characteristic reaction of persons who are incapable of integrating their experiences in a solid frame-work of unified sensibility. By repudiating the relevance of the vital context of lived experience, formalism emasculates art and leaves too many loose ends in aesthetic theory.

Emotion and aesthetic experience

Considering the fact that the word emotion frequently and universally figures in discussions of poetry and poetic experience it is necessary to define exactly its role and nature in the poetic response. As a convenient starting point I shall use Laurence Lerner's classification of theories about the role of emotion in poetic experience.[2] According to him, theoretically, we have five possibilities:

(1) Reading a poem we experience the aesthetic emotion alone.
(2) We experience the 'material' passion (real life emotions) alone.
(3) We experience the aesthetic emotion plus the material passion as it is.
(4) We experience the aesthetic emotion plus a special version of the material passion.
(5) We experience a special version of the material passion and nothing else.

---

1 Clive Bell, 'The "Difference of Literature" of Literature', *New Republic*, 29 November 1922, quoted by Morris Weitz, *Philosophy of the Arts* (Cambridge, 1950). p 9.

2 Laurence Lerner, *The Truest Poetry* (London, 1960), pp. 68-9. Lerner uses the distinction, made by Samuel Alexander, between 'formal passion' and 'material passion'.

Let us see whether the theory of *rasa* can be submerged under any of the foregoing alternatives. As has been pointed out earlier, the Indian theory makes a clear distinction between ordinary life emotions and the emotional content of aesthetic experience. Bharata's commentator Bhaṭṭa Lollata confused the two and led the discussion into a wrong track for a long time. He thought that when the ordinary life emotions were intensified *(upacit)* by the characters and situations in a poem they attained the state of *rasa*.[1] He did not care to verify the truth of their theory by referring it to the actual experience of poetry and drama. An emotion like anger, for instance, when intensified, only drives the subject to madness; it does not give him aesthetic delight. Their error resulted from establishing a crude and direct continuity between life and poetry, forgetting the mode in which the vibhāvās exist. *Rasa* is different from *sthāyin*.[2] It is true that Bharata sometimes says that *sthāyin* becomes rasa; but it is only due to analogy.[3] When the *vibhāvas*, etc., bring the *sthāyins* forth the latter lose their relations with the ego and therefore become impersonal. *Rasa* is the tasting of these impersonal *sthāyins*.

This distinction was not unknown in the west though its full significance has not been realised satisfactorily till recent times. Samuel Alexander makes a distinction between 'material passion' and 'formal passion'.[4] Cecil Day Lewis distinguishes between 'human emotion' and 'poetic passion'.[5] Isabel C. Hungerland in her book *Poetic Discourse* says that literature evokes emotions, but they are different from the real life emotions. 'They are spectator emotions,

---

1 *Abhinavabharati*, p. 272. tena sthāyi eva vibhāvanubhāvādibhir upacito, rasah.

2 *Abhinavabharati*, p. 284....na tu. carvanatiriktakālāvalambi sthāyivilaksana eva rasah.

3 *Abhinavabharati*, p.284. kevalam aucityād evamucyate sthāyi rasibhuta iti. Also see, *Dhvanynaloka Locana*, pp. 156-57: sthāyinastu rasibhāva aucityāducyate, tad vibhāvānubhāvo-cittavrittisamskarasundaracarvanodayāt.

4 *Beauty and Other Forms of Value*, p.54.

5 Cecil Day Lewis. *The Poetic Image* (London, 1955), p.20.

not participator emotions'.[1] Collingwood describes the peculiarity of the emotions in aesthetic experience in the following words:

> At the level of imaginative experience, the crude emotion of the psychical level is translated into idealised emotion or the so-called aesthetic emotion, which is thus not an emotion pre-existing to the expression of it, but the emotional charge on the experience of expressing a given emotion, felt as a new colouring which that emotion receives in being expressed.[2]

W.B. Yeats admits that this poetic emotion 'has nothing to do with action or desire'.[3]

An emotion is a disturbance, an agitation in the consciousness which tends to issue in action. The word is derived from the Latin prefix 'e' and the root 'moveo', and it means to stir and move out. In aesthetic experience emotions do stir in and agitate our mind, but they do not 'move out' in the form of action. When we respond to poetry the emotional states are not simply undergone and suffered; they are perceived and 'tasted'. The Sanskrit words to describe this process are *carvaṇa* which means masticating and *rasana* which means tasting. These words refer to the imaginative reconstruction of the meanings and identity of the poem by the reader and to his active enjoyment of the emotion even while they reverberate in his heart. In ordinary life we can control and even destroy an emotion by concentrating our attention on it. A detached contemplative mood is an enemy to the emotional disturbances in the mind. But in poetic experience, when we 'distance' the depicted emotions, they do not disappear; on the contrary we see them clearly and taste their individual flavours. The liberative function of poetry is partly an outcome of this peculiar nature of poetic experience. Once we are able to formulate and precisely define emotions and acquaint ourselves with their nature and internal differentiations we gain a kind of mastery over them. Poetic experience frees us from being a slave to emotions which are generally chaotic, discordant, powerful and blind. This is one of the meanings of the saying that poetry makes our insight into life keener.

---

1 Isabel Hungerland, *Poetic Discourse* (Berkeley, 1958), p.20.

2 R.G. Collingwood, *op.cit.*,p.273.

3 Quoted from George Whalley, *Poetic Process* (London, 1953), p.22.

Now, I think, we can go back to Lerner's classification referred to at the beginning of this section and see where the theory of *rasa* fits in. It is clear that the theory of *rasa* does not recognise any special 'aesthetic emotion'. It talks of eight or nine *sthāyins* which lie permanently embedded in the human psyche to be awakened by appropriate characters and situations. The 'aesthetic emotion' is certainly not one of them. The feeling of delight which accompanies all aesthetic experiences cannot be called an emotion. The Indian theory does not believe that we experience only life emotions — 'the material passions' — at the time of reading poetry. It raises the entire experience to the plane of *alaukikatva*, non-ordinariness, and insists that the intrusion of one's own personal material passions will only mar the poetic experience. Lerner's fifth view that what we experience is 'a special version of the material passion' is nearest to the Indian theory. The 'speciality' of the 'special version' is caused by the peculiar ontological status of a poem which transpersonalises the emotional experience.

'Alaukika' and Susanne K. Langer's ideas

In the light of the above discussion we may conclude that the naturalistic and isolationalist theories fail to do justice to the uniqueness of aesthetic experience. The former blurs the demarcation line between aesthetic experience and ordinary experiences in its justified effort to integrate art with life; the latter creates a chasm between life and art by denying any role to emotion in aesthetic experience. What we need is a theory which is free from the dogmatic either/or approach and which will establish the uniqueness of aesthetic experience without cutting it off from the vital emotions of human life. I believe the concept of *alaukika* helps us formulate such a theory. It strikes a middle path and reconciles the extremes of isolationalism and naturalism.

Why do we call aesthetic perception non-ordinary *(alaukika)*? Because it cannot be subsumed under any one of the modes of perception common in ordinary life. In the words of Abhinavagupta:

> With regard to the personages moving on the stage, one has neither the idea of being concerned with reality, nor of being concerned with a similitude — as in the case of two similar things — nor with an illusion, as when a piece of mother-of-pearl reminds one of a piece of silver —, nor with a super-imposition as when wrong knowledge follows the denying of the right —, nor with an ascertainment — as when one says, 'this peasant is a cow' (i.e. is as foolish as a cow) —, nor with a comparison — as

between a face and the moon —, nor with a copy — as in the case of a painted image —, nor with an imitation — as in the case of masters and disciples, who seek to explain the scriptures in the same way — nor with a sudden apparition — as in magic —, nor with a skillfully conjured-up apparition — as in a sleight-of-hand, etc. In all these cases, that which emerges does not appear, in fact, in a generalized form, and therefore, the subject does not actively share in what he sees. In consequences, the tasting of *Rasa* does not take place.[1]

Susanne K. Langer's theory of art as 'vital life' bears close affinity with the Indian concept of *alaukika*. A poem, according to her, is a non-discursive symbolic form: 'The feeling expressed by this form is neither his, nor his hero's, nor ours. It is the meaning of the symbol.'[2] It is interesting to compare Mammaṭa's statement on the same subject. He also says that the emotions expressed by the poem have no specific relation with any particular individual. They are independent of specifications such as concern or indifference.[3] Differentiating between ordinary experiences and poetic experience Susanne K. Langer says that the former are fragmentary, transient and often indefinite but 'the poet's business is to create the appearance of "experiences", the semblance of events lived and felt, and to organize them so they constitute a purely and completely experienced reality, a piece of *virtual life*.[4] The source of the subject-matter of poetry does not alter the nature of poetry as virtual experience. The poet may choose the subject-matter of his poem from some mythology or from his personal experiences. But this factor is irrelevant so far as the status of poetic experience is concerned. 'There is no trafficking with actualities in poetry, no matter how much the creator of the semblance has drawn on his own feelings, his deepest convictions, his memories and

---

1 *Abhinavabhārati*, p. 35., Gnoli's translation. See R. Gnoli, *Aesthetic Experience According to Abhinavagupta*, p. 76, note 2.

2 *Feeling and Form*, p. 211.

3 Mamaiva ite satroreva ite tātasthāryaiva ite Mammaṭa — *Kāvyaprakaśa*, ed. Satyavrat Singh (Banaras, 1955). p. 75.

4 *Feeling and Form*, p. 212.

secret wishes.[1]' It is this obvious affinity with the spirit behind the Indian theory which makes her pay the following tribute:

> Some of the Hindu critics, although they subordinate and even deprecate dramatic art in favour of the literary elements it involves, understand much better than their Western colleagues the various aspects of emotion in the theater, which our writers so freely and, banefully confuse: the feelings experienced by the actor, those experienced by the spectators, those presented as undergone by characters in the play, and finally the feeling that shines through the play itself — the vital feelings of the piece. This last they call *rasa*; it is a state of emotional knowledge, which comes only to those who have long studied and contemplated poetry[2].

Some of the supporters and opponents of the theory of *rasa* have tried to interpret the word *alaukika* in a quasi-mystical manner. *Alaukika*, in the context of poetics, has nothing to do with supernaturalism or mysticism. It does not mean 'otherworldly'. The prefix 'a' in *alaukika* has the meaning of a 'being similar and yet different'. We do not experience a different species of emotion. The emotions which are aroused in the poetic experience resemble the emotions in real life; but at the same time they are different in the sense that, while emotions in real life tend to issue in action, in poetic experience they are entertained without any such tendency and are 'tasted'. The dialectical unity of resemblance to and difference from ordinary experiences is best expressed by Viśvanātha who says that when we contemplate dramatic characters we have the feeling: 'It relates to some other and yet not quite the some other, it concerns me and yet does not concern me.[3]' It is because such a feeling is never experienced in ordinary life that poetic experience is considered non-ordinary *(alaukika)*.

---

1 *Ibid.*, pp. 256-57, cf. Otto Baensch: all feelings enter works of art as objectified feelings. 'As soon as they enter the work of art they therefore dissolve the ties with which they occurred in lived experience' (*Reflections on Art*, p. 32).

2 *Feeling and Form*, p. 323.

3 parasya na parasyeti mameti na mameti ca-*Sahitya Darpana*, III, 12, p. 120.

The paradox of 'tragic delight'

When we remind ourselves of the volume and ultimate futility of the discussions on the apparently paradoxical delight we get from the artistic portrayal of suffering we can clarify our point of view further. The question why tragedy delights arises from certain fallacious assumptions about the nature and function of poetry. It plagues all those who are victims of what I call the naturalistic fallacy, i.e., the belief that the function of poetry is to incite real life emotions in the reader. It began with Plato and his notion of poetry feeding and watering the passion. Aristotle's use of the term 'catharsis' to describe the emotional effect of tragedy has been explicated in a wide variety of ways. Escape from the insipid torpor of everyday existence into the excitement, awareness of the fictional framework, spirit of total resignation to fate, assertion of the will to live, the sense of reconciliation with the idea of eternal justice, satisfaction of sadistic and masochistic urges — these are some of the philosophical explanations of tragic delight[1].

Among the Indian theorists some maintain that all *rasas* give delight and others that only some evoke delight[2]. Dandin, Vamana, Lollata, Ramcandra, Gunacandra are prominent among those who accept the latter view. The theorists of the Central Tradition consider that such a view is untenable, our experience contradicts it. As Deshpande has pointed out, the view that some *rasas* give delight and others give sorrow is the inevitable conclusion of the argument that *rasa* is nothing but intensified *(upacit) sthāyins*[3]. Abhinavagupta starts from the premise that the emotions evoked in poetic experience are non-ordinary and transpersonal and therefore there is no question

---

1 See S. H. Butcher, *Aristotle's Theory of Poetry and Fine Art* (New York, 1953); F. L. Lucas, *Tragedy* (New York, 1962); P.K. Guha, *Tragic Relief* (London, 1932).

2 Nagendra, *Rasa-Siddhānta*, pp. 121, 133.

3 G. T. Deshpande, *Bhāratiya Sāhitya Sāstra* (Bombay 1960), pp. 337-41. Acharya Visveswara gives a wrong interpretation of Abhinavagupta's ideas on the problem. See *Hindi Abhinavabharati* (Delhi, 1960), pp. 222 ff. Abhinavagupta is talking about the delight and sorrow aroused by emotions in real life. The editor has, without any justification read 'rasa' in the place where sthāyi is mentioned.

of sorrow[1]. 'Drama always gives delight to the spectators, never sorrow.' Bharatamuni devised music and dance to remove such personal feelings which may arise in the minds of untrained and uncultured spectators[2]. The question why the depiction of suffering causes delight is irrelevant[3]. Sorrow is a symptom of agitation of the mind. In aesthetic experience there is a sense of rest, composure *(viśrānti)*. The feelings of sorrow, fear, disgust, wonder, etc., are merely colorations *(anurañjanā)*, or resonance of the transpersonal feelings which are the stuff of poetry[4].

We have had any number of explanations of this paradoxical phenomenon of tragic delight. But none of them seems to be satisfactory. The reason is that the question is based on a fallacy and therefore cannot have a satisfactory or correct answer. The fallacy is that there is a direct straight line relation between what is depicted in the poem and what is felt by the reader. We know that even in life there is no such straight line relation. Sufferings of personal enemies and enemy nations do not cause perverse delight only in those rare men of compassion. We are coldly indifferent to much suffering except when it obstructs our attempts at the gratification of desires. In life some emotions are pleasant, others unpleasant. We want to extend the range of pleasurable emotions like love and shrink away from the unpleasant ones like fear. But in poetry all our emotional reactions are strictly controlled by the aesthetic focus — the poem — which has non-ordinary existential status. The quality of our response is not determined by the pleasantness or unpleasantness of the emotions depicted but by the stylized and formalized object which has crystallized emotions and made them part of its structure. There is no question of our moving towards or away from these objects because they are not meant to help or hinder the gratification of our

---

1 *Abhinavabharati*, p. 289. Sāmājikānām hi harsaikaphalam nāṭyam na Śokadiphalam.

2 *Abhinavabharati*, p. 291. swagatakrodhasokadisankatahrdaya-granthi-bhanjanaya gitadiprakriya ca munina viracita.

3 Abhinavabhārati, p. 291. tatra codyam tāvad asat.

4 *Abhinavabharati*, p. 284... vibhavananubhavanasam-uparanjakatva-matrapranaih,...

desires by arousing pleasant or unpleasant emotions. The elements in the structure of tragedy, the human significance with which those elements are invested, the vision of the tragic artist — all of them might be different from and even superior to other genres of literatures. In descriptive and valuative criticism these topics can be profitably discussed. In aesthetics, when we discuss the qualities of aesthetic experience, the distinctions among genres lose their validity. As poetry, tragedy does not give us any delightful experience which is qualitatively different from that given by other genres. As poetry, tragedy delights us in the same way as any other literary genre, namely, by enabling us to feel the texture of emotional patterns and simultaneously understand their human significance. Therefore the question why tragedy delights is identical with why comedy delights or why poetry delights.

15

The Obstacles to Aesthetic Experience

Mohan Thampi

It is said that Moliére tried the worth of his plays on his cook. If the cook responded with interest, the success of the performance was assured. Every poet hopes that his poem will be read by a set of ideal readers who are competent enough to penetrate into the essential spirit of the poems and to realise fully the quality and intensity of the experience rendered in them. A published poem has its own life and destiny, and the poet has only as much control over it as an archer has over an arrow released from his bow. It may happen that the response is not proper, adequate, and satisfactory as it is governed by a number of factors. Just as there are constant factors in aesthetic experience there are also variable factors. The readers' social environment, the fund of real life experience, psychological temperament, degree of training, accidental influences, philosophical predilections, and emotional inhibitions are some of these variable factors. Aesthetic experience is transpersonal; but it occurs to a personal centre existing in a particular social cultural context and at a particular stage of the agent's life. In this chapter I propose to discuss how some of these variable factors may become obstacles in the realisation of a genuine aesthetic response.

The concept of sahr̥daya

There are many to whom the magic casement of poetry remains closed. Even among those who enjoy poetry, owing to several factors, the degree of adequacy with which the experience rendered in the poem is realized varies considerably. The *sahr̥daya* is the ideal reader. Literally, *sahr̥daya* means one whose sensibility is like that of the poet. He is *samānadharma*, of the nature of the poet himself. *Rasika* (one capable of relishing the *rasa* of poetry), and *sumanasah* (one whose mind is clear and concentrated), are two words roughly interchangeable with *sahr̥daya*. The heart of the ideal reader is perfectly attuned to the poet's heart. Even the subtlest and minutest vibrations of the poet's heart embodied in the poem produce sympathetic resonance of the same volume, pitch, and tone in the ideal reader's heart. Only the *sahr̥dayas* have the right of access to the spirit of poetry because only they have the proper intellectual and emotional equipment and training. Bharata gives a formidable list of qualifications demanded of an ideal audience of drama. The ideal spectators are men of good character; they are born in noble families; they are learned and desirous of fame and virtue. They are impartial, sufficiently mature, proficient in all the aspects of drama, attentive, honest and are conversant with various disciplines like grammar and prosody. They have a fine sense of the *bhavas* and the *rasas*. They are experts in debate and can detect flaws and appreciate merits. They have perfect sympathy with the feelings depicted. Bharata himself admits that all these qualities are not known to exist in the same spectator. Real spectators and real readers possess a combination of these various qualities in different proportions.

The sahṛdaya has two basic qualifications:

(1) He is a keen observer of situations and feeling-patterns in life and has a sufficient fund of experiences without which he cannot make the necessary inferences from the behaviour of the characters. No one can extract from a poem all the meanings it contains unless he is a keen student of life. The autonomy of poetic experience does not imply that we have nothing to take with us when we go to appreciate a poem. The stuff of poetry being experiences of life, a person ignorant of the relative significance of experiences and values of life cannot be a competent reader. If we go to the poem with an empty mind we shall gain very little. Experience can enrich a person's life and deepen his insight only if he is capable of making a significant whole of the hetero-geneous elements. Aldous Huxley has tellingly put it:

> Now experience is not a matter of having actually swum the Hellespont, or danced with dervishes, or slept in a doss house. It is a matter of sensibility and intuition of seeing and hearing the significant things, of paying attention at the right moments, of understanding and co-ordinating. Experience is not what happens to a man; it is what a man does with what happens to him.

There is significant difference between our response to Shakespeare in our boyhood and our adult response to him; this difference is the result of our gaining more life experiences and our stronger coordinating faculty which is a sign of maturity.

The *sahṛdaya* has a mirror-like sensibility cleansed, refined and purified by his constant acquaintance with poetry. The necessity to train our faculty for appreciation cannot be overstressed. Whenever we use our mental faculties for any purpose higher than that of mere animal existence we have to admit the necessity of training. Without this conscious training we are bound to miss much of what is there in a highly complex work of literature and substitute our own private notions and feelings irrelevantly and 'enjoy' the poem in a spurious manner. The response of a trained critical mind is superior to the 'spontaneous' facile experience of an untrained mind, because the former is fuller and more completely relevant than the latter. Unless we exercise rigorous discrimination in discovering the significance of experiential patterns and the textural qualities of a poem we shall be corrupted by the pressure of fashionable critical opinion.

In a fiercely competitive society opportunities to train such a poetic sensibility are certain to diminish. In such societies genuine cultural and spiritual values are sometimes suppressed, sometimes merely tolerated; they are never cultivated and promoted. There is always a lurking fear that a talent to create and appreciate genuine literature may cripple one's capacity to get on in this world where the number of automobiles and television sets is chief criterion to measure social success. The danger is great particularly in the developing nations where a lopsided emphasis on technological education will create a class of educated philistines to whom poetry and push pin will be of equal value. If poetry is appreciated by at least a minority in our country, it is only because the indomitable human spirit asserts itself despite the determined effort of the thoroughly illconceived educational system to smother and kill the spirit of poetry.

(2) The *sahṛdaya* is not just a passive reader. The word *pratibhā* (intuitive talent) is used to denote both the creative imagination of the poet and the receptive poetic sensibility of the competent reader. The *sahṛdaya* not only enjoys the poem but also discusses its merits and faults and formulates the basic principles of poetic creation and appreciation. He is a competent reader, critic and aesthetician all rolled into one. He can be called a 'complete reader' as F.R. Leavis uses the word.

Diversity of response

Discussing the concept of transpersonalisation, I tried to demonstrate that the postulation of a common emotional world and detachment from private interests necessitates the recognition of uniformity of response. But along with uniformity we have to recognise diversity of response. There is no doubt that the spirit of the ancient Greek tragedies is capable of pervading our consciousness when we read them or see them staged; but whether the plays stir us as completely and as deeply as they did the Greek audience is at least an open question. Our experiences are at the same time similar to and different from those of the ancient Greeks. The experiences are similar because the artist worked with 'instincts and attitudes which are an inseparable part of the common human emotional world and with values which are of significance for the entire mankind. At the same time the experiences are different because our social cultural environment, psychological traits and the kind of training our sensibility receives are different.

Though all men have at least potentially all the instincts, in some certain instincts will predominate and in others, certain other instincts will be prominent. Their likes, dislikes and perferences depend upon this fact. Young people tend to relish love poems; the learned take interest in intellectual topics, the seekers of wealth are particularly interested in stories about their kind and the contemplatives want to read poems dealing with *mokşa,* liberation. Heroic persons take delight in the presentation of *vira* (the heroic), *bibhatsa* (the disgusting) and *bhayānaka* (the terrible) *rasas*. Women, children and uncultured men take more interest in farce, costumes, etc.

This does not mean that we are inevitably and irrevocably predetermined to like only certain poems and dislike others. We can widen the area of our appreciation by conscious training. Sometimes it so happens that a reader confines his attention to one particular poetic tradition and excludes other traditions with the result that he remains narrow and parochial in his appreciation. Many critics have justly warned against superficial catholicity of taste. The sensibility which is capable of going into the same degree of rapture over *Śākuntalam* and *Naişadha* or Dostoievsky and Agatha Christie betrays its lack of subtlety and discrimination. The responses of a persons with such a 'catholic' sensibility are bound to be shallow and spurious. But this cannot be an argument to justify narrowness and exclusiveness of taste. Once we sympathetically understand the literary conventions and cultural traditions within which different poems were written we can appreciate them, though with differing degrees of interest and participation. Recognition of the poetic virtues of Donne need not necessarily create a blind spot in us for Shelley. The type of narrowness decried here is often propagated by some poet-critics who stress the importance of some poetic virtues which they try to embody in their work at the expense of other qualities which have equal or greater importance. The depth and intensity of a reader's response result partly from the complexity and breadth of his area of familiarity and appreciation.

Obstacles to poetics resonses

Anything which hampers the absolute contemplative concentration necessary to enter into the totality of the poem is extraneous to aesthetic response and therefore is *vighna* (obstacle). The following observations are based on a comparison between Abhinavagupta's formulations of *rasavighnas* (obstacles to *rasa*) and the ideas of I.A. Richards on the problem set forth in his *Practical Criticism.* Some obstacles flow from the poet's insufficient mastery over the theme and form of the poem and others from the reader's inability to respond to the poem with his total being. We are mainly concerned with the latter. First, I shall give a summary paraphrase of the obstacles as discussed by Abhinavagupta and I.A. Richards.

Abhinavagupta on the Seven Obstacles

(1) Improbability of events portrayed. Absence of adequate realisation of the subject-matter, images and characters. Poverty of *pratibhā*, intuitive talent, will prevent the reader from vividly recreating the content of the poem. Without such recreation, complete absorption in the poetic focus is impossible.

(2) Intrusion of spatial and temporal considerations. The absence of 'willing suspension' of spatial and temporal considerations will prevent the reader from transpersonalising his experience. He will apprehend the *bhavas* as related to himself or to others.

(3) Intrusion of personal feelings of pain and pleasure will damage the purity of aesthetic experience.

(4) Defective means of perception: inconsistent characterisation, obscure and unconnected imagery; the inability on the part of the reader to provide the necessary links.

(5) Obscurity: absence of clear aids to visualisation and other ways of immediate perception.

(6) Absence of a clear knowledge of the relative importance of the depicted elements.
(7) Doubts about the proper correlations among the *vibhavas,* etc.

Richards on the difficulties of the readers

(1) Inability to make out the plain meanings of the poem including sense, feeling, tone and intention; (2) difficulty in sensuous apprehension; (3) weakness of visual imagination; (4) erratic and irrelevant associations from private life; (5) stock responses; (6) sentimentality; (7) inhibitions; (8) doctrinal adhesions of the reader; (9) implicit or explicit technical presuppositions; (10) general critical pre-conceptions and the illegitimate expectations bred by theoretical prejudices.

Weakness of pratibhā

In all poetry sensuous imagery is a vital ingredient. The sensuous images function as vehicles of feeling. In some readers the capacity to reproduce imaginatively the patterns of visual and auditory images is weak. Sometimes they cannot capture the individual rhythm of a poem and consequently miss something of the intangible associations based on the rhythm. Dramatic representation on the stage removes this obstacle to some extent. Persons with powerful *pratibhā* (intuitive talent) can adequately realise all the *rasas* and *bhāvas* of a play even in reading. Acting, costumes, music, etc., make the realisation easy for those who do not have this capacity in sufficient measure. On the other hand, it also may happen that to persons with powerful imagination the stage representation is less satisfactory than their reading. The world of the play, when read, seems to be boundless; the suggestions thrown out by the poet can be carried to their farthest limits. In a visual representation he may experience a constriction of imagination. This often happens in films. No film version of a first rate novel or drama can be as rewarding as its reading. If unheard melodies are sweeter, unfilmed novels are better.

This weakness of imagination is aggravated by the absence of a sufficient fund of life experiences. We respond to a poem at a particular stage in the growth of our personality and the depth of our response is directly proportionate to the wealth of experience and observation which we bring to the appreciation. If the reader has been moving in a narrow groove his responses will lack vitality and variety. He develops only familiar easy stock-responses. He refuses to grow up because he has no experience of the exhilaration of confronting and assimilating challengingly disconcerting new attitudes. As Elizabeth Drew says, 'To the lazy mind the perfect soul-mate is Echo.' He is convinced that a poet's function is only to confirm him in his facile intellectual and emotional habits. Such imaginative lethargy will have a most debilitating influence on the spirit. The only way to overcome this obstacle is by never losing close contact with reality and by constantly exercising and sharpening our powers of observation.

Intrusion of personal feelings

It often happens that the reader's attention wanders and instead of concentrating on the aesthetic construct he indulges in private reminiscences and reveries. His private memories affect the feeling-tone of the aesthetic experience. When irrelevant they are impurities which vitiate the genuineness of the experience. Abhinavagupta says:

> This obstacle consists in the appearance of other forms of consciousness, due variously to the fear of being abandoned by these sensations of pleasure etc., to concern for their preservation, to a desire to procure other similar sensations, to the desire to get rid of them, give them open expression, hide them etc.

Henri Delacroix puts it as follows:

> It is very true with many people, aesthetic contemplation deviates into contemplation of themselves. To tell their own stories, to evoke in a game of ghosts their own potentialities, to dream of themselves — these are all the pleasures of art for many people....

The intrusion of personal feelings interfere with the free working of the poem. If the excitation is pleasurable the readers and spectators would want the experience to prolong; if it is painful — as it may happen when such persons read or witness a grim and harrowing tragedy — they would feel intense discomfort. Doctor Johnson could not endure the last scene of *King Lear*.

Excess of emotion

Romanticism and its later decadent form called aestheticism invented a cult of emotion which considered that indulging and luxuriating in 'tender' and 'soft' emotions is a value in itself. Sometimes readers wallow in emotions evoked by poems which specialise in 'melting' them. They forget the fact that it is always the significance of the situation in which the emotion is 'placed' in a poem that is important and not the emotion in itself. Such an excessive and over-facile emotional response which is inappropriate to the objective situation in the poem is called sentimentality. Richards thinks that, 'A person may be said to be sentimental when his emotions are too easily stirred, too light on the trigger. Condemning such sentimental response Stephen C. Pepper says that this gushing forth of emotion is objectionable on two counts. Firstly, the emotion is often false to the work of art and in that sense a false emotion. Secondly, a person who wanders with his emotions away from the work of art is not realising fully the event there presented. Pepper adds: 'A man who habitually flies off into emotional ecstasy in the presence of a work of art is likely to lack depth of appreciation, even if the emotion is relevant.' Every genuine aesthetic response is a total response; our entire being is awakened to new spiritual possibilities. Sentimental responses reduce the complexities of the poetic situations to the familiar crude stereotyped formulae. Repeated indulgence in such experiences will have disastrous effect on the readers: their sensibility is stunted; they gradually lose whatever capacity they have of comprehending the complexities of real and imagined situations. Their ability to discriminate between experiences and evaluate them is impaired beyond repair. Just as tears blur our physical vision sentimentality obscures our mental insight.

Emotional frigidity

Another obstacle to a full and genuine aesthetic experience is emotional frigidity which can be called the obverse of sentimental gush. Richards finds a 'widespread general inhibition of all the simpler expansive developments of emotion' among the educated population of England. The failure to evoke appropriate emotions may arise from the association of certain specific emotions with feelings of guilt or shame. It may also arise from the entirely mistaken notion that spiritual strength precludes any emotional response. It is an evidence of virtual denial of the vital springs of life. A cold intellectual response to poetry is a partial response. The Indians of the Classical Age were remarkably free from puritanical emotional inhibitions. The literature of the period shows that they did not let any of their emotional needs starve. The four *puruṣārthas* (the ends of human life) and the four *āśramas* (stages) were devised to satisfy all the legitimate human urges. Owing to a wrong one-sided emphasis on the emotion-negating aspects of certain Indian systems and to the influences of certain Victorian values which are not yet freed from puritanical prudery, the English-educated Indian intellectual suffers from emotional inhibitions and the resulting moral hypocrisy. His heart slowly dries up and poetry fails to move him. Suppression of emotion is not the same thing as its control and refinement. In life as in poetry there is need to strike a balance between excessive over-facile emotional reactions which blur our insight and cold intellectualism which devitalises our experiences by turning our heart into a wasteland.

Belief and poetic response

The current discussion in the west of the place of belief in poetic response, among other things, indicates the breaking down of systems of values. When a basic system of doctrines and values is widely believed in by the entire community such a problem does not assume serious importance. There were periods in the development of human civilisation, when the cultivated sections of the people possessed a common cultural and intellectual heritage. The Athens of Pericles, the England of Elizabeth I and the India of Chandragupta II may be cited as examples. Not that there were no stresses or tensions in those periods. But these stresses and tensions had a common tradition within whose framework they could contribute to the cultural fermentation of the period. Sometimes writers tied to invest their subject-matter with new meanings and values which made their readers uncomfortable (as did Euripides in Greece). Such tensions reach great heights during periods of social revolution. In our own times when the moribund and emergent forces are locked in a gigantic world-wide conflict it is natural that the established systems of beliefs and values should explode. It is not only that specific beliefs and values are challenged; the very bases of belief and values are questioned. Each group of interests seek to salvage its cherished illusions and beliefs from the universal wreckage. The acrimonious debate between C.P. Snow and F.R. Leavis over the 'Two Cultures' is one of the many amusing spectacles which confirm the schizophrenia of the western man.

In this century, the culmination of the process of the alienation of man which began with the maturing of the crisis of the capitalist society has made the writer an 'outsider'. The absence of an integrated approach to social reality disintegrates the self. Many writers find themselves outside the main current of mass movements which decide the destinies of peoples all over the world. No wonder that their gods fail. An acute sense of loneliness and isolation haunts them. The modern poet, in Stephen Spender's words, 'is in a cage with bars that are mirrors reflecting only himself, and there is no possibility of entering through the imaginations into the factual realities outside.' At present, when class divisions have assumed universal and explosive proportions, the shattering of the common basis of belief is only inevitable.

Both Eliot and Richards have tried to solve the problem of the place of belief in poetic response, each in his own way. It is difficult to know Eliot's exact position because he frequently shifts his ground and even makes contradictory statements. In his essay on Dante he makes a couple of distinctions. He wants us to separate what Dante believed as a poet from what he believed as a man. He makes another distinction between philosophical belief and poetic assent; in this, his position somewhat coincides with that of Richards who makes a distinction between intellectual beliefs and emotional beliefs. In his essay on Goethe he refers to the *Bhagavad Gita* and says that when he reads that poem he puts himself in the position of a believer. I do not think it proper to consider the *Gita* as a poem. It is merely a piece of dialogue which is a part of a vast epic; the idea therein cannot be discussed torn from its context in the *Mahābhārata*. Unless we can show that the meanings and values expressed in the *Gita* are realized more or less fully in the total poem we should imagine that it is not an organic part of the epic from the structural point of view. For a student of the poetry of *Mahābhārata,* the ideas of the *Gita* have only as much value as Tolstoy's ideas on historical processes have for a student of *War and Peace*.

Eliot says that when we read Dante we suspend both belief and disbelief. But he also says that when a reader is in agreement with the philosophy of the poet he enjoys his poetry more. He is unable to enjoy Shelley for the alleged childishness of the latter's beliefs. In his essay on Goethe he makes another distinction between the poet's philosophy and his wisdom. We are supposed to be able to accept the poet's wisdom even if we do not accept his philosophy. But Eliot does not clarify the exact nature of the relation between philosophical beliefs and wisdom. In his Dante essay he says that we are not called upon to believe what Dante believed 'for your belief will not give you a groat's worth more of understanding and appreciation.' But in his note to the same essay we find: 'So I can only conclude that I cannot, in practice, wholly separate my poetic appreciation from my personal beliefs'.

Thus we find that Eliot's ideas on the subject are confusing and contradictory. Let us see whether Richard's solution is acceptable. Richards cuts the Gordian knot by declaring that poetry is 'pseudo-statement'. He introduces in criticism logical positivist notions about the nature of language used in various disciplines and the verifiability of statements made in them. According to him pseudo-statements are not verifiable as propositions in scientific discourse. He has a pragmatic criterion of poetic truth: 'A pseudo-statement is "true" if it suits and serves some attitude or links together attitudes which on other grounds are desirable.' 'Language has two uses: referential and emotive. Poetry is the supreme form of emotive language.' 'The emotions and attitudes resulting from a statement used emotively need not be directed towards anything to which the statement refers.' Richards has put such a heavy stake on this distinction that he makes the claim: 'No revolution in human affairs would be greater than that which a widespread observance of this distinction would bring about.' Corresponding to this distinction in language he makes a distinction between scientific beliefs and emotive beliefs:

> Scientific belief we may perhaps define as readiness to act as though the reference symbolised by the proposition which is believed were true.
>
> [Emotive] beliefs are entertained only in the special circumstances of the poetic experience. They are held as conditions for further effects, our attitudes and emotional responses, and not as we hold beliefs in laws of nature, which we expect to find verified on all occasions.

These clearly formulated positions militate against Richard's own refusal to distinguish between aesthetic experience and ordinary experience. By the time he came to write *Practical Criticism* he considerably modified his views. Instead of 'scientific and emotive beliefs' he employs the terms 'intellectual and emotional beliefs'. Criterion of truth is relevant to scientific belief, but only internal logical consistency is required in intellectual belief. The major concession comes when he says: 'Most beliefs, of course, that have any strength or persistence are mixtures of intellectual and emotional belief or disbelief, in the intellectual sense, never arises when we are reading well.

We find that Richards's distinctions are invalidated both by his general theory of poetic response and by his admission that important beliefs are both intellectual and emotional. Psychologists are rapidly giving up the distinctions between the intellectual and emotional compartments of human mind.

In the classical, period, when the Indians believed in something, they believed in it, that was all; they never stopped to bother whether they intellectually believed in it or emotionally. The various aestheticians and critics were influenced by different philosophical systems in the general outlook; sometimes their considerations of aesthetic topics bear imprint of these systems. But the problem of belief, in the form in which it is posed by Eliot and Richards, did not present itself to them. Among the obstacles discussed by Abhinavagupta we have *sambhāvānaviraha*, improbability resulting from the weakness of imagination. This is not the improbability of response to poems containing unacceptable doctrinal beliefs. It deals with the absence of the internal consistency which links the images and actions rendered in the poem. The writer may depict extraordinary feats but only as achieved by extraordinary persons. This is not different from Aristotle's position that poets should prefer probable impossibilities to improbable possibilities. As the feudal base of Indian society had maintained the stability of its structure for a long time, people in general did not feel any self-division of their mental being. However, it may be necessary to point out that the Indian aestheticians linked *aucitya* (decorum or propriety) with *rasa*. The eighth canto of Kalidasa's *Kumārasambhava* has been criticised by some writers. The canto contains elaborate descriptions of the love-play of Śiva and Pārvati. The objection against the canto is that those who consider Śiva and Pārvati to be the father and mother of the universe cannot be expected to relish it. But even here the argument springs not from any rigid doctrinal positions but from a consideration of the principle of *aucitya* (propriety) in poetry.

To insist that beliefs have nothing to do with poetic appreciation will be as wrong as to insist that poetic appreciation is impossible unless the reader agrees with every belief contained in the poem. Though T.S. Eliot and Erich Heller criticise each other's ideas on the subject they agree at least on one point, i.e., perverse and puerile beliefs and good poetry are antagonistic. Eliot says:

> When the doctrine, theory, belief, or 'view of life' presented in a poem is one which the mind of the reader can accept as coherent, mature, and founded on the facts of experience, it interposes no obstacle to the reader's enjoyment, whether it be one that he accept or deny, approve or deprecate. When it is one which the reader rejects as childish or feeble, it may, for a reader of well-developed mind, set up an almost complete check.

Erich Heller also says:

> There are ideas and beliefs so prosaic, outlandish, or perverse in their innermost structure that no great or good poetry can come from them: for instance, Hitler's racialism. It is this negative consideration that to me finally proves the intimate positive relation between belief, thought and poetry. If there were no relation, there would be no reason either why the most perverse or idiotic beliefs should not be convertible into great poetry. They are not.

It is extremely difficult to analyse what we mean when we say that we believe in something. All beliefs can be expressed in the form of intellectual propositions; but our convictions and emotional attachment will have different degrees of mildness or intensity. We have a wide range from mild expectation to dead certainty. 'I believe the train leaves at 7.30', 'I believe that God exists', 'I believe that she loves me', 'I believe that life does not exist after death', 'I believe that it is glorious to die for one's country', etc., are statements uttered with different degrees of emotional intensity. In real life men and women are capable of entertaining contradictory beliefs. There are superstitious atheists and scientific theists. We have scores of religious and political sects with fanatical adherence to their doctrines. In spite of this we find that great writers are universally appreciated. How does it happen?

Poetry may contain propositions which warrant our assent or dissent, but poetry is not made of propositions. The New Critics are justified in their condemnation of the 'heresy of paraphrase' because propositions cannot be abstracted from poems which are patterns of 'resolved stresses' or 'dramas'. To appreciate Dante's *Inferno* we have to understand the Catholic eschatology, but we do not have to believe that we would be inmates of Hell after death. Poetry is the dramatic rendering of experience in terms of images and action. The beliefs expressed in poetry must be viewed as part of the character and action. The view consistently advocated in this book is that the reader's egoistic practical interests are kept in abeyance at the time of poetic experience. The corollary must be that the beliefs related to our personal interests are suspended during the experience of poetry.

What happens when we read the long Christmas sermon of Becket in *Murder in the Cathedral?* A Hindu or a Moslem is not converted to Becket's beliefs though the oration is powerful and persuasive. But he will be attentive because the passion with which the sermon is delivered deepens the tragic heroism of Becket's martyrdom. The theology underlying the sermon is unacceptable to the Hindu; but, since it is used to reinforce the moral and emotional significance of the dramatic context, he will not find it an obstacle in his response to the play.

But we cannot effect a total severance between poetry and belief. Erich Heller pointed out the incompatibility of fascism and good poetry. If a writer begins with the assumption that wanton cruelty to children is a laudable ideal, the basic humanity in us will revolt against his creation. Beliefs undergo a mutation when they enter poetry: they drop their status as propositions and assume the status of values. Beliefs outside poetry are sectarian propositions; in the poetry they are fused with value-situations. Most beliefs say directly or indirectly something about the human predicament. Literature is indifferent to those beliefs which have nothing to do with the value-situations in life. A poet need not be interested in the Second Law of Thermodynamics; but if he is indifferent to evil and its consequences he cannot create great poetry. Every belief implies, in practice, certain attitudes to certain specific situations in life. Beliefs may be private and sectarian; values are human and universal. It is the area where beliefs have a bearing upon value-situations in human life which is explored and illumined by the writer. In poetry beliefs become inextricably fused with the total meaning. As I tried to show earlier, during aesthetic experience we transcend the narrow cage of our egoistic interests and merge with the collective humanity. Only the value side of beliefs is relevant in our response to poetry. This value side is neither only intellectual nor only emotional. It is both, and appeals to the undivided humanity in the reader.

16

The Word and the World

Bimal Krishna Matilal

[Bimal Krishna Matilal's *The Word and the World* (1990) is an outstanding contribution to the study of comparative aesthetics. Although the author calls the book in his modesty India's contribution to the study of language, the language philosophy of India was a comprehensive discipline and it included linguistics, grammar, philosophy and literary criticism. The learned writer while doing justice to the synthetic nature of the subject, also relates it to contemporary discussions on language, cognition, meaning, ineffability of mystical experience and the ways it gets expressed by means of metaphor, paradox, negative dialectics etc.

The following two extracts from B.K. Matilal's *The Word and the World* discuss (i) the concept of *sphota* in the context of modern language philosophy and (ii) meaning in literary criticism with special reference to *Vakrōkti* and *dhwani.* The author explains in the first extract the two levels of language, Sphoṭa and *nada* according to Bhartṛhari and tells us how language is an activity — an activity which he would call 'languageing'. It may be further defined as vibration of consciousness. The articulated sound is *nada* and its earlier form is *sphoṭa* which has been differently translated as vibration, bursting etc. This *sphoṭa* is the cause of *nada.*

At this point the author also makes a distinction between 'the perceived world' and 'the interpreted world'. Though they form an indivisible whole, and we have to posit the existence of *śabda-brahman,* the eternal verbum, the ever-extending consciousness where everything is one, fused, for purposes of our understanding we have to admit (i) Sphoṭa, 'the inner speech' of the first vibration which is the causal basis of *upādānaśabda*, and (ii) *upādānaśabda* the designating of objects. The word-thought, the word-object relationship is not man-made or even God-made. It may be an instance of 'everything begins by referring back, that is to say, does not begin,' to put it in the words of J. Derrida. The second section of the same extract discusses Logocentrism and shows that Bhartṛhari was 'not guilty of it' in as much as he never anywhere condemns writing and secondly, even the Hindu scriptures are called *Sruti* which means that they have been 'heard'. There were perhaps difficulties in getting them written.

The same holistic view of things is seen in the second extract on meaning in literary criticism. Starting with an explanation of the stand taken by Ānandavardhana and Abhinava Gupta he describes the four powers or functions of words (1) *abhidha*, (2) *tātparya*, (3) *lakşhana* and (4) *dhwanana* or *vyañjana*. The author however seems to opt for the holistic frame work provided by Bhartṛhari and developed by Kuntaka. (In an earlier Chapter the author showed that to Bhartṛhari 'the nature of the self is nothing but identical with language-thought', in other words the *śabda* at the *para* stage is identified with the ultimate *Brahman*. The *Pasyanti* stage is said to be the subtle *sphoṭa* (*Vak* and *artha* are still one and fused). In the intermediate stage *Madhyama* the language and the thought it conveys are still one and undifferentiated, but at this preverbal stage (Shall we call it the language of silence? or *mauna vyākhya?*) the speaker sees them as differentiable — the verbal part as distinct and separable from *artha* (the meaning part). This stage impels him to speech (*vaikhari*) resulting in *nada sphota* of differentiation.

On the basis of the above philosophy the author rightly argues that *alaṃkāra* is not an embellishment, something added on to decorate, but part and parcel of the utterance itself. The utterance is the unit. In other words, the sentence is an unbreakable 'impartite whole'. It is by adopting the method of extraction and abstraction — *apoddhara* and allowing it to operate upon the given reality — of the whole sentence, — we get at individual words, roots etc. The author of *Vakroktijivita* also makes this clear when he says that what is said cannot be dissociated from the way it is said. The additional interest in the extract is the parallels it provides between the New Criticism in America and ancient Indian literary criticism, on the one hand, and the help it provides in understanding rhetorical terms like simile, metaphor, and concepts like poetry of statement and poetry of experience on the other. The common concern between the new Critics and the Indian aestheticians seems to be the reiteration of the indivisibility of form and content and more significantly, the pre-occupation with the way the language of poetry or poetic utterance deviates from normal utterance. The stress on obliqueness (*vakrata* in Kuntaka's thesis) and the claim that there cannot be any poem without *alaṃkāra* will strike a Western critic as an interesting parallel to the New Critical position. The author argues that the duality of *alaṃkāra* and *alaṃkārya* cannot be sustained. In this fused sense *alaṃkāra* itself is poetry even as for Cleanth Brooks metaphor *is* poetry. Ed.]

1. Translation and Bhartṛhari's concept of language (Śabda)

The received doctrine, which would be ascribed to the Nyāya realists, was that there is an inherent distinction between the word (signifier) and the object (signified). Surprisingly this was not very different from the general consensus among the traditional Western exponents of modern linguistics. Language is often uncritically thought to be a vehicle of thought or meaning. And from this flows the pervasive idea that in a multilingual world, the same thought is or can be conveyed by different expressions which are distinguishable parts of different languages. It is probably what a modern philosopher, Jacques Derrida, would call the metaphysicians' age-old desire to search for a 'transcendental signified', that is a concept independent of language, that forces upon us the duality and opposition of the signifier and the signified. The duality that is foisted upon us has generated the platitude that the *pure* signified is what remains constant between different translations just as in a change of currency the value of the money is supposed to remain intact. In the light of Bhartṛhari's idea, this is a platitude that we would do well to give up. For Bhartṛhari the signifier-signified duality (*vāk* and *artha*) is more a fiction than a reality. It is *vikalpa*, a convenient fiction, but it lacks the ultimate or absolute truth-value. The two are, for Bhartṛhari identical. The imagined duality is a useful ploy, to facilitate understanding. But its essence is given by its contextuality, hence beyond the context it loses its ultimate value. It is a ploy as well as a play. It is called a *vikalpa* in the sense of being a game or a play where we have rules which will have truth-values, but not when the game is over. Thus it is that Bhartṛhari's holistic doctrine of language, of which the identity of the *vācaka* (signifier) and the *vācya* (signified) is also a part, requires us to give up the search for any independent 'transcendent' meaning as the translational constant, as the invariant in variable languages, and yet the same view allows that there could be a situational meaning or *vācya* that would be correlated with different linguistic expressions or *vācakās* (signifiers) which would be deemed as intelligibly equivalent. Since linguistic expressions are not regarded in this theory as mere conveyor-belts for thoughts, there cannot be any absolute transposition of virgin thoughts from one language to another. Each thought is already a part and parcel of its so-called 'verbal' cloak. They are not separable. Like the mythical suit of armour which was 'in-born' with Karna in the *Mahābhārata*, thought and language are born together.

One may ask the obvious question: How are we to distinguish good translations from bad ones, how to determine distortion or even falsification by translation? For it would be extremely counter-intuitive to say that our translation is as good as any other. (For the moment, we are not talking about Quine's view of translation.) The tentative answer seems to be this. The goodness or badness of a translation, the distortion, falsity or correctness of it, would not be determined simply by the inter-linguistic or intra-linguistic semantic rules, but by the entire situations of each translation with all its uniqueness, that is, by the kind of total reactions, effects, motivations and preferences it generates on that occasion. It is a matter of common knowledge that a translator may deliberately or unconsciously choose the translational forms or expressions, in order to create the intended result, and within certain limits this choice may become tolerable. If it is intolerable the translation is bad. We can decide that the translation is bad or distorted to the extent it becomes intolerable.

I use 'signifier-signified', which is the terminology of modern linguists, for the Sanskrit '*vācaka-vācya*'. Despite obvious similarity, it is not fair to conflate the two terminologies and I am not attempting to compare or identify them. To introduce looseness in usage, I shall use 'signification' and 'designation' almost interchangeably. This will fit my purpose, for in Sanskrit we talk about only one word-object relation; *vācya-vācaka-bhavā.* There may simply be very distant resonance here of the rather technical use of the *signifier-signified* distinction of the Western linguists.

Bhartṛhari on *Śabda*

I shall present about a dozen verses from Bhartṛhari's text, *Vākyapadiya.* His theory of *śabda* (language) is a very complex one. For him language is an activity — a type of activity in which all human beings, in fact all sentient beings, engage. The Sanskrit name for this activity is *śabdanā* or *śabdana-vyāpāra.* It is 'languageing'. In Bhartṛhari's metaphor, it is the very vibration (*spanda)* of consciousness.

This theory has many facets. (1) Bhartṛhari tells us that language or *śabda* plays an indispensable part in our cultural life at different levels of consciousness. In fact, it makes the transaction between sentient beings possible. (2) He further asserts that *śabda* or language is the basis of the distinction between the sentient and the insentient. (3) All thought, all awareness is intertwined with 'languageing', for there cannot be any manifestation of awareness unless it is illuminated by *śabda* (see ch. 12). (4) There are two levels of language or *śabda* which all linguists must recognize, the implicit or the inner speech and the *articulate* noise. The former he called *spho ta*, the latter *nada*, 'sound', 'noise'. The former is more real, it is the causal basis of the latter (see ch.8). In another formulation, the latter is said to be the 'transformation' of the former. (5) Above all, Bhartṛhari propounds a cosmological thesis. The whole universe (or we should say the linguistic universe), consisting of two different types of things, the *vācyās*, bits and pieces of the constructed world to which language refers, and the linguistic expressions, the *vācaka* (signifiers), has evolved out of one principle called the Word-essence, *śabda-tattva*, the Eternal Verbum, *śabda-brahman*, the ever-extending consciousness of the sentient. We may discount this point as a theological or metaphysical bias, but there may be an important truth implicit in it here. Our perceived world is also an interpreted world. And this interpretation is invariably in terms of some language or other! Interpretation is 'languageing'. Bhartṛhari believes that both language and the 'world' it purports to refer to (and this 'world' by his own explicit admission may or may not coincide with the external, actual world) form an indivisible, unitary whole. In the light of such a theory it is easy to see how the *vācaka-vācya* (signifier-signified) distinction is artificial, provisional and ultimately collapsible into a unity from which it initially arises.

The first verse of the enormous text, *Vākyapadiya*, runs thus:

> The essence of *language* has no beginning and no end. It is the imperishable Brahman, the ultimate consciousness, which is *transformed* in the form of meanings and which facilitates the functioning of the world. (Verse 1.1)

An absolute beginning of language is untenable. Language is continuous and co-terminous with the human or any sentient being. A simple argument is formulated in support of this point. The argument is not very different from the early Mimāṃsaka argument against the conventionalists, the Naiyāyikas, who held that language is an arbitrary and conventional tool, and hence the word-object relationship is created by and learnt through convention for there does not exist any real connection between and word 'cow' and the object cow. According to Bhartṛhari, language is underived and the word-thought relationship is *given* to us; it is eternal. We cannot say that the word-thought relation was created by some humans or even by God in the long forgotten past, for we do not have any record of such convention. Besides, convention itself presupposes the prior presence of language, which is again sought to be derived from convention. This is patently circular. Invoking God does not help to avoid circularity because even God cannot make His intention known or create convention without using language. We may quote J. Derrida's epigram: 'Everything begins by referring back, that is to say, does not begin.'

The verses of Bhartṛhari quoted below make his idea of *śabda* clear. Some of these verses have been quoted and briefly commented upon in chapter 8. I will repeat them, nevertheless, to underline different aspects of their significance.

> Those who study *śabda* (linguists?) comprehend two types of *śabda* among the linguistic sounds (*upadana-śabda* as opposed to other noises). One is the causal basis for producing sounds and the other designates the object (= meaning). (Verse 1.44)

This may inadvertently be the beginning of the *sphoṭa-nāda* distinction that is very central to Bhartṛhari's view of language. There is another verse here which is omitted in the edited text but noted by the commentary. It is more explicit about this distinction:

> The *śabda* that is designative of meaning is an individual unit, a sequenceless whole, but it is revealed through the divided items (noisy realities produced in proper sequences). The latter gets intermixed with the object / meaning for it constitutes the very nature of the object / meaning. (Verse 1, 44)

Nāda, sometimes called *dhvani,* stands for the sound, the 'bang', the sonority of language, while *sphoṭa* by way of contrast means literally the language in the form of an 'explosive'— the explosive prior to the bang. For Bhartṛhari the latter is the real *śabda* 'language', of which the former is a causal transformation. Basically, the necessity of admitting *sphoṭa* arises in this way. How are we to explain the understanding of a complete meaning from sounds which are uttered in a temporal sequence (or, letters written in spatial sequence)?

sphoṭa is initially the 'Sanskrit grammarians' answer to this question. Between the two levels of language, *nāda* and *sphoṭa*, there is the relationship of the manifester and the manifested. *Nāda* makes *sphoṭa* manifest while it is also the causal transformation of the latter.

> Since *nāda* arises in sequence, *sphoṭa*, which has neither a former nor a latter stage, and which is sequenceless, is apprehended (or is born) as if having a sequence as well as parts. (Verse 1, 48)

The two levels are, however, not entirely separate, for the essential properties of one are transferred to the other, and thus they are two sides of the same *linguistic* coin.

> Just as the reflected image, although it resides in another place, seems to share the operation (i.e., movements of the waves in water), the *sphoṭa* and the *nāda* share the (linguistic) properties in the same way. (Verse 1, 49)

Bhartṛhari uses several analogies to explain the nature of language as he conceives it. I shall quote a couple of them here.

> The potentiality (*Kratu)* that is called language is like the yolk of the peahen's egg. It develops (being articulated) into the form of an act where it obtains parts and sequences. (Verse 1, 51).

The idea is that the original Kratu called language is a unity. Without parts and sequences. But when transformed it seems to have parts and sequences, even imperfections (due to pronunciation by human agents).

> Just as figure (the original model) is grasped by the painter's single awareness, and is painted upon the canvas as another complete, unitary figure, language or linguistic unit (*śabda)* has likewise all these three stages. (Verse 1, 52).

The idea is tentatively this: the original model = the original linguistic unit, a sentential expression along with what it conveys; the image grasped by the painter's mind = the linguistic reality in the speaker's mind; the painting = the speaker's articulation.

Bhartṛhari mentions some of his predecessors' views regarding the *sphoṭa-nāda* distinction. His own view seems to have crystallized out of explanation and criticism of these views. I have already discussed these views in chapter 8. Of the views examined, one (verse 93) says that *sphoṭa* is the universal or the linguistic type, sentence-type or world-type as opposed to their tokens (sounds), while another (verse 94) says that the *sphoṭa* or language is in fact *avikārya* 'unmodifiable' or 'immutable' and sounds which have modifications (good or bad, high or low, strong or weak) cause the perception or comprehension of the *sphoṭa* just as light causes perception of objects. In the course of his critique of these prevalent views, Bhartṛhari announces (Verse 121) how language has a pervasive influence on human behaviour.

> The idea that something is to be done in this world depends upon language. Even the child (when he acts) from the residual traces of his (previous) births has such understanding as is language-dependent. (Verse 1, 121)

It is also argued in the same context that unless the child has already the language in him he cannot make the effort to reproduce it thorough his vocal organs. Hence language is not learnt as a novel and external thing but it is an inherent constituent of our awareness, about which we become gradually conscious when the so-called learning procedure starts.

Bhartṛhari seems to assert that there is an inseparable connection between language and awareness. This thesis is explained as follows:

> There is no awareness in this world without its being intertwined with language. All cognitive awareness appears as if it is interpenetrated with language. (Verse 1, 123)

> If the language-impregnated nature of awareness went away from it, then a cognition would not manifest (any object), for that (language-impregnated nature) is the distinguishing nature of our cognitive awareness. (Verse 1, 124)

The above may imply the rather strong Bhartṛhari thesis:
(B1) All cognitive episodes are equivalent to verbal thoughts. Or, it may imply the weaker claim:

(B2) Most cognitive episodes with which we deal are invariably verbal thoughts at some implicit level.

There are two sides to this thesis. One is its epistemological implication, which I shall discuss elaborately in the next chapter. The other is a semantic issue: what happens to the semantic relation between word and object.

In terms of such loaded metaphors of 'illumination' and 'consciousness', one can put the matter as follows, the illuminative power of consciousness is always intertwined with its *vāg-rūpata or śabdanā* or 'languageing'. Taking some help from Kashmir Saivism (Utpala and Abhinava), one can round up this theory of awareness and say that each awareness-episode has two *natural* powers, the power to reveal or illuminate *(prakāśa)* and the power to discriminate or differentiate (*vimarśa).* The second power which is equivalent to 'languageing' or differentiation through verbalizability, is never found without the first. This seems to imply that if the pure sensory grasp is one where awareness is not isolatable from what one is aware of, and where what we are aware of is not conceptualizable or verbalizable, then such pure sensation is an impossibility. It is however well-known that some major philosophical traditions, among them the Buddhists and the sense-data theorists, argued that such awareness exists. Bhartṛhari's argument is that if the so-called sensory grasp penetrates into the level of awareness it already differentiates the grasped object through 'languageing' although at a very implicit level. For more on this, see the next chapter. The *vācya* cannot figure in any awareness without the presence of the *vācaka* already in it.

Bhartṛhari on word-object connection

The relation of *vācya* and *vācaka* has been the subject matter of discussion in various ways in Bhartṛhari's writing. I shall try to give a brief review of his position on this point. The said relation is one of identity, but from another point of view it may be called the 'signification' relation, for which the Sanskrit name is *vācya-vācaka-*bhavā. The first verse of chapter 3 of part III of *Vākyapadiya* says:

> From the utterance of words, the speaker's idea, the external object and the form of the word itself are understood. There stands (therefore) a relation between them (utterance of the word and the other three).

Immediately after this rather enigmatic statement, Bhartṛhari repeats the thesis that the word's own form is the most intimate *meaning* that is understood from the utterance of the word-token. This point was already established by elaborate argument in Part One of his book. The relation between the word and such a meaning of the word or any linguistic unit, a phrase or a sentence, is undoubtedly seen to be natural, non-derivative and eternally fixed. Hence if we take the first item as meaning, it is also not too much to say that the word and what it means are *identical*. The second item in this list offers more interesting possibilities. I believe this to be also Bhartrhari's own view, which may be stated as follows. The linguistic expression (and in Bhartṛhari's own view the primary unit is the sentence, not its word-constituents) designates or signifies the speaker's idea or thought, having first designated or signified its own form. The objects meant are assumed by the realist to constitute the external objects or the 'furniture' of the external world. But Bhartṛhari nowhere explicitly argues for this position although he mentions it as one of the standard views. He is not a realist in this sense. For him the object meant is what is grasped by the speaker's awareness. So it is the item that figures in his awareness. Our activities, which may be prompted by language, deal with external realities, a cow or a horse, but language does not *mean* or *signify* them. They are nevertheless understood at the utterance of the word because otherwise our activities will not be possible. Being asked for food we cannot very well present the speaker's 'mental' food! But nevertheless linguistic signification refers to a separate realm.

In this connection, Bhartṛhari develops an interesting critique of what is usually understood as the signification relation and of relation in general. This has been nicely dealt with by H. Herzberger and R. Herzberger (1981), who have called it 'Bhartṛhari's' paradox'. Bhartṛhari argued that the so-called signification relation is unsignifiable, for if we could signify it, we would turn it into an object and that would require a further signification relation. This follows from the general notion of relation which can be articulated as a general axiom about relation: no relation can be one of its relata. However, Bhartṛhari points out that the notion of signification relation enters into our consciousness through the use of genitive endings:

> This is the 'signifier' (*vācaka*) of that, that is the 'signified' (*vācya*) of this. The thatness (*tattva*) of connection between the word and

> what it means is thus understood from the genitive ending. Hence its own-nature (thatness) is 'designated'. (Verse III, 3.3)

A further point, which justifies the above thesis of unsignifiability, is this. An item is usually signified by a signifier, 'linguistic expression', on the basis of some property or aspect belonging to the signified object, but since the characters or aspects of the signification relation (or relation in general) are completely exhausted by its two relata, it is completely colourless — in fact too colourless to be signified at all.

> (But) there is no (proper) designator of the (said) relation (of signification) that speaks of (or designates) it on the basis of its own feature (*dharma*). (For) due to its being totally undermined by others (its two relata), its own feature is not designated. (Verse III, 3.4)

The signification relation is really unsignifiable and it is also a *natural* bond which makes the designator and the designated identical. Bhartṛhari also describes, with the help of some early semi-mythical accounts of language, how the designator and the designated remain in the mind of the sentient completely undifferentiated at the initial stage (called *paśyanti*) and how the duality articulates in the third stage through an intermediate stage (called *madhyamā* = intermediate), where the speaker (and not anybody else) 'sees' the difference although the two are not yet differentiated. Thus at the third level (called *vaikhari*) the audible speech is generated. Bhartṛhari argues repeatedly, however, that since the speaker utters (or even writes) the designator in order to convey or communicate the designated, each such utterance (or writing) carries an implicit assertion of the type 'this (the word) *is* (identical with) that (the thing)'. And this is cited as a *prŏof* of the inherent identity of the designator and the designated.

Logocentrism and the scriptic bias

After this rather sketchy account of Bhartṛhari's text, let me conclude by making some general comments. It would be relevant today to talk about the apparent opposition between the speech and the writing, the audible parts and the visible inscriptions that are supposed to represent language. Modern Western Linguists (notably Saussure and others) have been eloquent about the primacy of speech or spoken words (as opposed to writing) as the indispensable foundation of linguistics. Saussure condemned his nineteenth century predecessors, the grammarians, for their 'scriptism' which presumably conflated writing with language, letters with sounds. This has been called by Saussure 'the tyranny of writing' even a 'monstrosity' or distortion. In spite of this dire warning, some recent linguists (Harris, 1980, 8; Lyons, 1968, 9), have shown that this *scriptist bias* has persisted in many corners of the field of linguistics, for the temptation to analyse speech into writing (Lyons has called it the 'orthological dogma') is one to which many modern linguists have inadvertently succumbed. Anybody familiar with J. Derrida's writing, for example, knows the opposite view which regards logocentrism (particularly the centrality of speech or the sonic element in language) as a bias which has suppressed free thinking about language and retarded our reflection on the origin and status of writing and its proper place in our study of language. The purpose of this critique of the so-called Western metaphysics, the 'deconstruction' of the texts of Saussure, Rousseau, etc., to expose the dangers and destructive effects of logocentrism, has been to develop a science of writing called grammatology. But this is not to say that writing is better than speech. Rather, the attempt, as I understand it, is to show that the said opposition is an illusion since language, or the origin and development of language, has historically been as much involved with structured speech as with structured writing, 'for it is indeed history that one must stop in order to protect language from writing' (Derrida, 1976, 42).

From the point of view of Bhartṛhari's *sphoṭa* or the notion that language is an integral part of our consciousness, we may say that both speech and writing can alike be the 'illuminator' of the *sphoṭa*. One is not primary and the other does not particularly distort the *sphoṭa*. In fact both can equally 'distort' the *sphoṭa* in a non-pejorative sense. Both 'transform' (cf. *vikara*) the untrans-formable, unmodifiable *sphoṭa*, which is part and parcel of everybody's consciousness. In the light of Bhartṛhari's theory, therefore, both the translations and the original (whether vocal or written) are in some sense transformations.

In spite of Bhartṛhari's explicit use of *śabda* and speech, I would argue that he was not guilty of 'logocentrism' in Derrida's sense. In fact, in Indian tradition, where oral transmission of the *Vedas* (wrongly called the Scriptures, for the Sanskrit term is *Śruti* = something to be heard) was the norm, where oral recitation of the Buddha's dialogues (the Buddhist scriptures where each section always starts 'Thus, I have heard ...') lasted for centuries after the death of the Buddha (and the same is true of Jainism), and where oral transmission of other texts called *śāstras* continued for a long time and texts were first memorized by students before any explanation or understanding was attempted, it is no wonder that the word for language was the word for sound (*śabda*). All these facts of the Indian tradition might have been historically conditioned because scholars faced extreme difficulties due to climatic and other conditions, for example the monsoons, in preparing and preserving writing materials. But the tradition, I argue, is free from the *fault* of logocentrism. For logocentrism, as I see it, flourishes and derives nourishment from the explicit condemnation (and also 'damnation' — it has been called a *sin*) of writing, otherwise 'speech' cannot be promoted to the prime place. And for this point one can turn to Derrida. It is obvious to any reader of Derrida how this 'condemnation', in a paradoxical manner, provides ammunition for Derrida's deconstruction of the texts of Saussure and Rousseau. As far as I know, such condemnation of writing was conspicuous by its absence in the Indian tradition in which Bhartṛhari flourished. Hence the *sphoṭa* theory of language was not 'logocentric' in any damning sense. As I have said, both sonic and graphic symbols can be the 'illuminator' of the *sphoṭa*; and being the illuminator either of them can be identified with the illuminated. Both speech and writing can be in perfect harmony (where talk of 'violence' would be pointless) in Bhartṛhari's holistic view of language.

2. Meaning in Literary Criticism: *Vakrokti* and *Dhvani*

Philosophy, Lingustics and Literary Criticism — all these disciplines were, in classical India, intimately connected, and they were considered an integral part of the broader discipline, called *śastra*. Thus, interaction between them was more a rule then an exception. This appendix will illustrate the point.

Two theories of poetry

Poetryhood consists in ornamentation (of speech)' — this is one of the main theses of Kuntaka, a Kashmiri rhetorician of the eleventh century AD.

From early days, there were two main theories of poetry, that is, Sanskrit *Kāvya.* One regarded *alaṃkāra*, i.e., embellishment of speech and its meaning, by which was meant alliteration, paranomasia etc. (*śabdālamkara*) on the one hand, and simile, metaphor etc. (*arthālamkara*) on the other, as external means to beautify speech. The other regarded *alaṃkāra* as the very essence of poetry. The idea in the first theory was to compare a piece of poetry with a body to which *alaṃkāras* would be added to enhance its beauty. This body-metaphor itself suggests several other things. One is to accept that the body as such. i.e., the 'body unornamented', can also be beautiful by itself. This has led to the well known controversy about *svabhāvokti*, that even an unadorned speech, a natural description or an unembellished description of nature, would constitute poetry. A later Alaṃkārika has said, '*analamkrti punaḥ kvāpi*'[1]

The other point is that the body needs life or a soul in order to appear beautiful, and the question is what constitutes that soul, or as they put it, *śaririn*? The later writers' answer is that it is *rasa* or aesthetic rapture. But obviously *rasa* here stands for that property of poetic expression, by virtue of which such aesthetic enjoyment is evoked in the readers. All these later views hang together with an earlier view that was fundamental: *alaṃkāras* are external properties of the *kāvya*. Even Ānandavardhana's superlative genius and insight did not find this position unsatisfactory.[2]

In fact Ānandavardhana (c. AD 860) and Abhinavagupta (c. AD 980) turned further towards a different aspect of poetry, the meaning that is *shown* in poetry, but not *expressed* there explicitly. A third (or a fourth) power of the words was appealed to, the power of suggestivity, besides the primary power giving the lexical meanings and their constructs, and the secondary or indicative power giving the metaphorical meanings. (see ch.3)

In fact Abhinavagupta talks about three *well-recognized* 'powers' or 'functions' of words, instead of two (*abhidhā* 'denotative' that gives the lexical meanings, and *lakṣaṇā* 'indicative' that gives the metaphorical sense). In this, he seems to follow the Bhāṭṭa view of *abhihitānvaya* '(syntactic) connection after designation'. On this view, besides 'denotative' and 'indicative', there is another power called *tātparya-śakti* by virtue of which the isolated word-meanings given by *abhidhā* together generate a connected whole, the sentence-meaning. (See also ch. 10)

---

1 *Mammaṭa: Kāvyaprakāśa*. ed. V. Jhalkikar, Poona, 1965, Verse 4 ch.1

2 Ānandavardhana: Dhvanyāloka (with Abhinava's *Locana*, ed. P.Sastri, Banaras, C.S.S., 1940, second Uddyota, *verse* 17-19. See specially: '*Alaṃkāro hi bāhyālaṃ-karasamyād anginaś cārutva-hetur ucyate*' under verse 17. Also '*vivakṣā tatparatvena nangitvenakadacanā*' (*verse* 18 ab).

Having described these three powers, Abhinava says that suggestivity or *dhvani* is the fourth power or function (cf. *caturthyāmtu kaksāyam dhvanana vyāpāraḥ, Locana*, under 1.4). This is summed up as follows:

Therefore this is the fourth function distinct from the three *abhidhā, tātparya* and *lakṣaṇā*. It is understood from the designation of such and other terms: *dhvanana, dyotana, vyañjana, pratyāyana, avagamana.*[1]

Poetry, according to Ananda, *must* mean more than it says. And if what it *shows* i.e., the suggested sense, exceeds (*atiśaya*, i.e. is more attractive or more beautiful than) the expressed sense, then it constitutes a better variety of poetry. In verse 13 of Uddyota 1, Ānanda defines *dhvani* and argues in the *vṛtti* that the *suggested* sense must be dominant over the expressed sense (*vācyārtha*) in order that the piece of composition be the proper locus of *dhvani.*[2]

Abhinava carefully distinguishes the suggested emotive meaning of the poetic composition from the 'indicative' metaphorical extension (cf. *lakṣaṇā*) of the word's meaning. Metaphorical extension of the word-meaning is forced upon us (all hearers or readers) when the lexical meanings of two words forming a sentence do not fit, e.g., 'the village is on the river' or Newcastle-upon-Tyne'. The word 'river' by metaphorical extension should mean here 'the river-bank'. Abhinava says: *mukhyārtha-bādhāyāṃ lakṣaṇāyāḥ praklptiḥ* ('*lakṣaṇā* arises if the primary meanings are obstructed'), under 1.4 in *Locana*. The suggested emotive meaning or the poetic meaning flashes in the mind of the sensitive reader only after the literal or ordinary meaning of the sentence has been fully comprehended. Here the condition, i.e., the lack of fitness ('misfitting' = *ayogyatā*), for which the service of *lakṣaṇā* or metaphorical extension is required, is conspicuous by its absence.

Ānanda was more concerned with the emotive meaning of poetry — poetry being evocative of aesthetic pleasure in the sensitive reader. When emotions are 'suggested' (i.e. evoked obliquely) the beauty is all the more enhanced, the aesthetic rapture excels. *Alaṃkāras* etc. can only be subservient to this evocation of aesthetic enjoyment, called *rasa*. Thus, the first theory, we can say, was concerned with the depths of meaning and ambiguity of the literary composition.

---

1 *Locana, Ibid.*

2 Ibid., verse 13, and three *saṃgraha* śloka under it.

The second theory, however, regarded *alaṃkāras* as natural or essential properties of poetry. I have deliberately left *alaṃkāra* untranslated here. '*Alaṃakāra*' does not simply mean 'ornament'. An ornament is what adds to the beauty (cf. *alaṃkaroti*) but, in addition to that, *alaṃkāra* may be an *essential part* of the beauty itself. Vāmana (c. AD 800) inadvertently got it right in the first section of his first chapter. He used the term *alaṃkāra* in two distinguishable senses; in one sense, *alaṃkāra* stands for beauty or beautification in general. He says, 'poetry is understood to be attractive to us because of *alaṃkāra*' (1.1.1) and 'alaṃkāra' means beauty' (1.1.2).[1] Etymologically the word may mean making something beautiful or beautification (for alam = bhūṣaṇa).[2] But there is another sense, when we derive the word in the instrumental case that which beautifies (cf. alam kriyateanena). Then it will refer to the usual item, simile, alliteration, etc. It was Bhamaha[3] (c. AD 700) who was also aware of the second view and defended it explicitly. He implicitly accepted that *alaṃkāra* constitutes the nature of poetry. This consists in the composition of speech and its meaning in an 'oblique' (vakra) manner. It is not only what you say but also how you say it. He asserts (1.6): The embellishment of speech consists in the oblique composition of words and the oblique presentation of meaning. In Bhamaha's slightly loose terminology: vakrokti = atiśayokti = alaṃkāra. *Vakrokti* means strikingness in word and meaning. Atisayokti means a non-standard way of speech, something that is not 'the ordinary run of the mill' but speaks of a meaning that excels (vide II.81, 84, 85). In II.85, Bhamaha says that in all alaṃkāras there is 'strikingness in speech' (*vakrokti*). In this vein, he rejected the idea that a *vārtā*, a plain report such as 'The sun has set, the moon is up, birds go to their nests' can constitute poetry (II.87). Some scholars (Raghavan, etc.) have said that this is not a rejection of *vārtā*. But I believe Bhamaha meant it as such. Daṇḍin (c. AD 700) retorted, quoting the same example that this

---

1 Vāmana: *Kāvyālamkāra-sūtra-vṛtti*, ed. J. Vidyasagar, 3rd edn., Calcutta,1922, *Kāvyaṃgrāhyam alaṃkārat*, 1-1-1, *saundaryam alaṃkāraḥ*, 1.1.2.

2 As the lexicographer says: *Alaṃ bhūṣaṇa-paryāpti-śakti-vāraṇavācakam*.

3 See Bhāmaha: *Kāvyālaṃkāra*, ed. P.V. Naganath Sastry, Tanjore, 1927, for all the references below.

would be good poetry provided it suggests a special time or state. Daṇḍin's argument leaves no doubt that some alamkārikas did reject *vārtā*. Much later in the history, Mammaṭa (c. AD 1050) (5th chapter of *Kāvya*prakasa) argued that the words constituting the example of *vārtā* may suggest at least nine different meanings (to different types of persons).[1] The idea is that the said expression is highly suggestive, and if suggestivity constitutes good poetry this would be good poetry. Bhamaha explicitly rejected *hetu*, *sūkṣma* and *leśa* on the ground that they do not consist in the obliqueness of speech (*vakrokti*). Talking about *svabhāvokti*, Bhamaha hesitatingly says that some regard it (description of objects or events as they are, *tadavasthātvam*) as an alaṃkāra. This ('*kecit*' in Bhamaha) might have been a preliminary to the rejection of *svabhāvokti*. Here Daṇḍin contributes again. Daṇḍin defines and illustrates three types of *svabhāvokti* and argues that this could be an *alaṃkāra*. He argues that although 'telling as it is' (= *svabhāvokti*) is what dominates the *śāstras* (that is, a philosophical or scientific treatise as opposed to *kāvya*, poetry), it might be desirable (*ipsita*) in *kāvya* too. In fact, Daṇḍin in verse II.362 clearly divides 'poetic speech pattern' (*kāvya*) into two: natural and oblique. Hence 'telling as it is' cannot be ignored in *kāvya*, it does constitute an *alaṃkāra*, says Daṇḍin[2]

Under verse 1 of Uddyota 1, Ananda quotes a verse composed by (according to Abhinavagupta) Manoratha, a poet contemporary with Ananda, who argues that the so-called *dhvani*, is a figment of the imagination belonging to persons of lesser intelligence. It continues: the stupid people praise a piece of poetry as full of *dhvani* 'suggestivity', when it does not contain any meaning that pleases the mind, being devoid of *alaṃkāra* it does not consist of skilfully composed words and does not have any *vakrokti*. The mention of the word '*vakrokti*' here is significant. For if *vakrokti* were only a species of *alaṃkāra* it would not merit a separate mention. However, Manoratha may be referring to the view that regards *vakrokti* as the basis of all *alaṃkāras* as the essence of beautification in poetry. Abhinava's comment here is important.

---

1 See *Mammaṭa*, Ch. 5.

2 Daṇḍin: *Kāvyādarśa*, ed. R. Raddi, Sastri, Poona, 1938. See also V. Raghavan: *Some Concepts of the Alaṃkāra Śāstra*, Madras, 1942.

Abhinava says that the word *alaṃkāra* refers to the arthālaṃkāras, simile, etc. 'Skilfully composed words' refers to the *śabdālaṃkāras*, alliterations, etc. And '*vakrokti*' refers to the *guṇas* pertaining to the sound and sense. In other words, *vakrokti* refers to *utkṛṣṭa saṃghaṭina* — excellent arrangements of words, etc. It may refer to style or *rīti*. Abhinava notes further that there is an alternative explanation of *vakrokti* as the common property of all *alaṃkāras* However, if we accept this sense, the fault of repetition cannot be avoided.

Now let us consider Kuntaka. (c. AD 950) What P.V. Kane[1] vaguely called the *alaṃkāra* school, of which, according to him, Bhamaha was the 'oldest extant exponent' (p.83), may have had its last, and in my view, the most important, exponent in Kuntaka. Philosophically speaking, Kuntaka was a holist and an essentialist. For him, the *alaṃkāra* constiutes the very essence of poetry. And this is how he proves it. A *kāvya* 'poem' is something that a poet does or creates. What a poet makes is poetry. A poet makes 'ornamented speech'. Ornamentalism consists in introducing obliqueness or strikingness in speech such that it will rejoice or delight the reader (*tad-vid-āhlādakārin*, 1.7). Hence a piece of poetry = a poet's making = ornamented speech. Thus poetryhood is ornamnetalism = introduction of obliqueness, uncommonness, non-banality. Bhāmaha's insight was right. In every *alaṃkāra* (call it *alaṃkāra*$_2$, a term that denotes simile, metaphor, etc.) there is inherent obliqueness. It is what distinguishes poetry from ordinary speech, banal reports, newspaper reports, etc. Thus, the second view, instead of emphasizing the deeper meaning which a sensitive reader derives from poetry, concentrates on the medium through which the message is communicated and believes that the medium is inseparable from the message.

Kuntaka can be described as a holist. In this he was explicitly influenced by Bhartṛhari among the grammarians. He believed that the distinction between the *alaṃkāra* and the *alaṃkārya* the 'ornaments' and that which is being ornamented (remember our old body metaphor; a poem is like a body where ornaments are added for the sake of beauty), is totally artificial. The connection between them is one of inseparability. A poem is a whole, its beauty, or even the means for beautification, cannot be separated from it. To put it in

1 P.V. Kane: *History of Sanskrit Poetics*, Delhi, 1961,p. 372-8.

another way, if we can take *alaṃkāra*$_1$ out i.e., away from the poetic speech, then it loses its poetryhood (*kāvyatā*). A body, even a body where there is a soul, can remain as it is, without the beautifying ornaments. But a poem cannot remain a poem without the *alaṃkāra* (=ornamentation=the poet's making = *kavikarma*). This follows from the very comprehensive definition of *alaṃkāra* as *kavikarma*. In fact, it is wrong or misleading to equate *alaṃkāra*$_1$ with what is known in the West as a figure of speech in a formal scheme. Even Abhinava indirectly endorses Kuntaka's view of *alaṃkāra*, as the special charm invested in the composition by the poet's imagination.

The grammatical model for literary criticism

Now the question unavoidably arises, the question that is usually raised against any holistic framework: How are we supposed to study and analyse the *alaṃkāras* in the second sense, i.e., *alaṃkāra*$_2$ which activity constitutes the proper subject matter of *alaṃkāra śāstra*? We are supposed to discuss and classify similes, metaphors, alliterations, etc. But how? Kuntaka looked towards Bhartṛhari for the answer. Indeed, for Bhartṛhari and the Sanskrit grammarians, a sentence is an unbreakable, impartite whole (ch.8). But how then are we supposed to study words, their formation out of roots and affixes etc., which constitutes the proper subject matter of grammar? Bhartṛhari[1] answers this question by referring to what he calls the *apoddhāra* method. We follow the method of extraction and abstraction. We apply this method and operate it upon the given reality, a whole sentence. We reach individual words, and individual roots or suffixes through abstraction. We *artificially* constitute or create in this way words, roots and suffixes, the subject-matter of our study in grammar. The word 'artificially' means that they lack givenness or that their existence is a borrowed existence. Thus Bhartṛhari and other holists try to drive the point home by saying that the whole is real while parts are not, for they are constructs or abstracted bits. The natural home of a word is the sentence in which it occurs. Kuntaka refers to this argument of the holist, and on the basis of this analogy, he explains that although the *alaṃkāra* and the *alaṃkārya* are inseparable and constitute a whole, a distinction is made by the *apoddhāra*

[1] Bhartṛhari, *Vākyapadīya*, Kaṇḍa 2, verse 10.

method, only because it is instrumental (*upāya*) to our study and understanding of the nature of poetry, which constitutes the proper subject matter of *alaṃkāraśāstra*. The so-called *alaṃkāras* simile, etc., are therefore artificially abstracted from pieces of poetry much as the words are abstracted from the sentence. These *alaṃkaras* have only borrowed existence. They essentially belong to poetry; without poetry they have no *locus standi* outside. The expression 'a *gayal* is like a cow' is in this way not a case of *alaṃkāra* (although there is a simile) for it is not a piece of poetry. Similarly, 'There is fire on the hill because there is smoke' would not be a case of *hetu alaṃkāra*, although a reason is being assigned here, because it is a bland statement without any tinge of obliqueness or beauty. Kuntaka explains *apoddhṛtya* as *nikṛṣya,* i.e., *pṛthak pṛthag avasthāpya*, 'extracting, putting them separately (in awareness)'. He further glosses '*yatra samudāyarūpe tayor antarbhāvas tasmād vibhajya*', i.e., analysing or dividing them from the whole in which they inhere. The main point here is to understand the instrumental nature of this division. Every holist has to appeal to a form of instrumentalism as regards the extracted parts. Thus Kuntaka was no exception (cf. *tad-upāyataya*).

From what has now been said, we may still doubt whether Kuntaka was really a believer in the *alaṃkāra* theory, or to use Kane's expression, an exponent of the *Alaṃkāra* School. For on this theory, as I have already noted earlier, the 'body-metaphor' along with its various implications should be given up and the metaphor of the whole and 'naturalness' (essentiality or inseparableness) of *alaṃkāra* in poetry should be emphasized. The individual *alaṃkāras* do seem to be separable as a necklace is separable from the neck or the body. Kuntaka dispels this doubt in no uncertain terms[1]:

> This is the ultimate meaning (*paramārtha*) here: poetryhood, that is, the poet's making, belongs to something that is existent (*sataḥ*), where all parts have vanished into a whole (i.e., an impartite whole, *nirasta-sakalāvayava*) and which has *alaṃkāra* (as its essential constituent). Thus, the thesis is: poetryhood belongs to what has *alaṃkāra* 'ornaments', and it is not the case that *alaṃkā-ras* are added to, or connected (*yoga*) with, the poem.

---

1 Kuntaka, *Vaktokti-jivita*, ed. S.K. De, Calcutta. 1928. p.7, *vṛtti* under verse 6. Ch.1.

I have mentioned the Kuntaka thesis, which may be put as follows:

1. Obliqueness (*vakratā*) in speech underlies or pervades all *alaṃkāras*.

2. There cannot be any poem without such an *alaṃkāra*.

3. Therefore obliqueness in speech constitutes poetry.

And his argument is:

4. If poetry is what a poet makes, then we know that the poet makes or creates or introduces the required obliqueness in the middle of plain or banal expressions. Therefore, obliqueness = the property of being made by the poet = poetryhood.

Criticism of the theory of obliqueness in presentation

I shall now develop a critique of this thesis, which will include some traditional criticisms and some new ones.

(1) Daṇḍin hit the nail right on the head when he argued that even the plain expressions 'the sun is set, the moon is up, ...' can be part of some poetical composition in a suitably chosen context. This was promptly picked up by the later Dhvani theorists (e.g. Mammaṭa), as I have noted earlier. The problem is that banality or plainness in the composition of words and sounds does not imply plainness in meaning. Meaning is given by the context and the poet may of course use plain words in order to generate profoundly charming meaning. Kuntaka might have answered the charge as follows. Obliqueness in meaning (*artha*) is also a constituent of poetry. In verses 1, 9 and 10, Kuntaka explicitly states:

> Although many other words are there (to convey the same meaning), the (poetic) word is what uniquely conveys the sole meaning intended by the poet. The meaning is what beautifully vibrates and charms the hearts of the sensitive reader. Both (word and meaning are ornamented. This ornamentation of both is said to be the obliqueness in speech, a masterly way of speaking.

In other words Kuntaka can absorb the criticism of Daṇḍin and turn the counter-example into a proper example covered by his definition of poetry. His intention was to distinguish the ordinary mode of speech, or the cart drivers' language (*śākaṭika-vākya*), from the poetic language. But the problem is that even the cart drivers' plain or vulgar language can be accorded with beauty or obliqueness by setting it in an appropriate context. For example in the Viṣkambhaka in

Abhijñaśākuntala, the fisherman's as well as the policeman's plain and rough and ready speech became part of an excellent *dṛsyakāvya*. In short, we all know that the plain man's speech must be distinguished from *kāvya*, but the element of contextuality makes it impossible to a wholesale or blanket rejection of the plain man's speech.

(2) A *svabhāvokti*, as insisted upon by Daṇḍin, may be simply a graphic description and this may indeed be a piece of good poetry. Two well-known examples are often cited; one from *Abhijñāna-śākuntala: Grivābhangābhirāmam* etc. The other is *yaḥ kaumāra-haraḥ* etc. Kuntaka seems to tackle this objection in verses 1, 11-15. First, if the term *svabhāvokti* means description of the 'nature' (*svabhāva*) of the object or event, then any description can be such a description, for what else can we describe besides some 'nature of the object? If such a description is an *alaṃkāra* 'ornament' what it is that is being ornamented here? Second, an object that lacks a *svabhāva* 'nature', would be a fictitious object, a non-object, and in fact it would be indescribable, ineffable. Objects are denoted by words on the basis of their having some 'nature' or other. Hence any possibility of description in language implies description of 'nature' (*svabhāvokti*). Third, since one cannot climb upon one's own shoulder, the body' of a poem, the 'nature' (*svabhāva*) to be described, cannot ornament or adorn itself.

Kuntaka's argument is somewhat a priori. It is a dialectic based upon what is meant by *svabhāvokti* and what it is to be an *alaṃkāra*. But the underlying point is probably that the body metaphor, as well as the externalist view of *alaṃkāra* that goes along with it, is open to serious attack. The opponent in calling *svabhāvokti* an *alaṃkāra* has made his externalist position standing on its head, for the duality of *alaṃkāra* and *alamkarya* collapses.

(3) We should note that the well-known verses of Kālidāsa or *Śila-Bhaṭṭārika,* that are cited as examples of *svabhāvokti alaṃkāra* can be easily regarded as pieces of high-class poetry even by a follower of Kuntaka. It is not difficult to discover why such verses are charming to us and wherein lies the mastery of the poetic art (*kaver vyāpārah*) that introduces strikingness in the expression. So the dispute here is not about the *lakṣyas* or definienda, but about the defining or distinguishing characteristic itself (*lakṣaṇa*). Is it the obliqueness is speech? or, the profundity in the suggestiveness? or, the aesthetic rapture that it generates in the sensitive reader? Kuntaka opts for the first.

to be distinguished from what I have called the externalist view above. The 'externalist view', in my opinion, is that which regards *alaṃkāras* as external, and hence in principle separable, properties of *kāvya*. Some early *Ālaṃkārikas* seem to have upheld such a view. Kuntaka rejected it. But critics charge that Kuntaka was concerned only with the exterior of poetry, with *alaṃkāra*, *guṇa, rīti, doṣa*, etc. But this charge is unfounded. Kuntaka did not distinguish between 'exterior' and 'interior'. He was more concerned with the *vyāpāra* 'function' of the poet, with what is it that the poet does to the ordinary modes of speech (he also calls it *kavi-kauśala* (II.3, 4)). He was seriously concerned with *pratibhā*, the poetic genius or insight, that so-called 'philosopher's stone' which by its mere touch turns iron into gold, ordinary banalities into poetic expressions.

SECTION - III

Modern Indian Aesthetics

1

The Aesthetic Hypothesis

Mulk Raj Anand

The Hindu view of art proper may be said to lie in the aesthetic conception of *rasa*. A word of art may be said to be *rasavant* (a derivative adjective of *rasa*, meaning "having rasa"); the critic, connoisseur, or spectator who enjoys *rasa* may be called *rasikā*; the act in and through which the aesthetic emotion is enjoyed or contemplated may be technically styled *rasasvādana*.

A consideration of the sense in which the word *rasa* was used in the Vedas and the Upanishads might well prepare the way for the elucidation of its meaning in the hands of the rhetoricians and writers on poetics.

The word occurs in the *Rig-Veda* in the sense of juice (of the soma plant).[1] It is also used in the earlier hymns to signify water and milk.[2] And sometimes it is applied to mean flavour.[3] In the *Atharva-Veda, rasa* is used, not only in its earlier meaning as the juice of plants and herbs, but is also applied to the sap of grain,[4] and although it has come less to signify water and milk, one very interesting and important notion has become connected with it — that of "savour" or "taste." For instance the poet prays:

"May the satisfying savour of the honey mixed come to me."[5]

During the Upanishadic times the meaning of *rasa* developed, like that of most other Vedic conceptions, from the particular to the universal. From its signification as the essential element in concrete plants, grain, water, and milk, it has come to be an abstract idea of "essential element," or "essence."[6] For instance:

"Life breath or the vital air is the essence of the limbs."

---

1 IX. 63. 13. and IX. 65. 15.

2 VIII. 72. 13.

3 V. 44.13.

4 III. 31. 10.

5 III. i3. 15.

6 *Brh. Up.*, I. 3. 19.

It still continued, however, to be used for "savour" and "taste."[1] The philosophers declared that man "knows the taste by the tongue," and the word became a denominative verb, "to taste."[2] In the *Taittiriya* and the *Maiterya* Upanishads a great step forward was taken by the fusion of *rusa* as essence with a new meaning — the highest state of joy, an expression of the nature of the Supreme Being as reflected in the "self-luminous consciousness" of the Upanishadic seer.

"He is *Rasa*, having obtained Him the soul becomes full of bliss."[3]

Ananda Vardhana, a writer on poetics, refers to the second chapter of the *Ramayana* in support of his contention that he notion of *rasa* first came to be applied to literature through the poet Valmiki. The story is related that Valmiki was out one day gathering sacrificial wood and grass in the forest when he saw a pair of Kraunca birds joyfully twittering as they sat on the branch of a tree. An arrow came that very instant from an invisible hunter and struck the male bird, which instantily fell. The sage was filled with immense grief to reflect that only a moment ago the poor creature was happily singing, and now it lay dead in the dust, while its companion fluttered about it shrieking with anguish. Long did the incident trouble Valmiki's mind that day, and th epoignant tragedy lay heavy on his heart till he burst out in an ecstatic verse of exquisite melody and pathos, and became lost in the forgetfulness of pure bliss. This was the first *sloka* (verse) invented. The poet tried later introspectively to analyse the whole state of his mind from the moment when the original feeling arose to the time when he attained the boundless joy, and arrived at the conclusion that "that which proceeded from me who was overpowered by pathos shall be nothing but poetry or rhythmic expression" — *rasa*.

According to Ananda Vardhana, the various steps in the process which led to the utterance of rhythmic expression by Valmiki are:

---

1 *Ibid.*, III. 2. 4.

2 *Prasna. Up.*, IV. 2.

3 *Taittiriya Up.*, II. 7.

(1) the perceptual experience of the event; (2) the transference of the perceptual experience to the imagination, as the cause of that feeling of pathos which translated itself into (3) the outburst of poetry, and led to (4) the attainment of pure joy. This last blissful state Ananda Vardhana regarded as the feeling which poetry, or any sort of rhythmic expression, should evoke in the mind of the critic.

The science of poetry, which started when Valmiki analysed the nature of his rhythmic expression, came to be known as *Alamkāra-shastra*, or *Sahitya-shastra*. The first title means the science of the beautiful expression of the beautiful; the literal meaning of the second is that the science of the expression of beauty is the true companion of the soul. The systematic development of this scince went on for nearly two thousand years, i.e. from before the Christian era to the eighteenth century, and there are accounted some eight hundred and seventy-two major works on the aesthetics of poetry. But as my chief concern here is to explain the theory of *rasa* in its relation to art, I will not go into a detailed survey of all these books on poetics, but merely give an exposition of the meaning of *rasa*, the way it comes to be, and what its implications are when applied to a work of art.

What then is *rasa*, and how exactly is it evoked?

At the outset, it must be noted that it is difficult, if not impossible, to define the word *rasa* positively, because the conception implied in it is intuitively realised rather than sensibly experienced, but from its elaborate exposition, analysis, and classification by the sage Bharata in his *Natya-shastra*, in the various text-books culled from his pages, and in the commentaries based on him, its meaning may be suggested by saying that it is that state of bliss through the realisation of the inner worlds of faculty and experience which is aroused by the spectacle (dramatic, acrobatic, plastic, or pictorial) of a rhythmic expression and controlled emotion.

In an ordinary way it may be said to be caused by a work of art produced by the deliberate manipulation by an artist or poet of the emotions or feelings which formed the inspirational centre of his or her consciousness after he or she had envisaged a certain aspect or aspects of the universe. Let me illustrate the point by considering the history of a work of art. (1) The poet or the artist has been stirred, say, by the sight or thought of lovers embracing each other into recognising the presence of a feeling or emotion of love; (2) he is possessed by this emotion and sees it as a coherent experience with the inner eye; (3) then he translates his internal experience, or vision, as we may call it, into an external form, by speech if he is an actor, by the written word if he is a writer, by colours if he is a painter; (4) and then is produced (all things being perfectly assimilated) a perfect work of art, embodying the emotion of love, which the spectator or critic who has himself had the experience of being in love, and who retains impressions of that experience, is stimulated into enjoying as an abstract, universal experience, *rasa*, pure joy, irrespective of the emotion in the picture or the poem, or in his own experience.

This is very simply the process by which *rasa* may be evoked, but it is not quite so simple as it seems. For, first of all, the artist never knows when his creation might evoke *rasa* in the critic. Nor, indeed, does he care whether it will evoke that state. He is in love with his theme, and just dedicates himself to render it from sheer abundance of feeling, which makes it impossible for him to contain himself within himself. His work may evoke *rasa* through the *rasika's* own capacity to be delighted, "not from the character of the hero to be imitated, nor because the work aims at the production of aesthetic emotion."[1]

The demands that an artist must fulfil if his work is to be potentially capable of exciting *rasa* may, however, be noted. The artist is expected to have either a natural or acquired genius for noticing things. That is to say, he must have a very keen receptivity, acutely sensitive to life. And he should have a deep consciousness or vision of the illimitable resources in which he can mirror the Cosmos.[2]

The *karma* (good and bad deeds) of every man or the race in which he is born as well as the background of his experience determine his genius, but education and training also mould a man's powers. If he has the preliminary capacity to feel intensely, he can be helped to adumbrate the realities which cannot be humanly formulated through means of *Yoga* (contemplation) practices. I shall deal with the *Yoga*

---

1 *Dasarupa*, IV. 47.

2 "Creation comes from the depths — the mystic will say from God" (E.M. Forster).

method enjoined to artists in the next section. Meanwhile let me notice some other considerations which make a work of art capable of producing *rasa*.

Rasa is a very subtle state, requiring the manipulation of several different kinds of emotion, and a host of feelings, into a judicious fusion, before it may be evoked. The Hindu writers on poetics classified emotions into (1) lasting, (2) incidental or transitory. There are eight lasting emotions: (i) *Rati* (love), (2) *Hasa* (laughter), (3) *Soka* (sorrow), (4) *Krodha* (anger), (5) *Utsaha* (high-spiritedness), (6) *Bhaya* (fear), (7) *Jugupsa* (repugnance or disgust), (8) *Vismaya* (astonishment). A ninth class, not generally admitted is *Santa*, that mental state in which we regard the world as transitory or ephemeral.

Of the incidental emotions there are as many as thirty-three in number: self-disparagement; debility or weakness; apprehension of encountering what is desired and misgivings about obtaining the desired; indolence or aversion to activity; depression due to poverty or pain; painful reflection due to painful memories; perplexity or distraction; recollection; concentration or repose of the mind in contentment; shame or shrinking from pain or censure; unsteadiness or haste in constantly changing from one object to another; joy; agitation or flurry due to pleasant happenings; loss of faculty or activity, meaning disability to do any kind of work; arrogance; despair of success; impatience; drowsiness; possession of the self by a daemoniac fancy, or the influence on the self of some astrological phenomena; sleep; waking; impatience of opposition or rivalry; disguise of real feelings; sternness or cruelty; apprehension; sickness; absence of reflection or restraint; death; fear without cause; consideration or discussion.

Emotions, both lasting and transitory, manifest themselves in either of the following ways: (1) they precede or accompany a particular state of mind or body; (2) they appear as the external forms hwich indicate the existence of a mental state; and (3) they are involuntarily exhibited by the person who possesses them.

The eight lasting emotions in conjunction with their associated groups of feeling may evoke eight different forms of *rasa*. When we speak of eight different forms of *rasa*, however, we do not mean that *rasa* is either qualitatively or quantitatively divisible into eight species, but these eight are "the various colourings of one experience, and are arbitrary terms of rhetoric used only for convenience in classification; just as we speak of poetry categorically as lyric, epic, dramatic, etc., without implying that poetry is anything but poetry."[1] To enumerate the *rasas* corresponding to the emotions: (1) The emotion of love and the transitory feelings, longing, anxiety, raving, insanity, fever, stupor, death, are bound up with the *Sringara*, or the erotic *rasa*. (2) High-spiritedness and the incidental feelings, assurance, contentment, arrogance, and joy, are the signs of the *Vira*, or the heroic *rasa*. (3) Anger and the attendant feelings, indignation, intoxication, recollection, inconstancy, envy, cruelty, agitation, occur with the *Raudra rasa*, or the *rasa* of fury. (4) Mirth with its accompanying states, indolence, weariness, weakness, stupor, might evoke the *Hasya rasa*, or the *rasa* of comedy. (5) Astonishment and the feelings, joy, agitation, distraction, fright, may arouse the *Adbhuta rasa*, or the *rasa* of wonder. (6) The emotion of sorrow is conducive to the production of the *karuna rasa*, the *rasa* of pathos, so-called from Valmiki's experience of it on seeing the death of the Kraunca bird referred to above. (7) Disgust and the ephemeral feelings, agitation, sickness, provoke the *Bibhatsa rasa* or the *rasa* of indignation. The emotion of fear produces the *Bhayanaka rasa*, or the *rasa* of terror.[2]

The *rasas* are also identified with certain colours and with certain divinities. For instance, *Sringara*, or the erotic *rasa*, is associated with *shamya*, or dark colour, and the god Vishnu; *Hasya*, or the comic *rasa*, with the colour white and the god Rama; *Raudra*, the furious *rasa*, and *Vira*, the heroic *rasa*, go with the colours red and the gods Indra and Rudra respectively; *Karuna*, or the *rasa* of pity, is allied to the grey hue and the god Varuna; *Bhayanka*, or the terrible *rasa*, is ascribed a black colour and the presiding deity *Yama*; *Bibhatsa*, or the *rasa* of disgust, is connected with the blue colour and the god Siva, or Mahakala; *Adbhuta*, or the *rasa* of wonder, is assigned a yellow colour and the presiding deity Brahma.[3]

From the popular practice of representing *Ragas* and *Raginis* (musical modes) through the graphic arts which prevailed in India, it

---

1 Coomaraswamy, *Dance of Shiva*, P. 32.

2 Compare the analysis of emotions and their bearing on art in Sully's *Outlines of Psychology*, and Bain's *English Composition and Rhetoric*, Vol. II. Also Lord Cames' *Elements of Criticism*.

3 "It would be vain to deny that certain kinds and tones of colour have a real correspondence with emotional states of mind" (Laurence Binyon).

is evident that the Hindus firmly believed in the intimate relationship of the various arts in general, and of the graphic art and the art of music in particular. An anecdote on this question from an ancient *Silpa-shastra* (art-treatise) may be illuminating. A king once approached a sage and asked to be taught the methods of image-making. The following dialogue ensued:

KING: O Sinless One! Be good enough to teach me the methods of image-making.
SAGE: One who does not know the laws of painting can never understand the laws of image-making.
KING: Be then good enough, O Sage, to teach me the laws of painting.
SAGE: But it is difficult to understand the laws of painting without any knowledge of the technique of dancing.
KING: Kindly instruct me then in the art of dancing.
SAGE: This is difficult to understand without a thorough knowledge of the laws of instrumental music.
KING: Pray teach me the laws of instrumental music.
SAGE: But the laws of instrumental music cannot be learnt without a deep knowledge of the art of vocal music.
KING: If vocal music be source and end of all the arts, reveal then to me, O Sage, the laws of vocal music.[1]

It must be noted that the presence of the above mentioned permanent emotions among their respective groups of transitory feelings is absolutely essential if *rasa* is to be produced. The failure of the artist to weave the minor feelings into the central theme leads to a lack of unity and incoherence in his work. The sage Bharata says in his *Natya-shastra*:

> As a king to his subject, as a *Master* to his disciples,
> Even so the master-motif is the Lord of all other motives.

On no account, however, must a minor-motif be made the master-motif, unless there is a sheer weight of conviction and sincerity behind it, for "the extended development of a transient emotion tends

---

1 Reference may here be made to Schopenhauer's view popularised by Pater that "all arts constantly tend to attain the condition of music."

to the absence of *rasa*."[1] That is to say the work becomes sentimental.

Rasa may be evoked by any aspect of life treated by a great artist: "delightful or disgusting, exalted or lowly, cruel or kind, obscure or refined, actual or imaginary, there is no subject that cannot evoke *rasa* in man."[2] But here it must be noted that the treatement of life does not mean the imitation of nature. So far from being an imitation of nature, art is for the Hindus absolutely distinct from it: "In the limitless world of the poet's creation, the poet himself is the creator," says a well-known Indian rhetorician; "it (the world of his creation) lives and moves and has its being as it pleases him." "The poet's speech," says another famous Hindu writer on poetics, "creates a world which is not fettered by the laws of nature, which is of the very essence of joy, which is self-existent and not depending on anything else, and which brings into being a creation shining with the nine *rasas*." Art is thus for the Hindus essentially creative.

Of course, the elements from which the artist creates his work of art are taken from nature, but they are the alphabet out of which he moulds, by the deliberate exertion of his mind, the lines and forms by which he conveys his meaning.[3] If *rasa* is, then, supposed to be evoked by the treatment of life, it is supposed to be created by the deliberate treatment of that aspect of life.[4] The Hindus carried even further this conception of the deliberateness of art, and maintained that perfect spontaneity in a work of art is attained only by a perfectly deliberate treatment, a treatment that leaves nothing to chance. The actors and the dancers are enjoined, for instance, in a Hindu treatise on Dramaturgy, to cultivate as complete and sure a mastery of gesture as the puppet showman possesses over the limbs of his puppets; and the representations of the emotions of the hero to be portrayed should, it is declared, be absolutely mechanical, independent of the actor's or dancer's own feelings or emotions.

---

1 *Dasarupa*, IV. 45.

2 *Ibid.*

3 "Beauty is no quality either of trees or pigments, but like every other value only comes into being as the result of a spiritual activity. Its *esse is percipi*" (Croce).

4 " Art is the deliberate communication of feelings" (Tolstoy).

Hence there is said to be no difference between the actor and the audience, because the actor can enjoy the universal joy of *rasa* while he is playing a part in the same impersonal way as the spectators watching him. As Dr. Coomaraswamy renders the point: "If he is moved by what he represents, he is moved as a spectator, and not as an artist. ... Excellent art wears the airs of perfect spontaneity ... that is an art which conceals art."[1]

That this dictum is no mere theory is borne out by the fact that in the art of dancing and drama the Hindus had developed an exhaustive gesture language in which each little movement of the body was defined as a noun, pronoun, verb and tense, etc., just as ordinary language is defined in grammar. I will quote some of the rules of gesture later. Here I may quote the distinguished authority on Indian art, already referred to so many times, to show the actual works of Indian art that have come down to us, though apparently spontaneous, are in fact the result of a most careful and defined method. "The Ajanta frescoes," writes Dr. Coomaraswamy, "seem to show unstudied gesture and spontaneous pose, but actually there is hardly a position of the hand or of the body which has not a recognised name and a precise significance. The more deeply we penetrate the technique of any typically oriental art, the more we find what appears to be individual, impulsive, and natural is actually long inherited, well considered, and well bred. Under these conditions life itself becomes a ritual."[2]

On the analogy of a discussion of the degrees of excellence of different kinds of poetry in the various treatises on poetics, a principle might be laid down with regard to the degree of excellence achieved by different forms of art. Just as the highest poetry is that which gives in a beautiful form a message of deep meaning and overloaded significance, so that art is highest which suggests the profoundest vision in the most perfect style. And just as in inferior poetry the sense is lost in an exaggerated ornamentation and over-embroidery, and the result is a charming narrative lacking any very subtle meaning, so in inferior art, mere narrative and description being

---

1 Coomaraswamy and Dugrilla, *The Mirror of Gesture*, pp. 1-10.

2 *ibid.*

emphasised, there is a corresponding lack of significance. Therefore, we must guard againt the flowery rhetoric of narrative, and descriptive verse and art, and prefer the deep message of a simply wrought subject to the grandiloquent flummery of a work disguised in a scientifically elaborate metre and tricked out with all the hackneyed effusions of high-sounding poetry of "great" art.

The Hindus would seem, to the Western mind steeped in a strong belief in democracy, to expect rather too much from the *rasika*, the critic or the spectator. For *rasa* is enjoyed according to Dharmadatta "only by those who are competent." The ideal spectator is defined by Bharata as "one who is happy when the course of the drama is cheerful, melancholy when it is sorrowful, who rages when it is furious, and trembles when it is fearful."[1] In a word, he goes to the theatre to appreciate with sympathy what he sees.

The sensibility of the good critic as well as the artist may be either natural or acquired, or be a happy fusion of the two; but more often than not it is native, inherited through the *karma* (good or bad deeds of past life),[2] and with difficulty cultivated. Archaeologists or historians of art, like some of the most eager students of poetry, are seen not to have a right perception of *rasa*, and may, indeed, never have it, for instruction is not the purpose of art, but the evocation of joy in a mind potentially capable of realising it. "As for any man of simple intelligence," writes Dhanamjaya, "who says that from dramas, which distil joy, the gain is knowledge only, as in the case of history and the like, homage to him, for he has averted his face from what

---

1 *Natya-shastra*. "Picture, poetry, and every work of art produce no effect save on souls prepared to receive them" (Croce).

2 The Classical Hindu poet, Kalidasa, showed the influence of a man's *karma* (past life) on his capacity to enjoy the things of the present when he said: "The reason why on seeing beautiful objects and hearing harmonious sounds, even a happy man becomes full of longing and melancholy is that he remembers, without the experience rising to the surface of his working consciousness, the companionships and enjoyments which he had in previous births, and which are an integral portion of his treasury of emotions." A similar view was in Rossetti's mind when he wrote:

O born with me somewhere that men forget,
And though in years of sight and sound unmet,
Known for my soul's birth-partner well enough.

is delightful."[1]

Not only must the critic be sympathetic, but he must have a conscious desire to have *rasa* evoked in him. He must exert his imagination to create in himself a state conducive to the enjoyment of art. "Those devoid of imagination, in the theatre, are but as woodwork, the walls and the stones."[2] Sukracharya (the author of *Sukranitisara*, a sociological text containing a section on the craft of image-making), when he says, "the defects of images are constantly destroyed by the power of the virtue of the worshipper who has his heart always set on God"; and it is resuscitated by the poet Rabindra Nath Tagore: "In our country, those of the audience who are appreciative, are content to perfect the song in their own mind by the force of their own feeling."[3] And "if this attitude," says Dr. Coomaraswamy, "seems to us dangerously uncritical, that is to say dangerous to art, or rather to accomplishment, let us remember that it prevailed everywhere in all periods of great creative activity, and that the decline of art has always followed the decline of love and faith. Tolerance of an imperfect work of art may arise in two ways: the one uncritical, powerfully swayed by the sympathetic, and too easily satisfied with a very inadequate correspondence between content and form; the other creative, very little swayed by considerations of charm, and able by force of the true imagination to complete the correspondence of content and form which is not achieved or not preserved in the original. Uncritical tolerance is prettiness or edification, and recoils from beauty that is "difficult": creative tolerance is indifferent to prettiness or edification, and is able from a mere suggestion, such as an awkward 'primitive' or a

---

1 *Dasarupa*, I.6.

2 *Sahitya Darpana*.

"Some who have cold affections, sluggish imaginations, and no habits of observation can with difficulty discern beauty in anything; while others who are full of kindness and sensibility, and who have been accustomed to attend to all objects around, feel it almost in everything." Jeffrey, *Encyclopaedia Britannica*, article on "Aesthetics," 9th ed.

3 *My Reminiscences*, pp. 134-135.

"If one has not studied things with a partiality full of love, what one thinks about them is not worth saying" (Goethe).

broken fragment, to create or re-create a perfect experience."[1]

From my reference to the use of the word *rasa* in the Upanishads and the subsequent exposition of the way in which it comes to be, it may have become obvious that this conception of beauty is in the aesthetic world what *Ananda* is in the metaphysical, and *Ishvara* (God) in the religious. That it is really only the religio-philosophical hypothesis in a different dress, designed specifically to fit in with the experience of aesthetics, is confirmed by its frequent use in Indian literature interchangeably with its prototype.

The *Taittiriya Upanishad*, it might be recalled, had said: "He is *rasa*, having attained Him the soul becomes full of bliss." It is possible that the earliest writers on Poetics knew of this, and consciously desiring to establish their science on the secure foundations of the *sarva-vidya-pratistha* (the basis of all sciences), as *Brahma Vidya* (the science of the eternal) the knowledge of Brahman or philosophy had come to be known, they adopted the ideal *Ananda* of the mother science as *rasa* to be the ideal Poetics also. The philosopher of the *Bhagavad-Gita* had indeed made an overture to rhetoricians when he made Sri Krishna, the symbol of the All-pervasive Cosmic Life, say: "I am the splendour of splendid things," and "whatsoever is ... beautiful .... understand that thou to go forth from a fragment of my Splendour." Sankaracharya, the author of the Vedanta system of pure monism, had declared that "*Brahman* is *rasa*, *rasa* is bliss." And the definitions of *rasa* throughout the literature on poetics and rhetorics echo these statements. For instance, Vishvanatha says in the *Sahitya Darpana*: "It (*rasa*) is pure, indivisible, self-manifested, compounded equally of joy and consciousness, free of admixture with any other perceptions, the very twin brother of mystic experience (*Brahmasavadana Sahodarah*) and the very life of it is super-sensuous (*lokottara*) wonder."[2] Mammata, another rhetorician, talks of the "joy which is the crown of all the aims of life, which is immediately

---

1 Coomaraswamy, *Dance of Shiva*, p.34.

"In order to appreciate a masterpiece, we must have some knowledge of the terms which the artist has used and the principles he has followed. We know the terms only when we have ourselves used them and the principles when we have tried to follow them" (a recent European critic).

2 "Beauty belongs to the transcendental and metaphysical order" (Maritain, *Art and Scholasticism*).

produced by the relish of *rasa*, and which so fills the mind that one is aware of nothing else." While Jagannatha is still more explicit: "*rasa* is that shining forth of the bliss of the soul where the barriers to its self-expression are removed, the bliss being expressed through love and other emotional states."[1] Achutarya would seem to regard it as a mirror of the Cosmos when he says that *rasa* is a reflected bliss reflected as the beauty of woman in a polished mirror.[2]

The metaphysical Absolute was described in the Upanishads as the Ultimate Reality which is "the internal *Atman* of all created things." But, although it permeates the differentiated universe of *maya* (appearance) and we can feel it in the veins of existence, we cannot know it, materially, through the senses. As I have shown above, the same is true of *rasa*. It is an ideal state, a transcendental mode of consciousness, in which the essences of things are intuitively apprehended, by plunging back, as it were, into the *mysterium tremendum* of life, in the manner of the poet who sees the meaning of things by the sudden flash of a vision, or of the philosopher who realises the wholeness of experience in a moment.[3] In an ordinary human way the Hindu rhetoricians sought to describe *rasa*, qualitatively and quantitatively, as the Vedic seers described the Absolute ideal of their aspiration, but it is no more definable or provable logically than is the Supreme Reality (*Ananda*). Of it, it may be said that the proof of the pudding is in the eating. "God put it into my head, and I cannot put it into yours," says the man who experiences it. "*Rasa*, which by the predominance of *sattvaguna* is full of limitless and spontaneous self-consciousness and bliss, which is free from the taint of intruding objects, which is akin to Brahmic bliss, whose life is super-worldly and of exquisite charm, is enjoyed as a state of union of enjoyer and the enjoyed by fortunate and happy discerners of

---

1 "Beauty is the splendour of being shining from the proportioned parts of matter" (Maritain, *Art and Scholasticism*).

2 *Ibid.*

3 "Beauty is inexplicable; it is a hovering, floating, glittering shadow, whose outlines elude the grasp of definition" (Goethe).

delight."[1]

---

1 Visvanatha, *Sahitya Darpana*.

Similar views have been held at different times in Europe. For instance, Plotinus held: "That which sees must be kindred and similar to its object, before it can see it. The eye could never have beheld the Sun, had it not been Sunlike. The mind could never have perceived the beautiful, had it not first become beautiful itself. Everyone must partake of the Divine nature, before he can discern the Divinely beautiful."

Plato, dealing with the laws of beauty in the *Symposium*, says virtually the same thing: "He who would proceed aright in this matter should begin to visit beautiful forms. Soon he will perceive that the beauty of one form is akin to the beauty of another, and then if beauty of form is his general pursuit how foolish would he be not to recognise that beauty in every form is one and the same. Ane when he perceives this he will become a lover of all beautiful forms, and next he will consider that the beauty of the mind is more honourable than the beauty of things. ... At length the vision will be revealed to him of a single science which is the science of beauty everywhere ... a thing of wondrous beauty which is everlasting, not growing or decaying nor waxing nor waning ... but beauty Absolute, Separate, Simple, and Everlasting, which without diminution and without increase is imparted to the evergrowing and perishing beauties of all other things. ... He learns to use the beauties of earth as steps along which he mounts upwards; going from fair forms to fair practices, and from fair practices to fair notions, he arrives at the notion of Absolute Beauty, and at last knows what the essence of beauty is ... If man has ever eyes to see true beauty he becomes a friend of God and Immortal."

In the *Phaedrus* Plato declares Absolute Beauty to be "a super-sensuous, spiritual essence which is discerned by the mind when thrown into ecstasy."

Among the modern writers on aesthetics both Kant and Hegel would seem to echo a view identical with the Hindu: 'The beautiful," says the former, "is that which gives pleasure universally without a concept" (a concept being for him a form imposed by the faculty of judgment upon sense-data, making such sense-data knowable). "The outward shape by which the content is made perceptible," declares the latter, "is merely for the sake of the mind and the spirit."

2

Sakuntala: Its Inner Meaning

Rabindranath Tagore

Would'st thou the young year's blossoms
and the fruits of its decline,
And all by which the soul is charmed,
enraptured, feasted, fed,
Would'st thou the Earth and Heaven itself
in one sole name combine?
I name thee, O Sakuntala! and all at
once is said.

GOETHE.

Goethe, the master-poet of Europe, has summed up his criticism of *Sakuntala* in a single quatrain; he has not taken the poem to pieces. This quatrain seems to be a small thing like the flame of a candle, but it lights up the whole drama in an instant, and reveals its inner nature. In Goethe's words, *Sakuntala* blends together the young year's blossoms and the fruits of maturity; it combines heaven and earth in one.

We are apt to pass over this eulogy lightly as a mere poetical outburst. We are apt to consider that it only means in effect that Goethe regarded *Sakuntala* as fine poetry. But it is not really so. His stanza breathes not the exaggeration of rapture, but the deliberate judgment of a true critic. There is a special point in his words. Goethe says expressly that *Sakuntala* contains the history of a development — the development of flower into fruit, of earth into heaven, of matter into spirit.

In truth there are two unions in *Sakuntala;* and the *motif* of the play is the progress from the earlier union of the first Act, with its earthly unstable beauty and romance, to the higher union in the heavenly hermitage of eternal bliss described in the last Act. This drama was meant not for dealing with a particular passion, not for developing a particular character, but for translating the whole subject from one world to another — to elevate love from the sphere of physical beauty to the eternal heaven of moral beauty.

With the greatest ease Kalidas has effected this junction of earth with heaven. His earth so naturally passes into heaven that we do not mark the boundary-line between the two. In the First Act the poet has not concealed the gross earthiness of the fall of Ṣakuntala; he has clearly shown, in the conduct of the hero and heroine alike, how much desire contributed to that fall. He has fully painted all the blandishments, playfulness, and fluttering of the intoxicating sense of youth, the struggle between deep bashfulness and strong self-expression. This is a proof of the simplicity of Sakuntala; she was not prepared beforehand for the outburst of passion which the occasion of Dushyanta's visit called forth. Hence she had not learned how to restrain herself, how to hide her feelings. Sakuntala had not known Cupid before; hence her heart was bare of armour, and she could not distrust either the sentiment of love or the character of the lover. The daughter of the hermitage was off her guard, just as the deer there knew not fear.

Dushyanta's conquest of Sakuntala has been very naturally drawn. With equal ease has the poet shown the deeper purity of her character in spite of her fall — her unimpaired innate chastity. This is another proof of her simplicity.

The flower of the forest needs no servant to brush the dust of her petals. She stands bare; dust settles on her; but in spite of it she easily retains her own beautiful cleanliness. Dust did settle on Sakuntala, but she was not even conscious of it. Like the simple wild deer, like the mountain spring, she stood forth pure in spite of mud.

Kalidas has let his hermitage-bred youthful heroine follow the unsuspecting path of Nature; nowhere has he restrained her. And yet he has developed her into the model of a devoted wife, with her reserve, endurance of sorrow, and life of rigid spiritual discipline. At the beginning, we see her self-forgetful and obedient to Nature's impulses like the plants and flowers; at the end we see her deeper feminine soul — sober, patient under ill, intent on austerities, strictly regulated by the sacred laws of piety. With matchless art Kalidas has placed his heroine at the meeting-point of action and calmness, of Nature and law, of river and ocean, as it were. Her father was a hermit, but her mother was a nymph. Her birth was the outcome of interrupted austerities, but her nurture was in a hermitage, which is just the spot where nature and austerities, beauty and restraint are harmonized. There is none of the conventional bonds of society there, yet we have the harder regulations of religion. Her *gandharva* marriage, too, was of the same type; it had the wildness of nature joined to the social tie of wedlock. The drama *Sakuntala* stands alone and unrivalled in all literature, because it depicts how Restraint can be harmonized with Freedom. All its joys and sorrows, unions and partings, proceed from the conflict of these two forces.

Sakuntala's simplicity is natural, that of Miranda is unnatural. The different circumstances under which the two were brought up account for this difference. Sakuntala's simplicity was not girt round with ignorance, as was the case with Miranda. We wee in the First Act that Sakuntala's two companions did not let her remain unaware of the fact that she was in the first bloom of youth. She had learnt to be bashful. But all these things are external. Her simplicity, on the other hand, is more deeply seated, and so also is her purity. To the very end the poet shows that she had no experience of the outside world. Her simplicity is innate. True, she knew something of the world, because the hermitage did not stand altogether outside society; the rules of home life were observed here too. She was inexperienced though not ignorant of the outside world; but trustfulness was firmly enthroned in her heart. The simplicity which springs from such trustfulness had for a moment caused her fall, but it also redeemed her for ever. This trustfulness kept her constant to patience, forgiveness, and loving kindness, in spite of the cruellest breach of her confidence. Miranda's simplicity was never subjected to such a fiery ordeal; it never clashed with knowledge of the world.

Our rebellious passions raise storms. In this drama Kalidas has extinguished the volcanic fire of tumultuous passion by means of the tears of the penitent heart. But he has not dwelt too long on the disease — he has just given a glimpse of it and then dropped the veil. The desertion of Sakuntala by the amorous Dushyanta, which in real life would have happened as the natural consequence of his character, is here brought about by the curse of Durvasa. Otherwise, the desertion would have been so extremely cruel and pathetic as to destroy the peace and harmony of the whole play. But the poet has left a small rent in the veil through which we can get an idea of the royal sin. It is in the Fifth Act. Just before Sakuntala arrives at court and is repudiated by her husband, the poet momentarily draws aside the curtain from the King's love affairs. A woman's voice is heard singing behind the scene:

O honey-bee! having sucked the mango-blossoms in your search for new honey, you have forgotten the recent loving welcome by the lotus!

This tear-stained song of a stricken heart in the royal household gives us a rude shock, especially as our heart was hitherto filled with Dushyanta's love-passages with Sakuntala. Only in the preceding Act we saw Sakuntala setting out for her husband's home in a very holy, sweet, and tender mood, carrying with herself the blessings of the hoary sage Kanwa and the good wishes of the whole forest world. And now a stain falls on the picture we had so hopefully formed of the home of love to which she was going.

When the jester asked, "What means this song?" Dushyanta smiled and said "We desert our loves after a short spell of lovemaking and therefore I have deserved this strong rebuke from Queen Hansapadika." This indication of the fickleness of royal love is not purposeless at the beginning of the Fifth Act. With masterly skill the poet here shows that what Durvasa's curse had brought about had its seeds in human nature.

In passing from the Fourth Act to the Fifth we suddenly enter a new atmosphere; from the ideal world of the hermitage we go forth to the royal court with its hard hearts, crooked ways of love-making, difficulties of union. The beauteous dream of the hermitage is about to be broken. The two young hermits who are escorting Sakuntala, at once feel that they have entered an altogether different world, "a house encircled by fire!" By such touches at the beginning of the Fifth Act, the poet prepares us for the repudiation of Sakuntala at its end, lest the blow should be too severe for us.

Then comes the repudiation. Sakuntala feels as if she had been suddenly struck with a thunderbolt. Like a deer sticken by a trusted hand, this daughter of the forest looks on in blank surprise, terror and anguish. At one blow she is hurled away from the hermitage, both literal and metaphorical, in which she has so long lived. She loses her connection with the loving friends, the birds, beasts and plants, and the beauty, peace, and purity of her former life. She now stands alone, shelterless. In one moment the music of the first four Acts is stilled!

O the deep silence and loneliness that then surround her! She whose tender heart has made the whole world of the hermitage her own folk, to-day stands absolutely alone. She fills this vast vacuity with her mighty sorrow. With rare poetic insight Kalidas has declined to restore Sakuntala to Kanwa's hermitage. After the renunciation by Dushyanta it was impossible for her to live in harmony with that hermitage in the way she had done before ... She was no longer her former self; her relation with the universe had changed. Had she been placed again amidst her old surroundings, it would only have cruelly exhibited the utter inconsistency of the whole situation. A mighty silence was now needed, worthy of the mighty grief of the mourner. But the poet has not shown us the picture of Sakuntala in the new hermitage — parted from the friends of her girlhood, and nursing the grief of separation from her lover. The silence of the poet only deepens our sense of the silence and vacancy which here reigned round Sakuntala. Had the repudiated wife been taken back to Kanwa's home, that hermitage would have spoken. To our imagination its trees and creepers would have wept, the two girl friends would have mourned for Sakuntala, even if the poet had not said a word about it. But in the unfamiliar hermitage of Marichi, all is still and silent to us; only we have before our mind's eye a picture of the world-abandoned Sakuntala's infinite sorrow, disciplined by penance, sedate, and resigned — seated like a recluse rapt in meditation.

Dushyanta is now consumed by remorse. This remorse is *tapasya.* So long as Sakuntala was not won by means of this repentance, there was no glory in winning her. ... One sudden gust of youthful impulse had in a moment given her up to Dushyanta, but that was not the true, the full winning of her. The best means of winning is by devotion, by *tapasya.* What is easily gained is as easily lost. Therefore, the poet has made the two lovers undergo a long and austere *tapasya* that they may gain each other truly eternally. If Dushyanta had accepted Sakuntala when she was first brought to his court, she would have only occupied a corner of the royal household, and passed the rest of her life in neglect, gloom, uselessness.

It was a blessing in disguise for Sakuntala that Dushyanta abjured her with cruel sternness. When afterwards this cruelty reacted on himself, it prevented him from remaining indifferent to Sakuntala. His unceasing and intense grief fused his heart and welded Sakuntala with it. Never before had the King met with such an experience. Never before had he had the occasion and means of truly loving. Kings are unlucky in this respect; their desires are so easily satisfied that they never get what is to be gained by devotion alone. Fate now plunged Dushyanta into deep grief and thus made him worthy of true love made him renounce the role of a rake.

Thus has Kalidas burnt away vice in the eternal fire of the sinner's heart; he has not tried to conceal it from the outside. When the curtain drops in the last Act, we feel that all the evil has been destroyed as on a funeral pyre, and the peace born of a perfect and satisfactory fruition reigns in our hearts. Kalidas has internally cut right away the roots of the poison tree, which a sudden force from the outside had planted. He has made the physical union of Dushyanta and Sakuntala tread the path of sorrow, and thereby chastened and sublimated it into a moral union. Hence did Goethe rightly say that *Sakuntala* combines the blossoms of Spring with the fruits of Autumn, it combines Heaven and Earth. Truly in *Sakuntala* there is one Paradise Lost and another Paradise Regained.

The poet has shown how the union of Dushyanta and Sakuntala in the First Act as mere lovers is futile, while their union in the last Act as the parents of Bharata is a true union. The First Act is full of brilliancy and movement. We have there a hermit's daughter in the exuberance of youth, her two companions running over with playfulness, the newly flowering forest creeper, the bee intoxicated with perfume, the fascinated King peeping from behind the trees. From this Eden of bliss Sakuntala, the mere sweetheart of Dushyanta, is exiled in disgrace. But far different was the aspect of the other hermitage where Sakuntala, the mother of Bharata and the incarnation of goodness took refuge. There no hermit girls water the trees, nor bedew the creepers with their loving sister-like looks, nor feed the young fawn with handfuls of paddy. There a single boy fills the loving bosom of the entire forest-world; he absorbs all the liveliness of the trees, creepers, flowers, and foliage. The matrons of the hermitage in their loving anxiety, are fully taken up with the unruly boy. When Sakuntala appears, we see her clad in a dusty robe, face pale with austerities, doing the penance of a lorn wife, pure souled. Her long penances have purged her of the evil of her first union with Dushyanta: she is now invested with the dignity of a matron, she is the image of motherhood, tender and good. Who can repudiate her now?

The poet has shown here, as in *Kumara Sambhava* that the Beauty that goes hand in hand with Moral Law is eternal, that the calm, controlled, and beneficent form of Love is its best form, that beauty is truly charming under restraint and decays quickly when it gets wild and unfettered. This ancient poet of India refuses to recognize Love as its own highest glory; he proclaims that Goodness is the final goal of Love. He teaches us that the Love of man and woman is not beautiful, not lasting, not fruitful, so long as it is selfcentred, so long as it does not beget Goodness, so long as it does not diffuse itself into society over son and daughter, guests and neighbours.

The two peculiar principles of India are the beneficent *tie of home life* on the one hand, and the *liberty of the soul* abstracted from the world on the other. In the world India is variously connected with many races and many creeds; she cannot reject any of them. But on the altar of devotion (*tapaysa)* India sits alone. Kalidas has shown, both in *Sakuntala* and *Kumara Sambhava*, that there is a harmony between these two principles, an easy transition from the one to the other. In his hermitage a human boy plays with lion cubs, and the hermit spirit is reconciled with the spirit of the householder.

On the foundation of the hermitage of recluses Kalidas has built the home of the householder. He has rescued the relation of the sexes from the sway of lust and enthroned it on the holy and pure seat of asceticism. In the sacred books of the Hindus the ordered relation of the sexes has been defined by strict injunctions and Laws. Kalidas has demonstrated *that* relation by means of the elements of Beauty. The Beauty that he adores is lit up by grace, modesty, and goodness; in its intensity it is true to one for ever; in its range it embraces the whole universe. It is fulfilled by renunciation, gratified by sorrow, and rendered eternal by religion. In the midst of this beauty, the impetuous unruly love of man and woman has restrained itself and attained to a profound peace, like a wild torrent merged in the ocean of goodness. Therefore is such love higher and more wonderful than wild and untrained Passion[1].

---

1 This article was originally written by the author in Bengali and was translated into English by Professor Jadunath Sarkar.

3

The Soul of Poetic Delight and Beauty

Sri Aurobindo

The light of truth, the breath of life, great and potent things though they are, are insufficient to give poetry the touch of immortality and perfection, even a little of which is enough to carry it safe through the ages, unless the soul and form of delight and beauty take possession of the seeing of truth and give immortality to the breath and body of the life. Delight is the soul of existence, beauty the intense impression, the concentrated form of delight; and these two fundamental things tend to be one for the mind of the artist and the poet, though they are often enough separated in our cruder vital and mental experience. These twin powers meet, make a consonance of the perfect harmony of his work and are the first deities he serves, all the others only group themselves about them, strive to be admitted to the soul of delight and the privilege of beauty and have to make themselves acceptable to them before they can mix with them in a compelling and attracting oneness. For the poet the moon of beauty and delight is a greater godhead even than the sun of truth or the breath of life, as in the symbolic image of the Vedic moon-god Soma, whose plant of intoxication has to be gathered on lonely mountain heights in the moonlight and whose purified juice and essence is the sacred wine and nectar of sweetness, *rasa, madhu, amṛta* without which the gods themselves could not be immortal. A lightest trifle, if it manages to get itself saturated with this sweetness of poetic delight and beauty, will be preserved for its sake, while the highest strenuous labour of the thinking mind and the most forceful assertion of the life-power, if deprived of or deficient in this subtlest immortalizing essence, may carry on for a time, but soon drops, grows old, sinks into the gulf of oblivion or has at most a lifeless survival and belongs to the dead history of literature, not to its eternal present. But beauty and delight, whatever form it takes, — for we may speak here of the two as one, — has an unaging youth, an eternal moment, an immortal presence.

The imperative instinct for beauty and the aesthetic demand which set that among the first needs and was not satisfied with anything else if this were neglected or put second in importance, are now things, that are almost lost, nowhere general to the human mind, but once they were the sign of the poetic and artistic peoples and the great ages of art and poetry and supreme creation. The ancient communities who created those fine many-sided cultures which still remain the fountain-head of all our evolving civilization, had the instinct for beauty, the aesthetic turn of the temperament and formation of the mind almost, it would seem, from the beginning, planted in their spirit and their blood, colouring their outlook so that even before they got the developed intellectual consciousness of it, they created instinctively in the spirit and form of beauty and that is quite half the secret of the compelling and attractive power of the antique cultures. The earliest surviving poetry of ancient India was philosophical and religious, the Veda, the Upanishads, and our modern notions tend to divorce these things from the instinct of delight and beauty to separate the religious and the philosophic from the aesthetic sense; but the miracle of these antique writings is their perfect union of beauty and power and truth, the word of truth coming out spontaneously as a word of beauty, the revealed utterance of that universal spirit who is described in the Upanishads as the eater of the honey of sweetness, *madhvadam puruṣam;* and this high achievement was not surprising in these ancient deep-thinking men who discovered the profound truth that all existence derives from and lives by the bliss of the eternal spirit, in the power of a universal delight, Ananda. The idea of beauty, the spontaneous satisfaction in it, the worship of it as in itself something divine, became more intellectually conscious afterwards, was a dominant strain of the later Indian mind and got to its richest outward colour and sensuous passion in the work of the classical writers, while the expression of the spiritual through the aesthetic sense is the constant sense of Indian art, as it is also the inspiring motive of a great part of the later religion and poetry. Japan and China, more especially perhaps southern China, for the north has been weighted by a tendency to a more external and formal idea of measure and harmony, had in a different way this fusion of the spiritual and aesthetic mind and it is a distinguishing stamp of their art and culture. The Persian had a sort of sensuous magic of the transforming aesthesis born of psychic delight and vision. Ancient Greece did all its work of founding European civilization by a union of a subtle and active intelligence with a fine aesthetic spirit and worship of beauty. The Celtic nations again seem always to have had by nature a psychic delicacy and subtlety united with an instinctive turn for imaginative beauty to which we surely owe much of the finer strain in English literature. But there these spontaneous miracles of fusion end and in the mind of later peoples who come in and take possession with a less innate, a more derivative culture, the sense of beauty works with a certain effort and is clogged by many heavier elements which are in conflict with and prevent the sureness of the aesthetic perception. There is in their cruder temperament and intelligence a barbaric strain which worships rudely the power and energy of life and is not at home with the delight of beauty, an ethical and puritanic strain which looks askance at art and beauty and pleasure, a heavy scholastic or a dry scientific intellectual strain which follows after truth with a conscientious and industrious diligence, but without vision and fine aesthesis. And the modern mind, inheritor of all this past is a divided and complex mind which strives at its best to get back at the old thing on a larger scale and realize some oneness of its many strands of experience, but has not yet found the right meeting place; and it is besides still labouring under the disadvantage of its aberration into a mechanical, economical, materialistic, utilitarian civilization from which it cannot get free, though it is struggling to shake off that dullest side of it for which a naked and unashamed riot of ugliness could be indulged in without any prickings of the spiritual conscience but rather with a smug self-righteousness in the hideous, the vulgar and the ignoble. The day when we get back to the ancient worship of delight and beauty, will be our day of salvation; for without these things there can be neither an assured nobility and sweetness in poetry and art nor a harmonious perfection of the spirit.

An insufficiently profound and intimate perception of the real deep soul of poetic delight and beauty is the first obstacle to a recovery of the old strong soundness of the aesthetic sense and spontaneity of the aesthetic impulse. This comes from the peculiar character of the modern intelligence and its want of harmony between our internal selves and our external experience; there is little spontaneous joy of their meeting, an active labour to assimilate, but no happy, deep or satisfied possession either of self or life, a continual seeking but no repose in the thing found, a feverish restlessness without home and abiding-place. The spirit of man can make its home in either one of two things, the depths of our self arrived at through vision of self-knowledge, through power of self-mastery or through ecstasy, or a profound, a glad and satisfied acceptance of the truth, the delight and beauty of the world and life, of existence and experience. And either of these things can help too to bring in the other, — possess the inner self and life can become happy and illumined by a full sense of its hidden significance, or get hold of the complete delight and beauty of life and the world and you have then only a thin layer of shining mist to break through to get also at the self and spirit behind it, the eater of the honey of sweetness who is seated in the soul of man and extends himself through the universe. The ancient peoples had in a very large measure this foundation of satisfaction and harmony, took the greatest interest in the reality of the inner self, as once in India and China, the Atman, the Tao, and life and the world as its field of expression and self-experience or, like the Greeks, felt at once the naturalness and profundity of human existence and gave to it an immediate and subtle aesthetic response. The modern mind, on the contrary, looks little into our deepest self, takes little interest in sounding that depth and has hardly any confidence in its reality, and concentrates not on the truth and delight and beauty of life, but upon the stress of its results and circumstances, which in themselves have only an incidental and no satisfying and harmonious meaning, and on the agitating or attractive turmoil of the mind excited by their contact or their siege.[1] This difference results in a fundamental difference of aesthesis. The pure aesthetic spirit ought to be left free, trusted in, made master of its own action and creation and it will then create with greatness and beauty, in a calm and satisfied ecstasy, and yet safely harmonize its action with the other spiritual powers of our existence, the need of the life-soul, the insistent seeking of the thought-mind, the demand of the active will and the senses. But we now make the aesthetic sense and intelligence a servant of these other powers; it is condemned to serve first and foremost our external interest in life or our interest in thought or in troubled personality or the demand of the senses or passions and bidden to make them beautiful or vivid to us by an active aesthetic cerebration and artistic manufacture of the word or a supply of carefully apt or beautiful forms and measures. The secondary things are put in the

1 This is the result perhaps of an ill-assimilated Christian influence intervening on the external vitalism of the Teutonic temperament and on Latin intellectualism, and bringing in new needs and experiences which disturbed the mind and emotions without possessing the soul with peace or arriving at a harmony of spiritual emotion and spiritual self-knowledge.

first rank, the primary, the one thing needful has to get in as best it can to give some firm base to the creation. This aesthesis aided by the vast curiosity of the modern intelligence has done some great and much interesting work, but it arrives with difficulty at the readily fused harmonies and assured stamp of the perfect way of spiritual creation.

There is a profound intrinsic delight and beauty in all things and behind all experience whatever face it wears to the surface mind, which makes it to a spirit housed within us other than its first appearance, makes it, that is to say, no longer a thing exciting mental interest, pain, pleasure, but rather a revelation of the truth and power and delight of being and our feeling of it a form of the universal Ananda of the old philosophical thinkers, the calm yet moved ecstasy with which the spirit of existence regards itself and its creation. This deeper spiritual feeling, this Ananda is the fountain of poetic delight and beauty. It springs from a supreme essence of experience, a supreme aesthesis which is in its own nature spiritual, impersonal, independent of the personal reactions and passions of the mind, and that is why the poet is able to transmute pain and sorrow and the most tragic and terrible and ugly things into forms of poetic beauty, because of this impersonal joy of the spirit in all experience, whatever its nature. And as, therefore, the subject of the poet is all that he can feel of the infinite life of the spirit that creates in existence and all that he can seize of the infinite truth of God and Nature and our own and the world's being, so too what he brings out from his subjects is all that he can pour into speech of his vision of eternal and universal beauty, all that he can express of the soul's universal delight in existence. That is what he has to reveal, and to make others share in, to render more expressive and firmly present to them what experience they have of it and help the race towards its greater fullness in the soul of man and embodiment in our mind and life. This Ananda is not the pleasure of a mood or a sentiment or the fine aesthetic indulgence of the sense in the attraction of a form, superficial results and incidents which are often mistaken for that much deeper and greater thing by the minor poetic faculty, the lesser artistic mind, but the enduring delight which, as the ancient idea justly perceived, is the essence of spirit and being and the beauty which all things assume when the spirit lives in the pure joy of creation and experience.

The universality of this delight and beauty does not mean that we can take whatever we will straight from life and experience, just as it is, and by making it precise and vivid through word and image or dressing it in imaginative colour achieve poetic effect and beauty. That is the theory by which a great deal of our modern endeavour at poetry seems to be guided, as it is the ruling method of inferior poets and the mark too of the lesser or unsuccessful or only partially successful work of greater writers. The error made is to confuse the sources of poetic delight and beauty with the more superficial interest, pain and pleasure which the normal mind takes in the first untransmuted appeal of thought and life and feeling. That in its first crude form or a little deepened by sensitiveness of emotion and a reflective intelligence is the response to existence of the natural mind, the only instrument of the majority, and what it is apt to expect from the poet is that this is what he too shall give to the world and only think it more profoundly, feel it more sensitively, live it with a greater excitement and find for it beauty of word and attraction of rhythm. The poet has in him a double personality, a double instrument of his response to life and existence. There is in him the normal man absorbed in mere living who thinks and feels and acts like others, and there is the seer of things, the supernormal man, the super-soul or delight-soul in touch with the impersonal and eternal fountains of joy and beauty who creates from that source and transmutes by its alchemy all experience into a form of the spirit's Ananda. It is easy for him, if the demand of his genius is not constant or if he is not held back by a natural fineness of the poetic conscience, to subject this deeper and greater power to the lower and general demand and put it at the service of his superficial mental experience. He has then to rely on the charm and beauty of word and form to save the externality of his substance. But the genius in him when he is faithful to it, knows that this is not his high way of perfection nor the thing his spirit gave him to do; it is a spiritual transmutation of the substance got by sinking the mental and vital interests in a deeper soul experience which brings the inevitable word and the supreme form and the unanalysable rhythm. The poet is then something more than a maker of beautiful word and phrase, a favoured child of the fancy and imagination, a careful fashioner of idea and utterance or an effective poetic thinker, moralist, dramatist or story-teller; he becomes a spokesman of the eternal spirit of beauty and delight and shares that highest creative and self-expressive rapture which is close to the original ecstasy that made existence, the divine Ananda.

This rapture, the Platonic divine possession and enthusiasm, is born not of mental, but of soul experience, and the more the surface mind gets into the way, the more this divine passion is weakened and diluted by a less potent spirit. The surface mind is powerfully attracted by the stir of the outward passion and excitement the stress of immediate thought, life and action, hastens to embody it in speech or in deed and has no leisure to transmute life into those greater abiding values of which the soul in its depths is alone capable. But the higher faculties are given us as keys to a deeper experience; the seer, the poet, the artist, the children of the spirit's light and intuition are only true to themselves when they live in the depths of the soul, refuse to be hurried away by the surface call of mind and life and wait rather for their own greater voices. The poetry which insists on an external effectiveness, on immediate thought and life and experience, may seize very powerfully the ear of the moment, but is singularly frail in its affectation of power and even if it has strength of body, is hollow and null inside; it fails because it is concerned with immediately vital things perhaps, but not with that which is immortal. That is just why patriotic poetry, war poetry or poetry of the occasion and the moment are so difficult to write greatly and, although it would seem that these things are among the most dynamic and should move most easily to powerful utterance, are oftenest poor in poetic substance and inferior in value. For life they may be dynamic, but they are not so readily dynamic for art and poetry, and precisely because the vital interest, the life attraction is so strong that it is difficult to draw back from the external to the spiritual delight and the spiritual significance. A great poet may do it sometimes, because the constant instinct of his genius is to look beyond the surface and the moment to that which is universal and eternal behind the personal experience and the occasion is only for him an excuse for its utterance. The drama of action and mere passion is for the same reason short-lived in its gusto of vitality, fades in a century or less into a lifeless mask, while the drama of the soul abides, because it gets near to the subtler eternal element, the soul's essential aesthesis, the spirit's delight in self-creation and experience. Philosophical and religious poetry too fails so often by a neglect of the same fine distinction, because the interest of the thought pursued by the intellectual activity, the interest of the mind in its surface religious ideas and feelings get the upper hand and do not consent to sink themselves in the spiritual emotion of the seeing of truth and the abiding spiritual experience. The mental and vital interest, pleasure, pain of thought, life, action is not the source of poetic delight and beauty and can be turned into that deeper thing only when they have sunk into the soul and been transmuted in the soul's radiant memory into spiritual experience, — that perhaps was what the Greeks meant when they made Mnemosyne the eternal mother of the muses; the passions can only change into poetic matter when they have been spiritualized in the same bright sources and have undergone the purification, the *katharsis,* spoken of by the Greek critic; the life values are only poetic when they have come out heightened and changed into soul values. The poetic delight and beauty are born of a deeper rapture and not of the surface mind's excited interest and enjoyment of life and existence.

The ancient Indian critics defined the essence of poetry as *rasa* and by that word they meant a concentrated taste, a spiritual essence of emotion, an essential aesthesis, the soul's pleasure in the pure and perfect sources of feeling. The memory of the soul that takes in, broods over and transmutes the mind's thought, feeling and experience, is a large part of the process which comes by this aesthesis, but it is not quite the whole thing; it is rather only a common way by which we get at something that stands behind,the spiritual being in us which has the secret of the universal delight and the eternal beauty of existence. That which we call genius works or comes out from something deep within which calls down the word, the vision, the light and power from a level above the normal mind and it is the sense of the inrush from above which makes the rapture and the enthusiasm of illumination and inspiration. That source, when we know better the secrets of our being, turns out to be the spiritual self with its diviner consciousness and knowledge, happier fountains of power, inalienable delight of existence. The cultures that were able directly or indirectly to feel the joy of this self and spirit,got into the very strain of their aesthesis the touch of its delight, its Ananda, and this touch was the secret of the generalized instinct for beauty which has been denied to a later mind limited by intellectual activity, practical utility and the externals of life: we have to go for it to exceptional individuals gifted with a finer strain, but the wide-spread aesthetic instinct has been lost and has yet to be recovered for the common mind and recognized once more as a part of human perfection as indispensable as intellectual knowledge and at least as necessary to happiness as vital well-being. But this Ananda, this delight, this aesthesis which is the soul of poetic beauty works like other things, like poetic truth or the poetic breath of life on different levels, in different provinces of its actions with the same law that we have observed in the rest, of the emergence of a richer and profounder face of itself the more it gets inward and upward from the less to the more occult powers of its revelation. This finer soul of delight throws itself out on the physical mind and being, takes up its experiences and turns them by its own innate and peculiar power into things of beauty, fuses into itself the experiences of the life soul and transmutes to beauty their power and passion in the surge of its poetic ecstasy, takes up all life and form into the reflective thought-mind and changes them in the beauty and rapture of thought discovering and embodying new values of soul and Nature and existence. And in all its working there is felt its own essence of an intuitive delight which acts in these moulds and gets into them whatever it can of its own intimate and eternal delight values. But when that intuitive mind self-finding, self-seeing, self creating in a higher power of light and vision than is possible on the intellectual or other levels gets out into full play, and now there is some sign of this emergence, then we come nearer to the most potent sources of universal and eternal delight and beauty, nearer to its full and wide seeing, and its all-embracing rapture. This inner mind is the first native power of the self and spirit dropping its lower veils and the very life and aesthesis of the spirit in its creation is a life of self-experiencing spiritual delight and a luminous Ananda.

The beauty and delight of such a greater intuitive inspiration, a poetry of this spiritual Ananda making all existence luminous and wonderful and beautiful to us may be one of the gifts of the future. It is that of which we stand in need and of which there is some promise in the highest strains that we have now begun to hear. This change will mean that poetry may resume on a larger scale, with a wider and more shining vision the greater effect it once had on the life of the race in the noble antique cultures, At one time poetry was a revelation to the race of the life of the gods and man and the meaning of the world and the beauty and power of existence and through its vision and joy and the height and clarity of its purpose it became creative of the life of the people. Ananda, the joy of the spirit in itself carrying in it a revelation of the powers of its conscious being, was to the ancient Indian idea the creative principle, and ancient poetry did thus creatively reveal to the people its soul and its possibilities by forms of beauty and suggestions of power in a way we have to a great extent lost by our later pettier use of this always great art and medium. One might almost say that ancient India was created by the Veda and Upanishads and that the visions of inspired seers made a people. That sublime poetry with its revelation of godhead and the joy and power of life and truth and immortality or its revelation of the secrets of the self and the powers of its manifestation in man and the universe and of man's return to self-knowledge got into the very blood and mind and life of the race and made itself the fountain-head of all that incessant urge to spirituality which has been its distinguishing gift and cultural motive. The Mahabharata and the Ramayana revealing to it in forms of noble beauty and grandiose or beautiful or telling types of character the joy of its forms of life, the significance of its spiritual, ethical and aesthetic ideals, the powers and dangers of the human soul, its godheads and its titanisms have played a great and well recognized formative part second only to religion and the stress of religio-social training in the life of the Indian peoples. And even later the religious poetry of the Vaishnavas, Shaivas, Shaktas has entered powerfully into the life of the nation and helped to shape its temperament and soul-type. The effect of the Homeric poems in Greece, the intimate connection of poetry and art with the public life of Athens sprang from a similar but less steep height of poetic and artistic motive. The epic poems revealed the Hellenic people to itself in the lucid and clear nobility and beauty of an uplifting of life and an aesthetic sense of the humanity and divinity of man; the later art and poetry interpreted to Athens her religious ideas, her thought, her aesthetic instincts, the soul of grandeur and beauty of her culture.

And in all these instances, as in others like the art and poetry of Japan and of China, a more or less profoundly intuitive creation from the depths and expression through poetic delight of the soul of a people has been the secret of this effect and this power of creation or influence. But in other times and places poetry has been more a servant of aesthetic pleasure than a creative master of life and great spiritual agent; when it is at all great, it cannot fail to be that to a certain extent, but it has not so acted as a whole, centrally, in the same large and effective way or with the same high conscience of its function. It has leaned too much on the surface or external interests of life for the pleasure of the intellect and imagination and failed too much to create life from within by a deeper delight in the power of vision of the soul and spirit. The high energy of English poetry has done great and interesting things; it has portrayed life with charm and poetic interest in Chaucer, made thought and character and action and passion wonderful to the life soul in us in Shakespeare, seen and spoken with nobility and grandeur of vision and voice in Milton, intellectualised vigorous or pointed commonplace in Pope and Dryden, played with elegance and beauty on the lesser strings with the Victorians or cast out here and there a profounder strain of thought or more passionate and aspiring voice, and if the most spiritual strains have been few, yet it has dreamed in light in Shelley or drawn close in Wordsworth to the soul in Nature. And it may seem hard to say in the face of all this splendour and vigour and glow and beauty and of the undeniable cultural influence, that something was too often lacking which would have made the power of this poetry more central and intimate and a greater direct force on the life of the people, and yet this is, I think, true in spite of exceptions, not only here, but of almost all the later European literature. To get back to a profounder centre, to create from within in a more universal power of the spirit and its vision and delight of existence will supply the missing element and make poetry once again young and mighty and creative and its word deeply effective on life by the power of a greater Ananda.

The mind of man, a little weary now of the superficial pleasure of the life and intellect, demands, obscurely still, not yet perceiving what will satisfy it, a poetry of the joy of self, of the deeper beauty and delight of existence. A merely cultured poetry fair in form and word and playing on the surface strings of mind and emotion will not serve its purpose. The human mind is opening to an unprecedented largeness of vision of the greatness of the worlds, the wonder of life, the self of man, the mystery of the spirit in him and the universe. The future poetry must seek in that vision its inspiration, and the greater its universality of joy in existence, the more it seeks through intuitive sight and aesthesis the deepest fountains of poetic delight and beauty, the more it will become powerfully creative of a greater life for the race. The modern poet is perfectly right in a way in breaking down in whatever direction the bounds erected by the singers of the past around their magic palace and its grounds; he must claim all things in heaven or earth or beyond for his portion: but that care for a fine poetic beauty and delight which they safeguarded by excluding all or most that did not readily obey its law or turn to fair material of poetic shaping, he must preserve as jealously and satisfy by steeping all that he finds in his wider field in that profoundest vision which delivers out of each thing its spiritual Ananda, the secret of truth and beauty in it for which it was created; it is in the sense of that spiritual joy of vision and not in any lower sensuous, intellectual or imaginative seeing, that Keats' phrase becomes true for the poet, beauty that is truth, truth that is beauty and this all that we need to know as the law of our aesthetic knowledge. He is right too in wishing to make poetry more intimately one with life, but again in this sense only, in going back to those creative fountains of the spirits Ananda from which life is seen and reshaped by the vision that springs from a moved identity, — the inmost source of the authentic poet vision. The beauty and delight of all physical things illumined by the wonder of the secret spiritual self that is the inhabitant and self-sculptor of form, the beauty and delight of the thousand-coloured, many-crested million-waved miracle of life made a hundred times more profoundly meaningful by the greatness and the sweetness and attracting poignancy of the self-creating inmost soul which makes of life its epic and its drama and its lyric, the beauty and delight of the spirit in thought, the seer, the thinker, the interpreter of his own creation and being who broods over all he is and does in man and the world and constantly re-sees and shapes it new by the stress and power of his thinking, this will be the substance of the greater poetry that has yet to be written. And that can be discovered only if and so far as the soul of man looks or feels beyond even these things and sees and voices the eternal and knows its godheads and gets to some close inward touch of the infinite ecstasy which is the source of the universal delight and beauty. For the nearer we get to the absolute Ananda, the greater becomes our joy in man and the universe and the receptive and creative spiritual emotion which needs for its voice the moved tones of poetic speech.

APPENDIX

1. Sri Aurobindonean Aesthetics in Action

Sri Aurobindo is a poet, philosopher and yogi and his aesthetics is naturally comprehensive, synthetic and inclusive. It is rooted in the Vedas and Upanishads, but in the course of its development it has assimilated and accommodated many of the modern trends and his prophetic vision has outlined for us its future:

> The old habits of poetic speech still cling around and encrust or dilute the subtler subtlety, the more luminous light, the intenser intensities, the deeper depths sought for by the intuitive utterance .... These things however are already there and are shaping a new manner of speech, a basis for the more inner and illumined poetic language of the future .... (*Future Poetry 395*) .... The poetry of the future has to solve .... a problem new to the art of poetic speech, an utterance of the deepest soul of man and of the universal spirit in things not only with another and a more complete vision but in the very inmost language of the self experience of the soul and the sight of the spiritual mind .... (FP 398)

Talking of Vak the Rgvedic ṛṣi Uchatyaputra says,

> चत्वारि वाक् परिमिता पंदानि
> तानि विदु: ब्राहमणा ये मनिषिण:
> गुहा त्रीणि निहिता नेङ्गयन्ति
> तुरीयं वाचो मनुष्या वदन्ति

> Speech is measured out in four steps (planes). The Brahmanas who have the understanding (the wise who have knowledge of the mantras) know them. Concealed in the secrecy the first three do not move; only the speech in the fourth step (the last from above) men speak.

Another ṛṣi called Bṛhaspati observes;

> उतत्व: पश्यन् नददर्श वाचं
> उतत्व: श्रृण्वन् न श्रृणोत्येनां
> उतोत्वस्मै तन्वं विसस्त्रे
> जायेव पत्य उशती सुवासा:

> Vak, seeing one sees not; hearing one hears not; to another she disrobes herself as a loving well-drest wife lays bare the body to her husband.

Both of them were ṛṣis, Kavis, Seers or, even more accurately, *mantradrstarah*. The philosopher poet Bhartṛhari has given us a language philosophy which provides — so to say — a bridge between the pre-verbal states of an experience and the verbal expression of them in his concept of *sphoṭa* which may be rendered as utterance; and which is manifested through sounds temporally — though it is in itself beyond time. What is articulated by the speaker and heard by the listener is *dhvani* or sounds; but this dhvani (which is again of two kinds *Prākṛta* — the phonological structure — the sound pattern corresponding roughly to *Langue* and *Vaikhari* the individual instances of the utterance corresponding to *parole*) is only the manifesting agent of *sphoṭa*. The Western language philosophy stops with sounds/ meaningful sounds or words; but Bhartṛhari's *sphoṭa* — as he defines it — is a psychical (inner) entity which reveals itself through the articulated sounds. Cognition does not stop with an intellectual/ mental understanding of what the words say but consists in a direct intuitive perception of the whole — a knowledge by identity.

Sphoṭa and inner intuitive perception are the two most significant aspects of our aesthetics. Sri Aurobindo makes it clear that the word-rhythm is only part of what we hear; it is a support for the rhythm we listen to, behind in the Ear of the ear: श्रोत्रस्य श्रोत्रम् The ṛṣis of the Rgveda took it as their poetic function to be the hearers of Truth no less than seers of it: *Kavayah satyaśrutah*. Poetry thus involves *seeing* as well as hearing — inner seeing as well as inner hearing. Sri Aurobindo describes poetry therefore as Sight's sound-waves breaking from the soul's great deeps. The language of this criticism would appear certainly odd to those well read, well informed in and accustomed to the highly technical scientific language of the structuralists and post-structuralists who would examine a line of poetry / poem entirely on *semantic* and *epistemic* terms neglecting wholly the other dimensions of poetry such as rhythm / imagery and other sensuous components to which intuition alone can be responsive. Strictly speaking there is nothing much mysterious or esoteric or odd about the language of Sri Aurobindo or for that matter that of the Upanishadic seers. It has been the experience of all creative artists. Kathleen Raine's reference to the unwritten poem — the haunting pre-verbal rhythm to which the words should correspond or Eliot's remarks on the poetic process both in his *Music of Poetry* and in his *Three Voices of Poetry* must make it clear that the unexpressed pre-verbal state is a very real state. To this list of creative artists the name of A.E. Housman could also be added.

It is primarily the rhythm that takes us to the source of inspiration of the poem and determines the meaning of the words (both denotative and connotative). If tone and intonation alone can determine of the meaning of our day-to-day utterances, it is surely the 'rhythm' that must decide the meaning of the poem.[1] Hence it is not merely a question of choosing the most appropriate words (the best words) but putting them in the best order. Words in poetry are meant to convey a sense of realities not as they are *ordinarily* perceived but to bring out the *inner nature of a situation* as in the famous lines of *Macbeth*:

> Will all great Neptune's oceans wash this blood
> Clean from my hand? No, this my hand will rather
> The multitudinous seas incarnadine
> Making the green one red.

Here the melodious effect of both *multitudinous* and *incarnadine* is to create an impression of vividness on the eye; and reveal the soaring imagination of the speaker. The power of all Neptune's ocean is challenged, so to say, by the enormity of his crime. The polysyllabic '*multitudinous*' is balanced against the polysyllabic resonant word *incarnadine*. The inversion produces the effect of a grand *finale*. As with these words so with *one* connoting a whole total, single, undifferentiated thorough-going redness. In all successful poetry we have the best words in the best order — the order, the rhythm helping us to realize the richness of the diction and the diction reinforcing the word-music.

This does not mean that Sri Aurobindo is just the romantic-symbolic sort of poet-critic exalting 'pure poetry' making it just a cluster of musical sounds, sensational in their impact. Witness his remarks on Housman's appreciation of Shakespeare's song in *Measure for Measure*, 'Take, O take these lips away'. Housman found the notions expressed there (the semantic significance of the lyric) non-sensical; but found it wonderful poetry — since it appeals to our solar plexus and the essential work of the words and their music was not to *say* any thing intelligible but to transfuse emotion. But Sri Aurobindo observes that Housman ought to have said that the lyric transfuses emotionally a vision and a mood which are beyond *mind*.

Rhythm helps us not only to determine the meaning, realize the richness by drawing our attention to the overtones / undertones / association / suggestiveness of the diction but discriminate and fix the source of inspiration. Thus Chaucer's job, according to Sri Aurobindo, is to present *life* interestingly, *not* to interpret it. The ease, grace, lucidity and compactness of his expression are just adequate to help him to present his response to outward life, his kindly satisfaction, his lively sense of humour or light and easy pathos. His rhythm is close to prose because it is close to life, though he is still writing poetry since life is contemplated in a detached way from a subtle-physical level. His is an observing mind that makes itself a shining poetic mirror.

For passionate language and vitality one goes to Shakespeare. His rhythms evoke and communicate effectively the vital life and thrill of it. Profound as this poetry is, it cannot be called mystical, spiritual, even mental or intellectual.

A passage like the following one from *The Tempest*:

... we are such stuff
As dreams are made of,
And our little life is rounded with a sleep.

may be mistaken for spiritual or philosophic poetry because it talks about the transience of life. But Sri Aurobindo says that Shakespeare is not an intellectual nor a philosophical thinker or a mystic. For a truly mystical, spiritual poetry one may cite the following lines from Sri Aurobindo's "Nirvana":

Only the illimitable Permanent
Is here. A peace stupendous, featureless, still
Replaces all, ...
A silent unnamed emptiness content
Either to fade in the Unknowable
Or thrill with the luminous seas of the Infinite.

A poem does not become religious or mystical because terms like God or silence are used. It is the rhythm that makes the experience authentic and convincing. We hear the accent of higher experience in Shelley's

We look before and after
And pine for what is not...

Its exquisite melody and unsurpassable poignancy of pathos make it an expresssion welling out straight from psychic source. The rhythm reveals how the mind and the heart are working at their highest pitch. As with the above passage, so with the lyric:

I can give not what men call love.

The best instance of intuitive spiritual poetry is to be had in Wordsworth's

And I have felt
A presence that disturbs me with the joy
Of elevated thoughts; a sense sublime
Of something far more deeply interfused,
Whose dwelling is the light of the setting suns,
And the round ocean and the living air,
And the blue sky, and in the mind of man:
A motion and a Spirit, impels
All thinking things, all objects of all thought,
And rolls through all things.

We may contrast the tone and rhythm of these lines with passages from Dryden or Donne which are intellectual and mental though occasionally stirred by imagination. Hopkins, according to Sri Aurobindo, has vision, power and originality but occasionally his technique errs by excess.

Sri Aurobindo describes the characteristic movement of English poetry from the subtle physical poetry of Chaucer through the vitally energetic poetry of Shakespeare, to the poetic intelligance and mental poetry of the 18th century. He discerns also another movement which is mystical (which he calls the Celtic element as opposed to the Anglo-Saxon matter-of-factness) which is mystical and occult. The Romantic poets are called 'the poets of the dawn' inasmuch as their theme seems to be the 'unknown modes of being'. The late 19th century poetry is characterized by a many-sided intellectualism. One naturally recalls Matthew Arnold's survey of English poetry in his "Study of Poetry" and the critical canons by which he would judge the different kinds of poetry.

Poetry, like everything else in man, evolves and evolution means a bringing out of powers lying concealed. English poetry in its evolution, according to Sri Aurobindo, is progressing towards the kind of poetry which expresses itself in the Supreme rhythmic language which "seizes hold upon all that is finite and brings into each the light and voice of its own Infinite" (FP 392). The movement is spiral and the apparent fall from Blake's command over psychic realms, Wordsworth's spiritual experiences, Coleridge's supernaturalism, Shelley's imaginative transcendence, Keats's worship of Beauty and Byron's titanic energy, to the shallow but many-sided intellectualism of the Victorian age may seem to be rather shadowy but it is only apparent. We are in fact being prepared for the higher heights the glimpses of which are seen in the poetry of Whitman, Tagore and Yeats.

Sri Aurobindo's prophetic vision is based on, as we have seen, a sound linguistic philosophy which he has drawn from ancient Indian language philosophy and reinterpreted it for us. This is in sharp contrast to the assumptions of Bloomfieldian linguistics. The latter, in its preoccupation with data, ignored or neglected the creative urge and the creative potential of language which may transcend the langue-parole model which is posited. It is true that *langue* is the abstract system derived from a study of the *parole.* But it is located wholly at the level of sentence production. When a word becomes *Logos* or *the Word* is not the concern of either the structuralists or Chomskians. Indian language philosophy — starting from the *Word, sphoṭa* and *Pasyanti vak* coming down to *Vaikhari*, the articulated word — is comprehensive, providing for the descending and ascending movements — from the pre-verbal state which is the source of inspiration to the articulated word, and from the articulated word back to the inspiration and its source.

Note

1. The inspiration can come from any one of the following planes:

   (i) The overmind and its domains: some passages from the *Gita* and a good deal of the ṛks of Rgveda belong here. Among English poets Wordsworth's

The Cataracts blow their trumpets from the steep;
No more shall grief of mine the season wrong;
I hear the echoes through the mountains throng,
The winds come to me from the fields of sleep.

rises to this height — revealing concretely something that belongs to the realms of the spirit — an instance of *Pasyanti vak* or *the seeing word*.

(ii) The Higher Mental levels.
(iii) The psychic plane from which most of Shelley's poetry comes.
(iv) Mental.
(v) Poetic Intelligence.
(vi) Vital.
(vii) The Subtle physical: Browning, Dryden, Donne write mostly from the mental and poetic intelligence level; Shakespeare almost invariably from the vital and Chaucer from the subtle physical. Other terms, Sri Aurobindo employs, are piquancy, intensity, felicity and magnificence.

2. Indian Aesthetics: Its Role in the Teaching of Literature

There is very little of practical criticism in Sanskrit. We have indeed a lot of theory — a number of technical terms to indicate *Sabda* and *Arthālankaras*. But the alankarikas have not evolved a methodology which may be adopted in dealing with new poems or assessing older poems afresh from new points of view. [Except for a discussion of two or three slokas from *Kumarasambhava* and two or three verses from the *Rāmāyanā* (in the commentaries) there has been no consistent attempt at 'explication' in Sanskrit literary criticism. I am perhaps somewhat unfair here. One reason why we don't have much of the kind of practical criticism (popularized by the New Critics) in Sanskrit may be that the great teachers never bothered to record their oral elucidations of texts. Again, commentators like Mallinatha concentrated more on grammar and rhetoric indicating the nature of the alankaras employed than on explication. Arunagirinatha and Narayana were, of course, an exception. The great Bhashyas are philosophical, intellectual and rarely aesthetically satisfying.]

In recent years attempts have been made to provide an oriental slant to literary studies and criticism. Words like *rasa*, *riti*, *Vyañgya* are used along with words and phrases like art-emotion, style, suggestion etc. But the use or substitution of Indian terms for

English critical terms will not make the approach Indian. It is true that art-critics all over the world have held roughly the same view about the form and content of art; and one invariably has to employ the same terms. All that one can hope to do is to find out if the English terms adequately bring out the contents and implications of the Sanskrit terms; and then decide which term is nearer the concept we are trying to define. From the point of view of teaching literature this can be done only when both the teacher and the taught have some basic knowledge of the nature and function of art (in both traditions); and would like to analyse and compare. We can then proceed from the known to the unknown. Some of the *alankaras* like *upama rupaka*, *parinama*, *utpreksha*, *aprastutaprasamsa* are employed by all poets at all times. These terms have been defined by Sanskrit rhetoricians like Ruyyaka and Appayya Dikshita and they invite comparison with the corresponding terms in English rhetoric like simile, metaphor, allegory, analogy and metonymy. These belong to the category of *Arthalankara*. *Sabdalankaras* like *Anuprasa*, *yamaka*, *citra*, *slesa*, *vakrokti* and *punaruktabhasa* may be more easily understood if the examples are from Sanskrit or the literature of the native language. The English teacher in India would be well advised not to think of illustration from English since sensibility in this area is more difficult to acquire and open to dispute.

With this grounding the teacher may pass on to the level of *riti* — *style* as that which constitutes poetry (one may recall A.E. Housman's definition of poetry that it consists not in *what* you say but in *how* you say what you say) and then to *Vakrokti* which has been related to 'deviations' in linguistic criticism, and the 'oblique poetry' of Tillyard, or the irony and paradox of the New Critics. The fact that at this level it is possible to make use of Sanskrit critical terms to communicate goes to show that philosophers of aesthetics and rhetoricians all over the civilized societies have thought about these problems and probably arrived at similar, if not identical, formulations of concepts and the terms to define them.

At a deeper level in the matter of defining art experience as *Rasanubhava* (and this is born of a detached, aesthetically sensitive contemplation of life) there is a similarity. However the Indian approach stressed more the principle of *delight* (the poet's discovery of beauty and truth in *all* experiences) than the Western critic and that gave the poet a more honoured and important place. The delight referred to here is of a different order from the one described by Horace or Sidney. It is nearer to the romantic view of art. The poet was identified with the Creator (He was a Seer and Maker) since he had the Word: that is, he could *express* what seemed inexpressible and he had the resources. He could exploit the phonetic and semantic content of words, create new words — since he was 'inspired' and his *inspiration* gave him the power. All that he had to do was to make himself a fit medium for his inspiration, allow himself to be guided by it rather than by the 'meddling intellect'.

It is at this point that we come to the essentially Indian approach to art and poetry. Indian Art and poetry accepted *intuition*, *inspiration*, the *unknown modes* of being and all art could only be a product of a detached contemplation of any experience (life experiences or experiences beyond life or rational, even infra-rational ones). It is the poet's disinterestedness that helped him to communicate the *essence* of an experience and the delight that is associated with this *essence*.

Together with this basic concept of art went the concept of a *sahrdaya*; and the concept of the basic distinction between the *body* of poetry and the *soul* of poetry. The body-soul metaphor which defined art has to be understood in the context of the ideal reader as a *sahrdaya* who can, through a sensitive response to the body of poetry (*kavya*), get at the soul. The *sahrdaya* is not necessarily a great scholar nor a technical expert but one who by identity gets in a flash the *essence* or the *rasanubhava*. The Western aestheticians too, especially the moderns, have been talking about reader-oriented / reader-response criticism. But there is a difference, a vital difference. They (the critics of this school) do indeed start rightly from this end — (the end of the reader) with the words on the page, but they don't go beyond the words — the body — to the soul, for their skepticism, and their philosophy block the passage to the soul. Their sensitivity helps them to construct / deconstruct / reconstruct but in the process they miss the two essential things — the delight that the *soul* of kavya can communicate and its gift of integral knowledge. There is a lot of cleverness, what the rhetoricians would call *chamatkara* but very little of the *rasanubhava* which marks a sensitive critic and distinguishes him from a mere rhetorician who concentrates on the from.

Starting with Bharata who gave us the definition of *rasa*, almost all the Sanskrit critics have accepted the fact that art should give us primarily *delight* and *the peace that passeth understanding and sensation*. It is in the substratum of peace that one can contemplate even the most painful experience without any pathological consequence. This explains how *rasanubhava* and *rasanishpatti* are had only in a state of detachment, when, without involvement, the critic too can contemplate any experience. The joy of recollecting the painful experiences of poverty in one's early life when one is old and looking back is an instance in point. This experience of *rasa* is communicated through words. But the words, as the author of *Dhwanyaloka* puts it, are only pointers. They must take you beyond themselves. The rhetoricians may classify (and indeed they have classified) diction and the embellishments but they are of no value to a reader if they don't take him beyond. We have the example of the lamp that enables us to see the pot, and our interest is in the pot and the lamp is only a means to discover the pot though the light is still there and is as important. All the embellishments of poetry such as *sabda-alankara*, *artha-alankara*, *lakshanas* (metaphor), only form the body of poetry. But there is the soul, or to speak more concretely, the charm of the whole, called *lavanya* which is more than a sum of the parts.

I should consider the concept *rasa* a useful pedagogical tool, especially in teaching poetry and poetic drama. I say poetry and poetic drama deliberately. The stress on intuition and inspiration distinguishes the earlier Indian aestheticians from most literary critics in the West except perhaps the Romantics, notably Coleridge and Shelley. [This point is taken up again towards the close of this paper.] As teachers of drama we want the students to distinguish between the action-plot and the theme-plot, on the one hand and the elements that constitute the action plot such as the incidents/ characters, diction and imagery on the other. We can, no doubt, use the model of 'meaning' and 'the meaning of meaning' propounded by Richards and Ogden. The difficulty with Richards and Ogden, as with most practitioners of the distorted versions of the New Criticism, is that they are positivists and they stop with the emotive association of the words and the sensations they produce. The distinction made by E.D. Hirsch between meaning and significance is perhaps closer to the Indian view. Indian aestheticians believed in intuition and they felt that the experience of *dhwani* was a special kind of knowing which is distinct from all other types of knowing. It is not an implied meaning. The aestheticians, we noted, constantly employ the imagery of the light that discovers objects. The perception itself is described in terms of a flash of intuition, *pratibha*, sudden revelation. In bringing out the meaning or significance of a passage or text it is the concept of *suggestion* that can be legitimately exploited in helping our students to understand, for example, such valuable critical observations as the one made by Wilson Knight that the theme of *Macbeth* is the vision of Evil or that we have the experience of purgatorio and paradiso in *Lear*. These are the suggested meanings as opposed to our understanding of the events, characters, and the plot through the words on the page. The force of the story, characters and language is such as to take us beyond themselves and use them as pointers to the theme. The process may be described thus: There is the story of *Macbeth* which may be called *'Vastu'*. Macbeth starts with his 'vaulting ambition' which prompts him to kill Duncan, his kinsman, king and guest. His monstrous, ungrateful act leads him to further unnatural acts like contriving the death of Banquo, Macduff and his children. This is followed by the disintegration of his being, his realization of the emptiness of life and his final destruction. Whatever is indicated by this plot is reinforced by words and the images of light/ darkness, feasting/disruption, disease/healing, all suggesting the power of evil. In *King Lear* there is first the impulsive division of the kingdom and the disowning of Cordelia followed by the monstrous acts of the blinding of the father by the son (in the sub-plot) and the driving out of Lear himself. Lear soon dies to this world and to his old self. Cordelia comes to his rescue, and for a time Lear and Cordelia have the experience of the joy of reunion. But they don't have a place in this world of evil and they die. The theme is reinforced by the animal imagery and the imagery of trial in a court of law and finally that of the singing birds in prison. We proceed in the same way from the words, images and characters to the world of Denmark in *Hamlet* and then by a leap, to an awareness of the essentially painful nature of life and the impossibility of tackling evil while remaining in the world of evil. The very righteousness of Hamlet becomes self-righteousness and his attempt to set right what is wrong proves futile.

The experience of the emptiness of life that one feels when evil within prompts us to more acts of evil is the theme of *Macbeth*. His own destruction and the destruction of the world he creates for himself are the consequences made explicit by the play. Lear too is living in a world of monstrous evil, but his endurance leads him from the Inferno of evil through the Purgatory of suffering to the Paradise of joy.

Tagore's response to Kalidasa's *Sakuntala* helped him to see the play as the drama of three worlds: the world of sensuous beauty and earthly love, the world of asceticism and the world of harmony where earthly love is transformed into heavenly harmony. The evoked meaning however only works through the plot, characters and diction;

which is another way of saying that the literal sense is not set aside. It subserves the expressed meaning. It helps the Sahrdaya to make the interpretative leap. Hence the distinction made between the meaning of the whole work (*kavyartha*) as opposed to the lexical meaning of words and images (*sabdartha*). It is a kind of flash taking us into a 'non-space-dimension'. At this stage the Indian aesthetician also admitted that the poet himself has no full control over what his poem could invoke. The sensitive reader may experience more than what the poet intended. Thus it is true that the poet makes the *dhvani* structure in order to mediate his experience of reality. But once it is made, it is not the poet but his poem that speaks to the reader.

Terms like *vakrokti*, *riti*, *the gunas*, and *auchitya* may be used for explaining organic form. *Riti* is style in a very general sense which includes things like musical rhythm deviations in expression, appropriate diction, appropriate order, or 'keeping', to use the term employed by Robert Bridges. It is a sensitive response to these things that can take the reader to the heart and soul of poetry the *Kavya*.

But how to become a *sahrdaya*? What is the discipline for the *sahrdaya*? The word has not been properly rendered. He is not necessarily an intellectual. He is not a matter-of-fact scholar nor is he a sentimental reader. He is expected to achieve a kind of identity with the art and the artist. The Indian conditions were actually helpful in developing the reader's sensitivity in as much as he had very little knowledge of the writers and artists, their intentions, or even the historical circumstances in which the works of art were produced which deflect our attention from the text. So there was no chance for the Indian critic to commit the historical, biographical and intentional fallacies. He could respond only to the words on the page. His only training was in logic, grammar and rhetoric, which he got in reading the best works of art. He was expected to cultivate, in Wordsworth's phrase, 'wise passiveness' when he would be capable of the flash of intuition or what is called *sphurana*. The alert intellect must receive and not distort the intuition. Our language-philosophy helped him to see the limitations of *Vaikhari-Vak*, articulated words and his mind was ever ready to receive from other levels of Vak such as *Pasyanti* and *Madhyama* of which the *Vaikhari* (and the meaning it can convey) is only a fraction. The *sahrdaya* can respond to the hidden features and resources of *Vaikhari* (the creative artist, by exploiting these hidden features, forces *Vaikhari Vak* to yield more) and recreate for himself the experience in its entiretv.

Even a poem or a passage of poetry which may be apparently simple or plain, may have a significance often missed. Here is a passage from Wordsworth's *Michael:*

This not forgotten yet
The pity which was then in every heart
For the old man — and 'tis believed by all
That many and many a day he thither went,
And never lifted up a single stone.

Matthew Arnold said, "Nature herself seems, ... to take the pen out of his [Wordsworth's] hand, and to write for him with her own bare, sheer penetrating power. This arises from two causes; from the *profound* sincereness with which Wordsworth feels his subject, and also from the *profoundly* sincere and natural character of his subject itself ..."; and after quoting the line 'And never lifted up a single stone', he adds, "There is nothing subtle in it, no heightening, no study of poetic style, strictly so called at all, yet it is an expression of the highest and most *truly expressive kind...*" He is obviously *referring* to the suggestive power of the simplest of words. The context of the story (Vastu) and the words do cooperate with each other. There is the contrast on the one hand between the pity for the old man on the part of *every heart* and that between his *daily* visits *and his never lifting up a single stone* on the other. All the pity of the neighbours could not create in him any self-pity. In his last days Michael remained as dignified as he was when he was young and hopeful; and he keeps his word:

a Covenant
"Twill be between us; but, *whatever fate*
Befall thee I shall love thee to the last
And bear *thy memory* with me to the grave ...

Wordsworth could have used the word *But* in the place of '*And* in the line 'And never lifted up a single stone'. That, however, would have *altered Michael's* character. He never became a *hardened stoic* — neither had he any self-pity. He would go *everyday* resolving to build the sheep-fold; but his essential humanity, the education he had received from Nature helped him to maintain his dignity even in defeat and remain human. The words do *indeed* give us a lot more than they can normally do.

[Christopher Ricks has something very *perceptive* to say on this passage in his *Force of Poetry*. He tries to show that these simple words *and*, *up*, *down* contribute to the structure of the poem and their *force* helps us to realise the moral strength of Michael. My point is to show how the same word points beyond the plot and emotion to Michael retaining his *identity* with Nature and *deriving* all his strength from the education Nature gave him in his early years — 'the comfort in the strength *of love*' — in short, how *suggestive* even simple words can be. They take us *inward* into ourselves and we are made to feel with the character and to pass on from the expressed to the unexpressed *possibilities*.]

In Shelley it is not so much what is said but what is *not* said that is important. All his references to love in his poetry prepare our consciousness to grow, develop and reach a state of readiness for the *epiphany* of *self transcendence*. Sri Aurobindo said in *The Future Poetry* that Shelley "sings from the skies earthwards (and Keats looks from earth towards Olympus)." Light, Love and Liberty that Shelley talks about are spiritual qualities which he would bring down to earth without their losing their *intrinsic celestial* nature and shape. The negative method he adopts is to communicate the fact that the *truths* he sings about are difficult for mortal eyes to see and mortal *consciousness* to realize.

> What thou art we know not
> What is most like thee?
> From rainbow clouds there flow not
> Drops so bright to see
> As from thy presence showers a rain of melody.

"To bring his difficult significance home he lavishes inexhaustibly image on radiant image ... the sense floats in a storm of *coruscations* and dissolving star-showers." We have indeed in Shelley a pure poet, one who is all 'suggestion' and who has to go to his *imagination* or to some remote luminous experience of ideal world, for his medium. I may be permitted to conclude with a reference to three more poems, one by Keats, and the other two by Yeats. The poems are themselves metaphors and they take us from the particular to the general, from the material to the spiritual. The movement in Keats's *Grecian Urn* is from the lovers sculptured on the Urn to life and the contrast between life and art. One way of looking at the poem is to see it as presenting a dialectical tension. Another way is to see how through a contemplation of art we may be 'teased out of thought' and rise higher to a perception of Beauty-Truth identification. In Yeats's "Sailing to Byzantium" we start from Ireland and life and move to the world of 'artifice of eternity' where the speaker would, like the golden nightingale and its Emperor, spend his time listening to the song of the bird about the past or passing or to come. "Byzantium" shows that even that world is incomplete. Art can give us immortality, but not the warmth of life. The call of life is insistent and the bitter complexities, the mire and blood of human veins try to invade the world of Byzantium. They have of course to die into a dance, an agony of dance. They would swallow up the world of Essences. The raging sea of the world is lashing upon the pavement of Byzantium and it seems to be as endless as the process of purification. And the last words of the poem indicate the affirmation of time and life.

The Sanskrit poets wrote as they felt, expressing their vision in all its intensity and glory. The greater poets show indeed something of the awesome reticence and restraint that we find in passages of Shakespearean tragedy or the power and suggestive force of the best romantic poetry. That is why Indian epics and poetic drama, in spite of their being rooted in an authentic native culture, have a universal appeal and the critical theories deriving from them are so comprehensive and inclusive in their scope that they can be used to interpret all poets. (They are never prescriptive). Meaning to an Indian aesthetician *included* the cognitive/emotive/cultural significance of utterances. The Indian aesthetician was also a language philosopher and logician and so he was aware of the limitations of logic and the intellectual comprehension. His sensibility was *unified*; and his objective was to respond with his whole being.

It was Matthew Arnold who said that "an exclusive attention to the qualities of regularity, uniformity, precision and balance involved some repression and silencing of poetry, a touch of frost to the imaginative life of the soul and so the poetry of the XVIII Century lacked a high seriousness, a poetic largeness, freedom, insight, benignity." Referring to this statement and to Arnold's definition of poetry that it is at bottom 'a criticism of life', Eliot showed that Arnold's concern was with *great* poetry and not *pure* poetry. We may accept the distinction that in pure poetry we have the communication of *an experience in its entirety* (any experience), but in *great* poetry the experience itself is of a higher order, perhaps too high that it is not often easy for a poet who is not 'a bard' to find appropriate words for it. Indian aesthetics has provided for both kinds of poetry — rhetorical as well as bardic. If the alankarikas or the rhetoricians could respond to such poetry as the one found in this passage from Pope:

> Who but must laugh if such a/man there be
> Who would not weep it Atticus were he ...

passages like 'Ripeness is all ...' needed the sensibility of a critic of the Dhvani school. Ripeness is not just a metaphor — as we all know — its suggestive power is more far-reaching. And to contrast *Readiness is all* with *Ripeness is all* is to see the difference between the world of Hamlet and the world of Lear.

3. Schools of Criticism in Sanskrit

Depending on the emphasis and the relative importance the aestheticians attach to particular aspects of poetry, there are as many as eight different schools of criticism in Sanskrit.

1. The *Riti* School stresses *the manner*, the style, recalling the English poet A.E. Housman who said that poetry is seen *not* in what you say but in *how* you say what you say. Vamana is the principal exponent of this school.

2. The *Rasa* School considers that the soul of poetry lies in the *rasa* that it embodies.

3. The *Alankara* School concentrates on those factors that enhance the beauty of expression. It speaks of the various embellishments, *alankaras* that make an utterance truly poetic. The critics of the school discuss the *gunas* and *dosas* — the qualities and blemishes.

4. The *Vakrokti* School discusses the deviations that go to make an utterance impressive or poetic.

5. The *Dhwani* School attaches great importance to suggestion. It

brings in language philosophy, explains how the expressed sense/manifested forms must take us beyond to the soul of poetry.

6. *Auchitya* is emphasized by Kṣemendra. He declares, propriety, decorum alone can contribute to delight in poetry.

7. The *Guna* School has many things in common with the *Riti* school.

8. The *Anumāna* School stresses the element of *inference* and *logic* in the creation and appreciation of poetry.

Glossary

Abhidha: the primary meaning of a word; the literal sense of a word.

Abhinaya: gesture/movement of limbs in dance.

Adbhuta: wonder (See *Rasa)*

Alankāra: embellishment, ornament, a figure of speech.

Arthālankara: a figure of sense/semantically significant as opposed a figure of speech (called *Sabdalankara)* which depends for its pleasing effect on sound (rather than meaning) characterized by alliteration, rhyme etc.

Critics have classified as many as hundred odd figures under *arthālankara*. As Ānandhavardhana put it 'the great artists have revealed and used figures in thousands.' Some of them are (1) *upamā* (simile or comparison) (2) *paryāyokti* (a round about or periphrastic way of saying (3) *Yathasankhya* (order / enumeration) (4) *parikara* (significant way) (5) *samuccaya* (conjunction or grouping) (6) *punarukta* (iteration) (7) *Vyajastuti* (dissimulation) (8) *Samaskoti* (abridged or condensed expression) (9) *Virodha* (apparent contradiction). *Ullękha, Utpreksa, Atisayokti, dipaka, parinama* are others. There are in the main six varieties of *sabdalankara*: (1) *Anuprasa*; (2) *Yamaka;* (3) *Ctra*; (4) *Slesa*; (5) Vakrokti (as a figure of speech consisting in the use of evasive speech or reply either by means of a pun or by an affected change of *tone* and (6) *punaruktabhasa*.

Alankārika: a rhetorician as distinguished from an aesthetic philosopher or literary critic.

Alaukika: transcendental, beyond worldly experience.

Anubhava: experience.

Anubhāva: emotional response; external manifestation of emotion.

Angika: a term pertaining to *Abhinaya* (the movement of the limbs of the body).

Anumāna: inference.

Anuprāsa: alliteration.

Apahnuti: a figure of speech: denial of concealment of truth, using a simile in other than its true or obvious application.

Aprastutapraśamsa: implied or indirect meaning conveying the subject matter by means of that which is not the subject matter. A figure of speech which by describing the (which is not the subject matter) conveys a reference to the or subject matter.

Arthāntaranyāsa: A figure of speech: an illustration of a particular case by a general truth or of a general truth by a particular case.

Arthāntara sankramita vācya: literal meaning (that is twisted in getting) or retained in the suggestion (see *dhvani*).

Arthāpatti:

1) an inference from circumstances, presumptions, implication, one of the five sources of knowledge or modes of proof.
2) an inference used to account for an apparent inconsistency.
3) a figure of speech in which a relevant assertion suggests an inference not connected with the subject in hand.
4) postulation or immediate inference from negative concomitants/immediate inference based on the universal relation between the absence of the major and the absence of the middle terms.

Asamlaksya krama: order/sequence of stages not discerned.

Atisayokti: exaggeration, hyperbole.

Ativyāpti: fallacy of being too wide, wider than the term already defined.

Atyanta tiraskṛta vācya: expressed sense wholly concealed or rejected in the process of getting the suggested sense (see *dhvani*).

Aucitya: propriety, keeping, decorum.

Avivaksita vācya: the kind of *dhvani* or suggestion where the expressed sense is stultified; suggestive words whose primary sense is discarded (see *dhvani*).

Bhāva: the emotive meaning.

Bhāvakatva: the power of universalization, state of having a taste (the sensibility for that which is beautiful).

Bhāvana: aesthetic contemplation.

Bhayānaka: terror (see *rasa*).

Bhojakatwa: the power by which the *stayibhava* reaches its climax and is enjoyed by the spectators.

Bibhatsa: disgust (see *rasa*).

Citra: pictorial art.

Dhvani: Suggestion, resonance as different from —

(1) **Anumāna** (inference).

(2) **Arthāpatti** (Immediate inference base on universal relation between the absence of the major and the absence of the middle terms). (see above)

(3) **lakşaņā** (which is based on the primary sense of the word and is its extension).
(4) **tātparya** (the expressed sense).

Dhvani may be classified under —
(a) **avivakşita vācya** — where the literal meaning is not intended.
(b) **Vivaksitānyapara vācya** — where the literal meaning is intended but subserves the implied sense.
(c) **Vastudhvani** — where the suggested sense is the theme/ action etc.
(d) **alankāradhvani** — where the suggested sense is a figure of speech.
(e) **Samlkşyakrama vyangya** — instances where the stages of realizing the suggested sense from the expressed sense can be well perceived.
(f) **asamlakşya krama vyangya** — where the stages of realizing the suggested sense from the expressed sense are imperceptible.
(g) **Guņibhuta vyangya** — where the charm of the suggested sense is not more striking or subservient to than the expressed sense.

Guņa: quality, merit feature.

Guņa vritti: implication / indication.

Guņi bhūta vyangya: poetry where the suggested sense is subordinated (see *dhvani).*

Hāsya: humour (see *rasa).*

Kāku: (intonation) ironical.

Kānti: brilliance (of style).

Karuņa: compassion (see *rasa*).

Lakşaņa: the function of the word denoting a referent different from its normal and primary one but somehow related to it (some-times words like *upacarna, gauņi, vrtti, bhakti* are also used to refer to this secondary significative function of the word). It may also be rendered as metaphor or transfer, the conditions of the transfer being:
(1) the unsuitability of the primary meaning in the context,
(2) some relation between the primary and the actual referent; and

(3) the sanction for the metaphorical or transferred sense by popular usage.

Mādhurya: Sweetness (of style)

Pratibhā: flash of insight, intuition, creative imagination which helps one to see things as a whole.

Pratiyamāṇa: implied (sense/idea)

Paryāyokti: Periphrasis

Punarukti: iteration.

Rasa: essence, taste, aesthetic experience of an emotion (emotion resulting from contemplaton of life-emotion). They are basically nine in number: (1) sṛngāra — love; (2) hāsya — humour; (3) karuna — compassion/pathos; (4) raudra — wrath; (5) vira — heroism; (6) bhayanaka — terror; (7) bibhatsa — disgust; (8) adbhuta — wonder, the marvellous; (9) Śānta — peace.

The contributory factors that promote the realization of rasa are:

(1) **angika** — movements of the limbs of the body, abhinaya

(2) **vācika** — speech (words articulated)

(3) **āhārya** — dress

(4) **sāttvika** — expression of feelings.

Obstacles/barriers to the realization of *rasa**:

(1) Pratipattavayogyatā sambhāvana virahaḥ — lack of adequate realization of the *probability* or the reasonableness of things.

(2) Swagataparagatatva niyēmāna desa kāla viṣēsavesah — the presence of certain individualistic or distinctive features of time and place which enable the *sahṛdaya* to sever himself (detach himself?) from the objects described.

(3) nijasukādhi vivasibhava: undue assertion of self-regarding emotions, being under this spell of one's own individual pleasure or pain.

(4) pratityupāyavaikalyam — absence of adequate means of immediate realization.

---

* This part of the Glossary " Obstacles to the realisation of *rasa* " is taken from A.Sankaran, *Some Aspects of Literary Criticism in Sanskrit*, ed. by Dr. K. Kunjunni Raja (Madras: University of Madras, 1973)

(5) Sphutatwabhāvah — lack of clearness or perspicuity.
(6) apradhānata — absence of some element as the dominant factor; and
(7) samsaya yogha: doubt in general

Rasadhvani: suggestion as rasa

Riti: style, beautiful diction endowed with *guṇas (vaidharbi, gaudiya, panchali,* etc.). According to Vāmana *guṇas* endow beauty to the figures (alaṃkāras), enhance that beauty.

Rūdhi: established usage

Rūpaka: metaphor.

Sādhāraṇikaraṇa: powers of universalizing.

Sahṛdaya: perceptive reader, responsible and responsive; one who is capable of identifying himself with the poet.

Samāsokti: condensed expression / metaphor.

Sanghatana: poetic composition involving proper choice of diction and ordering of words.

Slēsa: paranomasia / pun, it is of three kinds

1. *abanga slesa* double meaning with the same word division;
2. *sabhanga slesa* double, meaning with different word division; and
3. *artha slesa,* a single meaning with different applications.

Sphoṭa: 'bursting forth'. That which flashes in the mind and realised as meaning when an utterance is made and heard. According to Bhartrhari the *sphoṭa* is the word or the sentence taken as a single meaningful unit.

Sthāyibhavā: permanent dominant emotions, the emotion that abide with us (see *rasa*).

Tātparya: purport, content.

Upacāra: see *lakṣaṇa*.

Utprēksa: a figure of speech, comparison in general, illustrative simile etc. A figure of speech which consists in supposing Upameya and Upamāna as similar to each other in some respects and in indicating a probability of their identity based on such similarity.

Vācya: that which is experessed, expressed sense.

Vācyartha: expressed sense.

Vaikhari: the heard *vak* as distinguished from the unheard: *para / pasyanti* and *madhyama vak.*

Vakrokti: deviation: Six varieties are distingished:*

1. *Varnavinayasa vakrokti* (corresponding to *sabdalankara*)
2. *pada purvardha vakrokti* (choice of terms)
3. *pratayaya vakrokti* (use of suffuxes)
4. Vakyavakrokti (all figures are brought in here)
5. *prakarana vakrokti* (choice of or changes made in the incidents of the plot)
6. *prabhandhavakrokti* (construction of the plot itself)

We may also distinguish a seventh type: a figure of speech equivocation / insinuation, innuendo (see *Alamkāra*)

Vastu: plot /idea / subject.

Vastudhvani: theme suggested.

Vibhāva: stimulus provided by charaters, excitants.

Vipralamba: (sṛngara) love in separation.

Vira: heroism (see rasa).

Virodha: contradiction.

Vyabhicāribhāva: passing moods, emotions.

Vyangya: suggestion (see *dhvani*).

Vyangyārtha: suggested sense (see *dhvani*).

Vyangyatva: suggestivity.

---

* The six types are as listed in A. Sankaran "*Some Aspects of Literarey Criticism in Sanskrit*".